Namibia

the Bradt Travel Guide

Chris McIntyre

edition
3

www.bradtguides.com

Bradt Travel Guides Ltd, UK
The Globe Pequot Press Inc, USA

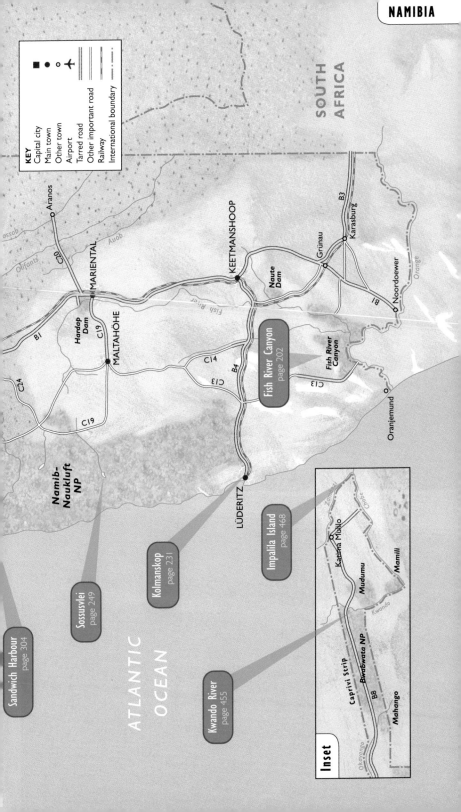

SOUTH AFRICA

Aranos

C10

Olifants

Auob

MARIENTAL

B1

Hardap
Dam

C19

MALTAHÖHE

C24

C19

Namib-
Naukluft
NP

Fish River

KEETMANSHOOP

Naute
Dam

Grünau

B3

Karasburg

B1

Noordoewer

Orange

C14

B4

C13

Fish River Canyon
page 202

Fish River
Canyon

C13

Oranjemund

LÜDERITZ

Sandwich Harbour
page 304

Sossusvlei
page 249

Kolmanskop
page 231

Impalila Island
page 468

Kwando River
page 455

ATLANTIC
OCEAN

KEY
Capital city
Main town
Other town
Airport
Tarred road
Other important road
Railway
International boundary

Inset

Zambezi

Chobe

Katima Mulilo

Mudumu

Mamili

Kwando

Caprivi Strip

Bwabwata NP

B8

Mahango

Okavango

Namibia
Don't
miss...

Etosha National Park
Male lion *Panthera leo*
(AZ) page 361

Sossusvlei
after extraordinary rains
(CM) page 249

Fish River Canyon
(CM) page 202

Culture
Bushmen lighting
a fire
(CM) page 16

Rock art
Twyfeltontein
(AZ) page 337

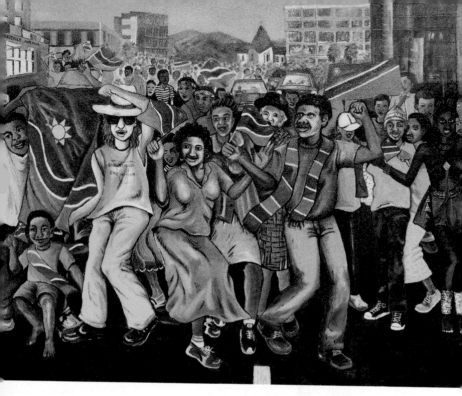

above **Independence mural, Windhoek** (AZ) page 119

below **Namib Desert** (CM) page 239

above **Clay castles, Skeleton Coast NP**
(CM) page 326

centre **Typical gravel road**
(CM) page 93

right **Kolmanskop**
(TH) page 231

above **Southern Namibia in flower after rain** (PS) page 216
below left **Kokerboom or quivertree** *Aloe dichotoma* (AZ) page 198
below right **Welwitschia** *Welwitschia mirabilis* (AZ) page 334
bottom right **Lithops, or living stones** (TL) page 303

Chris McIntyre went to Africa in 1987, after reading physics at Queen's College, Oxford. He taught with VSO in Zimbabwe for almost three years and travelled around extensively. In 1990 he co-authored the UK's first guide to Namibia and Botswana, published by Bradt, before spending three years as a shipbroker in London.

Since then, Chris has concentrated on what he enjoys most: Africa. He wrote the first guidebook to Zambia for Bradt in 1996, the first edition of this guide in 1998, a new Botswana guide in 2003, and co-authored a guide to Zanzibar in 2006. He is now managing director of Expert Africa – a specialist tour operator which organises a variety of high-quality trips throughout Africa, including Namibia – and regularly updates his guides.

He maintains a keen interest in development and conservation issues, acting as advisor to various NGOs and projects associated with Africa. He is a Fellow of the Royal Geographical Society and contributes photographs and articles to various publications, including *The Times*, *Wanderlust*, *BBC Wildlife* and *Travel Africa*. Based in west London, Chris lives with his fiancée, Susan Shand, and spends two or three months each year researching in Africa. He can usually be contacted by email on chris.mcintyre@expertafrica.com.

PUBLISHER'S FOREWORD *Hilary Bradt*

The first Bradt travel guide was written in 1974 by George and Hilary Bradt on a river barge floating down a tributary of the Amazon. It was followed by *Backpacker's Africa*, published in 1979. In the 1980s and '90s the focus shifted away from hiking to broader-based guides to new destinations – usually the first to be published on those places. In the 21st century Bradt continues to publish these ground-breaking guides, along with guides to established holiday destinations, incorporating in-depth information on culture and natural history alongside the nuts and bolts of where to stay and what to see.

Bradt authors support responsible travel, with advice not only on minimum impact but also on how to give something back through local charities. Thus a true synergy is achieved between the traveller and local communities.

* * *

I once spent a day in Namibia – or to be accurate in South West Africa – in the early 1970s. I was trying to hitchhike to the Fish River Canyon, but after 24 hours without seeing a single vehicle, George and I gave up and returned to South Africa.

Today Namibia is transformed, but I'm told that one thing remains unchanged: there are still very few cars on the roads. I'll be finding out for myself soon, when I visit all those places I've been reading about since the first edition of this guide in 1998: Etosha Pan, Sossusvlei, Okonjima ... Through his detailed and evocative descriptions, Chris McIntyre has successfully persuaded thousands of people to visit Namibia. I am thrilled that it's now my turn – and that I will have this classic guide with me.

Third edition May 2007   First published 1998

Bradt Travel Guides Ltd, 23 High Street, Chalfont St Peter, Bucks SL9 9QE, England.
www.bradtguides.com
Published in the USA by The Globe Pequot Press Inc, 246 Goose Lane,
PO Box 480, Guilford, Connecticut 06475-0480

Photographs Chris McIntyre (CM), Tricia Hayne (TH), Tracy Lederer (TL), Rebecca Johnson (RJ), Claire Scott (CS), Piet Swiegers (PS), Ariadne Van Zandbergen (AZ)
Front cover Oryx in desert, Sossusvlei (Jan Baks/Alamy)
Back cover Himba boy (RJ), Cheetah *Acinonyx jubatus* (CM)
Title page Flowering aloe (CM), Ballooning over the Namib Desert (CS), Caracal cub *Felis caracal* (CM)

Illustrations Annabel Milne, Carole Vincer   **Maps** Malcolm Barnes
Typeset from the author's disc by Wakewing
Printed and bound in Italy by Legoprint SpA, Trento

Major Contributors

This book, just as much as the previous editions, has been a team effort, and many have devoted their energy to it. Largest amongst the contributions to this third edition are from the following people.

TRICIA AND BOB HAYNE updated sections on Swakopmund and most of northern Namibia in great detail. As former editorial director of Bradt Travel Guides, Tricia is only too familiar with the minutiae of putting together a guidebook, although the distances of Namibia are in marked contrast to those covered for her own Bradt guide, to the Cayman Islands. Tricia and Bob have also helped to update Chris's guides to Botswana, Zambia and Zanzibar.

SUSAN SHAND joined the travel industry in 1999 and now manages the media and public relations for Classic Representation – a collection of some of Africa's finest independent safari camps and boutique hotels. In her spare time she co-authored Bradt's most recent Zanzibar guide. Susan spends several months each year in Africa with Chris McIntyre, and many more encouraging the press and public to visit; she can be contacted by email on susan.shand@blueyonder.co.uk.

TRACY LEDERER taught in the UK for 15 years, spending all of her holidays travelling the world. In 1993, she backpacked around Zimbabwe, Zambia and Malawi, kindling a love of Africa; since then she has travelled widely around the continent. She joined Expert Africa in 2004 and now specialises in organising offbeat and interesting trips to Namibia and Rwanda. Tracy spends several months each year travelling and researching in Africa.

GWYNNETH BEZUIDENHOUT was born in Namibia, and grew up in Windhoek. She trained in South Africa, where she got her first taste of working in the hospitality industry, before heading back to Windhoek in 2000 to join a company running camping trips for the adventurous. Gwynneth moved to the UK at the end of 2006, joining Wild about Africa to concentrate on arranging its small-group trips around Namibia.

However, this guide has been built very much on the solid foundations laid by contributions for the previous editions from:

Philip Briggs, Africa expert and author, who kindly gave an extensive and scholarly basis for the original wildlife section; **Purba Choudhury**, arts, press and PR professional, who researched and wrote the original arts and crafts section; **David Else**, expert author and old Africa hand, who kindly gave route descriptions for the Naukluft hiking section; **Sue Grainger**, traveller and writer, who wrote much original material for the Kaokoveld chapter, and commented on more besides; **Jonathan Hughes**, ecologist, who wrote most of the boxes on survival in the Namib, and gave other valuable critiques; and **Rob McDowell**, **Heather Tyrrell** and **Chantal Pinto** who have all worked with Chris at Expert Africa (or Sunvil Africa) over the years, and contributed to many sections, checked proofs and described many places seen on their travels.

Contents

LIST OF MAPS

Acknowledgements

This third edition couldn't have been written without the help of many people who have not yet been mentioned – some who helped with previous editions, and some with this one. Many names I have forgotten, others I never knew. I hope those who aren't named here will forgive me, but some who stand out for their help and input include the following.

The NTS team – Dave van Smeerdik, Anna Cassim, Sabina Hekandjo (both in Windhoek and later in London!), Sue Camp, Frieda Nefungo, Edna Mohrmann, Birgit Bekker, Regina Visher; the late Blythe Loutit, and the SRT team; the community at the remarkable Torra Conservancy, including Anna and Franz Coetzee; Chris Bakkes and MC; the team at Ground Rush, and Beth Sarro at Alter-Action, in Swakopmund; Jeanne Meintjes of Eco-Marine; Helen and Mike Warren from Erongo; Donna, Rosalea and Lisa at Okonjima; and, as ever, Kate and Bruno Nebe – without whom Swakopmund and its surroundings just wouldn't be the same.

Also Anja at Logufa, Gordon Campbell, Jenny Carvill, Hennie Fourrie, Retha Louise Hofmeyr, Dr Margaret Jacobsohn, Ruud Klep, Toya Louw, Ilvia McAdam, Arno and Estelle Oosthuysen, Barbara-Anne Parfitt, Leon and Anita Pearson, Nick Santcross, Kurt Schlenther, Amy and Marie Schoeman, Peter Ward and Dr Polly Wiessner.

The team at Expert Africa sends about 1,000 people to Namibia every year, and many of these have helped me with their personal perspectives on the country – through both discussions and reports after they return. Eric Carter, Michael Jones, and Andrew Pearson stand out, though for this edition special thanks are due to Irene and Alan Jessop, who have travelled regularly to Bushmanland; their feedback and comments have been invaluable. When I last visited the same area, Estelle Oosthuysen was generous with her time, and provided very detailed and accurate information that is the base for the map of Khaudum. (Expert Africa's travellers Paul Rankin and Debbie Shaw also take a bow here, for taking such a long trip to help Estelle map the park!)

Meanwhile, back in the office, Claire Scott, Maruska Adye and Sabina Hekandjo were always on hand to help with much information and experience, whilst the support of John, Noel and Dudley with my writing is always appreciated.

For this third edition, Bob and Tricia Hayne are particularly indebted to all those whose hospitality made travelling around Namibia so memorable. Thanks, too, to the many readers who kindly wrote in with update information, including Dave Armstrong, Kathleen Becker, Garry Brooks, Paul Cammaert, Jane Campion, Hilary Emberten, James Howett and Sasha Londono, Jenine Langrish, Julia Mason, Gillian and Alan Penny, Kate Rose, Peter and Rosemary Royle, Rita Teunissen, and Rob Thomson. Finally, special thanks to Marlien Van Zijl at Epupa Camp, Anita Devenish at Santorini Inn, Keith Irwin (www.namibia-1on1.com), and Anna Moores at Bradt Travel Guides, all of whose help was invaluable.

Immense gratitude, as usual, to those who worked on producing the book: Hilary Bradt, Sally Brock, Malcolm Barnes and, especially, Tricia Hayne – whose hard work made this book possible. It wouldn't have happened without her. That which is good and correct owes much to their care and attention, while errors and omissions remain my own.

Introduction

I first visited Namibia in 1989, as the South African administration started to relinquish its grip and the country prepared for independence. By then I had lived in Zimbabwe for several years and travelled widely. Namibia was rumoured to be wonderful; but nobody seemed to know any details. The world knew South West Africa (Namibia) only as a troubled place from news bulletins, nothing more.

So I hired a VW Golf and drove from Namibia's northeastern tip to its southern border in 12 days. Overseas tourism simply didn't exist then. Sesriem had one campsite with just 11 pitches for tents; the Fish River Canyon was deserted. The trip was terribly rushed, but Namibia captivated me. The scale of its wilderness was enchanting, and travelling was remarkably easy.

Six months later I returned to explore – and to research the first English guidebook to the country. Whilst I was there, Namibia's independence arrived, putting the country's troubles into the past. Optimism was tangible, justified by democracy, an implausibly reliable infrastructure and rich mineral resources. I delved a little deeper into its magic. Elsewhere in the world, Namibia disappeared from the television news.

Only in the late 1990s did it return – featuring on holiday programmes. Fortunately, though, Namibia is far from Europe or the Americas. It has no white sandy beaches, warm tropical waters or big hotels, so it has never appealed to mass tourism. However, it does have huge tracts of pristine wilderness, home to some stunning wildlife. Glance around. The Namib Desert has plants and animals found nowhere else on earth. Here is the world's oldest desert, where endemic wildlife has evolved to survive – like the contorted Welwitschia mirabilis that live for millennia, the elusive golden mole and the unique fog-basking beetles.

Namibia's population has always been tiny, a sprinkling of settlements founded by different peoples: some ancient, some colonial. Around these outposts, vast open areas remain protected as national parks, supplemented by conservancies where scattered local communities protect the wildlife in their own areas. Namibia has little industry and virtually no pollution, so you look up at the clearest stars you'll ever see.

Best of all, Namibia's wilderness is still easy to explore independently. Choose backroads here and you can drive for hours through endless plains, huge mountain massifs and spectacular canyons without seeing a soul. Even in Etosha, one of Africa's top game parks, driving around is easy, and you can stop beside the waterholes for as long as you like. As animals wander all around, you just sip a cold drink and focus your camera.

Namibia's not an ideal country for backpacking. However, if you can afford to hire a car, then the country is your oyster – and it's not expensive. Good food, wine, beer and cheap camping make the cost of living in Namibia lower than anywhere else in southern Africa. With just a little more cash to spare, and advanced bookings, you'll find Namibia's lodges, camps and guest farms cost a fraction of the price of similar places elsewhere in the region. Here you can afford comfort and expert guides who will help you discover their own areas, instructing you in everything from tracking black rhino to understanding the native flora.

Over the last 18 years I've been lucky enough to make dozens of trips back to Namibia. I've watched tourism gradually develop and change – and on the whole it's done so positively. While there are more visitors now, these are exploring more destinations within Namibia, so the country still seems empty. There are many new lodges and guest farms, but these are spread widely and most remain small, offering personal attention and unique attractions. Namibia is still not a mass-market destination, and there's no sign that it will be.

The contribution to the economy made by visitors is increasing, and the government recognises its importance – which is vital if the wild areas that attract visitors are to be conserved. Namibia's villagers, too, are benefiting from tourism. The Kaokoveld, in particular, is home to some thriving community projects – successes that are rare in most parts of Africa. Elsewhere, new conservancies are sprouting up, where neighbouring farms join forces and return wild game to their land, replacing domestic animals.

Just as Namibia is evolving, so are the ways to travel. Until recently, flying around was strictly the preserve of those who could afford to charter their own plane. They knew that Namibia's landscapes are often most spectacular from the air, and that flying around gives a whole new perspective on the country. Now it's becoming less expensive, with tour operators tailor-making fly-in trips around the country, and charging per seat, not per plane. These hops between lodges remain more costly than driving, but they are breathtaking, and allow easy access to even the remotest corners of the Skeleton Coast and Kaokoveld.

So Namibia and trips there are changing. But every time I go, I am again surprised at how easy the travelling is, and how remarkable the country.

NOTE ON DATUM FOR GPS CO-ORDINATES For GPS co-ordinates given in this guide, note that the datum used is WSG 84 – and you must set your receiver accordingly before copying in any of these co-ordinates.

All GPS co-ordinates in this book have been expressed as degrees, minutes, and decimal fractions of a minute.

Part One

GENERAL INFORMATION

Location Southwest Africa, astride the Tropic of Capricorn and beside the South Atlantic Ocean. Its main borders are with South Africa, Botswana and Angola, though it also adjoins Zambia.

Size 824,292km²

Climate Subtropical desert climate

Status Republic

Population 1,830,330 (2001 census) 2,044,147 (2006 estimate)

Population growth per year 0.59% (2006 estimate)

Life expectancy in years at birth 43 (2006 estimate)

Capital Windhoek, population 233, 529 (2001 census), 240,000 (2006 estimate)

Main towns Swakopmund, Walvis Bay, Lüderitz

Economy Major earners: mining, including uranium, diamonds and other minerals; agriculture; tourism

GDP US$7,400 per capita (2006 estimate)

Currency Namibian dollar (N$), equivalent to (and interchangeable with) South African rand

Rate of exchange £1 = N$14.07; US$1 = N$7.09, €1 = N$9.53 (April 2007)

Language English (official), Afrikaans, German, several ethnic languages (most in Bantu and Khoisan language groups)

Religion Christianity; traditional beliefs

International telephone code +264

Time Apr–Oct GMT +1, Oct–Mar GMT +2 (except Caprivi Strip: GMT +2 all year)

Electricity 220 volts, plugs with three round pins, as in South Africa

Weights and measures Metric

Flag Diagonal red stripe bordered by narrow white stripes separates two triangles: one green; one blue with a yellow sun motif.

Public holidays New Year's Day (1 January), Independence Day (21 March), Good Friday, Easter Monday, Workers' Day (1 May), Cassinga Day (4 May), Africa Day (25 May), Ascension Day (40 days after Easter Sunday), Heroes' Day (26 August), Human Rights Day (10 December), Christmas Day (25 December), Family Day (26 December)

Tourist information www.namibiatourism.com.na

History and Economy

HISTORY

PREHISTORY

Namibia's earliest inhabitants Palaeontologists looking for evidence of the first ancestors of the human race have excavated a number of sites in southern Africa. The earliest remains yet identified are Stone Age tools dated at about 200,000 years old, which have been recovered in gravel deposits around what is now the Victoria Falls. It is thought that these probably belong to *Homo erectus*, whose hand-axes have been dated in Tanzania to half a million years old. These were hunter-gatherer people, who could use fire, make tools, and had probably developed some simple speech.

Experts divide the Stone Age into the middle, early and late periods. The transition from early to middle Stone Age technology – which is indicated by a larger range of stone tools often adapted for particular uses, and signs that these people had a greater mastery of their environment – was probably in progress around 125,000 years ago in southern Africa. The late Stone Age is characterised by people who used composite tools, those made of wood and/or bone and/or stone used together, and by the presence of a revolutionary invention: the bow and arrow. This first probably appeared about 15,000 years ago, by which time the original Namibians were already roaming the plains of Damaraland and painting on the rocks at Twyfelfontein.

Africa's Iron Age Around 3000BC, late Stone Age hunter-gatherer groups in Ethiopia, and elsewhere in north and west Africa, started to keep domestic animals, sow seeds and harvest the produce: they became the world's first farmers.

By around 1000BC these new pastoral practices had spread south into the equatorial forests of what is now Congo, to around Lake Victoria, and into the northern area of the Great Rift Valley, in northern Tanzania. However, agriculture did not spread south into the rest of central/southern Africa immediately. Only when the technology, and the tools, of iron-working became known did the practices start their relentless expansion southwards.

The spread of agriculture and Iron Age culture seems to have been a rapid move. It was brought south by Bantu-speaking Africans who were taller and heavier than the existing Khoisan-speaking inhabitants of southern Africa.

BANTU COLONISATION

Khoisan coexistence By around the time of Christ, the hunter-gatherers in Namibia seem to have been joined by pastoralists, the Khoi-khoi (or Nama people), who used a similar language involving clicks. Both belong to the Khoisan language family, as distinct from the Bantu language family. These were pastoralists who combined keeping sheep, goats and cattle with foraging.

These stock animals are not native to southern Africa and it seems likely that some Khoisan hunters and gatherers acquired stock, and the expertise to keep

3

them, from early Bantu tribes in the Zimbabwe area. As the Bantu spread south, into the relatively fertile Natal area, the Khoisan pastoralists spread west, across the Kalahari into Namibia. Their traditional gathering knowledge, and ability to survive on existing plant foods, meant that they didn't depend entirely on their stock. Hence they could expand across areas of poor grazing which would have defeated the less flexible Bantu.

By around the 9th century another group, the Damara, are recognised as living in Namibia and speaking a Khoisan language. They cultivated more than the Nama, and hence were more settled. Their precise origin is hotly debated, as they have many features common to people of Bantu origin and yet speak a Khoisan language.

The first Bantu people By the 16th century the first of the Bantu-speaking peoples arrived from the east, the Herero. Oral tradition suggests that they came south from east Africa's great lakes to Zambia, across Angola, arriving at the Kunene River around 1550. However they got here, they settled with their cattle in the north of the country and the plains of the Kaokoveld. (Note that the Himba people living in the Kaokoveld today are a sub-group of the Herero, speaking the same language.)

Where the Herero settled, the existing people clearly had to change. Some intermarried with the incoming groups; some may even have been enslaved by the newcomers. A few could shift their lifestyles to take advantage of new opportunities created by the Herero, and an unfortunate fourth group (the Bushmen of the time) started to become marginalised, remaining in areas with less agricultural potential. This was the start of a poor relationship between the cattle-herding Herero and the Bushmen.

These iron-working, cattle-herding Herero people were very successful, and as they thrived, so they began to expand their herds southwards and into central Namibia.

The early explorers Meanwhile, in the 15th century, trade between Europe and the East opened up sea routes along the Namibian coast and around the Cape of Good Hope. The first Europeans recorded as stepping on Namibian soil were the Portuguese in 1485. Diego Cão stopped briefly at Cape Cross on the Skeleton Coast and erected a limestone cross. On 8 December 1487, Bartholomeu Diaz reached Walvis Bay and then continued south to what is now Lüderitz. However, the coast was so totally barren and uninviting that even though the Portuguese had already settled in Angola, and the Dutch in the Cape, little interest was shown in Namibia.

It was only in the latter half of the 18th century when British, French and American whalers began to make use of the ports of Lüderitz and Walvis Bay, that the Dutch authorities in the Cape decided in 1793 to take possession of Walvis Bay – the only good deepwater port on the coast. A few years later, France invaded Holland, prompting England to seize control of the Cape Colony and, with it, Walvis Bay.

Even then, little was known about the interior. It wasn't until the middle of the 19th century that explorers, missionaries and traders started to venture inland, with Francis Galton and Charles John Andersson leading the way.

Oorlam incursions By the second half of the 18th century, the Dutch settlers in the Cape of South Africa were not only expanding rapidly into the interior, but they were also effectively waging war on any of the indigenous people who stood in their way. In *Africa: A Biography of a Continent*, John Reader (see *Appendix 3*) comments:

Originating from the Cape, the Oorlam people were a variety of different groups, all speaking Khoisan languages, who left the Cape because of European expansion there. Some were outlaws, others wanted space far from the Europeans. Many broke away from fixed Nama settlements to join roving Oorlam bands, led by kapteins – groups which would hunt, trade and steal for survival.

Khoisan resistance hardened as the frontier advanced during the 18th century. [The] Government [of the Cape's] edicts empowered [commando groups of settlers]... to wage war against all the region's Khoisan, who were now to be regarded as vermin. Slaughter was widespread. Official records show that commandos killed 503 Khoisan in 1774 alone, and 2,480 between 1786 and 1795. The number of killings that passed unrecorded can only be guessed at.

By 1793 the settler population in the Cape totalled 13,830 people, who between them owned 14,747 slaves.

With this pressure from the south, it is no wonder that mobile, dispossessed bands of Khoisan, known as Oorlam groups, pressed northwards over the Orange River and into southern Namibia. They often had guns and horses, and had learned some of the Europeans' ways. However, they still spoke a Khoisan language, and were of the same origins as the Nama pastoralists who had already settled in southern Namibia.

At that time, the Nama in southern Namibia seem to have been settled into a life of relatively peaceful, pastoral coexistence. Thus the arrival of a few Oorlam groups was not a problem. However, around the start of the 19th century more Oorlams came, putting more pressure on the land, and soon regular skirmishes were a feature of the area.

In 1840 the increasingly unsettled situation was calmed by an agreement between the two paramount chiefs: Oaseb of the Nama, and Jonker Afrikaner of the Oorlam people. There was already much intermingling of the two groups, and so accommodating each other made sense – especially given the expansion of Herero groups further north.

The deal split the lands of southern Namibia between the various Nama and Oorlam groups, whilst giving the land between the Kuiseb and the Swakop rivers to the Oorlams. Further, Jonker Afrikaner was given rights over the people north of the Kuiseb, up to Waterberg.

Nama–Herero conflict By around the middle of the 18th century, the Herero people had expanded beyond Kaokoland, spreading at least as far south as the Swakop River. Their expansion south was now effectively blocked by Oorlam groups, led by Jonker Afrikaner, who won several decisive battles against Herero people around 1835 – resulting in his Afrikaner followers stealing many Herero cattle, and becoming the dominant power in central Namibia. From 1840, Jonker Afrikaner and his Oorlam followers created a buffer zone between the Hereros expanding from the north, and the relatively stable Nama groups in the south.

EUROPEAN COLONISATION

The missionaries In the early 1800s, missionaries were gradually moving into southern Namibia. The London Missionary Society and the German Rhenish and Finnish Lutheran Mission societies were all represented. These were important for several reasons. Firstly, they tended to settle in one place, which became the nucleus around which the local Nama people would permanently settle. Often the missionaries would introduce the local people to different ways of cultivation: a further influence to settle in permanent villages, which gradually became larger.

Secondly, they acted as a focal point for traders, who would navigate through the territory from one mission to the next. This effectively set up Namibia's first trade routes – routes that soon became conduits for the local Nama groups to obtain European goods, from guns and ammunition to alcohol. It seems that the missionaries sometimes provided firearms directly to the local people for protection. Whilst understandable, the net effect was that the whole area became a more dangerous place.

In 1811, Reverend Heinrich Schmelen founded Bethanie, and more missions followed. By December 1842, Rhenish missionaries were established where Windhoek now stands, surrounded by about 1,000 of Jonker Afrikaner's followers. The settlement soon started trading with the coast, and within a few years there was a steady supply of guns arriving.

Nama conflict In 1861 Jonker Afrikaner died while returning from a raid he had mounted on the Owambo people (a group of Bantu origin who had settled in the far north of the country and displaced some of the Hereros). Jonker's death left a power vacuum in central Namibia.

There were many skirmishes for control during the rest of the 1860s, and much politicking and switching of alliances between the rival Nama groups (some of Oorlam descent). The main protagonists included the Witboois from around Gibeon, the Afrikaners based in Windhoek, the Swartboois, the Blondelswarts, the Topnaar and the Red Nation.

The traders By around 1850 many hunters and traders were penetrating Namibia's interior, in search of adventure and profit – usually in the form of ivory and ostrich feathers. Amongst these, Charles John Andersson was particularly important, both for his own role in shaping events, and also for the clear documentation that he left behind, including the fascinating books *Lake Ngami* and *The River Okavango* (see *Appendix 3*) – chronicling his great journeys of the late 1850s.

In 1860 he bought up the assets of a mining company, and set up a centre for trading at Otjimbingwe, a very strategic position on the Swakop River, halfway between Walvis Bay and Windhoek. (Now it is at the crossroads of the D1953 and the D1976.) In the early 1860s he traded with the Nama groups in the area, and started to open up routes into the Herero lands further north and east. However, after losing cattle to a Nama raid in 1861, he recruited hunters (some the contemporary equivalent of mercenaries) to expand his operations and protect his interests.

In 1863 the eldest son of Jonker Afrikaner led a foolish raid on Otjimbingwe. He was defeated and killed by Andersson's men, adding to the leadership crisis amongst the Nama groups. By 1864 Andersson had formed an alliance with the paramount Herero chief, Kamaherero, and together they led a large army into battle with the Afrikaner Namas at Windhoek. This was indecisive, but did clearly mark the end of Nama domination of central Namibia, as well as inflicting a wound on Andersson from which he never fully recovered.

The peace of 1870 During the late 1860s the centre of Namibia was often in a state of conflict. The Hereros under Kamaherero were vying for control with the various Nama clans, as Charles Andersson and his traders became increasingly important by forming and breaking alliances with them all.

After several defeats, the Nama kaptein Jan Jonker led an army of Afrikaners to Okahandja in 1870 to make peace with Kamaherero. This was brokered by the German Wesleyan missionary Hugo Hahn – who had arrived in Windhoek in 1844, but been replaced swiftly after Jonker Afrikaner had complained about him, and requested his replacement by his missionary superiors.

This treaty effectively subdued the Afrikaners, and Hahn also included a provision for the Basters, who had migrated recently from the Cape, to settle at Rehoboth. The Afrikaners were forced to abandon Windhoek, and Herero groups occupied the area. Thus the Basters around Rehoboth effectively became the buffer between the Herero groups to the north, and the Namas to the south.

The 1870s was a relatively peaceful era, which enabled the missionaries and, especially, the various traders to extend their influence throughout the centre of the country. This most affected the Nama groups in the south, who began to trade more and more with the Cape. Guns, alcohol, coffee, sugar, beads, materials and much else flowed in. To finance these imports, local Nama chiefs and kapteins charged traders and hunters to cross their territory, and granted them licences to exploit the wildlife.

The Hereros, too, traded; but mainly for guns. Their social system valued cattle most highly, and so breeding bigger herds meant more to them than the new Western goods. Thus they emerged into the 1880s stronger than before, whilst the power of many of the Nama groups had waned.

THE SCRAMBLE FOR AFRICA In the last few decades of the 19th century the Portuguese, the British, the French, and Leopold II of Belgium were starting to embark on the famous 'Scramble for Africa'. Germany had long eschewed the creation of colonies, and Bismarck is widely quoted as stating: 'So long as I am Chancellor we shan't pursue a colonial policy.'

However, in March 1878 the English government of South Africa's Cape formally annexed an enclave around Walvis Bay. (The British had been asked earlier by missionaries to help instil order in the heartland of Namibia, but they didn't feel that it was worth the effort.)

In late 1883 a German merchant called Adolf Lüderitz started to buy land on the coast. He established the town named Lüderitzbucht – usually referred to now as Lüderitz – and began trading with the local Nama groups. (It was news of this act that was said to have finally prompted Britain to make Bechuanaland a protectorate.)

Faced with much internal pressure, Bismarck reversed his policy in May 1884. He dispatched a gunboat to Lüderitz and in July claimed Togo and Cameroon as colonies. By August Britain had agreed to Germany's claims on Lüderitz, from which sprang the German colony of South West Africa. Lüderitz itself was bought out a few years later by the newly formed German Colonial Company for South West Africa, and shortly after that the administration of the area was transferred directly to Germany's control.

In May 1884, Portugal proposed an international conference to address the territorial conflicts of the colonial powers in the Congo. This was convened in Berlin, with no Africans present, and over the next few years the colonial powers parcelled Africa up and split it between them. Amongst many territorial dealings, mostly involving pen-and-ruler decisions on the map of Africa, a clearly defined border between Britain's new protectorate of Bechuanaland and Germany's South West Africa was established in 1890 – and Britain ceded a narrow corridor of land to Germany. This was subsequently named after the German Chancellor, Count von Caprivi, as the Caprivi Strip.

German South West Africa After a decade of relative peace, the 1880s brought problems to central Namibia again, with fighting between the Hereros, the

Basters, and various Nama groups, notably the Afrikaners and the Swartboois. However, with German annexation in 1884 a new power had arrived. For the first five years, the official German presence in South West Africa was limited to a few officials stationed at Otjimbingwe. However, they had begun the standard colonial tactic of exploiting small conflicts by encouraging the local leaders to sign 'protection' treaties with Germany.

The Hereros, under Chief Maherero, signed in 1885, after which the German Commissioner Göring wrote to Hendrik Witbooi – the leader of the Witbooi Namas who occupied territory from Gibeon to Gobabis – insisting that he desist from attacking the Hereros, who were now under German protection. Witbooi wrote to Maherero, to dissuade him from making a 'pact with the devil' – he was, perhaps, ahead of his time in seeing this German move as an opening gambit in their bid for total control of Namibia.

In 1889 the first 21 German soldiers, Schutztruppe, arrived. More followed in 1890, by which time they had established a fort in Windhoek. That same year Maherero died, which enabled the German authorities to increase their influence in the internal politics of succession which brought Samuel Maherero to be paramount chief of the Herero. By 1892 the first contingent of settlers (over 50 people) had made their homes in Windhoek.

A fair trade? The 1890s and early 1900s saw a gradual erosion of the power and wealth of all Namibia's existing main groups in favour of the Germans. Gradually traders and adventurers bought more and more land from both the Nama and the Herero, aided by credit-in-advance agreements. A rinderpest outbreak in 1897 decimated the Herero's herds, and land sales were the obvious way to repay their debts. Gradually the Herero lost their lands and tension grew. The Rhenish Missionary Society saw the evil, and pressurised the German government to create areas where the Herero *could not* sell their land. Small enclaves were thus established, but these didn't address the wider issues.

THE 20TH CENTURY
Namibian war of resistance 1904–07 As land was progressively bought up, or sometimes simply taken from the local inhabitants by colonists, various skirmishes and small uprisings developed. The largest started in October 1903 with the Blondelswarts near Warmbad, which distracted most of the German Schutztruppe in the south. See *Appendix 3* for details of Mark Cocker's excellent *Rivers of Blood, Rivers of Gold* which gives a full account of this war.

The Herero nation had become increasingly unhappy about its loss of land, and in January 1904 Samuel Maherero ordered a Herero uprising against the German colonial forces. Initially he was clear to exclude as targets Boer and English settlers and German women and children. Simultaneously he appealed to Hendrik Witbooi, and other Nama leaders, to join battle – they, however, stayed out of the fight.

Initially the Hereros had success in taking many German farms and smaller outposts, and in severing the railway line between Swakopmund and Windhoek. However, later in 1904, the German General Leutwein was replaced by von Trotha – who had a reputation for brutal oppression after his time in east Africa. Backed by domestic German opinion demanding a swift resolution, von Trotha led a large German force including heavy artillery against the Hereros. By August 1904 the Hereros were pushed back to their stronghold of Waterberg, with its permanent waterholes. On 11 August, the Germans attacked, and the battle raged all day. Though not decisive, the Herero's spirit was beaten by the superior firepower and they fled east, into the Kalahari. Many perished. Sources conflict about exactly how many Herero lost their lives, but the battle at Waterberg certainly broke their resistance to the Germans.

Thereafter, somewhat late to be effective, Hendrik Witbooi's people also revolted against the Germans, and wrote encouraging the other Nama groups to do the same. The Red Nation, Topnaar, Swartbooi and Blondelswarts joined in attacking the Germans, though the last were largely incapacitated after their battles the previous year. The Basters stayed out of the fight.

For several years these Nama groups waged an effective guerrilla campaign against the colonial forces, using the waterless sands of the Kalahari as a haven in which the German troops were ineffective. However, in 1905 Hendrik Witbooi was killed, and January 1907 saw the last fighters sue for peace.

German consolidation With South West Africa under stable German control, there was an influx of German settler families and the colony began to develop rapidly. The settlers were given large plots of the country's most productive lands, the railway network was expanded, and many of the towns began to grow. The non-European Namibians were increasingly marginalised, and simply used as a source of labour.

The building of the railway to Lüderitz led to the discovery of diamonds around there in 1908, and the resulting boom encouraged an influx of prospectors and German opportunists. By that time the mine at Tsumeb was already thriving, and moving its copper produce south on the newly built railway.

The German settlers thrived until the declaration of World War I, and between 1907 and 1914 the colonists were granted self-rule from Germany, a number of the main towns were declared municipalities, and many of Namibia's existing civic buildings were constructed.

World War I At the onset of World War I, Britain encouraged South Africa to push north and wrest South West Africa from the Germans. In July 1915, the German colonial troops surrendered to South African forces at Khorab – a memorial now marks the spot. At the end of the war, Namibia became a League of Nations 'trust territory', assigned to the Union of South Africa as 'a sacred trust in the name of civilisation' to 'promote to the utmost the material and moral well-being of its inhabitants'. The Caprivi Strip was incorporated back into Bechuanaland (though it was returned 20 years later).

THE FINAL COLONISTS
South African rule After overcoming their initial differences, new colonists from South Africa and the existing German colonists soon discovered a common interest – the unabashed exploitation of the native population whose well-being they were supposed to be protecting.

Gradually more and more of the land in central Namibia was given to settler families, often Boers from South Africa rather than Germans from Europe. The native population was restricted to various 'native areas' – usually poor land which couldn't be easily farmed by the settlers: Bushmanland and Hereroland in the Kalahari, Damaraland and Kaokoland bordering on the Namib. Much of the rest of the black population was confined to a strip of land in the north, as far from South Africa as possible, to serve as a reservoir of cheap labour for the mines – which South Africa was developing to extract the country's mineral wealth.

In 1947, after World War II, South Africa formally announced to the United Nations its intention to annex the territory. The UN, which had inherited responsibility for the League of Nations trust territories, opposed the plan, arguing that 'the African inhabitants of South West Africa have not yet achieved political autonomy'. Until 1961, the UN insisted on this point. Year after year it was systematically ignored by South Africa's regime.

The struggle for independence Between 1961 and 1968, the UN tried to annul the trusteeship and establish Namibia's independence. Legal pressure, however, was ineffective and some of the Namibian people led by the South West African People's Organisation (SWAPO) chose to fight for their freedom with arms. The first clashes occurred on 26 August 1966.

In 1968, the UN finally declared the South African occupation of the country as illegal and changed its name to Namibia. Efforts by the majority of the UN General Assembly to enforce this condemnation with economic sanctions were routinely vetoed by the Western powers of the Security Council – they had vested interests in the multi-national companies in Namibia and would stand to lose from the implementation of sanctions.

The independence of Angola in 1975 affected Namibia's struggle for freedom, by providing SWAPO guerrillas with a friendly rearguard. As a consequence the guerrilla war was stepped up, resulting in increased political pressure on South Africa. But strong internal economic factors also played heavily in the political arena. Up to independence, the status quo had preserved internal inequalities and privileges. Black Africans (approaching 90% of the population) consumed only 12.8% of the gross domestic product (GDP). Meanwhile the inhabitants of European origin (10% of the population) received 81.5% of the GDP. Three-quarters of the agricultural production was in the hands of white farmers. Although average per-capita income was (and remains) one of the highest in Africa, whites earned on average over 17 times more than blacks. The white population clearly feared they had a great deal to lose if a majority government came to power and addressed itself to these racially based inequalities.

However, external South African economic factors had perhaps the greatest effect in blocking Namibian independence. South African and multi-national companies dominated the Namibian economy and carried massive political influence. Prior to independence, the Consolidated Diamond Mines Company (a subsidiary of Anglo-American) contributed in taxes 40% of South Africa's administrative budget in Namibia. Multi-nationals benefited from extremely generous facilities granted to them by the South African administration in Namibia. According to one estimate, the independence of Namibia would represent costs for South Africa of US$240 million in lost exports, and additional outlays of US$144 million to import foreign products.

In South Africa the official government view stressed the danger that a SWAPO government might present to Namibia's minority tribes (since SWAPO membership is drawn almost exclusively from the Owambo ethnic group), whilst taking few serious steps towards a negotiated settlement for Namibian independence.

On the military side, South Africa stepped up its campaign against SWAPO, even striking at bases in southern Angola. It also supported Jonas Savimbi's UNITA (National Union for the Total Independence of Angola) forces in their struggle against the Soviet/Cuban-backed MPLA (Popular Movement for the Liberation of Angola) government in Luanda. Meanwhile, Cuban troops poured into Angola and aggravated the situation further by threatening the South African forces in Namibia.

Resolution 435 On the diplomatic front, a proposal (Resolution 435) put forward by the UN security council called for, amongst other things, the cessation of hostilities, the return of refugees, the repeal of discriminatory legislation and the holding of UN-supervised elections. South Africa blocked this by tying any such agreement to the withdrawal of Cuban troops from Angola, and demanding guarantees that its investments in Namibia would not be affected. SWAPO refused to agree to special benefits for the European population and other minority groups, nor would it accept predetermined limitations to constitutional change following independence.

By 1987, all the states involved in the conflict were showing clear signs of wanting an end to hostilities. After 14 years of uninterrupted war, Angola's economy was on the brink of collapse. (The war is calculated to have cost the country US$13 billion.) On the other side, South Africa's permanent harassment of Angola, and military occupation of Namibia, were costing the regime dearly both economically and diplomatically.

In December 1988, after prolonged US-mediated negotiations, an agreement was reached between South Africa, Angola and Cuba for a phased withdrawal of Cuban troops from Angola to be linked to the withdrawal of South African troops from Namibia and the implementation of Resolution 435.

INDEPENDENCE The independence process began on 1 April 1989, and was achieved with the help of the United Nations Transition Assistance Group (UNTAG). This consisted of some 7,000 people from 110 countries who worked from nearly 200 locations within the country to ensure free and fair elections and as smooth a transition period to independence as was possible.

In November 1989, 710,000 Namibians (a 97% turnout) voted in the members of the National Assembly which would draft the country's first constitution. SWAPO won decisively, but without the two-thirds majority it needed to write the nation's constitution single-handedly, thereby allaying the fears of Namibia's minorities. The 72 elected members (68 men and four women) of the Constituent Assembly, representing between them seven different political parties, soon reached agreement on a constitution for the new Namibia, which was subsequently hailed as one of the world's most democratic. Finally, at 00.20 on 21 March 1990, I watched as the Namibian flag replaced South Africa's over Windhoek, witnessed by Pérez de Cuéllar, the UN Secretary-General, F W de Klerk, the South African President, and Sam Nujoma, Namibia's first president.

The country's mood was peaceful and, on the day, ecstatic. There was a tremendous feeling of optimism, as (arguably) Africa's last colonial territory had earned its independence – after sustained diplomatic pressure and a bitter liberation struggle that stretched back to the turn of the century.

POLITICS SINCE INDEPENDENCE Since the start there has been every indication that Namibia would stand by its constitution and develop into a peaceful and prosperous state. Walvis Bay, previously disputed by South Africa, was transferred to Windhoek's control on 28 February 1994, and its relations with neighbouring countries remain good.

In December 1994 general elections for the National Assembly returned SWAPO to power, with 53 out of 72 seats, and extended Sam Nujoma's presidency for a further five years. The main opposition among the remaining six parties continues to be the Democratic Turnhalle Alliance (DTA), although it is still haunted by the stigma of its co-operation with the former South African regime.

Under the terms of the constitution, which state that the president may serve only two terms in office, Sam Nujoma should have stepped down in 1999. Despite that, he went on to serve a third term, prompting concerns that the carefully crafted constitution was being pushed to one side. It wasn't until November 2004, when SWAPO was again returned to power with an overwhelming majority of the votes, that Nujoma made way for his chosen successor, while himself remaining head of the party. While SWAPO consolidated their position with 55 seats in the National Assembly, the other six parties between them shared just under a quarter of the vote.

The new president, Hifikepunye Pohamba, is generally considered to be both liberal and honest, and has pledged to continue his predecessor's policies. Controversially, particularly in the light of recent experiences in Zimbabwe, these include the redistribution of land. Namibia's commercial farmers have watched with concern in recent years as the president appeared to align himself with President Mugabe on the policy of land reform. Despite that, the government seemed until recently to have adopted a more even-handed approach than its neighbour. Until 2004, land purchased for redistribution was based on mutual agreement between buyer and seller. Since then, however, a new policy has been implemented under which reform is expected to be speeded up. Having said that, all of these land purchases have remained at market value, and are being financed largely with grants of aid money by Germany, and other donor nations. With compulsory purchase now on the agenda, President Pohamba has signalled that there will be no change of tack. This remains a hot political topic for activists within Namibia, and a source of concern for commercial farmers – but much less of an issue for most normal Namibians as the land issue here has never been as big an issue with normal people as it is in Zimbabwe.

GOVERNMENT AND CONSTITUTION

The Republic of Namibia's modern constitution, adopted on independence in 1990, was hailed as one of the world's most democratic. Its entrenched Bill of Rights provides for freedom of speech, press, assembly, association and religion. It also set up a bicameral Westminster-style parliament, with a strong executive and independent judiciary.

General elections for the first House of Parliament, the National Assembly, are held every five years. The members of the second House of Parliament, the National Council, are drawn from 13 Regional Councils, which are elected every six years. The constitution limits the president to a maximum of two terms of office – although Sam Nujoma's third term in office stretched this to breaking point in 1999.

ECONOMY

Before independence, the South African administration controlled the economy along traditional colonial lines. The country produced goods it did not consume but imported everything it needed, including food. Namibia still exports maize, meat and fish, and imports rice and wheat. However, although about 60% of the workforce is employed in agriculture, the country's commercial agriculture is limited by a lack of water, while large sections of the wetter northern regions are already farmed intensively by subsistence farmers.

Namibia inherited a well-developed infrastructure and considerable remaining mineral wealth. Mining is the mainstay of the economy, accounting for about 25% of the country's GDP. There are important reserves of uranium, lead, zinc, tin, silver, copper and tungsten, as well as very rich deposits of alluvial diamonds.

Tourism, albeit on a relatively small scale, also plays an important role in the formal economy. In the first years of independence, from 2003, the number of visitors grew steadily by about 15% per year. A decade later, however, the numbers had fallen, then settled, with statistics for arrivals from overseas in 2003 indicating

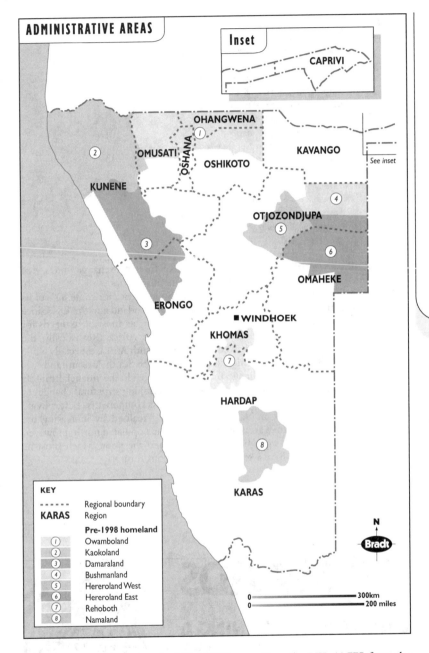

ADMINISTRATIVE AREAS

Inset

CAPRIVI

OHANGWENA
①

OMUSATI

OSHANA

OSHIKOTO

KAVANGO

See inset

②

KUNENE

③

OTJOZONDJUPA
⑤

④

⑥

OMAHEKE

ERONGO

■ WINDHOEK

KHOMAS
⑦

HARDAP

⑧

KARAS

KEY

- - - - - Regional boundary

KARAS Region

Pre-1998 homeland

①	Owamboland
②	Kaokoland
③	Damaraland
④	Bushmanland
⑤	Hereroland West
⑥	Hereroland East
⑦	Rehoboth
⑧	Namaland

N

Bradt

0	300km
0	200 miles

a total of 695,000 visitors, of which 19,291 were from the UK, 11,775 from the USA, and 58,036 from Germany. The potential for sustained growth in tourism, provided the increases are steady and well managed, remains significant.

Namibia's main attractions for visitors are stunning scenery, pristine wilderness areas and first-class wildlife. As long as the country remains safe and its wilderness areas are maintained, then the country's potential for quality tourism is unrivalled in Africa. Already tourism is a powerful earner of foreign exchange and a vital support for numerous local community-development schemes.

Economically, Namibia remains dependent on South Africa for some 80% of its trade; its other main trading partners are Germany, Switzerland and the UK. Since the country is still establishing its own industries, it meets most of its needs for manufactured goods by importing them from South Africa. Realistically, the economy is likely to stay closely involved with that of South Africa, especially while Namibia continues to peg its currency to the value of the South African rand.

The revenue and foreign exchange from mining provide the financial muscle for the government's agenda. The government is developing structural changes to make the economy more equitable, and to diversify its components. Better living conditions for the majority of Namibians are being realised by increasing the productivity of the subsistence areas, particularly in the populated north. However, there remains an enormous gap between the rich and the poor, which must be closed if the country is to have a secure and prosperous future.

2

People and Culture

PEOPLE

THE POPULATION At the time of the 2001 census, Namibia's population stood at 1,830,330, an increase of around 29% over the previous decade. That's a growth rate of a little less than 3% per year. By 2006, the population stood at an estimated 2,044,147, with the growth rate reduced to just 0.59% per year.

The effect of HIV/AIDS on the Namibian population has been devastating. In 2003, 21.3% of the population was said to be affected, with deaths linked to the disease during that year totalling around 16,000, and an estimated 57,000 children orphaned as a direct result. Statistics at the turn of the century indicated that the average life expectancy for a Namibian was 65 years, but this is now estimated at just 45 years. On a more positive note, Namibia's doctor/patient ratio is one of the best in Africa, with one doctor for every 3,390 people, and about five hospital beds per 1,000 people.

While the population is densest in the north (near the Angolan border), where rainfall is heaviest, and in the capital, Windhoek, the overall density is exceptionally low: only around two people per square kilometre. About 38.2% of Namibia's people are under 15 years of age, whilst only 3.7% are over 65. Around 87.5% of the population are black African in origin, and the remaining 12.5% are mostly of European or mixed race.

Of course, the statistics say nothing of the charm of many Namibians. If you venture into the rural areas you will often find that Namibians are curious about you. Chat to them openly and you will find most to be delightful. They will be pleased to help you where they can, and as keen to help you learn about them and their country as they are interested in your lifestyle and what brings you to their country.

A note on 'tribes' The people of Africa are often viewed, from abroad, as belonging to a multitude of culturally and linguistically distinct 'tribes' – which are often portrayed as being at odds with each other. Whilst there is certainly an enormous variety of different ethnic groups in Africa, most are closely related to their neighbours in terms of language, beliefs and way of life. Modern historians eschew the simplistic tags of 'tribes', noting that such groupings change with time.

Sometimes the word tribe is used to describe a group of people who all speak the same language; it may be used to mean those who follow a particular leader or to refer to all the inhabitants of a certain area at a given time. In any case, 'tribe' is a vague word that is used differently for different purposes. The term 'clan' (blood relations) is a smaller, more precisely defined, unit – though rather too precise for our broad discussions here.

Certainly groups of people or clans who share similar languages and cultural beliefs do band together and often, in time, develop 'tribal' identities. However, it is wrong to then extrapolate and assume that their ancestors will have had the same groupings and allegiances centuries ago.

In Africa, as elsewhere in the world, history is recorded by the winners. Here the winners, the ruling class, may be the descendants of a small group of intruders who achieved dominance over a larger, long-established community. Over the years, the history of that ruling class (the winners) usually becomes regarded as the history of the whole community, or tribe. Two 'tribes' have thus become one, with one history – which will reflect the origins of that small group of intruders, and not the ancestors of the majority of the current tribe.

ETHNIC GROUPS When the colonial powers carved up Africa, the divisions between the countries bore virtually no resemblance to the traditional areas of the various ethnic groups, many of which therefore ended up split between two or more countries. As you will see, there are cultural differences between the groups in different parts of Namibia, but they are only a little more pronounced than those between the states of the USA, or the regions of the (relatively tiny) UK.

There continues to be a great deal of inter-marriage and mixing of these various peoples and cultures – perhaps more so than there has ever been, because of the efficiency of modern transport systems. Generally, there is very little friction between these communities (whose boundaries, as we have said, are indistinct) and Namibia's various peoples live peacefully together.

In Namibia, which is typical of any large African country, historians identify numerous ethnic groups. The main ones are detailed below, arranged alphabetically. Apart from Afrikaans, their languages fall into two main families: Khoisan and Bantu. The population sizes given are based on surveys done during the 1980s, and adjusted according to estimated average growth rates since then.

Basters These Afrikaans-speaking people are descendants of indigenous Hottentot women and the Dutch settlers who first arrived at the Cape in the early 17th century. The original 'coloured' or 'bastard' children found themselves rejected by both the white and the black communities in the Cape, so keeping together they relocated themselves further north away from the colonialists. Proudly calling themselves 'Basters', they set up farming communities and developed their own distinct social and cultural structures.

During the 1860s, white settlers began to push into these areas so, to avoid confrontation, the Basters crossed the Orange River in 1868 and moved northwards once again. Trying to keep out of the way of the warring Hereros and Namas, they founded Rehoboth in 1871 and set up their own system of government under a Kaptein (headman) and a Volksraad (legislative council). Their support of the German colonial troops during the tribal uprisings brought them later protection and privileges.

Demands for self-rule and independence were repressed until the Rehoboth Gebiet was granted the status of an independent state in the 1970s. This move by the South African administration was made with the aim of reinforcing racial divisions amongst the non-whites – rather like in the South African 'independent homelands'.

Today, Namibia's Basters still have a strong sense of identity and make up just under 3% of the population. Most still live and work as stock or crop farmers in the good cattle-grazing land around Rehoboth. Their traditional crafts include products like *karosses* (blankets), rugs, wall-hangings and cushion covers made of cured skins.

Bushmen There is not another social/language group on this planet which has been studied, written about, filmed and researched more than the Bushmen, or San, of the Kalahari, although they currently comprise only about 3% of Namibia's population. Despite this, or indeed because of it, popular conceptions about them, fed by their image in the media, are often strikingly out of step with the realities. Thus they warrant a separate section devoted to them here.

The aim of these next few pages is to try and explain some of the roots of the misconceptions, to look at some of the realities, and to make you think. Although I have spent a lot of time with Bushmen in the Kalahari, it is difficult to separate fact from oft-repeated, glossy fiction. If parts of this discussion seem disparate, it's a reflection of this difficulty.

Recent scientific observations on the Khoisan Our view of the Bushmen is partly informed by some basic anthropological, linguistic and genetic research, mostly applying to the Khoisan, which is worth outlining to set the scene.

Anthropology The first fossil records that we have of our human ancestors date back to at least about 60,000 years ago in east Africa. These are likely to have been the ancestors of everyone living today.

Archaeological finds from parts of the Kalahari show that human beings have lived here for at least 40,000 years. These are generally agreed to have been the ancestors of the modern Khoisan peoples living in Botswana today. (The various peoples of the Khoi and the Bushmen are known collectively as the Khoisan. All have relatively light golden-brown skin, almond-shaped eyes and high cheekbones. Their stature is generally small and slight, and they are now found across southern Africa.)

Language research Linguists have grouped all the world's languages into around 20 linguistic families. Of these, four are very different from the rest. All these four are African families – and they include the Khoisan and the Niger-Congo (Bantu) languages.

This is amongst the evidence that has led linguists to believe that human language evolved in Africa, and further analysis has suggested that this was probably amongst the ancestors of the Khoisan.

The Khoisan languages are distinguished by their wide repertoire of clicking sounds. Don't mistake these for simple: they are very sophisticated. It was observed by Dunbar (see *Appendix 3*) that, 'From the phonetic point of view these [the Khoisan languages] are the world's most complex languages. To speak one of them fluently is to exploit human phonetic ability to the full.'

At some point the Khoisan languages diverged from a common ancestor, and today three distinct groups exist: the northern, central and southern. Languages gradually evolve and change as different groups of people split up and move to new areas, isolated from their old contacts. Thus the evolution of each language is specific to each group, and reflected in the classifications described later in this chapter.

According to Michael Main (see *Appendix 3*), the northern group are San and today they live west of the Okavango and north of Ghanzi, with representatives found as far afield as Angola. The southern group are also San, who live in the area between Kang and Bokspits in Botswana. The central group are Khoe, living in central Botswana, and extending north to the eastern Okavango and Kasane, and west into Namibia, where they are known as the Nama.

Each of these three Khoisan language groups has many dialects. These have some similarities, but they are not closely related, and some are different to the point where there is no mutual understanding. Certain dialects are so restricted that only a small family group speaks them; it was reported recently that one San language died out completely with the death of the last speaker.

This huge number of dialects, and variation in languages, reflects the relative isolation of the various speakers, most of whom now live in small family groups as the Kalahari's arid environment cannot sustain large groups of people living together in one place as hunter-gatherers.

In Namibia, the three main groups are the Haixom in the northern districts of Otavi, Tsumeb and Grootfontein; the !Kung in Bushmanland; and the Mbarankwengo in west Caprivi.

Genetic discoveries Most genetically normal men have an X and a Y chromosome, whilst women have two X chromosomes. Unlike the other 22 pairs of (non-sex) chromosomes that each human has, there is no opportunity for the Y chromosome to 'swap' or 'share' its DNA with any other chromosome. Thus all the information in a man's Y chromosome will usually be passed on, without change, to all of his sons.

However, very rarely a single 'letter' in the Y chromosome will be altered as it's being passed on, thus causing a permanent change in the chromosome's genetic sequence. This will then be the start of a new lineage of slightly different Y chromosomes, which will be inherited by all future male descendants.

In November 2000, Professor Ronald Davis and a team of Stanford researchers (see *Appendix 3*) claimed to have traced back this lineage to a single individual man, and that a small group of east Africans (Sudanese and Ethiopians) and Khoisan are the closest present-day relatives of this original man. That is, their genetic make-up is closest to his. (It's a scientific 'proof' of the biblical Adam, if you like.)

This is still a very contentious finding, with subsequent researchers suggesting at least ten original male sources ('Adams') – and so although this is interesting, the jury remains out on the precise details of all these findings. If you're interested in the latest on this, then you'll find a lot about it on the web – start searching with keywords: 'Khoisan Y chromosome'.

Historical views of the Bushmen Despite much evidence and research, our views of the Bushmen seem to have changed relatively little since both the Bantu groups and the first Europeans arrived in southern Africa.

The settlers' view Since the first Bantu farmer started migrating south through east Africa, the range of territory occupied by the foragers, whose Stone Age technology had dominated the continent, began to condense. By the time the first white settlers appeared in the Cape, the Khoisan people were already restricted to Africa's southwestern corners and the Kalahari.

All over the world, farmers occupy clearly demarcated areas of land, whereas foragers will move more and often leave less trace of their presence. In Africa, this made it easier for farmers, first black then white, to ignore any traditional land rights that belonged to foraging people.

Faced with the loss of territory for hunting and gathering, the foragers – who, by this time were already being called 'Bushmen' – made enemies of the farmers by killing cattle. They waged a guerrilla war, shooting poison arrows at parties of men who set out to massacre them. They were feared and loathed by the settlers, who, however, captured and valued their children as servants.

Some of the Khoisan retreated north from the Cape – like the ancestors of Namibia's Nama people. Others were forced to labour on the settlers' farms, or were thrown into prison for hunting animals or birds which had been their traditional prey, but which were now designated property of the Crown.

This story is told by Robert J Gordon in *The Bushman Myth: The Making of a Namibian Underclass* (see *Appendix 3*). He shows that throughout history the hunter-gathering Bushmen have been at odds with populations of settlers who divided up and 'owned' the land in the form of farms. The European settlers proved to be their most determined enemy, embarking on a programme of legislation and massacre. Many Bushmen died in prison, with many more shot as 'vermin'.

Thus the onslaught of farmers on the hunter-gatherers accelerated between the 1800s and the mid-1900s. This helped to ensure that hunter-gathering as a lifestyle continued to be practical only in marginal areas that couldn't be economically farmed – like the Kalahari. Archaeological evidence suggests that hunter-gatherer peoples have lived for about 60,000 years at sites like the Tsodilo Hills.

Western views Though settlers in the Cape interacted with Khoisan people, so did Europe and the US, in a very limited way. Throughout the 1800s and early 1900s a succession of Khoisan people were effectively enslaved and brought to Europe and the US for exhibition. Sometimes this was under the guise of anthropology, but usually it didn't claim to be anything more than entertainment.

One of the first was the 'Hottentot Venus' – a woman who was probably of Khoisan extraction who was exhibited around London and Paris from 1810 to 1815, as an erotic curiosity for aristocrats.

A string of others followed. For example, the six Khoisan people exhibited at the Coney Island Pleasure Resort, beside New York, and later in London in the 1880s and billed as the 'missing link between apes and men', and the 'wild dancing Bushman' known as Franz brought to England around 1913 by Paddy Hepston (see Parsons's piece in *Botswana Notes & Records*, detailed in *Appendix 3*).

In the 1950s a researcher from Harvard, John Marshall, came to the Kalahari to study the !Kung San. He described a peaceful people living in harmony with nature, amidst a land that provided all their needs. The groups had a deep spirituality and no real hierarchy: it seemed like the picture of a modern Eden (especially when viewed through post-war eyes). Marshall was a natural cameraman and made a film that follows the hunt of a giraffe by four men over a five-day period. It swiftly became a classic, both in and outside of anthropological circles.

Further research agreed, with researchers noting a great surfeit of protein in the diet of the !Kung San and low birth rates akin to modern industrial societies.

Again the Bushmen were seen as photogenic and sources of good copy and good images. Their lives were portrayed in romantic, spiritual terms in the book and film *The Lost World of the Kalahari* by Laurens van der Post (see *Appendix 3*). This documentary really ignited the worldwide interest in the Bushmen and led to subsequent films such as *The Gods Must Be Crazy*. All the images conveyed an idyllic view of the Bushmen as untainted by contact with the modern world.

The reality The reality was much less rosy than the first researchers thought. Some of their major misconceptions have been outlined particularly clearly in chapter 13 of John Reader's *Africa: A Biography of the Continent* (see *Appendix 3*). He points out that far from an ideal diet, the nutrition of the Bushmen was often critically limited, lacking vitamins and fatty acids associated with a lack of animal fat in their diet. Far from a stable population with a low birth rate, it seems likely that there had been a decline in the birth rate in the last few generations. The likely cause for this was periods of inadequate nourishment during the year when they lost weight from lack of food, stress and the great exertions of their lifestyle.

In fact, it seems likely that the San, whom we now see as foragers, are people who, over the last two millennia, have become relegated to an underclass by the relentless advance of the black and white farmers who did not recognise their original rights to their traditional land.

The Bushmen today and the media Though scientific thought has moved on since the 1950s, much of the media has not. The Bushmen are still perceived to be hot news.

The outpost of Tsumkwe is the centre for many of the Bushmen communities in Namibia. It's a tiny crossroads with a school and a handful of buildings, in a remote corner of northeastern Namibia. Despite its isolation, by 2001 this desert outpost was hosting no fewer than 22 film crews per year. Yes, really; that's an average of almost two full-scale film crews each month – not counting a whole host of other print journalists and photographers. These numbers are probably even greater now.

Talk to virtually any of the directors and you'll realise that they arrive with very clear ideas about the images that they want to capture. They all think they're one of the first, they think they're original, and they want to return home with images which match their preconceived ideas about the Bushmen as 'the last primitive hunter-gatherers'.

As an example, you'll often see pictures in the media of Bushmen hunters in traditional dress walking across a hot, barren salt pan. When asked to do these shoots the Bushman's usual comment is, 'Why? There's no point. We'd never go looking for anything there.' But the shots look spectacular and win prizes ... so the photographers keep asking for them. From the Bushmen's perspective, they get paid for the shots, so why not pose for the camera? I'd do the same!

Thus our current image of the Bushmen is really one that *we* are constantly recreating. It's the one that we expect. But it doesn't necessarily conform to any reality. So on reflection, popular thinking hasn't moved on much from Marshall's first film in the 1950s.

Current life for the Bushmen Looking at the current lifestyle of the Bushmen who remain in the more remote areas of the Kalahari, it's difficult not to lapse into a romantic view of ignoring present realities. There are too many cultural aspects to cover here, so instead I've just picked out a few that you may encounter.

Nomads of the Kalahari Perhaps the first idea to dispel is that the Bushmen are nomads. They're not. Bushmen family groups have clearly defined territories, called a *n!ore* (in the Ju/'hoansi language), within which they forage. This is usually centred on a place where there is water, and contains food resources sufficient for the basic subsistence of the group.

Groups recognise rights to the *n!ore*, which is passed on from father to first-born son. Any visiting people would ask permission to remain in these. Researchers have mapped these areas, even in places like the Central Kalahari.

Social system The survival of the Bushmen in the harsh environment of the Kalahari is evidence of the supreme adaptability of humans. It reflects their detailed knowledge of their environment, which provides them not only with food, but with materials for shelter and medicine in the form of plants.

Another very important factor in their survival is the social system by which the Bushmen live. Social interaction is governed by unwritten rules that bind the people in friendship and harmony, which must be maintained. One such mechanism is the obligation to distribute the meat from a large kill. Another is the obligation to lend such few things as are individually possessed, thereby incurring a debt of obligation from the borrower.

They also practise exogamy, which means they have an obligation to marry outside the group. This creates social bonds between groups. Such ties bind the society inextricably together, as does the system of gift exchange between separate groups.

Owing to the environmental constraints a group will consist of between 80 and 120 people, living and moving together. In times of shortage the groups will be much smaller, sometimes consisting of only immediate family – parents, grandparents and children. They must be able to carry everything they possess. Their huts are light constructions of grass, and they have few possessions.

Because no-one owns property, no-one is richer or has more status than another. A group of Bushmen has a nominal leader, who might be a senior member of the group, an expert hunter, or the person who owns the water rights. The whole group takes decisions affecting them, often after vociferous discussions.

Hunter-gatherers Any hunter-gatherer lifestyle entails a dependence on, and extensive knowledge of, the environment and the resident fauna and flora found there. In the Kalahari, water is the greatest need and the Bushmen know which roots and tubers provide liquid to quench thirst. They create sip wells in the desert, digging a hole, filled with soft grass, then using a reed to suck water into the hole, and send it bubbling up the reed to fill an ostrich egg. Water-filled ostrich eggs are also buried at specific locations within the group's 'area'. When necessary the Bushmen will strain the liquid from the rumen of a herbivore and drink that.

Researchers have observed that any hunting is done by the men. When living a basic hunting and gathering lifestyle, with little external input, hunting provides only about 20% of their food. The remaining 80% is provided largely by the women, helped by the children, who forage and gather wild food from the bush. By age 12 a child might know about 200 plant species, and an adult more than 300.

Hunting The Bushmen in the Kalahari are practised hunters, using many different techniques to capture the game. Their main weapons are a very light bow, and an arrow made of reed, in three sections. The arrowhead is usually poisoned, using one of a number of poisons obtained from specific plants, snakes and beetles. (Though most Bushmen know how to hunt with bows and arrows, the actual practice is increasingly uncommon when it's not done to earn money from observing visitors.)

All the hunters may be involved in the capture of large game, which carries with it certain obligations. The whole group shares in the kill and each member is entitled to a certain portion of the meat.

There are different methods for hunting small game, which only the hunter's family would usually share. One method for catching spring hares involves long, flexible poles (sometimes 4m) made of thin sticks, with a duiker's horn (or more usually now a metal hook) fastened to the end. These are rammed into the hare's hole, impaling the animal, which is then pulled or dug out.

Trance dancing Entertainment for the Bushmen, when things are good, usually involves dancing. During some dances, which may often have overtones of ritual or religion, the dancers may fall into a trance and collapse.

These trances are induced by a deliberate breathing technique, with a clear physiological explanation. Dances normally take place in the evening, around a fire. Then the women, children and old people will sit around and clap, whilst some of the younger men will dance around the circle in an energetic, rhythmic dance. Often this is all that happens, and after a while the excitement dies down and everyone goes to sleep.

However, on fairly rare occasions, the dancers will go into a trance. After several hours of constant exertion, they will shorten their breathing. This creates an oxygen deficiency, which leads to the heart pumping more strongly to compensate. Blood pressure to the brain increases; the dancer loses consciousness and collapses.

Caprivian The Caprivi people live in the fertile, swampy land between the Chobe and Zambezi rivers – at the eastern end of the Caprivi Strip. Their language is of the Bantu family. Like the Kavango and the Owambo, they farm a variety of crops, raise livestock, and fish. The agricultural potential of the area is one of the highest in Namibia. However, this potential has been largely unrealised. Before the war with Angola, and the heavy involvement of South African troops (which brought roads and infrastructure), the whole of the Kavango and Caprivi region was one of the least developed in Namibia.

Caprivians make up about 4% of Namibia's population, and most can be considered as members of one of five main groups: the Masubia and Mafwe groups, and the smaller Mayeyi, Matotela and Mbukushu. Their traditional crafts include extensive use of baskets (especially fish traps, and for carrying grain), wooden masks and stools, drums, pottery, leather goods and stone carvings.

Damara Along with the Nama and the Bushmen, the Damara are presumed to be the original inhabitants of Namibia, speaking a similar 'Khoi' click language (Khoisan family). Like the Nama, the Damara were primarily hunting people, who owned few cattle or goats. Traditionally enemies of the Nama and Herero, they supported the German colonial forces at Waterberg against the Herero uprisings and were awarded for their loyalty by an 'enlarged' homeland from the German authorities: Damaraland, the area adjacent to the Skeleton Coast (now the southern part of the Kunene province). Of the 80,000 Damara today, only a quarter manage to survive in this area – the rest work on commercial farms, in mines or as labourers in the towns. Damara women share the same Victorian style of dress as the Herero and Nama women.

They make up about 7.5% of Namibia's population, sharing their language with Namas. Traditionally Damara people had been thought of as miners, smelters, copper traders, stock farmers and tobacco growers, until the end of the 19th century when they moved to Damaraland and started practising agriculture.

Their traditional crafts include leather goods, glass and metal beadwork, wooden bowls and buckets, clay pipes and bowls, and more recently 'township art' such as wire cars.

Herero In 1904, the Herero and the Hottentots staged a massive uprising against the German colonial troops in South West Africa. It ended in a bloody massacre of over half the total Herero population at the battle of Waterberg. The few Herero that survived fled into the Kalahari, some crossing into what is now Botswana. The recently formed Herero People's Reparation Corporation, based in Washington, is currently suing the German government and two companies for £2.6 billion, with the case expected to be heard in the US courts during 2003.

Today, the Herero constitute the third-largest ethnic group in Namibia, after the Owambo and Kavango – about 8% of the present population. Their language is Bantu based. In Botswana, they are a minority group inhabiting Ngamiland, south and west of the Okavango Delta.

Traditionally pastoralists, the Herero prefer raising cattle to growing crops – prestige and influence are dependent on the number of cattle possessed. Today, the majority of Namibian Herero use their cattle-handling skills on commercial farms.

Herero women wear very distinctive long, flowing Victorian gowns and headdresses. Multiple layers of petticoats made from over 12m of material give a voluminous look (two women walking side by side occupy the whole pavement!). Missionaries, who were appalled by the Herero's semi-nakedness, introduced this style of dress in the 1800s. Now the Herero continue to wear these heavy garments and it has become their traditional dress – though they will admit just how hot it is if asked.

Traditional Herero crafts include skin and leather products, basketry, jewellery and ornaments, and dolls in traditional Victorian-style dress, which are a very popular curio for visitors.

Himba The Himba people share a common ethnic origin with the Hereros, having split from the main Herero group on the Namibia/Botswana border and moved west to present-day Kaokoland in search of available land. The place they found, however, is mountainous, sparsely vegetated and very arid. Cattle are central to their way of life, with the size of the herd an indication of wealth and prestige – but overgrazing of the poor soils is a major problem. The Himba are a minority group in Namibia (less than 1% of the population), and live almost entirely in their traditional areas in remote Kaokoland.

Traditional Himba crafts include work in skin and leather (headdresses, girdles and aprons), jewellery (copper-wire neckbands and bracelets), musical instruments, wooden neckrests, basketry and pottery.

Kavango The Kavango people share their name with the Okavango River, which forms the northern border of Namibia with Angola. Not surprisingly, they have based their traditional agricultural and fishing existence on the fertile land and good water supply afforded by this environment.

Many of the Kavango, who used to live on the northern side of the Okavango River in Angola, came south of the river into Namibia during the 1970s, '80s and early '90s. They fled from the civil war between South African-backed UNITA rebels and the Soviet/Cuban-backed MPLA regime. As a consequence, the Kavango population in Namibia more than doubled in size during the 1970s, and now forms the second-largest ethnic group in the country, making up almost 10% of the population.

Closely related to the Owambos, the Kavango people are traditionally fishermen, and crop and stock farmers. Their craftwork includes woodcarving (bowls, spoons, mortars, masks, boxes and furniture), basketry, pottery, jewellery (grass bracelets and copper-bead necklaces), mats, spears, daggers, pipes, musical instruments and headdresses.

Nama/Hottentot The Nama people are perhaps the closest in origin to the Bushmen, traditionally sharing a similar type of 'click' or Khoisan language, the same light-coloured yellow skin, and a hunter-gatherer way of life. One of the first peoples in Namibia, their tribal areas were traditionally communal property, as indeed was any item unless it was actually made by an individual. Basic differences in the perception of ownership of land and hunting grounds led in the past to frequent conflicts with the Herero people. The 50,000 or so Nama today live mostly in the area that was Namaland, north of Keetmanshoop in the south of Namibia, mainly working on commercial farms. Nama women share the same Victorian traditional dress as the Herero and Damara women.

The Nama people make up about 5% of Namibia's population, and are traditionally stock farmers. Their crafts include leatherwork (aprons and collecting bags), *karosses* (mantle of animal skins) and mats, musical instruments (eg: reed flutes), jewellery, clay pots and tortoiseshell powder containers.

Owambo The Owambo people (sometimes called Ovambo) are by far the largest group in Namibia and make up just over half the population. Their language, Oshivambo (sometimes known as Ambo or Vambo in Namibia), is Bantu based. The great majority live in their traditional areas – Owamboland – away from the

Comments here are intended to be a general guide, just a few examples of how to travel more sensitively. They should not be viewed as blueprints for perfect Namibian etiquette. Cultural sensitivity is really a state of mind, not a checklist of behaviour – so here we can only hope to give the sensitive traveller a few pointers in the right direction.

When we travel, we are all in danger of leaving negative impressions with local people whom we meet: by snapping that picture quickly, while the subject is not looking; by dressing scantily, offending local sensitivities; or by just brushing aside the feelings of local people, with the high-handed superiority of a rich Westerner. These things are easy to do, in the click of a shutter, or flash of a large dollar bill.

However, you will get the most representative view of Namibia if you cause as little disturbance to the local people as possible. You will never blend in perfectly when you travel – your mere presence there, as an observer, will always change the local events slightly. However, if you try to fit in and show respect for local culture and attitudes, then you may manage to leave positive feelings behind you.

One of the easiest, and most important, ways to do this is with **greetings**. African societies are rarely as rushed as Western ones. When you first talk to someone, you should greet him or her leisurely. So, for example, if you enter a shop and want some help, do not just ask outright, 'Where can I find … ?' That would be rude. Instead you will have a better reception (and better chance of good advice) by saying:

Traveller:	'Good afternoon.'
Namibian:	'Good afternoon.'
Traveller:	'How are you?'
Namibian:	'I am fine, how are you?'
Traveller:	'I am fine, thank you. (pause) Do you know where I can find … ?'

This approach goes for anyone – always greet them first. For a better reception still, learn these phrases of greeting in the local language. English-speakers are often lazy about learning languages, and, whilst most Namibians understand English, a greeting given in an appropriate local language will be received with delight. It implies that you are making an effort to learn a little of their language and culture, which is always appreciated.

main transport arteries in the remote far north of the country, straddled on the border with Angola. The area receives one of the highest rainfalls in the country, and supports a range of traditional crops as well as allowing good grazing for the extensive cattle herds.

Before independence, the existence of half a million indigenous Namibians on the border with (socialist) Angola seriously perturbed the South African administration. By investing money into the region, the administration hoped to establish a buffer against Angola to protect the areas in the interior. The policy backfired – Owamboland became the heartland of SWAPO during the struggle for independence. The consequent harassment by the South African Defence Force, and a rapid population increase (exacerbated by a large influx of refugees from Angola), have left the area over-pressurised and undeveloped. The SWAPO government has long pledged to redress this imbalance.

Most of the Owambo belong to one of eight tribes: the Kwanyama, Ndongo, Kwambi, Ngandjera, Mbalantu, Kwaluudhi, Nkolokadhi and Eunda. Most still live in Owamboland, and have traditionally been traders and businessmen.

Traditional Owambo craftwork includes basketry, pottery, jewellery, wooden combs, wood and iron spears, arrows and richly decorated daggers, musical

Very rarely in the town or city you may be approached by someone who doesn't greet you, but tries immediately to sell you something, or hassle you in some way. These people have learned that foreigners aren't used to greetings, so have adapted their approach accordingly. An effective way to dodge their attentions is to reply to their questions with a formal greeting, and then politely, but firmly, refuse their offer. This is surprisingly effective.

Another part of the normal greeting ritual is **handshaking**. As elsewhere, you would not normally shake a shop-owner's hand, but you would shake hands with someone to whom you are introduced. Get some practice when you arrive, as there is a gentle, three-part handshake used in southern Africa which is easily learnt – but not easily taught in a book.

Your **clothing** is an area that can easily give offence. Skimpy, revealing clothing is frowned upon by most Namibians, especially when worn by women. Shorts are fine for the bush or the beach, but dress conservatively and avoid short shorts, especially in the more rural areas. Respectable locals will wear long trousers (men) or long skirts (women).

Photography is a tricky business. Most Namibians will be only too happy to be photographed – provided you ask their permission first. Sign language is fine for this question: just point at your camera, shrug your shoulders, and look quizzical. The problem is that then everyone will smile for you, producing the type of 'posed' photograph which you may not want. However, stay around and chat for five or ten minutes more, and people will get used to your presence, stop posing and you will get more natural shots (a camera with a quiet shutter is a help). Note that care is needed near government buildings, army bases and similar sites of strategic importance. You must ask permission before snapping photographs or you risk people taking offence.

The specific examples above can teach only so much; they are general by their very nature. But wherever you find yourself, if you are polite and considerate to the Namibians you meet, then you will rarely encounter any cultural problems. Watch how they behave and, if you have any doubts about how you should act, then ask someone quietly. They will seldom tell you outright that you are being rude, but they will usually give you good advice on how to make your behaviour more acceptable.

instruments, fertility dolls, and ivory buttons (*ekipa*) – worn by women and conveying their status and indicating their husband's/family's wealth.

Other Namibians

Coloured Namibians The term 'coloured' is generally used in southern Africa to describe people of mixed (black–white) origin. These coloured people maintain a strong sense of identity and separateness from either blacks or whites – though they generally speak either Afrikaans or English (or frequently both) rather than an ethnic 'African' language. They are very different in culture from any of Namibia's ethnic groups, white or black.

Most coloureds in Namibia live in the urban areas – Windhoek, Keetmanshoop and Lüderitz. Those in Walvis Bay are mainly fishermen, and some in the south are stock farmers. Their traditional crafts centre mainly on musical instruments, like drums and guitars.

White Namibians The first whites to settle in Namibia were the Germans who set up trading businesses around the port of Lüderitz in 1884. Within a few years, Namibia formally became a German colony, and German settlers began to arrive in ever-increasing numbers. Meanwhile, white farmers of Dutch origin (the Boers, who first settled on the African continent at the Cape in 1652), were moving northwards in search of land free from British interference, following the cession of the Dutch Cape Colony to the British government.

Following the transfer of German Namibia to South African control after World War I, Boers (Afrikaners) moved into Namibia, and soon significantly outnumbered the German settlers. The Namibian whites collectively refer to themselves as 'Southwesters' after Namibia's colonial name of South West Africa.

Namibians of European descent live mainly in urban, central and southern parts of the country – though they also own and run most of the commercial farming operations. Virtually all of the tourism industry is managed by white Namibians. They came as missionaries, traders and hunters, though are now found throughout the economy. Perhaps a legacy of colonialism, they are normally amongst the more affluent members of society.

The crafts currently produced by the whites include leatherwork (shoes, handbags, belts), German Christmas and Easter decorations, needlework (including embroidery, patchwork and clothing), printed T-shirts, costume jewellery, greeting cards and various classical European art-forms.

Expatriates Distinct from white Namibians, there is a significant 'expat' community in Namibia. These foreigners usually come to Namibia for two or three years, to work on short-term contracts, often for either multi-national companies or aid agencies. Most are highly skilled individuals who come to share their knowledge with Namibian colleagues – often teaching skills that are in short supply in Namibia.

LANGUAGE

Namibia's variety of languages reflects the diversity of its peoples – black and white. Following independence, one of the new government's first actions was to make English Namibia's only official language (removing Afrikaans and German). This step sought to unite Namibia's peoples and languages under one common tongue ('the language of the liberation struggle'), leaving behind the colonial overtones of Afrikaans and German. This choice is also helping with international relations and education, as English-language materials are the most easily available.

While English is taught throughout the education system, Afrikaans is still the *lingua franca* amongst many of the older generation, and in rural areas Afrikaans tends to be more widely used than English (which may not be spoken at all) – despite the widespread enthusiasm felt for the latter. Virtually all black Namibians also speak one or more African languages, and many will speak several. Many white Namibians (especially those in the commercial farming communities of the central region) regard German as their first language, though they will normally understand English and Afrikaans as well.

Amongst the indigenous languages there are two basic language groups which bear no relation to each other: Bantu (eg: Owambo, Herero) and Khoisan (eg: Bushmen, Nama). Linguistics experts have identified at least 28 different languages and numerous dialects amongst the indigenous population. Although these different language groupings do loosely correspond to what might be described as Namibia's 'tribes', the distinctions are blurred by the natural linguistic ability of most Namibians. Thus, ethnic groupings provide only a rough guide to the many languages and dialects of Namibia's people.

EDUCATION

Since independence, the government has poured resources into an expansion of the education system, and at present about 89% of children (aged 6–16) attend school. In 2003, literacy was estimated at about 84%. There are small primary schools in the most rural of areas and large secondary schools in the regional centres. To help with this expansion, many foreign teachers came to Namibia with the help of NGOs and overseas aid agencies.

Children in secondary school study for the IGCSE (General Certificate of Secondary Education) and then move on to the HIGCSE. Lessons are taught almost exclusively in English, although some indigenous languages may also be taught.

RELIGION

Some 80–90% of the population follows a Christian religion. Dutch Reformed, Roman Catholic, Lutheran, Methodist and Presbyterian churches are all common. However, most people will also subscribe to some traditional African religious practices and beliefs.

ARTS, CRAFTS AND CULTURE

Namibia boasts some of the world's oldest rock paintings and engravings, which have been attributed to ancestors of Bushmen. The scenes are naturalistic depictions of animals, people, hunting, battles and social rituals. Local geology determined the colour usage in the paintings. Some are monochrome pictures in red, but many are multi-coloured, using ground-up earth pigments mixed with animal fat to produce 'paints' of red, brown, yellow, blue, violet, grey, black and white.

Rock engravings have also been found, often in areas where there is an absence of smooth, sheltered rock surfaces to paint on. Some of the best examples of paintings and engravings are in the Brandberg, Twyfelfontein and Erongo areas.

However, there is more to Namibian creativity than just rock paintings and engravings. Traditional arts and crafts include basketry, woodcarving, leatherwork, beadwork, pottery, music-making and dancing. More contemporary arts and crafts encompass textile weaving and embroidery, sculptures, print-making and theatre.

In 2003, Bank Windhoek came up with the sponsorship for an annual festival that draws together every aspect of the arts, from music, dance and drama to the visual arts and even creative writing.

Whilst events are held primarily in Windhoek, participants are selected from across the country. For details, see www.bankwindhoekarts.com.na.

For up-to-date information on cultural events, buy a copy of *The Namibian* (*www.nambian.com.na*) and read its 'Arts and Entertainment' section.

CRAFTS AND VISUAL ARTS To access the whole range of Namibian regional arts and crafts in one place, visit the Namibia Craft Centre (see page 147) in Windhoek. Housing numerous stalls under one roof, as well as the Omba Gallery, this is perfect for buying crafts if time is short. Outside of Windhoek, many towns have street markets selling curios, and numerous lodges have small outlets selling local arts and crafts, albeit sometimes at a rather inflated price. At grassroots level, the number of local communities that have set up small-scale craft projects is growing, bringing employment and attracting revenue back to where both are needed. Many of these are brought together within the fold of the Namibian Community-Based

Tricia Hayne

With the increasing incidence of AIDS among the local population, and poor standards of hygiene, there is a parallel increase in TB, which strikes as the immune system is lowered by HIV. And the problem is growing.

Lack of education means that there is almost total incomprehension about AIDS – put simply, it can't be seen, so it can't be there. This, in turn, means that many people are totally unaware that they have contracted the disease. When, on top of this, TB is diagnosed, and medication is handed out – anti-retroviral drugs are free at state hospitals and clinics – some patients will take all the tablets at once without understanding the implications for their health. Inevitably, complications set in, and many patients have died.

When Petra Illing first arrived in Windhoek from Germany, by way of Bosnia and Zaire, to work with a small medical organisation known as Tuberculosis Wurtzburg, she was confronted with a tuberculosis problem of epidemic proportions. In the ensuing years, she has put into practice her belief that 'people help people' – *tuyakula* – creating a scheme whereby TB patients are treated holistically. In essence, her aim was to offer patients a way out of the cycle of disease and poverty through a series of garden projects, which would then work outwards for the good of the community as a whole.

With the opening of the first of her 'garden clinics' in 1996, the *mosumbo* – 'white lady' – was deemed to be crazy. At that stage, standards of hygiene were so low that patients would simply defecate in the grounds of the clinic. Today, though, those grounds are transformed into neat rows of fruit, herbs and vegetables, such as cabbages, spinach, onions, lemons, oranges, grapefruits, grapes and tomatoes. Each is tended by a former TB patient, almost all of them women. In return for both remuneration and fresh fruit and vegetables, each is employed for about six months under the supervision of other ex-patients who are employed on a permanent basis.

There are seven garden clinics in the Tuyakula scheme in Windhoek, each with its own garden and children's play area, and there is sufficient food grown for everyone concerned with the projects. Directly related to the garden projects, three of the clinics now run feeding programmes for about 40 people at any one time. Each morning, at 08.30, patients on the feeding programme receive breakfast of bread, jam and butter, followed by their medication. At lunch, the process is repeated.

On average, TB patients weigh around 40–55kg when they first start attending hospital, and many can hardly stand. With good food and proper medication, they usually gain some 5–6kg in the following months. Most attend for about six months, first as inpatients in the TB hospital, next to the main Katutura hospital, then as outpatients at one of the city's clinics. Each of these clinics caters for up to 500 patients a day, with every conceivable ailment and complaint. It is here that TB patients become involved with the garden clinics.

In addition to those working in the gardens, some former patients are employed on craftwork, including making up soft furnishings for Petra's Tana Rose shop in Windhoek's Town Square, while others have come together to form a self-help group. With an improvement in health and a greater understanding of the importance of a good diet, former patients go out into the community to spread the news. Many have started to cultivate the land around their houses with food crops, and sometimes their neighbours follow suit, creating pockets of neatly tended vegetable plots. On the downside, maintaining the gardening project costs around N$120,000 a year, and funds – despite support from the German-based Johanniter International (*www.johanniter.de*) – are rapidly drying up.

Tourism Association, NACOBTA (*www.nacobta.com.na*), and are well worth seeking out,

For more details of Namibian arts and crafts, it may be worth contacting the Arts and Crafts Guild of Namibia (*PO Box 20709, Windhoek;* ✆ *061 223831;* f *061 252125*), which was established in 1992 to unite the various craftspeople under one umbrella group for promotional purposes.

Basketry Most baskets are made from strips of makalani palm leaves coiled into a shape that is determined by its purpose: flat, plate shapes for winnowing baskets, large bowl-shaped baskets for carrying things, small closed baskets with lids and bottle shapes for storing liquids. Symbolic geometric patterns are woven into a basket as it is being made, using strips of palm leaves dyed in dark browns, purples and yellows.

Recently, baskets have been made using strips of recycled plastic bags to wind around the palm-leaf strips or grasses. Baskets are typically woven by women and are part of the crafts tradition of the northern Namibian peoples – Caprivi, Himba, Herero, Kavango and Owambo.

The best examples are found in the northern arts and crafts co-operatives, which include Khorixas Community Craft Centre (page 335); Tsumeb Arts and Crafts (page 407); Mashi Crafts, beside the B8 in Kongola (page 456); and Caprivi Arts Centre in Katima Mulilo (page 465);

Woodcarving Woodcarving is usually practised by men in Namibia. Wooden objects are carved using adzes, axes and knives; lathe-turned work is not traditional. Carving, incising and burning techniques are used to decorate the wood. A wide range of woodcarving is produced: sculptural headrests, musical instruments such as drums and thumb pianos; masks, walking-sticks, toys, animal figurines, bows, arrows and quivers; domestic utensils including oval and round bowls and buckets as well as household furniture.

The northern Namibian peoples – Bushmen, Caprivians, Damara, Himba, Kavango and Owambo – have woodcarving traditions. Naturally the northern arts and crafts co-operatives have a good selection (see above), especially the Mbangura Co-operative (see page 442) which also specialises in wooden furniture. In addition the two street markets in Okahandja act as a national selling point for woodcarvings.

Leatherwork Leatherwork is practised by all the peoples of Namibia. The skins of cattle, sheep and game are tanned and dyed using vegetable materials, animal fat and sometimes red ochre. The goods crafted include carrying skins and bags, tobacco pouches, karosses (to be used as rugs or blankets) and traditional clothing – headdresses, girdles/aprons and sandals as well as more contemporary fashion accessories like shoes, boots, handbags, belts and jackets. The leatherworkers are usually women, though men also participate if large, heavy skins are being tanned or dyed. African Leather Creations (formerly Swakopmund Tannery; see page 282) is an interesting place to buy crafted leatherwork, but tanning is no longer carried out on the premises.

Beadwork Beadwork is traditionally the domain of the Bushman and Himba peoples. The Bushmen make beads from ostrich-egg shells, porcupine quills, seeds, nuts and branches; and also use commercially produced glass beads. The Himba people use iron beads and shells. In both peoples, men tend to make the beads and the women weave and string them into artefacts. These include necklaces, bracelets, armlets, anklets and headbands. The Bushmen also use beadwork to decorate their leatherwork bags, pouches and clothing – a particularly

2

Karakuls are central Asian sheep, the young of which have long been prized for their pelts. In 1902, a German fur trader called Paul Thorer shipped 69 of these from Uzbekistan to Germany in the hope of breeding them there. The damper European climes did not suit them, but in 1907 12 of those animals were shipped out to German South West Africa – as Namibia's climate was thought to be similar to that of the dry central Asian areas from where they had come.

They did well, and two years later 278 more animals were brought out from Asia. Later, the South Africans continued the work started by the Germans, when they took over as the reigning colonial power in Namibia. An experimental farm was started near Windhoek, to investigate the farming and breeding of karakuls.

Over the next 50 or 60 years Namibia gradually became one of the three main producers of karakul fur, or 'Persian lamb' as it is often known. Early on, selective breeding in Namibia had developed white pelts, which were not produced in either the USSR or Afghanistan – the competing countries. Then Namibia marketed its fur under the trade name of Swakara, for South West African karakul. Now, one firm markets these as Nakara, for Namibian karakul. See page 148.

This trade grew rapidly, and as early as 1937 the country exported over a million pelts for over £1,200,000. It grew to its peak in 1976, when about 2.8 million pelts earned some 50 million rand – before the anti-fur campaigns of the late '70s and '80s slashed the demand for fur, and the prices paid for pelts.

Then the market crashed, and the biggest single source of income for many farmers in southern Namibia was removed. Given that the fur came only from the slaughter of very young lambs (it is said to be at its softest when they are 36 hours old), it's not surprising that people felt unhappy about buying it.

However, these are tough sheep, well suited to Namibia's extremes of temperatures and semi-desert climate, so the loss of the market for their lambs' pelts was a major blow. Karakul wool carpets, woven in Swakopmund, are increasing the demand for the wool of adults. You can accelerate this trend by buying one as a souvenir, then perhaps karakuls will again be common in Namibia.

striking traditional design being the multi-coloured circular 'owl's-eye'.

Bushman crafts are best bought either locally in the Tsumkwe area or at the Tsumeb Arts and Crafts Centre (page 407). Alternatively, a more commercial outlet with a good selection is Bushman Art in Windhoek (page 147). Failing that, check for new outlets with the Nyae Nyae Development Foundation of Namibia (page 419).

The Himba people also make a traditional iron-bead and leather head ornament (*oruvanda*) that all women wear and belts (*epanda*) that only mothers wear. Authentic Himba crafts are easiest to find in Kaokoland, where you will often be offered crafts by local villagers.

Pottery Namibia's more renowned potters are women from the Caprivi, Kavango and Owambo peoples. Traditionally, geometric patterns of various colours decorate the vessels of different shapes and uses. Contemporary potters are experimenting with decoration by textures and a variety of sculptural motifs. The best selection of pottery is found at the Caprivi Arts Centre (see page 465).

Textiles Nama women traditionally used patchwork techniques when making dresses and shawls. Now these women utilise their sewing skills in the art of embroidery and appliqué, making table and bed linens, cushion covers and wall-hangings depicting Namibian animals and village scenes. Good places to buy these items include Penduka Gallery in Windhoek (page 147) and the Anin Project near Uhlenhorst (pages 190–1).

Another textile craft that has recently developed is the hand-weaving of pure karakul wool into wall-hangings and rugs. The designs are usually geometric patterns or Namibian landscapes, though almost any design can be commissioned. Among the best places to see and buy these rugs and wall-hangings are Karakulia and African Kirikara Art, both in Swakopmund (page 282) and Dorka Teppiche in Dordabis (see page 178).

Painting, sculpture and prints The work of contemporary Namibian artists, sculptors and print-makers is on display (and often available for sale) in the many galleries in the urban areas. The country's biggest permanent collection is at the National Art Gallery of Namibia (see page 155), which has over 560 works of art dating from 1864 to the present day. There are many landscapes and paintings of wild animals amongst the earlier works. Every two years the winning entries of the Standard Bank Biennale are exhibited here. Contemporary Namibian visual arts are exhibited at the following locations.

Omba Gallery Namibia Crafts Centre, 40 Tal St, Windhoek; ☏ 061 242 2222. Exhibits work of Namibian & international artists & craftspeople.
John Muafangejo Art Centre The Former Kitchen, Parliament Gdns, Windhoek; ☏ 061 231 160; f 061 240 930; e shipayo@mweb.com.na. This art school exhibits the work of young Namibian artists, as well as housing a small studio theatre.
Centre for Visual & Performing Arts University of

Namibia, Mandume Ndemufayo Rd, Pioneers Pk, Windhoek; ☏ 061 206 3804; f 061 206 3835
House of Art Maerua Mall, Windhoek; ☏ 061 251 700; f 061 225 012; e lucksa@iway.na
Engelhard Design 55 Sam Nujoma Av, Swakopmund; ☏ 064 404 606; e engel@mweb.com.na. A modern shop & gallery featuring contemporary Namibian art & jewellery, with exhibitions changing every 6 weeks or so.

It's worth noting that many professional artists choose to sell their work at street markets rather than pay a gallery commission on any items sold. So high-quality arts and crafts can be found by the roadside and on the pavements.

PERFORMING ARTS

Dance Traditional dancing in Namibia is a participatory activity at community gatherings and events like weddings. Hence, a visitor is unlikely to witness any, unless invited by a Namibian. Occasionally, public performances of traditional dancing are to be seen at local arts festivals, or even in traditional villages such as Lizauli (see pages 459–60), or – more formally – at the College for the Arts auditorium in Windhoek (see page 144). In Bushmanland, in villages surrounding Tsumkwe, traditional Bushmen dances are performed for tourists – usually for a fee. This is generally a relaxed, uncontrived affair.

Performances of European dance, including ballet, take place at either the National Theatre of Namibia or at the Franco-Namibian Cultural Centre (see page 144).

Music Most of the Namibian peoples have a music-making tradition – singing, and playing drums, bows, thumb pianos and harps. The Namas also have a tradition of religious singing in four-part harmony, a cappella. One group that has taken this to a wider audience is the University of Namibia Choir, which has gained an enviable reputation for performing a range of traditional music in both Namibian and European languages.

Pre-Independence colonial influences have resulted in many Namibian musicians performing in the Western tradition. Concerts are regularly performed by the Namibia National Symphony Orchestra, National Youth Choir and touring foreign musicians in the main auditorium of the National Theatre of Namibia (see page 144). Many smaller-scale concerts take place at the Franco-Namibian Cultural Centre (see page 144), and at Christus Kirche, Windhoek (ask at the church for concert details).

Jazz, reggae, *mbaganga* and pop bands perform at the 150-seater Warehouse Theatre (see page 144) and at the various bars, restaurants and clubs in Windhoek such as Club Thriller (see page 144). Bands and rock groups with a larger following usually perform at the Independence Arena in Katutura, which has the capacity for 4,000 people, or at the Windhoek Country Club (see page 157) which can accommodate audiences of over 1,000 people. Out of Windhoek, the national tour circuit includes large venues in Swakopmund, Walvis Bay and Okahandja.

On a more local level, Solitaire hosts a 'national' music festival each year; in 2006 this was held in November. The festival purports to feature bands from both Namibia and across southern Africa, but the reality is music with a predominantly country and western slant.

Theatre and film Namibian theatre companies come and go, as elsewhere, but there is no shortage of venues for performances – at least in the capital. Apart from the National Theatre of Namibia and the Warehouse Theatre, there are small studio-theatres at the John Muafangejo Arts Centre and the Space Theatre at the University of Namibia's Centre for Visual and Performing Arts. Both host avant-garde and experimental theatre performances.

The best of Namibian theatre (and other arts and crafts) can be seen at the annual Bank Windhoek Arts Festival (see page 27). More specifically, each year Windhoek plays host to the Wild Cinema International Film Festival, which gives Namibian film-makers the opportunity to showcase their art against films from the international arena.

SPORT

Sport is popular in Namibia, with football, rugby, hockey and netball all played in schools, and basketball being introduced in recent years. Increasingly successful in international rugby, the Namibian team has booked a place in the 2007 Rugby World Cup, to be held in France.

Athletics aficionados will be familiar with the name of Frankie Fredericks, the Namibian 200m sprinter. Slightly overshadowed by Michael Johnson, he has nevertheless brought home a string of international medals, the latest of which was in the Commonwealth Games held in Manchester in July 2002, which marked the finale of an international career that spanned well over a decade.

3

The Natural Environment

PHYSICAL ENVIRONMENT

The Republic of Namibia is located in southwest Africa, astride the Tropic of Capricorn and beside the South Atlantic Ocean. Its main borders are with South Africa, Botswana and Angola, though it also adjoins Zambia. Covering about 824,292km², the country is much larger than Kenya, and more than twice the size of Zimbabwe. In Western terms, Namibia is more than a third larger than the UK and Germany combined, or twice the size of California.

CLIMATE Most of Namibia is classified as an arid to semi-arid region (the line being crossed from semi-arid to arid when evaporation exceeds rainfall). Most of it has a sub-tropical 'desert' climate, characterised by a wide range in temperature (from day to night and from summer to winter), and by low rainfall and humidity. The northern strip follows the same pattern, but has a more moderate, less dry climate. Note that although the terms 'summer' (November to April) and 'winter' (May to October) are sometimes used, they are not as applicable as, say, in a European maritime climate.

Temperatures range widely from very hot to very cold, depending on the height of the land above sea level and the month. From April to September, in the 'dry season', it is generally cool, pleasant, clear and dry. Temperatures average around 25°C during the day, but nights are much colder. Frost is possible in the higher areas and the deserts. October and November are still within the 'dry season' but then the temperatures are higher, especially in the lower-lying and more northerly areas.

Most of Namibia's rain falls in the summer, from around December to March, and it can be heavy and prolonged in the northern regions of Owamboland and Caprivi. The further south or west you go, the drier it becomes, with many southern regions of the Kalahari and the whole of the coastal Namib Desert receiving no rainfall at all some years. In this 'rainy season' temperatures occasionally reach 40°C, and sometimes you may find it humid in the north.

Weather The beginning of the year, in January and February, is midsummer. Then it's hot and fairly damp with average maximum temperatures around 25–35°C and average minima around 10–20°C (depending exactly where you are). These averages, however, hide peaks of well over 45°C in the desert.

While prolonged rain may occur on occasion, on a typical day during the rains, the sky will start blue and by early afternoon the clouds will appear. In the late afternoon there will be an hour's torrential rain on some days. Such tropical storms are spectacular; everything feels terrifically fresh afterwards. However, you wouldn't want to be caught outside. By the early evening the sky will usually begin to clear again.

The frequency of the rains decreases, and they cease around March or April. From then the heat is waning and the land gradually cools and dries out. The nights quickly become cooler, accentuating the temperature difference between the bright, hot days and the clear nights. May is a lovely month: there is minimal chance of rain, nights are not yet too cold, and many of the summer's plants are still lush and green.

By June the nights are cold, approaching freezing in desert areas where night game drives can be bitter. July and August are winter, when the average maximum temperatures are around 15–25°C and the average minima are around 0–10°C. That said, you may still find yourself wearing shorts and a T-shirt during the day, and getting sunburnt if you are not careful. Clouds will be a rare sight for the next few months.

September is another super month, dry and clear, yet not too hot. By then most green vegetation is fading as the heat begins to build. Everything is dry. All through October the heat mounts, and by November it is very hot during the day. However, the humidity is still exceedingly low, so even the high temperatures feel quite pleasant.

By November the air seems pregnant with anticipation. Everything is dry, awaiting the rains. Though the clouds often build up in the afternoon, they won't usually deliver until at least December. When (and if) the rains do arrive, they are a huge relief, dropping the temperatures at a stroke, clearing the air and reviving the vegetation.

The coastal strip Temperatures on the Namibian coast follow a similar overall pattern, though it may seem very different from one day to the next. Here the climate is largely determined by the interaction between warm dry winds from inland and the cold Benguela Current. The sea is too cold for much evaporation to take place and, consequently, rain-bearing clouds don't form over the coast. Most of the coast is classified as desert – rainfall is an extremely low 15mm per annum on average, and in some years there may be none.

However, hot air from the interior mixes regularly with cold sea air to produce a moist fog that penetrates up to 60km inland. This happens regardless of season, and has done for millennia. It is this periodic morning fog which provides the

KIMBERLITE (DIAMOND) PIPES

Diamond is a crystalline form of ordinary carbon created under conditions of extreme pressure and temperature. In nature, such conditions are only found deep below the earth's surface in the lower crust or upper mantle. Under certain circumstances in the past (usually associated with tectonic activity) the rock matrix in which diamonds occurred was subjected to such great pressure that it became fluid and welled up to the earth's surface in a volcanic pipe of fluidised material. The situation is similar to a conventional volcanic eruption, except that instead of basaltic magma being erupted through fissures in the crust, the volcanic material is a peculiar rock called kimberlite. This contains a wide assortment of minerals (including diamond) in addition to large chunks of other rocks that have been caught up in the process.

The pipes are correctly termed kimberlite pipes, and occur throughout southern Africa from the Cape to Zaire. However, only a small proportion of those discovered have proved to contain diamonds in sufficient abundance to be profitably worked. Namibia's diamonds derive not from primary kimberlite pipes, but from secondary diamond deposits – areas where diamonds have been washed down and deposited by old rivers, which have eroded kimberlite pipes in the interior on their way.

THE FOSSIL DESERT

Though the Namib is one of the world's oldest deserts, many insist that the Kalahari doesn't qualify for the title 'desert' as it receives much more than 100mm of rain per year. However, the sand sheet that covers the Kalahari results in virtually no surface water, and evidence suggests that it may once have been much more arid than it is now. So although it is commonly called a desert, a better description of it would be 'a fossil desert'.

desert's only dependable source of moisture, and the Namib's endemic flora and fauna have evolved to take advantage of it.

GEOLOGY Geologically, Namibia forms part of an extremely old region, with Precambrian granitic and metamorphic rocks dating back over two billion years. These shield or 'basement' rocks are usually covered by more recent sedimentary rocks, mostly deposited during the Mesozoic era (65 to 235 million years ago). Tectonic activity or movement in the earth's crust over the last 100 million years or so created a number of rifts through which magma was able to reach the surface (see box, *Kimberlite (diamond) pipes* on previous page) and resulted in the uplifting of most of the area above sea level.

TOPOGRAPHY The topography of Namibia can be divided into four regions. At 2,000m, the highest land is the central plateau that runs roughly from north to south, from south of Keetmanshoop to north of Otjiwarongo. This is hilly, verdant country where most of Namibia's best farmland is concentrated.

To the west of this plateau, the land falls off in a dramatic escarpment down to the Namib Desert, one of the world's oldest deserts which stretches for 1,600km beside the Atlantic Ocean. The escarpment, and the incisions that have been cut through it by river action over the years, provides some of Namibia's most spectacular scenery. Below, the Namib is a flat coastal plain whose profile is broken only by shifting dunes and the odd towering inselberg (see page 241).

East of the central plateau, the land slopes off much more gradually, merging into the great sand-sheet of the Kalahari Desert. A plateau standing at about 1,000m, stretching from Namibia into Botswana and even beyond, this is rolling country with vegetated sand-dunes.

Sand-dunes Barchan, or crescentric, dunes arise wherever sand-laden wind deposits sand on the windward (upwind) slopes of a random patch on the ground. The mound grows in height until a 'slip-face' is established by sand avalanching down on the sheltered leeward (downwind) side. The resulting dune is therefore in a state of constant (if slow) movement – sand is continuously being deposited and blown up the shallow windward slope and then falling down the steep leeward slope. This slow movement, or migration, is more rapid at the edges of the dune (where there is less wind resistance) than in the centre, which results in the characteristic 'tails' of a mature barchan.

Fairly constant winds from the same direction are essential for the growth and stability of barchan dunes, which can migrate from anything up to 6m a year for high dunes to 15m a year for smaller dunes. Probably the best examples of barchan dunes occur in Namibia's Skeleton Coast, where some of the dune crests are highlighted by a purple dusting of garnet sand. You'll see them 'marching' across the road near where the D2345 turns from the main C34 coastal road.

Seif dunes Where the prevailing wind is interrupted by crosswinds driving in sand from the sides, a long seif or longitudinal dune is formed, instead of a swarm of barchans. The shape of seif dunes is that of a long ridge with high crests, parallel to the direction of the prevailing wind. They commonly occur in long parallel ranges, such as those south of the Kuiseb River which show up so clearly on satellite photographs.

Sand-sheets Sand-sheets occur when the land is vegetated with grass and scrub, or is covered with rocks and pebbles. Then the force of the wind is broken and it becomes less homogenous. In such situations poorly developed seif dunes or irregular barchans form, and may often join together to some extent, making an undulating sand sheet. From this platform of coarser sand, more erratic dunes often rise.

Sand-sheets, in one form or another, are the most common dune formation in southern Africa, since the 'text book' conditions needed to form perfect barchan or seif dunes are rare. However, the principles remain the same and 'imperfect' dunes of barchan or seif origin are widespread throughout the Kalahari and Namib deserts.

FLORA AND FAUNA

Despite its aridity, Namibia is full of fascinating wildlife. Its national parks and concession areas have protected their flora and fauna effectively and offer some superb big game, far from the tourist hordes of more conventional safari countries. Namibia has been the most successful country in the world at protecting its black rhino population, and has Africa's largest population of cheetahs.

Because the Namib is one of the world's oldest deserts, the extraordinary way that plants, animals and even human populations have adapted and evolved in order to survive here is fascinating. There are many endemic species: animals and plants not found anywhere else. From beetles and birds to big game like the famous 'desert elephants' and strange *Welwitschia* plants – Namibia has unique and varied wildlife.

VEGETATION TYPES As with animals, each species of plant has its favourite conditions. External factors determine where each species thrives, and where it will perish. These include temperature, light, water, soil type, nutrients, and which other species of plants and animals live in the same area. Species with similar needs are often found together, in communities which are characteristic of that particular environment. Namibia has a number of such communities, or typical 'vegetation types', within its borders – each of which is distinct from the others. East of the desert, some of the more common include the following.

Mopane woodland The dominant tree here is the remarkably adaptable mopane (*Colophospermum mopane*), which is sometimes known as the butterfly tree because of the shape of its leaves. It is very tolerant of poorly drained or alkaline soils and those with a high clay content. This tolerance results in the mopane having a wide range of distribution throughout southern Africa; in Namibia it occurs mainly in the higher, slightly wetter areas including Etosha, the northern Kaokoveld, Caprivi and the Kalahari.

Mopane trees can attain a height of 25m, especially if growing on rich, alluvial soils. However, shorter trees are more common in areas that are poor in nutrients, or have suffered from extensive fire damage. Stunted mopane will form a low scrub, perhaps only 5m tall. All mopane trees are deciduous, and the leaves turn beautiful shades of yellow and red before falling in September and October.

Ground cover in mopane woodland is usually sparse, just thin grasses, herbs and the occasional bush. The trees themselves are an important source of food for game, as the leaves have a high nutritional value – rich in protein and phosphorus – which is favoured by browsers and is retained even after they have fallen from the trees. Mopane forests support large populations of rodents, including tree squirrels (*Peraxerus cepapi*), which are so typical of these areas that they are known as 'mopane squirrels'.

Savanna This all-encompassing category refers to those areas of dry, thorny woodland that occur when trees and shrubs have invaded open grassland, often because of some disturbance like cultivation, fire or over-grazing. It could be subdivided further into 'thorntree', 'bush' and 'mixed tree and shrub' savanna.

Some form of savanna covers much of the Namibian highlands, and the dominant families of trees and bushes are the acacia, terminalia (bearing single-winged seeds) and combretum (bearing seeds with four or five wings), but many others are also present.

Teak forest In a few areas of the Kalahari (including some within Khaudum National Park), the Zambezi teak, *Baikaea plurijuga*, forms dry semi-evergreen forests on a base of Kalahari sand. This species is not fire-resistant, so these stands occur only where slash-and-burn cultivation methods have never been used. Below the tall teak is normally a dense, deciduous thicket of vegetation, interspersed with sparse grasses and herbs in the shadier spots of the forest floor.

Moist evergreen forest In areas of high rainfall, or near main rivers and swamps where a tree's roots will have permanent access to water, dense evergreen forest is found. This lush vegetation contains many species and is characterised by having three levels: a canopy of tall trees, a sub-level of smaller trees and bushes, and a variety of ground-level vegetation. In effect, the environment is so good for plants that they have adapted to exploit the light from every sunbeam. In Namibia, this occurs only as riparian forest (sometimes called riverine forest), which lines the country's major rivers.

Vlei A 'vlei' is a shallow grass depression, or small valley, that is either permanently or seasonally wet – though Namibia's vleis are drier than the areas that one would call vleis in countries further east. These open, verdant dips in the landscape usually support no bushes or trees. In higher valleys amongst hills, they sometimes form the sources of streams and rivers. Because of their dampness, they are rich in species of grasses, herbs and flowering plants. Their margins are usually thickly vegetated by grasses, herbs and smaller shrubs.

Floodplain Floodplains are the low-lying grasslands on the edges of rivers, streams, lakes and swamps that are seasonally inundated by floods. Namibia has only a few floodplains, in the Caprivi area. The best examples are probably beside the Okavango in Mahango, and near the Chobe and Zambezi rivers in the Impalila area. These contain no trees or bushes, just a low carpet of grass species that can tolerate being submerged for part of the year.

Pan Though not an environment for rich vegetation, a pan is a shallow, seasonal pool of water with no permanent streams leading into or from it. The bush is full of small pans in the rainy season, most of which will dry up soon after the rains cease. The Etosha and Nyae Nyae pans are just much larger versions, which attract considerable numbers of migrant birds when full.

DESERT FLORA Weighty tomes have been written on the flora of the Namib Desert, with its endemic plants and multitude of subtly different vegetation zones. One of the easiest to read is Dr Mary Seely's excellent book *The Namib* (see *Appendix 3*), which is widely sold in Namibia. This is well worth buying when you arrive, as it will increase your understanding and enjoyment of the desert immensely.

Distance from the coast and altitude are crucial to note when looking at the Namib's flora, as both are factors in determining how much moisture a plant receives by way of the fog. This is maximised at an altitude of about 300–600m above sea level, and extends up to about 60km inland. Thus the communities of vegetation can differ widely over very small distances: the plains full of delicate lichens in one place, but empty a kilometre away. Adaptations to the extremes are all around: wax-covered leaves to reduce transpiration, hollow stems to store water, low growth to avoid the wind, slow growth to take advantage of the infrequent moisture.

The species differ too widely to describe here, but are mentioned in the relevant chapters. Many will become familiar to even a casual observer; none could forget the prehistoric welwitschia (*Welwitschia mirabilis*), the kokerbooms silhouetted on rocky mountainsides, or the strange halfmen seen in the far south.

ANIMALS Namibia's large mammals are typical of the savanna areas of southern Africa, though those that rely on daily water are restricted in their distributions. With modern game capture and relocation techniques, you may well find animals far out of their natural ranges. (Bontebok and black wildebeest, for example, are native to South Africa but are now found on many ranches in Namibia.) Thus what you may see in a given area may be different from what 'naturally occurs'.

The large predators are all here in Namibia. Lion are locally common, but largely confined to the parks and the Caprivi area away from dense habitation. Leopard are exceedingly common throughout the country, and the central highlands provide just the kind of rocky habitat that they love. They are, however, very rarely seen naturally. Cheetah do exceptionally well in Namibia, which is said to have about 40% of Africa's population. This is mainly because commercial farmers eradicate lion and hyena relatively easily, and allow smaller buck, the cheetah's natural prey, to coexist with cattle. Hence the cheetahs thrive on large ranches – having problems only if the farmers suspect them of killing stock and try to eradicate them also.

Wild dog have a stronghold in the wild areas in and around Khaudum, but are seldom seen elsewhere. They need huge territories in which to roam, and don't survive well on commercially farmed land. Recent attempts to reintroduce them to Etosha have failed; it is hoped that some may succeed in the future.

The social spotted hyena is common in the north and northwest of the country, and even occurs down into the Namib's central desert areas and the Naukluft mountains – though it is not common here. Much more common and widespread is the solitary, secretive brown hyena, which can be seen by the coast, scavenging amongst the seal colonies.

Buffalo occur in protected national parks in the Caprivi, and have been re-introduced to Waterberg from South Africa, but are not found elsewhere in Namibia.

Elephant occur widely in the north, in Khaudum, Caprivi and Etosha. A separate population has its stronghold in the Kaokoveld. Many venture right down the river valleys and live in desert areas: these are the famous 'desert elephants'. They survive there by knowing exactly where the area's waterholes are, and where water can be found in the rivers. This ancestral knowledge, probably passed down the generations, is easily lost, although in recent years various conservation/development schemes in the area have been so successful that these 'desert-adapted' elephants are now thriving.

Black rhino occur in similar areas, but poaching now effectively limits them to some of the main national parks, and the less accessible areas of the Kaokoveld. Their numbers also are doing very well, and those in the Kaokoveld form one of Africa's only increasing black rhino populations: success indeed for an area outside any national park where only community conservation schemes stand between the poachers and their quarry. White rhino have been re-introduced to Waterberg and Etosha, where they seem to be thriving.

Antelope are well represented, with springbok, gemsbok or impala being numerically dominant depending on the areas. The rare endemic black-faced impala is a subspecies found only in northwestern Namibia and southern Angola.

Roan antelope are found in the Caprivi, Waterberg and Etosha. Sable occur only in the Caprivi, with excellent numbers often seen on the Okavango's floodplains on the edge of Mahango. In the Caprivi's wetter areas there are also red lechwe and the odd sitatunga.

Red hartebeest are widespread in the north and east, though common nowhere. Blue wildebeest are found in Etosha and the north, as are giraffe. Eland occur in Etosha and the Kalahari, whilst kudu seem the most adaptable of the large antelope, occurring everywhere apart from the coastal desert strip – and also eastwards to the Indian Ocean.

Amongst the smaller antelope, duiker are common everywhere apart from the desert, as are steenbok. Klipspringer occur throughout Namibia's mountains. Namibia's smallest antelope, the Damara dik-dik, is endemic to the area around the Kaokoveld and Etosha.

For further details of wildlife, see *Appendix 1*, pages 471–86.

BIRDLIFE Much of Namibia is very dry, and thus hasn't the variation in resident birds that you might find in lusher environments. However, many of those dry-country birds have restricted distributions, and so are endemic, or close to being so. Further, where Namibia's drier interior borders onto a wetter area, as within Mahango National Park, the species count shoots up.

In addition to its residents, Namibia receives many migrants. In September and October the Palaearctic migrants appear (ie: those that come from the northern hemisphere – normally Europe), and they remain until around April or May. This is also the peak time to see the intra-African migrants, which come from further north in Africa.

The coastal wetland sites, most notably around Walvis Bay and Sandwich Harbour, receive visits from many migrating species, as well as seabird species that aren't normally seen in the interior of southern Africa. So visits including the Caprivi and the coast, as well as the country's interior, make Namibia an excellent and varied destination for birding trips.

Inevitably the rains from December to around April see an explosion in the availability of most birds' food: seeds, fruits and insects. Hence this is the prime time for birds to nest, even if it is also the most difficult time to visit the more remote areas of the country.

FIELD GUIDES Finding field guides to plants, animals and birds whilst in Namibia is relatively easy; though it can be difficult outside of the country.

There are some comprehensive little hardback guides on the flora of various areas, including *Namib Flora* and *Damaraland Flora* published by Gamsberg Macmillan in Windhoek. These are sold in Namibia and marketed with visitors in mind as well as locals.

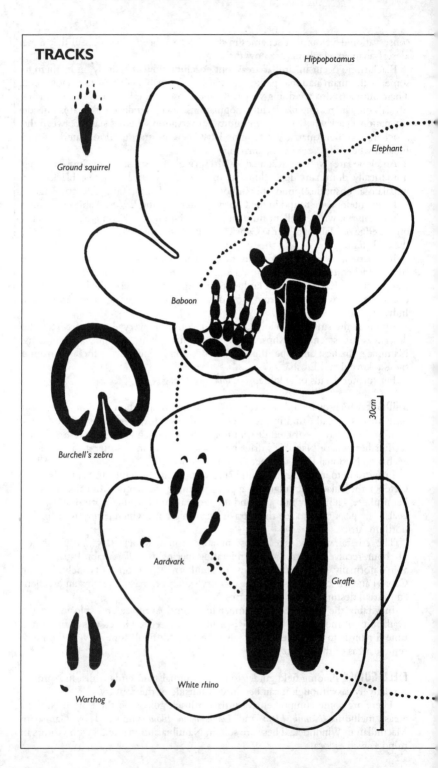

TRACKS

Ground squirrel

Hippopotamus

Elephant

Baboon

Burchell's zebra

Aardvark

Giraffe

Warthog

White rhino

30cm

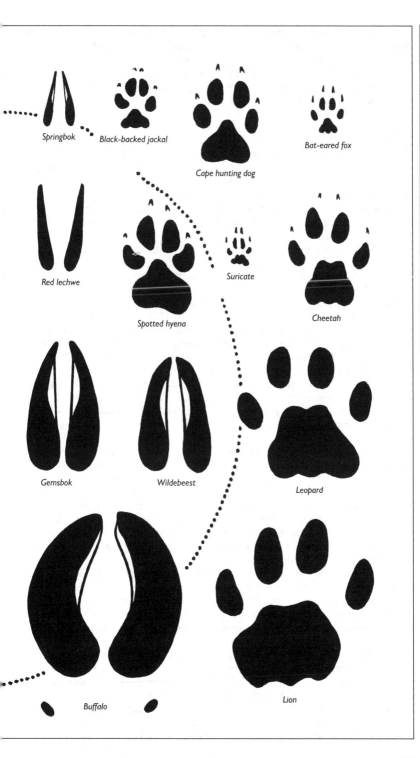

Springbok

Black-backed jackal

Cape hunting dog

Bat-eared fox

Red lechwe

Spotted hyena

Suricate

Cheetah

Gemsbok

Wildebeest

Leopard

Buffalo

Lion

The standard birding guide to travel with is still Newman's *Birds of Southern Africa,* which is widely available overseas. For mammals, Chris and Tilde Stuart's *Field Guide to Mammals of Southern Africa* is generally very good.

The Shell guides to *The Namib* and *Waterberg* are excellent for appreciating the area's flora and fauna. Doubtless more will appear for various other areas in due course. See *Appendix 3* for details of all these books.

CONSERVATION

A great deal has been written about conservation in Africa, much of it over-simplistic and intentionally emotive. As an informed visitor you are in the unique position of being able to see some of the issues at first hand, and to appreciate the perspectives of local people. So abandon your preconceptions, and start by appreciating the complexities of the issues involved. Here I shall try to develop a few ideas, touched on only briefly elsewhere in the book, which are common to most current thinking on conservation.

First, *conservation* must be taken within its widest sense if it is to have meaning. Saving animals is of minimal use if the whole environment is degraded, so we must consider conserving whole areas and ecosystems, not just the odd isolated species.

Observe that land is regarded as an asset by most societies, in Africa as it is elsewhere. (The Bushmen used to be perhaps a notable exception to this.) To 'save' the land for the animals and to use it merely for the recreation of a few privileged foreign tourists – whilst the local people remain in poverty – is a recipe for huge social problems. Local people have hunted game for food for centuries. They have always killed those animals that threatened them or ruined their crops. If we now try to proclaim animals in a populated area as protected, without addressing the concerns of the people, then our efforts will fail.

The only pragmatic way to conserve Namibia's wild areas is to see the *conservation* of animals and the environment as inseparably linked to the *development* of the local people.

In the long term one will not work without the other. Conservation without development leads to resentful local people who will happily, and frequently, shoot, trap and kill animals. Development without conservation will simply repeat the mistakes that most developed countries have already made: it will lay waste a beautiful land, and kill off its natural heritage. Look at the tiny areas of natural vegetation which survive undisturbed in the UK, the USA, or Japan, to see how unsuccessful they have been at long-term conservation over the last 500 years.

As an aside, the local people in Namibia – and other developing countries – are sometimes wrongly accused of being the only agents of degradation. Observe the volume of tropical hardwoods imported by the industrialised countries to see that the West plays no small part in this.

In conserving some of Namibia's natural areas, and helping its people to develop, the international community has a vital role to play. It could use its aid projects to encourage the Namibian government to practise sustainable long-term strategies, rather than grasping for the short-term fixes which politicians seem universally to prefer. But such strategies must have the backing of the people themselves, or they will fall apart when foreign funding eventually wanes.

Most Namibians are more concerned about where they live, what they can eat, and how they will survive, than they are about the lives of small, obscure species of antelope that taste good when roasted. To get backing from the local communities, it is not enough for a conservation strategy to be compatible with development: it must actually promote it and help the local people to improve their own standard of living. If that situation can be reached, then rural populations can be mobilised behind long-term conservation initiatives.

Governments are the same. As one of Zambia's famous conservationists once commented, 'governments won't conserve an impala just because it is pretty'. But they will work to save it *if* they can see that it is worth more to them alive than dead.

The best strategies tried so far on the continent attempt to find lucrative and sustainable ways to use the land. They then plough much of the revenue back into the surrounding local communities. Once the people see revenue from conservation being used to help them improve their lives – to build houses, clinics and schools, and to offer paid employment – then such schemes stand a chance of getting their backing and support. It can take a while ...

Carefully planned, sustainable tourism is one solution that can work effectively. For success, the local people must see that visitors pay because they want the wildlife. Thus, they reason that the existence of wildlife directly improves their income, and they will strive to conserve it.

It isn't enough for them to see that the wildlife helps the government to get richer; that won't dissuade a local hunter from shooting a duiker for dinner. However, if he benefits directly from the visitors, who come to see the animals, then he has a vested interest in saving that duiker.

It matters little to the Namibian people, or ultimately to the wildlife in general terms, whether these visitors come to shoot the animals with a camera or with a gun – as long as any hunting is done on a sustainable basis, so that only a few of the oldest 'trophy' animals are shot each year, and the size of the animal population remains largely unaffected. Photographers may claim the moral high ground, but should remember that hunters pay far more for their privileges. Hunting operations generate large revenues from few guests, who demand minimal infrastructure and so cause little impact on the land. Photographic operations need more visitors to generate the same revenue, and so may have greater negative effects on the country.

NATIONAL PARKS AND PRIVATE RESERVES In practice, there is room for both types of visitors in Namibia: the photographer and the hunter. The national parks are designated for photographic visitors, where no hunting is allowed.

Many private ranches now have game on their land and style themselves as 'hunting farms'. They are used mainly by overseas hunters (primarily from Germany and the USA) who pay handsomely for the privilege. The livelihood of these farms depends on hunting, and so it must be practised sustainably.

There are very few countries in Africa where land is being returned to a more natural state, with fewer livestock and more indigenous game, so Namibia is a great success story.

GOVERNMENT CONSERVATION POLICY In March 1995 the Namibian Cabinet passed a new policy on wildlife management, utilisation and tourism in communal areas (areas occupied by subsistence farmers rather than large-scale commercial ranches). Many interested groups, including the Integrated Rural Development and Nature Conservation (IRDNC; see box overleaf) were closely involved with the formulating of this policy, which enabled a whole new type of community project like Damaraland Camp to get off the ground.

The policy finally encouraged the linking of 'conservation with rural development by enabling communal farmers to derive financial income from the sustainable use of wildlife and from tourism'. It also aimed to 'provide an incentive to the rural people to conserve wildlife and other natural resources, through shared decision-making and financial benefit'.

Put simply, this gave a framework for local communities to take charge of the wildlife in their own areas for sustainable utilisation – with decisions made by the local communities, for the community.

Community Game Guard scheme This scheme (originally called the Auxiliary Game Guard scheme) started in the 1980s and has been behind the phenomenal recovery of the desert-adapted populations of elephant and black rhino in the area. In its simplest form, a community game guard is appointed from each community, and is paid to ensure that no member of the community hunts any animal that they are not allowed to hunt.

Community campsites These aim to enable local communities to benefit very directly from passing tourists. The community sets up a campsite, and then a central community fund receives the money generated – and the whole community decides how that revenue is spent. Once the tourists have stopped to camp, it also gives the community a chance to earn money by guiding the visitors on local walks, selling curios or firewood, or whatever else seems appropriate in the area.

There are now several community campsites in the Kaokoveld, and an increasing number in the Caprivi area.

TOURISM Namibia lies far from Africa's 'original' big-game safari areas of east Africa, Kenya and Tanzania, and from the newer destinations of Zimbabwe and Zambia. Aside from Etosha and Caprivi, Namibia doesn't have the density of game that visitors would expect for such a trip, or the warm tropical shores that they would expect for a beach holiday (anyone who has been to Lüderitz will surely agree). Thus the country doesn't generally attract first-time visitors who simply want to tick-off game, or see game and lie on a beach – a combination that accounts for much volume in the travel business. Therefore few cheap charter planes arrive in Namibia, and there is still only a small number of large hotels, most of which aim more for business people than tourists.

The main area of growth in Namibia's tourism is in individual self-drive trips and small-group tours. These are perfect for the small lodges and guest farms, and have encouraged many small-scale tourist ventures to develop and thrive – utilising not only the few famous national parks, but also old cattle ranches and otherwise unproductive sections of desert.

In the long term, this is a huge advantage for the country. With tourism continuing to grow slowly but steadily, it is hoped that Namibia will avoid the boom-then-bust experienced by countries like Kenya. Every month new small camps, lodges and guest farms open for visitors; most try hard to retain that feeling of 'wilderness' which is so rare in more densely populated countries, and much sought after by visitors. Namibia has so much space and spectacular scenery that, provided the developments remain small-scale and responsible, it should have a very long and profitable career in tourism ahead.

Perhaps Namibia's most promising developments in this field are its successes in linking tourism with community development projects. The Community Game Guard scheme has already safeguarded the populations of desert-adapted elephants and black rhino in the Kaokoveld, whilst a number of community campsites are thriving in the area.

Both projects are now extending their reach into the Caprivi area, assisted by trail-blazing individuals and organisations like the IRDNC. Tourism is a vital source of revenue for many of these projects and, if it helps to provide employment and bring foreign exchange into Namibia, this gives the politicians a reason to support environmental conservation.

Tourists' responsibility Visitors on an expensive trip to Namibia are, by their mere presence, making some financial contribution to development and conservation in Namibia. There are several things that they can do to maximise this.

If camping, they can seek out the community campsites, and support them. They can use the local people there for guides, and pay for the facilities. Even travellers on a lower budget can thus have a direct impact on some of Namibia's smaller, rural communities.

If staying in lodges, they can ask the lodge operator, in the most penetrating of terms, what he or she is doing to help local development initiatives. How much of the lodge's revenue goes directly back to the local community? How do the people benefit directly from the visitors staying at *this* camp? How much of a say do they have about what goes on in the area where *these* safaris are operated?

If enough visitors did this, it would make a big difference. All Namibia's operators would start to place development initiatives higher on their list of priorities. A few operators have really excellent forward-thinking ways of helping their local communities. The success of Damaraland Camp opened up the possibility for other ventures along similar lines, with recent initiatives including the newly opened Doro Nawas and Grootberg.

Some others make a form of 'charity' donation to local communities, but otherwise only involve local people as workers. Whilst this is valuable, much more is needed. Local people must gain greater and more direct benefits from tourism if conservation is going to be successful in Africa, and Namibia is no exception.

HUNTING Big-game hunting, where visiting hunters pay large amounts to kill trophy animals, is a practical source of revenue for many 'hunting farms' which accept guests. Some also accept non-hunters or 'photographic' guests.

It is interesting that the rich killing animals for sport is usually regarded as 'hunting', whilst the poor killing them for food is generally termed 'poaching'.

That said, though many find hunting distasteful, it does benefit the Namibian economy greatly, and encourages farms to cultivate natural wildlife rather than introduced livestock. Until there are enough photographic guests to fill all the guest farms used for hunters, pragmatic conservationists will encourage the hunters.

If you don't hunt, but choose to stay at these places, ensure either that you are comfortable with hunting *per se*, or that there are no hunters on the farm whilst you are there. Arguments over dinner are surprisingly common.

4

Planning and Preparation

Until 1990, most of Namibia's tourists were from South Africa. They came in their own vehicles, for the sea fishing and the game parks – which still have well-organised facilities. Following independence, greater numbers of visitors have arrived from overseas every year, some using the restcamp facilities which were developed for the South Africans. Generally, the overseas visitors have more money to spend; they want small lodges rather than large camps, and restaurants rather than self-catering facilities.

Thus Namibia is seeing a real boom in lodges and bushcamps, and many economically marginal farms are thriving again as guest farms. Such small, individual places don't suit large tours or high-volume tour operators, who use only large hotels for their big groups. Therefore, the future for Namibia, the way that tourism is growing, is in self-drive trips and fly-in safaris by independent visitors who visit the smaller lodges and guest farms, and don't want to be part of a large tour or a big group.

At the more economic end of the spectrum, there's also a boom in first-time visitors travelling around Namibia on a small-group camping trip, led by a driver/guide. This arrangement can offer great flexibility, and a real taste of the country at pretty low cost. Often people who first visit with a group like this will then often return for their own individual self-drive trip – or even fly-in safari.

Namibia is fortunate: its roads are good, its attractions well signposted, and its national parks well managed. Even the centralised booking system for the parks, based at Namibia Wildlife Resorts (NWR) in Windhoek, generally works well for advance bookings.

Despite its phenomenal growth, tourism to Namibia is still on a small scale, a fraction of that found in, say, South Africa or Kenya. So the feeling of wilderness has not been lost; you will still be the only visitors in many corners of the country.

WHEN TO GO

So, Namibia always seems deserted. That said, it becomes busier around Easter and from late July to the end of October. Then advanced bookings are *essential*. Many of the lodges and restcamps in and around Etosha, and in the Namib-Naukluft area, are fully booked for August by as early as the end of April.

Avoid coming during the Namibian school holidays if possible. These are generally around 25 April–25 May, 15 August–5 September and 5 December–15 January. Then many places will be busy with local visitors, especially the less expensive restcamps and the national parks.

The main season when overseas visitors come is from around mid-July to late October. Outside of this, you'll often find the lodges delightfully quiet and have some of the attractions to yourself.

While there really are neither any 'bad' nor any 'ideal' times to visit Namibia, there are times when some aspects of the country are at their best. You must decide what you are primarily interested in, and what's important to you, and then choose accordingly. See the *Climate* section, pages 33–5, for a more detailed discussion of the weather – perhaps the biggest influence on your decision. Then consider your own specific requirements, which might include some of the following.

PHOTOGRAPHY For photography, Namibia is a stunning country in any month. Even with the simplest of camera equipment you can get truly spectacular results. My favourite time for photography is April to June. Then the dust has been washed out of the air by the rains, the vegetation is still green, and yet the sky is clear blue with only a few wispy white clouds.

GAME VIEWING The latter parts of the dry season are certainly the best time to see big game. Then, as the small bush pools dry up and the green vegetation shrivels, the animals move closer to the springs or the waterholes and rivers. So the months between July and late October are ideal for game.

During and after the rains, you won't see much game, partly because the lush vegetation hides the animals, and partly because most of them will have moved away from the waterholes (where they are most easily located) and gone deeper into the bush. However, many of the animals you see will have young, as food (animal or vegetable) is at its most plentiful then.

BIRDWATCHING The last few months of the year witness the arrival of the summer migrant birds from the north, anticipating the coming of the rains. Further, if the rains are good the natural pans in Etosha and Bushmanland will fill with aquatic species, including huge numbers of flamingos. This is an amazing spectacle (see box on *Flamingos*, page 305). However, bear in mind that Namibia's ordinary feathered residents can be seen more easily during the dry season, when there is less vegetation to hide them.

WALKING Daytime temperatures occasionally top 40°C in October and November, and heavy rainstorms are likely during the first two or three months of the year. Hence walkers should try to come between about May and September, when the temperatures are at their coolest, and the chances of rain are minimised. Note that most of the long trails in the national parks are closed between November and March.

DRIVING AROUND Driving usually presents few problems at any time of year. However, visitors in January and February, and occasionally even March or exceptionally April, may find that flooding rivers will block their roads. These usually subside within a matter of hours, and certainly within a day or so, but do provide an extra hazard. A 4x4 may be useful at these times, although taking another route is usually a cheaper alternative! Those mounting 4x4 expeditions to the more remote corners of the country should certainly avoid these months, when large tracts of Bushmanland and Kaokoland, for example, become totally impassable in any vehicle.

For detailed coverage of driving in Namibia, see *Chapter 6*, pages 87–99. For suggested itineraries, see pages 95–9.

HOW TO TRAVEL

Obviously your style of travel around Namibia depends on your budget, though more expensive doesn't always guarantee a better trip.

BACKPACKING Backpacking around Namibia is very limiting. You need private transport to see most of the national parks, and will be missing out on a lot if you don't have it. However, if you can splash out on a few days' car hire here, and a couple of guided trips from a lodge there, you might get by on £20/US$36 per day for the rest of your time.

SELF-DRIVE TRIPS The best way to see the country is certainly to have your own vehicle. Whether you opt to use camps, lodges and restcamps, or bring your own camping kit, is then merely a matter of style. The questions of what, how and where to hire a vehicle, and how much it will cost, are extensively covered in *Chapter 6*, pages 87–91.

If you have a tight budget, a much better bet than backpacking would be to find four people to share the car, and camp everywhere. Then you could keep costs to around £40/US$72 per person per day.

For a less basic self-drive trip, with two people sharing the car and staying in a variety of small lodges and restcamps, expect a cost of about £80/US$145 each. If you choose more expensive lodges, with guided activities included, then this might rise to about £180–200 /US$320–60 per day each – but should guarantee a first-class trip.

GROUP TOURS Another option is to take a guided group tour around the country. These suit single travellers as they provide ready-made companions, those who may not feel confident driving, and those who really do want the input of a guide for their trip – without spending too much money. In either case, provided that you are happy to spend your whole holiday with the same group of people, such a trip might be ideal. Guided trips are generally more expensive than self-drive trips which follow the same itinerary and use the same accommodation. However, including some nights camping within a guided trip can help to bring its costs down substantially.

Generally, the smaller the vehicle used, the better and the more expensive the trip becomes. On a cheaper trip, expect to camp, with a group size of 12–15 people, for around £65/US$120 per day, based on a 12-day itinerary. For something less basic, using smaller minibuses, a trip of one to two weeks will cost around £120/US$215 a day, per person sharing, including all meals and activities. Several operators run small-group trips in Land Rovers, with professional guides rather than simply drivers. These can be excellent, but will cost more than a self-drive trip around the same itinerary. Expect to pay upwards of £150/US$270 per person per night.

PRIVATE GUIDED TRIPS If money is not so restricted, and especially if you're travelling in a small group with four or more people (eg: a family trip), you ought to consider a private guided trip. Your group would then have its own vehicle and guide for the whole trip. You might sleep in existing lodges and camps, or use camping kits supplied by your guide – or might even stay at luxury private tented camps set up just for you. The choice will be yours when you arrange the trip. This isn't a cheap way to travel, but can be well worth the price tag.

FLY-IN TRIPS Finally if your budget is very flexible (and especially if your time is very limited), then consider doing some or all of your trip as a fly-in safari. Small private charter flights can be arranged to many of the smaller lodges and guest farms; it's a very easy way to travel. It is also the only way to get to some of the more inaccessible corners, like the northern section of the Skeleton Coast.

A very popular combination is to fly down to the Sesriem area for three or four nights, hop up to Swakopmund, and then pick up a hire car to drive yourself north to Damaraland and Etosha. Another place commonly visited on short fly-in trips is the Fish River Canyon.

Gordon Rattray (www.able-travel.com)

A vast land of sand, strewn with rocks and pitted by rivers and ravines sounds inadvisable for people who have trouble walking, and downright impossible for wheelchair users. Surprisingly, the opposite is true. Namibia is one of Africa's most accessible destinations, with decent infrastructure, facilities catering to most needs and operators ranging from 'ready and efficient' to 'experienced and specialised'.

Granted, depending on your needs, a lot of research and effort may be necessary to get the best from your trip, but Namibians love a challenge and, as other travellers have shown, almost anything is possible.

ACCOMMODATION A quick surf of the internet will leave you awash with 'accessible' accommodation, but it pays to take care here. Although many proprietors are aware of this growing market and have ground-floor rooms with small steps and wide doorways, few have ideal, custom-built quarters. It is worth highlighting Tamboti Guest House in Windhoek, which has wheelchair-accessible rooms and roll-in showers. Although not everywhere can claim to be as accommodating, many proprietors are easily contactable by email so you can discuss your requirements beforehand.

Other hotels and lodges that are to some degree accessible are:

Windhoek and surrounds Tamboti Guest House (page 133), Gocheganas Nature Reserve (page 140), Midgard Lodge (page 167), Klein Windhoek Guest House (page 134)

Swakopmund & surrounds Hansa Hotel (page 272), Swakopmund Hotel & Entertainment Centre (page 272)

Near Tsumeb/Etosha Huab Lodge near Kamanjab (pages 345–6), Mokuti Lodge (page 370), !Uris Safari Lodge (pages 402–3)

Namib-Naukluft/South Rostock Ritz Desert Lodge (pages 259–60), Sossusvlei Lodge (page 252), Bahnhof Hotel, Aus (page 214)

For a more extensive list of accommodation with disabled access, contact the Hospitality Association of Namibia (\f+264 61 222904; e service@HANnamibia.com; www.hannamibia.com).

TRANSPORT

By air Windhoek's Hosea Kutako International Airport has wheelchairs, an aisle chair and staff to assist with transfers. It also has a roomy toilet for disabled people, although Graham Teager suggests that this appears to be an afterthought as it is located to the rear of the 'normal' toilet with three 90° turns required to get to it. More provincial airfields cannot guarantee such amenities.

Taxis I have yet to hear of a normal taxi company in Namibia that runs vehicles with facilities for people who prefer to stay in their wheelchairs. Having said that, drivers are happy to give people the time they need to enter and exit the car, and they are usually willing to help wheelchair users transfer from their chairs. However, it is important to remember that they are not trained in this skill – you need to fully explain the help you need and stay in control as the transfer proceeds.

Car hire Currently no company in Namibia has cars with basic hand controls, although

Colin Stewart managed to persuade Avis (page 91) to provide one, after 'prolonged negotiation' with their UK manager.

Your own vehicle Trish Thompson took hand controls with her on an extended tour of southern Africa, and fitted them to a car purchased on a one-year buy-back scheme. Although this worked, she says that despite several months of email conversations with the company prior to arrival, they still had to wait ten days in Cape Town dealing with unexpected paperwork.

By bus Namibia's buses are not adapted at all, so unless you can walk to some degree this method of transport will not be ideal.

By rail Currently, the only train with accessible bathrooms is the *Omugulu Gwombashe Star*, operating between Windhoek and Oshivelo in northern Namibia.

ACTIVITIES Going on safari is always possible, although the form this takes will depend on your ability and sense of adventure. In Walvis Bay, Levo Tours' (page 297) fishing, and seal and dolphin excursion boats can accommodate wheelchairs, and a special boarding ramp was built for this purpose. Scenic flights can be arranged through Capture Africa (↘ +264 64 404348; f +264 64 404249; e capture@mweb.com.na; www.captureafrica.com), and Trish Thompson says adrenalin sports such as Swakopmund's dune quad biking can be quite feasible for many disabilities.

HEALTH You must understand and be able to explain your own particular medical requirements, and rural hospitals are often basic, so take as much of your necessary medication and equipment with you. It is advisable to pack this in your hand luggage during flights in case your main luggage gets lost.

Namibia can be hot. If this is a problem for you, be careful to book accommodation with fans or air conditioning. A useful cooling aid is a plant-spray bottle.

SECURITY It is worthwhile remembering that if you are less mobile, then you are more vulnerable. Stay aware of who is around you and where your bags are, especially during car transfers and similar. These activities often draw onlookers, and the confusion creates easy pickings for an opportunist thief.

SPECIALIST TOUR OPERATORS
Endeavour Safaris ↘/f +27 (21) 556 6114; m +27 (73) 206 7733; e info@endeavour-safaris.com; www.endeavour-safaris.com. Specialists in accessible travel for disabled people.

Titch Tours ↘ +27 (21) 686 5501; f +27 (21) 686 5506; e titcheve@iafrica.com; http://titchtours.co.za. Operator running trips for disabled travellers.

Disabled Birders' Association e bo@fatbirder.com; www.disabledbirdersassociation.co.uk. Birdwatching trips worldwide for disabled people.

SandyAcre Safaris (page 125) Did the logistics for BBC television's *Beyond Boundaries* project, which involved a group of disabled people crossing Namibia. No specialist equipment but willing to cater to clients' needs to provide a feasible itinerary.

Big5Experience ↘ + 264 (0)62 581423; f + 264 (0)62 581423; e frikkie@big5experience.com; www.big5experience.com. No specialist equipment & little experience of disability, but an established operator that will attempt to accommodate all travellers.

FINALLY, SOME USEFUL ADVICE Pull wheelchairs backwards through soft sand! *(from Scott Hurd, who visited Namibia with a disabled friend).*

Expect to pay upwards of about £250/US$450 per person per night for a full fly-in trip, and note that your choice of lodges will be restricted to those that can arrange all your activities for you.

ORGANISING YOUR TRIP

Most visitors who come to Namibia for a holiday use the country's guest farms, lodges and restcamps – often combining them into a self-drive tour around the country.

Such trips are quite complex, as you will be using numerous hotels, camps and lodges in your own particular sequence. Many of these places are small (and so easily filled), and organise their own logistics with military precision. Finding space at short notice is often difficult.

To arrange everything, it's best to use a reliable, independent tour operator based in your own country. Although many operators sell trips to Namibia, few really know the country well. Insist on dealing directly with someone who does. Namibia changes so fast that detailed local knowledge is vital in putting together a trip that runs smoothly and suits you. Make sure that whoever you book with is fully bonded, so that your money is protected if they go broke; and, ideally, pay with a credit card. Never book a trip from someone who doesn't know Namibia personally: you are asking for problems.

Trips around Namibia are not cheap, though they are currently cheaper (and also better value in many cases) than in any other country in southern Africa. Expect to pay around the same to an operator as you would have to pay directly: about £550–1,100/US$990–1,980 per person per week, plus airfares. At this price you can expect a good level of service while you are considering the options and booking the trip. If you don't get it, go elsewhere.

Booking directly with Namibian safari operators or agencies is possible, but communication is more difficult and you will have no recourse if anything goes wrong. European/US operators usually work on commission for the trips that they sell, which is deducted from the basic cost that the visitor pays. Thus you should end up paying about the same whether you book through an overseas operator or talk directly to someone in Namibia, but the former is a lot easier.

TOURIST INFORMATION The national tourist board, Namibia Tourism (☏ +264 61 290 6000; f +264 61 254848; e info@namibiatourism.com.na; www.namibiatourism.com.na), based in Windhoek, is worth contacting for information – with plenty of brochures and a good tourist map – before your trip.

TOUR OPERATORS Until relatively recently, most tour operators overseas have overlooked Namibia. Now that it is better known, many are hastily putting together programmes without knowing what they're doing. Often they are just selling tours that someone in Namibia has designed and marketed. Few have spent much time in the country themselves, and fewer still can give detailed first-hand guidance on all of the country, let alone a wide range of guest farms, camps and lodges.

Don't be talked into thinking that there are only a handful of places to visit and a few camps to stay in. There are many, all individual and different. Ask about ones mentioned in these chapters; a good operator will know the vast majority of them and be able to describe them to you.

Here I must, as the author, admit a personal interest in the tour-operating business: I organise and run the southern African operations of the UK operator Expert Africa (☏ 020 8232 9777; e info@expertafrica.com) and Wild about Africa (☏ 020 8758 4717; e safari@wildaboutafrica.com). In Namibia, Expert Africa concentrates on flexible self-drive trips and fly-in safaris; our self-drive safaris start at about £1,400/US$2,520 per person for two weeks, including flights from London, car hire, all accommodation and some meals. Wild about Africa focuses on guided small-group trips, which start at around £1,000/US$1,800 per person for ten days, including flights from London, all transport, accommodation and meals.

I believe that between Expert Africa and Wild about Africa, we have by far the best and most interesting programme of varied trips to Namibia – and will happily send you a detailed map of Namibia and our brochures to demonstrate this. Just call us.

UK For a fair comparison, UK tour operators that feature Namibia include:

Aardvark Safaris RBL Hse, Ordnance Rd, Tidworth, Hants SP9 7QD; ☏ 01980 849160; e mail@aardvarksafaris.com; www.aardvarksafaris.com. Small, upmarket operator featuring much of Africa & Madagascar.

Abercrombie & Kent St George's Hse, Ambrose St, Cheltenham, Glos GL50 3LG; ☏ 0845 0700 610; f 0845 0700 607; e info@abercrombiekent.co.uk; www.abercrombiekent.co.uk. Long-established, large & posh operator worldwide, with a wide choice of Africa trips – though often focuses on selling its own lodges in Africa.

Africa Explorer 5 Strand on the Green, London W4 3PQ; ☏ 020 8987 8742; e john@africa-explorer.co.uk; www.africa-explorer.co.uk. Tiny but knowledgeable company, run by the jovial John Haycock.

Africa Travel Centre 21 Leigh St, London WC1H 9EW; ☏ 0845 450 1520; e info@africatravel.co.uk; www.africatravel.co.uk. Featuring east & southern Africa, the Africa Travel Centre has a special emphasis on golfing holidays, & trips for sportspeople to Africa.

Cazenove & Loyd 9 Imperial Studios, 3–11 Imperial Rd, London SW6 2AG; ☏ 020 7384 2332; e info@cazloyd.com; www.caz-loyd.com. Old-school, established tailor-made specialists to east/southern Africa, the Indian Ocean Islands, & Central/South America.

Cedarberg African Travel 5 Oriel Ct, The Green, Twickenham TW2 5AG; ☏ 020 8755 7917; e web@cedarberg-travel.com; www.cedarberg-travel.com. South African specialist with some knowledge of Namibia.

Cox & Kings Gordon Hse, 10 Greencoat Pl, London SW1P 1PH; ☏ 020 7873 5000; e cox.kings@coxandkings.co.uk; www.coxandkings.co.uk. Old company renowned for India, now also featuring Latin America, Indian Ocean, Middle East, China, Asia & Africa, including some Namibian trips.

Expert Africa 9 & 10 Upper Sq, Old Isleworth, Middx TW7 7BJ; ☏ 020 8232 9777; e info@expertafrica.com; www.expertafrica.com. Started trips to Namibia in 1992, & now have the most comprehensive programme to the country, run by Chris McIntyre – this book's author.

Explore! Nelson Hse, 55 Victoria Rd, Farnborough, Hants GU14 7PA; ☏ 0870 333 4001; e res@explore.co.uk; www.explore.co.uk. A relatively large company specialising in escorted small-group tours throughout the world. Currently has a choice of three Namibia-only tours.

Gane & Marshall Northway Hse, 1379 High Rd, London N20 9LP; ☏ 020 8445 6000; e holidays@ganeandmarshall.com; www.ganeandmarshall.com. Small-group trips to South & Central America and the Galápagos, plus the Far East & most of Africa, from Ethiopia to Namibia.

Guerba Wessex Hse, 40 Station Rd, Westbury, Wilts BA13 3JN; ☏ 01373 826611; e info@guerba.co.uk; www.guerba.co.uk. Long-standing overland truck company that's branched out in recent years into other trips worldwide; takes a very responsible approach to African travel.

Hartley's Safaris The Old Chapel, Chapel Lane, Hackthorn, Lincs LN2 3PN; ☏ 01673 861600; e info@hartleys-safaris.co.uk; www.hartleys-safaris.co.uk. Old-school, established tailor-made specialists to east/southern Africa & Indian Ocean islands.

Nomad African Travel 14 Sharpe's Hill, Barrow, Bury St Edmunds IP29 5BY; ☏/f 01284 810101; e nomad@microlink.zm; www.nomadafricantravel.co.uk. Set-itinerary camping safaris around southern Africa, including Namibia.

Okavango Tours & Safaris Marlborough Hse, 298 Regent's Park Rd, London N3 2TJ; ☏ 020 8343 3283; e info@okavango.com; www.okavango.com. Small, long-established specialists to east/southern Africa, Madagascar & the Indian Ocean islands.

Rainbow Tours 305 Upper St, London N1 2TU; ☏ 020 7226 1004; e info@rainbowtours.co.uk; www.rainbowtours.co.uk. Established operator to southern, east & central Africa, the Indian Ocean & Madagascar. Recently expanded into Oman.

Safari Consultants Orchard Hse, Upper Rd, Little Cornard, Suffolk CO10 0NZ; ✆ 01787 228494; ℮ bill@safariconsultantuk.com; www.safari-consultants.co.uk, www.safariconsultantuk.com. Old-school tailor-made specialists to the Indian subcontinent, east/central/southern Africa, including Namibia, & the Indian Ocean islands.

Safari Drive Windy Hollow, Sheepdrove, Lambourn, Berks RG17 7XA; ✆ 01488 71140; ℮ info@safaridrive.com; www.safaridrive.com. Operate expedition-style trips using equipped Land Rovers, mainly in Botswana & Tanzania though also covers Namibia.

Scott Dunn World Fovant Mews, 12 Noyna Rd, London SW17 7PH; ✆ 020 8682 5000; ℮ africa@scottdunn.com; www.scottdunn.com. Worldwide luxury operator featuring Asia, Latin America, ski chalets, Mediterranean villas & Africa, including Namibia.

Steppes Travel 51 Castle St, Cirencester, Glos GL7 1QD; ✆ 01285 650011; ℮ africa@steppestravel.co.uk; www.steppestravel.co.uk. Originally founded as Art of Travel, this posh tailor-made specialist now features much of Asia, as well as most of east, central &

southern Africa, plus Mauritius & the Seychelles.

Tim Best Travel 68 Old Brompton Rd, London SW7 3LQ; ✆ 020 7591 0300; ℮ info@timbesttravel.com; www.timbesttravel.com. Bespoke operator concentrating on South America, the Indian Ocean islands & Africa — including Namibia.

Wild about Africa Sunvil House, Upper Sq, Old Isleworth, Middx TW7 7BJ; ✆ 020 8758 4717; ℮ safari@wildaboutafrica.com; www.wildaboutafrica.com. Sister-company of Expert Africa offers a wide choice of small-group guided trips in Namibia & some of Botswana from inexpensive camping trips to privately guided expeditions.

Wildlife Worldwide Long Barn South, Sutton Manor Farm, Bishops Sutton, Hants SO24 0AA; ✆ 0845 130 6982; ℮ sales@wildlifeworldwide.com; www.wildlifeworldwide.com. Wide-ranging small operator with programmes across the globe, including options that feature Namibia.

Zambezi Safari & Travel Ermington Mill, Ivybridge, Devon PL21 9NT; ✆ 01548 830059; ℮ info@zambezi.com; www.zambezi.com. Web-based tailor-made specialist to a range of African destinations.

Overland specialists

Dragoman Camp Green, Debenham, Stowmarket, Suffolk IP14 6LA; ✆ 01728 861133; ℮ info@dragoman.co.uk; www.dragoman.co.uk. Budget overland truck tours worldwide, including Africa.

Exodus Grange Mills, 9 Weir Rd, London SW12 0NE; ✆ 020 8673 0859; ℮ info@exodus.co.uk; www.exodus.co.uk. Budget overland truck & set tours worldwide, including Africa.

US

Africa Adventure Company 5353 N Federal Highway, Suite 300, Fort Lauderdale, FL 33308; ✆ 954 491 8877, 1 800 882 9453; f 954 491 9060; ℮ noltingaac@aol.com; www.africa-adventure.com

Ker & Downey 6703 Highway Bd, Katy, Texas 77494; ✆ 0800 423 4236; ℮ info@kerdowney.com; www.kerdowney.com

South Africa

Jenman African Safaris 7 Lancaster Rd, Kenilworth, Cape Town 7702; ✆ 021 683 7826; ℮ info@jenmansafaris.com; www.jenmansafaris.com

Pulse Africa PO Box 2417, Parklands 2121, Johannesburg; ✆ 011 325 2290; ℮ info@pulseafrica.com; www.pulseafrica.com

NATIONAL PARKS Namibia Wildlife Resorts (NWR) is the government department responsible for all the national parks. It is generally efficient, if sometimes apparently over-zealous about its bureaucracy. Its system insists that advance bookings for accommodation are made through the Windhoek office.

You can, theoretically, reserve accommodation by post or fax. However, you must pay for it in advance. From overseas this may require a telex transfer of money. To start this process, write to Namibia Wildlife Resorts (*Central Reservations Office, P Bag 13267, Windhoek;* ✆ *061 285 7200;* f *061 224900;* ℮ *reservations@nwr.com.na, nwr@mweb.com.na; www.nwr.com.na*). If you are booking fewer than 25 days ahead, then you must pay for everything in full. This system is most easily mastered by visiting the office in person in Windhoek (see page 124 for directions to the office). Alternatively book in advance through a tour operator that understands the system.

Entry permits for most parks are available at the gates, provided you're there before they close and there is space left. The exceptions are permits for the Naukluft, Terrace Bay and Torra Bay, which can be obtained only from Windhoek. Permits to drive through the Namib section of the Namib-Naukluft Park are available at most tourist offices.

Entrance to the major national parks – Etosha, Namib-Naukluft (Sesriem entrance), Waterberg, Ai-Ais Transfrontier, and the Skeleton Coast – is currently N$80 per person (under 16s free), plus N$10 per vehicle. At other parks, the entrance fee is N$40 per person, but the fee for vehicles remains N$10. NWR revise their prices every year.

If you have booked accommodation in advance through the NWR, it's worth confirming this just before your trip. Despite the best of intentions, there have been occasions when visitors have arrived to find pre-booked accommodation closed for reasons such as flooding or a presidential visit, so it's wise to be cautious. Note that accommodation fees do not include park entrance fees; both are payable.

PUBLIC HOLIDAYS During Namibia's public holidays the towns shut down, though the national parks and other attractions just carry on regardless.

New Year's Day	1 January
Independence Day	21 March
Good Friday	
Easter Monday	
Workers' Day	1 May
Cassinga Day	4 May
Africa Day	25 May
Ascension Day	40 days after Easter Sunday
Heroes' Day	26 August
Human Rights Day	10 December
Christmas Day	25 December
Family Day	26 December

GETTING THERE AND AWAY

✈ BY AIR

From Europe There are several airlines flying to Namibia from Europe. Some are direct, and all are reliable. Most fly overnight, so you can fall asleep on the plane in London, and wake in southern Africa ready to explore. The time difference between western Europe and Namibia is minimal, so there's no jet lag.

In July 2005 Air Namibia (☎ 0870 774 0965) introduced a direct flight from London Gatwick to Windhoek. Flights depart from Gatwick on Sunday, Wednesday and Friday, returning from Windhoek on Saturday, Tuesday and Thursday. Another option to Windhoek with Air Namibia is from Frankfurt, with connections to London on British Airways. Currently flights depart from Frankfurt for Windhoek on Monday, Tuesday, Thursday and Saturday evenings. Northbound they leave Windhoek for Frankfurt on Tuesday morning, and also Wednesday, Friday and Sunday evenings. Air Namibia also operates connecting flights to/from Johannesburg and Cape Town to link up with most of these intercontinental flights to/from Windhoek.

If you consider flying via Johannesburg, then there's a whole host of other options, from many European airports. British Airways and South African Airways have daily services from London, and both operate add-on connections to Windhoek, run by their subsidiaries, though these take longer and are more expensive than flying direct.

Virgin also services the Johannesburg route, though their add-on prices to Windhoek are not usually as competitive. If cost is an issue, you could fly to Johannesburg, hire a car there (where car-hire prices are significantly lower than in Namibia), and drive to Namibia, though it's a very long journey (800km to Fish River Canyon), so only for the absolutely determined or those with lots of time on their hands.

Expect to pay from around £550/US$825 return. Prices rise significantly for departures during Easter, July, August, and peak from mid-December to mid-January, when you can expect to pay up to £950/US$1,425. The quietest periods are mid-April to the end of June, and November.

Finding cheap tickets, and the right flights, is an art in itself. All the airlines will help you with information, but they sell their own seats at the 'published' fares. These are considerably above what you can expect to pay if you shop around. If you plan to hire a car or arrange some accommodation in advance, then speak to one of the UK's specialist tour operators (see pages 52–4) *before* you book your flights. They will often offer to arrange everything together, and quote one cost for your whole trip – flights, car and accommodation. This may seem a lot, but compare it with the cost and hassle of putting the various components together yourself and you'll find that the better operators offer excellent deals.

However, if you're on a very tight budget and want to fly in and backpack around, then talk to a flight-only specialist. In the UK, look in the classified adverts in the Sunday papers (start with the *Sunday Times*). You'll quickly learn what's available and how much the tickets cost. Flight specialists usually know nothing about Namibia; they just want to sell you flight tickets quickly. In London, they include Trailfinders (✆ 020 7938 3939; *www.trailfinders.com*) and Travel Bag (✆ 0870 814 6645; *www.travelbag.co.uk*).

From the Americas South African Airways operates direct flights between Atlanta and Johannesburg, code-sharing with Delta, which connect with numerous regional flights to Windhoek. Alternatively, many travellers from the US approach southern Africa using connections via Europe, joining Air Namibia's flights in Frankfurt, or travelling on one of the many carriers servicing Johannesburg, and then connecting through to Windhoek. Start your research by looking in the classified section of the *New York Times*, which has a good section on discount flight specialists.

Given the duration of these flights, travellers often include a few days in Europe as they transit. This highlights the possibility of booking a return USA–London flight (from US$440 return) with an American travel specialist, and a return London–Windhoek flight (from US$800 return) with a London specialist. This means that you can use discounted fares for both legs and make a considerable saving. However, do allow a day or so in London between the flights, as your flights will not technically 'connect' – and if one is late you don't want to miss the other.

Travellers in Central and South America might use the Atlanta or European gateways, or the direct flights between São Paulo and Johannesburg, run by South African Airways (code-share with Varig) five times a week.

From elsewhere From the Far East, there are flights between Johannesburg and most of the major centres in the region, including Hong Kong (with South African Airways or Cathay Pacific) and Singapore (South African Airlines and Singapore Airlines). From Australasia, the best route is probably one of the flights from Perth to Johannesburg, with South African Airways or Qantas, connecting to Windhoek.

BY LAND If you are not flying in, then entering over one of Namibia's land borders is equally easy. Namibia has fast and direct links with South Africa – good tarred roads and railway service.

Crossing borders Namibia's borders are generally hassle-free and efficient. If you are crossing with a hired car, then remember to let the car-hire company know as they will need to provide you with the right paperwork before you set off. Opening hours at the borders are currently as follows (see also *www.namibweb.com/gi.htm*):

With Botswana
Buitepos – on the Gobabis–Ghanzi road	08.00–22.00
Impalila Island – over the river from Kasane	07.00–18.00
Ngoma Bridge – between Caprivi and Kasane	08.00–18.00
Mohembo – on the southern side of Mahango	08.00–17.00

With Zambia
Wenella – just north of Katima Mulilo	07.00–18.00

With Angola
Oshikango – on the main road north	08.00–18.00
Ruacana – near the hydro-electric station	08.00–18.00
Rundu – cross the river to go north	08.00–17.00

With South Africa
Hohlweg – on the D622 southeast of Aroab	08.00–16.30
Klein Menasse – on the Aroab–Rietfontein road	08.00–22.00
Ariamsvlei – on the Karasburg–Upington road	24 hours
Noordoewer – on the Windhoek–Cape Town road	24 hours
Oranjemund – the bridge over the Orange River	06.00–22.00
Velloorsdrif – on the C10 southeast of Karasburg	08.00–16.30

VISAS AND ENTRY REQUIREMENTS

DOCUMENTS Currently all visitors require a passport which is valid for at least six months after they are due to leave, and an onward ticket of some sort. In practice, the second requirement is rarely even considered if you look neat, respectable and fairly affluent.

At present, British, Irish and American citizens can enter Namibia without a visa for 90 days or less for a holiday or private visit, as can nationals of the following countries: Angola, Australia, Austria, Belgium, Botswana, Brazil, Canada, Cuba, France, Germany, Iceland, Italy, Japan, Kenya, Lesotho, Liechtenstein, Luxembourg, Malaysia, Mozambique, the Netherlands, New Zealand, Portugal, Russia and the CIS, Scandinavian countries, Singapore, South Africa, Spain, Swaziland, Switzerland, Tanzania, Zambia and Zimbabwe.

That said, it is *always* best to check with your local Namibian embassy or high commission before you travel. If you have difficulties in your home country, contact the Ministry of Home Affairs in Windhoek on the corner of Independence Avenue and Kasino Street (*P Bag 13200, Windhoek;* ✆ *061 292 2111*).

The maximum tourist visa is 90 days, but this can be easily extended by application in Windhoek. You will then probably be required to show proof of the 'means to leave', like an onward air ticket, a credit card, or sufficient funds of your own. The current cost of a tourist or business visa is N$207.

ⓔ NAMIBIAN EMBASSIES AND HIGH COMMISSIONS A list of the foreign embassies in Windhoek can be found on pages 150–1. Namibia's diplomatic representatives overseas include:

Angola 37 Rua Dos Coqueiros, PO Box 953, Luanda;
🕿 +244 2 395483; f +244 2 339234;
e embnam@netangola.com

Belgium Av de Tervuren 454, B1150 Bruxelles;
🕿 +32 2 771 1410; f +32 2 771 9689;
e nam.emb@brutele.be

Botswana PO Box 987, 2nd Floor, Debswana Hse,
Gaborone; 🕿 +267 390 2181; f +267 390 2248;
e nhc.gabs@info.bw

France 80 Av Foch, 17 Square de l'Av Foch, Paris
75016; 🕿 +33 1 4417 3265/76; f +33 1 4417
3273; e namparis@club-internet.fr

Germany 2nd Floor, 5 Wichmannstrasse, 10787
Berlin; 🕿 +49 30 254 0950; f +49 30 254
09555; e namibiaberlin@aol.com

Russia 2nd Kazachy Lane, Hse No 7, Moscow;
🕿 +7 95 230 3275; f +7 95 230 2274;
e namembrf@online.ru

South Africa PO Box 29806, Sunnyside 0132, 702
Church St, Arcadia, Pretoria; 🕿 +27 12 481 9100;
f +27 12 343 7294; e secretary@namibia.org.za

Sweden Luntmakargatan 86–8, PO Box 19151, SE-
104 32 Stockholm; 🕿 +46 8 612 7788; f +46 8
612 6655; e info@embassyofnamibia.se

UK 6 Chandos St, London W1G 9LU; 🕿 +44 20
7636 6244; f +44 20 7637 5694; e namibia-
highcomm@btconnect.com

USA 1605 New Hampshire Av NW, Washington, DC
20009; 🕿 +1 202 986 0540; f +1 202 986
0443; e info@ namibianembassyusa.org;
http://www.namibianembassyusa.org/

Zambia 30B Mutende Rd, PO Box 30577, Woodlands,
Lusaka; 🕿 +260 1 260407/8; f +260 1 263858;
e namibia@coppernet.zm

Zimbabwe 31A Lincoln Rd, Avondale, PO Box 7166,
Harare; 🕿 +263 4 885841; f +263 4 885800;
e namhighcom@primenet.co.zw

IMPORTS AND EXPORTS Since Namibia is a member of the Southern African Customs Union (SACU), there are few import and export restrictions between Namibia and either Botswana or South Africa. If you wish to export animal products, including skins or legally culled ivory, make sure you obtain a certificate confirming the origin of every item bought. Remember: even with such a certificate, the international CITES convention prohibits the movement of some things across international borders. Do consider the ethics of buying any animal products that might be covered by CITES.

$ MONEY AND BANKING

CURRENCY The Namibian dollar (N$) is divided into 100 cents. This is freely convertible in Namibia; there's no black market and no customs regulations applicable to moving it across borders. It is currently tied to the South African rand (R) so that N$1 = R1. Rand can be used freely in Namibia – nobody even notices – though it is often difficult to change Namibian dollars once you leave Namibia. Even in South Africa, you must change the dollars at a bank, and may be charged a small premium for doing so.

Many banks overseas know only the exchange rate for rand, and don't supply Namibian dollars, or even quote a rate for it. If that's the case, you can bring rand to Namibia, and use that instead.

If the rand plummets in the future, perhaps as the result of negative developments in South Africa, then Windhoek may take full control of its currency, and allow it to float free from the rand. Its economy is probably strong enough to make this a very positive move. Check the latest situation with one of the bigger banks before you leave.

For most of the late 1990s the rand slowly, but steadily devalued: it slipped from about £1 = R6 in 1996 to £1 = R12 in 2001. Then in late 2001 it tumbled down to almost £1 = R20, only to recover back to £1 = R12 in 2003. It has remained around the £1 = R11–12 since then, until dropping a little in 2006. It could easily move either way in the future. Currently, in April 2007, the rates of exchange are:

£1 = N$14.07
US$1 = N$7.09
€1 = N$9.53

Despite the volatility, travel in Namibia for the Western visitor remains good value compared with the rest of the region.

HOW TO TAKE YOUR MONEY Cash in the form of Namibian dollars or South African rand is essential for buying petrol and small items, and in remote areas.

The major credit cards (Visa, MasterCard and Diners Club) are widely accepted by lodges, hotels, restaurants and shops, and often transactions in Namibia take time to appear on your statement. There are reports, though, that American Express cards are increasingly difficult to use in both shops and banks. Even the smaller towns now have ATMs, either as part of a bank, or inside supermarkets, and withdrawing cash by this means is usually no harder than at home. That said, Visa cards are easier than most, while Switch/Cirrus cards often do not work in these machines. It's important to remember that there are long distances between towns and lodges, so be sure to assess your needs thoroughly in advance.

Some travellers still prefer to take some of their money as travellers' cheques (sterling or US dollars). Banks in the cities will cash travellers' cheques, and both American Express and Barclays Visa cheques are well recognised, and replacements are issued if cheques are stolen. Away from the banks travellers' cheques which are not in Namibian dollars or South African rand can be difficult to use. Wherever you are, remember that petrol stations always require cash.

The best system is always to have some cash Namibian dollars (or rand – remember they are interchangeable) with you, whilst conserving these by using credit cards where you can. You can gradually withdraw more money from your credit or debit cards, or by cashing travellers' cheques, as your trip progresses. However, always make sure that your Namibian dollars will last out until you can get to a bank. For details of changing money, see below.

BANKING Changing money at any of the commercial banks is as easy and as quick as it is in Europe. Normal banking hours are 08.30–15.30 weekdays and sometimes 08.30–11.00 Saturdays, depending upon the town, though there are a few places that are open seven days a week. Banks will cash travellers' cheques or give cash advances on credit cards, though the clearance required for a cash advance may take 30 minutes or so. Note that you may need to take a passport, even just to change currency.

ATMs work with Visa and MasterCard cards, though whether you are using a debit card or a credit card, you should enter 'credit card account' and not 'bank account' when prompted about where you want your money to come from.

Note that at the end of the month, when many government employees are paid, the queue at the bank can be several hours long.

BUDGETING Namibia genuinely offers something to suit travellers of every budget, with accommodation ranging from backpackers' hostels to luxurious lodges with everything in between. For an indication of budgeting for various styles of trip, see *How to travel*, pages 48–52.

TIPPING Tipping is a very difficult and contentious topic – worth thinking about carefully; thoughtlessly tipping too much is just as bad as tipping too little.

Ask locally what's appropriate; here I can only give rough guidance. Helpers with baggage might expect a couple of Namibian dollars for their help. Restaurants will often add an automatic service charge to the bill, in which case an additional tip is not usually given. If they do not do this, then 10% would certainly be appreciated if the service was good.

At upmarket lodges, tipping is not obligatory, despite the destructive assumptions of some visitors that it is. If a guide has given you really good service, then a tip of about N$100 (US$5–10/£2–5) per guest per day would be a generous reflection of this. If the service hasn't been that good, then don't tip. Always tip at the end of your stay, not at the end of each day/activity, which can lead to the guides only trying hard when they know there's a tip at the end of the morning. Such camps aren't pleasant to visit and this isn't the way to encourage top-quality guiding. Give what you feel is appropriate in one lump sum, though before you do this find out if tips go into one box for all of the camp staff, or if the guides are treated differently. Then ensure that your tip reflects this – with perhaps as much again divided between the rest of the staff.

WHAT TO TAKE

This is difficult advice to give, as it depends upon how you travel and your own personality. If you intend to do a lot of hitching or backpacking, then you should plan carefully what you take in an attempt to keep things as light as possible. If you have a vehicle for your whole trip, then weight and bulk will not be such an issue.

CLOTHING On most days you will want light, loose-fitting clothing. Cotton (or a cotton-rich mix) is cooler and more absorbent than synthetic fibres. For men, shorts (long ones) are usually fine, but long trousers are more socially acceptable in towns and especially in rural settlements and villages. For women, knee-length skirts or culottes are best. Namibia has a generally conservative dress code. Revealing or scruffy clothing isn't respected or appreciated by most Namibians.

For the evenings, especially for chilling rides in the back of safari vehicles, and during rainstorms, you will need something warm. Night-time temperatures in the winter months can be very low, especially in desert areas. If possible, dress in layers, taking along a light sweater (polar-fleeces are ideal) and a long-sleeved jacket, or a tracksuit, and a light but waterproof anorak. Note that some excellent cotton safari-wear is produced and sold locally. Try the department stores in Windhoek.

Finally, don't forget a squashable sunhat. Cotton is perfect. Bring one for safety's sake, even if you hate hats, as it will greatly reduce the chance of your getting sunstroke when out walking.

OTHER USEFUL ITEMS See *Camping and walking in the bush*, pages 107–13, for a discussion on what type of camping equipment to take, and *Medical kit*, pages 73–4, for other health-related items. In addition, here are a few of my own favourites and essentials, just to jog your memory:

- sunblock and lipsalve for vital protection from the sun
- sunglasses – essential – ideally dark with a high UV absorption
- insect repellent, especially if travelling to the north or during the rains
- 'Leatherman' multi-purpose tool. Never go into the bush without one of these amazing assistants
- electrical insulating tape – remarkably useful for general repairs
- binoculars – essential for watching game and birds
- camera, film and long lenses (see *Photography* box, pages 62–3)

- basic sewing kit, with at least some really strong thread for repairs
- cheap waterproof watch (leave expensive ones, and jewellery, at home)
- couple of paperback novels
- large plastic 'bin-liner' (garbage) bags, for protecting your luggage from dust
- simple medical kit (see page 73)
- magnifying glass, for looking at some of the smaller attractions

And for backpackers, useful extras might include:

- concentrated, biodegradable washing powder
- long-life candles
- nylon paracord (20m) for emergencies and washing lines
- good compass and a whistle
- more comprehensive medical kit (see pages 73–4)
- universal plug

MAPS AND NAVIGATION A reasonable selection of maps is available in Europe and the USA from specialised outlets. The Michelin map of east and southern Africa (sheet 995) sets the standard for the whole subcontinent, but is not really detailed enough for Namibia. The Freytag & Berndt map of Namibia looks good, though adds little to the free map issued by the tourist board. Much better is the Globetrotter Travel Map, published by New Holland in London.

Imported maps are obtainable in Europe from Stanfords in Long Acre, London (↘ 020 7836 1321; www.stanfords.co.uk) or Geocenter in Stuttgart, Germany (↘ 711 490 722 10; www.geokatalog.de). In the USA try Map Link, Santa Barbara, California (↘ 805 692 6777; http://catalog.maplink.com).

Namibia has an excellent range of detailed, albeit very old, 'Ordnance Survey' type maps available cheaply in Windhoek, from the Surveyor General's office on Robert Mugabe Avenue. See *Windhoek*, page 122, for details. If you are planning a 4x4 expedition, then you may need to buy some of these before you head out into the bush. Expeditions to Kaokoland should also pick up a copy of the Shell map of Kaokoland. It's better than anything else to that area, and does have good general information about the area in the back.

However, for most normal visitors on self-drive or guided trips, all the Ordnance Survey maps are *far* too detailed and unwieldy to use. Much better is the map distributed by the tourist board, which is perfectly adequate for self-drive trips on Namibia's roads. It is probably the best map available, with a useful distance table, and a street plan of Windhoek. It is available free at most tourist centres and information offices in Namibia. Overseas, most Namibian tourist offices will supply them, as will some of the better specialist tour operators (pages 52–4).

GPS systems If you are heading into the more remote parts in your own vehicle, then consider investing in a small GPS: a global positioning system. Under an open, unobstructed sky, these can fix your latitude, longitude and elevation to within about 100m, using 24 American military satellites that constantly pass in the skies overhead. They will work anywhere in the world.

Commercial units cost from around £100/US$160 in Europe or the USA, although their prices are falling (and features improving) as the technology matures. Even the less expensive models will store 'waypoints', enabling you to build up an electronic picture of an area, as well as working out basic latitude, longitude and elevation. So, for example, you can store the position of your camp, and the nearest road, enabling you to leave with confidence and be reasonably sure of navigating back. This is invaluable in remote areas where there are few landmarks.

Beware though: a GPS isn't a substitute for good map-work and navigation. Do not come to rely on it, or you will be unable to cope if it fails. Used correctly, a GPS will help you to recognise minor errors before they are amplified into major problems. Finally, note that all these units use *lots* of battery power, so bring spares with you and/or a cigarette-lighter adaptor.

ELECTRICITY Sockets usually supply alternating current at 220/240V and 50Hz. The plugs are the old standard British design, with three round pins. These are available in all the towns, though adaptors are less easy to find. Often taking a

PHOTOGRAPHIC TIPS

Ariadne Van Zandbergen

EQUIPMENT Although with some thought and an eye for composition you can take reasonable photos with a 'point-and-shoot' camera, you need an SLR camera if you are at all serious about photography. Modern SLRs tend to be very clever, with automatic programmes for almost every possible situation, but remember that these programmes are limited in the sense that the camera cannot think, but only make calculations. Every starting amateur photographer should read a photographic manual for beginners and get to grips with such basics as the relationship between aperture and shutter speed.

Always buy the best lens you can afford. The lens determines the quality of your photo more than the camera body. Fixed fast lenses are ideal, but very costly. A zoom lens makes it easier to change composition without changing lenses the whole time. If you carry only one lens, a 28–70mm (digital 17–55mm) or similar zoom should be ideal. For a second lens, a lightweight 80–200mm or 70–300mm (digital 55–200mm) or similar will be excellent for candid shots and varying your composition. Wildlife photography will be very frustrating if you don't have at least a 300mm lens. For a small loss of quality, tele-converters are a cheap and compact way to increase magnification: a 300 lens with a 1.4x converter becomes 420mm, and with a 2x it becomes 600mm. Note, however, that 1.4x and 2x tele-converters reduce the speed of your lens by 1.4 and 2 stops respectively.

For wildlife photography from a safari vehicle, a solid beanbag, which you can make yourself very cheaply, will be necessary to avoid blurred images, and is more useful than a tripod. A clamp with a tripod head screwed onto it can be attached to the vehicle as well. Modern dedicated flash units are easy to use; aside from the obvious need to flash when you photograph at night, you can improve a lot of photos in difficult 'high contrast' or very dull light with some fill-in flash. It pays to have a proper flash unit as opposed to a built-in camera flash.

DIGITAL/FILM Digital photography is now the preference of most amateur and professional photographers, with the resolution of digital cameras improving all the time. For ordinary prints a 6 megapixel camera is fine. For better results and the possibility to enlarge images and for professional reproduction, higher resolution is available up to 16 megapixels.

Memory space is important. The number of pictures you can fit on a memory card depends on the quality you choose. Calculate in advance how many pictures you can fit on a card and either take enough cards to last for your trip, or take a storage drive onto which you can download the content. A laptop gives the advantage that you can see your pictures properly at the end of each day and edit and delete rejects, but a storage device is lighter and less bulky. These drives come in different capacities up to 80GB.

screwdriver to rewire your appliance on to a local plug is the easiest way to ensure that it will work.

PHOTOGRAPHY

Namibia's scenery and wildlife are a big draw for photographers, but the country's harsh environment creates its own problems.

CAMERA INSURANCE Most travel insurance policies are poor at covering valuables, including cameras. If you are taking a valuable camera abroad, then include it in your house insurance policy, or cover it separately with a specialist.

Bear in mind that digital camera batteries, computers and other storage devices need charging, so make sure you have all the chargers, cables and converters with you. Most hotels have charging points, but do enquire about this in advance. When camping you might have to rely on charging from the car battery; a spare battery is invaluable.

If you are shooting film, 100 to 200 ISO print film and 50 to 100 ISO slide film are ideal. Low ISO film is slow but fine grained and gives the best colour saturation, but will need more light, so support in the form of a tripod or monopod is important. You can also bring a few 'fast' 400 ISO films for low-light situations where a tripod or flash is no option.

DUST AND HEAT Dust and heat are often a problem. Keep your equipment in a sealed bag, stow films in an airtight container (eg: a small cooler bag) and avoid exposing equipment and film to the sun. Digital cameras are prone to collecting dust particles on the sensor which results in spots on the image. The dirt mostly enters the camera when changing lenses, so be careful when doing this. To some extent photos can be 'cleaned' up afterwards in Photoshop, but this is time-consuming. You can have your camera sensor professionally cleaned, or you can do this yourself with special brushes and swabs made for the purpose, but note that touching the sensor might cause damage and should only be done with the greatest care.

LIGHT The most striking outdoor photographs are often taken during the hour or two of 'golden light' after dawn and before sunset. Shooting in low light may enforce the use of very low shutter speeds, in which case a tripod will be required to avoid camera shake.

With careful handling, side lighting and back lighting can produce stunning effects, especially in soft light and at sunrise or sunset. Generally, however, it is best to shoot with the sun behind you. When photographing animals or people in the harsh midday sun, images taken in light but even shade are likely to be more effective than those taken in direct sunlight or patchy shade, since the latter conditions create too much contrast.

PROTOCOL In Namibia, as elsewhere, it is unacceptable to photograph local people without permission, and many people will refuse to pose or will ask for a donation. In such circumstances, don't try to sneak photographs as you might get yourself into trouble. Even the most willing subject will often pose stiffly when a camera is pointed at them; relax them by making a joke, and take a few shots in quick succession to improve the odds of capturing a natural pose.

Ariadne Van Zandbergen is a professional travel and wildlife photographer specialising in Africa. She runs the Africa Image Library. For photo requests, visit www.africaimagelibrary.co.za or contact her on e ariadne@hixnet.co.za.

4

HOTELS, PENSIONS, LODGES AND CAMPS The hotels here are without exception fairly clean and safe. Unless you choose a really run-down old-style hotel in one of the smaller towns, you're unlikely to find anywhere that's dirty. Generally you'll get what you pay for, with the level of choice outside Windhoek and Swakopmund improving year on year.

Establishments are licensed by the local authority as hotels, lodges, restcamps, etc, according to their facilities, though the distinction between a hotel and a lodge depends on its location – a hotel must fall within a municipal area; a lodge will be outside. Similarly, a guest farm must be a working farm, otherwise it will be classified as a lodge. They are also graded by stars, from one to five, but the system is more a guide to their facilities and size than the quality or service. The 'T' that appears alongside the star rating indicates that the place has been judged suitable for tourists, while the number of 'Y's reflects the type of licence to serve alcohol (three 'Y's being a full licence).

Most bush camps and lodges are of a high standard, though their prices – and atmosphere – vary wildly. Price is a guide to quality here, though not a reliable one. Often the places that have better marketing (ie: you've heard of them) cost more than their less famous neighbours which are equally good.

GUEST FARMS These are private farms which host small numbers of guests, usually arranged in advance. They are often very personal and you'll eat all your meals with the hosts and be taken on excursions by them during the day.

Most have some game animals on their land and conduct their own game drives. One or two have interesting rock formations, or cave paintings to visit. Some encourage mainly 'photographic' visitors – that is visitors with a more general interest in the place and its wildlife. Most of these guest farms have been included in this guide. Others, which concentrate mainly on hunters coming to shoot trophy animals, have generally not been included.

Many guest farms concentrate on German-speaking visitors, though those mentioned in this guide also welcome English-speaking guests (and many will make enormous efforts to make you feel at home).

Their prices vary, but are rarely less than N$450 per person – and usually nearer N$750. They generally include all your meals, and often some trips around their farm.

CAMPING Wherever you are in Namibia, you can usually find a campsite nearby. In the more remote areas, far from settlements, nobody bothers if you just sleep by the road. The campsites which are dotted all over the country generally have good ablution blocks, which vary from a concrete shed with toilets and cold shower, to an immaculately fitted-out set of changing rooms with toilets and hot showers. The more organised ones will also have facilities for washing clothes.

Prices are frequently per site, which theoretically allows for 'a maximum of eight persons, two vehicles and one caravan/tent'. In practice, if you've a couple of small tents you will not often be charged for two sites, so travelling in a small group can cut costs considerably.

CHILDREN Many of Namibia's hotels, lodges and camps offer special rates for children, which can range from discounts to free accommodation to those sharing a room with their parents. Some go out of their way to cater for children, too, perhaps with a family room that has loft accommodation. Conversely, a few venues are not suitable for youngsters. It's always worth checking for any special deals when making your initial enquiries, as well as ensuring that your chosen location is safe for your family.

✗ FOOD AND DRINK

FOOD Traditional Namibian cuisine is rarely served for visitors, so the food at restaurants tends to be European in style, with a bias towards German dishes and seafood. It is at least as hygienically prepared as in Europe, so don't worry about stomach upsets. Restaurant prices are generally lower than you would expect for an equivalent meal in Europe, with a light lunch with drink at N$35–50, and main courses at N$70 being fairly standard in Windhoek and Swakopmund restaurants (assuming that you're not splashing out on a seafood platter).

Namibia is a very meat-orientated society, and many menu options will feature steaks from one animal or another. However, there is usually a small vegetarian selection in most restaurants, and if you eat seafood you'll be fine. Most lodge chefs will go out of their way to prepare vegetarian dishes if given notice. If you are camping then you'll be buying and cooking your own food anyway.

In the supermarkets you'll find pre-wrapped fresh fruit and vegetables (though the more remote the areas you visit, the smaller your choice), and plenty of canned foods, pasta, rice, bread, etc. Most of this is imported from South Africa. You'll probably be familiar with some of the brand names.

Traditional foodstuffs eaten in a Namibian home may include the following:

eedingu	dried meat, carrots and green beans
kapana	bread
mealie pap	form of porridge, most common in South Africa
omanugu	also known as mopane worms (*Imbrassia belina*), these are fried caterpillars, often cooked with chilli and onion
oshifima	dough-like staple made from millet
oshifima ne vanda	millet with meat
oshiwambo	spinach and beef

DRINK

Alcohol Because of a strong German brewing tradition, Namibia's lagers are good, the Hansa draught being a particular favourite. In cans, Windhoek Export is one of a number to provide a welcome change from the Lion and Castle which dominate the rest of the subcontinent.

The wine available is mainly South African, with little imported from elsewhere. At its best, this matches the best that California or Australia have to offer, and at considerably lower prices. You can get a bottle of palatable wine from a *drankwinkel* (off licence) for N$55, or a good bottle of vintage estate wine for N$80.

Soft drinks Canned soft drinks, from Diet Coke to sparkling apple juice, are available ice cold from just about anywhere – which is fortunate, considering the amount that you'll need to drink in this climate. They cost about N$5 each, and can be kept cold in insulating polystyrene boxes made to hold six cans. These cheap containers are invaluable if you have a vehicle, and are not taking a large cool box with you. They cost about N$50 and are available from some big hardware or camping stores. If you are on a self-drive trip, these are an essential buy in your first few days.

Water The water in Namibia's main towns is generally safe to drink, though it may taste a little metallic if it has been piped for miles. Natural sources should usually be purified, though water from underground springs and dry riverbeds seldom causes any problems. (See *Chapter 5*, page 76, for more detailed comments.)

SHOPPING FOR CRAFTS

With rich deposits of natural minerals, Namibia can be a good place for the enthusiast to buy **crystals and gems** – but don't expect many bargains, as the industry is far too organised. For the amateur, the desert roses (sand naturally compressed into forms like flowers) are unusual and often cheap, while iridescent tiger's eye is rare elsewhere and very attractive. If you're really interested, forget the agates on sale and look for the unusual crystals – in Windhoek the House of Gems (see pages 147–8) is a must, and in Omaruru Johnston's Gems is fascinating (see page 381).

In Kavango and Caprivi, you'll find good **woodcarvings** sold by the side of the road on small stalls. However, the best selection is at the co-operative which has huge stands either side of Okahandja. There are also some good buys to be had in Windhoek, both behind the information kiosk opposite the Kalahari Sands Hotel and in Post Street Mall.

In the Kalahari regions, **Bushman crafts** are some of the most original and unusual available on the continent, often using ostrich eggshell beads with very fine workmanship. Outside a few expensive shops in the major towns, by far the best source for this is the mission in Tsumkwe.

For details of other crafts, see *Chapter 2*, pages 27–31.

ℓ COMMUNICATIONS AND MEDIA

COMMUNICATIONS

Post The post is efficient and reasonably reliable. A postcard or airmail letter to Europe or the US costs about N$3.40; delivery to Europe takes about a fortnight. For larger items, sending them by sea is much cheaper, but it may take up to three months and isn't recommended for fragile items.

Post offices are normally open Monday to Friday 08.00–16.30, and those in towns on Saturdays also, 08.00–12.00.

Telephone, fax and email Dialling into Namibia, the country code is 264. Dialling out, the international access code is 00. In both cases, omit the first 0 of the area code. You can dial internationally, without going through the operator, from any public phone box, provided you've enough coins or a phonecard (although note that most public phones take only cards). Phonecards (Telecards) are available in denominations of N$10, N$20 and N$50 from post offices and several shops, including many supermarkets.

Namibia's telephone system has been almost entirely upgraded, with many remote areas converted from old manual exchanges to direct-dial numbers. Generally three-digit area codes – like 061, 064 and 063 – are exceedingly easy to reach, whilst some of the remaining manual country exchanges, and party lines, can prove a nightmare.

If faxing from abroad, always dial the number yourself, with your fax machine set to manual. Wait until you are properly connected (listen for a high-pitched tone), and then try to send your fax.

Note that 'a/h' written next to a phone number means 'after hours' – ie: a number where the person is reachable in the evenings and at weekends. Often this is included for emergency contact, not for casual enquiries.

Mobile phones will work in many areas of central Namibia, though not in the more remote corners of the country. You may need to 'enable' this function with your service provider before leaving home. If you're planning to use your mobile for more than just emergencies, it's far cheaper to buy a local SIM card on arrival in Namibia and use this for the duration of your trip. The main Namibian service provider is Tango, which provides excellent coverage in all the major towns, but reception on any network is almost non-existent when you get off the beaten track. If you plan to visit the more remote regions independently, it may be worth considering taking a satellite phone for emergencies (to hire a phone, try Be Local Tourism – see page 155).

Email is common, but don't expect swift responses to all your emails to Namibia. There are plenty of internet cafés in major towns, and many hotels and backpackers' lodges have internet facilities too.

MEDIA

The press There are no official press restrictions in Namibia, and generally there's a healthy level of debate and criticism in some of the media, although that's not to say that important issues don't sometimes escape public scrutiny because of powerful pressures on editors. In short, it's just like back home!

There is a choice of about seven commercial newspapers, which are easiest to obtain in the larger cities. Getting them elsewhere often means that you will be a few days out of date. The *Namibian* and the *Windhoek Advertiser* are probably the best during the week, and the *Windhoek Observer* on Saturday is also good. One or two of the others are written in Afrikaans and German.

Radio and television The government-sponsored Namibia Broadcasting Corporation (NBC) accounts for most of the radio and all of Namibia's normal TV stations. They broadcast radio in six languages from Windhoek, and in three languages from transmitters in the north of the country.

There are currently five local commercial radio stations in Windhoek, all of which are primarily music based: Radio Wave, Radio Kudu, Radio Kosmos, Radio Energy and Radio 99. Away from Windhoek and the larger centres, the radio and public television can be difficult to receive. If you're travelling around in a car, make sure you bring lots of music tapes.

NBC broadcasts one public television channel, and there are several commercial networks. These satellite channels offer a variety of international news, sport and movie channels – the same the world over. By far the most common is the South African-based Mnet TV, which is installed in many of the larger hotels.

5

Health and Safety

with Dr Felicity Nicholson and Dr Jane Wilson-Howarth

There is always great danger in writing about health and safety for the uninitiated visitor. It is all too easy to become paranoid about exotic diseases that you may catch, and all too easy to start distrusting everybody you meet as a potential thief – falling into an unfounded us-and-them attitude towards the people of the country you are visiting.

As a comparison, imagine an equivalent section in a guidebook to a Western country – there would be a list of possible diseases and advice on the risk of theft and mugging. Many Western cities are very dangerous, but with time we learn how to assess the risks, accepting almost subconsciously what we can and cannot do.

It is important to strike the right balance: to avoid being excessively cautious or too relaxed about your health and your safety. With experience, you will find the balance that best fits you and the country you are visiting.

BEFORE YOU GO

TRAVEL INSURANCE Visitors to Namibia should always take out a comprehensive medical insurance policy to cover them for emergencies, including the cost of evacuation to another country within the region. Such policies come with an emergency number (often on a reverse charge/call collect basis). You would be wise to memorise this, or indelibly tattoo it in as many places as possible on your baggage.

Personal effects insurance is also a sensible precaution, but check the policy's fine print before you leave home. Often, in even the best policies, you will find a limit per item, or per claim – which can be well below the cost of a replacement. If you need to list your valuables separately, then do so comprehensively. Check that receipts are not required for claims if you do not have them, also that the excess which you have to pay on a claim is reasonable.

Annual travel policies can be excellent value if you travel a lot, and some of the larger credit-card companies offer excellent policies. However, it can often be better to get your valuables named and insured for travel using your home contents insurance. These year-round policies will try harder to settle your claim fairly as they want your business in the long term.

IMMUNISATIONS Having a full set of immunisations takes time, normally at least six weeks, although some protection can be had by visiting your doctor as late as a few days before you travel. Ideally, see your doctor or travel clinic (see pages 71–3) early on to establish an inoculation timetable.

Legal requirements No immunisations are required by law for entry into Namibia, unless you are coming from an area where **yellow fever** is endemic. In that case, a vaccination certificate is mandatory. To be valid the vaccination must be obtained at least ten days before entering the country.

Recommended precautions Preparations to ensure a healthy trip to Namibia require checks on your immunisation status: it is wise to be up to date on **tetanus**, **polio** and **diphtheria** (now given as an all-in-one vaccine, Revaxis, that lasts for ten years), and hepatitis A. Immunisations against meningococcus and rabies may also be recommended. Immunisation against cholera is not required for trips to Namibia.

Hepatitis A vaccine (Havrix Monodose or Avaxim) comprises two injections given about a year apart. The course costs about £100, but may be available on the NHS; it protects for 25 years and can be administered even close to the time of departure. **Hepatitis B** vaccination should be considered for longer trips (two months or more) or for those working with children or in situations where contact with blood is likely. Three injections are needed for the best protection and can be given over a three-week period if time is short. Longer schedules give more sustained protection and are therefore preferred if time allows. Hepatitis A vaccine can also be given as a combination with hepatitis B as 'Twinrix', though two doses are needed at least seven days apart to be effective for the hepatitis A component, and three doses are needed for the hepatitis B.

The newer injectable **typhoid** vaccines (eg: Typhim Vi) last for three years and are about 85% effective. Oral capsules (Vivotif) are currently available in the US (and soon in the UK); if four capsules are taken over seven days it will last for five years. This is encouraged unless you are leaving within a few days for a trip of a week or less, when the vaccine would not be effective in time. **Meningitis** vaccine (ideally containing strains A, C, W and Y, but if this is not available then A+C vaccine is better than nothing), is recommended, especially for trips of more than four weeks (see *Meningitis*, pages 81–2).

Vaccination against **rabies** is unnecessary for most visitors, but would be wise for those who travel for extended periods (four weeks or longer), or stay in rural areas (see *Rabies,* page 82). Ideally three injections are taken over a minimum of 21 days, though even taking one or two doses of vaccine is better than none at all. Contrary to popular belief these vaccinations are relatively painless.

Experts differ over whether a BCG vaccination against **tuberculosis** (TB) is useful in adults: discuss this with your travel clinic.

In addition to the various vaccinations recommended above, it is important that you should be properly protected against malaria. For detailed advice see below.

Ideally you should visit your own doctor or a specialist travel clinic (see pages 71–3) to discuss your requirements if possible at least eight weeks before you plan to travel.

MALARIA Malaria is the most dangerous disease in Africa, and the greatest risk to the traveller. It occurs in northern, and occasionally central, Namibia (see map, page 81), so it is essential that you take all possible precautions against it. Broadly, anti-malarial tablets are recommended for the northern third of the country from November to June, and for the Okavango and Kunene rivers all year round.

Malaria prevention Prophylaxis regimes aim to infuse your bloodstream with drugs that inhibit and kill the malaria parasites which are injected into you by a biting mosquito. This is why you must start to take the drugs *before* you arrive in a malarial area – so that they are established in your bloodstream from day one. Unfortunately, malaria parasites continually adapt to the drugs used to combat them, so the recommended regimes must adapt and change in order to remain effective. None is 100% effective, and all require time to kill the parasites – so unless there is a medical indication for stopping, it is important to complete the course after leaving the area as directed (usually one to four weeks depending on the regime). Falciparum (cerebral) malaria is the most common in Africa, and usually fatal if untreated, so it is worth your while trying to avoid it.

Seek current advice on the best antimalarials to take: usually mefloquine, Malarone or doxycycline. If mefloquine (Lariam) is suggested, start this two-and-a-half weeks (three doses) before departure to check that it suits you; stop it immediately if it seems to cause depression or anxiety, visual or hearing disturbances, severe headaches, fits or changes in heart rhythm. Side effects such as nightmares or dizziness are not medical reasons for stopping unless they are sufficiently debilitating or annoying. Anyone who has been treated for depression or psychiatric problems, has diabetes controlled by oral therapy or who is epileptic (or who has suffered fits in the past) or has a close blood relative who is epileptic, should probably avoid mefloquine.

In the past doctors were nervous about prescribing mefloquine to pregnant women, but experience has shown that it is relatively safe and certainly safer than the risk of malaria. That said, there are other issues, so if you are travelling to Namibia while pregnant, seek expert advice before departure.

Malarone (proguanil and atovaquone) is as effective as mefloquine. It has the advantage of having few side effects and need only be continued for one week after returning. However, it is expensive and because of this tends to be reserved for shorter trips. Malarone may not be suitable for everybody, so take advice from a doctor. The licence in the UK has been extended for up to three months' use and a paediatric form of tablet is also available, prescribed on a weight basis.

A third alternative is the antibiotic doxycycline (100mg daily). Like Malarone it can be started one day before arrival. Unlike mefloquine, it may also be used in travellers with epilepsy, although certain anti-epileptic medication may make it less effective. In perhaps 1–3% of people there is the possibility of allergic skin reactions developing in sunlight; the drug should be stopped if this happens. Women using the oral contraceptive should use an additional method of protection for the first four weeks when using doxycycline. It is also unsuitable in pregnancy or for children under 12 years.

Chloroquine and proguanil are no longer considered to be effective enough for Namibia but may be considered as a last resort if nothing else is deemed suitable.

All tablets should be taken with or after the evening meal, washed down with plenty of fluid and, with the exception of Malarone (see above), continued for four weeks after leaving.

Despite all these precautions, it is important to be aware that no anti-malarial drug is 100% protective, although those on prophylactics who are unlucky enough to catch malaria are less likely to get rapidly into serious trouble. In addition to taking anti-malarials, it is therefore important to avoid mosquito bites between dusk and dawn (see *Avoiding insect bites*, pages 77–8).

There is unfortunately the occasional traveller who prefers to 'acquire resistance' to malaria rather than take preventive tablets, or who takes homeopathic prophylactics thinking these are effective against killer disease. Homeopathy theory dictates treating like with like so there is no place for prophylaxis or immunisation in a well person; bone fide homeopathists do not advocate it. Travellers to Africa cannot acquire any effective resistance to malaria, and those who don't make use of prophylactic drugs risk their life in a manner that is both foolish and unnecessary.

➕ TRAVEL CLINICS AND HEALTH INFORMATION A full list of current travel clinic websites worldwide is available from the International Society of Travel Medicine on www.istm.org. For other journey preparation information, consult www.tripprep.com. Information about various medications may be found on www.emedicine.com. For information on malaria prevention, see www.preventingmalaria.info.

UK

Berkeley Travel Clinic 32 Berkeley St, London W1J 8EL (near Green Park tube station); ☏ 020 7629 6233

Cambridge Travel Clinic 48a Mill Rd, Cambridge CB1 2AS; ☏ 01223 367362; e enquiries@ travelcliniccambridge.co.uk; www.travelcliniccambridge.co.uk. *Open Tue–Fri 12.00–19.00, Sat 10.00–16.00.*

Edinburgh Travel Clinic Regional Infectious Diseases Unit, Ward 41 OPD, Western General Hospital, Crewe Rd South, Edinburgh EH4 2UX; ☏ 0131 537 2822; www.link.med.ed.ac.uk/ridu. Travel helpline (*0906 589 0380*) open weekdays 09.00–12.00. Provides inoculations & antimalarial prophylaxis, & advises on travel-related health risks.

Fleet Street Travel Clinic 29 Fleet St, London EC4Y 1AA; ☏ 020 7353 5678; www.fleetstreetclinic.com. Vaccinations, travel products & latest advice.

Hospital for Tropical Diseases Travel Clinic Mortimer Market Bldg, Capper St (off Tottenham Ct Rd), London WC1E 6AU; ☏ 020 7388 9600; www.thehtd.org. Offers consultations and advice, and is able to provide all necessary drugs & vaccines for travellers. Runs a healthline (*0906 133 7733*) for country-specific information and health hazards. Also stocks nets, water purification equipment & personal protection measures.

Interhealth Worldwide Partnership Hse, 157 Waterloo Rd, London SE1 8US; ☏ 020 7902 9000; www.interhealth.org.uk. Competitively priced, one-stop travel health service. All profits go to their affiliated company, InterHealth, which provides health care for overseas workers on Christian projects.

Liverpool School of Medicine Pembroke Pl, Liverpool L3 5QA; ☏ 051 708 9393; f 0151 705 3370; www.liv.ac.uk/lstm

MASTA (Medical Advisory Service for Travellers Abroad) Moorfield Rd, Yeadon, Leeds LS19 7BN; ☏ 0870 606 2782; www.masta-travel-health.com. Provides travel health advice, anti-malarials & vaccinations. There are over 25 MASTA pre-travel clinics in Britain; call or check online for the nearest. Clinics also sell mosquito nets, medical kits, insect protection & travel hygiene products.

NHS travel website www.fitfortravel.scot.nhs.uk. Provides country-by-country advice on immunisation & malaria, plus details of recent developments, & a list of relevant health organisations.

Nomad Travel Store/Clinic 3–4 Wellington Terrace, Turnpike Lane, London N8 0PX; ☏ 020 8889 7014, travel-health line (office hours only) ☏ 0906 863 3414; e sales@nomadtravel.co.uk; www.nomadtravel.co.uk. Also at 40 Bernard St, London WC1N 1LJ; ☏ 020 7833 4114; 52 Grosvenor Gdns, London SW1W 0AG; ☏ 020 7823 5823; and 43 Queens Rd, Bristol BS8 1QH; ☏ 0117 922 6567. For health advice, equipment such as mosquito nets & other anti-bug devices, & an excellent range of adventure travel gear.

Trailfinders Travel Clinic 194 Kensington High St, London W8 7RG; ☏ 020 7938 3999; www.trailfinders.com/clinic.htm

Travelpharm The Travelpharm website, www.travelpharm.com, offers up-to-date guidance on travel-related health & has a range of medications available through their online mini-pharmacy.

Irish Republic

Tropical Medical Bureau Grafton Street Medical Centre, Grafton Bldgs, 34 Grafton St, Dublin 2; ☏ 1 671 9200; www.tmb.ie. A useful website specific to tropical destinations. Also check website for other bureaux locations throughout Ireland.

USA

Centers for Disease Control 1600 Clifton Rd, Atlanta, GA 30333; ☏ 800 311 3435; travellers' health hotline ☏ 888 232 3299; www.cdc.gov/travel. The central source of travel information in the USA. The invaluable *Health Information for International Travel*, published annually, is available from the Division of Quarantine at this address.

Connaught Laboratories PO Box 187, Swiftwater, PA 18370; ☏ 800 822 2463. They will send a free list of specialist tropical-medicine physicians in your state.

IAMAT (International Association for Medical Assistance to Travelers) 1623 Military Rd, 279, Niagara Falls, NY 14304-1745; ☏ 716 754 4883; e info@iamat.org; www.iamat.org. A non-profit organisation that provides lists of English-speaking doctors abroad.

International Medicine Center 920 Frostwood Dr, Suite 670, Houston, TX 77024; ☏ 713 550 2000; www.traveldoc.com

Canada

IAMAT Suite 1, 1287 St Clair Av W, Toronto, Ontario M6E 1B8; ☏ 416 652 0137; www.iamat.org

TMVC Suite 314, 1030 W Georgia St, Vancouver, BC V6E 2Y3; ☏ 1 888 288 8682; www.tmvc.com. Private clinic with several outlets in Canada.

Australia, New Zealand, Singapore

IAMAT PO Box 5049, Christchurch 5, New Zealand; www.iamat.org

TMVC ↘ 1300 65 88 44; www.tmvc.com.au. Clinics in Australia, New Zealand & Singapore, including:
Auckland Canterbury Arcade, 170 Queen St, Auckland; ↘ 9 373 3531
Brisbane 6th floor, 247 Adelaide St, Brisbane, QLD 4000; ↘ 7 3221 9066
Melbourne 393 Little Bourke St, 2nd Floor, Melbourne, VIC 3000; ↘ 3 9602 5788
Sydney Dymocks Bldg, 7th Floor, 428 George St, Sydney, NSW 2000; ↘ 2 9221 7133

South Africa & Namibia

SAA-Netcare Travel Clinics P Bag X34, Benmore 2010; www.travelclinic.co.za. Clinics throughout South Africa.

TMVC 113 D F Malan Dr, Roosevelt Pk, Johannesburg; ↘ 011 888 7488; www.tmvc.com.au. Consult website for details of other clinics in South Africa & Namibia.

Switzerland

IAMAT 57 Chemin des Voirets, 1212 Grand Lancy, Geneva; www.iamat.org

MEDICAL KIT Pharmacies in the main towns in Namibia generally have very good supplies of medicines, but away from these you will find very little. If you're venturing deep into the wilds, then you should take with you anything that you expect to need. If you are on an organised trip, an overlanding truck, or staying at hotels, lodges or safari camps, then you will not need much, as these establishments normally have comprehensive emergency kits. In that case, just a small personal medical kit might include:

- alcohol-based hand rub or bar of soap in plastic box
- antihistamine tablets
- antiseptic, eg: iodine or potassium permanganate (don't take antiseptic cream)
- aspirin or paracetamol
- blister plasters (if you plan any serious walking)
- condoms or femidoms and contraceptive pills
- impregnated bed-net or permethrin spray
- insect repellent
- lipsalve (ideally containing a sunscreen)
- malaria prophylaxis
- Micropore tape (for closing small cuts – and invaluable for blisters)
- moisturising cream
- sticking plaster (a roll is more versatile than pre-shaped plasters)
- sunscreen

However, if you are likely to end up in very remote situations, then you should also consider taking the following – and know how to use them:

- burn dressings (burns are a common problem for campers)
- antibiotics: ciprofloxacin or norfloxacin, for severe diarrhoea
- antibiotic eye drops, for sore, 'gritty', stuck-together eyes (conjunctivitis)
- injection swabs, sterile needles and syringes
- lint, sterile bandage and safety pins
- oral rehydration sachets
- steristrips or butterfly closures
- strong painkiller (eg: codeine phosphate – also use for bad diarrhoea)
- tweezers (perhaps those on a Swiss army knife)
- water purification equipment (2% tincture of iodine and dropper is ideal)
- a good medical manual (see *Appendix 3*, page 490).
- tinidazole for giardia or amoebic dysentery (see below for regime)
- malaria diagnostic kits (5) and a digital thermometer (for those going to remote areas)

Dr Jane Wilson-Howarth

Long-haul air travel increases the risk of deep vein thrombosis (DVT). Although recent research has suggested that many of us develop clots when immobilised, most resolve without us ever having been aware of them. In certain susceptible individuals, though, clots form on clots and when large ones break away and lodge in the lungs this is dangerous. Fortunately this happens in a tiny minority of passengers.

Studies have shown that flights of over five-and-a-half-hours are significant, and that people who take lots of shorter flights over a short space of time can also form clots. People at highest risk are:

- Those who have had a clot before – unless they are now taking warfarin
- People over 80 years of age
- Anyone who has recently undergone a major operation or surgery for varicose veins
- Someone who has had a hip or knee replacement in the last three months
- Cancer sufferers
- Those who have ever had a stroke
- People with heart disease
- Those with a close blood relative who has had a clot

Those with a slightly increased risk are:

- People over 40
- Women who are pregnant or have had a baby in the last couple of weeks
- People taking female hormones, the combined contraceptive pill or other oestrogen therapy
- Heavy smokers
- Those who have very severe varicose veins

If you wear glasses, bring a spare pair. Similarly those who wear contact lenses should bring spare ones, also a pair of glasses in case the dust proves too much for the lenses. If you take regular medication (including contraceptive pills) then bring a large supply with you – much easier than hunting for your usual brand in Namibia. Equally, it's worth having a dental check-up before you go, as you could be several painful days from the nearest dentist.

IN NAMIBIA

HOSPITALS, DENTISTS AND PHARMACIES Should you need one, Namibia's main hospitals are good and will treat you first and ask for money later. However, with comprehensive medical insurance as part of your travel cover, it is probably better go to one of the private clinics. The main ones are in Windhoek and Otjiwarongo, and these are capable of serious surgery and a good quality of care. Outside of these, there are private medical facilities in Karibib, Swakopmund, Tsumeb and Walvis Bay.

If you've a serious problem outside of Windhoek, then **International SOS** organise medical evacuations from anywhere; they can be contacted from a landline toll free on ℩ 0800 911911, or on ℩ 061 230505. If you're calling from a mobile, the number is m 081 707. They do insure individual travellers, but many lodges are members, covering you while you are staying there, and the best car-hire

- The very obese
- People who are very tall (over 6ft/1.8m) or short (under 5ft/1.5m)

A deep vein thrombosis is a blood clot that forms in the deep leg veins. This is very different from irritating but harmless superficial phlebitis. DVT causes swelling and redness of one leg, usually with heat and pain in one calf and sometimes the thigh. A DVT is only dangerous if a clot breaks away and travels to the lungs (pulmonary embolus). Symptoms of a pulmonary embolus (PE) include chest pain that is worse on breathing in deeply, shortness of breath, and sometimes coughing up small amounts of blood. The symptoms commonly start three to ten days after a long flight. Anyone who thinks that they might have a DVT needs to see a doctor immediately who will arrange a scan. Warfarin tablets (to thin the blood) are then taken for at least six months.

PREVENTION OF DVT Several conditions make the problem more likely. Immobility is the key, and factors like reduced oxygen in cabin air and dehydration may also contribute. To reduce the risk of thrombosis on a long journey:

EXERCISE BEFORE AND AFTER THE FLIGHT
- Keep mobile before and during the flight; move around every couple of hours
- Drink plenty of water or juices during the flight
- Avoid taking sleeping pills and excessive tea, coffee and alcohol
- Perform exercises that mimic walking and tense the calf muscles
- Consider wearing flight socks or support stockings (see www.legshealth.com)
- Ideally take a meal each week of oily fish (mackerel, trout, salmon, sardines, etc) ahead of your departure. This reduces the blood's ability to clot and thus DVT risk. It may even be worth just taking a meal of oily fish 24 hours before departure if this is more practical.

If you think you are at increased risk of a clot, ask your doctor if it is safe to travel.

firms, like Avis, will automatically cover you with International SOS if you have one of their cars. Finally, it may be that your insurers overseas would ultimately pick up the International SOS bills if their services were needed.

Pharmacies in the main towns stock a good range of medicine, though often not in familiar brands. Bring with you a repeat prescription for anything you may lose or run out of.

STAYING HEALTHY Namibia is probably the healthiest country in sub-Saharan Africa for visitors. It has a generally low population density and a very dry climate, which means there are comparatively few problems likely to affect visitors. The risks are further minimised if you are staying in good hotels, lodges, camps and guest farms, where standards of hygiene are generally at least as good as you will find at home.

The major dangers in Namibia are car accidents caused by driving too fast on gravel roads, and sunburn. Both can also be very serious, yet both are within the power of the visitor to avoid.

The following is general advice, applicable to travelling anywhere, including Namibia.

Food and storage Throughout the world, most health problems encountered by travellers are contracted by eating contaminated food or drinking unclean water. If you are staying in safari camps or lodges, or eating in restaurants, then you are unlikely to have problems in Namibia.

However, if you are backpacking and cooking for yourself, or relying on local food, then you need to take more care. Tins, packets, and fresh green vegetables (when you can find them) are least likely to cause problems – provided that clean water has been used in preparing the meal. In Namibia's hot climate, keeping meat or animal products unrefrigerated for more than a few hours is asking for trouble.

Water and purification Tap water in Namibia's major towns and borehole water used in many more remote locations is perfectly safe to drink. However, even the mildest of the local microbes may cause slight upset stomachs for an overseas visitor. Two-litre bottles of mineral water are available from most supermarkets; these are perfect if you're in a car.

If you need to purify water for yourself in the bush, then first filter out any suspended solids, perhaps by passing the water through a piece of closely woven cloth or something similar. Then bring it to the boil, or sterilise it chemically. Boiling is much more effective, provided that you have the fuel available.

Tablets sold for purification based on either iodine or chlorine are normally adequate. Just follow the manufacturer's instructions carefully. Iodine is the most effective, especially against the resilient amoebic cysts which cause amoebic dysentery and other prolonged forms of diarrhoea.

A cheaper alternative to tablets sold over the counter is to travel with a small bottle of medical-quality tincture of iodine (2% solution) and an eye dropper. Add four drops to one litre of water, shake well, and leave to stand for ten minutes. If the water is very cloudy (even after filtering) or very cold, then either double the iodine dose, or leave to stand for twice as long.

This tincture of iodine can also be used as a general external antiseptic, but it will stain things deep brown if spilt – so seal and pack its container exceedingly well.

Heat and sun Heatstroke, heat exhaustion and sunburn are often problems for travellers to Namibia, despite being easy to prevent. To avoid them, you need to remember that your body is under stress and make allowances for it. First, take things gently; you are on holiday, after all. Next, keep your fluid and salt levels high: lots of water and soft drinks, but go easy on the caffeine and alcohol. Third, dress to keep cool with loose-fitting, thin garments – preferably of cotton, linen or silk. Finally, beware of the sun. Hats and long-sleeved shirts are essential. If you must expose your skin to the sun, then use sun blocks and high-factor sunscreens (the sun is so strong that you will still get a tan). Be especially careful of exposure in the middle of the day and of sun reflected off water, and wear a T-shirt and lots of waterproof suncream (at least SPF15) when swimming. The glare and the dust can be hard on the eyes, too, so bring UV-protecting sunglasses and, perhaps, a soothing eyebath.

Eye problems Bacterial conjunctivitis (pink eye) is a common infection in Africa; people who wear contact lenses are most open to this irritating problem. The eyes feel sore and gritty and they will often be stuck together in the mornings. They will need treatment with antibiotic drops or ointment. Lesser eye irritation should settle with bathing in salt water and keeping the eyes shaded. If an insect flies into your eye, extract it with great care, ensuring you do not crush or damage it otherwise you may get a nastily inflamed eye from toxins secreted by the creature. Small elongated red-and-black blister beetles carry warning colouration to tell you not to crush them anywhere against your skin.

Prickly heat A fine pimply rash on the trunk is likely to be heat rash; cool showers, dabbing dry, and talc will help. Treat the problem by slowing down to a relaxed schedule, wearing only loose, baggy, 100%-cotton clothes and sleeping naked under a fan; if it's bad you may need to check into an air-conditioned hotel room for a while.

Skin infections Any mosquito bite or small nick in the skin gives an opportunity for bacteria to foil the body's usually excellent defences; it will surprise many travellers how quickly skin infections start in warm humid climates and it is essential to clean and cover even the slightest wound. Creams are not as effective as a good drying antiseptic such as dilute iodine, potassium permanganate (a few crystals in half a cup of water) or crystal (or gentian) violet. One of these should be available in most towns. If the wound starts to throb, or becomes red and the redness starts to spread, or the wound oozes, and especially if you develop a fever, antibiotics will probably be needed: flucloxacillin (250mg four times a day) or cloxacillin (500mg four times a day). For those allergic to penicillin, erythromycin (500mg twice a day) for five days should help. See a doctor if the symptoms do not start to improve within 48 hours.

Fungal infections also get a hold easily in hot, moist climates so wear 100%-cotton socks and underwear and shower frequently. An itchy rash in the groin or flaking between the toes is likely to be a fungal infection. This needs treatment with an antifungal cream such as Canesten (clotrimazole); if this is not available try Whitfield's ointment (compound benzoic acid ointment) or crystal violet (although this will turn you purple!).

Avoiding insect bites The most dangerous biting insects in parts of Namibia (see map, page 81) are mosquitoes, because they can transmit malaria, yellow fever and a host of other diseases.

Research has shown that using a mosquito net over your bed, and covering up exposed skin (by wearing long-sleeved shirts, and tucking trousers into socks) in the evening, are the most effective steps towards preventing bites. Bed-net treatment kits are available from travel clinics; these prevent mosquitoes biting through a net if you roll against it in your sleep, and also make old and holey nets protective. Mosquito coils and chemical insect repellents will help, and sleeping in a stream of moving air, such as under a fan, or in an air-conditioned room, will help to reduce your chances of being bitten.

DEET (diethyltoluamide) is the active ingredient in many repellents (Repel have an excellent range), so the greater the percentage of DEET, the stronger the effect. However, DEET is a strong chemical. Just 30% is regarded as an effective, non-toxic concentration. It will dissolve some plastics and synthetic materials, and may irritate sensitive skin. Because of this, many people use concentrated DEET to impregnate materials, rather than applying it to themselves. An alternative to this is to use Bug Guards – wrist and ankle bands containing 100% DEET in capsule form. The capsules break on movement, but the chemical never touches the skin. One pack contains four bands, which when used, last for two weeks. Mosquito nets, socks and even cravats can be impregnated and used to deter insects from biting. Eating large quantities of garlic, or cream of tartar, or taking yeast tablets, are said to deter some biting insects, although the evidence is anecdotal – and the garlic may affect your social life.

Mosquitoes and many other insects are attracted to light. If you are camping, never put a lamp near the opening of your tent, or you will have a swarm of biters waiting to join you when you retire. In hotel rooms, be aware that the longer your light is on, the greater the number of insects will be sharing your accommodation.

Aside from avoiding mosquito bites between dusk and dawn, which will protect you from elephantiasis and a range of nasty insect-borne viruses, as well as malaria (see page 80), it is important to take precautions against other insect bites. During the day it is wise to wear long, loose (preferably 100%-cotton) clothes if you are pushing through scrubby country; this will keep off ticks and also tsetse and day-biting *Aedes* mosquitoes which may spread viral fevers.

Tsetse flies hurt when they bite and it is said that they are attracted to the colour blue; locals will advise on where they are a problem and where they transmit sleeping sickness.

Minute pestilential biting blackflies spread river blindness in some parts of Africa between 190°N and 170°S; the disease is caught close to fast-flowing rivers since flies breed there and the larvae live in rapids. The flies bite during the day but long trousers tucked into socks will help keep them off. Citronella-based natural repellents (eg: Mosi-guard) do not work against them.

Tumbu flies or putsi, often called mango flies, are a problem where the climate is hot and humid. The adult fly lays her eggs on the soil or on drying laundry and when the eggs come into contact with human flesh (when you put on clothes or lie on a bed) they hatch and bury themselves under the skin. Here they form a crop of 'boils' each with a maggot inside. Smear a little Vaseline over the hole, and they will push their noses out to breathe. It may be possible to squeeze them out but it depends if they are ready to do so as the larvae have spines that help them to hold on.

In putsi areas either dry your clothes and sheets within a screened house, or dry them in direct sunshine until they are crisp, or iron them.

Jiggers, or sandfleas, are another flesh-feaster, which can be best avoided by wearing shoes. They latch on if you walk barefoot in contaminated places, and set up home under the skin of the foot, usually at the side of a toenail where they cause a painful, boil-like swelling. They need picking out by a local expert.

Snakes, spiders and scorpions Encounters with aggressive snakes, angry spiders or vindictive scorpions are more common in horror films than in Namibia. Most snakes will flee at the mere vibrations of a human footstep whilst spiders are far more interested in flies than people. You will have to seek out scorpions if you wish to see one. If you are careful about where you place your hands and feet, especially after dark, then there should be no problems. You are less likely to get bitten or stung if you wear stout shoes and long trousers. Simple precautions include not putting on boots without shaking them empty first, and always checking the back of your backpack before putting it on.

Snakes do bite occasionally, and you ought to know the standard first-aid treatment. First, and most importantly, *don't panic*. Most snakes are harmless and even venomous species will only dispense venom in about half of their bites. If bitten, you are unlikely to have received venom; keeping this fact in mind may help you to stay calm.

Even in the worst of these cases, the victim has hours or days to get to help, and not a matter of minutes. He/she should be kept calm, with no exertions to pump venom around the blood system, whilst being taken rapidly to the nearest medical help. The area of the bite should be washed to remove any venom from the skin, and the bitten limb should be immobilised. Paracetamol may be used as a painkiller, but never use aspirin because it may cause internal bleeding.

Most first-aid techniques do more harm than good: cutting into the wound is harmful and tourniquets are dangerous; suction and electrical inactivation devices do not work. The only effective treatment is antivenom. In case of a bite, which you fear may be both serious and venomous then:

- Try to keep calm. It is likely that no venom has been dispensed.
- Stop movement of the bitten limb by applying a splint.
- If you have a crêpe bandage, wrap it around the whole limb (eg: all the way from the toes to the thigh), as tight as you would for a sprained ankle or a muscle pull.
- Keep the bitten limb below heart height to slow spread of any venom.
- Evacuate the victim to a hospital that has antivenom.
- *Never* give aspirin. You may offer paracetamol, which is safe.
- *Do not* apply ice packs.
- *Do not* apply potassium permanganate.

If the offending snake can be captured without any risk of someone else being bitten, take it to show the doctor. But beware, since even a decapitated head is able to dispense venom in a reflex bite.

When deep in the bush, heading for the nearest large farm or camp may be quicker than going to a town: it may have a supply of antivenom, or facilities to radio for help by plane.

DISEASES AND WHEN TO SEE A DOCTOR

TRAVELLERS' DIARRHOEA There are almost as many names for this as there are travellers' tales on the subject. Firstly, do resist the temptation to reach for the medical kit as soon as your stomach turns a little fluid. Most cases of travellers' diarrhoea will resolve themselves within 24–48 hours with no treatment at all. To speed up this process of acclimatisation, eat well but simply: avoid fats in favour of starches, and keep your fluid intake high. Bananas and papaya fruit are often claimed to be helpful. If you urgently need to stop the symptoms, for a long journey for example, then Lomotil, Imodium or another of the commercial anti-diarrhoea preparations will do the trick. They stop the symptoms, by paralysing the bowel, but will not cure the problem. They should be used only as a last resort and never if you have bad abdominal cramps with the diarrhoea.

If the diarrhoea persists for more than two days, or the stools contain blood, pus or slime, and/or you have a fever, you must seek medical advice. There are as many possible treatments as there are causes, and a proper diagnosis involves microscopic analysis of a stool sample, so go straight to your nearest hospital. The most important thing, especially in Namibia's climate, is to keep your fluid intake up. If it is not possible to reach medical help quickly then a dose of norfloxacin or ciprofloxacin repeated twice a day until reaching medical help may be appropriate (if you are planning to take an antibiotic with you, note that both norfloxacin and ciprofloxacin are available only on prescription in the UK). If the diarrhoea is greasy and bulky and is accompanied by sulphurous (eggy) burps the likely cause is giardia. This is best treated with tinidazole (four x 500mg in one dose, repeated seven days later if symptoms persist).

The body's absorption of fluids is assisted by adding small amounts of dissolved sugars, salts and minerals to the water. Sachets of oral rehydration salts give the perfect biochemical mix you need to replace what is pouring out of your bottom but they do not taste so nice. Any dilute mixture of sugar and salt in water will do you good so, if you like Coke or orange squash, drink that with a three-finger pinch of salt added to each glass. The ideal ratio is eight level teaspoons of sugar and one level teaspoon of salt dissolved in one litre of water. Palm syrup or honey make good substitutes for sugar, and including fresh citrus juice will not only improve the taste of these solutions, but also add valuable potassium.

Drink two large glasses after every bowel action, and more if you are thirsty. If you are not eating you need to drink three litres a day *plus* whatever you are sweating *and* the equivalent of what's going into the toilet. If you feel like eating, take a bland diet; heavy greasy foods will give you cramps.

If you are likely to be more than a few days from qualified medical help, then come equipped with a good health manual and the selection of antibiotics which it recommends. *Bugs, Bites & Bowels* by Dr Jane Wilson-Howarth (see *Appendix 3*, page 490) is excellent for this purpose.

MALARIA You can still catch malaria even if you are taking anti-malarial drugs so you should do everything possible to avoid mosquito bites. Untreated malaria is likely to be fatal, but even strains resistant to prophylaxis respond well to prompt treatment. Because of this, your immediate priority upon displaying possible malaria symptoms – including a rapid rise in temperature (over 38°C), and any combination of a headache, flu-like aches and pains, a general sense of disorientation, and possibly even nausea and diarrhoea – is to establish whether you have malaria, ideally by visiting a clinic.

A definite diagnosis of malaria is normally possible only by examining a blood sample under the microscope. It is best to get the problem properly diagnosed if possible, so don't treat yourself if you can easily reach a hospital first. Even if you test negative, it would be wise to stay within reach of a laboratory until the symptoms clear up, and to test again after a day or two if they don't. It's worth noting that if you have a fever and the malaria test is negative, you may have typhoid or paratyphoid, which should also receive immediate treatment.

If (and only if) medical help is unavailable, then self-treatment is fairly safe, except for people who are pregnant or under 12 years of age. Should you be travelling to remote parts of Namibia, you would be wise to carry a course of treatment to cure malaria, and a rapid test kit. With malaria, it is normal enough to go from feeling healthy to having a high fever in the space of a few hours (and it is possible to die from falciparum malaria within 24 hours of the first symptoms). In such circumstances, assume that you have malaria and act accordingly – whatever risks are attached to taking an unnecessary cure are outweighed by the dangers of untreated malaria.

There is some division about the best treatment for malaria, but either Malarone or Coarthemeter are the current treatments of choice. Discuss your trip with a specialist either at home or in Namibia.

DENGUE FEVER This mosquito-borne disease – and other similar arboviruses – may mimic malaria but there is no prophylactic medication available to deal with it. The mosquitoes that carry this virus bite during the daytime, so it is worth applying repellent if you see any mosquitoes around. Symptoms include strong headaches, rashes, excruciating joint and muscle pains and high fever. Dengue fever only lasts for a week or so and is not usually fatal. Complete rest and paracetamol are the usual treatment. Plenty of fluids also help. Some patients are given an intravenous drip to keep them from dehydrating. It is especially important to protect yourself if you have had dengue fever before. A second infection with a different strain can result in the potentially fatal dengue haemorrhagic fever.

SEXUALLY TRANSMITTED DISEASES AIDS is spread in exactly the same way in Africa as it is at home, through body secretions, blood and blood products. The same goes for the dangerous hepatitis B. Both can be spread through sex.

Remember that the risks of sexually transmitted disease are high, whether you sleep with fellow travellers or locals. About 80% of HIV infections in British heterosexuals are acquired abroad. If you must indulge, use condoms or femidoms,

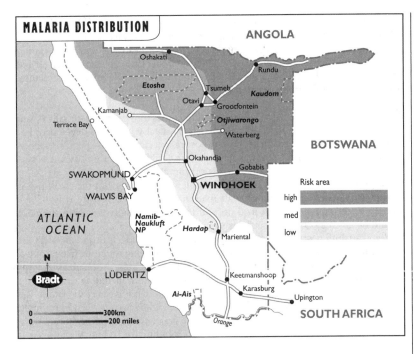

which help reduce the risk of transmission. If you do have unprotected sex, visit a clinic as soon as possible; this should be within 24 hours, or no later than 72 hours, for post-exposure prophylaxis. And if you notice any genital ulcers or discharge, get treatment promptly.

HEPATITIS This is a group of viral diseases which generally start with Coca-Cola-coloured urine and light-coloured stools. It progresses to fevers, weakness, jaundice (yellow skin and eyeballs) and abdominal pains caused by a severe inflammation of the liver. There are several forms, of which the two most common are typical of the rest: hepatitis A (or infectious hepatitis) and hepatitis B (or serum hepatitis).

Hepatitis A, and the newly discovered hepatitis E, are spread by the faecal-oral route, that is by ingesting food or drink contaminated by excrement. They are avoided in the same ways you normally avoid stomach problems: by careful preparation of food and by drinking only clean water. But as there are now excellent vaccines against hepatitis A it is certainly worth getting inoculated before you travel. See *Recommended precautions* on page 70.

In contrast, the more serious but rarer hepatitis B is spread in the same way as AIDS (by blood or body secretions), and is avoided the same way as one avoids AIDS. There is a vaccine which protects against hepatitis B, but three doses are needed over a minimum of four weeks. It is usually considered necessary only for medical workers, people working closely with children or if you intend to travel for eight weeks or longer. There are no cures for hepatitis, but with lots of bed rest and a good low-fat, no-alcohol diet most people recover within six months. If you are unlucky enough to contract hepatitis of any form, use your travel insurance to fly straight home.

MENINGITIS This is a particularly nasty disease as it can kill within hours of the first symptoms appearing. The telltale symptoms are a combination of a blinding headache (light sensitivity), a blotchy rash and a high fever. Immunisation (see page 70) protects against the most serious bacterial form of meningitis. Although other forms of meningitis (usually viral) exist, there are no vaccines for these. Local papers normally report localised outbreaks. A severe headache and fever should make you run to a doctor immediately. There are also other causes of headache and fever; one of which is typhoid, which occurs in travellers to Namibia. Seek medical help if you are ill for more than a few days.

RABIES Rabies is contracted when broken skin comes into contact with saliva from an infected animal. The disease is almost always fatal when fully developed, but fortunately there are excellent post-exposure vaccines. It is possible, albeit expensive, to be immunised against rabies before you travel. You are advised to take this if you intend working with animals or you are travelling for four weeks or more to remote areas. Rabies is rarely a problem for visitors, but the small risk is further minimised by avoiding small mammals. This is especially true of any animals acting strangely. Both mad dogs in town and friendly jackals in the bush should be given a very wide berth, as should ground squirrels.

If you are bitten, scratched or licked over an open wound, clean and disinfect the wound thoroughly by scrubbing it with soap under running water for five minutes, and then flood it with local spirit or diluted iodine. This helps stop the rabies virus entering the body and will guard against wound infections, including tetanus.

Seek help immediately, ideally within 24 hours, though it is never too late, as the incubation period for rabies can be very long. Those who have not been immunised will need a full course of injections. The vast majority of travel health advisors, including WHO, recommend rabies immunoglobulin (RIG), but this product is expensive (around US$800) and may be hard to come by – another reason why pre-exposure vaccination should be encouraged. Tell the doctor if you have had pre-exposure vaccine, as this should change the treatment you receive. The later stages of the disease are horrendous – spasms, personality changes and hydrophobia (fear of water). Death from rabies is probably one of the worst ways to go.

TICKBITE FEVER African ticks are not the rampant disease transmitters they are in the Americas, but they may spread tick-bite fever and a few dangerous rarities in Namibia. Tickbite fever is a flu-like illness that can easily be treated with doxycycline, but as there can be some serious complications it is important to visit a doctor.

Ticks should ideally be removed as soon as possible as leaving them on the body increases the chance of infection. They should be removed with special tick tweezers that can be bought in good travel shops. Failing that you can use your fingernails: grasp the tick as close to your body as possible and pull steadily and firmly away at right angles to your skin. The tick will then come away complete, as long as you do not jerk or twist. If possible douse the wound with alcohol (any spirit will do) or iodine. Irritants (eg: Olbas oil) or lit cigarettes are to be discouraged since they can cause the ticks to regurgitate and therefore increase the risk of disease. It is best to get a travelling companion to check you for ticks; if you are travelling with small children, remember to check their heads, and particularly behind the ears.

Spreading redness around the bite and/or fever and/or aching joints after a tick bite imply that you have an infection that requires antibiotic treatment, so seek advice.

BILHARZIA OR SCHISTOSOMIASIS Though a very low risk in Namibia, bilharzia is an insidious disease, contracted by coming into contact with contaminated water. It is caused by parasitic worms which live part of their lives in freshwater snails, and part of their lives in human bladders or intestines. A common indication of an infection is a localised itchy rash – where the parasites have burrowed through the skin – and later symptoms of a more advanced infection may include passing bloody urine. Bilharzia is readily treated by medication, and only serious if it remains untreated.

The only way to avoid infection completely is to stay away from any bodies of fresh water. Obviously this is restrictive, and would make your trip less enjoyable. More pragmatic advice is to avoid slow-moving or sluggish water, and ask local opinion on the bilharzia risk, as not all water is contaminated. Generally bilharzia snails do not inhabit fast-flowing water, and hence rivers are free of it. However, dams and standing water, especially in populated areas, are usually heavily contaminated. If you think you have been infected, don't worry about it – just get a test done on your return at least six weeks after your last possible exposure.

Avoiding bilharzia If you are bathing, swimming, paddling or wading in fresh water which you think may carry a bilharzia risk, try to get out of the water within ten minutes.

- Avoid bathing or paddling on shores within 200m of villages or places where people use the water a great deal, especially reedy shores or where there is lots of water weed.
- Dry off thoroughly with a towel; rub vigorously.
- If your bathing water comes from a risky source try to ensure that the water is taken from the lake in the early morning and stored snail-free, otherwise it should be filtered or Dettol or Cresol added.
- Bathing early in the morning is safer than bathing in the last half of the day.
- Cover yourself with DEET insect repellent before swimming: it may offer some protection.

SLEEPING SICKNESS OR TRYPANOSOMIASIS This is really a cattle disease, which is rarely caught by people. It is spread by bites from the distinctive tsetse fly – which is slightly larger than a housefly, and has pointed mouth-parts designed for sucking blood. The bite is painful. These flies are easily spotted as they bite during the day, and have distinctive wings which cross into a scissor shape when they are resting. They are not common in Namibia, but do occur occasionally in Bushmanland and the Caprivi. Note that not all tsetses carry the disease.

Prevention is easier than cure, so avoid being bitten by covering up. Chemical insect repellents are also helpful. Dark colours, especially blue, are favoured by the flies, so avoid wearing these if possible.

Tsetse bites are nasty, so expect them to swell up and turn red – that is a normal allergic reaction to any bite. The vast majority of tsetse bites will do only this. However, if the bite develops into a boil-like swelling after five or more days, and a fever starts two or three weeks later, then seek immediate medical treatment to avert permanent damage to your central nervous system. The name 'sleeping sickness' refers to a daytime drowsiness which is characteristic of the later stages of the disease.

Because this is a rare complaint, most doctors in the West are unfamiliar with it. If you think that you may have been infected, draw their attention to the possibility. Treatment is straightforward, once a correct diagnosis has been made.

RETURNING HOME

Many tropical diseases have a long incubation period, and it is possible to develop symptoms weeks after returning home (this is why it is important to keep taking anti-malaria prophylaxis for the prescribed duration after you leave a malarial zone). If you do get ill after you return home, be certain to tell your doctor where you have been. Alert him/her to any diseases that you may have been exposed to. Several people die from malaria in the UK every year because victims do not seek medical help promptly or their doctors are not familiar with the symptoms, and so are slow to make a correct diagnosis. Milder forms of malaria may take up to a year to reveal themselves, but serious (falciparum) malaria will usually become apparent within four months.

If problems persist, get a check-up at one of the hospitals that specialise in tropical diseases. Note that to visit such a hospital in the UK, you need a letter of referral from your doctor.

For further advice or help in the UK, ask your local doctor to refer you to the Hospital for Tropical Diseases (see page 72), or in the US to the Centers for Disease Control (see page 72).

SAFETY

Namibia is not a dangerous country, and is generally surprisingly crime-free. Outside of the main cities, crime against visitors, however minor, is exceedingly rare. Even if you are travelling on local transport on a low budget, you are likely to experience numerous acts of random kindness, but not crime. It is certainly safer for visitors than the UK, USA or most of Europe.

That said, there are increasing reports of theft and muggings, in particular from visitors to Windhoek, so here as in any other city it is important not to flaunt your possessions, and to take common-sense precautions against crime. A large rucksack, for example, is a prime target for thieves who may be expecting to find cameras, cash and credit cards tucked away in the pockets. Provided you are sensible, you are most unlikely to ever see any crime.

Most towns in Namibia have townships, and often these are home to many of the poorer sections of society. Generally they are perfectly safe to visit during the day, but tourists would be wise to avoid wandering around with valuables. If you have friends or contacts who are local and know the areas well, then take the opportunity to explore with them a little. Wander around during the day, or go off to a nightclub together. You'll find that they show you a very different facet of Namibian life from that seen in the more affluent areas. For women travellers, especially those travelling alone, it is important to learn the local attitudes about how to behave acceptably. This takes some practice, and a certain confidence. You will often be the centre of attention, but by developing conversational techniques to avert over-enthusiastic male attention, you should be perfectly safe. Making friends of the local women is one way to help avoid such problems.

THEFT Theft is rarely a problem in Namibia – which is surprising given the poverty levels amongst much of the population. The only real exception to this rule is theft from unattended vehicles, which is common in Windhoek (especially) and the larger towns. If you leave your vehicle with anything valuable on view, then you will probably return to find a window smashed and items stolen. Aside from this, theft is really very unusual.

If you are the victim of a theft then report it to the police – they ought to know. Also try to get a copy of the report, or at least a reference number on an official-looking piece of paper, as this will help you to claim on your insurance policy when you return home. However, reporting anything in a police station can take a long time, and do not expect any speedy arrests for a small case of theft.

ARREST To get arrested in Namibia, a foreigner will normally have to try quite hard. However, even though most Namibians are not paranoid about spies, it is always wise to ask for permission to photograph near bridges or military installations. This simple courtesy costs you nothing, and may avoid a problem later.

One excellent way to get arrested in Namibia is to try to smuggle drugs across its borders, or to try to buy them from 'pushers'. Drug offences carry penalties at least as stiff as those you will find at home – and the jails are worse. Namibia's police are not forbidden to use entrapment techniques or 'sting' operations to catch criminals. Buying, selling or using drugs in Namibia is just not worth the risk.

Failing this, argue with a policeman or army official – and get angry into the bargain – and you may manage to be arrested. It is *essential* to control your temper; stay relaxed when dealing with officials. Not only will you gain respect, and hence help your cause, but you will avoid being forced to cool off for a night in the cells.

If you are careless enough to be arrested, you will often only be asked a few questions. If the police are suspicious of you, then how you handle the situation will determine whether you are kept for a matter of hours or days. Be patient, helpful, good-humoured and as truthful as possible. Avoid any hint of arrogance. If things are going badly after half a day or so, then start firmly, but politely, to insist on seeing someone in higher authority. As a last resort you do, at least in theory, have the right to contact your embassy or consulate, though the finer points of your civil liberties may end up being overlooked by an irate local police chief.

BRIBERY Bribery may be a fact of life in some parts of Africa, but in Namibia it is very rare. Certainly no normal visitor should ever be asked for, or offer, a bribe. It would be just as illegal as offering someone a bribe back home.

SAFARI DRIVE

The ultimate way to explore Namibia

www.safaridrive.com
Tel: 01488 71140

Safari Drive has been organising tailor-made, self drive safaris in Namibia since 1993. With expert knowledge of the roads, conditions, routes and regions, Safari Drive gives you the freedom and security to embark on the adventure of a lifetime.

- Versatile, independent safaris with the freedom to explore at your own pace
- Personal itineraries tailored to your budget and trip requirements
- Expedition-level Land Rover Defenders equipped for up to four people to camp in comfort
- A range of accommodation options from luxury lodges to wilderness camping
- Comprehensive safety measures including in-country briefing, highly detailed trip book and satellite phone back-up
- Extensive kit list including roof tents, water tanks, GPS and all camping gear

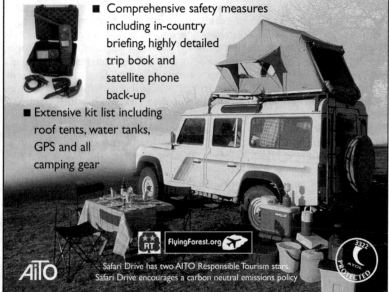

Safari Drive has two AITO Responsible Tourism stars.
Safari Drive encourages a carbon neutral emissions policy

FlyingForest.org

6

Getting Around Namibia

DRIVING

Driving yourself around Namibia is, for most visitors, by far the best way to see the country. It is much easier than driving around Europe or the USA: the roads are excellent, the traffic is light, and the signposts are numerous, clear and unambiguous.

Further, if you choose to visit private camps or concession areas, you can then use the skills of the resident guides to show you the wildlife. You're not restricted to the car, to be in it every day. Driving yourself gives you freedom to explore and to go where you like, when you like.

It's generally easiest to hire a vehicle for your whole time in Namibia, collecting it at the airport when you arrive, and returning it there when you depart. This also removes any worries that you may have about bringing too much luggage (whatever you bring is simply thrown in the boot on arrival).

However, if your budget is very tight then you may think about taking a vehicle for just a few days, perhaps from Windhoek to Swakopmund via the Sesriem area, or to drive around Etosha. However long you keep the vehicle, the type you choose and the company you hire from can make an enormous difference to your trip.

HIRING A VEHICLE Think carefully about what kind of vehicle to hire, and where to get it from, well before arriving in the country. It is usually better to organise this in advance. Check out the deals offered by overseas operators *before* you buy your flights. Arranging flights, car and accommodation with one operator, based in your home country, can sometimes be cheaper and easier than making all the bookings separately. The normal minimum age to hire a car is 23, though the occasional operator will accept drivers of 21.

Hiring a car in one city and dropping it off elsewhere is perfectly possible with the major car-hire companies. Expect to pay a drop-off fee. Although these vary widely, depending on the distance and location, you'll probably be looking at a figure of at least N$600.

There are four big car-hire companies in Namibia: Avis, Budget, Europcar and Imperial (which is associated with Hertz). Their prices tend to be similar, as do their conditions of hire, which leaves quality and availability as appropriate criteria for choosing between them.

Having used all four, I now generally hire from Europcar. They have the youngest and largest fleet, as well as a wide back-up network in Namibia, so any problems get sorted out fast. There is the further advantage that they are well represented throughout the subcontinent, so it is easy to arrange one-way trips between South Africa or Botswana and Namibia – which adds a lot of flexibility to your choice of route.

Aside from these four large firms, there is a plethora of smaller, local car-hire companies in Windhoek (see page 91), some of which are good. Others have more dubious reputations, and even buy their cars from the big companies, which dispose of their vehicles after one or two years. This makes their rates cheaper. However, compromising on the quality of your vehicle is crazy when you rely upon it so completely. Economise on accommodation or meals – but rent the best vehicle you can.

Hiring a 4x4 requires similar logic to the above, but more money. Most car-hire companies offer 4x4s, but because of their expense fleets are often much smaller, and so they must be booked even further in advance.

Typical 'per day' on-the-road prices from the more reputable companies, based upon 7–13 days' rental with unlimited mileage and their maximum insurance (see *Insurance, CDWs and gravel roads*, pages 89–90), are:

Group B	Corolla 1.6 or similar	£33/US$54
Group J	VW Golf Chico	£29/US$47
Group W	Nissan 4x4 D/cab	£74/US$122

Slightly cheaper deals are available from smaller local firms, but none has the same back-up support as the big companies. Neither will you have the same chance of redress if there are any problems. The cost of adding in a second driver is usually N$120 (under 23: N$130).

If time is not in short supply but money is, consider just hiring for a few days at a time to see specific sights – which would not be too expensive if you are planning on sitting by waterholes in Etosha all day.

No matter where you hire your vehicle, do give yourself plenty of time when collecting and dropping it off to ensure that it is properly checked over for damage etc. Make sure, too, that you get the *final* invoice before you leave the vehicle, or you may return home to an unexpected credit-card bill.

A warning Before you sign up for any car hire, see the section on insurance and CDWs on pages 89–90. There is often fine print in these agreements which may mislead the unwary.

2WD or 4x4? Whether you need to hire a 2WD or a 4x4 vehicle depends on where you want to go. For virtually all of the country's main sights and attractions, and many of the more offbeat ones, a normal saloon 2WD car is ideal.

The only real exception to this advice is if you're travelling anywhere during the rains, around January to March, when you might consider taking a 4x4, just in case you need to ford any shallow rivers that block the road. Additional advantages of a 4x4 vehicle are:

- You relax more on gravel roads, knowing the vehicle is sturdier.
- You may be higher up, giving a slightly better view in game parks.
- It's easier to cross shallow rivers or sand patches if you encounter them.

However, the main disadvantages are:

- The cost of hiring a 4x4 is about double that of hiring a 2WD.
- 4x4s are generally heavier to handle, and more tiring to drive.
- A 4x4's fuel consumption is much higher.
- 4x4s have higher centres of gravity, and so tend to roll more easily.
- There's usually no secure boot (trunk), where luggage is not on view, so you can't safely leave bags in the 4x4 when you are not there.

Despite the disadvantages, if you want to get up to the northern Kaokoveld, further than Tsumkwe in Bushmanland, or to any of the really offbeat areas in the Caprivi

– then you'll *need* a high-clearance 4x4. The main point to remember is that in most of these areas, just one 4x4 vehicle simply isn't enough. Your party needs to have a *minimum* of two vehicles for safety, and you should have with you a couple of experienced bush-drivers. These areas are very dangerous if you drive into them alone or ill-equipped.

What kind of 2WD? This is really a question of budget. A simple 'Group J' or 'Group B'– usually a basic 1.3 or 1.6 VW Golf, Toyota Corolla or Mazda Midge – is fine for two adults and most trips. (The harder suspension of the Golf is probably best on Namibian roads.)

If you've any flexibility in your budget, then get one up from the basic car if you can. A 'Group B' normally comes with air conditioning and a radio/tape player, both of which can be useful. A larger vehicle is superfluous for two people, unless you need an automatic gearbox, want the sheer luxury of the space, or plan to drive huge distances.

For three or four people, look to a larger saloon, typically a Group C, like a VW Jetta 1.6. This has a cavernous boot (trunk) for luggage, and power steering is added to its refinements. If budget allows, then the Toyota Camry is excellent – and in many ways better than the more expensive Mercedes 220 which is sometimes offered.

Five or six people on a budget should consider a Toyota Condor, which is very spacious, or something similar. If your budget is flexible, then consider either two small cars, or a VW Microbus (combi). Two cars will give more flexibility if the group wants to split up on occasions. These combis have lots of space to move around, and six window seats for game viewing. Their main disadvantage is that they lack a secure, hidden boot. Like most 4x4s, you can't safely leave the vehicle alone with any luggage in it. A further alternative is a group S vehicle, such as a Nissan X Trail or similar,which looks like a 4x4 and has good ground clearance, but is actually a 2WD.

What kind of 4x4? In order of increasing cost, the choice normally boils down to a single-cab Nissan or Toyota Hilux, a double-cab Nissan or Toyota Hilux, or a Land Rover 110. Occasionally you'll find Mazdas used instead of Toyotas, but their design and limits are very similar. The only relevant difference is that Toyotas are more common, and hence their spares are easier to obtain.

For two people, the single-cab Toyota Hilux is fine. This has just two seats (sometimes a bench seat) in the front and a fibreglass canopy over the pick-up section at the back. This is good for keeping the rain off your luggage, but it will not deter thefts. That said, it's worth noting that a twin-cab will afford you a lot more space to move around and enable you to store cameras and drinks within easy reach.

For three or four people, you'll need the double-cab or the Land Rover. The double-cabs are lighter vehicles, generally more comfortable and faster on tar. However, the Land Rovers are mechanically more simple, and easier to mend in the bush – *if* you know what you're doing. Further, your luggage is inside the main cab, and so slightly safer, easier to access, and will remain a little less dusty. Five or more people will need the flexibility of two vehicles – more than four people in either of these is really quite squashed.

INSURANCE, CDWS AND GRAVEL ROADS Wherever you hire your vehicle, you must read all the fine print of your hire agreement very carefully. The insurance and the collision damage waiver (CDW) clauses are worth studying particularly closely. These spell out the 'excess' that you will pay in the event of an accident. The CDW excesses vary widely, and often explain the difference between cheap rental deals and better but more costly options.

In the last decade Namibia has proved to be a very bad country for accidents. The problem is that the gravel roads are too *good*. If they had lots of pot-holes, then people would go slowly. But instead they are smooth, even and empty – tempting people to speed. This results in an enormous damage and write-off rate amongst the car-hire fleets. One large company with 70 cars complained to me that clients had written off 10% of its fleet in the last month.

Generally this isn't due to collisions, but to foreign drivers going too fast on gravel roads and losing control on a bend, or losing concentration and falling asleep on a long, straight, tar road. There is usually no other reason than carelessness and ignorance. This phenomenon affects 2WDs and 4x4s equally.

Because of this, car-hire companies have very high excesses (ie: the amounts that you pay if you have a major accident). A maximum 80% CDW is normal – which means that you will always pay 20% of the cost of any damage. The bill for a major accident in a small Group A or B would normally be £1,300/US$2,080.

However, beware: the fine print will often state that you will still pay for *all* of the damage if you have an accident due to *negligence, or where no other vehicles are involved and you are driving on a gravel road*.

Some companies will offset some of this risk for you for an additional cost – the extra charge of their additional collision damage waiver (ACDW). Even after you have paid that, many will still hold you liable for 20% of the cost of any damage which occurs on an untarred road – and all of the cost if the accident is caused by 'negligence'. In short, the Namibian companies simply can't get totally comprehensive cover for their rental cars.

The only way around this is the solution found by a UK-based company that specialises in fly-drive trips to Namibia: Expert Africa (↘ *020 8232 9777; www.expertafrica.com*). They offer their travellers a full 100% CDW – with no excesses in the event of a major accident, even if it occurs on a gravel road with no other vehicle involved. They insure their vehicles in the UK, not in Namibia, hence they can get this full cover.

This also gives them the lowest rental rates around, whilst using the best car-hire companies in Namibia. Expert Africa offers this to UK-based clients who book a whole trip with them: flights, car hire and accommodation. Their trips are flexible, good value, and well worth considering.

DRIVING OVER BORDERS If the car-hire companies have offices in Botswana and South Africa, then you can *usually* take cars into these countries. You will need to advise the company in advance, as they need a few days to apply for the right permits and insurances – which may cost an extra N$150 or so.

If you are planning to drive into Botswana, you will surrender your cross-border permit at the control post, then pay for a short-term permit and road safety levy fee for a total of P60 (60 pula) (£5/US$9). On your return, you will need to purchase a new cross-border permit for N$140 (£10/US$16.50).

If you want to do a one-way hire, this is also possible, but expect a one-way drop-off fee of around N$600 (£48/US$86) for distances between 150 and 350km, up to N$1,200 (about £96/US$173) for distances exceeding 500km. For pick ups and drop offs that are not at an airport location there will be an additional delivery and collection charge of around N$110. For a vehicle hired in Windhoek and dropped off in Botswana at Kasane Airport, there will be a fee of N$3,500 (£280/US$504), which is made up of a one way fee of N$2,500 and a collection fee of N$1,000. A fee of N$3,300 (approx £264/US$475) will apply to cross-border rentals between South Africa and Namibia.

Note that car hire is generally cheaper in South Africa, and about the same price in Botswana. Thus for a long trip a one-way hire from South Africa into Namibia is usually slightly cheaper than vice versa.

Taking vehicles across Zimbabwe's borders is trickier, and has only become possible in the last few years. It is generally very expensive to do one-way hires that pick up or drop off in Zimbabwe (though Botswana's Kasane is very close).

CAR-HIRE COMPANIES There is a voluntary grouping of the more responsible members of the car-hire trade, the Car Rental Association of Namibia (CARAN) (*PO Box 80368, Windhoek;* \f *061 242375;* e *caran@iway.na; www.caran.org*). This lays down guidelines for standards and provides an informal arbitration service if things go wrong.

The following car-hire companies are based in Windhoek, though many will also have branches in other Namibian towns:

Larger companies

Avis \ 061 233166; f 061 223072; www.avis.co.za
Budget \ 061 228720 (Eros Airport), 062 540225 (Windhoek International Airport), 061 228720 (town centre); e reservations@budget.co.za; www.budget.co.za. CARAN member.
Hertz Hosea Kutako International Airport, Windhoek; \ 061 255 4115; f 061 540117; www.hertz.co.za

Imperial \ 061 227103; m 081 124 0364; f 061 222721; e wdhcity@imperial.ih.co.za; www.imperialcarrental.co.za. CARAN member.
National/Alamo \ 061 377217; f 061 271064; e reservations@national-namibia.com; www.national-namibia.com

Smaller local companies These include:

Andes 25 Voigts St; \ 061 256334; m 081 129 1259; f 061 256337, e info@andescarrental.com; www.andescarrental.com. CARAN member.
Asco 191 Mandume Ndemufayo Av; \f 061 377200; e info@ascocarhire.com; www.ascocarhire.com. CARAN member.
Britz 4 Eros Rd, Eros; \ 061 250654; f 061 250653; e britznam@britz.com.na
Camel 18 Edison St, Southern Industrial, Windhoek; \ 061 248818; m 081 128 6353, 081 124 1282; f 061 248819; e info@camelcarhire.com.na; www.camelcarhire.com.na. CARAN member.
Camping Car Hire 36 Joule St, Southern Industrial; \ 061 237756; m 081 127 2020; f 061 237757; e carhire@mweb.com.na; www.campingcarhire.com.na. CARAN member.
Caprivi Fidel Castro St; \ 061 256323; m 081 129 3355; f 061 256333; e info@caprivi.com.na, info@kessler.com.na; www.kessler.com.na, www.caprivicarhire.de. CARAN member.
Easycar.com www.easycar.com/car-hire/destination/Namibia
Kalahari 109 Daan Bekker St, Olympia; \ 061 252690; m 081 124 0374; f 061 253083;

e kalahari@natron.net
Leopard \ 061 236113; f 061 236111; e leopard@leopardtours.com; www.leaopardtours.com. CARAN member.
Into Namibia 340 Sam Nujoma Dr, Klein Windhoek; \ 061 253591; m 081 128 8899; f 061 253593
Kessler See *Caprivi, above.*
Namibia Leisure Rentals \ 061 224712, 250725; f 061 224217; e reservations@resdes.com.na; www.namleisurent.com.na
Odyssey 12 Joule St; \ 061 223269; m 081 127 2222; f 061 228911; e odyssey@iway.na; www.odysseycarhire.com. CARAN member.
Pegasus 81 Daan Bekker St; \ 061 251451; m 081 124 4375; f 061 254165; e pegasus@mweb.com.na; www.pegasuscar-namibia.com. CARAN member.
Tempest 43 Werner List St & at Hosea Kutako Airport; \ 061 227103; f 061 222721; e tempestcarhire.co.za; www.tempestcarhire.co.za.
V A 24 Sanderburg St, Pioneers Park; \ 061 233577; m 081 124 4612, 081 128 3494; f 061 241682; e nameagle@iway.na; www.natron.net/tour/vacar/main.html

ON THE ROAD Almost all of Namibia's major highways are tarred. They are usually wide and well signposted, and the small amount of traffic on them makes journeys easy. Less important roads are often gravel, but even these tend to be well maintained and easily passable. Most of the sights, with the exception of Sandwich Harbour, are accessible with an ordinary saloon car (referred to as 2WD in this book). Only those going off the beaten track – into Khaudum, Bushmanland or the Kaokoveld – really need to join an organised group.

The only safe alternative to such a group trip is a convoy of two 4x4s with at least as many experienced bush drivers. Don't be fooled into thinking that a 4x4 will get you everywhere, and solve all your problems. Without extensive experience of using one on rough terrain, it will simply get you into dangerous situations which you have neither the skill nor the experience to cope with. See *4x4 driving*, pages 94–5, for further discussion.

While some sources advise that an International Driving Permit is required if you wish to drive here, driving on a normal overseas driving licence with the requisite passport generally seems to be fine. You'll often be asked to produce documentation at roadblocks etc, so keep these to hand. With a British licence, an international permit can be obtained in the UK from the RAC, or in the USA from Triple A.

Driving is on the left.

EQUIPMENT AND PREPARATIONS Driving around Namibia is usually very easy – much easier than driving at home. But because the distances are long, and some areas remote, a little more preparation is wise.

Fuel Petrol and diesel are available in all the major towns, and many more rural corners too. For most trips, you just need to remember to fill up when you have the opportunity. Prices will depend to a certain extent on where you are, but leaded petrol costs around N$5.49 per litre, unleaded around N$5.50, and diesel a little less at N$5.33. In a major emergency, many farms will be able to help you – but you shouldn't let yourself finish up in need of such charity.

If you are taking a small expedition into the northern Kaokoveld, Bushmanland, or the more obscure corners of the Caprivi, then you will need long-range fuel tanks and/or a large stock of filled jerrycans. It is essential to plan your fuel requirements well in advance, and to carry more than you expect to need. Remember that using a vehicle's 4x4 capability, especially in low ratio gears, will significantly increase your fuel consumption. Similarly, the cool comfort of a vehicle's air conditioning will burn your fuel reserves swiftly.

It's worth knowing that if you need to transfer petrol from a jerrycan to the petrol tank, and you haven't a proper funnel, an alternative is to roll up a piece of paper into a funnel shape – it will work just as well.

Spares Namibia's garages are generally very good, and most larger towns have a comprehensive stock of spares for most vehicles. (Expect to pay over £60/US$96 for a new tyre for a small 2WD saloon.) You'll often find several garages specialising in different makes of vehicle. In the bush you'll find that farm mechanics can effect the most amazing short-term repairs with remarkably basic tools and raw materials.

NAVIGATION See the section on *Maps and navigation* in *Chapter 4* for further comments. The free map of the country issued by the tourist board is probably the best for driving. Note that many of the road numbers have changed in recent years, and continue to change, with several D roads being upgraded to C roads with entirely different numbers. The current tourist-board map indicates some of these changes but local signposts may not match, so it's wise to take particular care in out-of-the-way places.

Those mounting expeditions may want to think about buying more detailed maps from the Surveyor General's office (see page 122). If you are heading to the sand tracks of Bushmanland or the wilds of eastern Caprivi, then consider taking a GPS system.

DRIVING AT NIGHT Never drive at night unless you have to. Both wild and domestic animals frequently spend the night by the side of busy roads, and will actually sleep on quieter ones. Tar roads are especially bad as the surface absorbs all the sun's heat by day, and then radiates it at night – making it a warm bed for passing animals. A high-speed collision with any animal, even a small one like a goat, will not only kill the animal, but will cause very severe damage to a vehicle, and potentially fatal consequences to you.

2WD DRIVING

Tar roads All of Namibia's tar roads are excellent, and a programme of tarring is gradually extending these. Currently they extend to linking most of Namibia's larger towns. Most are single carriageways (one lane in either direction), and it's an effort to rein back the accelerator to remain within the speed limit of 120km/h.

Remember that even on these you will find hazards like animals crossing. These roads are not as insulated from the surrounding countryside as the motorways, freeways and autobahns back home. So don't be tempted to speed.

On main roads, regular picnic sites with a shaded table and benches give the opportunity to stop for a break on long journeys.

Strip roads Very occasionally there are roads where the sealed tar surface is wide enough for only one vehicle. This becomes a problem when you meet another vehicle travelling in the opposite direction ... on the same stretch of tar. The local practice is to wait until the last possible moment before you steer left, driving with two wheels on the gravel adjacent to the tar, and two on the tar. Usually, the vehicle coming in the opposite direction will do the same, and after passing each other both vehicles veer back on to the tar. If you are unused to this, then slow right down before you steer on to the gravel.

Gravel roads Most roads in Namibia are gravel, and most of these are very good. Virtually all are fine for 2WD vehicles. They don't normally suffer from pot-holes, although there may be slight ruts where others have driven before you.

You will occasionally put the car into small skids, and with practice at slower speeds you will learn how to deal with them. Gravel is a less forgiving surface on which to drive than tar. The rules and techniques for driving well are the same for both, but on tar you can get away with sloppy braking and cornering which would prove dangerous on gravel.

The main problem with Namibia's gravel roads is that they are too good. Drivers are lulled into a false sense of security; they believe that it is safe to go faster, and faster. Don't fall for this; it isn't safe at all. See the *Insurance, CDWs and gravel roads* section on pages 89–90, and promise that you'll never drive faster than 80km/h on gravel. That way you'll return from a self-drive trip still believing how safe and good the roads are! A few hints for gravel driving in a 2WD vehicle may be helpful:

- **Slowing down** If in any doubt about what lies ahead, always slow down. Road surfaces can vary enormously, so keep a constant lookout for pot-holes, ruts or patches of soft sand which could put you into an unexpected slide.

- **Passing vehicles** When passing other vehicles travelling in the opposite direction, always slow down to minimise both the damage that stone chippings will do to your windscreen, and the danger in driving through the other vehicle's dust cloud. If the dust cloud is thick, don't return to the centre of the road too fast, as there may be another vehicle behind the first.
- **Using your gears** In normal driving, a lower gear will give you more control over the car – so keep out of high 'cruising' gears. Rather stick with third or fourth, and accept that your revs will be slightly higher than they might normally be.
- **Cornering and braking** Under ideal conditions, the brakes should only be applied when the car is travelling in a straight line. Braking whilst negotiating a corner is dangerous, so it is vital to slow down before you reach corners. Equally, it is better to slow down gradually, using a combination of gears and brakes, than to use the brakes alone. You are less likely to skid.

Salt roads For details of driving on salt roads, see page 309.

4X4 DRIVING If you have a high-clearance 4x4, it can extend your options considerably. However, no vehicle can make up for an inexperienced driver – so ensure that you are confident of your vehicle's capabilities before you venture into the wilds with it. You really need extensive practice, with an expert on hand to advise you, before you'll have the first idea how to handle such a vehicle in difficult terrain. Finally, driving in convoy is an essential precaution in the more remote areas, in case one vehicle gets stuck or breaks down. Some of the more relevant techniques are outlined below.

Driving in sand If you start to lose traction in deep sand, then stop on the next piece of solid ground that you come to. Lower your tyre pressure until there is a distinct bulge in the tyre walls (having first made sure that you have the means to re-inflate them when you reach solid roads again). A lower pressure will help your traction greatly, but increase the wear on your tyres. Pump them up again before you drive on a hard surface at speed, or the tyres will be badly damaged.

Where there are clear, deep-rutted tracks in the sand, don't fight the steering wheel – just relax and let your vehicle steer itself. Driving in the cool of the morning is easier than later in the day because when sand is cool it compacts better and is firmer. (When hot, the pockets of air between the sand grains expand and the sand becomes looser.)

If you do get stuck, despite these precautions, don't panic. Don't just rev the engine and spin the wheels – you'll only dig deeper. Instead stop. Relax and assess the situation. Now dig shallow ramps in front of all the wheels, reinforcing them with pieces of wood, vegetation, stones, material or anything else which will give the wheels better traction. Lighten the vehicle load (passengers out) and push. Don't let the engine revs die as you engage your lowest ratio gear, and use the clutch to ensure that the wheels don't spin wildly and dig themselves further into the sand.

Sometimes rocking the vehicle backwards and forwards will build up momentum to break you free. This can be done by intermittently applying the clutch and/or by getting helpers who can push and pull the vehicle at the same frequency. Once the vehicle is moving, the golden rule of sand driving is to keep up the momentum: if you pause, you will sink and stop.

Driving in mud This is difficult, though the theory is the same as for sand: keep going and don't stop. That said, even the most experienced drivers get stuck. Some areas of Namibia (like the omurambas in Khaudum National Park) have very fine soil known as 'black-cotton' soil, which can become totally impassable when wet.

If you are unlucky enough to need to push-start your vehicle while it is stuck in sand or mud, then there is a remedy. Raise up the drive wheels, and take off one of the tyres. Then wrap a length of rope around the hub and treat it like a spinning top: one person (or more) pulls the rope to make the axle spin, whilst the driver lifts the clutch, turns the ignition on, and engages a low gear to turn the engine over. This is a difficult equivalent of a push start, but it may be your only option.

Rocky terrain Have your tyre pressure higher than normal and move very slowly. If necessary passengers should get out and guide you along the track to avoid scraping the undercarriage on the ground. This can be a very slow business, and is often the case in the highlands of the northern Kaokoveld.

Crossing rivers The first thing to do is to stop and check the river. You must assess its depth, its substrate (type of riverbed) and its current flow; and determine the best route to drive across it. This is best done by wading across the river (while watching for hippos and crocodiles, if necessary). Beware of water that's too deep for your vehicle, or the very real possibility of being swept away by a fast current and a slippery substrate.

If everything is OK then select your lowest gear ratio and drive through the water at a slow but steady rate. Your vehicle's air intake must be above the level of the water to avoid your engine filling with water. It's not worth taking risks, so remember that a flooded river will often subside to much safer levels by the next morning.

Overheating If the engine has overheated then the only option is to stop and turn the engine off. Don't open the radiator cap to refill it until the radiator is no longer hot to the touch. Even then, keep the engine running and the water circulating, while you refill the radiator – otherwise you run the risk of cracking the hot metal by suddenly cooling it. Flicking droplets of water onto the outside of a running engine will cool it.

In areas of tall grass keep a close watch on the water temperature gauge. Grass stems and seeds will get caught in the radiator grill and block the flow of air, causing the engine to overheat and the grass to catch fire. You should stop and remove the grass seeds every few kilometres or so, depending on the conditions.

DRIVING NEAR BIG GAME The only animals which are likely to pose a threat to vehicles are elephants (see box *Driving near elephants: avoiding problems* page 96 for details). So, treat them with the greatest respect and don't 'push' them by trying to move ever closer. Letting them approach you is much safer, and they will feel far less threatened and more relaxed. Then, if the animals are calm, you can safely turn the engine off, sit quietly, and watch as they pass you by.

If you are unlucky, or foolish enough to unexpectedly drive into the middle of a herd, then don't panic. Keep your movements, and those of the vehicle, slow and measured. Back off steadily. Don't be panicked, or overly intimidated, by a mock charge – this is just their way of frightening you away. Professionals will sometimes switch their engines off, but this is not for the faint-hearted.

SUGGESTED ITINERARIES If you're organising a small 4x4 expedition, then it is assumed that you know exactly what you're doing, and where you want to go, and hence no 4x4 itineraries have been included here.

The suggested itineraries here, for 2WDs, are intended as a framework only, and the time spent at places is the *minimum* which is reasonable – if you have less time,

Elephants are the only animals that pose a real danger to vehicles. Everything else will get out of your way, or at least not actively go after you, but if you treat elephants wrongly there's a chance that you might have problems.

To put this in perspective, most drivers who are new to Africa will naturally (and wisely) treat elephants with enormous respect, keeping their distance – simply out of fear. Also, in the more popular areas of Etosha, where the elephants are habituated to vehicles, you'd have to really annoy an already grumpy elephant for it to give you trouble.

To give specific advice is difficult, as every elephant is different. Each is an individual, with real moods and feelings – and there's no substitute for years of experience to tell you what mood they're in. However, a few basics are worth noting.

Firstly, keep your eyes open and don't drive too fast. Surprising an elephant on the road is utterly terrifying, and dangerous for both you and the elephant. Always drive slowly in the bush.

Secondly, think of each animal as having an invisible 'comfort zone' around it. (Some experts talk of three concentric zones: the fright, flight and fight zones – each with a smaller radius, and each more dangerous.) If you actively approach then you breach that zone, and will upset it. So don't approach too closely: keep your distance. How close depends entirely on the elephants and the area. More relaxed elephants having a good day will allow you to get within 25m of them; bad-tempered ones that aren't used to cars may charge at 250m! You can often approach more closely in open areas than in thick bush. That said, if your vehicle is stationary and a relaxed, peaceful elephant approaches you, then you should not have problems if you simply stay still.

Thirdly, never beep your horn or flash your lights at an elephant (and if at night, you shouldn't be driving yourself anyhow!). Either is guaranteed to annoy it. If there's an elephant in your way, just sit back, relax and wait; elephants always have right of way in Africa! The more sound and fury – like wheel spins and engine revving – the more likely that the elephant will assume that you are attacking it, and this is especially the case with a breeding herd.

Finally, look carefully at the elephant(s):

- Are there any small calves around in the herd? If so expect the older females to be easily annoyed and very protective – keep your distance.
- Are there any males in 'musth' around? These are fairly easy to spot because of a heavy secretion from penis and temporal glands and a very musty smell. Generally these will be on their own, unless they are with a cow on heat. Such males will be excitable; you must spot them and give them a wide berth.
- Are there any elephants with a lot of seepage from their temporal glands, on the sides of their heads? If so, expect them to be stressed and easily irritable – beware. This is likely to have a long-term cause – perhaps lack of good water, predator pressure or something as random as toothache – but whatever the cause that animal is under stress, and so should be given an extra-wide berth.

then cut places out rather than quicken the pace. With more time to spare, consider taking the same routes, and exploring each area in greater detail.

When planning your own itinerary, try to intersperse the longer drives between more restful days. Avoid spending each night in a new place, as shifting your base can become tiring. Try to book hire cars and accommodation as far in advance as you can; that way you'll get the places you want, exactly when you want them.

Included here are two very loose categories: 'budget' and 'indulgent'. These broadly reflect the cost of the choices made. Most of the places on the budget itinerary allow camping. The odd place that doesn't, like Zebra River Lodge, is such good value that it'd be wasteful not to use it.

Two weeks
Southern–central Namibia

Night		Budget	Indulgent
I	Fly overnight to Namibia		
2	In/near Windhoek	Tamboti Guesthouse	Eningu Clayhouse Lodge
3–4	Mariental area	Hardap Restcamp	Bagatelle Game Ranch
5–6	Fish River Canyon area	Ai-Ais Restcamp	Cañon Lodge
7–8	Lüderitz	Kratzplatz	The Nest
9	Helmeringhausen area	Hotel Helmeringhausen	Dabis G'stfarm
10–11	Namib-Naukluft area	Desert Homestead	Wolwedans Dune Lodge
12–13	Namib-Naukluft area	Zebra River Lodge	Sossusvlei W'ness Camp
14	Fly overnight out of Namibia		

There is a wide choice of places in the NamibRand, Sesriem and Naukluft areas for the last four nights of this trip. It really depends on how much time you want to spend exploring the mountains and walking, compared with investigating the area's dunes and desert.

Central Namibia–Etosha

Night		Budget	Indulgent
I	Overnight flight to Namibia		
2	In/near Windhoek	Rivendell Guesthouse	Heinitzburg Hotel
3–4	Swakopmund	Brigadoon	Hansa Hotel
5	Skeleton Coast	Die Oord Restcamp	Cape Cross Lodge
6–7	Damaraland	!Gowati Lodge	Damaraland Camp
8	Etosha/Damaraland	Okaukuejo Restcamp	Damaraland Camp
9	Etosha	Okaukuejo Restcamp	Ongava Lodge
10	Etosha	Halali Restcamp	Ongava Lodge
11–12	Etosha	Namutoni Restcamp	Onguma Tented Camp
13	En route to Windhoek	Okonjima Main Camp	Okonjima Bush Camp
14	Fly overnight out of Namibia		

This trip is better in a 'clockwise' direction, as below, because then the best game-viewing (at Etosha) is saved until near the end. This route could easily be expanded by a few days to visit the Sesriem area, by slotting it in after Windhoek and before Swakopmund.

Even on an unrestricted budget, many would rather stay inside Etosha, at the basic Okaukuejo and Halali restcamps, rather than outside it – regardless of how comfortable the outside lodges are.

Three weeks
Southern–central–Etosha

Night		Budget	Indulgent
I	Overnight flight to Namibia		
2–3	Mariental area	Hardap Restcamp	Bagatelle
4–5	Fish River Canyon area	Ai-Ais Restcamp	Cañon Lodge
6–7	Lüderitz	Kratzplatz	Zum Spergebiet Sea View
8	Namib-Naukluft area	Hotel Helmeringhausen	Wolwedans

DISTANCE CHART
Distances in kilometres

Distances between towns are only one part of the equation when calculating travelling times. More important are the type of road (tar, gravel, salt) and the terrain, both of which must be taken into consideration.

Aus
989 **Buitepos**
898 115 **Gobabis**
1145 777 657 **Grootfontein**
798 786 630 645 **Henties Bay**
1156 783 688 425 345 **Kamanjab**
346 1010 895 1142 1115 1153 **Karasburg**
876 501 388 403 242 414 873 **Karibib**
1422 1533 1418 767 1404 1156 1901 1252 **Katima Mulilo**
211 802 687 934 907 945 208 665 1693 **Keetmanshoop**
149 777 662 419 234 113 1147 317 1150 982 **Khorixas**
125 1136 1021 1268 1268 1249 471 923 1279 999 2027 **Lüderitz**
249 692 498 549 540 555 583 334 1273 332 829 374 **Maltahöhe**
432 381 466 713 686 724 429 506 1101 221 718 555 111 **Mariental**
1226 863 738 167 677 506 1223 484 926 1015 500 1458 814 905 **Namutoni**
442 1101 991 1238 1211 1249 147 969 1997 304 1286 609 636 525 1319 **Noordoewer**
764 393 276 381 395 392 761 112 1140 553 430 889 443 332 487 857 **Okahandja**
1128 753 640 397 579 2621 1125 386 1128 917 256 1253 807 696 123 1221 364 **Okaukuejo**
937 562 339 342 254 353 934 61 1101 726 256 1060 616 505 448 1030 173 325 **Omaruru**
1401 708 913 342 852 681 1398 659 989 1190 675 1524 1080 969 245 1494 637 368 598 **Oshakati**
1174 683 568 87 507 336 1053 404 846 845 330 1179 735 524 170 1449 292 308 253 345 **Otavi**
938 565 450 207 389 218 935 197 966 727 212 1061 617 506 288 1031 174 190 135 463 118 **Otjiwarongo**
1011 638 523 280 462 145 1008 269 1011 800 139 1134 690 576 361 1104 247 117 208 436 191 73 **Outjo**
606 407 292 539 512 550 603 270 1298 395 729 285 174 620 699 158 522 331 795 450 332 405 73 **Rehoboth**
1553 1180 1065 494 1143 272 1550 686 1253 1342 377 1676 1232 1121 469 1646 798 534 750 152 497 688 876 876 **Ruacana**
1393 1020 905 248 893 645 1390 741 511 1182 639 1516 1072 961 415 1486 629 617 590 335 455 500 787 742 **Rundu**
1389 1016 921 658 578 233 1386 233 1389 1178 346 1512 1068 957 739 1482 625 495 586 569 451 378 783 323 878 **Sesfontein**
434 877 921 771 356 709 725 472 1530 517 615 559 185 296 852 821 390 754 533 682 637 992 564 261 981 1019 1015 **Sesriem**
1051 676 563 578 67 412 1048 175 1337 840 318 731 482 619 659 1144 287 561 236 834 489 371 444 445 684 826 645 297 **Swakopmund**
1237 746 631 60 570 399 1116 377 819 907 367 1242 798 687 107 1241 355 345 316 282 63 181 228 513 434 308 632 745 552 **Tsumeb**
700 709 913 256 901 581 1398 659 974 1190 675 1524 1080 938 349 1494 637 653 598 563 343 476 536 795 750 545 914 1027 824 316 **Tsumkwe**
1401 700 594 690 98 443 1079 206 1458 814 349 938 451 650 866 1175 318 593 267 521 403 476 521 866 715 947 676 266 31 673 946 **Walvis Bay**
693 320 205 452 466 463 466 181 1211 482 457 816 181 71 435 363 242 708 245 708 363 245 318 87 860 700 696 319 356 426 708 389 **Windhoek**

9	Namib-Naukluft area	Desert Homestead	Wolwedans
10–11	Namib-Naukluft area	Desert Homestead	Kulala Desert Lodge
12–13	Swakopmund	Sea Breeze	Swakopmund Hotel
14–15	Damaraland	Twyfelfontein Lodge	Doro Nawas
16–17	Etosha	Okaukuejo Restcamp	Ongava Lodge
18–19	Etosha	Halali Restcamp	Mushara Lodge
20	En route to Windhoek	Waterberg Restcamp	Waterberg Wilderness Lodge
21	Fly overnight out of Namibia		

Trans-Caprivi Strip

Night		Budget	Indulgent
1	Overnight flight to Victoria Falls		
2–3	Victoria Falls area	Waterfront	Tongabezi
4–6	Chobe River area	Camping in Kasane	Impalila Island
7–8	Katima–Mudumu area	Camp Kwando camping	Lianshulu
9–10	Popa Falls area	Popa Falls Restcamp	Ndhovu Lodge
11	Rundu	n'Kwazi camping	Hakusembe
12–13	Etosha	Namutoni Restcamp	Etosha Aoba
14–15	Etosha	Okaukuejo Restcamp	Ongava Lodge
16	Southern Kaokoveld	Aba Huab Restcamp	Huab Lodge
17	Southern Kaokoveld	Ongongo campsite	Huab Lodge
18	Southern Kaokoveld	Ongongo campsite	Etendeka
19	Southern Kaokoveld	Brandberg Restcamp	Etendeka
20	En route to Windhoek	Erongo Wilderness Lodge	Okonjima
21	Fly overnight out of Namibia		

This trans-Caprivi route is intrinsically more expensive than spending the same length of time just in Namibia. Victoria Falls and the Chobe/Kasane are both relatively costly, Botswana's national park fees are relatively high, and there would also be a one-way drop-off fee levied on the car hire. Such a trip is better suited to a second or third visit to Namibia, rather than the first.

✈ BY AIR

Namibia's internal air links are good and reasonably priced, and internal flights can be a practical way to hop huge distances swiftly. The scheduled internals are sufficiently infrequent that you need to plan your trip around them, and not vice versa. This needs to be done far in advance to be sure of getting seats, but does run the risk of your trip being thrown into disarray if the airline's schedule changes. Sadly, this isn't as uncommon as you might hope. See *Chapter 8*, page 148, for the contact details of airline head offices in Windhoek.

Increasingly private charter flights are being used for short camp-to-camp flights. These are expensive, though the DuneHopper (see pages 101 and 126) is an attempt to cut these prices.

REGIONAL FLIGHTS **Air Namibia** (*www.airnamibia.com.na*) operates regular and reliable flights around the region. Return fares from Windhoek are around £117/US$222 to Maun, £258/US$466 to Victoria Falls, £200/US$361 to Luanda, and £135/US$223 to Johannesburg or Cape Town. In general, you will find these to be the same price if you buy them locally or overseas. However, if you travel between Europe and Namibia with Air Namibia, and book your regional flights at the same time, then these routes become much cheaper. Prices and timetables of internal flights change regularly.

CLASSIC AIR FLIGHTS

Walking over the tarmac in the late 1990s at Hosea Kutako Airport to board your flight to Victoria Falls, you may have been surprised to find a silver, black, white and turquoise Fish Eagle in front of you – a glistening old propeller-driven plane. Aviation enthusiasts would recognise this as a vintage Douglas DC-6B, powered by four Pratt & Whitney R-2800 engines. It is one of two classic DC-6Bs which belonged to the privately owned Namibia Commercial Aviation (NCA).

In fact these two were the very last aircraft to roll off the production line in 1958. Initially they had a little less than three years of European commercial operations with JAT, of Belgrade, before they were transferred to the Yugoslav Air Force. The Fish Eagle was then used exclusively as the personal transport of the Yugoslav leader, Marshall Tito. For this it was fitted out in style with wood and leather, extra soundproofing, a kitchen/galley, and even six beds.

Over a decade later, in 1975, both aircraft were donated to the Zambian Air Force, where Marshall Tito's plane became President Kaunda's personal transport for several years, before falling out of favour. Then it was left to languish on the ground in Lusaka for 15 years. Finally, in 1992, the Zambian Air Force decided to sell 40 tonnes of DC-6 spares, and a condition of sale was that the buyers would agree to take away and dispose of these two aircraft. NCA bought the spares and, after a week working on the first of the planes, the engineers had restored one of the aircraft, the Fish Eagle, sufficiently for it to be flown out to Rundu, their base in Namibia. This has now been sold, but the second aircraft, the Bateleur, was restored during 1998 and is still in use for private charters all over Namibia.

The main regional airports (with their international city codes) are Cape Town (cpt); Johannesburg (jnb); Livingstone, Zambia (lvi); Maun, Botswana (mub); Victoria Falls, Zimbabwe (vfa); Windhoek, International (wdh).

South African Airways (*www.flysaa.com*) and **Comair** (a subsidiary of **British Airways**, *www.comair.co.za*) also operate links to Jo'burg and Cape Town, and **Air Botswana** (*www.airbotswana.co.bw*) links Maun with Windhoek.

INTERNAL FLIGHTS

Scheduled internal flights Namibia has a reasonable network of scheduled internal flights, run by **Air Namibia** from Windhoek's Eros Airport (ERS). The number of destinations available has been cut significantly in recent years, and are currently just: Katima Mulilo, M'pacha (mpa); Lüderitz (lud); Ondangwa (ond); Oranjemund (omd) and Walvis Bay (wvb). Flights depart the hub of Windhoek, using the capital's Eros Airport (ers).

Prices and timetables of internal flights change regularly. Generally, though, these flights are not too expensive. As an example, Lüderitz to Windhoek, a distance of 816 miles, costs N$2,760 return (£197/US$325), excluding airport tax.

Chartered internal flights

Namibia Commercial Aviation ❏ 061 223562; f 061 234583; www.nca.com.na. Runs a superb DC6 dating from 1958. Currently in use for private charters, it used to form part of Air Namibia's normal schedule on the routes to/from Victoria Falls.

Wings over Africa ❏ 061 255001/2; m 081 128 3334, 250 5562; f 061 255002; e wrld@ iafrica.com.na; www.flyinafrica.com

FLEXIBLE FLY-IN TRIPS In the last few years, there have been an increasing number of light aircraft flights around Namibia, arranged by small companies using small four- and six-seater planes. These are particularly convenient for linking farms and lodges which have their own bush airstrips. If you have the money, and want to make the most of a short time in the country, then perhaps a fly-in trip would suit you. Now it's possible to visit Namibia in the same way that you'd see Botswana's Okavango Delta, by flying from camp to camp. This is still the only way to see the northern wilderness area of the Skeleton Coast. Any good tailor-made specialist tour operator (see pages 52–4) could put together such a trip for you – but expect it to cost at least £250/US$375 per person per night.

One particularly popular option is to take one of the scheduled flights that link Windhoek and Swakopmund with the properties around Sesriem and Wolwedans. This is usually arranged as part of a package through a tour operator, or one of the lodges. It's not cheap, but is a fast way to get into the dunes if time is limited. One company organising such trips is DuneHopper (*www.dunehopper.com*), which offers scheduled packages ranging from two to five nights to the NamibRand and Sossusvlei, with daily departures from Windhoek and Swakopmund. As an indication of costs, a return three-night trip from Windhoek or Swakopmund to Wolwedans Dunes Lodge currently costs N$11,930 per person, based on a minimum of two passengers, and including all full board and activities.

Of course, if you've a private pilot's licence and an adventurous streak, then Namibia's skies are marvellously open and free of hassles – but you'll have to spend a day in Windhoek sorting out the paperwork and taking a test flight.

BY RAIL

Generally, Namibia's trains cater better for freight than visitors (*Desert Express* and *Omugulu Gwombashe Star* excepted). Although there is an extensive network of tracks connecting most of Namibia's main towns, many of these are freight only, and there is no through service into South Africa either – the only passenger train to cross the border terminates at Upington, where there is no through connection into the South African rail network (the next mainline station, De Aar, is 415km away). Even within Namibia, routes have been curtailed in recent years, with no passenger trains now running north of Otjiwarongo.

The dedicated Starline passenger rail service is run by TransNamib (*www.transnamib.com.na/Starline.htm*). Trains are pleasant and rarely full, but they are slow and stop frequently. Travelling by train is not for those in a hurry but, while most visitors without their own vehicle prefer long-distance coaches or hitchhiking, travelling by train affords the opportunity to meet local people rather than other visitors.

TransNamib (061 298 2600) has recently addressed the issue of speed, with the introduction of a new, faster train between Windhoek and Swakopmund/Walvis Bay, and between Windhoek and Ondangwa in the north. Called the *Omugulu Gwombashe Star*, it's a luxury train. It departs on Friday only from Windhoek to Swakopmund and Walvis Bay, leaving Windhoek at 14.00, and arriving in Swakopmund at 20.30; the return journey to Windhoek is on Sunday, leaving Walvis Bay at 13.00, and Swakopmund at 13.49, and arriving in Windhoek at 19.30. Tickets cost N$95 in economy or N$135 in business class. On the northern route, trains also depart from Windhoek on a Friday, at 17.30, returning from Ondangwa on Sunday at 13.00. Fares on this route are N$105 one way in economy class.

With the exception of the route from Keetmanshoop to Upington, and the *Omugulu Gwombashe Star*, all train journeys are overnight. This means that there's no chance of enjoying the view, but, on the plus side, it allows travellers to get a night's sleep while in transit, saving on accommodation costs and perhaps 'gaining' a day at their destination. Carriages are divided into 'economy' and 'business' sections, some with sleeper compartments that convert to seating in the daytime, and tickets come with a numbered seat reservation. There are vending machines dispensing snacks and soft drinks on most (but not all) trains, which also have water fountains; videos are shown through the journey.

Passengers need to check in half an hour before the train departs. Only two pieces of luggage may be carried free of charge; bicycles are not allowed.

FARES Overall, fares for TransNamib's trains or buses are low (the 370km journey between Swakopmund and Otjiwarongo, for instance, costs N$61 in economy class, one way), but the tariff can appear amazingly complex. There are various combinations of two classes of travel, three different tariffs (off-peak periods, peak periods and high-peak periods), and occasional discounts (33%) for travel on Tuesdays and Wednesdays. There is in fact a grid that underlies the pricing structure; once you have decided on the various components, then it's just a matter of checking your journey against that grid. Copies are available at the station in Windhoek.

The most expensive permutation, for travel between Windhoek and Keetmanshoop during a high-peak period, in business class, would cost N$92, while economy is N$71. All train prices quoted are for one-way fares.

SCHEDULES TransNamib services cover the following routes (for details, see individual chapters):

Windhoek – Okahandja – Karibib – Usakos – Swakopmund – Walvis Bay (depart daily exc Sat at 19.55)
Walvis Bay – Swakopmund – Usakos – Karibib – Okahandja – Windhoek (depart daily exc Sat at 19.00)

Windhoek – Rehoboth – Kalkrand – Mariental – Gibeon – Asab – Tses – Keetmanshoop (depart daily except Sat at 19.40)
Keetmanshoop – Tses – Asab – Gibeon – Mariental – Kalkrand – Rehoboth – Windhoek (depart daily except Sat at 18.50)

Keetmanshoop – Grünau – Karasburg – Ariamsvlei – Upington (depart Wed, Sat at 08.50)
Upington – Ariamsvlei – Karasburg – Grünau – Keetmanshoop (depart Sun, Thu at 05.00)

Windhoek – Omitara – Witvlei – Gobabis (depart Sun, Tue, Thu at 21.50)
Gobabis – Witvlei – Omitara – Windhoek (depart Mon, Wed, Fri at 20.50)

Windhoek – Okahandja – Karibib – Omaruru – Otjiwarongo (depart Mon, Wed, Fri at 18.15)
Otjiwarongo – Omaruru – Karibib – Okahandja – Windhoek (depart Mon, Wed, Fri at 18.15)

Otjiwarongo – Omaruru – Usakos – Arandis – Swakopmund – Walvis Bay (depart Mon, Wed, Fri at 16.20)
Walvis Bay – Swakopmund – Arandis – Usakos – Omaruru – Otjiwarongo (depart Mon, Wed, Fri at 16.15)

The complete Starline timetable is available online at www.transnamib.com.na/Starline.htm. Aside from these train services, Starline also run some passenger services by bus. See page 105 for details.

BOOKING All Starline trains and buses may be booked at any station. Main station telephone numbers for passenger enquiries are as follows:

Grootfontein	067 249 2200	**Mariental**	063 249200
Karasburg	063 271 1200	**Okahandja**	062 503315
Keetmanshoop	063 229200	**Omaruru**	064 570006

| Otjiwarongo ☎ 067 305200 | Walvis Bay ☎ 064 208505 |
| Swakopmund ☎ 064 463538 | Windhoek ☎ 061 298 2175/2032/2083 |

A booking fee of N$6 will be charged for ticket collection after 16.00 or on a Sunday.

THE DESERT EXPRESS The *Desert Express* (*P Bag 13204, Windhoek;* ☎ *061 298 2600;* f *061 298 2601;* e *desert.express@transnamib.com.na; www.desertexpress.com.na/main.htm*) was introduced in 1998, the result of years of planning and work. The whole train was designed, built and fitted for this trip. It offers a luxurious overnight trip with interesting stops en route, and currently makes the journey between Windhoek and Swakopmund twice a week, with different stops in each direction. One-way tickets cost N$1,850/2,400 per person sharing/single.

The train has 24 air-conditioned cabins (making advance booking vital). Each is small but ingeniously fitted: beds that pull down from the walls, washbasins that move, and various switches cleverly hidden away. Each has its own en-suite facilities and will sleep up to three people, though two in a cabin is ideal. It's a super way to be whisked between Windhoek and Swakopmund in comfort, perfect for a trip's start or end.

Check-in is 30 minutes before departure; if you've free time around Windhoek station then take advantage of the wait to visit the TransNamib Museum (see pages 154–5).

Westbound, it leaves Windhoek on Friday afternoon at 12.00 in winter (first Sunday in April to first Sunday in September), or 13.00 in summer. After about an hour it reaches the Okapuka Ranch, where travellers disembark for a short excursion to see the ranch lions being fed. Continuing on the train, a sundowner drink and nibbles are served before an impressive dinner, after which the train stops in a siding, Friedrichsfelde, for the night. It starts moving early in the morning, catching the spectacular sunrise over the desert and passing through the Khan Valley before stopping in the dunes between Swakopmund and Walvis Bay, for travellers to take a short walk in the desert. It arrives in Swakopmund at 10.00 after a good breakfast.

Eastbound, it departs from Swakopmund on Saturday afternoon at 15.00, winter and summer. After a few hours it stops at Ebony siding from where passengers are transported to Spitzkoppe, where there's a chance to explore in search of rock paintings, or have a sundowner drink. Everyone is back on the train about three hours later, after which dinner is served. At 08.00, the train reaches Okapuka Ranch for an hour's stop to see the ranch lions being fed, before continuing with breakfast and arriving at Windhoek station by 10.30.

There are also occasional four-day all-inclusive trips between Windhoek and Etosha (*N$5,555/4,995 sgl/pp sharing*). Dates in 2007 are 5–8 July and 25–28 October, and six-day trips between Swakopmund and Etosha, via Windhoek (*N$8,000/7,150 sgl/pp sharing*). In 2007, these are scheduled for 1–6 June, 27 July–1 August and 5–10 October. For details of future dates, keep an eye on the *Desert Express* website.

Bookings for all trips can be made through good overseas operators, local agents, or with *Desert Express*, including through their website.

 BY BUS

In comparison with Zimbabwe, east Africa or even South Africa, Namibia has few cheap local buses that are useful for travellers. That said, small Volkswagen **combis** (minibuses) do ferry people between towns, usually from townships, providing a good fast service, but they operate only on the busier routes between centres of population. Visitors usually want to see the more remote areas – where local people just hitch if they need transport. As an indication of fares, you could expect to pay around N$150–170 between Windhoek and Swakopmund (£10–12/US$18–20).

COACHES

Intercape Mainliner The South African coach company, Intercape Mainliner (☏ +27 21 380 4400 24 hrs; 061 227847 office hrs; f 061 228285; e info@ intercape.co.za; www.intercape.co.za), operates luxury vehicles on long-distance routes covering many of the main towns. These are comfortable, with refreshments available, as well as music, videos, toilets and air conditioning.

Reservations for all coaches should be made at least 72 hours in advance, either via Intercape's website, or at one of their offices, or through one of the agents listed below. The exception to this is the journey between Windhoek and Rehoboth, where tickets may be bought only on the bus prior to departure. Tickets may be bought online with a credit card, or through Intercape's reservations office at the Galilei Street depot in Windhoek, off Jan Jonkers. Alternatively, get in touch with one of their **booking agents**:

Gobabis Boekhou & Sekretariële; ☏ 062 562470
Grunau Country House; ☏ 063 262001
Katima Mulilo Tutwa Travel & Tourism; ☏ 066 252739
Keetmanshoop JJ's Supermarket, Bakery & Take-Aways; ☏ 063 225251
Lüderitz Lüderitz Safari & Tours; ☏ 063 202719

Swakopmund Sure Ritz Travel; ☏ 064 405151; f 064 405131; e dunjaw.ritzswp@galileosa.co.za
Swakopmund Trip Travel; ☏ 064 404031
Tsumeb Tourism Services, 1551 Omeg Allee; ☏ 067 220728; f 067 220916; or Tsumeb Aviation Services, Jordaan St; ☏ 067 220520; f 067 220821
Windhoek Harvey World Travel; ☏ 061 253528

and in South Africa:

Cape Town Intercape; ☏ (27) 21 386 4400

Johannesburg Intercape; ☏ (27) 11 333 9618

Timings given in this guide for Mainliner services are local winter time (April–October), which is one hour ahead of summer time. Schedules have changed little over the years, but they do vary slightly from year to year so it's as well to use the information in the individual chapters as a guide, and to check the latest timetables before planning a trip. Buses are run on the following routes:

Windhoek – Okahandja – Karibib – Usakos – Swakopmund – Walvis Bay (four times a week, departing Mon, Wed, Fri, Sun)
Windhoek – Okahandja – Otjiwarongo – Otavi – Tsumeb – Grootfontein – Rundu – Katima Mulilo – Victoria Falls (four times a week, departing Mon, Fri, Sat, Sun)
Windhoek – Rehoboth – Mariental – Keetmanshoop – Grünau – Cape Town (four times a week, departing Mon, Wed, Fri, Sun)
Windhoek – Rehoboth – Mariental – Keetmanshoop – Grünau – Upington (four times a week, departing Mon, Wed, Fri, Sun; note that tickets between Windhoek and Rehoboth cannot be pre-booked)

Fares Intercape's fares, like airline fares, are no longer charged at a fixed rate. The figures quoted in this guide are based on the cost of a 'Full Flexi' ticket in January 2007, but 'Flexi' and 'Saver' tickets are also on offer, and fares vary according to factors such as the direction of travel, seat availability and, one assumes, profitability of the route. For example, at the time of going to press, a Full Flexi ticket from Windhoek to Swakopmund was quoted online at N$145 one way, but from Swakopmund to Windhoek was N$140. Note that booking agents usually charge a handling fee on each ticket of around N$10.

Up-to-date schedules and fares may be obtained on www.intercape.co.za. Fares are quoted one way, and vary quite significantly according to the type of ticket. The following gives an indication of one-way fares:

Windhoek to Rehoboth	N$175 approx (must be purchased on the bus)
Windhoek to Okahandja	N$170
Windhoek to Swakopmund	N$140
Windhoek to Walvis Bay	N$140
Windhoek to Otjiwarongo	N$150
Windhoek to Grünau	N$260
Windhoek to Rundu	N$495
Windhoek to Cape Town	N$520
Windhoek to Johannesburg	N$685
Windhoek to Victoria Falls	N$495

Starline services Part of the TransNamib group, which operates most of the country's railway service, Starline also operate buses on a few routes nationwide, linking some of the areas that used to be serviced more regularly by the rail network. These often leave from railway stations, and most of the routes are designed for local traffic, often with just one service a week and a minimal length of time at the destination. Unfortunately, the most useful service for visitors, which linked Lüderitz with Keetmanshoop, is no longer operational, but there are still services linking Mariental with towns to the east.

For booking details and costs, see TransNamib's rail stations, pages 102–3. Current timetables are available online at www.transnamib.com.na/Starline.htm.

Namib-Naukluft Lodge Shuttle African Extravaganza run a useful minibus shuttle service between Windhoek, Swakopmund and their Namib-Naukluft Lodge, near Solitaire (see page 258). Though in practical terms this limits you to staying at their lodge, unless you can arrange for another to collect you, it is a convenient way to see part of the desert if you don't want to drive.

The shuttle departs from both towns at 14.00 (13.00 Apr–Sep), arriving at the lodge just before sunset. After a day at Sossusvlei, the return shuttle leaves the lodge early in the morning on day three to reach Windhoek or Swakopmund at around 12.30. The trip costs N$3,500 per person sharing, or N$3,930 single, for a return trip; or N$4,200 per person sharing, N$4,630 single, if you want to start from Windhoek and end at Swakopmund, or vice versa. This includes accommodation and meals, drinking water en route, park entrance fees, and medical evacuation insurance.

LOCAL TRANSPORT

Private **taxis** operate in the larger towns, and are useful for getting around Windhoek, Swakopmund and Walvis Bay. They are normally summoned by phoning, rather than being hailed from the street.

Minibuses serve the routes between the townships and the centre, usually leaving only when (very!) full. Unless you know where you are going, and have detailed local advice about which ones to take, you're unlikely to find these very useful.

HITCHHIKING

Hitchhiking is a feasible way to travel independently around Namibia, provided that you're patient and don't have a tight schedule to keep. It is certainly one of the best ways to meet people, and can be speedy and cheap. How fast you get lifts is determined by how much traffic goes your way, where you stand, and how you dress. Some of the gravel roads have very little traffic, and you will wait days for even a single car to pass. The important part is to set off with enough food and (especially) water to be able to wait for this long, or to choose very carefully the lifts that you take, and where they leave you.

For the sake of courtesy, and those who come after you, it's important not to abuse people's kindness. Offer to help with the cost of fuel (most people will refuse anyhow) or pay for some cold drinks on the way. Listen patiently to your host's views and, if you choose to differ, do so courteously – after all, you came to Namibia to learn about a different country.

7

Camping and Walking in the Bush

CAMPING

Many manuals have been written on survival in the bush, often by military veterans. If you are stranded with a convenient multi-purpose knife, then these useful tomes will describe how you can build a shelter from branches, catch passing animals for food, and signal to the inevitable rescue planes which are combing the globe looking for you – whilst avoiding the attentions of hostile forces.

In Namibia, camping is usually less about surviving than about being comfortable. You will usually have much more than the knife: at least a bulging backpack, if not a loaded vehicle. Thus the challenge is not to camp and survive, it is to camp and be as comfortable as possible. Only practice will teach you this, but a few hints might be useful for the less experienced African campers.

WHERE YOU CAN CAMP In national parks and areas that get frequent visitors, there are designated camping sites, usually at restcamps. Most people never need to venture away from these.

Outside the parks, you should ask the local landowner, or village head, if they are happy for you to camp on their property. If you explain patiently and politely what you want, then you are unlikely to meet anything but warm hospitality from most rural Namibians. They will normally be as fascinated with your way of life as you are with theirs. Company by your camp fire is virtually assured.

CHOOSING A SITE Only experience will teach you how to choose a good site for pitching a tent, but a few points may help you avoid problems if you're in a very remote area:

- Avoid camping on what looks like a path through the bush, however indistinct. It may be a well-used game trail.
- Beware of camping in dry riverbeds: dangerous flash floods can arrive with little or no warning.
- Near the coast, and in marshy areas, camp on higher ground to avoid cold, damp mists in the morning and evening.
- Camp a reasonable distance from water: near enough to walk to it, but far enough to avoid animals which arrive to drink.
- If a storm with lightning is likely, make sure that your tent is not the highest thing around.
- Finally, choose a site that is as flat as possible; it will make sleeping much easier.

CAMP FIRES Camp fires can create a great atmosphere and warm you on a cold evening, but they can also be damaging to the environment and leave unsightly piles of ash and blackened stones. Deforestation is a cause for major concern in much of the developing world, including parts of Namibia, so if you do light a fire then use wood as the locals do: sparingly. If you have a vehicle, then consider buying firewood in advance from people who sell it at the roadside in the more verdant areas.

If you collect it yourself, then take only dead wood, nothing living. Never just pick up a log: always roll it over first, checking carefully for snakes or scorpions.

Experienced campers build small, highly efficient fires by using a few large stones to absorb, contain and reflect the heat, and gradually feeding just a few thick logs into the centre to burn. Cooking pots can be balanced on the stones, or the point where the logs meet and burn. Others will use a small trench, lined with rocks, to similar effect. Either technique takes practice, but is worth perfecting. Whichever you do, bury the ashes, take any rubbish with you when you leave, and make the site look as if you had never been there. (See *Appendix 3* for details of Christina Dodwell's excellent *Explorer's Handbook – Travel, Survival and Bush Cookery*.) Finally, a practical warning: cooking after dark, especially in the rainy season, by any form of artificial light poses its own hazards in the form of flying insects. Unless you want mopane moths in with the stir fry, it's best avoided.

Don't expect an unattended fire to frighten away wild animals – that works in Hollywood, but not in Africa. A camp fire may help your feelings of insecurity, but lion and hyena will disregard it with stupefying nonchalance.

Finally, do be hospitable to any locals who appear – despite your efforts to seek permission for your camp, you may effectively be staying in their back gardens.

USING A TENT (OR NOT) Whether to use a tent or to sleep in the open is a personal choice, dependent upon where you are. In an area where there are predators around (specifically lion and hyena) then you should use a tent – and sleep *completely* inside it, as a protruding leg may seem like a tasty take-away to a hungry hyena. This is especially true at organised campsites, where the local animals have got so used to humans that they have lost much of their inherent fear of man. At least one person has been eaten while in a sleeping bag next to Okaukuejo's floodlit waterhole, so always use a tent in these restcamps.

Outside game areas, you will be fine sleeping in the open, or preferably under a mosquito net, with just the stars of the African sky above you. On the practical side, sleeping under a tree will reduce the morning dew that settles on your sleeping bag. If your vehicle has a large, flat roof then sleeping on this will provide you with peace of mind, and a star-filled outlook. (Hiring a vehicle with a built-in roof-tent would seem like a perfect solution, until you want to take a drive whilst leaving your camp intact.)

CAMPING EQUIPMENT If you intend to camp in Namibia, then your choice of equipment will be affected by how you are travelling; you'll have more room in a vehicle than if you just carry a backpack. A few things to consider are:

Tent Mosquito-netting ventilation panels, allowing a good flow of air, are essential. Don't go for a tent that's small; it may feel cosy at home, but will be hot and claustrophobic in the desert. That said, strength and weatherproofing are not so important, unless you're visiting Namibia during the height of the rains.

Mat A ground mat of some sort is essential for comfort, warmth and protecting the tent's groundsheet from stony ground (put it underneath the tent). The ubiquitous closed-cell foam mats are good and readily available. Genuine Karrimats and Therm-a-Rests (combination air-mattress/foam mats) are quite expensive, but much stronger and more durable – worth the investment.

Sleeping bag A three-season down sleeping bag is ideal, being the smallest and lightest bag that is still warm enough for winter nights. Synthetic fillings are cheaper, but for the same warmth are heavier and more bulky. They do have the advantage that they keep their warmth when wet, unlike down, but clearly this is not so vital in Namibia's dry climate.

Sheet sleeping bag Thin pure-cotton sheet sleeping bags are good protection for your main sleeping bag, keeping it cleaner. They can, of course, be used on their own when your main sleeping bag is too hot.

Stove 'Trangia'-type stoves, which burn methylated spirits, are simple to use, light, and cheap to run. They come complete with a set of light aluminium pans and a very useful all-purpose handle. Often you'll be able to cook on a fire with the pans, but it's nice to have the option of making a brew in a few minutes while you set up camp. Canisters for gas stoves are available in the main towns if you prefer to use these, but are expensive and bulky. Petrol- and kerosene-burning stoves are undoubtedly efficient on fuel and powerful – but invariably temperamental, messy, and unreliable in the dusty desert. If you're going on a long hike then take a stove and fuel, as firewood may not always be available in the drier areas.

Torch (flashlight) This should be on every visitor's packing list. Find one that's small and tough, preferably water- and sand-proof. Head-mounted torches leave your hands free, which is especially useful when cooking. Relatively new LED bulbs consume remarkably little power and are well worth the investment; even Maglite-type torches can now be upgraded to use such bulbs. These are not widely available in Namibia.

Water containers For everyday use, a small two-litre water bottle is invaluable – however you are travelling. If you're thinking of hiking, you should bring a strong, collapsible water-bag for times when you will be away from a close source of water. Ten litres is a useful size, and probably the most you'll ever consider carrying on top of your normal kit. (Ten litres of water weighs 10kg.) Large plastic containers for the car can be bought when you arrive.

See *Chapter 4*, pages 60–1, for a memory-jogging list of other useful items to pack.

DANGERS FROM WILDLIFE Camping in Africa is really very safe, though you may not think so from reading this. If you have a major problem while camping, it will probably be because you did something stupid, or because you forgot to take a few simple precautions. Here are a few general basics, applicable to anywhere in Africa and not just Namibia.

Large animals Big game will not bother you if you are in a tent – provided that you do not attract their attention, or panic them. Elephants will gently tiptoe through your guy ropes while you sleep, without even nudging your tent. However, if you wake up and make a noise, startling them, they are far more likely to panic and step on your tent. Similarly, scavengers will quietly wander round, smelling your evening meal in the air, without any intention of harming you.

- Remember to use the toilet before going to bed, and avoid getting up in the night if possible.
- Scrupulously clean everything used for food that might smell good to scavengers. Put these utensils in a vehicle if possible, suspend them from a tree, or pack them away in a rucksack inside the tent.

- Do not keep any smelly foodstuffs, like meat or citrus fruit, in your tent. Their smells may attract unwanted attention.
- Do not leave anything outside that could be picked up – like bags, pots, pans, etc. Hyenas, amongst others, will take anything. (They have been known to crunch a camera's lens, and eat it.)
- If you are likely to wake in the night, then leave the tent's zips a few centimetres open at the top, enabling you to take a quiet peek outside.

Creepy crawlies As you set up camp, clear stones or logs out of your way with extreme caution: underneath will be great hiding places for snakes and scorpions. Long moist grass is ideal territory for snakes and Namibia's many dry, rocky places are classic sites for scorpions.

If you are sleeping in the open, note that it is not unknown to wake and find a snake lying next to you in the morning. Don't panic; it has just been attracted to you by your warmth. You will not be bitten if you gently edge away without making any sudden movements. (This is one good argument for using at least a mosquito net!)

Before you put on your shoes, shake them out. Similarly, check the back of your backpack before you slip it on. Just a curious spider, in either, could inflict a painful bite.

WALKING

Walking in the African bush is a totally different sensation from driving through it. You may start off a little unready – perhaps even sleepy for an early morning walk – but swiftly your mind will awake. There are no noises except the wildlife's, and your own. So every noise that isn't caused by you must be an animal; or a bird; or an insect. Every smell and every rustle has a story to tell, if you can understand it.

With time, patience and a good guide you can learn to smell the presence of elephants, and hear when impala are alarmed by a predator. You can use ox-peckers to lead you to buffalo, or vultures to help you locate a kill. Tracks will record the passage of animals in the sand, telling what passed by, how long ago, and in which direction.

Eventually your gaze becomes alert to the slightest movement, your ears aware of every sound. This is safari at its best. A live, sharp, spine-tingling experience that's hard to beat and very addictive. Be careful: watching animals from a vehicle will never be the same for you again.

WALKING TRAILS Namibia has several long hikes suited to those who are both fit and experienced in Africa. These include unaccompanied trails along the Fish River Canyon, in the Naukluft Mountains and on Waterberg Plateau, and guided trails on Waterberg, along the Ugab River, at Tok Tokkie Trails in the Namib, and in the Canyon Natura Park.

There are also hundreds of shorter hikes, varying from half an hour's stroll to a few days, and many areas which cry out to be explored on foot. None involve much big game, though you may come across larger animals; all are more about spending time in the environments to increase your understanding of them.

SAFETY OF GUIDED WALKS In many areas where guided game walks are undertaken, your chances of being in a compromising situation with seriously dangerous game – namely lion, buffalo or elephant – are almost zero. There are many first-class guided walks in the desert and the mountains, showing you superb scenery and fascinating areas, which don't have these risks to contend with.

Generally Namibia isn't the place for a walking safari which concentrates on big game (as always, there are exceptions – Hobatere springs to mind, as do Palmwag Rhino Camp and Ongava). Hence many guides don't need to carry a gun, or know how to use one. This is fine for most of Namibia.

However, in areas where you may meet lion, buffalo or elephant, you need extra vigilance. A few lodges will take chances, and send you out walking with a guide who doesn't have big game experience. Don't let them. If lion, buffalo or elephant are present, then you need a professional guide who carries a loaded gun and knows how to use it.

This applies especially in Mahango, Mamili and Mudumu, which have thick vegetation cover and healthy game populations. Don't accept the logic that 'experience and large stick' will be good enough. It will be for 99.9% of the time ... but you don't want it to become the 0.1%. Don't walk in such areas unless your guide has experience of big game and a rifle.

Further east, in Zambia and Zimbabwe where walking safaris have been refined, the guides must pass stringent exams and practical tests before they are licensed to walk with clients.

GUIDED WALKING SAFARI If you plan to do much walking, and want to blend in, try to avoid wearing any bright, unnatural colours, especially white. Muted shades are best; greens, browns and khaki are ideal. Hats are essential, as is sun-block. Even a short walk will last for two hours, and there's often no vehicle to which you can retreat if you get too hot.

Cameras and binoculars should be immediately accessible – ideally in dust-proof cases strapped to your belt. They are of much less use if buried at the bottom of a camera bag.

With regard to safety, your guide will always brief you in detail before you set off. S/he will outline possible dangers, and what to do if they materialise. Listen carefully: this is vital.

FACE-TO-FACE ANIMAL ENCOUNTERS Whether you are on an organised walking safari, on your own hike, or just walking from the car to your tent in the bush, it is possible that you will come across some of Africa's larger animals at close quarters. Invariably, the danger is much less than you imagine, and a few basic guidelines will enable you to cope effectively with most situations.

Firstly, don't panic. Console yourself with the fact that animals are not normally interested in people. You are not their normal food, or their predator. If you do not annoy or threaten them, you will be left alone.

If you are walking to look for animals, then remember that this is their environment, not yours. Animals have been 'designed' for the bush, and their senses are far better attuned to it than yours are. To be on less unequal terms, remain alert and try to spot them from a distance. This gives you the option of approaching carefully, or staying well clear.

Finally, the advice of a good guide is more valuable than the simplistic comments noted here. Animals, like people, are all different. So whilst we can generalise here and say how the 'average' animal will behave – the one that's glaring over a small bush at you may have had a really bad day, and be feeling much more grumpy than average.

Here are a few general comments on how to deal with some potentially dangerous situations.

Buffalo This is probably the continent's most dangerous animal to hikers, but there is a difference between the old males, often encountered on their own or in small groups, and large breeding herds.

Lone male buffalo are easily surprised. If they hear or smell anything amiss, they will charge without provocation – motivated by a fear that something is sneaking up on them. Buffalo have an excellent sense of smell, but fortunately they are short-sighted. Avoid a charge by quickly climbing the nearest tree, or by side-stepping at the last minute. If adopting the latter, more risky, technique then stand motionless until the last possible moment, as the buffalo may well miss you anyhow.

The large breeding herds can be treated in a totally different manner. If you approach them in the open, they will often flee. Occasionally though, they will stand and watch, moving aside to allow you to pass through the middle of the herd. Neither encounter is for the faint-hearted or inexperienced, so steer clear of these dangerous animals wherever possible.

Black rhino The Kaokoveld has one of the world's best populations of black rhino – a real success story for Namibian conservation. However, if you are lucky enough to find one, and then unlucky enough to be charged by it, use the same tactics as you would for a buffalo: tree-climbing or dodging at the last second. (It is amazing how fast even the least athletic walker will scale the nearest tree when faced with a charging rhino.) If there are no trees in the vicinity, you have a problem. Your best line of defence is probably to crouch very low, so you don't break the skyline, and remain motionless.

When tracking black rhino in Namibia, you'll almost always be in the company of two or three professional guides/trackers, usually staff of Save the Rhino Trust. I've often been out with them; and the experience can be amazing. On one occasion, we were joined by visitors sporting bright outdoor clothing, who proved disastrously poor at listening to instructions. Having been told to remain dead still because a rhino with a calf was close, one of the group ignored this, stood up and clicked a camera. The rhino charged – it was so fast; this was a very dangerous situation.

Seconds later, as it approached, the trackers all jumped up in unison, shouting and clapping. The rhino changed direction almost instantly, and carried on running into the distance with its calf for miles. It was a tense situation and we were lucky. The one most harmed was the rhino – running for its life, followed by its calf, in 35° heat. We'd put the calf's life in danger, because one visitor couldn't listen to his guide.

Elephant Normally elephants are only a problem if you disturb a mother with a calf, or approach a male in musth (state of arousal). So keep well away from these. However, after decades of persecution, Namibia's 'desert elephants' have a reputation for almost unprovoked aggression. Many people (mostly local villagers) are killed by them each year. The moral is to give these elephants a very wide berth, and to be extremely cautious when in areas where they are likely to be found.

Normally, if you get too close to an elephant, it will first scare you with a 'mock charge': head up, perhaps shaking; ears flapping; trumpeting. Lots of sound and fury. This is intended to be frightening, and it is. But it is just a warning and no cause for panic. Just freeze to assess the elephant's intentions, then back off slowly.

When elephants really mean business, they will put their ears back, their head down, and charge directly at you without stopping. This is known as a 'full charge'. There is no easy way to avoid the charge of an angry elephant, so take a hint from the warning and back off slowly as soon as you encounter a mock charge. Don't run. If you are the object of a full charge, then you have no choice but to run – preferably round an anthill, up a tall tree, or wherever.

Lion Tracking lion can be one of the most exhilarating parts of a good walking safari. Sadly, they will normally flee before you even get close to them. However, it can be a problem if you come across a large pride unexpectedly. Lion are well camouflaged; it is easy to find yourself next to one before you realise it. If you had been listening, you would probably have heard a warning growl about 20m ago. Now it is too late.

The best plan is to stop, and back off slowly, but confidently. If you are in a small group, then stick together. *Never* run from a big cat. Firstly, they are always faster than you are. Secondly, running will just convince them that you are frightened prey worth chasing. As a last resort, if they seem too inquisitive and follow as you back off, then stop. Call their bluff. Pretend that you are not afraid and make loud, deep, confident noises: shout at them, bang something. But do not run.

John Coppinger, one of Africa's most experienced guides, adds that every single compromising experience that he has had with lion on foot has been either with a female with cubs, or with a mating pair, when the males can get very aggressive. You have been warned.

Leopard Leopard are very seldom seen, and would normally flee from the most timid of lone hikers. However, if injured or surprised, they are very powerful, dangerous cats. Conventional wisdom is scarce, but never stare straight into the leopard's eyes, or it will regard this as a threat display. (The same is said, by some, to be true with lion.) Better to look away slightly, at a nearby bush, or even at its tail. Then back off slowly, facing the direction of the cat and showing as little terror as you can. As with lion – loud, deep, confident noises are a last line of defence. Never run from a leopard.

Hippo Hippo are fabled to account for more deaths in Africa than any other animal (ignoring the mosquito). Having been attacked and capsized by a hippo while in a dug-out canoe on the Okavango, I find this very easy to believe. Visitors are most likely to encounter hippo in the water, when paddling a canoe or fishing. However, as they spend half their time grazing ashore, you'll sometimes come across them on land. Out of their comforting lagoons, hippos are even more dangerous. If they see you, they will flee towards the deepest channel nearby – so the golden rule is never to get between a hippo and its escape route to deep water. Given that a hippo will outrun you on land, standing motionless is probably your best line of defence.

Snakes These are really not the great danger that people imagine. Most flee when they feel the vibrations of footsteps; only a few will stay still. The puff adder is responsible for more cases of snakebite than most other venomous snakes because, when approached, it will simply puff itself up and hiss as a warning, rather than slither away. This makes it essential always to watch where you place your feet when walking in the bush.

Similarly, there are a couple of arboreal (tree dwelling) species which may be taken by surprise if you carelessly grab vegetation as you walk. So don't.

Spitting cobras are also encountered occasionally; they will aim for your eyes and spit with accuracy. If the spittle reaches your eyes, you must wash them out *immediately* and thoroughly with whatever liquid comes to hand: water, milk, even urine if that's the only liquid that you can quickly produce.

CANOEING

There is comparatively little canoeing done in Namibia, though operations do run on the country's borders: down the Orange River, on the eastern side of the

Kunene, and occasionally on the Kwando, the Chobe and the Zambezi. The main dangers for canoeists are:

HIPPO Hippos are strictly vegetarians, and will attack a canoe only if they feel threatened. The technique for avoiding hippo problems is first of all to let them know that you are there. Bang your paddle on the side of the canoe a few times (most novice canoeists will do this constantly anyhow).

During the day, hippopotami congregate in the deeper areas of the river. The odd ones in shallow water, where they feel less secure, will head for the deeper places as soon as they are aware of a nearby canoe. Avoiding hippos then becomes a simple case of steering around the deeper areas. This is where experience and knowing the river become useful.

Trouble starts when canoes inadvertently stray over a pod of hippos, or when a canoe cuts a hippo off from its path of retreat. Either situation is dangerous, as hippos will overturn canoes without a second thought, biting them and their occupants.

CROCODILES Crocodiles may have sharp teeth and look prehistoric, but are of little danger to a canoeist ... unless you are in the water. Then the more you struggle and the more waves you create, the more you will attract their unwelcome attentions. They become a major threat when canoes are overturned by hippos – making it essential to get out of the water as soon as possible, either into another canoe or onto the bank.

When a crocodile attacks an animal, it will try to disable it. It does this by getting a firm, biting grip, submerging, and performing a long, fast barrel-roll. This disorients the prey, drowns it, and probably twists off the bitten limb. In this dire situation, your best line of defence is to stab the reptile in its eyes with anything sharp that you have. Alternatively, if you can lift up its tongue and let the water into its lungs while it is underwater, then a crocodile will start to drown and will release its prey.

There is one very reliable report of a man surviving an attack in the Zambezi. The crocodile first grabbed his arm and started to spin backwards into deep water. The man wrapped his legs around the crocodile, to spin with it and avoid having his arm twisted off. As it spun, he tried to poke his thumb into its eyes, but this had no effect. Finally he put his free arm into the crocodile's mouth, and opened up the beast's throat. This worked. The crocodile left him and he survived with only a damaged arm. Understandably, anecdotes about tried and tested methods of escape are rare.

MINIMUM IMPACT

When you visit, drive through, or camp in an area and have 'minimum impact' this means that the area is left in the same condition as – or better – than when you entered it. Whilst most visitors view minimum impact as being desirable, spend time to consider the ways in which we contribute to environmental degradation, and how these can be avoided.

DRIVING Use your vehicle responsibly. If there's a road, or a track, then don't go off it – the environment will suffer. Driving off-road leaves unsightly tracks which detract from the 'wilderness' feeling for subsequent visitors. In the drier western areas these tracks can also crush fragile desert plants, and scar the desert for decades.

HYGIENE Use toilets if they are provided, even if they are basic long-drop loos with questionable cleanliness. If there are no toilets, then human excrement should always be buried well away from paths, or groundwater, and any tissue used should be burnt and then buried.

If you use rivers or lakes to wash, then soap yourself near the bank, using a pan for scooping water from the river – making sure that no soap finds its way back into the water. Use biodegradable soap. Sand makes an excellent pan-scrub, even if you have no water to spare.

RUBBISH Biodegradable rubbish can be burnt and buried with the camp fire ashes. Don't just leave it lying around: it will look very unsightly and spoil the place for those who come after you.

Bring along some plastic bags in which to remove the rest of your rubbish, and dump it at the next town. Items which will not burn, like tin cans, are best cleaned and squashed for easy carrying. If there are bins, then use them, but also consider when they will next be emptied, and if local animals will rummage through them first. Carrying out all your own rubbish may still be the sensible option.

HOST COMMUNITIES Whilst the rules for reducing impact on the environment have been understood and followed by responsible travellers for years, the effects of tourism on local people have only recently been considered. Many tourists believe it is their right, for example, to take intrusive photos of local people – and even become angry if the local people object. They refer to higher prices being charged to tourists as a rip-off, without considering the hand-to-mouth existence of those selling these products or services. They deplore child beggars, then hand out sweets or pens to local children with outstretched hands.

Our behaviour towards 'the locals' needs to be considered in terms of their culture, with the knowledge that we are the uninvited visitors. We visit to enjoy ourselves, but this should not be at the expense of local people. Read *Cultural guidelines*, pages 24–5, and aim to leave the local communities better off after your visit.

LOCAL PAYMENTS If you spend time with any of Namibia's poorer local people, perhaps staying at one of the community campsites, then take great care with any payments that you make.

Firstly, note that most people like to spend their earnings on what *they* choose. This means that trying to pay for services with beads, food, old clothes or anything else instead of money isn't appreciated. Ask yourself how you'd like to be paid, and you'll understand this point.

Secondly, find out the normal cost of what you are buying. Most community campsites will have a standard price for a campsite, an hour's guided activity, or whatever. Find this out before you sleep there, or accept the offer of a walk. It is then important that you pay about that amount for the service rendered – no less, and not too much more.

As most people realise, if you try to pay less you'll get into trouble – as you would at home. However, many do not realise that if they generously pay a lot more, this can be equally damaging. Local rates of pay in rural areas can be very low, and a careless visitor can easily pay disproportionately large sums. Where this happens, local jobs can lose their value overnight. (Imagine working hard to become a game scout, only to learn that a tourist has given your friend the equivalent of your whole month's wages for just a few hours' guiding. What incentive is there for you to carry on with your regular job?)

If you want to give more – for good service, a super guide, or just because you want to help – then either buy some locally made produce (at the going rate), or donate money to one of the organisations working to improve the lot of Namibia's most disadvantaged. The Nyae Nyae Foundation (page 419), IRDNC (page 44) and Save the Rhino Trust (page 343) would all be delighted to suggest a worthwhile home for your donation – where every cent of your money will be put to good use, without causing any damage to the people that you are trying to help.

Part Two

THE GUIDE

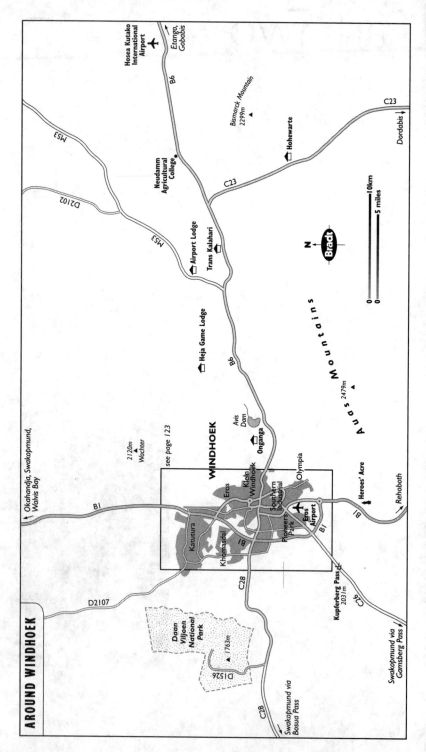

AROUND WINDHOEK

Okahandja, Swakopmund, Walvis Bay

M53

D2102

Hosea Kutako International Airport

Etango, Gobabis

B6

Bismarck Mountain 2299m

Hohewarte

C23

Dordabis

Neudamm Agricultural College

C23

Airport Lodge
Trans Kalahari

M53

N

Bradt

0   5 miles
0   10km

Heja Game Lodge

B6

Avis Dam

2120m
Wachter

see page 123

WINDHOEK

Onganga

A u a s   M o u n t a i n s

2479m

B1

Eros

Klein Windhoek

Katutura

Khomasdal

B1

Southern Industrial

Pioneers Park

Eros Airport

Olympia

Heroes' Acre

Rehoboth

B1

Kupferberg Pass 2031m

C26

Swakopmund via Gamsberg Pass

C28

D2107

Daan Viljoen National Park

1763m

D1526

Swakopmund via Bosua Pass

C28

8

Windhoek

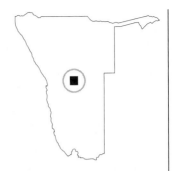

Namibia's capital spreads out in a wide valley between bush-covered hills and appears, at first sight, to be quite small. Driving from the international airport, you pass quickly through the suburbs and, reaching the crest of a hill, find yourself suddenly descending into the city centre.

As you stroll through this centre, the pavement cafés and picturesque old German architecture conspire to give an airy, European feel, whilst street-vendors remind you that this is Africa. Look upwards! The office blocks are tall, but not skyscraping. Around you the pace is busy, but seldom as frantic as Western capitals seem to be.

Leading off Independence Avenue, the city's main street, is the open-air Post Street Mall, centre of a modern and rapidly growing shopping complex. Wandering through here, between the pastel-coloured buildings, you'll find shops selling everything from fast food to fashion. In front of these, street-vendors crouch beside blankets spread with jewellery, crafts and curios for sale. Nearby, the city's more affluent residents step from their cars in shaded parking bays to shop in air-conditioned department stores. The atmosphere is relaxed, to the extent that visitors tend to forget that this is a capital city. As in any city, it is important to remember that tourists tend to stand out, and as such are potentially vulnerable to crime. So it makes sense to keep any valuables well hidden, and to keep a watchful eye on bags or rucksacks. Similarly, if you're in your own vehicle, keep the doors locked – even when you're just getting out to open a gate – and be aware of what's going on around you.

Like many capitals, Windhoek is full of contrasts, especially between the richer and poorer areas, but it lacks any major attractions. For casual visitors the city is pleasant; many stop for a day or two, as they arrive or leave, though few stay much longer. It is worth noting that the city all but closes down on Saturday afternoons (although some shops open on a Sunday morning), so be aware of this if you plan to be in town over a weekend. Note, too, that during the holiday season, from Christmas to around 10 January, large numbers of locals head for the coast, leaving many shops, restaurants and tourist attractions closed. That said, this is the centre of Namibia's administration, and the hub of the country's roads, railways and communications. If you need an embassy, good communications, or an efficient bank, then Windhoek is the right place for you. And to prepare for a trip into the bush, Windhoek is by far the best place in Namibia to get organised and buy supplies.

HISTORY

At an altitude of about 1,650m, in the middle of Namibia's central highlands, Windhoek stands at the head of the valley of one of the Swakop River's tributaries. The Nama people named this place Ai-gams ('fire-water') and the Herero called it Otjomuise ('place of steam'), after the group of hot (23–27°C) springs, now situated in the suburb of Klein Windhoek.

The springs were long used by the original Khoisan hunter-gatherer inhabitants. However, the first recorded settlement here was that of the important chief Jonker Afrikaner and his followers, around 1840. (Jonker had gradually moved north from the Cape, establishing himself as the dominant power in the centre of the country, between Nama groups in the south and Herero to the north.) Many think that the name Windhoek was bestowed on the area by him, perhaps after Winterhoek, his birthplace in the Cape. Others suggest that Windhoek is simply a corruption of the German name for 'windy corner'. Jonker Afrikaner certainly used the name 'Wind Hoock' in a letter to the Wesleyan Mission Society in August 1844, and by 1850 the name 'Windhoek' was in general use.

By December 1842, Rhenish missionaries Hans Kleinschmidt and Carl Hahn had established a church and there were about 1,000 of Jonker's followers living in this valley. The settlement was trading with the coast, and launching occasional cattle-rustling raids on the Herero groups to the north. These raids eventually led to the death of Jonker, after which his followers dispersed and the settlement was abandoned.

The Germans arrived in 1890, under Major Curt von François. They completed the building of their fort, now known as the Alte Feste – Windhoek's oldest building. This became the headquarters of the *Schutztruppe*, the German colonial troops. Gradually German colonists arrived, and the growth of the settlement accelerated with the completion of the railway from Swakopmund in 1902.

In 1909 Windhoek became a municipality. The early years of the 20th century saw many beautiful buildings constructed, including the landmark Christus Kirche, constructed between 1907 and 1910. Development continued naturally until the late 1950s and '60s, when the South African administration started implementing policies for racial separation: the townships began to develop, and many of Windhoek's black population were forced to move. This continued into the '70s and '80s, by which time rigid separation by skin colour had largely been implemented. The privileged 'whites' lived in the spacious leafy suburbs surrounding the centre; black residents in Katutura, which means 'the place where we do not like to (or 'will not') live' (see box, page 156); and those designated as 'coloured' in Khomasdal. Even today, these divisions are largely still in place.

The 1990s, following independence, saw the construction of new office buildings in the centre of town. More recently, impressive new government buildings, including a new Supreme Court building, have been constructed on the east side of Independence Avenue, while the open spaces between the old townships and the inner suburbs are gradually being developed as modest, middle-income housing.

GETTING THERE AND AWAY

Most visitors passing through Windhoek are either driving themselves around or are members of a group trip. Relatively few will need to rely on the local bus, coach or train services detailed here, despite their efficiency.

BY AIR Windhoek has excellent international air links with the UK, Germany, South Africa, Zimbabwe and Zambia, as detailed in *Chapter 4, Planning and preparation*, pages 55–6. More general information on air travel around Namibia is also included in *Chapter 6*, pages 100–1. From Windhoek there are regular flights to:

Katima Mulilo	N$1,931	Oranjemund	N$2,880
Lüderitz	N$2,760	Swakopmund	N$1,160
Ondangwa	N$2,040	Walvis Bay	N$1,160

Travellers should note that Windhoek has two airports, and check which one is used for each of their flights. Hosea Kutako International Airport tends to be for larger aircraft and most international flights, while Eros, near the Safari Hotel, caters mostly for internal flights and light aircraft, and just a few international flights. Both are small by international standards and are modern and pleasant – at least as airports go. For airline contact details, see page 148.

Windhoek's Hosea Kutako International Airport is 42km east of town, along the B6 towards Gobabis. In the passenger area inside the airport are two small bureaux de change open for incoming flights, as well as a useful ATM, a post office and a café that overlooks the arrivals hall. There's also a tourist-information kiosk.

Inside the departure lounge, beyond customs, there's plenty of seating, a bar, a couple of souvenir shops, and a larger duty-free shop that also has a range of souvenirs, safari clothes and books. This last shop accepts Namibian dollars, credit cards and some foreign currency. You will probably get your change in South African rand, and the staff here will also exchange N$100 notes for the equivalent in rand, if asked.

The larger car-hire companies (see page 91) have their own offices at the airport, and others will meet you there on request, so picking up a hired car on arrival is straightforward.

If you don't plan to have your own vehicle, and have made no other arrangements, you can pre-book one of the services run by local companies. Operators include:

Camelthorn Transfer & Tours ☏ 061 219017
Dial a Driver ☏ 061 259677; f 061 259679

Exclusive Transfers ☏/f 061 260367; m 081 122 9844
Transfer Excellence ☏/f 061 244949

Alternatively, a taxi to/from the airport should cost from around N$250, depending on the number of passengers. If you've asked a porter to carry your bags to your car or taxi, a tip of around N$1–2 is about right.

Eros International Airport stands near the main B1 road on the way south to Rehoboth, about 500m from the Safari Hotel. It is even smaller than the international airport – positively bijou. Eros is used for most of Air Namibia's internal flights, a few regional services (and sometimes Cape Town flights) and a steady stream of light aircraft traffic. It has a few car-rental desks, including Avis (but hardly ever anyone there), and a small café, and is usually refreshingly informal. There's no public transport to/from here, but as it's relatively close (4km) to the centre of town, taxis are easily summoned by phone (see page 124). Failing that, the Safari Court Hotel and its cheaper partner, the Safari Hotel, are just a few minutes' walk away, with a regular shuttle running between them and the airport at N$120 per person.

BY BUS/COACH Intercape Mainliner (☏ 061 227847; f 061 228285; www.intercape.co.za) coaches depart from the big parking area behind the tourist-information kiosk opposite the Kalahari Sands Hotel. These head south for Upington (with connections to Jo'burg) and Cape Town on Monday, Wednesday, Friday and Sunday. Westbound coaches head to Walvis Bay via Okahandja, Karibib, Usakos and Swakopmund, on Monday, Wednesday, Friday and Sunday. There is also a service between Windhoek and Victoria Falls four times a week. See *Chapter 6*, pages 104–5, for more precise details and costs.

Townhoppers (☏ 064 407223; m 081 210 3062; e townhoppers@iway.na) operate a daily shuttle service between Windhoek and Swakopmund. Buses leave from the tourist information centre on Independence Avenue at 14.30, with a one-way fare costing N$160 from Windhoek centre, or N$280 from the airport.

BY TRAIN Windhoek is at the hub of TransNamib's relatively slow services around the country, with regular services from the city's railway station (*off Bahnhof Street;* \ *061 298 2032*). Departures to Otjiwarongo are on Monday, Wednesday and Friday at 18.15; to Keetmanshoop daily (except Saturday) at 19.40; to Swakopmund and Walvis Bay daily (except Saturday) at 19.55; to Gobabis on Sunday, Tuesday and Thursday at 21.50; and to Upington on Wednesday and Saturday at 19.40. See *Chapter 6*, pages 101–3. A recently introduced service, the *Omugulu Gwombashe Star*, is a faster tourist train that links Windhoek with Swakopmund and Ondangwa. For details, see page 101.

The capital is also a terminus for the *Desert Express's* trips (see page 103) across the Namib, aimed specifically at visitors. This leaves from Windhoek station on Friday at 12.00 (13.00 in summer), arriving in Swakopmund at 10.00 the following morning. Its air-conditioned cabins have en-suite facilities and cost N$1,850 per person sharing a twin cabin. This includes excursions, dinner and breakfast. Each year there are also occasional four-day all-inclusive trips to Etosha (N$5,050/4,540 sgl/pp sharing); for details of current dates, see www.desertexpress.com.na/main.htm.

ORIENTATION

Under South African rule, Windhoek grew like most large South African cities, forming an 'atomic' structure. Its nucleus was the central business district and shopping areas, surrounded by leafy, spacious suburbs designed for whites with cars. Beyond these, the sprawling, high-density townships housed Windhoek's non-white population.

In modern Windhoek, 16 years after independence, this basic structure is still in place, though the colour divisions have blurred. The leafy suburbs are still affluent, though are now more mixed, and new suburbs have sprung up in the southern parts of the city. Meanwhile, Khomasdal and Katutura remain crowded, poorer and have very few white residents.

The rapid growth in traffic within Windhoek has resulted in considerable development in the road infrastructure, with flyovers now carrying through traffic over the city's more congested areas. This can make orientation for the driver – particularly someone who has visited the city on a previous occasion – quite a challenge, so do get an up-to-date map (see below) and keep an eye on the signposts.

In common with other towns in Namibia, Windhoek undergoes occasional road name changes to reflect the prominence of local or international figures. Recent changes include the following, though it is likely that both names will remain in use for a considerable period of time:

Bülow Street   renamed Frans Indongo Street
Stübel Street   renamed Werner List Street
Peter Müller Street   renamed Fidel Castro Street

MAPS For most visitors, the free map available from the tourist board is the best around. Overall, it is good and reasonably accurate.

For detailed maps, head for the Surveyor General's office on Robert Mugabe Avenue (\ *061 245056/7/8/9;* f *061 227312; closed lunchtime*), between Dr May and Lazarett streets. Ordnance Survey maps are around N$50 each. The 1:1,000,000 map of the whole country is wall-sized and shows all commercial farms and their

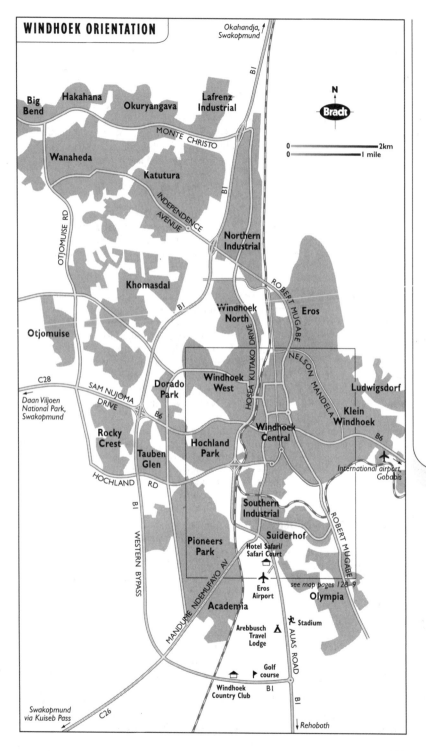

WINDHOEK ORIENTATION

Okahandja,
Swakopmund

B1

N

Bradt

0 —————— 2km
0 —————— 1 mile

Big
Bend

Hakahana

Okuryangava

Lafrenz
Industrial

MONTE CHRISTO

Wanaheda

Katutura

OTJOMUISE RD

INDEPENDENCE
AVENUE

B1

Northern
Industrial

Khomasdal

B1

Windhoek
North

Eros

ROBERT MUGABE

Otjomuise

C28

Daan Viljoen
National Park,
Swakopmund

SAM NUJOMA
DRIVE

Dorado
Park

Windhoek
West

HOSEA KUTAKO DRIVE

NELSON MANDELA

Ludwigsdorf

Klein
Windhoek

B6

B6

Rocky
Crest

Tauben
Glen

Hochland
Park

Windhoek
Central

International airport,
Gobabis

HOCHLAND RD

B1

Southern
Industrial

Suiderhof

ROBERT MUGABE

WESTERN BYPASS

Pioneers
Park

Hotel Safari/
Safari Court

Eros
Airport

see map pages 128–9

Olympia

MANDUME NDEMUFAYO AV

Academia

Arebbusch
Travel
Lodge

Stadium

AUAS ROAD

Golf
course

Windhoek
Country Club

B1

B1

Swakopmund
via Kuiseb Pass

C26

Rehoboth

names. The 1:250,000 maps are good for vehicle navigation in the wilder areas, while the 1:50,000 series suits walkers. Most of the surveys were originally made in 1979, so despite being recently printed these maps are old. However, they are the best available.

GETTING AROUND

PRIVATE TAXIS In and around Windhoek it's usually best to walk, as everything is central and close together. It's not a good idea to hail a taxi on the street, particularly for women on their own, so pre-book from a reliable source, or try one of the following reliable companies below. In general, agree the fare before you take the taxi.

Celestial Transfers ↘ 061 235898
Dial a Driver ↘ 061 259677; f 061 259679
Exclusive Transfers ↘/f 061 260367; m 081 122 9844
A Kasera Dial-a-Cab ↘ 061 240557; m 081 124 7040
L&C Transfers & Chauffeurs ↘ 061 272129; m 081 124 7040

Prime Radio Taxis ↘ 061 272221; m 081 127 7575
Taxi Express & Shuttle ↘ 061 239739
Transfer Excellence ↘/f 061 244949
White Rhino Taxi ↘ 061 221029; m 081 129 9903. Small but very reliable.

HIRED CAR Windhoek is extremely easy to navigate, with just a few main roads, good signposting, and surprisingly little traffic, even at so-called 'peak' times of the day. Parking for a short period is straightforward, too: there are meters along Independence Avenue and some side roads, costing N$0.50 for 20 minutes near the Thuringer Hof Hotel, rising to N$0.50 for just ten minutes as you get nearer to the post office. Parking is free after 18.00 Monday to Friday, or after 13.00 on Saturday and all day Sunday. Car guards – easily recognised by their orange or yellow vests – are regularly on duty on main roads. Ask them to keep an eye on your car in return for a tip of around N$1–2 for half a day, or up to N$4 in the evening. How vigilant they are is a matter for guesswork, of course, but their presence affords some sense of protection for your vehicle.

If you're shopping in the centre of town, secure and shaded parking is available in the multi-storey car park behind the Kalahari Sands Hotel (turn down Fidel Castro Street off Independence Avenue, then left again into Werner List Street; the entrance to the car park is on the left). Parking here costs N$2.60 per hour.

For details of car-hire companies, see page 91.

SHARED TAXIS AND MINIBUSES Shared minibuses and taxis do shuttle runs between the centre of town and both Katutura and Khomasdal. These are primarily for workers from the townships, and as such are mostly at the beginning and end of the working day, though some do run at other times. They are crowded and inflexible, but very cheap. If you want to take one, ask locally exactly where the taxi you need stops in town.

ℹ TOURIST INFORMATION AND TOUR OPERATORS

Your best source of information will often be the people that you meet. Meanwhile, if you're just starting to get to grips with the country, then begin at the office of **Namibia Wildlife Resorts (NWR)** (*Erkraths Bldg, Independence Av;* ↘ *061 285 7200;* f *061 224900;* e *reservations@mweb.com.na, nwr@mweb.com.na; www.nwr.com.na; open Mon–Fri 08.00–17.00*). This is where you book accommodation in the national parks, and get (limited) information about them, either in person or by fax, email or phone. Credit cards are accepted. To book a campsite, you need to pay a deposit of

10%, with the balance payable 60 days before arrival. Alternatively, you can take a chance and turn up at campsites – if there's space, you can pay direct. This is also the place for any dealings with the **MET** (Ministry of Environment and Tourism: *www.met.gov.na*), who have a desk in the same office.

TOURIST INFORMATION For information on Windhoek itself, and the surrounding area, or to find a guide to take you off the beaten track, check out the excellent **tourist information bureau** for the city in the centre of Post Street Mall (*PO Box 59;* ☎ *061 290 2092/2058;* f *061 290 2203/2/8;* e *maj@windhoekcc.org.na; www.cityofwindhoek.org.na; open Mon–Fri, 07.30–13.00 & 14.00–16.30*). The bureau also operates a smaller information kiosk opposite the Kalahari Sands Hotel on Independence Avenue (*open Mon–Fri, 07.30–13.00 & 14.00–16.30*).

Namibia Tourism (☎ *061 290 6000;* f *061 254848;* e *info@namibiatourism.com.na; www.namibiatourism.com.na*) is based on the corner of Frans Indongo and Fidel Castro streets, in the centre of Windhoek, close to Independence Avenue. There's also an information office at Jenny's Place (see page 141) in Klein Windhoek.

TRAVEL AGENTS There is a list of Windhoek's travel agents in the current *Welcome to Namibia*, published annually by the tourist board, but it is unlikely to be comprehensive, with old ones ceasing to trade and new ones starting up with alarming regularity. Have a look, too, at *Namibia Holiday & Travel*, published by Venture Publications and widely available in Namibia. You could also pop into the Namibia Tourist Board, on the corner of Fidel Castro and Werner List streets, for advice.

Most arrangements are best made as far in advance as possible. Unless you are travelling independently and camping everywhere, this usually means booking with a good specialist operator before you leave (see pages 52–4). This will also give you added consumer protection, and recourse from home if things go wrong. However, if you are in Windhoek, and need to arrange something on the spot, then try one of the following general agents:

African Extravaganza Mandume Ndemufayo St, Southern Industrial; ☎ 061 372100; f 061 215356; e afex@afex.com.na; www.african-extravaganza.com

Africa Tourist Info 40 Beethoven St; ☎ 061 228717; f 061 250258; e infotour@iafrica.com.na; www.infotour-africa.com

Chameleon Safaris Voigt St; ☎ 061 247668 f 061 220885; e chamnam@mweb.com.na; www.chameleonsafaris.com

Ondese Travel & Safaris ☎ 061 220876; fax; 061 239700; e info@ondese.com; www.ondese.com

SandyAcre Safaris ☎ 061 248137; f 061 238707; e info@sandyacresafaris.com; www.sandyacresafaris.com

Sense of Africa ☎ 061 275300; f 061 263417; e info@sense-of-africa.com.na; www.sense-of-africa.com

SWA Safaris ☎ 061 221193, 237567, f 061 225387; e swasaf@swasafaris.com.na; www.swasafaris.com

Tou Safaris ☎ 061 241183; f 061 241936; e tristan@tou-safaris.com; www.tou-safaris.com

For budget options, which for two or three people may work out no more expensive than self-drive, the following are recommended:

Cardboard Box Travel Shop Kaiserkrone Centre, Post Street Mall; ☎ 061 256580; f 061 256581; e info@namibian.org; www.namibian.org. General agents, ideal for short-notice trips.

Thimbi Thimbi ☎ 061 224461; f 061 227743; e thimbi@mweb.com.na; www.thimbi-safaris.com.

Sister company to Chameleon. Adventure camping safaris.

Wild Dog & Crazy Kudu Safaris ☎ 061 257642; f 061 240802; e info@wilddog-safaris.com; www.wilddog-safaris.com. Small-group guided trips.

Specialist tour operators

DuneHopper ✆ 061 234793; f 061 259316;
e info@naturefriend.com.na; www.dunehopper.com.
Two- to five-night fly-in trips from Eros Airport to
Sossusvlei & the NamibRand Nature Reserve.

The Trail Hopper ✆ 061 264521; f 061 264389;
e hiking@mweb.com.na; www.trailhopper.com.
Specialises in hiking, including Brandberg & Naukluft
mountains, and Fish River Canyon.

For companies operating local excursions, see pages 155–7.

WHERE TO STAY

Windhoek has a range of places to suit different budgets, from four-star hotels to
backpackers' dorms. Hardly any are run down or seedy, so you are unlikely to find
yourself in a dive. Prices range upwards from about N$150 per person, sharing a
double room with en-suite toilet and bathroom. Single travellers will usually pay
about 30–50% more. Dormitory beds at backpackers' lodges cost around N$70–80.

The dividing line between hotels and pensions/guesthouses used here is
somewhat artificial: one of atmosphere rather than title or price. Hotels tend to be
larger and more expensive, but often have more amenities: you can be more
anonymous and blend into the scenery. Windhoek's pensions and guesthouses are
smaller, often family-run, and usually more friendly and personal. See also the
general comments in *Chapter 4*, page 64. The larger hotels invariably put on
extensive spreads for their meals. Eat-as-much-as-you-can buffet meals, especially
breakfasts, are the norm.

HOTELS

⌂ **Windhoek Country Club Resort** (152 rooms) Western
Bypass, Windhoek South; ✆ 061 205 5911; f 061
252797. Central reservations ✆ +27 11 806 6888;
e hotels@legacyhotels.co.za; www.legacyhotels.co.za.
Managed by the South African chain Legacy Hotels &
Resorts, the Country Club is Windhoek's grandest hotel.
It is situated on the B1 bypass that skirts the city,
about 1.5km off the road to Rehoboth & almost right
next to the industrial area of Prosperita & the newly
developed residential area of Cimbebasia.

Its cavernous, vaulted entrance hall is made of
mock-stone blocks, & lined with various small shops.
Opposite reception is the cave-like entrance to the
casino, where rows of people fill slot machines with
money or gamble at tables from 10.00 right
through to 04.00 the next morning.

The resort's rooms are plush & well designed,
with AC, heating, Mnet TV, minibar/fridge, phone,
hairdryer, safe, & a balcony or patio. Each has a
toilet, & separate bath & shower en suite; one is
specially adapted for paraplegics. In the public areas,
surveillance systems have been installed for added
security.

Outside, at the back of the hotel, there's a fast-
flowing circular river, surrounding a pool & poolside
bar, shaded by another design in rough-hewn rocks.
Beyond is an 18-hole golf course, with special rates
for guests (see page 157).

Buffet lunch in the main restaurant, the
Kokerboom, is N$115 (N$125 on Sunday); dinner is
N$152. Above the casino is a very good Chinese
restaurant, Chez Wou, which attracts a busy trade
from outside the hotel for both lunch & dinner.

The Country Club is a good hotel, but it is
expensive & could be anywhere in the world.
*From N$1,290/1,540 sgl/dbl, up to presidential suite
N$6,000, all B&B.*

⌂ **Kalahari Sands Hotel** (173 rooms) Gustav Voigts
Centre, 129 Independence Av, PO Box 2254; ✆ 061
280 0000; f 061 222260; e ksands@sunint.co.za;
www.suninternational.com. Dominating the city's
skyline in the centre of Independence Av, the
Kalahari Sands Hotel is a large hotel owned by the
Sun International group. Escalators whisk you
through the shopping arcade below to its lobby,
which is pretty much like the lobby of any other
4-star hotel. The rooms are above the lobby,
reached by one of several lifts, so most have good
views of the city. All are carpeted & well furnished,
with AC, direct-dial phones, Mnet TV, & en-suite
toilet, bath & shower. Twin beds, or a king-sized
double, are the norm. Facilities include the Dunes
restaurant, Oasis bar, Sands Casino, a small gym &
spa & a rooftop pool. Generally regarded as
Windhoek's best hotel, the Kalahari Sands lacks
character & feels like a good Sheraton. That said, it

works well & is convenient for walks around the centre of town.

Standard N$1,380, deluxe N$1,710, executive suite N$3,600, presidential suite N$5,300. B/fast N$105, lunch buffet N$125, dinner N$135.

🏠 **Safari Court Hotel** (252 rooms) Aviation Rd; 📞 061 296 8000; f 061 235652; e safari@safarihotel.com.na, reservations@safarihotel.com.na; www.safarihotel.com.na. This international-standard hotel has grown up alongside the older Hotel Safari (see below) over the past few years. Although it still shares the Safari's entrance from the road, & guests may take advantage of the expansive pool, the Safari Court is altogether more exclusive than its lowlier sibling, with its own vaulted reception area, & a separate restaurant & bar.

The hotel's modern, elegant rooms are of a high standard, with en-suite toilets, baths & superb, powerful showers. They also have tea/coffee-making facilities, a fridge with minibar, direct-dial phones, TVs with Mnet & a large lockable section to the wardrobes. If you're arriving in the morning, perhaps from nearby Eros Airport, then an early check-in is normally possible. A regular shuttle connects the 2 hotels with Eros Airport, while transfers to the international airport cost around N$120 pp.

The elegant Acacia restaurant is open for breakfast & dinner only, serving an international cuisine including Namibian oysters, ostrich steak & seafood, & an extensive buffet.

N$628/738 sgl/dbl, B&B.

🏠 **Hotel Safari** (192 rooms) Aviation Rd; 📞 061 296 8000; f 061 235652; e safari@safarihotel.com.na; www.safarihotel.com.na. About 3km from the centre of town, just off the B1 road to Rehoboth & close to Eros Airport, the Hotel Safari covers several acres & includes a large pool set in the grounds. Its younger (& larger) sister hotel, the Safari Court, is adjacent.

Public areas & bedrooms have been extensively renovated, & there are 2 styles of accommodation. Budget rooms are laid out motel style, while slightly more expensive 'business-class' rooms are housed in a separate 2-storey block.

All the Safari's rooms are a good standard, with en-suite toilet & shower/bath, direct-dial telephone, minibar/fridge, tea/coffee maker, & a TV. An excellent breakfast is included, & drinks & snacks (tasty toasted sandwiches, burgers, etc) are served beside the pool throughout the day – making this a popular venue for a mid-afternoon bite to eat. The hotel also has its own restaurant & grill bar.

If you've no transport, then the complimentary minibus is convenient for trips to/from town, leaving opposite the Kalahari Sands, on Independence Av. *Business N$568/668 sgl/dbl, budget N$418/508sgl/dbl, all B&B.*

🏠 **Hotel Fürstenhof** (33 rooms) Frans Indongo St; 📞 061 237380; f 061 228751; e furstenhof@proteahotels.com.na; www.proteahotels.com/furstenhof. Less than 1km west of the centre, the Fürstenhof is perched slightly above the city off Frans Indongo St. It is now owned by the Protea group, but retains lots of individuality & a traditional German character – emphasised by heavy velour fabrics, old furnishings & lots of deep, dark colours. Its spacious rooms all have AC, minibar/fridges, phones, satellite TV, digital safes, hairdryers & en-suite toilets with a shower or bath. The hotel now has a swimming pool.

The restaurant (see page 142) is good but expensive, & has changed little in recent years. *Standard & deluxe rooms N$334/980 sgl/dbl, luxury N$988/1,220 sgl/dbl, family (2 adults/2 children) N$1,846, all B&B.*

🏠 **Hotel Heinitzburg** (16 rooms) 22 Heinitzburg St; 📞 061 249597; f 061 249598; e heinitz@mweb.com.na; www.heinitzburg.com. This distinctive white turreted fort, built at the turn of the 19th century, is a member of the Relais et Châteaux group. Set high on a hill, it is quiet & secluded, yet easily seen from Independence Av. Drive about 1km from the centre, along Sam Nujoma Dr, towards the airport. Take a right on to Heinitzburg St and the Castle, No 22, is reached via a short but steep drive on the right.

Owned by Beate Raith, previously the proprietor of the Fürstenhof, this is one of the most stylish places in town. Its rooms are all different; alongside amenities such as satellite TV & fridge/minibar & gilded bathrooms, expect impressive furniture with expanses of beautiful, solid wood & lots of space. With four-poster beds, dreamy white quilts & sumptuous fabrics, this is a truly romantic hideaway. Outside, a rose terrace commands super views of the city below – an attraction in its own right for non-residents who come for afternoon tea & cakes – & there is a sheltered pool area with sun loungers.

The Heinitzburg's restaurant, Leo's, offers a contrast in style. Small, modern & sophisticated, its menu is the creation of the hotel's own French chef (see page 142). Delicious lunches are served on the terrace.

Deluxe N$1,170/1,755 sgl/dbl, poolside deluxe N$1,373.48/ 2,298.93, all B&B.

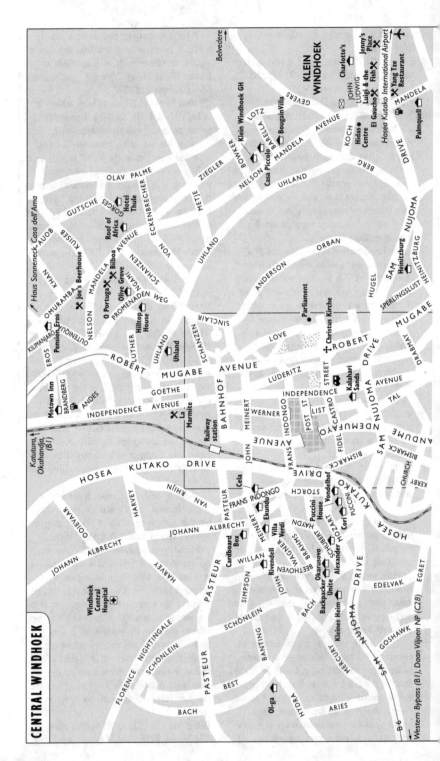

CENTRAL WINDHOEK

KLEIN WINDHOEK

128

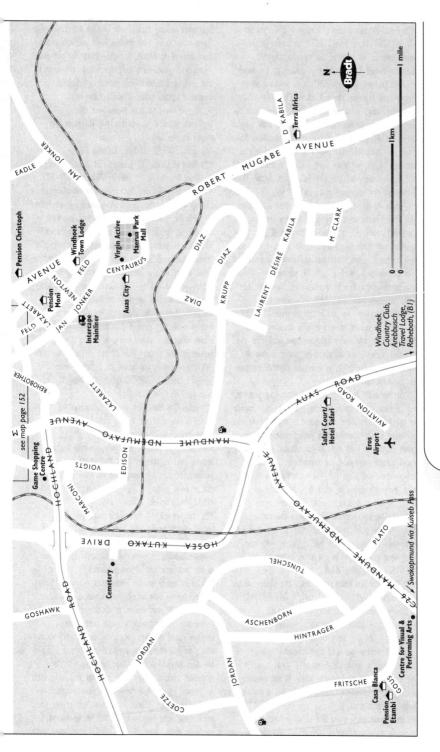

see map page 152

Pension Christoph

Windhoek
Town Lodge

Virgin Active
Maerua Park
Mall

CENTAURUS

Auas City

Pension
Moni

Intercape
Mainliner

EADLE

IAN JONKER

AVENUE

NEWTON

JONKER

LAZARETT

FELD

FELD

REHOBOTHER

ROBERT MUGABE AVENUE

L D KABILA

Terra Africa

M CLARK

DIAZ

DIAZ

KRUPP

DIAZ

LAURENT DÉSIRÉ KABILA

Windhoek
Country Club,
Arebbusch
Travel Lodge,
Rehoboth, (B1)

AUAS ROAD

AVIATION ROAD

Safari Court/
Hotel Safari

Eros
Airport

NDEMUFAYO AVENUE

MANDUME

LAZARETT

EDISON

VOIGTS

MARCONI

Game Shopping
Centre

HOCHLAND

HOSEA KUTAKO DRIVE

NDEMUFAYO AVENUE

MANDUME

PLATO

TUNSCHEL

Swakopmund via Kuiseb Pass

C26

Cemetery

HOCHLAND ROAD

GOSHAWK

JORDAN

JORDAN

ASCHENBORN

HINTRAGER

Centre for Visual &
Performing Arts

Casa Blanca

Pension
Etambi

GOUS

FRITSCHE

COETZE

1km

1 mile

0

0

N

Bradt

Hotel-Pension Thule (14 rooms) 1 Gorges St; 061 250146; f 061 250759; e thule@mweb.com.na. In spite of the appellation, the German-owned Thule is clearly aiming at the hotel market. Opened in April 2002, it is situated in a prime spot high on the hill above Eros, with sweeping views across the city. To get here from the airport, follow Nelson Mandela Av to the traffic lights after the BP garage, then turn right into Metje St. Take the third left into Olaf Palme St, then left at the top of the hill into Gorges (later Gutsche) St. At the top of the next hill, turn left again, & the Thule is behind the imposing gates on the left.

From its flag-festooned entrance past tall palms, the Thule oozes style. Airy, light & very modern, its carpeted rooms are a blend of chrome & glass with opulent soft furnishings that would make a film star feel at home. Each room has AC/heating & boasts two double beds, with a safe, TV, phone, minibar/fridge, coffee & tea facilities, hairdryer. En-suite facilities have both bath & shower, with underfloor heating for maximum comfort. In addition, VIP rooms have a sofa & dressing room. There is also one room designed specifically for the disabled. Views come as standard, either across the mountains at the back, or over the central fountain to the city beyond.

In the main building, & the surrounding grounds, no expense has been spared to maximise the impact of the hotel's location. This is not a place for vertigo sufferers, or for families with young children. Varying levels feature a pool with elegant tables & chairs, a small formal courtyard, the restaurant & – at the top – the Sundowner bar. The restaurant, with its wide curved expanse of glass & terrace beyond, is open for b/fast & dinner, with a set menu on request. The bar, a great place for a sundowner, opens to the public from 16.30 to 21.30. And if you look over the edge of the hill at sunset, you may even spot guinea fowl in the trees below. *N$845/1,190 sgl/dbl B&B.*

Thüringer Hof Hotel (40 rooms) cnr Independence Av & Bahnhof St; 061 226031; f 061 232981; e thuringerhof.reservations@olfitra.com.na; www.namibsunhotels.com.na. This member of the Namib Sun chain is very close to the railway station, & across the road from the main police station. Popular with the German & local business markets, it tends to be quite noisy. It has recently undergone a complete facelift & now has a stylish, light reception area.

Double or twin rooms are clean & functional, if generally unremarkable: all have direct-dial phones, tea/coffee-making facilities, & TV. One attraction of the hotel is its lively beer garden. Here you can order food as well as drinks, & choose from the pub-grub menu, with good-value daily specials. In the front is the popular Butcher's Grill, with its traditional no-nonsense square tables & white tablecloths.

If you want to stay somewhere that's straightforward & convenient, the Thüringer Hof might fit the bill. *N$565/730/775–850 sgl/dbl/suite B&B.*

Roof of Africa (27 rooms) 124 Nelson Mandela Av, Klein Windhoek; 061 254708; m 081 124 4930; e info@roofofafrica.com; www.roofofafrica.com. Clearly visible as you're entering Windhoek on Nelson Mandela Av, Roof of Africa has its main entrance in Gusinde St. Originally set up as a new-generation backpackers' place, it has undergone something of a transformation & is now more of a well-equipped hotel, albeit with a lively bar & restaurant that has freshly cooked buffets daily. Each of its rooms has AC, phone, wireless internet connection, TV & electronic safe, while additional luxuries are a solar-heated swimming pool & private sauna. The on-site travel office is a useful extra, as is the shuttle service to the airport (N$100 pp) & the city centre (N$10 pp); prices are based on 2 people min. *Jan–Jun, Dec N$520/730 sgl/dbl, Jul–Nov N$570/795 sgl/dbl, all DBB.*

Auas City Hotel (24 rooms) Centaurus Rd, Maerua Park; 061 239768; f 061 239826; e auascityhotel@mweb.com.na; www.auascityhotel.com. This new, no-frills hotel almost next to Maerua Park Mall is geared to the business market. All rooms are en suite with AC, & dbl or twin beds. *N$330/420 sgl/dbl; b/fast N$40.*

Motown Inn (60 rooms) cnr Brandberg & Independence Av; 061 234646; m 081 128 1871; f 061 234646; e reservations@motown.namibia.na; www.motown.namibia.na. Located at the northern end of Independence Av, this inn focuses primarily on the backpacker market & those looking for no-frills accommodation at a sensible price. Clean & comfortable, it offers good security – rooms are accessed with a swipe card, there is a security guard on duty round the clock, every room has a safe, & there's secure parking. Internet facilities are also exceptional, with four computers in the reception area, & a free daily internet slot for guests.

Rooms cater for a range of accommodation needs. Some have shared bathrooms, others are en suite; some have fans, others have AC. All except economy rooms have TV. The hotel has its own pizza restaurant, a cafeteria & lounge, with room service available. There are also laundry facilities & a coin-operated laundrette.

Economy (shared facilities) N$254.55; en suite N$335.74; executive N$457.83; self-catering. N$550.

PENSIONS AND B&BS The proliferation of pensions and guesthouses in recent years has spawned plenty of lookalike establishments each catering for the same market. Most are situated in the suburban areas surrounding Windhoek. The more centrally located are mostly clustered in the area just to the west of Independence Avenue (helpfully known as West Windhoek), within a reasonable walking distance of shops and other facilities. One of the most popular areas for visitors is to the northeast, incorporating Eros and Klein Windhoek. Here, in addition to plenty of accommodation, there is a good choice of restaurants and bars. In Olympia, to the southeast of the city, pensions are relatively scarce. Those that are here are usually quiet, often with views over the rolling hills to the south. Then to the southwest are the open spaces of Pioneers Park.

Unless otherwise stated, all rooms have en-suite shower and toilet facilities.

Central Windhoek and Windhoek West

⌂ **Hotel-Pension Alexander** (13 rooms) 10 Beethoven St; ⌕/f 061 240775. Between Schubert & Mozart streets, Pension Alexander is 15 minutes' walk from the centre, & is owned and run by the eponymous Alexander. It aims for simple, affordable accommodation, & rooms all have cool tiled floors, fans, direct-dial telephones, TV with Mnet, & a bath or shower. There's a small but pleasant pool outside & the rooms are quite spread out, with safe off-street parking available.
N$280/400/500 sgl/dbl/ family (4 people), B&B.

⌂ **Hotel-Pension Cela** (18 rooms) 82 Frans Indongo St; ⌕ 061 226295/4; f 061 226246; e cela@ mweb.com.na, info@hotelcela.com; www.hotelcela.com. This suburban pension, just beyond the Handke near John Meinert St, seems rather jaded, but its rooms are reasonably well equipped, with fridge/minibar, phone & Mnet TV. With a small swimming pool at the back, & off-street parking, it makes a fairly central base, though it is a shame that the seating areas outside the rooms are dominated by concrete rather than plants & lawns.
N$360/495/595 sgl/dbl/trpl, B&B.

⌂ **Pension Cori** (16 rooms) 8 Puccini St, Windhoek West; ⌕ 061 228840; m 081 127 7397; f 061 225806; e cori@cyberhost.com.na; www.pension-cori-namibia.com. It's not difficult to spot this lilac-&-blue pension near the corner of Hosea Kutako Dr & Puccini St, some 5 mins' walk from the centre of Windhoek. Owner Rini lives on the premises & has run her hospitable pension since the late 1990s. Each well-appointed twin room has a private entrance from the garden, & features a TV, radio/alarm, coffee/tea-making facilities & a fan.

The attractive garden offers plenty of shady trees, with a swimming pool, & a thatched seating area & braai. Dinner — usually a braai — is available on request, or guests may make use of the grill facilities for their own cooking. There is secure parking for guests' vehicles. Airport collection can be arranged for N$150 per trip, or Rini will collect you from the airport shuttle stop in Windhoek.
N$300/400/555 sgl/dbl/trpl, B&B.

⌂ **Ekundu Guesthouse** (8 rooms) 10 Johann Albrecht St; ⌕ 064 253440, f 064 253565; e ekundu@mweb.com.na. Opened in 1999, this small, central guesthouse with its distinctive green-&-cream colour scheme has bright, modern rooms with pine furniture & Mnet TV. It's inexpensive, there's a cheerful b/fast area, & the kitchen is also available for guest use. Secure parking is available, too. The drawback? It's on a busy road, so can be noisy.
N$310/425/495 sgl/dbl/family, inc continental b/fast.

⌂ **Hotel-Pension Handke** (10 rooms) 3 Rossini St; ⌕ 061 234904; f 061 225660; e pensionhandke@ iafrica.com.na; www.natron.net/handke. Just out of the centre, the inexpensive Handke is within about 5 mins' walk of the centre of town — ideal if you've no car. A dedicated mother-&-son team, Amanda & Ernst Kipka, offer a warm welcome. Handke's rooms are small & simple, yet good value, particularly those at the back which are quieter than the others All have en-suite shower/toilet, ceiling fan & direct-dial phone. There's little space around the rooms, but the tree-shaded garden is a pleasant place to sit, & the TV lounge & breakfast area offer real home comfort. Convenient off-street parking in front of the pension is a major advantage if you have a car (if so, approach via John Meinert St). Internet facilities are available.

N$310/470 sgl/dbl, family room N$195 pp (min 3 people), all B&B; 10% surcharge on credit cards.

⌂ **Hotel-Pension Kleines Heim** (14 rooms) 10 Volans St, Windhoek West; ☎ 061 248200; f 061 248203; e kleiheim@iafrica.com.na; www.kleinesheim.com. Kleines Heim is about 5 mins' drive from the centre of town, or a 15-min walk. To reach it, take Sam Nujoma Dr west, then right onto Bach St, left onto Mercury St, & left again onto Volan St. Parking is off the street & within the pension's grounds.

Run by Henk & Adrée Mudge, Kleines Heim has a beautiful setting. Its individually decorated rooms, with many personal touches, lead onto lawns, which surround a swimming pool under impressive palm trees. All the rooms are very comfortable & spacious, with direct-dial phones, TVs, tea/coffee-making facilities, en-suite shower/toilets (three with bath), & all have underfloor heating for winter (a big bonus, when many small pensions can be cold) & ceiling fans for summer. Dinner, prepared by the Damara chef, can be provided on request.

From N$525/345 sgl/pp sharing.

⌂ **Okarusuvo** (3 rooms) 17 Beethoven St; ☎ 061 232252; m 081 241 7817; e riben@ mweb.com.na; www.natron.net/tour/okarusuvo. Erda Iben opened this small guesthouse, which is a 15–20-min walk from the city centre, in 2000. This is very much a B&B establishment, suitable for holidaymakers rather than backpackers. Erda will arrange transfers to the airport & lifts into town.

N$260/350 sgl/dbl.

⌂ **Ol-ga** (4 rooms) 91 Bach St, PO Box 20926, West Windhoek; ☎ 061 235853; f 061 255184; e olgaguest@iway.na; www.olga-namibia.de. Gesa Oldach claims that her home is one of the oldest B&Bs in Windhoek. Located about 2.5km west of the centre of the city, this is a guesthouse that will appeal particularly to birdwatchers, for numerous species are attracted to its mature trees. Pine-furnished rooms are small but well appointed, with local art adorning the walls, & TV, kettle with tea & coffee & mosquito nets. There is a barbecue available for guests.

N$220/300 sgl/dbl, B&B.

⌂ **Puccini Guest House** (15 rooms) 4 Puccini St; ☎/f 061 236355; e info@puccini-namibia.com; www.puccini-namibia.com. Between Sam Nujoma & Hosea Kutako drives, just beyond the railway, Puccini St is less than 10 mins' walk from town. An affordable guesthouse, this has a pool, sauna, secure parking, & a well-equipped kitchen, as well as a lapa with an old

wood-burning stove & a pizza oven. Rooms are either en suite or with shared bathroom. Rates include a light breakfast, though more substantial fare can be provided at extra cost. The owner, Christelle, together with her Jack Russells, provides a relaxed atmosphere & can help with booking trips or car hire.

Shared bathroom N$175/250 sgl/dbl; en suite N$275/320/500 sgl/dbl/family, all inc light b/fast.

⌂ **Rivendell** (8 rooms) 40 Beethoven St; ☎ 061 250006; f 061 250258 e havens@mweb.com.na. Under new management since 2003, this guesthouse offers a homely, comfortable, clean & relaxed place to stay to the west of the city, about 15–20 mins' walk from the centre. Rooms are either en suite or with shared bathrooms, & some are situated around the swimming pool. Extra beds can be added if required. There is also a self-catering flat with a bedroom, lounge & kitchenette. In addition to a communal lounge with TV, internet access, metered phone & laundry services are available. Prices include b/fast, but guests are welcome to use the self-catering kitchen.

En suite N$350/200 sgl/pp sharing, shared facilities N$270/160 sgl/pp sharing, all B&B.

⌂ **Schwalbenheim** (8 self-catering apts) 14 Bismarck St; ☎ 061 222829; e info@ schwalbenheim.com.na; www.schwalbenheim.com.na. Opened in 1998, this Namibian-run accommodation, in a quiet location, comprises 5 apts with 4 beds, 2 with 2 beds & 2 sgls. Each apt has its own self-catering facilities, en-suite bathroom & small patio & grassed area. Although some guests stay for longer periods, the owner is happy to cater for overnight stops. It's a good place for families.

From N$280/340/390 sgl/dbl/trpl; largest apt N$490.

⌂ **Hotel-Pension Steiner** (16 rooms) 11 Wecke St; ☎ 061 222898; f 061 224234; e steiner@ iafrica.com.na; www.steiner.com.na. This small, quiet pension, built on several levels, is a convenient short walk from the centre, squeezed into a cul-de-sac off Trift St, between Sam Nujoma Dr & Fidel Castro St. Its recently renovated rooms have tiled floors, Mnet & German TV channels, phones, minibar/fridges, ceiling fans, & radios, as well as en-suite toilets & either baths or showers.

Behind the building is a thatched bar overlooking a deep swimming pool, around which tables for light lunches are set. In winter months, the open fire in the lounge bar is particularly welcome.

Steiner is particularly popular with German and French visitors, & its atmosphere is one of helpful efficiency.

N$390/595/710/775, sgl/dbl/trpl/qudpl, all B&B.

🏠 **Tamboti Guesthouse** (15 rooms) 9 Kerby St; ☎ 061 235515; f 061 259855; e tamboti@ mweb.com.na. This friendly guesthouse, 15 mins' walk from the centre of town, benefits from 2 swimming pools, a patio where you can watch the sunset, & secure parking. Each of the varied rooms, including a family room with its own lounge area, has its own small shaded area with a bench or chairs & umbrella, & guests also benefit from tea/coffee facilities & an honesty bar. Facilities for the disabled are said to be excellent.
N$320/450 sgl/dbl, inc continental b/fast.

🏠 **Vondelhof Guesthouse** (8 rooms) 2 Puccini St; ☎ 061 248320; f 061 240373; e vondelhof@ mweb.com.na; www.vondelhof.com. The new Vondelhof, with its tall turret, ochre-washed walls & large pool set in attractive gardens, is close to the centre of Windhoek. Each room is individual – with a private patio, or a desk, or interconnecting for families – but all have TV, phone, minibar, safe, fan & coffee/tea facilities. Dinner & light lunches are available, & there's internet access for guests.
N$525/750/895 sgl/dbl/trpl, B&B.

🏠 **Villa Verdi** (13 rooms, 1 luxury suite) 4 Verdi St; ☎ 061 375300; e villaverdi@

Eros and Klein Windhoek

🏠 **Belvedere Guesthouse** (9 rooms) 78 Gever St, Ludwigsdorf; ☎ 061 258867; m 081 128 4241; e belvedere@mweb.com.na; www.belvedereguesthouse.com. This new guesthouse sets out to attract both tourists & business travellers, with a heated swimming pool surrounded by a wooden deck, & a floodlit tennis court, as well as private areas within the garden for individual barbecues. Along with this, each of the tasteful & well-appointed rooms has all the facilities of a good hotel: DSTV, desk with phone & internet access, AC & heating, bath or shower, minibar, coffee/tea facilities, hairdryer & safe.
N$600/650 sgl/dbl B&B.

🏠 **Pension BougainVilla** (5 rooms) 66 Barella St, Klein Windhoek; ☎ 061 252266; f 061 252260; e bougainvilla@mweb.com.na; www.pensionbougainvilla.com. On the corner of Nelson Mandela St, just after the turning into Barella St beyond the traffic lights as you come into Windhoek from the airport, this is the large white building with dark pink decoration; it's not difficult to spot.

Double rooms with queen-sized beds each have TV, AC, phone with internet connection, private bar & hairdryer, Outside, tranquil, flower-decked gardens

leadinglodges.com; www.villa-verdi.com. Reservations ☎ 061 375300; f 061 375333; e res@leadinglodges.com; www.leadinglodges.com. In many ways this place off John Meinert St set the standards for small hotels in Windhoek in 1994. The stylish use of ethnic décor & African art broke the mould of the standard, traditional German pensions, & made this instantly into Windhoek's artiest &, arguably, best small pension. Now it is under the umbrella of the upmarket company, Leading Lodges of Africa.

All the rooms have a different theme, mostly following Namibia's different tribes. All are non-smoking. Each has double or twin beds, bath or shower, TV with Mnet, direct-dial phones, minibar/fridge, & electric blankets for the winter. AC is planned in the near future for half the rooms. Snacks are available all day by the small splash-pool, & dinner is included in the rates. As Villa Verdi is often booked up, advance reservations are essential.
Standard N$610/490 sgl/pp sharing, luxury N$740/610 sgl/pp sharing, B&B.

surround the swimming pool. There's secure parking for those with a car (though the centre of town is just 15 mins' walk away), & barbecue facilities as well. Evening meals are available by arrangement.
N$491.40/608.40 sgl/dbl.

🏠 **Casa Piccolo** (9 rooms) 6 Barella St, Klein Windhoek; ☎ 061 221155; f 061 221187; e casapiccolo@iafrica.com.na; www.natron.net/tour/casapiccolo. Opposite Pension BougainVilla, the bright yellow of Casa Piccolo's walls gives the place a sunny atmosphere that permeates through the tiled floors & simple white décor of its twin-bedded rooms. Claudia Horn has run this place since 2000, mostly catering for the South African business market, though holidaymakers would be just as much at home with bright, clean facilities that include fan, AC/heater, fridge, minibar, coffee- and tea-making facilities, phone & TV. Off-street parking will add to peace of mind if you have a vehicle.
N$380/550 sgl/dbl, B&B.

🏠 **Hotel-Pension Eros** (21 rooms) 21 Omuramba Rd, Eros Pk; ☎ 061 227020; m 081 242 0676; f 061 242919; e eros@iway.na. Just south of Eros St, this successful pension near Joe's Beerhouse is very good value. Modern rooms, in several blocks adjacent to a padlocked parking area, all have direct-dial phone, TV

& minibar/fridge. Efficiency is the hallmark here, as you would expect from a pension that is geared almost exclusively to the business market. *N$310/410 sgl/dbl, B&B.*

⌂ **Hilltop House** (6 rooms) 12 Lessing St; ☎/f 061 249116; e hilltop@iafrica.com.na. This spacious, airy B&B overlooking Windhoek's rolling northern suburbs has gained a reputation as one of the best of its kind in the city. From the airport, turn right off the B6 into Nelson Mandela Av, continue along this road and then turn left into Schanzen Rd & again right into Promenaden Rd. Head up the hill, & turn left at the 'stop' sign into Lessing St; No 12 is on the left. From here, the centre of Windhoek is just a 15-min stroll, or a couple of minutes by car.

Each of the wooden-floored bedrooms looks out over the secluded garden & beyond across to the surrounding hills. Tasteful cream décor, offset by dark-wood furniture, is enlivened by numerous personal touches: traditional woodcarvings, hand-filled jars of hand cream & shampoo, plants & wrought iron give a hint of Africa juxtaposed with real comfort. All rooms have an en-suite stone-tiled shower with two washbasins & hairdryer, & other mod cons include TV with DSTV, AC, phone, coffee/tea-making facilities, & fridge with (affordable) minibar.

Breakfast at Hilltop is a meal to be savoured, served in your room or by the small pool in the early morning sun. Diehard aficionados of bacon & egg will not be disappointed, but for the very best try the 'healthy eating' option — it's unbeatable. Light meals are also available on request if you're too tired to venture out. *N$700/1,170/1,600 sgl/dbl/trpl, B&B.*

⌂ **Klein Windhoek Guesthouse** (9 rooms, 2 self-catering flats) 2 Hofmeyer St, Klein Windhoek; ☎ 061 239401; m 081 226 2883; f 061 234952; e kwgh@iway.na; www.kleinwindhoekguesthouse.com. Situated in a quiet area next to the Klein Windhoek River, this guesthouse is on the point of expansion, with new rooms to be built both on site & across the road, & a new restaurant/bar. At present, each light & airy room has its own little garden area, & there's a breakfast room with lounge area, fronted by a swimming pool. A separate 2-bedroom flat sleeps 4 people. *N$386.61/488.35 sgl/dbl, B&B, self-catering N$702 per room.*

⌂ **Casa dell'Ama** (2 rooms) 66 Amasonietstreet, Eros Pk; ☎ 061 234131; m 081 278 5975; f 061 234683; e marutscaeuronovelties.net; www.euronovelties.net. In the heights of Eros Pk, the striking russet walls of Casa dell'Ama conceal a lovely, spacious retreat. This is Marutsca Breitenmoser's chic home & it's very much a place to be part of the family. Fine art hangs on the walls, sweet incense fills the halls, fresh herbs are collected for cooking & an air of calm pervades. There's a modern, open-plan kitchen/dining room, where tasty fresh meals are made on request, a bar-cum-chill-out area filled with books & a TV, & a huge communal deck with superb mountain (and distant power plant) views & a large swimming pool. There are only 2 bedrooms here but they are some of the largest in Windhoek, & certainly some of the most original in décor. Sissal carpets, apricot walls, huge picture windows & solid wooden furniture are teamed with leather chairs, lovely African throws on the beds & trendy orange paper lanterns for sidelights. Both rooms have modern, tiled en-suite bathrooms with both a bath & shower. *N$500 pp, B&B.*

⌂ **Haus Sonneneck** (8 rooms) 1 Robyn St, Eros; ☎/f 061 225020; m 081 127 3353; e haussonneneck@mweb:com.na; www.haussonneneck.com. Located beyond the MediClinic at Eros, on the corner of Eros Way & Robyn St (but with the main entrance on Eros Way), Haus Sonneneck is well established as one of Windhoek's best pensions. German owners, Gisela & Rudolf, and their playful dachshund, ensure that all runs smoothly throughout the pension & are a good source of local knowledge The rooms here line the long entrance drive amid an oasis of bougainvillea, bananas, palms & even a stunning white pepper tree. Iron bird sculptures, a few trickling water features & plenty of resident birdlife make this a thoroughly pleasant & peaceful retreat, only a few mins' drive from downtown Windhoek. The rooms are all single-storey & spacious, if a little clinical in feel. They have bright, white-tiled interiors & deep-pile rugs, AC, minibar/hot drinks, digital safe, satellite TV, phone, & a small, private patio garden with table & chairs. Two rooms also feature a small open-plan kitchenette, & for families there's a very large room with a dbl & a sgl bed, & a $^3/_4$-size futon (with a cot available on request). There's a large breakfast room (no other meals are served) & bar area, an inviting chemical-free swimming pool, & self-drivers will welcome the plentiful secure parking. *N$450/740/920/1,050 sgl/dbl/family (3)/family (4), B&B.*

⌂ **Olive Grove** (10 rooms, 1 suite) 20 Promenaden Weg, Klein Windhoek; ☎ 061 239199; f 061 234971; e info@olivegrove.com.na;

www.olivegrove.com.na. This smart new guesthouse is located in a renovated old house about 10 mins' walk from the centre of Windhoek. To get there from the airport, turn right off the B6 into Nelson Mandela Av, then left into Schanzen St, & right near the end of the road into Promenaden Weg; the Olive Grove is on the right, on the corner of Ngami St.

Friendly yet professional, it boasts excellent service & good food (dinner N$140 pp), prepared in an open-plan kitchen that creates an air of informality. Stylish, minimalist décor throughout, including the lounge area, is softened by Moroccan lanterns & old wooden doors of Indonesian origin. Each of the rooms, with AC, minibar, TV & plenty of other mod cons, has twin beds set on grey cement plinths, with the same theme running through into large, well-appointed bathrooms (some with bath, others with shower, or even both). There's also a wrought-iron table & two chairs, & French windows to a shared balcony area with more of the same. In one corner of the courtyard, a small raised terrace incorporates a pool shaded by the signature olive tree, while above, well away from prying eyes, lie a freshwater spa pool & lounging area. This is a good spot for the start or finish of any holiday. *N$735–890/615–735 sgl/pp sharing, B&B.*

🏠 **Hotel-Pension Palmquell** (10 rooms) 60 Jan Jonker Rd; 🌧 061 234374; **m** 081 127 1036; **f** 061 234483; **e** hotel.palmquell@iafrica.com.na; www.palmquell.com. If you're coming from the airport, the Palmquell is clearly signposted to the left off Sam Nujoma Dr. Follow Jan Jonker Rd past the junction with Nelson Mandela Av, and you'll find it on the right. It's a bit too far to walk into Windhoek, but ideal if you have a car – there is secure parking available.

Olympia and southeast Windhoek

🏠 **Hotel-Pension Christoph** (12 rooms) 33 Heinitzburg St; 🌧 061 240777; **f** 061 248560: **e** christoph@mweb.com.na; www.natron.net/tour/christoph. Taken over in 2001 by a friend of the eponymous Christoph's daughter, the atmosphere here has changed. Situated on the southeast corner of Robert Mugabe & Heinitzburg streets, the pension is 10–15 mins' walk from the centre. At the heart of Christoph is a pool, surrounded by lawns to laze on (with loungers) & overlooked by the rooms. Nearby is a bar for sundowners, complete with sizeable woodcarvings & space to park off-road. Christoph's well-equipped rooms have tiled floors, ceiling fans, shower/toilet, tea/coffee makers, Mnet & satellite TV,

Austrian-owned, this upmarket pension offers a quiet setting among the palm trees that give it its name. Relax in the sauna, lounge by the pool, or take a cool dip, perhaps followed by a drink at the bar. Double & family rooms are simply furnished, but very well equipped, with AC & underfloor heating, telephone, TV & a wall safe; paintings by Namibian artists provide an individual touch. Although meals are not available in the evening, there are plenty of restaurants locally. And the hotel does boast a good range of South African wines! *N$565/457 sgl/pp sharing, B&B.*

🏠 **Hotel-Pension Uhland** (14 rooms) 147 Uhland St; 🌧 061 229859; **f** 061 229108; **e** info@hotelUhland.com; www.hotelUhland.com. Situated on the northeast side of town, off Independence Av, this friendly, pink-painted pension stands on the side of a hill, making it an airy spot when it's hot. The centre of town is a 10–15-min walk away, though Uhland has plenty of secure parking if you have a car.

The new owners have completely renovated this small pension, with evident pride. Cane furniture complements the carpeted rooms, which each have TV, clock/radio, phone, mosquito nets, ceiling fans, tea/coffee-making facilities & minibar. There's also separate internet access for the guests, with wireless LAN available. The comfortable living room with TV & stereo adjoins the breakfast room, while outside is a patio with a pool, & a thatched bar area. Some rooms have a couch which turns into 2 beds, and even small kitchens, all for the same price, so ask what's available when you book or check in. Coffee & homemade cake in the afternoon, & à-la-carte dinners focusing on game complete the package. *N$350/480/590 sgl/dbl/trpl, inc buffet b/fast.*

minibar/fridges, safe-boxes, phones, & small digital clocks to wake you from your slumber. *From N$351/468 sgl/dbl, B&B.*

🏠 **Hotel-Pension Moni** (13 rooms, 3 family units) 7 Rieks van der Walt St; 🌧 061 228350; **f** 061 227124; **e** reswhk@monihotel.com; www.monihotel.com. Within 20 mins' walk of the city centre, & 10 mins' walk from Maerua Park Mall, this pension is easiest to reach from the Ausspannplatz roundabout (recently renamed the August Neto Gdns), at the south end of Independence Av. From there take Jan Jonker, then first left on to Lazarett, first right onto Feld, & then first left into Rieks van der Walt St.

Everything in this quiet, friendly pension, run by new owner Marita Schneider, is immaculately kept –

from the gardens to the accommodation, which overlooks a central pool area. Redecorated in 2005, its rooms are bright & cheerful, with original paintings on the walls, & direct-dial phones, radio/alarms, fans, TV with Mnet & tea/coffee-making facilities. Dinner is not automatically available, but can be prepared for groups, & sandwiches or snacks are also available on request.
N$404/567/700/785 sgl/dbl/trpl/qudpl, B&B.

⌂ **Terra Africa** (9 rooms) 6 Kenneth McArthur St, Olympia; ☎ 061 252100; 📱 081 249 2520; f 061 252020; e terra@africaonline.co.na; www.terra-africa.com. Terra Africa is set in a residential road behind a gate adorned with bougainvillea. The rather utilitarian square building belies the care that has being lavished on the modern interior since new owner Rolf Hannsen & his two partners took over in November 2006. They have renovated & redecorated throughout, & have commissioned artwork from Namibia & Uganda to adorn the walls. Stone-flagged floors lead into a spacious lounge with dining area for b/fast & dinner, & big picture windows overlooking tree-shaded gardens, recently relandscaped, with a small pool & courtyard area.

Be careful when you're booking: although most of the rooms overlook the hills, those upstairs (both self-catering) are not cushioned from traffic noise on Robert Mugabe Av. Dinner (N$45–150) is available on request for guests and non-residents alike. *N$400/350 sgl/pp sharing, B&B.*

⌂ **Windhoek Town Lodge** (20 rooms) Ballot St; ☎/f 061 252536. The angular design of this quiet lodge just 15 mins' walk from Windhoek centre, or 5 mins from Maerua Pk, reflects its no-frills attitude. To get here, follow Independence Av to Ausspannplatz, then turn left into Lazarett St, right into Feld St, & left into Ballot St. The lodge is on the right.

En-suite dbl rooms are located on two storeys. Their simple pine furniture is offset by tiled floors; each room has a free-standing fan, TV & tea/coffee-making facilities, while the self-catering units come with fridge, 2-plate stove, sink & table & chairs.
N$260/375/445 sgl/dbl/family. No b/fast served.

Pioneers Park and southwest Windhoek

⌂ **Hotel-Pension Etambi** (11 rooms) 6 Gous St; ☎ 061 241763; f 061 242916; e etambi@ mweb.com.na; www.etambi.com. As Etambi is 10 mins' drive from the city centre, you really need your own vehicle to stay here. To get there, take Marconi St westwards, before turning onto Jordan St, following the signs for Pioneers Pk. The road sweeps around to the right, & after about 1km you take the third left onto Hintrager St. After a further kilometre, take first right onto Fritsche St, & the left after the shopping centre onto Gous St. Etambi is on the right.

Run by Peter & Elke Young, Etambi caters a lot for independent businesspeople — so has phones & TVs in the rooms, each of which has its own entrance off the garden. It's a friendly & efficient little pension, with the owners' hallmark clearly imposed. The rooms are large & comfortable with modern furnishings. Each has a kettle, minibar/fridge & a room safe. There is an outside braai for guests to use, a small pool, & a cool, vine-covered terrace area. Secure parking is available.
N$340/440/640 sgl/dbl/family (4), B&B.

⌂ **Casa Blanca Hotel** (13 rooms) 52 Fritsche St (cnr Gous St), Pioneers Pk; ☎ 061 249623; f 061 249622; e casa@iway.na; www.casablancahotelnamibia.com. Just next to Etambi, & under the same ownership, the turreted Casa Blanca with wrought-iron finishing has a slightly classier atmosphere. Still geared to the business market, & with a small conference room/bar, it is located on the main road so at busy periods rooms at the front can be quite noisy.

Comfortable, stylish rooms, grouped round a small, Italian-style courtyard, have king or twin beds with carefully chosen curtains & furnishings, & examples of Peter's photography adorning the walls. Each also has its own desk with plug for a laptop computer. To the front is Elke's domain: a mature garden with numerous indigenous plants & areas where guests can relax, while at the side is a small pool & bar area. Meals are available at Etambi on request.
N$450/600 sgl/dbl, B&B.

HOSTELS AND CAMPING Windhoek has a thriving number of backpackers' hostels. Until relatively recently, these were mostly confined to the north and west suburbs. Now, while the Cardboard Box is still the favourite choice of younger travellers, the newer brigade of Chameleon City Lodge and Backpacker Unite, with en-suite private rooms as well as dorms, are increasingly successful. Being newer and, generally, better equipped, they often demonstrate a willingness to help visitors (with free lifts from the city, and the like) and tend to have one eye on a more mature market. The city's only dedicated campsite, Arebbusch, is just south of town, so of benefit only to those with vehicles. Campers without transport can pitch a tent at some of the backpackers' hostels.

⚲ Arebbusch Travel Lodge (26 chalets, 52 rooms, camping) Olympia; ✆ 061 252255; f 061 251670; e atl@mweb.com.na; www.arebbusch.com. Less than 10km south of the centre, between the Safari Hotel & Windhoek Country Club, this is Windhoek's only dedicated campsite; it is clean, spacious & very impressive. There are 12 pitches for caravans, & 40 for tents, as well as budget & 'B&B' rooms & self-catering chalets. B&B rooms with twin or dbl beds are en suite, & come with AC, DSTV, phone, fridge, linen. Chalets also boast a stove, crockery & braai facilities. Budget rooms utilise the camping ablution facilities. All are clean, comfortable, & serviced daily. Arebbusch's security is tight – with an electric fence & guard on the gate.

There's also a spotless restaurant on site, with a good range of steaks & salads, some vegetarian options & a kids' menu (closed Sun except for b/fast). Added to this are a laundry, a bar & a good pool. The only snag is that you need a car to get here.
Budget N$284.87/203.48 sgl/ pp sharing, self-catering N$488.35/366.26 sgl/pp sharing. Camping N$75 pp.

⌂ Backpacker Unite (89 beds) 5 Greig St; ✆ 061 259485; m (day): 081 129 8093; e magicbus@iafrica.com.na. Between Bach & Beethoven streets, Backpacker Unite is about 10 mins' walk from the centre. The zebra-striped exterior walls may be appealing, but the razor wire hanging from them certainly isn't. This is a rather soulless establishment, with simple, clean rooms & 4 bathrooms. Visitors can use the pool & sauna, & there is a pool table, too.
N$60 dorm bed, N$195 dbl, B&B. Camping N$40 pp.

⌂ Cardboard Box (43 dorm beds, camping) 15 Johann Albrecht St; ✆ 061 228994; f 061 256581, e ahj@iafrica.com.na; www.namibian.org. On the corner of John Meinert St, a short uphill walk from town, this large & rather scruffy backpackers' lodge has been the capital's favourite for younger independent travellers for quite a while – despite its size & noisy dorms. Visitors have use of a small pool, pool table, washing machines, internet access, & crockery/cutlery in the kitchen.
N$65 dorm bed, N$180 private room. Camping N$50 pp.

⌂ Chameleon City Backpackers Lodge (12 dorm beds, 16 rooms, 1 honeymoon suite) 5–7 Voigt St North, Windhoek Central; ✆ 061 244347; f 061 220885; e chamnam@mweb.com.na, info@chameleon.com.na; www.chameleonbackpackers.com. An offshoot of the original Chameleon Backpackers, City Lodge was opened in 2001 & has proved a considerable success. Guests with advanced bookings are collected off incoming buses at the terminal in central Windhoek by the tourist information kiosk, opposite the Kalahari Sands Hotel. Those who are walking from the stop should head north up Independence Av, then turn right on Sam Nujoma & left onto Mandume Ndemufayo, where the Chameleon sign will be above you to the left (turn left, then left again into Trift St, & finally left into Voigt St).

City Lodge is set to become the benchmark for backpackers' hostels. Bright, cheerful & clean, its small, well-decorated dormitories are comfortable & well thought out, while dbl rooms offer a degree of privacy, with their own washbasins or own en-suite bathrooms. All rooms are fitted with electronic safes. Other facilities include a fully equipped kitchen, TV & video, & a secure cage for luggage, not to mention phone, bar, & internet access. There's a barbecue area too, next to the large & inviting swimming pool. And for N$45 they'll do your laundry! Secure parking is also available.
Dorm beds N$80 in 6-bed room, en-suite room N$230–60 twin/dbl per room, rooftop tent N$60 pp, N$300 honeymoon suite, all B&B.

JUST OUTSIDE TOWN Lodges and guest farms have proliferated in the area around Windhoek, and many of these make good alternatives to staying in the city on the way to or from the airport.

To the east (towards the airport) There are quite a few places to stay along the road between Windhoek and Hosea Kutako International Airport. The benefits of staying out of town in relatively rural surroundings are self-evident, and there are many different styles of accommodation from which to choose. Those below are listed in order of their distance from Windhoek.

Hotel-Pension Onganga (10 rooms) 11 Schuckmann St, Avis; ☎ 061 241701; m 081 127 3494; f 061 241676; e onganga@mweb.com.na; www.onganga.com. This simple, modern pension near Avis Dam is signposted to the left off the B6 airport road, shortly after leaving Windhoek. Built on several levels, it has quiet twin & dbl rooms, each with en-suite shower, AC, DSTV, phone, minibar/fridge & tea/coffee-making facilities. Screened doors & windows mean that guests can take advantage of the breeze afforded by Onganga's hillside position. Owner Steffi has decorated the place in a cheerful yellow & white, with cane furniture in the breakfast room, & an open fire for chilly winter evenings. A new restaurant offers a full menu.

Outside, the small pool facing the mountains is surrounded by a grassy area set with umbrellas, overlooked by a rustic bar with a barbecue, while behind the pension is a 20-min walking trail. There's also a small craft shop with postcards. Airport collection is N$120 pp (2+) while trips to Windhoek cost N$30 – or you can get a lift with someone from the guesthouse.
N$380/540 sgl/dbl, B&B.

Heja Game Lodge (26 rooms) ☎ 061 257151/2; f 061 257148; e heja@namib.net.com; www.hejalodge.com. Signposted off the B6 airport road, just 13km from Windhoek, this family-run lodge is 3km along a tarred road past Otjihase Mine, then a further 3km on a gravel track through land grazed by a variety of game animals. Wildebeest, springbok, blesbok, oryx, ostrich & warthog are just some of the animals to be spotted as you drive through.

Rooms are functional, with AC, satellite TV & phone. Activities include game drives, & 1hr horserides with a guide, & there's the possibility of longer drives into Namibia's third-highest mountain. The restaurant is open daily, with an à-la-carte menu, except Sun. There is even a private church on site for weddings etc. While this is not a place to linger, it makes a carefree stopover for families & is well frequented by the German market. Heja is particularly popular with day trippers on Sundays, when there's a buffet lunch from 12.00–14.00 and you'll need to book. Short game drives, very short horse rides & the swimming pool overlooking the dam are added Sun attractions, & there's a trail around the dam that takes about 1hr to walk.
N$330/580 sgl/dbl, B&B.

Airport Lodge (6 bungalows) ☎ 061 231491/243192; f 061 236709; e airport@ mweb.com.na; www. natron.net/tour/airport. Run by Brian & Hermine Black, Airport Lodge is signposted halfway between Windhoek's main international airport & the city, about 600m from the B6 main road, down the MR53 turning. Set well apart in extensive bush, each of the lodge's ethnic-décor thatched bungalows has 3 sgl beds (children will love the third, set high up in its own 'loft' area), en-suite toilet/shower, mini-kitchen, satellite TV, direct-dial phone, mosquito nets & AC/ceiling fan, not to mention a small veranda. There's a large swimming pool with outside & inside bars, a braai, and an open fire for winter evenings. Dinner is served à la carte. This is a peaceful & convenient stop before & after a flight (airport transfers N$165 per trip).
N$360/410/460/750/860 sgl/dbl/tpl/family (4)/family (6). B/fast N$38.

Trans Kalahari Caravan Park (9 rooms) ☎ 061 222877; f 061 220335; e woodway@ namibnet.com, grimm@transkalahari.com; www.mietwagen-namibia.de. Set back above the main airport road, just 21km from the airport (a little closer than Airport Lodge), this is more than just a caravan park, with large, simply furnished, en-suite rooms, some with AC, catering mainly for the German market. Pitches at the campsite have electricity, water & a grill area, & a toilet block with hot-water showers.

The main building features a rustic bar and restaurant with lounge area & a good range of crafts for sale – ideal for last-minute souvenirs – & the restaurant serves Namibian–German cuisine, with the emphasis on game. Some may be put off by the owner's dogs, which include a Doberman, or by the lack of TV; others will appreciate the privacy. Airport transfers are N$125 pp.
N$210/350–380 sgl/dbl. Camping N$30 pp & N$40 per pitch.

Hohewarte Guest Farm ☎/f 062 540420; e howarte@mweb.com.na, www.natron.net/hohewarte. Follow the airport road for about 28km, then turn right towards Dordabis. Hohewarte is 15km down this road, to the left. Once a German colonial police station, Hohewarte farm now stands in an area of some 10,000ha, at the foot of the 2,299m Bismarck Mountain.
N$663/578 sgl/ pp sharing.

🏠 **Etango Guest Farm** (6 rooms) ☎ 062 540423/51; 📱 081 129 3007, 124 4848, 283 3438; f 062 540410; e etangoranch@mweb.com.na; www.anvo.com. The family-run Etango is just 3.5km from the international airport; to get there, drive just 150m east of the airport on the B6, then turn right through a gate & continue 2km or so down a sandy track until you come to the farm. Owned by Volker & Anke Grellmann & managed by their son, Robert, it is in the Namatanga Conservancy. All rooms are en suite with AC, while some — more simple — have

To the north and west

🏠 **Elisenheim Guest Farm** (8 rooms, camping) ☎/f 061 264429; e awerner@mweb.com.na; www.natron/net/tour/elisenheim. Just 15km north of the centre of Windhoek, Elisenheim is signposted to the left of the main B1 as it leaves the city. Follow the track for a further 6km, then turn right just before Namibia tannery. The farm, set in grounds of some 5,000ha at the foot of the mountains, offers German hospitality & a place to relax under the care of Andreas & Christina Werner.

The comfortable rooms all have en-suite showers & toilets, while outside is a tree-shaded swimming pool surrounded by a grassy area. Weaver birds nest in the bamboo that shelters the house. Close by is a small campsite, with 5 pitches & its own pool. Campers need to be totally self-sufficient, as nothing is available here except firewood.

Dinner is usually a 2-course set menu based on game, & lunches can also be prepared. Visitors are welcome to explore the area, which is home to kudu, warthog & steenbok, & plenty of baboons 'looking for work', or to take a sundowner trip into the mountain (min 4 people).
N$345.90/559, sgl/dbl, B&B. Camping N$45 pp. Closed 1 Dec–15 Jan.

🏠 **Sundown Lodge** (11 rooms) ☎ 061 247017; f 061 232541; e sundown@iafrica.com.na; www.sundown-lodge.abc-interndetdesign.de. Sundown Lodge is a purpose-built stopover, providing a basic night's rest in attractive surroundings near Windhoek. It is well signposted just off the main B1, about a 25km drive north of the city, on the D1474. (Though this has been omitted from some maps, it's easy to find as it's right by the police roadblock.)

self-catering facilities, & a family room is planned. A large lounge/dining room allows for dining en famille. There are opportunities for birdwatching & nature drives or walks on the farm, which has a range of endemic wildlife such as kudu, oryx & hartebeest, & a group of mountain zebra. With its rural location close to the airport, this is an ideal spot for the beginning or end of a trip. Lunch/dinner approx N$50/100. Scenic drive N$130 pp.
N$640/960/1,125 sgl/dbl/family (2 adults, 2 children), DBB.

Expect your room to have its own phone/desk, fridge, kettle & tea/coffee facilities, en-suite toilet & shower, & a small patio for sitting outside. Lunch & dinner are available; alternatively, there are braai facilities. Guests are welcome to use the swimming pool with adjacent bar, or to explore the surrounding bush. Transfers to Windhoek International Airport available.
N$370/500 sgl/dbl, B&B.

🏠 **Immanuel Wilderness Lodge** (9 rooms) ☎ 061 260901; 📱 081 277 2301; f 061 260903; e immanuel@wilderness-namibia.de; www.namibia-accommodation.com. Marianne & Ralph Eder & their two children came to Namibia from Germany in 1999. Soon after their arrival they adopted a Namibian boy called John Immanuel, after whom their attractive lodge is named. It is approached down the same drive as Sundown Lodge (above), & set in 10ha of land. Cats, dogs, rabbits & horses are part of the homestead, & horseriding is a possibility if booked in advance. There's also a pool to cool off in & a nature trail.

Dbl & twin rooms are in 3 separate thatched bungalows, with simple rustic furniture — some of it homemade — and en-suite showers. Each has a ceiling fan &, outside, a small patio with chairs; 3 have a minibar. Lunch & 3-course dinner are available on request at N$40–45 & N$105 respectively. Don't come here expecting luxury, but for genuine hospitality & warmth, it would be hard to beat.
N$330/520–540 sgl/dbl; dbl with 2 extra sgls for children 8–12 N$650, quadpl N$720, all B&B.

Additional options in this direction, but within relatively easy reach of Windhoek, are:

Okapuka (see page 168)

Düsternbrook (see pages 167–8)

To the south

🏠 **Constance Lodge GocheGanas** (16 rooms) ☎ 061 224909; f 061 224924; e info@gocheganas.com; www.gocheganas.com. Drive 20km south of Windhoek on the B1 then turn left onto the D1463; GocheGanas is on the right after a further 9km. This self-styled 'wellness village' is set on a hill overlooking a private 6,000ha reserve. With both outdoor & heated indoor pools, cave sauna, fitness suite & gym, & 11 treatment rooms, there's all you could wish for in the pampering stakes, complemented by a fruit & juice bar & a hilltop restaurant. Rooms are large & smart, with great views across the reserve; each is kitted out with AC, TV, DVD/video, minibar, internet port, bath & shower as well as outdoor shower. Twin beds are the norm, but 5 superior suites have dbls — as well as a private terrace & generally greater luxury. There's also a crown suite catering for up to 4 people, with a spacious master bedroom, as well as a living/dining room with sofa bed, & a kitchenette.

The reserve boasts 21 large game species, affording the opportunity for relaxing game drives. N$1,900/1,650 sgl/pp sharing Jan–Jun, N$2,185/1,895 sgl/pp sharing Jul–Oct.

🏠 **Auas Game Lodge** (15 rooms) ☎ 061 240043; f 061 248633; e auas@iafrica.com.na; www.auas-lodge.com.na. Auas is about 44km southeast of Windhoek into the Kalahari. To reach it, take the B1 or the C23 roads heading south, then turn left onto the gravel D1463 — the road may not be viable in a 2WD in the rainy season, so do check in advance if this is likely to be a problem. The lodge is 22km from the B1, or 16km from the C23.

Auas stands on a game farm, whose residents include black wildebeest, giraffe, & a leopard in a separate enclosure. The active will appreciate the swimming pool, walking trails, & opportunities for mountain-bike rides, while more sedentary guests can relax on their own veranda. Dinner N$120. N$644/925 sgl/dbl, inc B&B, coffee & cake.

Other accommodation possibilities to the south of Windhoek include the following:

🏠 **Amani Lodge** (page 163) This French-owned lodge 26km southwest of Windhoek on the C26 offers an excellent dinner.

🏠 **Eningu Clayhouse Lodge** (pages 178–9) A stylish lodge within an hour of the airport, this should be top of your list.

✖ WHERE TO EAT

Windhoek has lots of cafés and restaurants, though you'll often have more success searching for European cuisine than African specialities. Note that many places are closed on Sundays. Not surprisingly, as a spin-off from the burgeoning restaurant scene, there are plenty of fast-food places, particularly in the new shopping malls. Pies, burgers and the like are freely available at points right across the city, including Nando's on Independence Avenue, just up from the station, while in the shopping malls, particularly at Maerua Park, pizza parlours proliferate.

CAFÉS AND LIGHT MEALS Eating out at lunch is something of an institution in Windhoek, and there's no shortage of options throughout the city, particularly in the central shopping malls or out at Maerua Park. Prices are reasonable: for a light lunch with a drink, expect to pay around N$50 – and less in a fast-food outfit. Most are open from breakfast until late afternoon, with shorter hours at weekends. Those listed here are particularly recommended.

✖ **Craft Centre Café** 40 Tal St; ☎ 061 249974. The pick of the bunch, this popular café with open-air balcony is one of Windhoek's best eateries, even if the view isn't up to much. Frequented by locals & visitors, it serves a great range of homemade quiches, salads, cakes & puddings, not to mention fresh lemonade & all sorts of other goodies. It's

on the same premises as the excellent Craft Centre — though open slightly longer hours (if the Craft Centre is closed, take the stairs to the left in what looks like a red steel tower). Open Mon–Tue 09.00–17.30, Wed–Fri 09.00–19.30, Sat–Sun 09.00–16.00.

✖ **Café Zoo** Independence Av; ☎ 061 215169. Set at

the bottom of Zoo Park, the elegant & more central Café Zoo has a shaded terrace overlooking Independence Av. Specialising in delicious cakes & light meals, it is now also open for dinner (see below).

✗ **Zoo Park Restaurant** ☏ 061 258484. Up the hill, at the top of the park, this simple establishment, not to be confused with Café Zoo (above) overlooks the amphitheatre (see page 145). With its popular pool table, it's by no means a tourist Mecca, but has a more authentic feel as a result. Burgers, sandwiches & daily lunchtime specials. *Open 09.00–21.00 or 22.00 (Sun from 12.00).*

✗ **Brix Bistro** Independence Av; ☏ 061 257971. Part of the Elephant Crossing near the Kalahari Sands, this is a good place to combine shopping for crafts with eating out.

✗ **Katiti Joe's** Post Street Mall; ☏ 061 225316. This central café-cum-delicatessen spills out onto the pavement, with wooden bench-tables surrounded by huge beer barrels. It's a lively venue, & a great place to watch the world go by. For something more substantial, try The Gourmet next door (see below).

⬛ **Levinson Arcade** Off Independence Av, leading to Post Street Mall. Two established cafés here, the **Schneider** and the **Central**, are good places to watch the world go by.

⬛ **Ins Wiener** Wernil Pk. A traditional German coffee shop that has stood the test of time in its location at the bottom of Wernil Park Mall. It also serves light lunches such as Greek, tuna or chicken salad.

⬛ **Mugg & Bean Café** Town Sq. Next door to Ocean Basket, this is a fairly functional place geared to shoppers & office workers.

⬛ **Brazilian Coffee Bar** Frans Indongo Gdns & Maerua Pk. Serves light meals, good coffee & Italian-style snacks.

✗ **Jenny's Place** 78 Sam Nujoma Dr, Klein Windhoek; ☏ 061 269152. East of the centre, this popular coffee shop serves everything from excellent cakes to sandwiches & light meals in a surprisingly spacious, tree-shaded courtyard. Freshly squeezed fruit juice & a range of coffees & milkshakes are also on offer throughout the day. Jenny's also has a good gift & craft shop, as well as a tourist information office.

RESTAURANTS Like any capital, Windhoek has dozens of restaurants to choose from – you should have no problem finding something good to eat. Until the late 1990s, most served fairly similar fare, often with a German bias, but now there is a lot more variety. There are Italian, Portuguese, Indian and even Ethiopian specialities, to name just a few. Many reach a very high standard, and few are expensive in European or American terms.

Eating at the very best, and without restricting your choices, you would have to try very hard to make a meal cost more than N$200 per person. Here's a selection of favourites.

✗ **Abyssinia** Feld St; ☏ 061 254891/2. This very smart restaurant at the southern end of the city specialises in Ethiopian cuisine, complete with the traditional coffee ceremony, with meals served either in Ethiopian style or at Western tables. It's an excellent option for vegetarians.

✗ **Restaurant Africa** Alte Feste, Robert Mugabe Av; ☏ 061 247178. The setting, in one of Windhoek's historical buildings & with a balcony overlooking the city, is part of the attraction here. With traditional dishes from Namibia & the rest of Africa, and little concession to Western ideas of tender meat, the service & food can be somewhat hit-and-miss, so it's an authentic experience. Delicacies – for the truly adventurous – include *omanugu*, or mopane worms. *Open daily 07.00–22.00.*

✗ **African Roots** Hidas Centre, Sam Nujoma Dr; ☏ 061 232796. Near the junction at Klein Windhoek, the name says it all.

✗ **Café Zoo** Independence Av; ☏ 061 215169. The already popular lunchtime venue with elegant surroundings & friendly but professional service has now branched out with an interesting evening menu that should be popular with locals & tourists alike.

✗ **Cattle Baron** Maerua Park; ☏ 061 254154. Situated within this new shopping complex, the Cattle Baron has two restaurants next to each other, namely the Lounge & Grill House. The former has a more formal setting with round tables encircled by black leather seating, while the Grill House has a more relaxed family atmosphere. Primarily grills, but there's a separate children's menu.

✗ **La Cave** Carl List Bldg, Fidel Castro St; ☏ 061 224173. The unprepossessing entrance opposite the Sanlam Centre is more akin to a storeroom than a smart restaurant. But continue downstairs & you'll find a tiled, modern restaurant with separate sports bar & a couple of slot machines. The smallish eating area is cool & modern, but the adjoining bar maintains the original décor so appears somewhat old-fashioned. The menu is along German lines with fish & game prominent, & a lunchtime special is available most days at about N$30. *Closed Sun.*

✗ **Chez Wou** see page 126 (Windhoek Country Club).

✗ **Délices de France** Square Pk, Hebenstreit St, Ludwigsdorf; ☎ 061 235705. For those who love French cuisine, this is particularly attractive in summer when you can sit outside.

✗ **The Gourmet** Kaiserkrone, off Post Street Mall; ☎ 061 232360. In the Kaiserkrone Centre, on the left of Post Street Mall as you walk from Independence Av, this established favourite has now moved into the centre of town. Good food, with the emphasis on German dishes & pizzas/pasta, is served either indoors or in the pleasant, tree-shaded courtyard. There's a car park for diners. *Open Mon–Fri 07.30–22.00, Sat 08.00–22.00.*

✗ **Hotel Fürstenhof** Romberg St, Windhoek; ☎ 061 237380. West of the centre, one of Windhoek's grandest restaurants has quite a formal atmosphere. For men, a jacket & tie wouldn't be out of place. The food is classic French/German style, varying from seafood through to game & a daily vegetarian dish. The wine list is grouped by grape variety, & most bottles are around N$80. The choice is competent, but neither inspired nor outstanding value. The Fürstenhof seems to be resting on its laurels.

✗ **Gathemann** 175 Independence Av; ☎ 061 223853. This grand old establishment must have the best position of the capital's restaurants, on a first-floor balcony in the centre of town, with commanding views over Zoo Park. If the rather stiff atmosphere isn't to everyone's taste, the traditional German cuisine (with a bias towards game) remains good. Prices are higher than average for Windhoek, though not excessive. The wine list is extensive, & therefore good in parts. *Open lunch & dinner.*

✗ **El Gaucho Argentine Grill** Sam Nujoma Dr; ☎ 061 255 503. The lively saloon-style bar & restaurant at Klein Windhoek has a glass wall between the restaurant & kitchen, so diners can see the large fire where lamb & beef are cooked on the spit & grill. Good-value meals with options of seafood & salads as well as meat. There's often live guitar music with Argentinian tunes.

✗ **Grand Canyon Spur** 251 Independence Av; ☎ 061 231003. Situated above street level, opposite the Bank Windhoek, the Spur offers American burgers, steaks & a host of side orders, together with Windhoek's best serve-yourself salad bar. The atmosphere is lively, not dissimilar to a Hard Rock Café. *Open daily, early until late.*

✗ **Itumba** ☎ 061 275 4710/4888; ⓔ itumba@tgi.na. A little way south of the city, about 5 mins' drive from Windhoek Country Club, this new venue offers the atmosphere of a traditional bush boma, with meat & vegetables cooked over an open fire to order. It's fun during the summer but can get quite cold in the winter months.

✗ **Joe's Beerhouse** 160 Nelson Mandela Av; ☎ 061 232457; ⓔ joes@iafrica.com.na; www.joesbeerhouse.com. The cavernous thatched premises that house Joe's Beerhouse seat over 200 people in a rustic environment set around a large bar area. Joe's cuisine is good value & has been strictly for serious 'carnivores', with lots of game & huge portions, though veggies are now getting a look in too. Beers & spirits are excellent, but wines are mediocre. Service can be slow & lackadaisical. There's also a small craft shop with postcards. Joe's reputation goes before it, & the place is almost always full; booking is usually essential.

✗ **Leo's at the Castle** 22 Heinitzburg St; ☎ 061 249597. The Heinitzburg's stylish restaurant, Leo's, is one for the elite. Small, modern & sophisticated, it is open for dinner only, masterminded by the hotel's French chef. In addition to the carefully selected à-la-carte menu, which is dominated by fish & game (but vegetarians are well catered for on request), there is a 4-course gourmet menu. The Heinitzburg boasts the largest wine cellar in Namibia, so be prepared to linger over the wine list.

✗ **Luigi & the Fish** 90 Sam Nujoma Dr; ☎ 061 256399; ⓔ luigi@iafrica.com.na. About 2.5km from the centre, Luigi's is on the left of Sam Nujoma Dr, about 100m after the junction with Nelson Mandela Av, at Klein Windhoek. Its atmosphere is relaxed, with plenty of seating both inside & out under the trees. Food here is a feast for fish lovers (though there's plenty of meat & some good veggie options as well), while starters have a Mexican slant. Service is friendly, but can be slow when it's busy. There is sometimes live music in the courtyard, & upstairs is a popular bar that's open till late.

✗ **La Marmite** 383 Independence Av; ☎ 061 248022; ⓜ 081 244 5353. This small, friendly restaurant north of the main shopping area specialises in west & central African food. Owned & run by its Cameroonian chef, Martial, it's well worth a visit, with excellent food, especially on the vegetarian front, & very reasonable prices. Perhaps surprisingly, it has a good wine list, too. *Normally closed Sun. No credit cards.*

✗ **nice** 2 Mozart St; cnr Hosea Kotako Dr; ☎ 061 300710; www.nice.com.na. The brains behind

Wolwedans have come up with the Namibian Institute of Culinary Education, with a view to training chefs in a professional restaurant setting. Renovation of an old house to the west of the city has created a series of stylish dining options, from the strictly formal to the sophistication of a sushi bar, and a rather more accessible courtyard. It's all going live in May 2007; is Windhoek ready for the Jamie Oliver approach?

✗ Ocean Basket ✆ 061 253507; The popular South African seafood chain now has a branch in Town Sq. *Open Mon–Sat 11.00–22.00, Sun 11.00–21.00.*

✗ O Portuga 151 Nelson Mandela Av; ✆ 061 272900. This friendly and relaxed Portuguese/Angolan restaurant at Eros has a Mediterranean flavour. The wide-ranging menu is particularly strong on seafood, & you can expect huge portions. South African wines are fairly standard; Portuguese are very expensive. It's a popular place with a mixed clientele, but service can be very slow when the place is busy.

✗ Primi Piati Maerua Mall. Along with good pasta & meat dishes, Primi Piati serves a great range of cocktails. *Open daily till late.*

✗ Sardinia Pizzeria 39 Independence Av; ✆ 061 225600. This relaxed café/restaurant serves genuine Italian cuisine. Owned & run by the Solazzi family, it's worth a second glance, for behind the café-style front is a simple restaurant area — though you'll have to book to get a table here in the evenings. The wine list is reasonable, although Italian favourites come at a price. *Closed Tue.*

✗ Taal 416 Independence Av; ✆ 061 221958; e taal@mac.com.na. Windhoek at last has an Indian restaurant, serving good, authentic food, albeit under bright lights. Don't come in a hurry, though.

✗ Am Weinberg Jan Jonker St, Klein Windhoek; ✆ 061 236050. This smart, stylish restaurant is in a renovated old house near Klein Windhoek. Open for lunch (with daily specials) & dinner, it's on the pricy side, but serves consistently good food from a broad menu, with some oriental influence.

✗ Yang Tze Sam Nujoma Dr; ✆ 061 234779. A large, efficient restaurant, situated above Spar near the junction with Nelson Mandela Av, this prepares probably the best Chinese food in town. Equally well suited to a business lunch or a relaxing dinner, it also has a take-away service. *Open daily till 23.00.*

✗ Sushi & Teppanyaki Grill Maerua Mall; ✆ 061 301700. Japanese restaurant with a range of dishes. *Open daily from 11.00.*

ENTERTAINMENT AND NIGHTLIFE

Windhoek is not famous for its nightlife. Most visitors choose to go to a restaurant for a leisurely dinner and perhaps a drink, and then retire for an early start the next day. But if you feel livelier, there are cinemas and a few nightclubs, as well as the occasional concert. Friday is usually the best night, better than Saturday. Similarly, weekends at the start/end of the month, when people have just been paid, are busier than those in the middle. For details of what's on, keep an eye out for posters around the city, or check the list of current happenings outside the tourist information kiosk opposite the Kalahari Sands Hotel. It may also be worth looking at the *Big Issue*, which has made an appearance on Windhoek's streets.

BARS Namibia doesn't have the 'pub' culture of the UK. In the poorer areas, especially in the old townships, there are some illegal *shebeens* (so-called *cuca-shops*), geared purely to serious drinking. It's worth noting that here, as in most traditional cultures in southern Africa, respectable women are rarely seen in bars.

If you're intent on finding somewhere relaxing to drink, then look no further than the hotel bars. All the bigger hotels have bars, including the relaxed beer garden at the **Thüringer Hof**, though places like the **Fürstenhof**, or smaller establishments, may restrict their use to residents only. One of the best places for a sundowner is the bar of the **Thule Hotel**, and those at the **Heinitzburg Hotel** and the **Wine Bar** are not bad either. See the section on *Hotels*, pages 126–40.

If you're thinking of somewhere with more life, then **Joe's Beerhouse** is your best bet. Slightly further out, at Klein Windhoek, there's a popular bar above **Luigi & the Fish** which is open every day.

In the other direction, Maerua Park Mall off Centaurus Avenue is quite a hive of activity in the evenings, with many shops open till quite late, and several bars, cafés and informal restaurants where you can while away the evening. Among these, the bar at **Mike's Kitchen** is a comfortable place for a relaxed evening, while the more trendy can try the cocktails at **Hemmingway** (✆ 061 300222) or **Primi Piati**.

NIGHTCLUBS Windhoek normally has a couple of clubs running at any one time, some of them cosmopolitan and fun. As in most cities, clubs go in and out of fashion in a matter of months, so anything written here is probably already out of date. Ask for up-to-date local advice on what's currently good and safe. If you're thinking of a club in one of the townships, you should go with a local, or get a reliable taxi that will take you and collect you. At the time of writing, the best venues are:

☆ **Bump** In the southwest of Windhoek, near Keppler St, this is one of the most popular nightclubs. Open Wed, Fri & Sat 22.00 till late. Fri is particularly busy. Cover charge around N$20 pp.

☆ **Da Vinci** Wright St, Southern Industrial area. Another very popular venue, and a good place if you're into rock & techno music. Sometimes have DJs from South Africa releasing new CDs.

☆ **Ladidas** Off Lazarett St. Plays good music & is particularly popular with the local community. Also

has lounge bar upstairs if you do not fancy dancing downstairs.

☆ **Club Thriller** Katutura; ✆ 061 216669. An old favourite that has operated since before independence. It plays a bit of everything but mostly African music, & is open almost till dawn. You should have a guide &/or taxi to come here.

☆ **Kiepies** Close to the Bump; specialises in country music.

Although there are numerous so-called 'casinos' that flaunt row upon row of one-armed bandits, there are only two real casinos, one at the Windhoek Country Club, the other at the Kalahari Sands Hotel. Both are open until the small hours.

CINEMAS Windhoek's three-screen multiplex, the **Maerua Park Cinema** (✆ 061 248980/249267) in Maerua Park Mall on Centaurus Road (where Robert Mugabe Avenue meets Jan Jonker), has five screens. Although this is the capital's only cinema, prices are low compared with Europe or the US: tickets are N$40 but on Wednesdays they're just N$20 and it's a very popular day to go but prepare yourselves for lots of teenagers. Films shown are very much the latest Hollywood releases, and drinks and snacks are available too.

THEATRES AND CONCERTS Windhoek's most relaxed venue for the performing arts and live theatre is the **Warehouse Theatre** (48 Tal St; ✆ 061 225059; f 061 220475). Housed in the Old Breweries Building, it has a modern mix of local and visiting artists, with music from jazz and funk to rock and roll. It's a safe place, with a relaxed atmosphere – trendy, arty and highly recommended. Cover charge varies with the band. Snacks are available, but eat elsewhere before you arrive, and there's a bar open until late. See the papers for the latest information.

There are several more formal options. Concerts, opera, theatre, ballet and contemporary dance are performed at the **National Theatre of Namibia** (corner of Robert Mugabe Av/12 John Meinert St; ✆ 061 237966; f 061 237968) and the **College of the Arts** auditorium (contact the principal at 41 Fidel Castro St, PO Box 2963; ✆ 061 225841; f 061 229007). The **Franco-Namibian Cultural Centre** (FNCC) (118 Robert Mugabe Av, PO Box 11622, Windhoek; ✆ 061 222122; f 061 224927; e fncc@mweb.com.na) is primarily a language centre, but has a small cinema and holds various concerts and cultural events, usually with a francophone bent. All three are worth checking to see if there are any productions while you're around. Information is advertised at the back of newspapers, especially the Friday

Windhoek Observer which covers the weekends. Otherwise, ask at your hotel or pension for details.

For more unusual and experimental theatre, try the **Space Theatre** at the University of Namibia's Centre for Visual and Performing Arts at Pioneers Park, close to the Country Club (*contact Ann Namupala on* ↘ *061 206 3802*), or the small studio theatre at the **John Muafangejo Art Centre** (see page 32).

Twice a month, **Theatre in the Park**, under the auspices of the College of the Arts, puts on live shows in Parliament Gardens. In addition, they have initiatives that range from children's theatre to the promotion of African films. Ad hoc performances at lunchtime and weekends may also take place. Details are available at the Windhoek city information office.

Finally, there's the **amphitheatre** in Zoo Park, which gets booked for a variety of concerts and productions. For details, look out for posters around town or at the adjacent Zoo Park restaurant.

SHOPPING

Shopping in Windhoek was revolutionised when the Town Square shopping mall was opened right in the centre. Open seven days a week (morning only at weekends), it's a top-notch mall with plenty of choice and sets the standard for shops throughout the capital. Around this, most of the area is pedestrianised, incorporating Post Street Mall, Mutual Platz, Levinson Arcade and the Wernhil Centre. At weekends in particular it's a busy, bustling place.

Parking in the centre is still relatively straightforward, with a couple of car parks clearly marked. Alternatively, if you want to stay for an hour at most, use one of the meters on Independence Avenue. However, if you're looking for something specific, then phone around first – it's much quicker than scouring the city by foot or car.

Beyond the centre, a new wing was opened in 2006 at Maerua Mall near the swimming pool in the southeast of the city, giving this popular place a new lease of life – and there's plenty of free parking. Then to the east of town, in Klein Windhoek, a new mall focusing on arts and crafts has also just opened.

BOOKS AND MUSIC Imported books are generally expensive in Namibia, and even those published locally are subject to a heavy sales tax. But if you want something specific on Namibia, then often you'll get titles here which are difficult to find abroad. The best places to look are:

CNA Gustav Voigts Centre, 129 Independence Av & Wernhil Centre. A large South African book chain with a section on the latest titles. Very mainstream.
Der Bücherkeller Carl List House, Fidel Castro St, PO Box 1074; ↘ 061 231615; f 061 236164. Recently under new management, & now linked to Swakopmund Buchhandlung, this large shop has plans to broaden its stock considerably from the current selection, which is dominated by novels & coffee-table books, but with some Namibia-specific natural history books. Many of the books are in German, but there's a reasonable selection in English.
Onganda Y'Omambo Books On the north side of Post Street Mall; ↘ 061 235796; f 061 235278. This shop has a wide selection of books (new &

secondhand), with a particularly good selection on Namibian history & culture, & by Namibian authors.
RC Bookshop Frans Indongo St (corner of Werner List St). This bookshop is in front of St Mary's Cathedral & sells mainly religious books. It also has a small coffee bar.
Uncle Spike's Book Exchange Garten St, on the corner of Tal St; ↘ 061 226722. Has a more eclectic range. Good for swapping paperbacks.
Windhoek Book Den Frans Indongo Gardens; ↘ 061 239976
Zum Bücherwurm 11 Kaiserkrone; ↘/f 061 255885; e bucherwurm@namibnet.com. Although this specialises in German books, there's a small but interesting selection of books on Namibia in English.

For a selection of African music CDs, try Universal Sounds (✆ *061 230 4520*) on the corner of Independence Avenue and Post Street Mall or Musica (✆ *061 227037*) in Post Street Mall, who also have an outlet in Maerua Mall.

CAMERAS, FILM AND OPTICS Most of the main brands of film are now available in Windhoek, including a range of slide film. Ideally, buy film from the specialists in Windhoek, rather than waiting until you're at a remote game lodge, whose limited film supplies are out of date, having been on a hot shelf for years. If you're looking for anything outside the 100/200/400 ISO range, or have very specific needs, then bring all your own supplies with you.

Similarly, most popular cameras can be found here, though they are often more expensive than they would be in Europe or the US. There are numerous places that will develop your snaps – often within the hour – or sell you a film, but Windhoek's best specialists are:

FotoWorld Independence Av, opposite Shoprite; Ø 061 223191. Has equipment & film, including Fuji Velvia slide film for those diehards using traditional cameras.
Nitzsche-Reiter At the front of the Sanlam Centre,

on Independence Av; ✆ 061 231116
Photo World 246 Independence Av, opposite Frans Indongo St; ✆ 061 223223
Gerhard Botha Independence Av, opposite Sardinia Restaurant; ✆ 061 235551

CAMPING KIT

To rent It is easy to arrange to hire camping kit in Windhoek, provided that you can return it there at the end of your trip. Both the following companies have a comprehensive range, from tents and portable toilets to full 'kitchenboxes', gaslights and jerry cans. They are best contacted at least a month in advance, and can then arrange for a pack incorporating what you want to be ready when you arrive. The minimum rental period is three days. They usually request a 50% deposit to confirm the order, with full payment due on collection of equipment.

Camping Hire Namibia 78 Malcolm Spence St, Olympia, PO Box 80029, Windhoek; ✆/f 061 252995; e camping@iafrica.com.na; www.orusovo.com/camphire. Payment may be made either in cash or by credit card (Visa or MasterCard).

Adventure Camping Hire 74 Laurent Desiré Kabila St, PO Box 20179, Windhoek; ✆/f 061 242478; m 081 129 9135; e adventure@natron.net; www.natron.net/tour/adventure

To buy If you need to buy camping kit in Namibia, then Windhoek has the best choice. Items from South Africa are widely available, but kit from Europe or the US is harder to find. The best places are:

Cape Union Mart Upstairs in Town Square & Maerua Park Mall; ✆ 061 220424. Has a wide range of camping equipment, safari clothes & shoes.
Cymot 60 Mandume Ndemufayo Av; ✆ 061 295 7000; f 061 234921; e greensport@cymot.com; www.cymot.com.na. Cymot gets bigger every year, & their expanding range is the best around: everything from spare parts for cars (✆ 061 226242), to a good range of cycles and spares (✆ 061 236536), to tents and outdoor equipment. Branches throughout the country.
Nomad Town Square; ✆ 061 259674. Safari clothes (and good souvenirs), albeit a little pricy.

Safari Den In the middle of Post Street Mall. In their plush shop they've binoculars, knives (including Swiss Army and Leatherman tools), and a useful range of tents, sleeping bags & other camping kit. Their main branch is at 20 Bessemer St (✆ 061 231934), in the southern industrial area.
Safariland (Holtz) Gustav Voigts Centre, 129 Independence Av, PO Box 421, Windhoek; ✆ 061 235941. Has a similar variety of safari & bush wear.
Trappers Trading Co Wernhil Park, PO Box 9953; ✆ 061 223136. Has an outlet on the mall, close to Safari Den. It's good for practical bush wear – cotton clothes are cheaper here than in Europe, &

the quality's reasonable though rarely excellent. Also has a small shop at the Windhoek Country Club Hotel (✆ 061 233749).

Le Trip At the bottom of the Wernhil Park Centre; ✆/f 061 233499. Something of a one-stop shop for campers, with everything from tents & rucksacks to bicycle equipment, & a full range of useful extras such as the invaluable polystyrene containers that keep canned drinks refreshingly cold.

CRAFTS AND CURIOS The Post Street Mall normally hosts one of the capital's largest craft and curio displays, as street traders set out their wares on blankets in front of the shops. Similarly, sellers of basketwork and carvings can usually be found at the western end of Fidel Castro Street near the tourist information kiosk, which is almost opposite the Kalahari Sands on Independence Avenue. There is also a wide variety of commercial craft shops in the centre of town, all aiming at tourists and often presenting similar crafts in a more upmarket setting, with higher prices. Of note are the following:

Namibia Craft Centre 40 Tal St (next to the Warehouse Theatre); ✆/f 061 242 2222; e ncc@ rf.com.na. Well worth a visit. This houses the Omba Gallery, with regular exhibitions of Namibian & other African art, a café (see page 140), & numerous stalls selling different arts & crafts including paintings, sculptures, designs in copper, hand-painted fabrics, carvings, basketwork, jewellery & much else. Many of the exhibitors are members of NACOBTA — the Namibia Community-Based Tourism Association — that was founded in 1995 with the aim of improving living standards among Namibia's rural communities. Members welcome visitors to their sites without advance notice. For details, contact them direct (18 Liliencrone St, PO Box 86099, Windhoek; ✆ 061 220558; f 061 222647; e nacobta@ iafrica.com.na; www.nacobta.com.na). Open Mon–Fri 09.00–17.30, Sat & Sun 09.00–13.30.

Master Weavers Wernhil Park; ✆ 061 221895. Offer a fine variety of handmade rugs for sale, though they are imported from South Africa & visitors may prefer to buy Namibian rugs direct from the factories in Swakopmund, Lüderitz, or Karibib.

Bushman Art Gallery Erkraths Bldg, 187 Independence Av; ✆ 061 228828/229131; e bushmanart@iafrica.com.na; www.bushmanart.com. Despite the name, this is primarily a shop, albeit with an unusually large selection. At the front it is purely a curio/gift shop, with a good selection of books on Namibia (in German & English), as well as T-shirts, jewellery, gemstones, cards, hats & even socks. At the back, however, among artefacts on sale from all over Africa, are small displays of Bushman tools, clothing, etc, various African masks & Karakul carpets. Open Mon–Sat 09.00–17.30, Sun 10.00–13.00.

Penduka ✆ 061 257210/251445; e penduka@ namibnet.com; www.penduka.com. Out beyond Katutura, overlooking the Goreangab Dam, this co-operative employs local women in a village setting to produce a range of crafts, including textiles & baskets. To get there, follow Independence Av north through Katutura, cross over Otjomuise Rd, then bear left onto Green Mountain Dam. The centre is down a dirt track to the left. Alternatively, join one of the half-day excursions that cover this area (see page 155). Visitors may watch crafts being made, & buy them in the on-site shop, or have a cup of coffee & slice of cake. With advance notice, it's also possible to arrange guided tours of Katutura, or dinner & overnight accommodation on site.

Tana Rose Town Square; ✆ 061 258583. If it seems strange to include a smart home-furnishing shop under 'crafts', it's for good reason. Tana Rose is run by Petra Illing who sells fabrics & other goods imported from her native Germany. What makes this shop worthy of support is that orders for soft furnishings are made up by women working with the Tuyakula project (see box, page 28).

Gemstones Given the incredible minerals and precious stones that are mined in Namibia, it's a wonder that there aren't better gemstones for sale as curios. Sadly many of the agates and semi-precious stones seen in curio shops on Independence Avenue are imported from as far away as Brazil.

The exception to the rule is **House of Gems** (✆ 061 225202; f 061 228915). Tucked away at 131 Werner List Street, near John Meinert Street, it is run by Sid

Peters (one of the country's leading gemmologists). It is a real collector's place, packed with original bits and pieces. Even if you're not buying, it is worth visiting. Some of the stones are from Sid's own tourmaline mines (claimed to produce the world's best tourmaline). Here you can see them sorted, cut, faceted and polished on the premises.

Leatherwork Windhoek is a good place to buy leatherwork. You'll see lots of ostrich, game and karakul leathers. Don't expect any give-aways, but if you know what you want then there are good deals to be had. The standard varies greatly; you will find some local work aiming at export markets of a very high standard, while other products are not so good. As with anywhere, shop around. The highest-quality sources are in the centre of town, like **Pelzhaus** on Independence Avenue, over the road from the main post office, and **Nakara** for *Namibian karak*ul leathers, near Gathemann Restaurant on Independence Avenue. (Previously this was Swakara, for *South West African karak*ul leathers!)

It's also worth visiting the **Okapuka Tannery**, about 20km north of Windhoek. To find it, take the main road to Okahandja, then turn off at the signs for Elisenheim, and follow this road for about 6km.

FOOD AND DRINK The age of the supermarket has certainly reached Namibia, though there remain some good small food shops around town. If you are stocking up for a long trip into the bush, then seek out the best large stores. Most central is **Checkers** in the basement of the Gustav Voigts Centre on Independence Avenue – the car park is behind the Kalahari Sands Hotel (see page 126). A little further away is **Shoprite** on Independence Avenue itself, towards the Thuringer Hof Hotel. For fresh fruit and vegetables, it's worth a trip to **Fruit & Veg City**, a specialist supermarket behind the Kalahari Sands Hotel; rather surprisingly, it also boasts a deli and serves fresh smoothies and good ice cream. Further out of town, but most convenient for drivers, are the large supermarket in the new **Game** shopping centre at the junction of Bismarck and Hochland roads, and Checkers at **Maerua Park Mall**. For those staying at Klein Windhoek, the most convenient store is probably OK Foods in the **Hidas Centre**, at the junction of Sam Nujoma and Nelson Mandela.

PHARMACIES There are numerous pharmacies throughout the city, many of them open seven days a week, and most with a range of goods and drugs that is equal to anything in western Europe or the USA. The pharmacy in the Erkraths Building on Independence Avenue is on 24-hour call (m *081 129 4422*).

OTHER PRACTICALITIES

AIRLINES Most of the airlines have town offices somewhere around the Sanlam Centre, near the Kalahari Sands Hotel.

✈ **Air Namibia** Gutenberg Platz, Werner List St; ☎ 061 299 6444; www.airnamibia.com.na
General reservations ☎ 061 299 6146
Eros International Airport ☎ 061 299 6500. Mostly domestic & regional flights.
Hosea Kutako International Airport ☎ 061 299 6600 The main airport for international arrivals & departures.
✈ **British Airways** Sanlam Centre, 154 Independence Av; ☎ 061 248528; f 061 245529. Comair, the South African regional carrier, is now owned by British Airways & shares the same premises in the Sanlam Centre; ☎ 061 226662; f 061 227923
✈ **Lufthansa** Sanlam Centre, 154 Independence Av; ☎ 061 226662; f 061 227923; e wdhgg@dlh.de
LTU ('Germany's other airline'), Gustav Voigt Centre; ☎ 061 302220; f 061 302225; e ltu.whk@kuehne-nagel.com

✈ **South African Airways (SAA)** Carl List Hse, Independence Av; ☎ 061 273340; f 061 235200

✈ **TAAG Angolan Airlines** Sanlam Centre, Independence Av (near SAA); ☎ 061 226625/236266; f 061 227724

BANKS AND MONEY The centre of town has all the major banks in the country. All have ATMs and are generally very efficient; service is likely to be quicker than at the smaller branches in the suburbs, or outside the capital. There are also ATMs in the various shopping malls across the city. If you need anything complex, like an international money transfer, go to the largest branch possible. In any event, remember to take your passport with you.

Banks The city's main branches of Namibia's largest four banks are all very near the centre:

$ **First National Bank** 209 Independence Av; ☎ 061 299 2101; f 061 225994; e info@fnbnamibia.com.na; www.fnbnamibia.com.na. This is in the centre of Independence Av, opposite the post office. It has close links to Barclays in the UK, & is best for Visa transactions.

$ **Standard Bank** Gustav Voigt Centre, Independence Av; ☎ 061 278200; f 061 236128; e info@standardbank.com.na; www.standardbank.com.na. If you're using MasterCard rather than Visa, then Standard is probably the best bank to deal with.

$ **Bank Windhoek** 262 Independence Av; ☎ 061 299 1122; f 061 299 1541; e info@bankwindhoek.com.na; www.bankwindhoek.com

$ **Nedbank** 27 Independence Av; ☎ 061 295 9111; f 061 295 2269; www.nedbank.com

Changing money Rates for exchanging money are the same at most of the banks, though expect to get considerably lower rates from a hotel. Outside of normal banking hours, the bureau de change at Nedbank on Independence Avenue, opposite the tourist information kiosk, is open Saturday and Sunday, 08.00–19.00 (and also accepts American Express cards), while the bureaux de change at the airport are opened for incoming flights. Money can also be changed at the post office (see below). Thomas Cook are based at Namibia Bureau de Change, Levison Arcade, off Independence Avenue (☎ *061 229667*).

HOSPITALS In an emergency, phone ☎ **211111** in Windhoek, which will put you through to an operator who can reach the ambulance or fire services. In case of difficulty getting through, phone 1199. If you have a mobile phone, then call ☎ 112. For an ambulance from the private International SOS, call toll free on ☎ 0800 911911, or on ☎ 061 230505. If you're calling from a mobile, the number is m 081 707. The police can be reached on ☎ 10111.

The city's main public hospital is Windhoek Central Hospital, on Florence Nightingale Street (☎ *061 222886*). This is good, but with huge demands from the local population, it can become very busy. If you've a serious medical condition then it's better to use your medical travel insurance, and contact one of the private hospitals (each of which is open 24 hours and has an accident and emergency department):

✚ **Medi Clinic** Heliodoor St, Eros Pk; ☎ 061 222687. Windhoek's most expensive clinic, reached via Nelson Mandela Dr & then Omuramba Rd.

✚ **Catholic Mission Hospital** 92 Werner List St (between Frans Indongo & John Meinert streets);

☎ 061 237237. Much more central, but not quite so plush.

✚ **Rhino Park Private Hospital** Hosea Kutako Dr; ☎ 061 225434. This aims to provide affordable healthcare, but has no casualty department.

If you've a serious problem outside Windhoek, then contact **International SOS** (see pages 74–5).

POST AND COMMUNICATIONS The **main post office** (*open Mon–Fri 08.00–16.30, Sat 08.00–12.00*) is in the centre of Independence Avenue, between Daniel Munamava Street and Zoo Park. It's cheap and easy to send packages overseas from here, and it has an efficient poste restante facility; it also sells phonecards. Aside from this, the office has a foreign-exchange desk, a good philately counter, a place to make international phone calls or send faxes, plus access to the internet.

Internet facilities The proliferation of internet facilities worldwide is not lost on Windhoek. In addition to dedicated internet cafés such as those listed below, many backpackers' hostels and hotels allow internet access to their guests. While prices at individual venues vary slightly, the norm is N$10 for 30 minutes.

🖳 **Communication Service Centre & Internet Café** 452 Independence Av. *Open Mon–Sat 08.00–20.00, Sun 09.00–21.00.*
🖳 **i café** Daniel Munamava St
🖳 **Town Square** There's an internet café on the lower level of the mall.

🖳 **World Connect** Cnr Fidel Castro & List streets. Fast internet connection (though not the cheapest), & friendly staff.
🖳 **Post office** Internet facilities are in the main post office on Independence Av. Opening hours as for the post office itself.

Mobile phones By far the most economical means of using a mobile phone in Namibia is to buy a local SIM card on arrival. These are available from one of the MTC outlets around the city, including Post Street Mall and Maerua Park. There are plenty of smaller shops too.

Mobile phones can be rented for your trip from a number of locations, including Windhoek International Airport and Walvis Bay Airport. In Windhoek try Budget Cellular (*18 Mutual Platz;* 📞 *061 239746;* f *061 239744*).

VISAS AND IMMIGRATION For visa extensions or anything to do with immigration, you need the Department of Civic Affairs (📞 *061 292 9111*), within the Ministry of Home Affairs. This is currently in the Cohen Building, on the corner of Kasino Street and Independence Avenue. Office opens Monday to Friday 08.00–13.00.

FOREIGN EMBASSIES AND HIGH COMMISSIONS Namibia's diplomatic missions abroad can be found on pages 57–8. Foreign missions in Namibia, all of which are in Windhoek, include:

🇪 **Angola** (embassy) Angola Hse, 3 Dr Agostinho Neto St, Box 6647, Windhoek; 📞 061 227535; f 061 221498; telex: 897 wk
🇪 **Belgium** (consulate) HKW Stewart Scott Bldg, Ground Floor, 6879 Bismark St, PO Box 22584, Windhoek; 📞 061 238295; f 061 236531
🇪 **Botswana** (embassy) 101 Klein, PO Box 20359, Windhoek; 📞 061 221941/2–7; f 061 236034; telex: 894 wk
🇪 **Brazil** (embassy) 52 Bismarck St, Windhoek West, PO Box 24166, Windhoek; 📞 061 237368; f 061 233389; telex: 498 bremb wk
🇪 **Canada** (consulate) Suite 1118, Sanlam Centre, Independence Av, PO Box 239, Windhoek; 📞 061 251254; f 061 251686; e canada@mweb.com.na
🇪 **Denmark** (consulate) 7 Best St, PO Box 24236,

Windhoek; 📞 061 237565; f 061 237614; e cn@ibis.org.na
🇪 **Egypt** (embassy) 10 Berg St, PO Box 11853, Klein, Windhoek; 📞 061 221501/2; f 061 228856
🇪 **France** (embassy) 1 Goethe St, PO Box 20484, Windhoek; 📞 061 276700; f 061 231436; telex: 715 wk
🇪 **Germany** (embassy) 6th Floor, Sanlam Centre, 154 Independence Av, PO Box 231, Windhoek; 📞 061 273100; f 061 22 2981; e info@german-embassy-windhoek.org; www.german-embassy-windhoek.org; telex: 482 wk
🇪 **Ghana** (high commission) 975 Nelson Mandela Av, Klein Windhoek, PO Box 24165; 📞 061 221341; f 061 221343
🇪 **Italy** (embassy) Cnr Anna & Gervers St, PO Box

240065, Ludwigsdorf, Windhoek; ☏ 061 228602;
f 061 228659; e ambitwin@iafrica.com.na; telex:
620 wk
🅴 **Kenya** (high commission) 5th Floor, Kenya Hse,
Robert Mugabe Av, PO Box 2889, Windhoek; ☏ 061
226836; f 061 221409
🅴 **Netherlands** (embassy) 2 Crohn St, PO Box 564,
Windhoek; ☏ 061 223733; f 061 223732;
e nlgovwin@mweb.com.na
🅴 **Nigeria** (high commission) 4 Omuramba Rd, Eros,
PO Box 23547, Windhoek; ☏ 061 232103/5; f 061
221639
🅴 **Norway** (consulate) 39 Schanzen Weg, PO Box
X13303, Windhoek; ☏ 061 258278; f 061 230528;
e irenew@mweb.com.na
🅴 **Portugal** (embassy) 24 Robert Mugabe Av , PO
Box 443, Windhoek; ☏ 061 237928; f 061 237929
🅴 **South Africa** (embassy) RSA Hse, 48 Jan Jonker
Rd, PO Box 23100, Klein Windhoek; ☏ 061 205
7111; f 061 224140; e sahcwin@iafrica.com.na
🅴 **Spain** (embassy) 58 Bismarck St, PO Box 21811,

Windhoek; ☏ 061 223066; f 061 223046;
e embespna@mail.mae.es
🅴 **Sweden** (embassy) 9th Floor, Sanlam Centre, 154
Independence Av, PO Box 23087, Windhoek; ☏ 061
2859111; f 061 2859222;
e ambassaden.windhoek@foreign.ministry.se
🅴 **Switzerland** (consulate), PO Box 9298, Eros,
Windhoek; ☏ 081 127 9388; f 061 220104
🅴 **UK** (high commission) 116 Robert Mugabe Av,
PO Box 22202; ☏ 061 274800; f 061 228895;
e general.windhoek@fco.gov.uk;
www.britishhighcommission.gov.uk/namibia
🅴 **USA** (embassy) 14 Lossen St, P Bag 12029,
Windhoek; ☏ 061 221601; f 061 229792;
emergencies (out of working hours only) m 081
127 4384
🅴 **Zambia** (high commission) 27 Sam Nujoma Dr, PO
Box 22882, Windhoek; ☏ 061 237610; f 061 228162
🅴 **Zimbabwe** (high commission) Cnr Independence Av
& Grimm St, PO Box 23056, Windhoek; ☏ 061
228134; f 061 226859

WHAT TO SEE AND DO

Although Windhoek isn't the planet's liveliest capital, there are some beautiful old buildings, a couple of museums and art galleries, and some tours worth taking.

WINDHOEK'S HISTORICAL BUILDINGS: A WALKING TOUR Most of Windhoek's historical buildings date from around the turn of the 20th century, and are close to the centre of town. Walking is the obvious way to see these. Starting in the Post Street Mall, here is one suggested sequence, taking about two or three hours.

In the middle of the mall is a sculpture incorporating 33 **meteorites** that fell around Gibeon, some 300km south of Windhoek. These were part of what is thought to have been the world's heaviest shower of meteorites, which occurred around 600 million years ago. About 77 meteorites, with a total mass of 21 tonnes, have been recovered so far; many of these are in museums around the globe.

At the junction of the mall with Independence Avenue is a replica of the **clock tower** that was once on the old Deutsche-Afrikabank. The original was constructed in 1908.

Now turn southeast, towards Christus Kirche, and cross Independence Avenue into Zoo Park. From here, you can get a good view of three fine buildings on the west side of Independence Avenue. They were designed by Willi Sander, a German who designed many of Windhoek's older landmarks. The right-hand one of the three, **Erkraths Building**, was built in 1910: a business downstairs, and a place to live upstairs. **Gathemann House**, the building in the middle, was designed for Heinrich Gathemann, who was then the mayor of Klein Windhoek, and built in 1913 to a basically European design, complete with a steep roof to prevent any accumulation of snow! Again, it originally had living quarters above the business. **Kronprinz Hotel** was designed and built by Sander in 1901 and 1902. It was extended in 1909, and refurbished and extended in 1920. It is now overshadowed by the Sanlam building, but a plan has been made to modernise the shops (one of which is Nakara, see page 148) whilst preserving the façades.

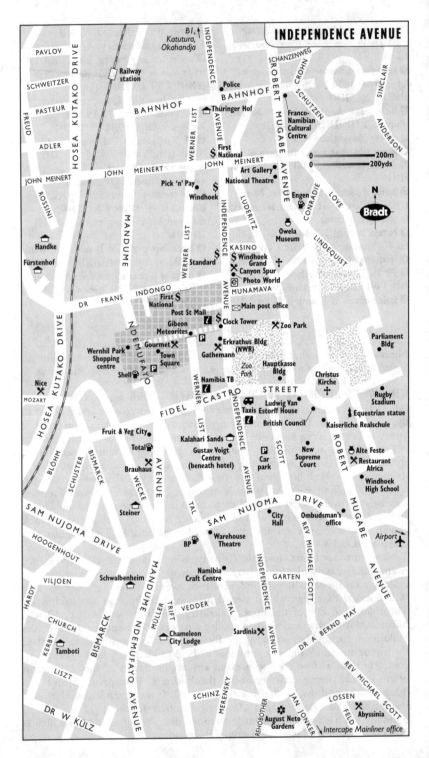

INDEPENDENCE AVENUE

Continuing into **Zoo Park**, on green lawns under its palm trees (among the Christmas decorations!) you will find two features of note. A sculptured **Elephant Column** over a metre high marks the place where primitive tools and elephant remains, dated to about 5,000 years ago, were found. Scenes of an imagined elephant-hunt kill are depicted in bas-relief (by Namibian sculptress Dörte Berner), and a fossilised elephant skull tops the column.

On the south side of the elephant column is the **war memorial**, about a century old, crowned by an eagle, and dedicated to German soldiers killed while fighting the Nama people. As yet there is no memorial for the Nama people, led by Hendrik Witbooi. (Recently the Namas killed have been remembered as part of the general monument at Heroes' Acre; see page 160.)

Now head south on Independence Avenue a short way until your first left turn, up Fidel Castro Street. On the other side of the corner are Windhoek's best street-sellers for baskets, and a tourist information kiosk, as well as the bus and taxi terminus. On the left, on the far corner of Lüderitz Street, you will see the **Hauptkasse**. Used as the house of the Receiver of Revenue, as well as officers' quarters and even a hostel, it is now the Directorate of Extension Services, within the Ministry of Agriculture. Opposite the Hauptkasse, on the south side of Fidel Castro Street, **Ludvig Van Estorff House** was simply built in 1891, as a canteen, and is named after a commander of the Schutztruppe who lived here in 1902–10. It is now the National Reference Library.

Nearby, in a commanding position on its own roundabout, the **Christus Kirche**, a 'fairytale' Evangelical Lutheran church, is Windhoek's most famous building. It was designed, by Gottlieb Redecker, in art nouveau and neo-Gothic styles, and built between 1907 and 1910 of local sandstone. Kaiser Wilhelm II donated the stained-glass windows; his wife, Augusta, gave the altar Bible. Originally this church commemorated the peace at the end of various wars between the German colonists and the indigenous people of Namibia, and inside are plaques dedicated to the German soldiers who were killed. (As yet, there's no mention of the losses of the indigenous people.) The church is now normally locked, but if you wish to see inside, the key can be borrowed during office hours (07.30–13.00) from the church offices, just down the hill at 12 Fidel Castro Street.

On the west side of Robert Mugabe Avenue, just near Christus Kirche, the **Kaiserliche Realschule** is now part of the National Museum. However, it was built in 1907–8 as a school, and became Windhoek's first German high school.

Walking further south along Robert Mugabe Avenue, you'll see the new Bank of Namibia building. On your right, just before crossing Sam Nujoma Drive, is the **Office of the Ombudsman**. Built as a dwelling for the chief justice and his first clerk, this was originally erected in 1906–7, and has much decorative work typical of the German 'Putz' style of architecture. The original stables are now a garage and outbuilding.

Now turn around and walk back towards Christus Kirche, on the right (east) side of Robert Mugabe Avenue.

The large building on the right is the old fort, **Alte Feste**, built by the first Schutztruppe when they arrived here around 1890. It is strategically positioned, overlooking the valley, though its battlements were never seriously besieged. A plaque on the front maintains the colonial view that it was built to 'preserve peace and order' between the local warring tribes – which is as poor a justification for colonialism as any. Inside is now the main historical section of the National Museum (see page 154 for details).

To the left of the Alte Feste is the **Equestrian Statue**, a large statue of a mounted soldier, commemorating the German soldiers killed during the wars to subdue the Nama and Herero groups, around 1903–7. (Here, too, there's no mention of the Nama or Herero people who died.)

Once back at the Christus Kirche, turning right (east) leads you to what were originally the administrative offices of the German colonial government, the **Parliament** (formerly **Tintenpalast**). The building became known as the Tintenpalast, or Ink Palace, for the amount of bureaucracy that went on there, and has housed successive governments since around 1912. The Germans occupied it for only about a year, before losing the colony to South Africa after World War I. Now this beautiful double-storey building is home to Namibia's parliament. Tours of the building, which could integrate well into this short walking tour (perhaps 1½–2 hours after the start), take place Monday–Friday 09.00–10.00, 10.00–11.00 and 15.00–16.00. If you'd like to visit out of hours, try phoning ↘ 061 288 2583 or ↘ 061 202 8097, or you can find out more on www.parliament.gov.na. Even if you don't take a tour, do make time for the lovely formal gardens and fountain that grace the area in front.

As you continue north along Robert Mugabe Avenue, on the left is the president's official residence, the **State House**. This was built as recently as 1958, on the site of the old German governor's residence. Until 1990, this was used by South Africa's administrator general.

It is now a short walk left, down Daniel Munamava Street, back to join Independence Avenue by the main post office.

MUSEUMS, GALLERIES AND LIBRARIES
Windhoek has, perhaps after Swakopmund, some of the country's best museums, galleries and libraries, though even these state collections are limited. The South African regime, which controlled the museums until 1990, had a polarised view of the country's history, understandably, and undesirably, slanted towards their involvement in it. It remains difficult to find out much of the history of Namibia's indigenous peoples. That said, the museums are gradually redressing the balance.

Alte Feste and State Museum
(*Robert Mugabe Av;* ↘ *061 293 4362. Open Mon–Fri 09.00–18.00, Sat &Sun 10.00–12.30, 15.00–18.00. Admission free, but donations actively encouraged*) This is the capital's best museum, concentrating on Namibia's history over the last few centuries. A number of old wagons and even a steam engine adorn the terrace in front of the building. Inside the fort is an exhibition of historical photographs, and displays of household implements of the missionaries and the country's indigenous peoples. There's also a special exhibit on the independence process, and the transition to majority rule in 1990. In a separate wing is an excellent display covering Namibia's rock art, with a smaller exhibition on beadwork. Whether or not you have time to visit one of the sites mentioned, it's well worth spending a bit of time here. Of particular interest is the visual explanation of how some of the paintings developed over time through layering and overpainting. Outside, on the terrace overlooking the city, are a number of old wagons, and to the side a steam engine.

Owela Museum
(*Robert Mugabe Av;* ↘ *061 293 4358. Open Mon–Fri 09.00–18.00, Sat & Sun 10.00–12.30, 15.00–18.00. Admission free*) North of State House, almost opposite Conradie Road, Owela Museum houses the natural history sections of the State Museum, with a good section on cheetah conservation, and a little on the country's traditional cultures.

TransNamib Museum
(*Bahnhof St;* ↘ *061 298 2186. Open Mon–Fri 08.00–13.00, 14.00–17.00. Admission N$5 per adult*) Housed upstairs in the old railway station

building, this museum is run by the parastatal transport company, TransNamib. It shows the development of transport in the country over the last century, with particular emphasis on the rail network. Ring the bell when you arrive; the museum is probably open, even if the gate is locked!

National Art Gallery of Namibia (*Robert Mugabe Av & John Meinert St;* ✆ *061 231160;* f *061 240930. Open Tue–Fri 09.00–17.00, Sat 09.00–14.00. Closed Sun, Mon. Admission free, but donations encouraged*) Namibia's small National Gallery (also see page 31) has a permanent exhibition of Namibian art – some historical, some contemporary – and also hosts a variety of visiting exhibitions. It's well worth checking out.

National Reference Library (*11 Fidel Castro St;* ✆ *061 293 4203*) Housed in Ludvig Van Estorff House (see page 153), this is really of more relevance to serious researchers than casual visitors.

KATUTURA Windhoek's northern township, Katutura (see box on page 156), is becoming more accessible to visitors, in a similar way to Johannesburg's Soweto.

For the visitor, streets in the township are very confusing, and it's easy for an outsider to get lost, so it's best to stick to the main thoroughfares. Nevertheless, it's safe enough here in the daytime, though at night it is not advisable to come without a guide. Some of the city tours (see below) include Katutura on their itineraries.

There are two markets in Katutura: Soweto on Independence Avenue, and Kakukaze Mungunda Market on Mungunda Street. To find out about opening times for the markets, contact the Windhoek city information office in Post Street Mall (✆ *061 290 2565*). Beyond the townships is the Penduka Co-operative (see page 147).

OTHER OPTIONS Various small agencies offer tours of the city, some walking, some by vehicle. Often an afternoon tour will be combined with driving out onto some of the mountains overlooking Windhoek for a sundowner drink. It is also possible to visit the township of Katutura as part of a Windhoek city tour, though these aren't as popular as Jo'burg's tours of Soweto. Other alternatives include half- or full-day trips to one of the outlying game farms, or to Daan Viljoen National Park, and – a recent introduction – 4x4 trail driving.

The companies running day trips seem to change often. Current favourites are:

Local tour operators

Be Local Tourism 3 Hoba St; m 081 275 2257; f 061 241716; e info@be-local.com; www.be-local.com. In addition to cultural tours of central Windhoek & Katutura (N$280 pp), Be Local specialises in 4x4 trail drives, & runs courses in off-road driving techniques in either a 2WD or 4x4 (N$310–630 per vehicle). This is also the place to hire a satellite phone (N$78 per day, exc talk time), or to organise a sundowner trip out of the city.

Camelthorn Transfers & Tours ✆ 061 255490; f 061 255490; e camelthorn@africaonline.com.na. Dinah & her husband offer some of the best township & city tours, along with WanderZone (see below). They collect & drop off clients from/at their accommodation, with each 3hr tour departing daily at 09.00 & 14.00.

Focus Travel Centre ✆ 061 257825; f 061 257826; e focus@iafrica.com.na. Focus offer a range of ¹/₂-day trips, from city-centre walks & visits to Katutura (N$185 pp) to afternoon hikes or mountain biking (N$460 pp). Additional options include caving (N$685) and game drives (N$685–995).

Pack Safari 109 Papageienweg; ✆ 061 231603; m 081 124 6956; f 061 247755; e info@packsafari.com; www.packsafari.com. Pack Safari runs a range of day tours (min 2 people), including a 3hr city tour (N$340 pp) taking in historical buildings, the affluent suburb of Ludwigsdorf and the less affluent Katutura, where a development project is visited. Other options include a ¹/₂-day visit to Daan Viljoen (N$370 pp), a full day to the Gamsberg Trail (N$1,580) or a visit to the cats at Amani

Tricia Hayne

Until the middle of the 20th century, there was little in the area to the northwest of Windhoek to indicate what the future might hold. Since 1913, most black people in the city had lived in what is now known as the Old Location, to the west of Independence Avenue around Hochland Park. When, during the 1950s, the authorities decided to build a new location as part of the Union National Party's enforced apartheid, they were met with stiff resistance, culminating in riots on the night of 10 December 1959. The Old Location was duly abolished, and the people forcefully resettled to Katutura and the neighbouring townships of Khomasdal, Wanaheda and Okuryangava.

Although the line dividing the white areas of Windhoek from the black townships was effectively Hosea Kutako Avenue, the real division came earlier, at the point where Independence Avenue crosses the railway line. During the years of apartheid, workers heading into the centre of town needed to show a kopf (or 'head') card to be allowed over the bridge; in the evening, the gate was closed at 18.00, preventing further movement in and out of the centre of Windhoek by black Namibians.

In the early days, there was strict segregation in the townships by tribe, with houses labelled D for Damara, H for Herero, O for Owambo, etc. Even now, house numbers indicate tribal affiliations, each in different areas. After the declaration of independence in 1990, the government invited Namibians from the north to come to the capital to work, with promises of a house, a garden, a job and even a car. Thousands of people accepted the invitation, and the population of the townships swelled – even if the reality did not necessarily match up to the promises. Today, the population of Katutura is officially around 40,000, but unofficial estimates place that figure far higher, at up to 200,000.

At first, long houses were built to meet the needs of large, extended families of farm workers. Later, small corrugated-iron 'box' houses formed the second phase of development. The third phase, with the best of intentions, was the construction by various NGOs of modern houses. Most of the people who moved into the area came from traditional kraals in the north of the country, and were ill-equipped to cope with the challenges of urban life. Where there were small houses, families of eight to 12 people would move in, and Western-style kitchens were left empty as the tradition of cooking in the open air was continued in the small yards.

It would be unsurprising if the streets of Katutura were strewn with litter, but by and large the reverse is the case. It is striking that, in spite of the sprawling nature of the township, and the density of housing, it is both orderly and clean. Water pipes are stationed every 300–400m. In some areas, bougainvillea lines some of the streets, and there are occasional sunflowers in the gardens. Maize, too, is grown, though this is almost exclusively for *tombo* – maize beer – not to eat. There is little in the way of cultivation of food, and malnutrition is rife.

Perhaps unexpectedly, there is no shortage of schools. These are government run, but most were built by donations from overseas charities and governments. Although, in theory, education is compulsory, the reality is not so straightforward. Aside from the cost of schooling, each child must have a uniform. As wages in the black community are significantly lower than those for white workers, many families cannot afford to provide this uniform, and their children remain on the streets. For the post-school generation, there are a number of training opportunities provided by the Church, hospitals and schools, as well as the government, in fields that include nursing and waitressing.

(N$830). There are also scheduled and guided tours through the region.
WanderZone Tours Pelican Sq; \/f 061 300558; m 081 214 8404; www.wanderzonetours.com. In addition to city & township tours where 'you won't feel like a tourist', WanderZone offer the chance to try out the nightlife of Windhoek with a local guide, or to have dinner at Club Thriller in Katutura.

If you prefer to drive yourself, and want to head off the beaten track, it is worth contacting the Windhoek tourist information office in Post Street Mall (see page 125), who can arrange for a local community guide to accompany you. Guides are accredited by the City of Windhoek. The office should also be able to put you in touch with another company, Otweau, run by local people and specialising in tours of Katutura.

SPORTS FACILITIES

GYM
Virgin Active (*Centaurus Rd, just off Jan Jonker, by Maerua Mall. Open Mon–Thu 05.00–21.00, Fri &Sat 07.00–20.00*) The city's biggest gym has a large indoor pool, plus a large gym with lots of training machines, an aerobics studio, several glass-backed squash courts, and steam and sauna rooms. Day membership as a casual visitor is N$50, so if you need to relax and have a shower in town before travelling, this is the perfect place. Note that the car park is patrolled, but don't leave your luggage unattended in a car outside.

Nucleus (*Old Brewery Building, Tal St. Open Mon–Thu 06.00–21.00, Fri 06.00–20.00, Sat &Sun 09.00–13.00, 16.00–19.00. N$50 per day, N$120 per month*) Centrally located by the Namibia Craft Centre, this fitness gym has been operating since the early 1990s. It's at the top of several flights of stairs (getting there is a workout in itself), and offers full changing facilities, basic running/cycling machines and general fitness apparatus.

GOLF
Windhoek Golf and Country Club (↘ *061 205 5223;* f *061 205 5220;* e *wcc@ iafrica.com.na; www.wccgolf.com.na. Hotel residents N$70/140 9/18 holes; non-affiliated N$200/180 9/18 holes; driving range N$15/30 30/60 balls*) This 18-hole golf course next to Windhoek Country Club Resort offers the usual facilities you might expect from such an upmarket club: a resident professional, motorised caddies, a driving range and a well-equipped pro-shop. The clubhouse has a bar area and a restaurant, the Eagle's Nest (open Wed–Sun). Next door is the Windhoek Bowls Club, which has its own clubhouse, bar and swimming pool.

HORSERIDING There are several game farms that offer horseriding to guests, including Immanuel Wilderness Lodge just outside Windhoek (see page 139), but you'll need to book this well in advance.

SWIMMING Following the demise of the old swimming pool near Maerua Park, a new Olympic-size swimming pool has been opened, rather aptly in the district of Olympia, on the corner of Sean McBride and Frankie Fredericks streets.

EXCURSIONS OUTSIDE WINDHOEK

AVIS DAM Just outside Windhoek on the road to the international airport, Avis Dam is something of a let-down. As you would expect, there's a manmade lake here, created by a dam across the Klein Windhoek River, and it's popular with locals for fishing, birdwatching, picnics, canoeing and bike rides, but there's little of any scenic interest to attract visitors. On the other hand, it's a pleasant spot for a picnic on the way to or from the airport. If you've more time, Daan Viljoen National Park is a far better bet.

Canoes are sometimes available for hire at weekends from Nokki's Canoe Hire (m 081 128 5231) at the thatched building on the opposite side of the main road.

DAAN VILJOEN NATIONAL PARK *(Entrance N$40 pp, under 16s free, plus N$10 per car, all payable at the park. Open daily sunrise to sunset; day visitors must leave by 18.00)* This small game park, some 20km west of the city, has good facilities, is accessible all year to 2WD vehicles and makes an easy, half-day excursion from the capital (though you'll need longer for some of the hikes). It encompasses some of the hills of the Khomas Hochland and, with its thorn trees and dry scrub vegetation, the environment is typical of the central highland area around Windhoek. This rolling landscape has been a park since 1962, and even before then some parts were protected.

The park has good populations of Hartmann's mountain zebra, blue wildebeest, kudu, gemsbok and springbok, as well as klipspringer (as you would expect from the hilly terrain), red hartebeest, impala and even eland. Baboons and rock hyrax (dassies) are often quite visible, and you may spot a family of warthog too.

Over 200 bird species have been recorded here, and Daan Viljoen is a good place for several species endemic to this north-central area of Namibia. These include the lively rockrunner, or Damara rockjumper, which warbles a distinctive song in the morning and evening, and is often seen jumping around with its tail high in the air. The white-tailed shrike is black, white and grey and tends to bounce along the ground, often in groups making lots of noise. Montiero's hornbill is quieter, and more difficult to spot, and Rüppel's parrot and the rosy-faced lovebird are particularly 'cute' species often seen here.

During the middle of the week – and even sometimes at weekends – Daan Viljoen is quiet, attracting just a few locals out from Windhoek to sit by the lake formed by Augeigas Dam, perhaps with a barbecue. There's a **6.5km game drive** marked on the ground as 'Detour' – it's a one-way route, leading from the entrance up to the park office, so if time is tight it's better to do this when you arrive. On the other hand, as there is no really dangerous game here, take the opportunity to walk around by yourself, following one of the shorter of the park's marked trails (see below). Your chances of spotting some game are good.

Getting there Take Sam Nujoma Drive out of town, then follow the signs onto the C28 towards Swakopmund. The park is well signposted, about 24km from town, on a good tar road. If you don't have a vehicle, call one of the companies running city tours; most offer day trips here (see pages 155–7).

Where to stay Accommodation needs to be booked in advance at the NWR in Windhoek, but for day visits you can complete the formalities at the gate.

Rondavels and luxury suites are set around the shores of the lake, and there's also a campsite, with plenty of ablution blocks. Rondavels have two single beds, hotplates, fridges, bedding, washbasins and towels, and shared showers and toilets, while the communal kitchen for campers has its own fridge. Note, though, that the restaurant is a significant distance from the campsite. Rates include park entrance fees for up to four people (additional group members pay the standard entrance fee). *Rondavel N$200/300 sgl/dbl, B&B (3 visitors or more N$85 pp), suite N$750, camping N$150 per site (max 8 people, 1 caravan or tent, 2 vehicles).*

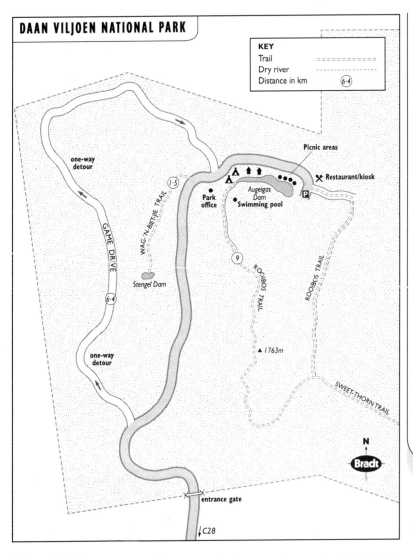

DAAN VILJOEN NATIONAL PARK

KEY

Trail	=========
Dry river	---------
Distance in km	(6·4)

one-way detour

Picnic areas

✗ Restaurant/kiosk

GAME DRIVE

WAG-'N-BIET-JIE TRAIL

(1·5)

Park office

Augeigas Dam
Swimming pool

(9)

ROOIBOS TRAIL

ROOIBOS TRAIL

(6·4)

Stengel Dam

one-way detour

▲ 1763m

SWEET-THORN TRAIL

N

Bradt

entrance gate

↓C28

Other facilities There's a restaurant which opens for meals, 07.00–09.00, 12.00–14.00 and 19.00–21.00, as well as a small kiosk selling snacks and soft drinks and absolute essentials – oil, soup, sugar and corned beef (perversely, it's closed at lunchtimes during the week). Some distance from these is a large swimming pool. There is no petrol station.

Hiking The game park excludes elephant, buffalo and lion, so you can safely walk alone on the short game trails. There are several routes, foremost among which are:

Wag-'n-biet-jie Trail is an easy 3km stroll, following the Augeigas River. It's named after the Afrikaans for the buffalo thorn, meaning 'wait-a-bit'. This common tree is all around, and can be distinguished by the curved thorns pointing backwards on its branches. These snag anyone who is caught by the tree's main thorns and tries to pull free – forcing them to 'wait a bit'. The trail follows the river upstream until it reaches a lookout point over the Stengel Dam, after which it returns along the same route back to the camp.

Rooibos Trail is a more strenuous 9km hike, starting at the swimming pool from where it winds up to the region's highest point (1,763m) after about 3km. The views are worth the climb, and you can usually see Windhoek in the distance. Then it gradually descends to cross part of Choub River, and wind round across it again, though there is apparently an alternative route which follows the riverbed left until the trail rejoins it.

Sweet-thorn Trail is a 32km, two-day hike, which must be booked in advance through Windhoek's NWR. Only one group of 3–12 people is allowed on the trail per day, starting at 09.00 from the restcamp office. This trail also follows the dry Choub River for part of the time, but strikes out into the otherwise unseen north and east sections of the park. There's a fee of around £10/US$16 per person, and you must supply your own food and equipment, though there is a simple hut halfway along for the overnight stop.

Alternatively, you can just follow the wild game trails from the restcamp area. You are unlikely to get lost unless you try to. Before you set off walking, see if you can get a copy of the guide to the local birdlife, *Birds of Daan Viljoen National Park,* from the park's kiosk. This excellent little booklet contains a species checklist, an identification guide to some of the more common birds, and short descriptions of the habitats found in the park.

HEROES' ACRE About 15km south of the city, to the left of the B1 as you head south from Windhoek, Heroes' Acre is a N$61 million monument to 'the Namibian peoples' struggle for independence and self-emancipation'. It was completed in August 2002, in time for the annual Heroes' Day, 26 August, and boasts a restaurant, a pavilion with a seating capacity of 5,000 people and a platform for dignitaries.

One of its main features is an 8m-high wall-panel, depicting various scenes from Namibia's popular revolts and uprisings, including the Nama people's uprising under Kaptein Hendrik Witbooi, resistance to the forced removal of people to Katutura, and the armed liberation struggle. Whilst only Namibian stones were used in the site's construction, the panel and various bronze statues, including one of a soldier weighing about four tonnes, were imported from North Korea.

GAME LODGES AND GUEST FARMS Even if you're staying in Windhoek, you may like to spend half a day or so visiting a local game lodge or guest farm. Places within easy reach of the centre that welcome day visitors include Midgard (see page 167), Auas Game Lodge (see page 140), Amani Lodge (page 163) and Hohewarte Guest Farm (see page 138).

OTHER POSSIBILITIES Within relatively easy reach of Windhoek is Okahandja (about 1½ hours by car), with its woodcarvers' markets and the nearby Von Bach Recreational Resort and Gross Barmen Hot Springs (see page 169). Or if you just want to escape the city for a day, you could try some watersports at Lake Oanob Resort (see page 181).

9

The Central Corridor

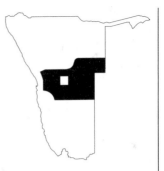

Despite Windhoek's dominance of the country's central region, remember that it occupies only a small area. The city doesn't sprawl for miles. Drive just 10km from the centre and you will be on an open highway, whichever direction you choose. The recent completion of the Trans-Kalahari Highway means that you can drive directly from Walvis Bay right across this region to South Africa's northern heartland, without leaving tarmac. In time, this may have a major impact on the area.

This chapter concentrates on this central swathe of Namibia, working outwards from Windhoek – to the edges of the Namib-Naukluft National Park in the west, and to the border with Botswana in the east.

WEST FROM WINDHOEK: TO THE COAST

Travelling from Windhoek to the coast, there's a choice of three obvious roads: the main tarred B2, the C28 and the more southerly C26. If speed is important, then you must take the B2: about four hours of very easy driving, although be aware that, to the north of Okahandja, there are pot-holes over a distance of about 20km. Both the 'C' road options are gravel, and will take at least six hours to drive. However, they are more scenic.

Note that some of the side-roads off these three main roads are used very little. The D1412, for example, is a narrow, slow road whose crossing of the Kuiseb is wide and sandy. It would probably be impassable during the rainy season.

GUEST FARMS AND LODGES Between the B2 to the north and the C26 to the south are several good guest farms and lodges. Details of these are given under the route itself (see pages 163–4), or under the relevant town.

Between the C28 and the B2, Tsaobis Leopard Nature Park (page 171) and Etusis Lodge (page 171) are probably better as stops when travelling north–south, as they are somewhat off-piste between Windhoek and Swakopmund.

Rooisand (page 259), at the foot of the Gamsberg Pass, would make an excellent stop on the C26. In the same area are Corona and Weissenfels guest farms, and several farms which cater to parties in their own 4x4 vehicles, who want challenging 4x4 driving and hiking. Of these, some allow you to follow trails across their land and neighbouring farms, and on to the Gamsberg itself.

THE C28 The shortest of the gravel roads, the C28, goes through beautiful scenery, but is also tortuous, with numerous cattle grids along its route. Around halfway along, you drive (slowly!) through the steep gradients (20%) of the Bosua Pass – where the central Namibian Highlands start to give way to granite kopjes of rounded boulders before the low, flat Namib.

CENTRAL CORRIDOR

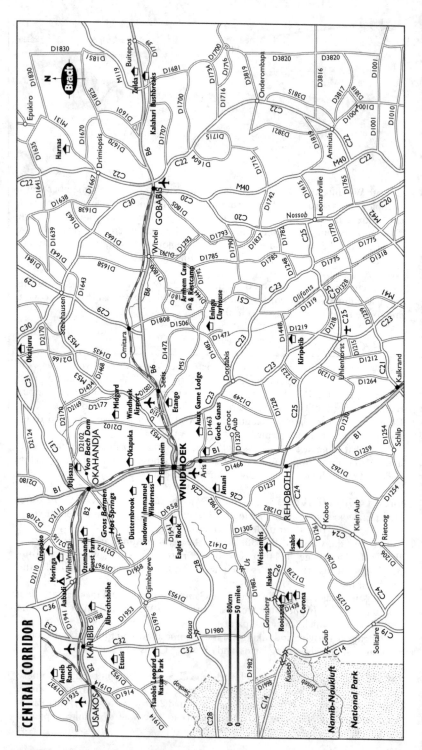

Guest farms and lodges along the C28

🏠 **Eagles Rock Leisure Lodge** (5 bungalows) ✑/f 061 257116; f 061 257187; e erllodge@ mweb.com.na; http://resafrica.net/eagles-rock-leisure-lodge. A 45-min drive (38km) west of Windhoek, Eagles Rock is 3km along the D1958, after its junction with the C28. Being so close, Eagles Rock makes a good stop for those who want to stay near, but not actually in, Windhoek – & Matthias & Rosanna Bleks are fascinating hosts.

The lodge is set amidst trees & lawns, with a pool for the heat, & a cosy (& eclectic) library inside for cool winter evenings. Double-bedded bungalows have en-suite shower/toilet & plenty of space, & there's also a family suite. Rosanna's Italian background influences the food, which is excellent.

If you are staying for a few days then game drives, nature walks, visits to nearby Bushman paintings, & even horseriding can be organised. Matthias has been at Eagles Rock since childhood & is involved in a training centre nearby, run by his father, Helmut Bleks. This includes vocational training for weaving, tannery, brick-laying, market gardening & the hospitality industry – & visits here can be arranged if you have a special interest in what's going on.
N$587.06/968.34 sgl/pp sharing, DBB.

THE C26 The C26 is much longer than the C28, but just as scenic. Just after its start, it drops steeply through the Khomas Hochland Mountains (the Kupferberg Pass), then later passes through the remarkable folded mountains of the Gamsberg Pass, which itself involves 20km of twists and turns, and 40 minutes' driving if you go gently (admiring the fine views). Further on still, the Kuiseb Pass sees the road wind down into the river's valley, cross on a small bridge, and then gradually climb back on to the desert plain (discussed in *Chapter 12*).

Guest farms and lodges along the C26

🏠 **Amani Lodge** (5 chalets) ✑ 061 224712; f 061 224217; e reservations@resdes.com.na; www.amani-lodge-namibia.com. Some 28km southwest of Windhoek on the C26, just over the Kupferberg Pass, Amani Lodge stands at an altitude of 2,150m. It's perhaps best known as the highest lodge in Namibia. Amani is run by Alain & Olivier Houlet, who are originally from France. The accommodation has been built to a high standard – with touches of French style: individual mountain chalets with twin beds, en-suite showers & superb views. The main house includes a breakfast area, & there's also a communal bar & lounge/dining area, while outside is a pool.

The lodge's major attraction lies in its big cats: three convalescent leopards that have been nursed back to relative health, & orphaned cheetahs that were unable to survive in the wild, & are now monitored by conservationists, including the Cheetah Conservation Fund.

Aside from this, activities include hiking in the mountains & stargazing: the lodge has its own telescope.
N$1,255/1,100 sgl/pp sharing, inc DBB & visiting the cats.

🏠 **Weissenfels Guest Farm** (11 rooms, camping) ✑ 062 572112; f 062 572102; e rowins@ iafrica.com.na; www.orusovo.com/weissenfels. Weissenfels is 120km west of Windhoek on the C26 – just west of the D1265, & east of the Gamsberg Pass. It covers 40km² acres of rolling highlands & has been a guest farm since 1992. Now it is run by Winston Retief & Rosi Rohr, who have retained a fairly traditional feel to it.

Accommodation is in either 'budget' dbl rooms, which share bathrooms, or en-suite dbl rooms. There's also a larger family room. (Because of its location, Weissenfels does cater for occasional small tour groups.)

Weissenfels makes a good stopover for a snack or lunch if you're travelling on the C26, but if you decide to stay for longer then there are some pleasant hiking trails (which you can follow with a guide, or on your own), & there's a fair amount of game around. Alternatively, 4x4 game drives & horseriding (from N$352/hr) are possible, as are picnics at the farm's various rock pools, & a trip to the top of the Gamsberg in a specially converted 4x4. The lodge also offers a range of massage & therapy treatments, from N$80.
En suite N$450/750 sgl/dbl, shared facilities N$350/575, family N$750–950, all DBB. Camping N$100 pp.

🏠 **Rooisand** (see page 259)

🏠 **Corona Guest Farm** (10 rooms, 4 tents) ✑/f 062 572127; f 062 572147; e corona@iway.na; www.natron.net. Corona is about halfway between Windhoek & Walvis Bay, 20 mins south of the C26. To reach it, take the D1438 turn-off (which is about

31km east of the C14/C26 junction north of Solitaire) south for 18km.

Corona now boasts 4 family-size suites, 6 dbl rooms & 4 safari tents – each with its own bathroom. There are also several verandas, small lounges, a bar (with satellite TV), a reading corner, & an outdoor swimming pool with sundeck under some lovely jacarandas.

Activities include various farm pursuits plus horseriding, nature drives & hiking. There are various shelters containing rock art on the farm, & from here it's possible for hikers to climb the Gamsberg Mountain, making use of Corona's 'mountain hut' as their base for a night if they wish.

Tent N$550 pp sharing, room N$650, suite N$750, inc DBB, coffee & cake

🏠 **Hakos Guest Farm** *(7 rooms, 2 private campsites)* ✆f 062 572111; e hakos@mweb.com.na; www.natron.net/tour/hakos. Run by Johann Straube, this small guest farm is signposted 7km to the left (if you're heading east) from the top of the Gamsberg Pass. There are great views over the surrounding mountains, various hiking trails on the farm & a 4x4 route over the mountains. More unusual attractions include the indoor swimming pool & a small observatory with a 'roll-off roof' which has mirror & lens telescopes on a heavy mount with automatic tracking. That said, Johann encourages amateur astronomers to bring their own equipment, & enthuses about the clarity of the night sky.

N$585/490 pp sharing, DBB. Camping N$45 pp.

HORSE TRAILS Reit Safari (✆ *061 250764, 061 257465;* m *081 127 0248;* f *061 256300;* e *info@reitsafari.com; www.reitsafari.com*), run by Albert and Waltraut Fritzsche, organises adventurous trips on horseback, from the central highlands to Swakopmund. They travel across the escarpment and through the desert. With a few nights to get used to the horses, and one at the end to relax, these are full 12-day trips. Participants must be fit, have extensive experience of riding and horses, and be totally at ease on the back of a cantering horse. Riders camp throughout the trip and trucks transport the equipment ahead of the party.

Dates are fixed ahead, with five trips organised for 2007, all listed on their website. Other trips are arranged on an occasional basis. Rates, in euro, are from €2,500 pp for the whole trip, including all meals, but excluding drinks.

THE MAIN B2 The B2 heads north from Windhoek to Okahandja, about 71km, before turning west for the coast. Although the distance to Swakopmund is 358km, the road is flat and the tarred surface means that – despite a relatively poor surface just north of Okahandja – it is around four hours of very easy driving.

Okahandja This small town is 71km north of Windhoek. It has some reasonable shops, a couple of banks, 24-hour fuel, two of the country's best open markets for curios, an excellent shop for *biltong* (dried meat), and quite a lot of old buildings and history – if you've the time to stop and take a look around.

History Okahandja is the administrative centre for the Herero people (see *Chapter 2*, pages 22–3), despite being considerably southwest of their main settlements. Missionaries first reached the area in the late 1820s, but it wasn't until 1849 that the first of them, Friedrich Kolbe, settled here. He remained for less than a year, driven away by the attacks of the Namas, under Jonker Afrikaner.

He fled with good reason as, on 23 August of the following year, about 700 men, women and children were killed by the Namas at the aptly named Blood Hill. It is said that after the massacre, the women's arms and legs were chopped off in order to take their copper bangles.

The small kopje of Blood Hill can be seen just to the east of the main Windhoek–Swakopmund road. Jonker Afrikaner lies peacefully in his grave, next to several Herero chiefs, opposite the church on Kerk Street.

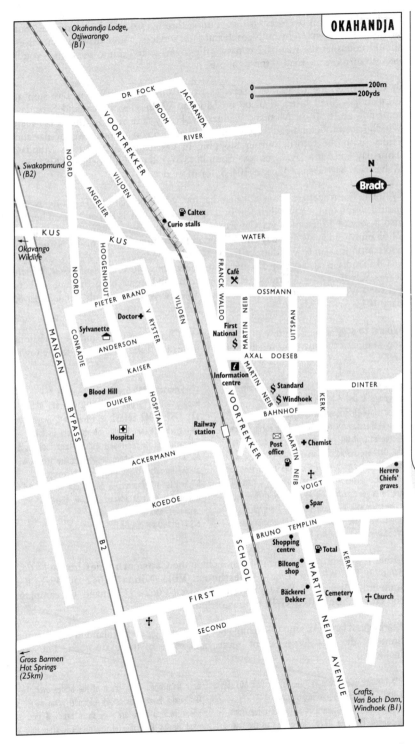

Okahandja Lodge,
Otjiwarongo
(B1)

DR FOCK

BOOM

JACARANDA

VOORTREKKER

RIVER

200m
200yds

N

Bradt

NOORD

ANGELIER

VILJOEN

KUS

Caltex

Curio stalls

WATER

Swakopmund
(B2)

KUS

FRANCK WALDO

Café

OSSMANN

Okavango
Wildlife

NOORD

HOOGENHOUT

PIETER BRAND

Doctor +

V RYSTER

MARTIN NEIB

First
National
$

UITSPAN

CONRADIE

Sylvanette

ANDERSON

KAISER

VILJOEN

AXAL DOESEB

Information
centre

MARTIN NEIB

$ Standard

$ Windhoek

DINTER

Blood Hill

DUIKER

HOSPITAAL

VOORTREKKER

BAHNHOF

KERK

Hospital

Railway
station

Post
office

+ Chemist

MARTIN NEIB

Herero
Chiefs'
graves

ACKERMANN

+

VOIGT

KOEDOE

Spar

BYPASS

B2

BRUNO TEMPLIN

Shopping
centre

Total

Biltong
shop

Bäckerei
Dekker

Cemetery

MARTIN NEIB AVENUE

KERK

+ Church

SCHOOL

FIRST

+

SECOND

Gross Barmen
Hot Springs
(25km)

Crafts,
Van Bach Dam,
Windhoek (B1)

Getting there Most overseas visitors coming through Okahandja are driving, but the town is also served by both coach and train services. Those driving themselves should note that the main B2 bypasses the town, so to go into the centre you'll need to turn off the road at the signposts.

By coach Intercape Mainliner's services from Windhoek to Walvis Bay stop at Okahandja's Shell Ultra at 07.00 on Monday Wednesday, Friday and Saturday, returning at 16.50 on Monday, Wednesday, Friday and Sunday. Buses between Windhoek and Victoria Falls reach Okahandja at 17.55 on Monday, Wednesday and Friday, with the return journey stopping in Okahandja at 04.30 on Monday, Thursday, and Saturday. Fares cost around N$70–130 to Windhoek, and N$125 to Walvis Bay. See *Chapter 6*, pages 104–5, for more details.

By train Trains depart from Okahandja for Windhoek at 05.10, daily except Saturday, and on the same days for Swakopmund and Walvis Bay at 22.05. There is also a service to Tsumeb via Omaruru and Otjiwarongo, leaving Okahandja at 21.55 on Monday, Wednesday and Friday, and returning at 04.00 on the same days and continuing on to Windhoek. Trains are very slow.

Okahandja is also a stop for the faster new *Omugulu Gwombashe Star*, which leaves Windhoek on a Friday, returning from Ondangwa on a Sunday. Tickets between Windhoek and Okahandja cost N$68 one way. For details, see *Chapter 6*, page 101.

🏠 **Where to stay** There are few places to stay in Okahandja itself, and most visitors stay at one of the surrounding guest farms instead. All the same, close to the town are:

🏠 **Okahandja Lodge** (22 rooms, 2 family units, camping) ☏ 062 504299; f 062 502551; e okalodge@africaonline.com.na; www.okahandjalodge.com. About 2km north of town, to the east of the road just after the turn-off to the Okahandja Wildlife Gardens, this is one of a number of lodges around Namibia's towns that cater for coach parties. Its en-suite rooms – 6 have AC – are in large, thatched blocks partially circling an open lawn with a nearby pool. They are pleasant inside, with fans & DSTV, if somewhat unoriginal. N$550/900 sgl/dbl, B&B. Camping N$55 pp.

🏠 **Sylvanette B&B Guesthouse** (9 rooms) 311 Hoogenhout St; ☏ 062 501213/501078; m 081 127 3759; f 062 501852; e sylvanette@iway.na; www.sylvanette.com. In the suburbs close to town, Sylvanette has double rooms with en-suite facilities & AC, an airy lounge where sundowners are served, & a cosy breakfast room. There's a fully equipped kitchen for self caterers, & dinner can be arranged if you request it in advance. Outside, there's a swimming pool & secure parking. N$310/480 sgl/dbl, B&B.

Other less-inspiring options in town include the **Capricorn Guesthouse** (☏ 062 504672; m 081 279 1988), **Guesthouse Villa Nina** (☏ 062 502497), the uninviting Andreas Kukuri Conference Centre (☏ 062 503331) and, for camping, the **Horseshoe Pub & Grill** to the north of town.

🏠 **Nearby guest farms** Around Okahandja lies some of the best farmland in the country. Some of the local farms accept guests, and some of those are good. The best include:

🏠 **Otjisazu Guest Farm** (13 rooms) ☏ 062 501259; f 062 501323; e otjisazu@iway.na; www.otjisazu.com. Otjisazu is an hour's drive from Windhoek. Take the D2102 signposted to the Von

Bach Dam about 1km south of the bridge over the Okahandja River. After about 4.5km & again at about 16.5km there are very sharp bends, & the road crosses a number of dry riverbeds. (This isn't a road to drive for the first time when it's dark.) It reaches Otjisazu after about 27.5km. The area around is rolling acacia scrub/bush – typical of the central plateau around Windhoek.

The farm stands in pleasant, well-watered gardens with a good stone braai & stone counter, & shaded tables. There is also a separate outside boma dining area & bar, overlooking a good-size pool. Inside, the farmhouse is comfortable & spacious. The furniture's neither antique nor very modern – despite the building dating from 1878, when it was originally built as a mission. The twin rooms are comfortable, solidly constructed & all en suite: most seem purpose-built.

Nature drives are available around the farm – lasting an hour or so in the evening. With luck you'll spot a few of the farm's kudu, gemsbok, springbok, duiker, steenbok, or (it is claimed) eland. Horseriding is available on request (N$65 for around 2 hrs), and there are also mountain bikes. Otjisazu has always been quite a nice guest farm, & its owners seem determined to make staying here good value.
From N$528.52 pp, DBB.

Midgard Lodge (46 rooms) ↘ 062 503888; f 062 503818; e midgard@mweb.com.na; www.namibsunhotels.com.na. Run by the Namib Sun Hotel group, Midgard is about 85km from Windhoek on the D2102. It covers 65km², which includes a large swimming pool, tennis courts, horseriding & hiking trails. Midgard is popular for an outing from town for Sunday lunch, though it is better suited to conferences than casual visitors. This is reflected in the style & layout of its rooms, which have all the accoutrements of a good business hotel.
Standard N$530–590/740–825 sgl/dbl low–high season; VIP N$645–720/970–1,075 sgl/dbl low–high season, all B&B.

Okatjuru Guest Farm (6 rooms) ↘ 062 549121; f 062 594120; e jhein@iway.na; www.jhein.iway.na; reservations ↘ 061 224712; f 061 224217; e okatjuru@reservation-destination.com. Although a considerable distance from Okahandja, that's the easiest point of access. Take the B1 out of town for 10km, then the C31 towards Hochfeld for 107km, before turning right onto the D2166 for the last 8km to the farm. It's a traditional farm, with guest accommodation – all en suite – shared between a thatched chalet, a loft & a guesthouse. The farm is stocked with plenty of game, making game drives a good option to see giraffe, black rhino, waterbuck, kudu, oryx, zebra & eland, among others.

Photographers will appreciate hides overlooking the waterholes. There's also the possibility of rhino-tracking on foot for small groups.
N$80.87 pp sharing, DBB. Rhino tracking N$135 pp, game drive or nature walk N$75 pp.

Oropoko Lodge (30 rooms, 3 suites) ↘ 062 503871; f 062 503842; e oropoko@iafrica.com.na; www.oropoko.com. Oropoko is reached by taking the main B2 west from Okahandja for about 41km, before turning north onto the D2156. It is well signposted 18km along this road.

Oropoko is a grand lodge with a stunning situation on a small mountain, whose top was flattened to make way for it. Its large outdoor pool has an impressive view, & the lodge's bar & dining room are of a similar scale. Meals are extensive affairs: large buffet breakfasts, & heavy à-la-carte dinners. The bar has numerous large leather armchairs. Guest rooms at Oropoko are large, square & modern, each with an en-suite bathroom, twin beds, minibar/fridge, phone, & its own safe.

The lodge aims for the most affluent travellers, & caters for hunting as well as photographic guests. It also has its own shooting school, which might explain the zeal of the security force manning the gate.

The game area surrounding the lodge buildings is about 11,000ha, and is home to white rhino, giraffe, waterbuck and nyala, as well as the more normal antelope for this area like gemsbok, kudu, & steenbok. Game drives (N$100 pp) & guided walks (N$25 pp) can be organised.
N$670/995/1,490 sgl/dbl/trpl, B&B. Dinner N$140.

Düsternbrook Guest Farm (5 rooms, 2 safari tents, camping) ↘ 061 232572; f 061 234758/232572; e dbrook@mweb.com.na; www.duesternbrook.net. To reach Düsternbrook, turn west off the B1, about 30km north of Windhoek, onto the D1499, & then follow the clear signs for another 18km. Düsternbrook's venerable claim to fame is its leopards & cheetah, which are kept in several large enclosures, the smallest being 10 acres, & can be viewed from a vehicle. It also has a much larger area of land for game drives & 4 well-marked walks to view less dangerous game, including zebra, waterbuck, hartebeest, giraffe, eland, oryx, kudu, white rhino & smaller buck, not to mention a rich birdlife. Horseriding with game-viewing & a mountain drive into the Khomas Mountains are added attractions.

The main building is a large old colonial farmhouse dating from 1910. Its walls are adorned with paintings & hunting trophies: limited & sustainable trophy hunting provides meat for the table. There's also a large pool, & a range of books on wildlife & natural history.

Düstenbrook was one of Namibia's first guest farms. Its hospitable owners speak English, German, French & Afrikaans.

N$740–890 pp sharing, inc DBB, leopard/cheetah viewing & a game drive. Sgl supplement N$396. Camping N$75. Leopard feeding N$199 pp.

🏠 **Okapuka Ranch** (29 rooms, 1 suite) ✆ 061 257175; f 061 234690; e okapuka@iafrica.com.na; www.natron.net/okapuka. Okapuka has an imposing set of gates on the eastern side of the main B1 road, about 40km south of Okahandja and 30km north of Windhoek. Its 2.5km drive winds through 120km² of well-stocked game ranch, protecting herds of sable, giraffe & blue wildebeest as well as gemsbok, kudu, ostrich & crocodile. The lodge's major attraction, though, is the 3km² enclosure containing a pride of lion, which are fed regularly for the benefit of observers (I'll ignore here any discussion of the ethics of keeping, & breeding from, a pride of lion described by the owner as 'problem animals').

The lodge itself has been stylishly built on a rise above the surrounding country, & lavishly equipped with a sauna, floodlit tennis courts, & a chic swimming pool, for the use of residents only.

Accommodation is split across 2 sites: most of the thatched rooms are set together at the edge of the park, while an entirely separate mountain lodge has its own 4 rooms & broad views across the bush. Individual en-suite rooms are attractively designed, with karakul floor rugs & original artwork on the walls. Each boasts AC/heating, minibar, kettle & phone, as well as a private terrace.

The large, thatched bar/lounge area is beautiful, though more imposing than relaxing. Alongside, the restaurant caters for both residents & day visitors. On Sun, there is a 3-course lunchtime buffet; at other times, there is an à-la-carte menu focusing on game.

Okapuka encourages day visitors, offering daily 1½hr game drives, as well as lion feeding, helicopter flights, horseriding & other activities. There are also 2 walking trails of 2 & 6hrs duration respectively. Note that the ranch regularly hosts guests from the *Desert Express* train (see page 103) to watch a lion feed, which inevitably brings the occasional influx of visitors.

N$750/1,050 sgl/pp sharing, inc b/fast & lion-feeding tour. Dinner N$125.

✗ Where to eat Okahandja has several good small take-aways dotted along Main Street, including a good coffee shop just by the Shell fuel station as you come into the town from Windhoek. Just on the northern outskirts of town (at the turn-off of the D2110 from the B1) is the **Okakango Wildlife Restaurant & Garden Centre** (✆ *062 523280*). Alongside an established plant nursery (perfect if you need to buy a house plant during your travels) is a busy restaurant that overlooks a small area set aside for game, and a children's play area. It makes a good stopover, especially for families, and the car park seemed a relatively safe place to leave things – though you might be wise to ask the security guard to keep a special watch on your car if there's any luggage on view.

Getting organised Okahandja has a scattering of 24-hour **fuel stations** alongside its main roads. The town's **post office** is almost opposite its pharmacy, and if you need a **bank** then there are branches of Standard Bank and First National on the main Martin Neib Avenue, and Bank Windhoek on the corner of Bahnhof Avenue, all with ATMs.

For **food and provisions**, there's a large supermarket, and the town's grocery shops are reputed to have some of the country's best fresh vegetables. There's also a renowned outlet for biltong on the eastern side of Martin Neib Avenue (the main B1 from Windhoek), near the bakery – Bäckerei Dekker.

In an emergency, the police are reached on ✆ 062 10111, whilst the ambulance is on ✆ 062 503030, the hospital ✆ 062 503039, and the fire service ✆ 062 5001052 (after hours m 081 253 7309).

What to see and do By the side of the railway line, on Voortrekker Street, is a large open-air **curio market** run by the Rundu-based Namibian Carvers' Association. This and its sister outlet on the southern side of town are probably the two best places in the country for carvings. See *Chapter 2*, page 29.

Craftsmen here specialise in large wooden carvings. These include some beautiful thin, wooden giraffes (some 2m or more high), huge 'tribal' heads, cute flexible snakes, and wide selections of more ordinary carved hippos and bowls. Do stop for a wander around as you pass, especially if you're on the way to Windhoek airport to leave – this is the perfect spot for last-minute present shopping, and it's open on Sundays. A word of caution, though: the traders here have become quite aggressive in their sales tactics, and some of the prices quoted appear extortionate. If you're not prepared for the hassle, and to bargain fairly hard, then a curio shop could be a better bet.

Historical sites The town has many historical sites, including the **graves** of a number of influential leaders, such as Jonker Afrikaner, the powerful Oorlam leader; Chief Hosea Kutako, an influential Herero leader who campaigned against South African rule in the 1950s; and Chief Clemens Kapuuo, once president of the DTA, who was assassinated in 1978. Note that casual visitors cannot access these graves.

Close by is the **Church of Peace**, a Lutheran-Evangelistic church built in 1952 and now enclosed by a high fence, and also the **house of Dr Vedder**, one of the oldest in town.

Just south of the post office, on Hoof Street, is a building known as **the old stronghold**, or the old fort. This was the town's old police station, started in 1894, though now it is empty and falling into disrepair. Meanwhile to the west, **Blood Hill**, scene of the 1850 massacre, is found between Kaiser and Duiker streets, although there's little to see now.

AROUND OKAHANDJA There are two resorts close to Okahandja, both run by the NWR. These are primarily used as weekend get-aways by the local urbanites – though if you are passing and need somewhere cheap to stay, they are fine.

Von Bach Recreational Resort Von Bach Dam supplies most of the capital's water, and is surrounded by a nature reserve. It is signposted a few kilometres along the D2102 just south of Okahandja, and 1km south of the bridge over the Okahandja River. The environment here is thorn-scrub and particularly hilly, supporting game including kudu, baboon and leopard, as well as Hartmann's mountain zebra, springbok, eland and even ostrich. However, with only one road through the park they are all very difficult to spot. Don't come here just for the game. (↘ 062 501475. Admission N$40 pp per day, plus N$10 per car; under 16s free. Open all year: gates open at sunrise and close at sunset.)

Where to stay

🏠 **Von Bach Campsite** Visitors have the option of a couple of very basic 2-bed huts, without bedding or facilities (you must use the campers' communal ablution blocks), or camping. Reservations can be made through the NWR in Windhoek, & day visitors must phone in advance if they want to drop in. *Camping N$110 per pitch; N$100 per hut. Park fees extra.*

Gross Barmen Hot Springs This busy resort has a shop, restaurant, filling station and tennis courts, as well as the mineral spa fed by the hot thermal springs. It is built around a dam about 25km southwest of Okahandja, on the banks of the Swakop River, and is easily reached from the town's southern side along the C87. Note that day visitors must phone ahead to book. (↘ 062 501091. Entry N$80 per day, plus N$10 for car; under 16s free. Open all year.)

What to see and do Gross Barmen's main attraction is its **mineral spring and swimming baths**. The fountain here, clearly visible, wells up at about 65°C. It feeds the inside 'thermal hall' with its sunken baths for overnight visitors, as well as the cooler outside pools (for children and adults) which are used mainly by the day visitors, who are especially numerous at weekends.

Additional attractions are some gentle walks in the surrounding hillsides and, especially for birdwatchers, a good little path cut right through the reedbeds. These all make pleasant strolls, and a couple of benches make good vantage points over the dam while you rest.

Where to stay

Gross Barmen Restcamp Accommodation includes 4-bed bungalows, 2-bed bungalows or rooms, & campsites. All have a fridge/kettle, hotplate, en-suite shower & toilet, & linen & bedding provided; 'luxury' 4-bed suites also have DSTV. The 2-bed bungalows also have field kitchens.

Book through the NWR in Windhoek, and note that day visitors must phone in advance, to arrange their visits.
N\$580–800 4-bed bungalow, N\$350 2-bed. Camping N\$50 per site (max 8 people). Park fees extra.

KARIBIB

For over 90 years, this small town on the railway line from Windhoek to Swakopmund, 112km from Okahandja on the B2, has been known mainly for the very hard, very high-quality marble which comes from the Marmorwerke quarry nearby. This produces about 100 tonnes of finished stone per month – mainly kitchen/bathroom tiles and tombstones.

More recently, in the late 1980s, South Africa's Anglo-American Corporation opened the open-cast Navachab Gold Mine on the south side of town, to mine low-grade ore.

There's a lot of small-scale mining in the area, especially for gemstones. Amethyst, tourmaline, aquamarine, quartz, silver topaz, citrine and garnets are just some of the minerals found in the region around here. See the tumbled stones on the floor display of the Namib i centre (see Henckert Tourist Centre, below) for an idea of what is around – they all come from the local area.

Trains between Windhoek and Tsumeb, and between Windhoek and Walvis Bay, all call at Karibib. For details, see *Chapter 6*, pages 101–3.

Where to stay

In town there's the choice of a backpackers' lodge and a country club, but there are several guest farms nearby.

Irmi's Lodge (11 rooms) 310 Hidipo Hamutenya St; ✆ 064 550081; f 064 550240; e imstrobl@ iway.na. Just at the eastern entrance to town on the B2, the refurbished Irmi's is next to the Engen garage. With its painted walls & mature trees, it has a welcoming appearance, & is popular with backpackers. It also has a pool and braai area. N\$260/420/500 sgl/dbl/trpl, B&B, dorm bed N\$110 pp.

Klippenberg Country Club & Guesthouse ✆ 064 170732; m 081 124 8730, 081 216 6066. Near the mountainous outcrop known as Klippenberg, this is signposted on the main road. It has tennis courts, squash, a swimming pool, a small golf course & a bar/restaurant that is popular with some of Karibib's residents. It's not really geared to tourists, but is hospitable enough if you drop by. N\$230/460 sgl/dbl, B&B.

Nearby guest farms There are several guest farms and lodges in this area, including:

Albrechtshöhe Guest Farm (5 rooms) ✆/f 062 503363; e meyer@iafrica.com.na; www.natron.net/tour/albrechtshoehe/index.html. Albrechtshöhe is off the D1988, about 2km south of the main B2, 92km west of Okahandja, & 26km from Karibib. It's a traditional guest farm, run by

Paul-Heinz & Ingrid Meyer, which started life as a railway station. Because of the natural springs of the area, the Schutztruppe completed Albrechtshöhe in 1906 to provide water for horses & steam trains. Today these historic, fortified buildings house the guest farm. Activities include bush walks & game drives as well as expeditions to search for gems & explore the local mountains; on site, there's a small swimming pool. Like many Namibian guest farms, this is also a hunting farm. *From N$500 pp, DBB.*

⌂ **Tsaobis Leopard Nature Park** (8 bungalows, camping) ` 064 550811/244712; f 064 550954/224217; e tsaobis@iafrica.com.na. This private 37,000ha game reserve is in beautiful hilly country, 11km west of the C32, on the south bank of the Swakop River. The animals here include leopard, cheetah, wild dog, aardwolf, caracal, zebra & gemsbok. The lodge also supports a research project into the baboons that inhabit the area. Most of the animals seen by guests are kept in enclosures near the main house & bungalows.

This is a good area for hiking; there are several trails & 2-way radios are available. Scenic & sundowner drives take guests into the surrounding desert, & a 6hr drive can be arranged with at least a month's notice to find out about the area's geology, including a visit to an old aquamarine mine.

Tsaobis is more like a restcamp than a guest farm & accommodation is in simple self-catering bungalows, or at the adjacent spotlessly clean campsite with private, open-air, hot showers, but no electricity. Meals are available on request. Outside, a lapa offers welcome shade in the heat of the day, and there is a swimming pool for cooling off. Note that there is no fuel or supplies at Tsaobis, & neither activities (walks or guided wildlife drives) nor meals are automatically available: all should be pre-arranged when you book your accommodation. *N$304.74/203.48 self-catering bungalow sgl/pp sharing (2 people). Camping N$50 pp.*

⌂ **Etusis Lodge** (7 bungalows, 6 tents) ` 064 550826; f 064 550961; e etusis@iway.na; www.etusis.com. The turning for Etusis is signposted from the C32, about 19km south of Karibib. The lodge itself is 16km from the road, standing at the foot of the Otjipatera Mountains: a range of white marble.

Solid, comfortable bungalows with exposed wooden beams & attractive thatch have en-suite toilets & showers. Each sleeps up to 4 people, & has 220V electricity, solar-heated water & a ceiling fan. Simple 'luxury' tents on a concrete base stand nearby, sharing clean communal facilities.

Central to the lodge is a bar & dining area, with small curio shop & TV/lounge — all under a large thatched building overlooking a small swimming pool. The lodge also has limited conference facilities.

Activities include game drives — in search of impala, kudu, mountain zebra, leopard, jackal & blesbok — & the opportunity to hike unguided in the mountains behind the lodge. There are also options for horseriding, rock climbing, kite-flying, target shooting & various other sports. *N$975/850 bungalow sgl/pp sharing, N$650 tent pp, all DBB, inc N$50 towards protection of Hartmann's mountain zebra.*

⌂ **Aabadi Bush Camp** ` 061 224712/250725; f 061 224217; e Aabadi@reservation-destination.com. This community-run bush camp just outside Wilhelmstal, off the B2 before Karibib, has been set up next to a natural waterhole in the bush. Overnight visitors have their own camp with ablution block, but the place is also open to day visitors. It's an original concept, with local dishes such as Herero *potbrood* (pot-baked bread) & Nama *skaapkop* (sheep's head) served, while the 'souvenir hut' allows visitors to join with their hosts to make their own crafts — or to purchase items previously made. Guided walks in the morning & afternoon include an overnight stay & meals as appropriate. *N$80 camping. N$250 ½-day day visitors. Guided walk from N$375, inc dinner & overnight camping (own tent).*

✗ **Where to eat** In addition to the hotels above, there's Die Grüne Ecke craft shop/café, and the Karibib Bakery and Café, through the OK supermarket. There's also the slightly dubious-looking Western Restaurant, next to the eponymous gambling club and bar. If it's just a drink and a snack you're after, though, head for the simple café at the Henckert Tourist Centre (see below).

Getting organised Karibib boasts an OK **supermarket** next to Irmi's Lodge, and a couple of **fuel stations**, as well as a **post office** and, for **banks**, a branch of the First National. There's also a garage on the main road where staff can carry out vehicle repairs. **In an emergency**, the police are reached on ` 064 10111, the ambulance and private clinic (located behind the First National Bank) on ` 064 550073, and the fire service on ` 064 550126/550254.

What to see and do Your first stop here should be the **Henckert Tourist Centre** (see below), but if you have more time then the town is dotted with several **historic buildings** dating from the early 1900s. Then Karibib was an important overnight stop on the railway between Windhoek and Swakopmund, as well as a trade centre. Ask at the information centre for their brief guide to the town.

There is a small **shooting range** and a few **hiking trails** into the rolling landscapes south of town, behind the country club. In town itself, the Club Western Gambling and Entertainment Centre, and its adjacent Club Western Restaurant, seem to be the focus of local excitement, although as an alternative, the town's cemetery is beautifully lit at night!

The local branch of the Wildlife Society has a '**vulture restaurant**' with twice-weekly feedings, and the **gold mine** has occasional site tours. Horseriding trips may also be available. For any of these, enquire at the information centre (in advance, if possible), which is the main stop for visitors passing through.

Henckert Tourist Centre (38 Hidipo Hamutenya; ☎ 064 550700; f 064 550720; e tourist@henckert.com; www.henckert.com; open Mon–Fri 08.00–17.00, Sat & Sun 09.00–16.00) On the main street, this is a landmark – a first-class curio shop that doubles as a Namib i information centre. This fascinating shop began as a small gem shop in 1969. Now it has a very large range of carvings and curios, one of the country's best selections of Namibian semi-precious stones and gemstones, a facility to change money if necessary, and a friendly café serving drinks and snacks. There's even a children's corner with eye-catching stones.

There is also a weaving centre, employing about 25 people. Visitors can watch, and account for some 70% of the rugs and crafts sold. This demonstrates the importance of tourism here, and the vital role that you play in the local economy when you spend money in Namibia.

USAKOS This small town, 147km from Swakopmund, used to be the centre of the country's railway industry, though now it's little more than a stop on the line between Windhoek and Walvis Bay, with banks and fuel to tempt those who might otherwise pass right through. The Namib i information office is useful if you're planning to do much exploration of the local area.

Where to stay and eat For casual snacks as you pass through on your way to Swakopmund, **Namib Wüste Farm Stall** is the best in town – and it also has a restcamp (☎/f 064 530283). It is almost always open (closing at 20.00, even on Sundays) for a good range of take-away foods, biltong and chilli bites.

Most visitors staying in the area will use the guest farms around here and Karibib, but if you need to stay in Usakos itself, your other two options are:

⌂ **Bahnhof Hotel** (14 rooms) Theo-Ben Gurirab St; ☎ 064 530444; f 064 530765; e websmith@ iway.na; www.erongominerals.com/bahnhof. The 2-star Bahnhof, located next to the post office, is fully licensed with an à-la-carte restaurant, bar, beer garden & undercover off-street parking. Each room has AC, satellite TV, telephone & en-suite bathroom. Internet & conference facilities are available. Birdwatching & local Bushman art are on offer at the nearby Mansfield farm, next to Usakos. N$280/420 sgl/dbl, B&B.

⌂ **Usakos Hotel** (10 rooms) Theo-Ben Gurirab St; ☎/f 064 530259. This plain hotel has a simple restaurant, & off-street parking. All the rooms have en-suite bathroom & some have AC. There's a restaurant & bar, & a swimming pool to cool off after the day's drive. If you've no transport then you can arrange day trips from here to Spitzkoppe (see page 329) with the owner. N$100–120/200–240 sgl/dbl.

Nearby guest farms

🏠 **Ameib Ranch** (10 rooms, camping) 📞 064 530803; **f** 064 530904; **e** ameib@natron.net; www.natron.net/tour/ameib/main.html. Ameib has been accepting guests for years, & is quite idiosyncratic, but it does have superb rock formations & excellent rock art, so is worth a visit.

Approaching from Windhoek or Otjiwarongo, turn right towards Swakopmund in the centre of town, then immediately right again, onto the D1935. This turning can be inconspicuous: there's a small sign to Ameib on your right as you turn, & a hospital on your left. (From Swakopmund on the B2, look for a small sign to the left. If you reach the main junction in the centre of town, you have missed it.) From here, follow the gravel D1935 for 12km to a signposted right turn onto the D1937. The landscape is beautiful: a little like Damaraland's vegetation, with sparse cover on the hillsides, & lush river valleys. About 5km further (on poor gravel) you reach Ameib's imposing gates. Then 11km later, the ranch is set amongst rounded granite boulders in the Erongo Mountains.

Its rooms are large & clean, with en-suite facilities, but uninspiring décor: they are functional, but not beautiful. The campsite has a pool, & braai area.

Visitors come here mainly for the excellent rock paintings. Many are within Phillip's Cave, a large eyelash-shaped cave made famous by Abbé Breuil's *Rock Paintings of Southern Africa* (see *Appendix 3*). It's a classic site for Bushman art, and the paintings here include a famous elephant, giraffe, & red stick-like people. Getting there is a 1.8km drive from the ranch itself, followed by a 30-min trail (15 mins at a fast, serious hiking pace). If possible, do this in the cool of the morning.

There are also unusual rock formations, like the Bull's Party — a group of large rounded boulders which (allegedly) look like a collection of bulls talking together. These are about 5.2km from the main ranch, and around them are lots of unusually shaped rocks, including mushroom-shaped & balancing boulders — worth exploring for an afternoon. N$495 pp sharing, B&B. Camping N$70 pp.

Getting organised If you need money then there's a First National Bank, and for supplies try the mini market at Engen, Lewis Stores or the Usakos Self-help (which is a shop, not a therapy group). These, like the fuel stations, are all on Theo-Ben Gurirab Street – the erstwhile Bahnhof Street.

In an emergency, the police are reached on 📞 064 10111, whilst the ambulance and fire service are on 📞 064 530023 – or **m** 081 251 5518 after hours. The hospital is 📞 064 530013/530067.

EAST FROM WINDHOEK

GOBABIS This busy town, standing at the centre of an important cattle farming area on the western edges of the Kalahari, forms Namibia's gateway into Botswana via the Buitepos border post, about 120km east. It's an ideal place to use the banks, fill up with fuel or get supplies before heading east towards Ghanzi, where most goods aren't so easily available. However, it's less interesting as a stopover.

Getting there

By car The main tar road, west to Windhoek and east into Botswana, is part of the trans-Kalahari route designed to link Walvis Bay with South Africa's Gauteng Province (the area around Johannesburg and Pretoria). This means that shipments from Europe or the USA can be sent via Walvis Bay, and trucked across this road to Gauteng – which should be far faster than shipping them to Durban, and moving them by road from there. Whilst certainly helping Gauteng's economy, its benefit for Namibia or the Kalahari is less obvious. It is expected to herald an increase in traffic on this route over the next few years.

By coach Intercape Mainliner used to run a good service linking Windhoek and Jo'burg, which stopped at Gobabis. However, this has now ended – it runs through Upington instead – so there are currently no coaches passing through Gobabis.

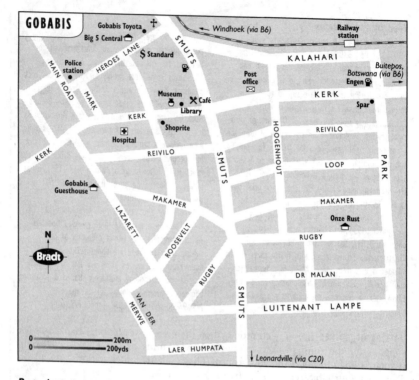

GOBABIS

By train Gobabis is linked to Windhoek by a train service, which arrives from there around 05.25 on Tuesday, Thursday and Sunday, and departs again at 20.50 on Monday, Wednesday and Friday. It is very slow, taking almost eight hours to get to Windhoek. See *Chapter 6*, pages 101–3, for details, or call the TransNamib in Gobabis (☏ 061 562416).

🏠 **Where to stay and eat** For snacks during the day there's a take-away at the back of the general store – just to the right of the Municipal Offices on the main street. More substantial is Erni's Bistro & Pub (*29 Quinto Cuanavale Av;* ☏ *062 565222*), where you can dine on 'lady's rump' or bubblegum milkshake under the watchful eye of Erni himself. If you want to stay in the area for a few days, then consider Arnhem Restcamp, or the excellent Eningu Clayhouse Lodge, just west of here, near Dordabis: see pages 178–9. However, if you need to be nearer town, then there are four possibilities:

🏠 **Big 5 Central Hotel** (16 rooms, camping) Heroes' Lane; ☏ 062 562094/5; f 062 564902; e big5gbs@iway.na; www.big5namibia.com. This old town hotel has had a makeover, designed to appeal to the South African market on the move. All rooms are en suite, with fan or AC, TV & fridge, & there's a separate campsite. In addition to a restaurant & bar, there's a bottle store, freezer, & braai facilities. *Standard N$180/280 sgl/dbl, AC N$200/300 sgl/dbl, family N$130 pp, all B&B. Camping N$20 pp.*

🏠 **Gobabis Guest House** (6 rooms) 8 Lazarett St; ☏ 062 563189; m 081 129 2471; f 062 564125; e gghnam@iafrica.com.na; www.swiftcentre.com/gobabisguest. To find this from the main road, turn right down Kerk St, then left down Lazarett St; the guesthouse is on the right. The rooms are clean & modern with AC, DSTV, phone, fridge & small veranda. As well as secure parking, there's a swimming pool & private braai area.
N$250/350 sgl/dbl, B&B.

🏠 **Goba-Goba Lodge & Rest Camp** (7 rooms, 2 chalets, camping) ☎ 062 564499; f 062 564466; e goba@mweb.com.na; www.namibweb.com/gobagoba.htm. This new accommodation option overlooking the Black Nossob River caters for a range of travellers passing through Gobabis. Rooms at the lodge have all the usual accoutrements – TV, AC, phone, tea-making facililties – while the chalets have those plus a view. The restcamp has both a campsite & simple rooms, all sharing a single ablution block & kitchen. Guests not wishing to self-cater can dine in the à-la-carte River Restaurant. There's also a pool and a tennis court. N$419/594/670/724 sgl/dbl/family/chalet (max 5 people). Restcamp N$155 pp, camping N$115 (2 people).

🏠 **Onze Rust Guesthouse** 95 Rugby St; ☎ 062 562214; f 062 565060; e onzerust@iafrica.com.na; www.natron.net/tour/onzerust/main.html. The centrally located Onze Rust is set in pretty gardens, with secure parking. Its en-suite rooms with sgl, dbl & family permutations have AC & private braai facilities. N$200/300 sgl/dbl. B/fast N$25 pp.

Getting organised The main **banks** are all here: Bank Windhoek and First National are both on Church Street, whilst Standard Bank is on Heroes' Lane. As you drive around the small centre, Gobabis will strike you as a prosperous community, with many small, busy shops and businesses. This means that it's a good place to stop for last-minute supplies if you are on the way to Botswana – start at the Spar at the crossroads of Kerk and Park streets. Several **24-hour fuel stations** line the main road, and **garages** include the useful Gobabis Toyota on Heroes' Lane and Pottie's Repairs & Services for Hyundai on Reivilo Street. For **tourist information** on the region, try the small Gobabis Information Centre (*Church St;* ☎ *062 564954; f 062 564952; e omaheketour@mweb.com.na*).

In an emergency, the police are reached on ☎ 062 10111, whilst the ambulance and hospital are on ☎ 062 566200, and the fire service on ☎ 062 566666.

🏠 **Nearby guest farms** There is an assortment of fairly offbeat guest farms within reach of Gobabis, and several places geared up to catch people taking overnight stops on the Trans-Kalahari Highway. These include:

🏠 **Kiripotib Guest Farm** (3 rooms, 2 chalets) ☎/f 062 581419; e hans@kiripotib.com; www.kiripotib.com. The engaging Hans Georg and Claudia von Hase run this friendly guest farm, about 2 hours' drive from Windhoek airport on the D1448. It's the base not only for a thriving little arts and crafts business, but also for African Kirikara Safaris – which offers various mobile safaris around the subcontinent. Kiripotib's spacious accommodation is split between the guesthouse, which has 3 pleasant rooms with en-suite bathrooms, and 2 new brick-built chalets set in open grassland. ,These each sleep 3 people, and have en-suite shower, minibar and a private veranda. Meals, including home-grown produce, are served in a thatched lapa, or around the fire under the stars, For winter evenings, a cosy sitting room has a small library and a TV.

Perhaps the most interesting aspect of Kiripotib is the variety of arts and crafts practised on site. There's a spinning workshop and weavery, where the team on the farm produces a variety of unique Namibian carpets made from karakul wool. You can see all the stages between the sheep and the carpets, and there's a small exhibition of these that are for sale at around N$1,500 per m². If you're planning on buying a carpet, then it costs no more to bring colours and fabric samples to Kiripotib, where the team can make up one of their designs to match your colours and sizes as closely as possible. (Obviously this takes time, but they do send regular shipments to Europe, so delivery is easily arranged.) Thanks to Claudia's training as a goldsmith, there's also a well-equipped small jewellery workshop which, when in full production, makes fascinating viewing. From an arts and crafts perspective, one of the most interesting trips is to see the Anin embroidery project at the Jena farm (see pages 190–1), which is about 80km south of Kiripotib.

More local activities include farm drives (usually integrated with a general tour of the weavery), walking trails, and visits to nearby farms with their own attractions. For example, with a little advanced notice, you can visit Tivoli Star Lodge, based on the neighbouring farm, which has a small observatory with a sliding roof and a computer-controlled reflecting telescope. Alternatively another nearby farm has plenty of game in a classic Kalahari landscape (shame the big cats are caged), or it's possible to arrange a drive and half-day walk in the Karubeams Mountains. There it takes about 30 mins to climb on to a lovely plateau, and there's a fair chance of seeing oryx, kudu and klipspringer.

Chalet N$599/498 sgl/pp sharing; room N$499/425 sgl/pp sharing, all B&B, inc farm tours, sundowner drive (exc drinks), tea, coffee and cake. Lunch N$75, dinner N$110. Closed 20 Dec–20 Jan.

🏠 **Kalahari Bushbreaks** (8 rooms, camping) 📞 062 568936; f 062 569001; reservations 📞 061 226979; f 061 226999; e enquiries@ kalaharibushbreaks.com; www.kalaharibushbreaks.com. About 87km east of Gobabis, and 26km west of the border with Botswana at Mamuno, Kalahari Bushbreaks is some 3km south of the main B6. It is owned & run by Ronnie & Elsabe Barnard, who have lived here since 1982. The lodge has 40km^2 under game, including eland, oryx, giraffe, kudu, red hartebeest, warthog, zebra (both Burchell's & Hartmann's mountain) & blue wildebeest. Several species of antelope which wouldn't normally be found in the Kalahari are also here, including waterbuck & blesbok (both normal & albino). The predators include cheetah, leopard & caracal.

Accommodation is in attractively decorated rooms, 2 with double beds, and all with en-suite facilities. When I last visited there was talk of 2 new bungalows which will each have 2 twin rooms. The standard is generally good, with lots of wood, reeds & leather. A campsite with 10 pitches is geared to travellers on the Trans-Kalahari, who are welcome to take part in activities and meals at the guesthouse.

The main lodge building consists of a warm, enclosed lounge & dining area with high thatched ceiling. Above this are 3 en-suite bedrooms. There's also a large, doughnut-shaped thatched boma area, with a fireplace in the middle, which is used for outdoor eating when temperatures are warm. Reflecting Ronnie's profession of architecture, it's all been well & carefully designed with solid wood on a large scale. Be aware that there is a sprinkling of animal trophies on the walls, & that the farm is occasionally used for hunting.

Although many visitors simply stop over here, activities can be arranged revolving around game & birdwatching drives. They can also encompass visiting rock paintings (some San, and some alleged to be of a different origin), bush walks with a guide & horseriding for experienced riders (who don't mind riding feisty working horses) without a hard hat.

N$480/575 sgl/ pp sharing, DBB. Tent N$60 pp; camping N$40 pp. Lunch N$69, dinner N$115. Game drive/guided walk N$100 pp. Open all year.

🏠 **Zelda Game & Guest Farm** (16 rooms) 📞 062 560427; f 062 560431; e zelda.guestfarm@ iafrica.com.na; www.zelda-game-and-guestfarm.com. Zelda is about 90km east of Gobabis, & 20km west of the Buitepos border, on the north side of the main B6 Trans-Kalahari Highway. This farm started in 1946, and started accepting guests in 1997. It covers about 100km^2, of which half is dedicated to game, & the rest to cattle farming.

Most people use the farm, with its 'Baboona' bar, restaurant, souvenir shop & pleasant, leafy garden, as a stopover. For action, there's volleyball, or a cool swimming pool for those hot Kalahari days. Rather more interesting are farm trails to be walked in the company of a local Bushman tracker, or an opportunity to visit the !Xhananga village to learn more about the traditions of these people.

N$500/390 sgl/pp sharing, B&B.

🏠 **Good Hope Country House** (4 rooms) 📞/f 062 563700; e goodhope@sanworld.com.na; www.sanworld.com.na. Run by James & Christine Chapman – descendants of James Chapman, the famous Victorian explorer – this is a small guesthouse whose simple rooms benefit from AC. It is often used as a base for safaris run by the family.

When researching I wasn't able to get in touch with Good Hope, although it seems to have a generally good reputation. I'd welcome news about it from passing visitors.

N$350/990 sgl/dbl B&B.

🏠 **Harnas Guest Farm** (3 cottages, 3 'igloos', camping) PO Box 548, Gobabis; 📞 062 682035/6; f 062 683037; e harnas@iway.na; www.harnas.de Almost 100km northeast of Gobabis, Harnas probably has the highest profile of any guest farm in the region. To get here, take the B6 east from Gobabis & turn left after about 6km onto the C22. The first 12.5km of this is tar, but then it reverts to being a wide gravel road for about 30km until it reaches a Harnas sign at Drimiopsis, when you take a right. About 7.5km further on the road branches & you keep left. Continue for a further 38km & the entrance to Harnas is on the left.

Harnas farm was once a cattle farm, but has gradually changed into a sanctuary for injured & orphaned animals – including several wild dogs – and now houses over 200 of them. That's why it's so well known. The Harnas Wildlife Foundation has several projects, which also include the rehabilitation & reintroduction of animals wherever possible.

Several farms, often driven by kind individuals with the very best of motives, have set up 'orphanage' or 'rehabilitation' programmes in Namibia for injured/unwanted animals. Harnas, Kaross and Okonjima spring to mind as the high-profile examples – but they are not the only ones.

Before visiting, it's perhaps worth considering the logic of some of the arguments for this, and perhaps discussing the issues with your hosts while there.

Some aim just to keep alive damaged or orphaned animals, some of which can be rehabilitated and released, though others can't be. The problems of keeping, say, a small orphaned antelope like a bushbuck are minimal. However, the problems caused by big cats are more major. Keeping such carnivores is difficult, as they need to be in very secure pens. Further, animals need to be killed to feed them. If it's a kindness to keep an injured lion alive, what about the horses, cows or antelope that are slaughtered to feed it? Why is the lion's life more valuable than the herbivores'?

Demand for visitors to see big cats and other 'sexy' species close up makes keeping habituated big cats a potentially lucrative draw for a guest farm. (Note that I don't use the term 'tame' as neither lions nor leopards ever seem to become anything like truly tame.) So is this why it's done?

Cynics claim that it's far from pure compassion. They question why there's a paucity of rescue centres for, say, black-faced impala, a species that is seriously endangered and rare. They're very beautiful and well worth preserving – but are they sexy enough to attract guests? Probably not, the cynics observe.

Pragmatic conservationists have lots of time for projects to preserve species, but many argue that individual animals are much less important. And as neither lions nor leopards are anything like rare – nor will they be in the near future – they really don't fall into this bracket at all. Most conservationists don't see the point in spending time and money keeping a lion alive when the same money could go towards preserving a whole ecosystem elsewhere.

One could argue, however, that when well run, such projects generate large incomes from visitors. This cash can then be used to fund serious, necessary (but perhaps less attractive) research programmes, or education programmes, which really do benefit Africa's wildlife on a much broader scale. That's a fine argument – but if it's the case, and this is their rationale for keeping caged animals as an attraction to raise money, then the cynics argue that it's time such organisations came clean.

Another key element of the farm's activities is a medical outreach project focusing on AIDS prevention & bringing specialist services such as cataract operations to the local people.

There's a variety of accommodation, all spread around quite a large grassy area. Brick-built cottages, which overlook a waterhole, & stone igloo-style bungalows are well equipped with en-suite facilities, AC, kitchenettes & braai areas. Backing this up is a campsite with 6 pitches, each with power, & a central ablution block. Visitors have use of a restaurant (with simple set menus), though many self-cater, & there's a large swimming pool available. Activities centre around morning & evening animal feeding tours, night drives & – by prior arrangement – horseriding.

N$792–858 pp sharing, DBB; camping N$148. Game drives N$90 pp, & animal feeding N$120–198 pp; night drive N$60 pp; horseriding N$70 pp/hr. Open all year.

CROSSING THE BORDER INTO BOTSWANA The Buitepos border opens 08.00–22.00 and is suitable for 2WD vehicles. There's little on the other side apart from a border post until you reach the small Kalahari cattle farming town of Ghanzi.

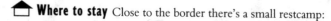

Where to stay

Close to the border there's a small restcamp:

East Gate Rest Camp (9 bungalows, 12 cabins, camping) ☏ 062 560405; f 062 450406; e eastgate@namib.net.com; www.namibweb.com/eastgate.htm. Turquoise-painted chalets set out in neat rows & a grassy campsite attract visitors to break a long journey. En-suite bungalows all have AC, but vary in standard & size, from 1 bedroom with kitchen to 2 bedrooms with TV & phone, sleeping 6. Simple cabins have just 2 sgl beds, & shared facilities. In addition, the camp has fuel & a shop, a swimming pool, bar & restaurant. *Bungalow N$300 (2 people)–700 (6 people), depending on standard; cabin N$90 pp; camping N$40 pp.*

Hitching Gobabis is probably the best place for hitching from Namibia into Botswana, as many trucks pass this way. Don't accept anything that will stop short of the border at Buitepos, and do carry plenty of food and water.

DORDABIS AND ENVIRONS

The small town of Dordabis, at the end of the tarred C23 to the southeast of Windhoek, is closer to the capital than Gobabis. Set in a beautiful valley covered with tall acacia trees, and between rounded, bush-covered hills, there's a police station, a petrol station (fuel available 08.00–20.00 only) and a shop selling a limited selection of food and drink. There is a township just outside the centre and the people when we last passed through were very friendly.

In recent years the area has attracted attention as the base for several artists and craftspeople, especially weavers. **Dorka Teppiche**, situated on the farm Peperkorrel 294 (*PO Box 9976, Dordabis;* ☏ *062 582581*) welcomes visitors, and here you can see how the textiles are woven, as well as buy the results.

Where to stay

Many of the guest farms in the area around Dordabis and Gobabis promote hunting rather than just watching game, though there are two excellent exceptions. Both are unusual, and worth a visit:

Eningu Clayhouse Lodge (9 chalets) ☏ 062 581880; f 062 581577; e juiced@mweb.com.na; www.eningu.com.na. Just an hour's drive (65km) south of the international airport, Eningu is surrounded by bush-covered dunes on the fringes of the Kalahari. Expect lots of masked weaverbirds in hanging nests, round eroded hills, & perhaps a little Kalahari sand when the grass dies down. It is one of Namibia's most original small lodges, and remains consciously arty – though in a very unpretentious manner – under the enthusiastic new ownership of Kate Dunston. The work of many artists can be seen around the lodge & there's a lovely curio shop filled with driftwood products & assorted porcupine ornaments – the latter made by the lodge's 'adopted' AIDS orphans & sold as a means to generate pocket money & school fees.

The offbeat nature of Eningu stretches beyond the shop, though. Here gentle opera drifts through the restaurant, local speciality meals include the likes of cactus parfait & springbok sushi; an underground 'cellar' is the venue for intimate cheese & wine tastings, the waterhole is lit in red to avoid animal disturbance & porcupines are fed daily at 22.00.

There are 8, semi-detached cottages & a separate honeymoon suite, all constructed, as the name suggests, of Kalahari clay bricks, though the apricot adobe effect & boxy design give it more than a suggestion of Mexico. Each has a cool, rustic interior, comfortably furnished with batik bedding, gourd lampshades & smooth concrete bases to ensure the beds are scorpion- & snake-free. The 'crazy-paving' effect floors are dotted with locally woven rugs, & natural objets d'art & paintings add a homely touch. There are heaters for winter & fans for summer, though the gauze windows are effective at catching the cool evening breeze. A small thatched veranda, mosquito nets, sun hats & a tea/coffee station are there for your comfort & energy saving lightbulbs are a small indication of the environmental efforts being made here. There are en-suite showers rather than baths in the rooms, with plans for an outdoor shower in the honeymoon suite.

Activities include 3 beautifully marked walking trails, archery, volleyball & badminton, though relaxing in the hammocks amongst the banana trees (or lounging by the swimming pool & whirlpool-jacuzzi) is also popular. If you stay for more than one night, then you may also do trips to a local sculpture studio, a local leatherworking shop & craft centre, or even Arnhem Cave. This is a super, idiosyncratic lodge, perfect for a first/last night in Namibia. *N$750/640 sgl/pp sharing, DBB.*

⌂ **Arnhem Cave & Restcamp** (4 chalets, camping) \/f 062 581885; m 081 124 5177; e arnhem@ mweb.com.na; www.natron.net/arnhem-cave/index.html. Arnhem is signposted from the D1808, about 4km south of its junction with the D1506. From the airport take the B6–M51–D1506–D1808; from Gobabis turn left at Witvlei onto the D1800–D1808.

The main attraction here is a cave system. It's claimed to be the longest in Namibia & the sixth-longest so far discovered in Africa, with about 4,500m of passages. It's thought to have been a home for bats for around 9,500 years, & still probably contains about 15,000 tonnes of bat guano, despite it being mined on & off for the last 70 years. Six species of bat have been identified here, including the giant leaf-nosed bat – the world's largest insectivorous bat. There are also shrews, spiders, beetles, water-shrimps & various invertebrates, some of which are endemic to the cave.

Though very dusty, & not at all fun for claustrophobics, there's a marked trail through the cave. Visitors are advised to dress in old clothes & bring torches (which can be hired).

The small restcamp here has good, purpose-built, thatched 4-bed chalets (with fridges) as well as grassy camping sites & a swimming pool. Wood is for sale, & braai facilities are provided, but meals should be booked in advance. *Chalet N$450/350 sgl/pp sharing, B&B; self-catering N$380 pp; camping N$75 pp. Guest visits to cave N$60 pp.*

SOUTH FROM WINDHOEK

REHOBOTH Just north of the Tropic of Capricorn and 87km south of Windhoek on the tarred B1, Rehoboth is the centre of the country's Baster community (see *Chapter 2*, page 16), which is quite different from any of Namibia's other ethnic groups, and jealously guards its remaining autonomy. However, there are few reasons to stop here, other than the museum, and most people pass on through.

Getting there Most visitors just slow down as they drive through on the main road, but if you're without a vehicle and want to stop, it's possible to get to Rehoboth by train or coach. Note that long-distance coaches won't pre-book the short Windhoek–Rehoboth legs, but you may be able to board on a stand-by basis. Perhaps this explains the relative prevalence of hitchhikers around Rehoboth.

By coach Intercape Mainliner's services from Windhoek to South Africa stop at the Echo service station, at 17.55 on Monday, Wednesday, Friday and Sunday, then from South Africa to Windhoek (stand-by only) at 04.10 on Monday, Tuesday, Thursday and Saturday. These cost around N$510 to Cape Town and a very steep N$175 from Windhoek. See *Chapter 6*, pages 104–5, for more details.

By train Trains depart from Rehoboth for Windhoek at 04.25 daily, except Saturday, and for Keetmanshoop at 22.10. However, not only are the trains very slow – see *Chapter 6*, pages 101–3, for details – but the station is too far north of the town to walk, so this is rarely a good option for visitors.

⌂ **Where to stay** In the centre of town, the **Suidwes Hotel** (*Annes Christians St; \ 062 522238*) lies just to the east of the main road, and appears to rent rooms by the hour or the night. Better options are the Reho Spa, and Lake Oanob Resort (see page 181):

⌂ **Reho Spa** (21 bungalows) \ 062 522774; f 062 522769; e reservations@nwr.com.na; www.nwr.com.na. Run by the NWR, this small restcamp is built around the town's hot-water

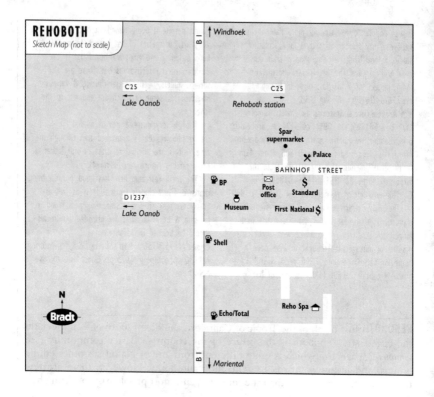

↑ Windhoek

C25
Lake Oanob

C25
→
Rehoboth station

Spar
supermarket

✕ Palace

BAHNHOF STREET

🔧 BP

✉ Post office

$ Standard

D1237
Lake Oanob

Museum

First National $

🔧 Shell

N

Bradt

Reho Spa ⌂

🔧 Echo/Total

↓ *Mariental*

---

springs. Although it's signposted from the B1, it's not quite as easy to find as you'd expect. The simplest approach is to turn east off the B1 at the Echo/Total garage. Follow this to the end, then turn left; Reho Spa is on the left. There's a memorable indoor jacuzzi of thermal spring water the size of a swimming pool (open 07.00–18.00), as well as a large outdoor pool & some good bungalow accommodation. The place can be marvellously empty if you avoid the weekends & holidays, when it's popular with day visitors. All the bungalows have a fridge, cooker, washbasin, toilet & bath or shower, & campsites are available.

4-bed bungalow N$450, 2-bed bungalow N$299. Camping N$90 per site, with powerpoint, up to 4 people, plus N$10 per additional person up to a max 8. Day visitors N$30 pp, plus N$10 per vehicle. Spa N$20/15 adult/child. Picnic site N$25.

Getting organised Though there's infinitely less choice here than in Windhoek, Rehoboth does have a couple of **grocery shops**, including a Spar, and the marvellously named Pick-Mor Bazaar. There are also branches of the First National and Standard **banks**, and several casinos and nightclubs – none very exclusive. On the road through town are various 24-hour **fuel stations**. And if you're looking for somewhere to eat, you could try **Le Palace Restaurant** (*Bahnhof St;* ☎ *062 523831*), close to the Spar supermarket.

In an emergency, the police are reached on ☎ 062 10111/523223, whilst the ambulance is on ☎ 062 523811 or ☎ 522006 after hours, the hospital on ☎ 062 522006/7 or ☎ 524502, and the fire service on ☎ 062 522091 or after hours on ☎ 062 524097/522950.

What to see and do Rehoboth's only real attraction for visitors is its small **museum** (*P Bag 1017, Rehoboth;* ☎ *062 522954; www.rehobothmuseum.com; admission N$5/2 adult/child. Open Mon–Fri 09.00–12.00, 14.00–16.00, Sat 09.00–12.00*), just behind the post office. It has good local history exhibits on the origins of the Baster community, and the flora and fauna in the surrounding area, as well as a rather surprising but interesting section on bank notes. Of interest in the vicinity is Lake Oanob, an attractive manmade lake which makes a pleasant place to relax for those driving through.

If you're heading towards Sesriem, then note that south of Klein Aub (on the C47 southwest of Rehoboth) is a road sign showing a cup and saucer, 1km off the road. This is Connie's Restaurant, which serves excellent coffee, biscuits and light snacks.

Lake Oanob West of Rehoboth is Lake Oanob, created by the construction of the highest dam in Namibia. Completed in 1990, it is also one of the country's newest dams. There is a display at the lookout point showing 'before' and 'after' photos of the dam's construction, as well as some of the technical drawings used. It's an amazing thought that such a small body of water as this has a catchment area of about 2,700km².

To reach the dam, take the D1280 west of the B1, about 8km before Rehoboth, and follow this road for around 7km. There is an entrance fee of N$10 pp.

Lake Oanob Resort (9 rooms, 6 chalets, camping) \ 062 522370; f 062 524112; e oanobresort@ iway.na. Built to cater for the numerous city dwellers who use the place as a weekend escape, Lake Oanob Resort has expanded in recent years, adding a small number of rooms & self-catering chalets overlooking the lake to the simple campsite here. En-suite dbl & family rooms have rustic furnishings, and each has a small veranda – ideal for checking out the night sky – while the chalets are extremely well equipped for a longer stay. There's an outside bar/restaurant on site that is relaxed & friendly, & an enclosed dining area for chilly winter evenings.

Fishing is available on the lake, & watersports enthusiasts are catered for with a range of facilities that include waterskiing, aqua-biking & kayaking. On land, there are short walking trails & bridle paths (horses available) around the lake. It's a pretty good place for birdwatching, too, with fish eagles & pelicans frequenting the area, & plans are under way to reintroduce game to the park, with springbok, blesbok, giraffe, zebra, hartebeest, wildebeest, oryx, impala & ostrich already in residence. As a short stop on the way south from Windhoek, this is well worth investigating.

N$570/690/870 sgl/dbl/family, B&B; 2-bedroom chalet from N$900, 3-bedroom chalet from N$1,440. Camping N$60 pp.

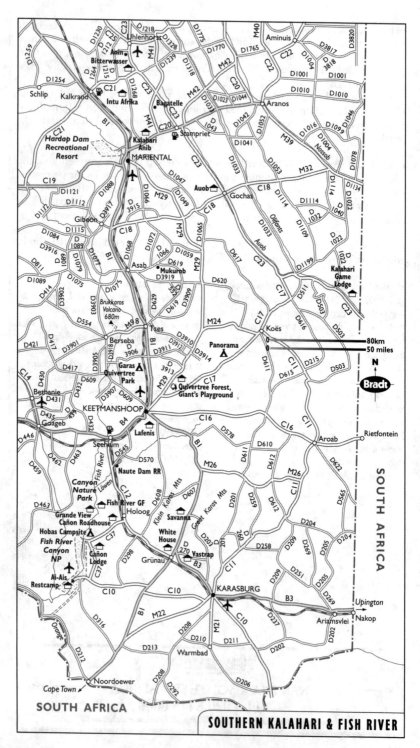

SOUTHERN KALAHARI & FISH RIVER

10

The Southern Kalahari and Fish River Canyon

If you have journeyed north from South Africa's vast parched plateau, the Karoo, or come out of the Kalahari from the east, then the arid landscapes and widely separated towns of southern Namibia will be no surprise. Like the towns, the region's main attractions are far apart: the Fish River Canyon, Brukkaros, the Quivertree Forest, and scattered lodges of the Kalahari.

Perhaps because of their separation, they receive fewer visitors than the attractions further north, so if you want to go hiking, or to sleep out in a volcano, or just to get off the common routes – then this southern side of the country is the perfect area to do it.

MARIENTAL

Despite being the administrative centre of the large Hardap Region, which stretches from the Atlantic coast to Botswana, Mariental still avoids being a centre of attention by having remarkably few attractions. It is central and has a sprinkling of efficient businesses, ranging from Desert Optics optometrist to the PP supermarket on the north side of town, serving the prosperous surrounding farmlands. By and large it contains very little of interest though, and there's an increasing amount of low-level, but nonetheless persistent, hassle and begging. Visitors view it as a place to go through, rather than to, often skirting around the town on the main B1 – stopping only for petrol and cold drinks at the Engen petrol station, if they stop at all.

Standing on the edge of the Kalahari Desert, in an area which has long been a centre for the Nama people of Namibia, Mariental gained its name from the area's first colonial settler, Herman Brandt, who called it 'Marie's Valley', after his wife.

When we last visited in 2006, Mariental and its immediate surroundings were recovering from serious flooding. Despite that, this area receives virtually no rain in some years. As a result, Namibia's successful commercial farmers have diversified in order to survive. The (welcome) current trend towards managing native game rather than farm animals, and earning income directly from tourism, is just an example of this. Similarly, the shrinking trade in pelts of karakul sheep – once so important to southern Namibia – seems to be concentrating around the town, while an ostrich abattoir has established Mariental as an important centre for the country's ostrich farming, which is expanding rapidly as markets open up around the world for the ostrich's lean, low-fat meat.

GETTING THERE

By car Approaching by car you can't miss Mariental. It's set slightly back, adjacent to the main B1, and is very well signposted. There are two main turnings for the town centre: one south of the larger side-roads to Stampriet and Hardap Dam, and the other just north of the tarred C19 to Maltahöhe. Between the two is the modern, efficient Trek garage, which incorporates a Wimpy restaurant and small supermarket.

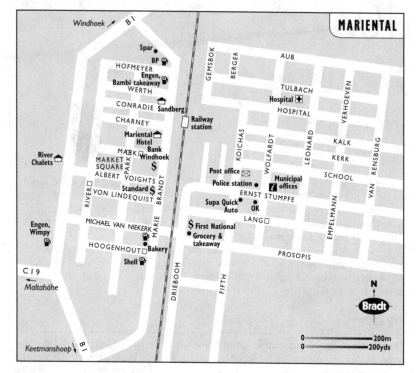

MARIENTAL

By bus The Intercape Mainliner service between Windhoek and Cape Town stops at Mariental, at the Engen station, at 20.15 on Monday, Wednesday, Friday and Sunday heading south, and then at 02.30 on Monday, Wednesday, Friday and Saturday going north. Tickets cost around N$490 to Cape Town, N$140 to Keetmanshoop and N$175 to Windhoek, and must be booked in advance. See pages 104–5 for details.

Starline buses link Mariental with Gochas on Wednesday, leaving Mariental at 08.00 and returning at 15.30. There are also buses on Monday and Thursday to Maltahöhe, departing at 08.00 and returning at 15.00, and east to Aranos via Stampriet, leaving Mariental on Tuesday and Friday at 08.00, and returning at 16.30.

By train Mariental is linked to Windhoek and Keetmanshoop by a slow, overnight train service. It departs daily except Saturday for Keetmanshoop at 02.20 and for Windhoek at 00.20. See *Chapter 6*, page 102, for details, or call TransNamib (℡ *066 29202*).

WHERE TO STAY If distances dictate that you stop around Mariental, then the hotels in town are convenient and generally cheaper than the nearby lodges. If you've more time, or are on a pre-arranged itinerary, then Kalahari Anib Lodge, Intu Afrika, or the resort at Hardap Dam are possibilities. See below for all three. Note that, without an advanced booking, you're more likely to find rooms in town. The Mariental and Sandberg hotels are both on the main Marie Brandt Street, two blocks apart, while the Guglhupf is on a side road.

⌂ **Mariental Hotel** (18 rooms) Marie Brandt St, PO Box 619, Mariental; ℡ 063 242466/7/8; ℡ 063 242493. Since before independence, this has been the best hotel in town by far. It was renovated a few years ago, when a small swimming pool & fairly well-equipped (for its location) gym were added, &

all the rooms were brought up to the same standards. All now have en-suite bathroom, AC, clock-radio, coffee station & a direct-dial telephone. The hotel continues to be kept spotlessly clean, & the staff are friendly & helpful, even when the place is totally booked by businessmen, which is not uncommon. There is a reasonable restaurant serving pasta & steak meals for around N$60, & a convenient car park at the back of the property. *N$300/400 sgl/dbl, B&B.*

🏠 **Sandberg Hotel** (14 rooms) Marie Brandt St. Following serious flooding in 2006, the Sandberg was forced to close. The disreputable public bar remains open, & at some stage the rooms may be refurbished & operational again. If the Mariental Hotel is full & you're forced to stay in town, it may be worth visiting the Sandberg to check on progress.

🏠 **River Chalets** (10 chalets) PO Box 262, Mariental; ☎ 063 240515; m 081 128 2601; f 063 242418. Sadly, the cheerful yellow & blue self-catering cottages at River Chalets were destroyed by floods in 2006. In excess of 1.7m of muddy water filled every building in a matter of hours & the pragmatic owners have been forced to completely rebuild as a result. The new chalets are likely to have been erected by the time you read this, in which case it's a well-priced option located on the west side of the main B1, as it effectively bypasses Mariental. The rooms will continue to concentrate on families & small groups, with each accommodating 3 or 5 people, & all having braai facilities.

✖ **WHERE TO EAT** If you're staying at one of the hotels, then it is easiest to eat there: both have (or had) restaurants in keeping with their general styles. For those just passing through, the three main garages have facilities to bite-and-run. The Engen garage at the north end of town has the **Bambi** take-away adjacent to it, serving pies and simple meals; the virtually neighbouring BP garage now boasts a **Star** take-away; while on the main road the slick Engen garage has a more extensive **Wimpy** with tables and menus. This serves what you'd find in any Wimpy across the world, opens late into the evening, and is arguably the smartest place in town.

GETTING ORGANISED Mariental is an efficient market town, with banks, garages, post office, police station and a couple of supermarkets, including a large Spar at the entrance to town by the BP garage and an OK Grocer supermarket on Ernst Stumpfe Road to the east of the railway line. It is worth remembering that virtually everything in town is closed over the weekend, with the exception of the OK Grocer and the fuel stations.

The railway line from Windhoek south bisects the town, allowing only one crossing point (Michael van Niekerk Street). Two of the **banks**, the Bank Windhoek and the Standard Bank, are on the western side, while the First National Bank is just over the tracks. There is an additional First National ATM at the Engen petrol station on the B1.

Most of the **fuel stations** are on the west side of town, close to the B1, but there is also a **Supa Quick Auto centre** across the railway line, at the junction of Fifth Street and Ernst Stumpfe Road. Having crossed the tracks, you take a left on to Drieboom Street, then follow the road round onto Ernst Stumpfe Road. Turn left onto Khoicas Street, just before the magistrates court, to reach the **post office**, and turn left just after the magistrates court and police **station** (☎ 063 10111) onto Wolfaardt Street to get to the **hospital** (☎ 063 242092), imaginatively located on Hospital Street. There is a **tourist information office** (*open Mon–Fri only*) housed within the municipal offices.,

HARDAP DAM RECREATIONAL RESORT

(*Entry N$40 per adult per day, & N$10 per car, under 16s free*) About 250km from Windhoek, and less than 25km from Mariental, lies the Hardap Dam, creating Namibia's largest manmade lake. This dams the upper reaches of the Fish River to

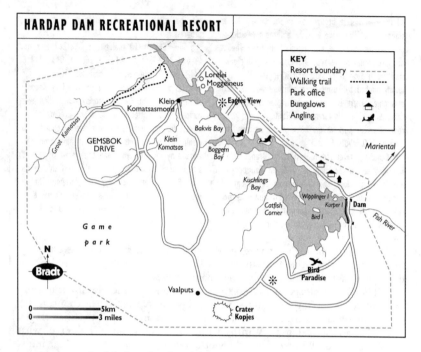

HARDAP DAM RECREATIONAL RESORT

KEY
- Resort boundary `-------`
- Walking trail `·········`
- Park office
- Bungalows
- Angling

Labels on map: Lorelei, Moggeineus, Klein Komatsasmond, Eagles View, Bakvis Bay, Boggem Bay, Groot Komatsas, GEMSBOK DRIVE, Klein Komatsas, Kuchlings Bay, Catfish Corner, Wipplinger I, Kurper I, Bird I, Dam, Fish River, Mariental, Game park, N, Bradt, Vaalputs, Bird Paradise, Crater Kopjes

Scale: 0—5km / 0—3 miles

---

provide water for Mariental and various irrigation projects. It is surrounded by a small reserve, complete with restcamp.

GETTING THERE Hardap has clear signposts from the main B1, about 10km north of Mariental. The entrance gate is 6km from the road, and then the office is a further 3km. There is no public transport here, though in the high season hitchhiking in and out of the restcamp from the B1 turn-off should prove straightforward.

THE DAM The origin of Hardap's name is uncertain. It is probably derived from a Nama name for a big pool that was flooded by the dam, though the word also means 'nipple' (or possibly 'wart') in the Nama language – and one of the rounded hills around the dam is said to resemble a female breast.

The dam wall is 39.2m high and 865m long and was completed in 1963. It holds a maximum of about 300 million cubic metres of water, and covers around 25km². Though it doesn't often fill, it will when the rains are exceptional. It filled to 97.7% of its capacity in early 1997, forcing the sluice gates to be opened for the first time in 20 years. If they had remained shut, it would have flooded Mariental with the next rains. (This same 1997 season also saw Sossusvlei flooded for the first time in a decade.)

Far more serious consequences arose in 2006, when the exceptional rains in February caused the dam waters to rise so high that the authorities feared that the wall would burst. The decision was taken to open the gates to ease the pressure, but too much water was released, flooding the surrounding plain and leaving Mariental under about 1.7m of water, with massive consequential damage.

FLORA AND FAUNA Hardap stands in the central highlands of Namibia, and its rolling hilly landscape is mostly covered in low-growing bushes and stunted trees. Its river courses tend to be thickly vegetated, often having dense, taller stands of camelthorn and buffalo-thorn trees.

The most interesting birds to be seen here are often Cape species, at the northern edge of their range, like the cinnamon-breasted warbler, the Karoo eremomela or the uncommon Sclater's lark. Others are Namibian species towards the southern edge of their ranges, like the delightful rosy-faced lovebirds.

Hardap's larger game includes Hartmann's mountain zebra, oryx, kudu, springbok, eland and red hartebeest, most concentrated in the mountainous section of the park. Cheetah used to occur, but they thrived and escaped onto neighbouring farms, so now they have been excluded. This is classic leopard country, hilly and thickly bushed – so these are the dominant predators, though they are seldom seen. There are no lion, elephant or buffalo.

A handful of black rhino were relocated to Hardap from Damaraland in 1990, and they have settled up towards the north of the park. They were introduced to the west side of the lake, but one has been reported as crossing the lake to settle into a territory on the eastern side.

THE RESORT Surrounding the lake is about 251km² of protected national park, home to a variety of game. The lake itself is about 30km long, and effectively splits this area into two. On the northeast shore is a narrow strip within which the restcamp perches, on cliffs overlooking the lake. A scenic drive links several picnic sites and lookout points along its length. Within the park, watch out for deep sand on the roads, which can make driving – especially in a 2WD – quite hazardous.

On the southwest side of the lake, the reserve stretches far from the lake's shore, and is game park, veined by game drives and a few short hiking trails. Note that Hardap becomes very hot during the summer, and very cold during the winter. From chilly recollections of its windy campsite in September, I'd hate to camp here when it's *really* cold!

Where to stay and eat

🏠 **Hardap Dam Restcamp** (50 bungalows, camping) 📞 063 240381; f 063 242285; reservations 📞 061 2857200; f 061 224900; e reservations@ nwr.com.na; www.nwr.com.na. There has been little change here in over a decade, & no apparent investment in upgrades, yet things have not degenerated either, & rooms remain clean & functional. The camp tends to be used by university groups & Windhoek residents escaping for a weekend's fishing. Accommodation ranges from a dormitory to several 2-bed bungalows with a kitchen area, fridge, hotplate, shower & carport, to 5-bed suites with AC, equipped kitchen, TV & phone.

Bedding & towels are provided, but no crockery or cutlery. Private braai sites with lovely views across the dam do much to make up for the non-matching furniture, old floor tiles & basic motel interiors. If self-catering isn't your thing, there is a restaurant with superb views over the lake (open 07.00–09.00, 12.00–14.00, 18.00–21.00; meals must be ordered at least 30 mins before closing time). A kiosk by the adjacent pool sells drinks & crisps 08.00–17.00.
2-bed bungalow N$300, 4-bed chalet N$400, 4-bed luxury suite N$800; camping N$50 per site plus N$30/15 per adult/child (max 8 people)

Getting organised Unlike some resorts, Hardap is open all year and doesn't lock its guests out at night. You can enter and leave at any hour of the day or night – though you can pay for accommodation only during office hours.

There's a fuel station, a small shop, and the kiosk mentioned above. However, if you intend to cook, then stock up in Mariental.

What to see and do Hardap can get busy at the weekend, with city dwellers escaping for a weekend of fishing or relaxing, but it's generally quiet during the week. The game park is small but quite good, and the hike is excellent. In the past, a ferry service has run across the lake, but this is currently not operational.

Namibia's native fish When paying your entry fees at reception, don't forget to take a glance at the aquaria there – displaying some of Namibia's freshwater fish, including those in the lake.

If you have a special interest in fish, then Namibia's Freshwater Fish Institute is just near the park entrance, on the left as you drive in. This is not a tourist sight, but a research and breeding centre, where the scientists sometimes welcome visitors who are fascinated by fish. Given that several Namibian species are endemic to small areas, even just to one lake or pan, this work of protecting and monitoring fish species is important.

The game park If larger vertebrates are of more interest, then head for the game park. This means leaving the restcamp and taking a right turn before getting to the gates to the park – then driving over the dam wall. Get a map from the park office, as there are over 60km of gravel roads for game drives.

Branching off the far circular game drive in the Great Komatsas area (the Gemsbok Drive) is a marked hiking trail of 15km. This isn't strenuous and takes about four to five hours – though there is a shorter variation, using a shortcut, of 9km which takes two to three hours. There is no dangerous game around apart from a few black rhino – so keep vigilant for the thud of heavy feet, and read the *Rhino* section on page 112 before starting.

EAST OF MARIENTAL AND THE B1: THE KALAHARI

The Kalahari Desert often surprises people when they first see it. It is very different from the Namib. First of all, remember that the Kalahari is not a true desert: it receives more rain than a true desert should. The Kalahari is a *fossil* desert. *Chapter 3*, page 35, gives a more complete explanation, but don't expect to find tall Sossusvlei-style dunes devoid of greenery here. The Kalahari's dunes are very different. They are often equally beautiful, but usually greener and less stark, and with this vegetation comes the ability to support more flora and fauna – including bat-eared foxes – than a true desert.

Thus a few days spent in a Kalahari environment adds another dimension to a trip to Namibia, and provides game-viewing away from the ever-popular Etosha, or the lush reserves of the Caprivi.

GUEST FARMS AND LODGES To the east of Mariental, on the Kalahari side, there are several excellent lodges/guest farms, as well as the flying centre at Bitterwasser, which is a major attraction in its own right for accomplished glider pilots.

When the Namibian–South African border is reopened at Mata Mata, then the area southeast of Mariental will open up to guests, as more people pass though. The huge Kgalagadi Transfrontier Park is Africa's first 'Peace Park' – a truly integrated trans-national wildlife reserve – although perhaps to the chagrin of the Kalahari Gemsbok's small band of existing devotees, who have always regarded this out-of-the-way corner as one of the best national parks on the subcontinent.

Kalahari Anib Lodge (55 rooms, camping) 061 230066; f 061 251863; e info@ gondwana-desert-collection.com; www.gondwana-desert-collection.com. This once privately run small lodge set among the Kalahari dunes has been reinvented in recent years, creating a large new lodge attracting both tour groups & independent travellers. It is situated about 10km north of Mariental, around 23km east of the B1, on the C20 towards Stampriet & Aranos.

The restaurant & chalets are arranged around a shaded courtyard with a large swimming pool. Of the rooms, 36 with a private veranda are available for tour groups. The remaining rooms, for independent travellers, are set slightly apart, with views of the open Kalahari savanna & with a separate swimming pool. For campers, there are 3 exclusive sites equipped with private bathrooms & BBQ facilities. Two hours before sunset, a sundowner game drive allows guests to witness the attractions of the Kalahari.

N$580/465 sgl/pp sharing , B&B; camping N$100 pp. Lunch N$70, dinner N$150. Game drive N$125 pp.

🏠 **Bagatelle Kalahari Game Ranch** (10 rooms)
📞 063 240982; f 063 241252; e info@bagatelle-kalahari-gameranch.com; www.bagatelle-kalahari-gameranch.com; reservations 📞 061 224712; 061 224217; e reservations@resdes.com.na; www.resdes.com.na. Owned & run by the delightful Fred & Onie, Bagatelle is a homely ranch, where they farmed sheep & cattle until recently building the lodge & creating a 7,000ha game reserve. Straddling the B1268, 50km north of Mariental, it's a convenient & comfortable stop amid rolling, linear dunes. The original farmhouse has been converted into a cosy lounge, restaurant & library area, & there is a pool & boma for lazy afternoons & casual dining. Four of the chalets are wooden & raised on stilts atop a russet sand ridge, whilst the others line the inter-dune 'street' & are imaginatively constructed using insulating bales of straw. The interiors are similar in both locations: dark leather furniture, African objets d'art, wicker lampshades, comfortable beds, wooden chests, animal-print fabrics & an honesty bar. The only notable difference is that baths are found only in the ridge rooms; the others have just showers. The Strohbale rooms, used as family rooms, have a convertible sofa bed which can sleep 2 younger children or 1 adult.

Nature drives take place morning & afternoon, giving guests the opportunity to see springbok, kudu, oryx (including a very relaxed one hanging out in the shady carport), hartebeest, giraffe, eland, steenbok, wildebeest & ostrich. There are also 4 cheetah kept in a 12ha enclosure beside the main lodge, as part of a Cheetah Conservation Fund project. For many, however, the game highlight at Bagatelle is the habituated meerkat population which parades around the chalets in search of grubs, providing engaging pre-breakfast entertainment & great photo opportunities.

Dune chalet N$850, straw-bale chalet N$750, both pp sharing, B&B; children 6–14 N$450; under 6 N$350. Lunch N$75, dinner N$135. Scenic drive N$120 pp. Guided walk N$95 pp.

🏠 **Intu Afrika Kalahari Game Reserve** 📞 061 375300; f 061 375333; e intu@leadinglodges.com; www.intu@leadinglodges.com. The small (10,000ha)

private reserve of Intu Afrika has been fortunate in having backing to promote & sustain a sizeable wildlife reserve, as well as to develop an interesting project with the help of a small Bushman community. It is located on the D1268, 110km north of Mariental, just south of the C21 (or north of the C20), & is clearly signposted from the B1 whether heading north or south.

There are 3 accommodation options: Zebra Kalahari Lodge, Camelthorn Lodge & the newly renovated Suricate Tented Lodge. Each is run individually, with its own kitchen, bar & management, though activities are common to all.

The original Zebra Lodge building is substantial, with comfortable furniture in its large airy lounge, a well-stocked bar, & enormous tree-trunk carvings adorning the reception area. At the front is a stylish swimming pool, overlooked by some marvellously knurled old *Acacia erioloba* trees. There are 4 twin rooms on either side of the main building, each modern & functional with a minimum of clutter. The floors are tiled, the bathroom's en suite, & there's a phone in each room. Set a short distance away are 5 luxurious split-level bungalows, each with a sitting area & a bedroom — popular with small families, or as suites.

The landscape at Intu Afrika is classic Kalahari: deep red longitudinal dunes, usually vegetated, separated by lighter clay inter-dune valleys covered in grass, trees & shrubs. The area's larger game includes giraffe, oryx, blue & black wildebeest, Burchell's zebra, & springbok — but it is the smaller animals that are the stars. The reserve seems to have a high density (or at least a visible number) of bat-eared foxes, & some entertaining groups of meerkats (suricats); the sight of a group of meerkats foraging under the guard of 'sentries' is a real delight. The sentries balance upright on their hind legs, while their keen eyes scan the area around. Neither of these social creatures is common, yet they seem to thrive here. Game drives & related activities such as birdwatching trips are available from all parts of the reserve, including the campsite.

One other aspect of the lodge that it promotes is its Bushman project — set up by anthropologists Bets & Michael Daiber. In late 1996, a small community of about 40 !Xoo Bushmen decided to support this project, & relocated to the reserve. The project's aim was to: 'empower the [Bushmen] community to regain their dignity and pride by creating employment and cultural activities which utilise traditional Bushmen skills in order to generate money for their community ... including game guiding, tracking, camp supervising and craft making.'

For the visitor, interactions with Bushmen start by being guided on early morning walks by community members, who not only can point out some of the wildlife, but also explain their traditional way of life, including collecting & storing food. You can also buy their crafts at Zebra Lodge. Six families now live here, & many of the children go to a nearby school, while other members of the community are employed on the reserve.

Compared with other lodges in the region, rates at Intu Afrika are very high, a reflection as much on its location in a beautiful private reserve as on the standards that prevail overall.
Zebra Lodge N$810–1,480 DBB; Suricate Tented Lodge N$1,050–1,250, all pp sharing. Sgl supplements apply at lodges.

🏠 **Bitterwasser Lodge & Flying Centre** (22 bungalows, 13 rondavels) P Bag 13003, Windhoek; ☏ 063 265300; f 063 265355; e bitterwa@ mweb.com.na; www.bitterwasser.com. South of Uhlenhorst, on the C15, about 59km from the B1, this specialist lodge caters to glider pilots up to world-class level. Note that this is not a school for gliding – it is a place for those who know how. Pilots often stay for weeks, & have broken so many records that there's an avenue of palm trees lining the way to the airfield, where each palm was planted to commemorate a record. Every year, the avenue grows.

Bitterwasser has a range of aircraft available for hire, but most pilots prefer to ship out their own craft by container for the season, which runs from Oct–Feb (though the lodge is open all year round). Gliding aside, there are opportunities for swimming, hot-air ballooning & game drives.

The lodge has a range of comfortable bungalows sleeping up to 4 people; all have en-suite facilities, AC & 24-hour electricity. Rondavels are more basic, with simple furniture & a central ablution block. There are also rooms in the adjacent Dune House. If you're a serious glider, then email them for precise details of their facilities & prices, or check out their website – though note that much of this is in German.
Bungalow € 155–219/110–155 sgl/pp sharing. Rondavel € 78/67 sgl/pp sharing. B/kfast € 5, dinner € 15. Note that rates are quoted in euro.

🏠 **Auob Lodge** (26 rooms) ☏ 063 250101; f 063 250102; e auob@ncl.com.na; www.namibialodges.com; central reservations ☏ 061 240375/374750; f 061 256 598. Situated on the C15, about 6km north of Gochas, Auob Lodge stands in the Kalahari, close to the dry River Auob, within 80km² of its own land. It also has its own airstrip, co-ordinates S24.49 E18.46. Despite the name, the place has the atmosphere of a continental hotel, with heavy furniture, a bar, pool room, lounge & separate restaurant. Rooms, located around a swimming pool, are comfortable, with ceiling fans & en-suite shower & toilet, but don't expect much in the way of frills. The lodge offers horseriding (not suitable for novices), quad-biking, & game drives amongst typical Kalahari game species, including giraffe & wildebeest, plus blesbok, introduced from South Africa.
N$515/380 sgl/pp sharing, B&B. Dinner N$120.

UHLENHORST North of Mariental, this dot on the map seems little more than a large farm. It marks a petrol station and a general farm store, even if the latter has the farm's own workers in mind, rather than the odd lost tourist. However, you might be surprised to learn that in the 1930s and '40s there were two hotels, several shops, a post office and a bank here. Uhlenhorst is typical of many small Namibian towns that were once important, but faded with the advent of communications and good roads into mere shadows of themselves. If you come this way, then stop at the store for excellent homemade *biltong* – and perhaps to see the owners' large collection of pet ducks and even a few swans. Not the obvious pets in the Kalahari. With more time to spare, seek out the nearby farm, Jena, which is on the west side of the C15 or MR33 between Uhlenhorst and Hoachanas. From here Heidi von Hase runs a cottage embroidery industry, the **Anin project** (*anin* means 'birds' in the local Nama language), employing about 300 women of the 'Red Nation' Nama people. They handmake a wide and intricate range of embroidery and linen, including bed linen and tableware. All work from home and come from in and around the tiny village of Hoachanas – nearby at the junction of the C21 and C15 (MR33). Crafts like these are increasingly benefiting the economies of some of Namibia's poorer areas – so go on, buy something while you're here! For details, or to make an appointment to visit the farm shop, contact Anin Namibia (*P Bag 13094, Windhoek;* \ *063 265331;* f *063 265332;* e *anin@mweb.com.na; www.anin.com.na*). If you're not passing through, seek out their stall at the craft centre in Windhoek, or at Casa Anin in Swakopmund.

STAMPRIET TO GOCHAS Stampriet itself has nothing of interest to drivers except a small fuel station – useful should you be running low – and Gochas likewise, but the C15 road between the two small towns makes an interesting alternative to the B1 if you're driving south from one of the above lodges. Running parallel to the Auob River, it passes through a fertile stretch of farmland. Perhaps of greatest interest, though, are the ground squirrels that inhabit the banks lining the road; it's a great place to stop and watch these intriguing animals as they go about their daily routines. From Gochas, it is a straight drive on the C18, a good, empty road, to rejoin the B1 near Gibeon.

For those without a vehicle who are tempted in this direction, Starline runs a bus from Mariental to Gochas via Stampriet every Wednesday, arriving in Stampriet at 09.30 and Gochas at 11.00, and departing at 12.30 and 14.30 respectively. A second service links Mariental with Stampriet and then further east to Aranos on Tuesday and Friday, again arriving in Stampriet at 09.30, but leaving at 15.30.

THE ROAD FROM MARIENTAL TO KEETMANSHOOP

Between Mariental and Keetmanshoop is a 221km stretch of tar road that most visitors see at speed. However, a few places are worth knowing about as you hurry past.

GIBEON About 6km west of the B1, this sprawling community lies in a valley. Its sole claim to fame is as the site of what is thought to be the world's heaviest shower of meteorites some 600 million years ago. Many of these are now displayed in Windhoek's Post Street Mall (see page 151), while a smaller specimen may be seen at the museum in Rehoboth.

ASAB Almost halfway between Mariental and Keetmanshoop is a tiny place beside the road: Asab. There's a fuel station, although supplies cannot be guaranteed, and a sparsely stocked shop. It's a useful spot for emergencies, and the place to branch off the main road if you are heading to Mukurob.

MUKUROB Known as 'the Finger of God', Mukurob was once an immense rock pinnacle, which balanced on a narrow neck of rock and towered 34m above the surrounding plains. It collapsed around 8 December 1988, leaving a sizeable pile of rubble. Its demise caused much speculation at the time, as the finger's existence was linked to divine approval – and the country was in the process of becoming independent. Initially it was claimed that God was displeased with contemporary developments in this independence process. Later, right-wing extremists were blamed rather than God. Eventually, though, theories linked its fall firmly with the shock waves from the large Armenian earthquake of 7 December. To drive to where it stood, turn east off the B1 onto the D1066, just south of Asab, and follow the signs for about 23km. To see it as it once was, drop into the tourist information office at Keetmanshoop and have a look at the replica.

TSES Two-thirds of the way towards Keetmanshoop, opposite the turning to Berseba and Brukkaros, Tses is a small township of around 1,000 inhabitants on the east of the road, and a stop on the line for both Intercape Mainliner buses and the Starline train between Windhoek and Keetmanshoop. As in any small, poor country township, visitors passing through are treated as something of a curiosity, but made welcome. There's a post office, a small trading store across the railway, a Catholic school, and a fuel station – which occasionally runs out, so don't let your fuel supply run too low in this area.

BRUKKAROS Rising to 650m, the volcanic crater of Brukkaros towers over the expanse of bare, flat plains that surround it. It's a classic volcano shape, easily visible west of the B1. Early this century the Germans used the eastern side of the crater as the base for a heliograph. Then later, in the early 1930s, the Smithsonian Institute built a solar observatory on the western side, taking advantage of the clear air and lack of artificial lights nearby. Both the Germans and the observatory have now gone, and the skies are as clear as ever – so it's a great place to explore and possibly camp.

Getting there About 80km north of Keetmanshoop, and just south of the turning to Tses, turn west onto the M98 (signposted simply 'Berseba'). The road crosses the Fish River after about 19km, and it's worth a short stop to check out the waterbirds, including sacred ibis, that congregate here. In late afternoon, you may even spot a family of baboons crossing the river. After a further 19km, just before you reach Berseba, turn north towards the volcano onto the D3904. Though this looks like a short distance, it'll be 9km or so on a flat road until you are at the gates, and only then do you start to climb the volcano near the end of the road. Getting here without your own vehicle would mean taking the twice-weekly bus to Berseba (arriving from Keetmanshoop at 11.00 on Monday and Friday, and departing at 12.15) but you'd almost certainly have to walk from there.

There's an entrance fee of N$15 pp for day visitors, plus N$10 for a vehicle. The money collected benefits the people of the surrounding villages.

Where to stay

Brukkaros Campsite Reservations ☎ 061 255977; f 061 222647; e office@nacobta.com.na; www.nacobta.com.na. Before the road deteriorates, there's a small campsite with individual BBQ places, basic toilets & bucket showers. Above this, you need a 4x4 to reach the second camping area. Neither firewood nor water are available so come fully equipped – there's a small store in Berseba if you're out of the basics. There's also a public telephone at the gate in case of emergency. *N$35 pp.*

What to see and do From the 4x4 campsite, a footpath leads to the eroded edge of the southern crater's southern lip. The path here was made while the observatory was being constructed, and it goes over the lip and into the crater, taking about 40 minutes, then continues up to the old observatory just below the western rim after an hour or so. The rim itself is a very short scramble away. Guided walks are in theory available for a small fee.

You can hike around here, or just sit and watch the dust-devils twist their way for miles around as the sun goes down. It is a superb place to sleep out under the stars, which you will probably never see more clearly.

BERSEBA The nearest town to Brukkaros, Berseba is one of the region's oldest settlements – notable for having had a Rhenish missionary, Samuel Hahn, based there as early as 1850. Now it remains a large though poor settlement, surviving by subsistence farming. This area often receives very little rain, and agriculture of any kind is difficult. There are a couple of shops for essentials and a fuel pump at the end of the road, though don't rely on the latter.

Continuing south on the B1, the road remains level and straight. If you're camping and hoping to stop before Keetmanshoop, it may be worth considering Susan Hulme's somewhat unusual site 22km to the north of the town:

🏠 **Garas Quivertree Park & Restcamp** \/f 063 223217; e morkel@namibnet.com. There's a great sense of humour here, with numerous model figures lining the 1km drive from the B1 to the campsite. Although there *is* a campsite, with some very basic (but nevertheless clean) toilet & shower facilities, the real appeal is the rather eclectic mix of traditional huts & other artefacts that are displayed around the place almost in junkyard fashion. There are quivertrees too, as you would expect from the name, & several aloe plants. Wood & water are available, but otherwise you need to be entirely self sufficient. *Camping N$35 pp. Day visitors N$10 pp plus N$5 per vehicle.*

KEETMANSHOOP

Pronounced 'Keet-mans-verp', which is often shortened in slang to just 'Keetmans', Keetmanshoop lies about 480km south of Windhoek at an altitude of 1,000m. The tar roads from Lüderitz, South Africa and Windhoek meet here, making it the hub of southern Namibia's road network, as well as the administrative centre of this region.

Originally there was a Nama settlement on the banks of the seasonal Swartmodder River here, also known as Swartmodder. Then, in 1866, the Rhenish Missionary Society sent Johan Schröder here from their established station at Berseba. He organised the building of a church and named it Keetmanshoop (which means 'Keetman's hope'), after Johan Keetman, one of the rich benefactors who had paid for the building.

In 1890 that church was swept away by a freak flood, but a new one, built on higher ground, was completed five years later. This was disused for years, but restored and declared a monument in 1978. Now it shelters the town's museum, so at least visit this, even if you see nothing else here.

GETTING THERE

By air Keetmanshoop's small airport is found by following Sam Nujoma Drive (Kaiser Street) west and north through town, past the caravan park, and out the other side. There are currently no scheduled flights, although it is possible for charters to land here. In case the situation should change, it is worth checking with Air Namibia (see page 148).

By car Keetmanshoop is situated at the hub of the road network in southern Namibia, linked to Windhoek, South Africa and Lüderitz by good tar roads.

By bus Intercape Mainliner runs a good service linking Windhoek and Cape Town, via Keetmanshoop. Buses leave the Engen Garage on Lafenis at 22.45 on Monday, Wednesday, Friday and Sunday heading south, and then at midnight on Monday, Wednesday, Friday and Saturday going north. Fares cost around N$430 one way to Cape Town and N$255 to Windhoek, and tickets must be booked in advance, either at the local office at the Engen garage on Lafenis Avenue or through another agent (see pages 104–5 for details).

The Starline bus service that used to link Keetmanshoop with towns throughout the south is no longer operational, leaving towns to the west of the town effectively cut off from public transport.

By train Keetmanshoop is linked by train services to Windhoek and also to Ariamsvlei, on the South African border, and through to Upington. Trains run

10

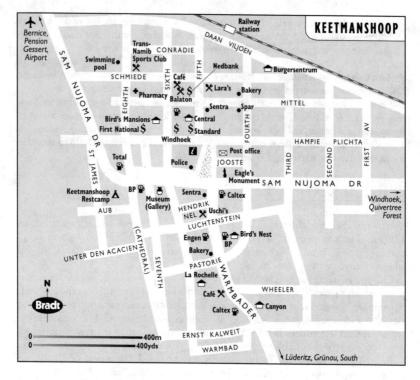

between Keetmanshoop and Windhoek every day except Saturday, arriving at 16.30 and departing at 18.50. On two days per week, Wednesday and Saturday, trains depart for Ariamsvlei at 08.50, arriving back the following day at 16.30. See *Chapter 6*, pages 101–3, for details, or call TransNamib in Keetmanshoop (✆ *063 292202/2209230*).

WHERE TO STAY

🏠 **Central Lodge** (19 rooms) Fifth Av; ✆ 063 225850; f 063 223532; e clodge@iway.na; www.central-lodge.com. When George Roux opened the elegant Central Lodge in 2001, he plugged a big gap in the market. A breath of fresh air in Keetmanshoop, the Central is just that – central. Its narrow entrance leads through the restaurant to a spacious courtyard, complete with fountain, around which are set light, welcoming rooms. Each is well appointed, with en-suite shower, TV, phone, AC/heating, telephone & tea/coffee-making facilities. Three luxury rooms also boast a jacuzzi.

Beyond the courtyard is a swimming pool surrounded by a grassy area with tables & chairs. In the main building, the stylish & modern restaurant serves the standard fare of steaks, fish & crayfish. Alongside is a small bar, while outside, secure parking is available for visitors' vehicles. *N$240–260/380–400 sgl/dbl, B&B.*

🏠 **Canyon Hotel** (70 rooms) Warmbader Rd; ✆ 063 223361; f 063 223714; e info@canyon-namibia.com; www.canyon-namibia.com. Time has not dealt kindly with Keetmanshoop's best hotel, but when visited in 2006 it was being renovated. In the meantime, the service remains friendly, & the rooms, whilst they could be anywhere in the world, are comfortable, with TVs, direct-dial telephones, AC & simple coffee machines. En-suite bathrooms have showers &, downstairs, hairdryers.

Around the hotel you'll find a restaurant, a bar, & a bistro serving light meals. There's also a large outdoor pool & a gym, & an internet café is in hand. *From N$425 pp sharing, B&B.*

🏠 **Bird's Mansions Hotel** (23 rooms) Sixth Av; ✆ 063 221711; f 063 221730; e birdsmansions@iway.na; www.birdsaccommodation.com. In the centre of town, Bird's Mansions is linked to Bird's Nest B&B, & friendly service is the hallmark. Large rooms

with new carpets & fans are off the courtyard at the back, while others are located in the main building. All share the same facilities, though: TV, phone & AC. The airy restaurant offers a varied menu of fish, game, steak & pasta, while at the rear of the hotel is a new lapa with heated swimming pool, eating area & dance floor. There's also an internet café, & off-street parking behind the hotel (entrance on Seventh St).
N$370/520/700 sgl/dbl/family, B&B.

⌂ **Bird's Nest B&B** (10 rooms) 16 Pastorie St; ☎ 063 222906; e birdnest@iafrica.com.na; www.birdsaccommodation.com. The Bird's Nest is an excellent little B&B close to the centre of Keet, & under the same ownership as Bird's Mansions. Rooms are fairly small, but light & modern, with attractive fabrics & en-suite showers or baths. All have AC/heating, ceiling fans, TV, phone & facilities for making hot drinks. Outside, the gardens are well tended, underlying the care that goes into this place.
N$340/480/660 sgl/dbl/family, B&B.

⌂ **La Rochelle** (7 rooms) 12 Sixth Av; ☎ 063 223845; m 081 235 1871/081 216 7979; f 063 224208. The cheerful new paint job on this 100-year-old house reflects the new ownership of Petro & Joubert de Witt, who took it over in 2006. Rooms vary in size, & include 2 family units — one sleeping 4 in one room, the other with 2 separate bedrooms each with their own bathroom & interleading door. All are en suite, with remote TV, tea/coffee facilities, & AC. Outside is a small pool & a pleasant rocky garden, plus secure parking.
N$150/300/380–420 sgl/dbl/family. B/fast N$30 pp.

⌂ **Pension Gessert** (7 rooms) 138 13th St, Westdene; ☎/f 063 223892; e gesserts@

iafrica.com.na. This quiet little residential B&B with its pretty garden is in the Westdene suburb. To reach it, head west & then northwest on Sam Nujoma Dr (Kaiser St), crossing the railway line. Then turn sharp left into Westdene, & right into 19th Av. 13th St is the third turning on the left. The place is friendly & professional.

Attractive rooms have en-suite facilities & AC, & there is a small swimming pool that you can use. B/fast is provided, & other meals are available on request.
N$330/460/590 sgl/dbl/family, B&B.

⌂ **Bernice Beds** (5 rooms) 129 10th St; ☎ 063 224851; m 081 124 6278; f 063 224852, e bernice@iway.na. Also in the suburb of Westdene, this small pension set in attractive gardens has been taken over recently as well, by Stef & Christi Coetzee. As for Pension Gessert, above, take the road to the northwest towards the airport, cross over the bridge & turn left at the lights, then left again into 10th St. Dbl & family rooms all have TV, AC/heating & en-suite showers, & there's safe parking. Pleasant & welcoming, this place offers good-value accommodation.
N$190/290 sgl/dbl, family N$390 (sleeps 3), N$480 (sleep 4) & N$550 (sleeps 5), all B&B.

⌂ **Keetmanshoop Restcamp** Eighth Av; ☎ 063 221265; f 063 222835. This has been one of Namibia's best municipal sites for years. Inside protective coils of razor wire lie clean ablution blocks surrounded by grass lawns (easily pierced by tent-pegs), & there's lots of space for cars & caravans on the gravel drives that surround the grass. It's a very good site, if you are happy to camp in town.
N$46 per site, plus N$23 per vehicle.

✖ **WHERE TO EAT** Keetmanshoop's best place for a good meal is the **Central Lodge** (see page 194). Both the **Canyon Hotel** and **Bird's Mansions** also have restaurants, the former rather soulless and typical of a large hotel. Both have wide-ranging menus that include a couple of vegetarian options.

Once you've run the gauntlet of the very austere bar at the front, **Lara's Restaurant** (☎ 063 222233; open Mon–Sat 10.00–14.00), at the corner of Fifth Avenue and Schmiede Street, is an unexpectedly cheerful spot without any pretensions. Portions are huge, and it's chips with everything, but the steaks are excellent and prices are reasonable. **Uschi's** (☎ 063 222445; open Mon–Thu 07.00–20.00, Fri 08.00–20.00, Sat 08.00–13.00), at the corner of Hendrik Nel Street and Fifth Avenue, offers a variety of snacks and light meals, including an adventurous pizza menu – but don't come in a hurry for the latter. **Balaton** (☎ 063 222539) on Mittel Street opens all day as a take-away and simple restaurant serving spicy Hungarian cuisine: very warming and ideal for cold winter evenings. The Germanic **Trans-Namib Sports Club** on Schmiede Street serves pub grub and draught beer.

On the snack front, most of the proliferation of garages have some form of café attached, serving pretty standard fare of pies, burgers and cold drinks – useful if you're pushed for time.

GETTING ORGANISED Keetmanshoop could well be vying for the record for the greatest number of **fuel stations** per head of population! It's also a good place to visit banks and shops and get organised. If you enter on Sam Nujoma Drive (Kaiser Street), then you will find most of these one block over to your right, on Hampie Plichta (Fenschel) Street – which runs parallel to Sam Nujoma Drive. Here are the First National, Bank Windhoek and Standard **banks**, while the main **supermarkets**, including Sentra and Spar, are on Mittel Street, one block to the north, as is Nedbank. Next to Uschi's restaurant is a second branch of Sentra. **Camping supplies** are available from LTL on Hampie Plichta Street, opposite Central Lodge. For souvenirs, it may be worth checking out the craft stalls laid out by the side of the road as you leave the B1.

If you want to stop for a brief break, then the small grassy park standing between the tourist office and the post office is ideal. You can relax and watch both the townspeople and your vehicle at the same time.

In an emergency, the main hospital (✆ 063 223388) is on the main road as you're heading out of town; this is also the number for the ambulance. The town's pharmacy, Khabuser Apteek, is on Mittel Street (✆ 063 223309), and the police may be contacted on ✆ 063 10111.

Tourist information Southern Tourist Forum (STF) (*Fifth St;* ✆ *063 221266;* f *063 223818; open Mon–Fri, 07.30–12.30 & 13.30–16.30*) Opposite the main post office, over a grassy square, this bears a grand name for a tourist office, but it aims to promote the whole region and the staff can be helpful. If you do pop in, look out for the replica of Mukurob, the Finger of God (see page 191).

WHAT TO SEE AND DO Like many of Namibia's provincial towns, Keetmanshoop doesn't have a wealth of attractions in the town, though you could while away a couple of lazy hours visiting its museum, and the tourist office, which resides in perhaps the town's most historic building, the **Kaiserliches Postamt** – or Imperial Post Office. This was built in 1910 and is now a national monument.

Keetmanshoop Museum (*Sam Nujoma Dr;* ✆ *063 221256; open Mon–Fri 07.30–12.30, 13.30–16.30, but closed 16.00 on Fri; admission free, but donations welcome*) This centrally located old Rhenish Mission Church was built in 1895 to replace the original one that the floods destroyed. Now it is surrounded by rockeries and used as the town's museum. Don't ignore these rockeries though, as they are dotted with native plants, as well as old wagons, machinery and even a Nama hut. If you're not visiting the Quivertree Forest, then take a close look at the small trees here in the museum's garden.

Inside the church is a beautiful pulpit and an interesting collection of local memorabilia, including a selection of early cameras, photographs, and various implements that were used by past townspeople.

NEARBY GUEST FARMS AND LODGES

🏠 **Quivertree Forest Restcamp** (7 rooms, 8 bungalows, camping) 📞/f 063 222835; e quiver@iafrica.com.na. Some 14km from Keetmanshoop is the Quivertree (or Kokerboom) Forest (see opposite), which stands on privately owned farmland. To get here, take the C16 road towards Koës, & turn off on to the M29 (marked just 29 on the road).

The farm itself is owned by Coenie & Ingrid Nolte, who are helpful & informative hosts. Accommodation options are varied. En-suite rooms, including a family room, are in 2 separate houses, each with its own lounge & minibar, & one with a kitchen. In addition, there are comfortable self-catering bungalows, of a wonderful igloo design, all of which have en-suite facilities. Nearby is a BBQ area, tree-house style. There is also a tree-shaded campsite adjacent to the Quivertree Forest, with BBQ facilities & electricity.

It's also a great place for children, with a swimming pool, ingeniously converted from a large farm tank, & a trampoline, not to mention a family of meerkats & a pet warthog & a pet eland. Don't be put off by the cage behind the farm buildings; this is a holding area for cheetahs, which are permanently housed in separate enclosures of 15ha & 37ha respectively. Staying here is a good alternative to Keetmanshoop, & makes it easier to see the forest & the rocks around dawn & dusk, when the light is at its best for photography. N$465/770/1,035/1,625 sgl/dbl/trpl/family, DBB; N$365/560/735/1,125, B&B, N$273/385/458/663, self-catering. Camping N$70 pp.

⚑ Panorama Campsite (4 pitches) ✆ 063 225050. Campers seeking something a little more remote

may be interested in this simple site some 40km from Keetmanshoop on the C17 towards Koës. Each pitch has a table, hot water & braai, with ablution blocks close by & wood available on site, though you will need to bring all other provisions with you. There is a 16km 'high-vehicle' trail around the site, & a guided fossil 'trail', taking in the fossils of the huge mesosaurus that inhabited the freshwater lakes of Gondwanaland 270 million years ago. Stands of quivertrees are also a feature of this landscape, as are the giant dolorite rock formations. N$65 pp

⌂ Lafenis Lodge (19 bungalows, camping) ✆/f 063 224316; f 063 224309; e lafenislodge@iway.na. Just south of Keetmanshoop on the B1, about 2km from the junction with the B4 for Lüderitz, this is a simple, friendly restcamp with a rather unlikely Wild West theme and a small game park. It caters adequately for overnight stops. There's a campsite with electric hook-ups, a swimming pool & a small restaurant, & each of the small bungalows has AC. Bungalows from N$225 (1-bed) to N$730 (6-bed), B&B; backpackers N$125. Camping N$75 per site, plus N$55/25 per adult/child under 13.

EXCURSIONS FROM KEETMANSHOOP If you prefer to base yourself in a town, then the **Fish River Canyon** and **Brukkaros** can both become day trips from Keetmanshoop. However, each is a destination in its own right, and so they are covered separately. The two obvious excursions from town, the Quivertree Forest and the Giant's Playground, are almost adjacent. A little further afield, on the way to the Fish River Canyon via Seeheim, is Naute Dam, recently declared a recreational area.

Quivertree Forest and Giant's Playground (*Entrance N$20 pp, plus N$20 per car*)
Also known as the 'Kokerboomwoud', the Quivertree Forest is a dense stand of *Aloe dichotoma* tree-aloes, just 14km away from Keetmanshoop on the land of Gariganus Farm, owned by Coenie and Ingrid Nolte.

Take the B1 north for about one kilometre, then the C17 towards Koës, then left again onto the M29 shortly after this. These trees are found all over southern Namibia and the northern Cape, but in few places are so many seen together. (A second is a few kilometres south of Kenhardt, on the R27 in South Africa.)

Ideally drop in here around sunset or sunrise, when the light is at its best. These skeletal 'trees' make particularly striking photographs when the lighting of a fill-in flash is balanced against flaming sunset behind.

Just 5km further down the M29 are some marvellous balancing basalt rocks known as the Giant's Playground. Reminiscent of formations in Zimbabwe's Matobo Hills, these are more limited but still interesting.

Naute Dam Recreational Resort
Surrounded by low hills, and overlooked by the Klein Karas mountains, the lake created by Naute Dam is about 26km long and, at its widest, some 7km. The 470m-long dam was opened in 1972. Standing 37m above the riverbed, it holds back the water from the Naute River as it feeds into the Fish River to the southwest. From the main entrance, where there are picnic

QUIVERTREES

The quivertree or kokerboom, *Aloe dichotoma*, occurs sporadically over a large area of southern Namibia and the northern Cape, usually on steep rocky slopes. Its name refers to its supposed use by the Bushmen for making the quivers for their arrows – the inside of a dead branch consists of only a light, fibrous heart which is easily gouged out to leave a hollow tube.

The quivertree is specially adapted to survive in extremely arid conditions: its fibrous branches and trunk are used for water storage, as are its thick, succulent leaves, whilst water lost through transpiration is reduced by waxy coatings on the tree's outside surfaces. Additionally, in common with most desert-adapted flora, its growth rate is very slow.

tables and a small snack kiosk, there is a good vantage point over both the dam itself and the lake beyond with its cluster of small islands.

Not surprisingly, the lake has become a focus for numerous birds. There are opportunities for birdwatching from the viewpoint, but it is the reed-fringed sandy lakeshore to the south of the main entrance that is the real haven for waterbirds, with pelicans, herons, little egrets, cormorants and sacred ibis all in evidence. On the margins can be seen plenty of other species, including the blacksmith plover, African darter and African red-eyed bulbul.

Perhaps surprisingly, the game park remains in its infancy, but it is probably just a matter of time before this becomes an attraction in its own right.

Despite its obvious attractions, it seems that little investment has been put in to development of the resort to date. Instead, efforts have been concentrated on an irrigation project fed by water from the dam, leading to the production of dates for worldwide markets.

Getting there From Keetmanshoop, take the B4 west to Seeheim, then turn south onto the C12. The entrance to the resort is to the left, about 25km from Seeheim, just before the dam itself. Further south, just beyond the dam, is a second turning onto the D545, signposted Nautedam, which leads towards the southern lakeshore. This road heads straight towards the mountains for 13km, then you turn right by a farm, signposted 'camping area'. From here, you can choose whether to head for the lake (take the left fork) or the game park. Alternatively you can drive along the B4 for 31km, then turn left onto the B545 (before the Seeheim turn-off).

 Where to stay Although an area around the lake is officially designated as a campsite – there's a sign to that effect, anyway –there are no facilities here at all, so if you plan to camp you will have to bring everything with you. That said, it's a peaceful spot right by the lake, and a wonderful place for birdwatching. A small camping fee is payable at the main entrance.

THE DEEP SOUTH

South and east of Keetmanshoop, Namibia's central highlands start to flatten out towards the South Africa's Karoo, and the great sand-sheet of the Kalahari to the east. Many of the roads here are spectacular: vast and empty with enormous vistas. The C10 between Karasburg and the B1, and the D608, are particular favourites.

The towns here seem to have changed little in years. They vary from small to minute, and remind the outsider of a typical South African *dorp* (a small town). Expect some of them to be on the conservative side.

BETWEEN KEETMANSHOOP AND GRÜNAU

Where to stay The long straight road between the two towns is characterised by farmland, backed to the east by the Karas Mountains. In recent years, a number of guest farms along the road between Keetmanshoop and Grünau have opened their doors to visitors. The most established of these is the White House (which is also closest to Grünau), but others are worth considering. The following are listed in order of distance from Keetmanshoop.

Savanna Guest Farm (5 rooms) ☎/f 063 683127; f 063 262050; e savanna@iway.na. This 2,000ha farm in a beautiful setting at the foot of the Great Karas Mountains is run by Erich & Zelda von Schauroth. The turning is off the B1, 42km north of Grünau, opposite the D203.

En-suite rooms with AC are comfortable, though not luxurious, & have self-catering facilities. Many guests stay for days or even weeks at a time, for this is a place to discover for yourself the environment of a working sheep farm. Don't come expecting to be entertained, but if you enjoy walking & getting away from it all, this could be an ideal location. For added relaxation, there is a heated swimming pool, & in the evening a 3-course dinner with traditional farm cooking is available by arrangement. N$440/380 sgl/pp sharing, DBB. Self-catering & long-term rates available on request.

White House Guest Farm (5 rooms, 3 bungalows) ☎/f 063 262061; e withuis@iway.na. The turn-off to the White House has a clear signpost, about 11km north of Grünau, on the B1. The house itself lies 4km from the main road, on a working 15,000ha sheep farm which stretches to the distant mountains.

The best accommodation here is in a stunning old farmhouse with Oregon pine floors, high wooden ceilings, wide verandas, a huge kitchen & even an old radiogram. It was built in 1912 for £2,500, & bought by the present owner's grandfather in 1926 for £3,500. After its being used as a school, amongst other things, & falling into disuse, the present owners, Dolf & Kinna De Wet, began to renovate the house in 1995. They have done a superb job. Just sit down quietly to soak up the atmosphere & journey back to the first half of the 19th century.

Guests normally stay in one of a handful of beautiful old rooms here on a self-catering basis; the kitchen has a large fridge, gas cooker, & all crockery & utensils. This isn't luxurious (though it would have been 60 years ago), but it is comfortable & very authentic. At the back, there's a small separate studio flat with its own fridge & dining table in the one room, & little shower-toilet adjacent.

In the grounds of the main house are 3 relatively new self-catering bungalows. Comfortable & well equipped, each unit sleeps 4 people in a dbl bed & 2 bunks, with en-suite shower & outside braai, so is ideal for families. If you decide on this option, do ask for the sgl chalet; the dbl one has paper-thin walls. Camping is also available. Excellent meals may be ordered in advance: come with a good appetite!

The White House is a beautiful old place which is excellent value & well worth a visit (though the historical aspect will pass you by if you're not in the main house). Those with an interest in geology will also be attracted by the rose quartz mine on the farm. N$150 pp, under 12s half price. B/fast N$30, dinner N$60, braai pack N$50.

GRÜNAU Grünau is a crossroads, where the railway from Upington in South Africa crosses the main B1. Trains stop on Sundays and Thursdays at 11.25 en route to Keetmanshoop, while the Intercape Mainliner bus between South Africa and Windhoek departs from the Shell truck stop in Grünau for Windhoek on Tuesday, Thursday, Friday and Sunday at 21.45 (N$260 one way), returning to Upington at 00.30 on Monday, Tuesday, Thursday and Saturday (N$185).

The little town also, more or less, marks the spot where the main tarred B3 from the central and eastern parts of South Africa meets with the B1 coming from the Cape. Thus it is strategically positioned for overnight stops between South Africa and Namibia – but isn't a destination of note in its own right.

Where to stay There is a choice of places to stay in and around Grünau itself, including several on the B1 to the north (see above).

🏠 **Grünau Country House** (10 rooms, 4 bungalows, camping) Old Main Rd; 🕾 063 262001; f 063 262009; e grunauch@iway.na; www.grunauch.iway.na. When Altus & Izane took over the former Grünau Hotel in 2001, they changed the name, & set about renovations, including partial rebuilding, refurbishment of the rooms, & enlargement of the private ladies' bar, the whole now enclosed by a security fence.

All rooms are now en suite, with 3 of them, & the main building, having wheelchair access. Bungalows share their own ablution block. Over 30 trees have been planted on the site, particularly around the campsite, where 4 pitches have electricity & water points. All meals are available in the fully licensed à-la-carte restaurant. The lodge is an agent for the Intercape Mainliner bus service, & runs a shuttle between here & the bus terminus. *N$175.250/360 sgl/dbl/family; bungalow N$75 pp, camping N$30 pp.*

🏠 **Grünau Motors** (5 chalets, camping) 🕾 063 262026; f 063 262017; e willa@iafrica.com.na. Just on the north side of Grünau is a 24hr Shell petrol station, with a simple restcamp attached. The small bungalows are clean & well appointed, with AC, en-suite bathroom, TV & kitchenette. The surroundings, though, are flat & characterless, albeit with secure parking. The shop sells snacks & basic foodstuffs, & has a simple restaurant which closes at 20.00, though if you're there out of hours, there's also a 24hr kiosk. *N$170/290. Camping N$80 per pitch, plus N$10 pp.*

🏠 **Vastrap Guest Farm** (6 rooms) 🕾/f 063 262063; e vastrap@mweb.com.na; www.vastrapguestfarm.com. Around 5km from Grünau on the B3 to Karasburg is a sign to the attractive Vastrap Guest Farm, which is about 2km from the road, on a farm belonging to Rean & Hettie Steenkamp. The design is unusual, as these are rooms within old farmstead buildings that have been linked together rather than in separate bungalows. Rooms are simple but cheerful, with en-suite showers. There is also a dining room where home-cooked meals are served on request, & guests can make use of both braai & freezer facilities. Outside is a new swimming pool, & there's the opportunity for day trips on the farm & to the Fish River Canyon. *N$300/400/420/480 sgl/dbl/trpl/family (4). B/fast N$45, dinner N$65.*

KARASBURG

KARASBURG Karasburg is really a bigger version of Grünau – a convenient overnight stop on a long journey. Trains, too, stop here between Upington and Keetmanshoop, on Sunday and Thursday at 11.20, as do the Intercape Mainliner buses between Windhoek and South Africa, heading north from the Total and Engen garages at 20.45 on Tuesday, Thursday, Friday and Sunday, and returning south at 01.00 on Monday, Tuesday, Thursday and Saturday.

The town has several 24-hour **fuel stations**, while for **supplies**, there is a Spar supermarket next to the Total garage.

There's a **post office** on Park Street, a **Bank Windhoek** on 9th Avenue and a **First National Bank** on Main Street – so if Namibia's dollar ever floats free from South Africa's rand, you can expect these to be busy. The **hospital** is on 🕾 063 270167. Signposts to Lordsville and Westerville point the way to Karasburg's old-style satellite townships.

🏠 **Where to stay and eat** There is just one hotel in town, plus a few bed and breakfasts. The places listed here all have their own restaurants, or you could try Hanzell's (🕾 *063 270484/270485*), next to the Engen garage on Main Street.

🏠 **Kalkfontein Hotel** (17 rooms, camping) 🕾/f 063 270172; f 063 270457; e kalkfont@iway.na. This is a typical small-town hotel. Its bar is the local meeting place, & its rooms are spread around yards & courtyards at the back. They're pretty basic, & their furniture is old & somewhat battered, but they are clean & well kept, with en-suite bath or shower. *N$150 pp sharing, B&B.*

🏠 **Jeanie's B&B** (5 rooms) 88 Kalkfontein St; 🕾 063 270349; e maggievw@iway.na. Each of Jeanie's rooms is en-suite & has a ceiling fan, twin or dbl beds & a water cooler. Breakfast & dinner are served in the dining area in the main house, with lunch available on request. Outside is a small pool, & a BBQ area under lots of shady trees. *N$150/250 sgl/dbl B&B.*

🏠 **Accommodation Zebra** 🕾/f 063 270378, m 081 235 2926. Plans are in hand for this new lodge which is expected to open towards the end of 2007.

WARMBAD About 48km south of Karasburg, Warmbad (the name means 'warm bath' in German) features some hot springs, as well as what is reputed to be the oldest existing house in Namibia. The town was also the centre of the Nama-German war in the early 19th century.

The springs have recently been purchased by the government, with a view to developing them into a tourist attraction, together with simple accommodation, but this is unlikely to progress without private funding.

KOËS This small outpost lies about 124km northeast of Keetmanshoop, deep in the Kalahari Desert. It is the centre for the local Afrikaans farming community, and has a **Bank Windhoek**, a few small shops and a hotel.

⌂ Where to stay

⌂ **Hotel Koës** (8 rooms, 1 chalet) 2 Fontein St; \/f 063 252716; e khoibos @ mweb.com.na. Some of the rooms at this small, basic hotel are en suite; other share facilities. It's perhaps not going to be the highlight of your holiday, but might be useful in an emergency.
N$170 pp, B&B.

⌂ **Kalahari Game Lodge** (7 chalets, camping) \ 063 693105. Reservations \ 061 222281; f 061 251556; e kgl @ africaonline.com.na; www.kalaharigamelodge.com. This simple restcamp on a 27,000ha estate is on the C15, almost 100km east of Koës, near the Mata Mata gate into the enormous Kgalagadi Transfrontier Park. If & when that gate reopens, this is bound to become a popular spot to stop overnight, but until then it will probably remain hard to get to & rarely visited. Those who do make it this far east can partake in game drives tracking the reserve's family of lion, which have collar transmitters, or perhaps cheetah & wild dog which are also to be found here. Accommodation is in rustic rooms, 3 with en-suite facilities.
N$560/490 sgl/pp sharing, B&B; camping N$65 pp.

NOORDOEWER This small settlement on the Orange River stands a few kilometres from the main crossing point for Namibia–Cape traffic at Vioolsdrif. If you're crossing into Namibia from that point, you're advised to get there early; it's open 24 hours but tends to get busy after about 10.00. There is reliable fuel in the town, and a branch of Bank Windhoek and a Standard Bank agency could be useful for changing Namibian dollars before crossing into South Africa.

Noordoewer also lies on the edge of the newly created Ai-Ais-Richtersveld Transfrontier Conservation Park, and is the embarkation point for several canoeing and rafting trips down the Orange. These are based in, and organised from, Cape Town (see page 217). A final point of interest is that, thanks to a ready supply of water, there are several large-scale irrigation projects in the area, some producing table-quality grapes like those on the Orange further east in South Africa.

⌂ Where to stay

⌂ **Orange River Lodge & Camping Site** (7 rooms, 1 cabin, camping) Main Rd; \ 063 297012, 297422; f 063 297013; e orlodge @ iway.na; www.orlodge.iway.na. About 1km or so from the border, next to the BP station in Noordoewer, this small lodge is set in attractive grounds. All its rooms each have a private bathroom & AC, TV & tea/coffee-making facilities; dbl rooms are self-catering, & the other can each sleep a family of 4. Camping is on the banks of the river, as is a river cabin set in a more private location than the rooms. It's a good place for an overnight stop or to relax for a little longer, with à-la-carte meals served in a thatched lapa, & activities that include fishing & canoeing.
N$195/295 sgl/dbl; additional guests N$60 pp. B/fast N$30.

⌂ **Camel Lodge** (18 rooms, camping) National Rd; \ 063 297171; f 063 297134. In the centre of Noordoewer, 3km from the border with South Africa, Camel Lodge is a convenient stopover – although at the time of writing we understand that it is temporarily closed. Should it reopen, it may be worth knowing that some rooms have en-suite facilities & TVs, while others share a bathroom, but all have AC. à-la-carte & take-away meals are available, & there's a swimming pool.

Å Abiqua River Camp (camping) \/f 063 297255; e abiqua@amanzitrails.co.za; www.amanzitrails.co.za. Abiqua River Camp is a grassy, shady campsite on the Orange River with views onto the lovely Geelkrans cliffs. Situated 16km downstream from the Noordoewer border post, it is easily accessible via a tarred road. Canoeing, fishing & birdwatching are popular activities. Electricity, wood & ice are available. *N$50 pp.*

There is also **Fiddler's Inn**, located in the 'no man's land' area between Noordoewer and the South African border.

FISH RIVER CANYON

At 161km long, up to 27km wide, and almost 550m at its deepest, the Fish River Canyon is probably second in size only to Arizona's Grand Canyon – and is certainly one of Africa's least-visited wonders.

This means that as you sit dangling your legs over the edge, drinking in the spectacle, you're unlikely to have your visit spoiled by a coach-load of tourists, or to leave feeling that the place is at all commercialised. In fact, away from the busier seasons, you may not see anyone around here at all!

GEOLOGY The base rocks of the Fish River Canyon, now at the bottom nearest the river, are shales, sandstones and lavas which were deposited about 1,800 million years ago. Later, from 1,300 to 1,000 million years ago, these were heated and strongly compressed, forming a metamorphic rock complex, which includes intrusive granites and, later, the dolorite dykes which appear as clear, dark streaks on the canyon.

A period of erosion then followed, removing the overlying rocks and levelling this complex to be the floor of a vast shallow sea, covering most of what is now southern Namibia. From about 650 to 500 million years ago various sediments, limestones and conglomerates were deposited by the sea onto this floor, building up into what is now referred to as the Nama Group of rocks.

About 500 million years ago, the beginnings of the canyon started when a fracture in this crust formed a broad valley, running north–south. Southward-moving glaciers deepened this during the Dwyka Ice Age, around 300 million years ago. Later faults and more erosion added to the effect, creating canyons within each other, until a mere 50 million years ago, when the Fish River started to cut its meandering way along the floor of the most recent valley.

HISTORY Situated in a very arid region of Namibia, the Fish River is the only river within the country that usually has pools of water in its middle reaches during the dry season. Because of this, it was known to the peoples of the area during the early, middle and late Stone Ages. Numerous early sites dating from as early as 50,000 years ago have been found within the canyon – mostly beside bends in the river.

Around the beginning of this century, the Ai-Ais area was used as a base by the Germans in their war against the Namas. It was finally declared a national monument in 1962. Ai-Ais Restcamp was opened in 1971, though it has been refurbished since then.

GETTING THERE Detailed routes to the various lodges and camps are given below. Note that you can't drive between the west and the east sides of the canyon quickly. If you are approaching the east side from the north during the rainy season, and the C12 is blocked by flooding, then try taking a shortcut from the B4, on-to the D545

AFRICA'S LARGEST CANYON?

Pedants cite Ethiopia's Blue Nile Gorge as being Africa's largest canyon. It is certainly deeper than the Fish River Canyon, at about 1,000m, but it is also narrower (about 20km wide at its widest), and probably shorter as well. Like many vague superlatives, 'largest' is difficult to define. In this case, we would have to measure the volume of the canyon – and even then there would be questions about exactly where it begins and ends. Suffice to say that both are too large to take in at one sight, and both are well worth visiting.

and then the C12. If the water pouring over the retaining wall is too fast to cross, then a detour to your left will bring you to a crossing on top of a dam wall – avoiding the need to ford the torrent. Alternatively, take the longer tar route on the B1 and C10.

WHERE TO STAY Seeing the canyon as a day trip from a base some way off is practical, particularly as the diagonal rays of early morning or late evening light do little for photographers' hopes of capturing the depths of the canyon. Keetmanshoop is one possibility, or for a less urban setting you could opt for somewhere around Karasburg or Grünau to the east, or Seeheim to the north. However, if only to minimise your driving, stay closer if you can – at Hobas Campsite, Ai-Ais or one of the private lodges nearby, offering a good range of choice.

Private lodges

Cañon Lodge (30 twin bungalows) 061 230066; f 061 251863; e info@gondwana-desert-collection.com; www.gondwana-desert-collection.com. Cañon Lodge is one of several accommodation options that lie within the 102,000ha Gondwana Reserve. The reserve, which borders on the national park, was established by Manni Goldbeck in 1996 from 7 commercial sheep farms, with the aim of reclaiming the land from overgrazing & returning it to its natural state. Close to the canyon's northern viewpoints, the lodge is just 2km off the C37, which itself is 7km south of the junction to the Fish River Canyon.

The lodge centres on an old farmhouse, built in 1904, which has been restored & now functions as the reception, well-stocked bar, coffee & restaurant area. Adjacent is an open terrace where tables are shaded by an old false pepper tree (the seeds of which must have been imported with horse feed for the German Schutztruppe).

All around the lodge are stone kopjes – small hills made from bare stone boulders. Amongst these, ingeniously spread out, are beautiful bungalows, containing dbl or twin beds, an en-suite toilet & shower or bath, within raw stone walls under thatched roofs. These are rustic in concept, but comfortable & innovative, & surprisingly cool during the heat of the day.

Both guests & day visitors are catered for in the large but intimate restaurant, which in summer spills out onto the terrace, but on chilly winter evenings is warmed by blazing open fires. Meals are substantial, with considerably more choice than you might expect in such an out-of-the-way place. Much of the reason for this lies in the lodge's self-sufficiency project, for a hefty proportion of the fresh food consumed comes from their own farm. Already, the place produces almost all its own bacon, milk, eggs & salad vegetables, not to mention fresh herbs, & homemade bread & salamis, thus obviating the necessity to bring in expensive & tired products from markets as far away as South Africa. While a significant aspect of trial & error lies behind this success, there is no doubting the value of the achievement, both in terms of local employment & the environment – not to mention the taste!

In addition to the obvious attractions of the canyon itself across the plain, there is plenty to do while here, & some visitors stay for several days. Climb up a kopje (which is easy) & you'll find a spot for a sundowner, overlooking a wide plateau &, 20km away, the main viewpoint of the canyon. Stay at the bottom, & you can spend time watching the colony of dassies on those same rocks as they bask

Tricia Hayne

The peace of the canyon is disturbed for just a few moments by the sound of a light aircraft as it sweeps across the apparently endless plateau to the east and suddenly soars over the edge of the canyon. Just five passengers share the tiny cockpit of the Cessna 210 with the pilot. Since this is a top-wing aircraft, everyone on board has unimpeded views over the landscape unfolding below and plenty of opportunity for photography.

This may be the Fish River, but from the air the word 'snake' comes more readily to mind as it winds down the canyon in a series of tortuous switchbacks. Even in the dry season, pools of green water reflect back the shadow of the plane as it follows the river on its course through towering canyon walls whose turreted edges have been eroded over countless millennia. Among the broad bands of browns and dull reds, the occasional bright flower clings to bare rock, but it is the sheer scale of the spectacle that makes a flight worthwhile. For all too brief a time, passengers have the chance to share the perspective of the magnificent black eagle that occasionally circles overhead.

As the plane weaves down the canyon, the edges soften and the landscape takes on the more familiar pattern of a mountainous environment. Towards Ai-Ais, the riverbed widens and the aircraft veers away, following parallel to the canyon before returning to Cañon Lodge.

Weather permitting, flights are run daily from Cañon Lodge. For details, and current prices – which are tied to the US dollar, so fluctuate constantly – contact the lodge direct (see page 203).

in the evening sun. Guided walks & drives are offered around the reserve at various times of day, &, for the more adventurous, there are flights down the canyon (see box, above), as well as guided horseriding trips (hard hats are provided). There's even a small swimming pool set a short distance from the lodge itself where you can relax in complete privacy.
N$805/645 pp sharing, B&B. Dinner N$145, lunch N$70, lunchpack N$50.

🏠 **Cañon Roadhouse** (9 rooms, camping) 🌭 063 683111. Reservations as for Cañon Lodge, above. Cañon Roadhouse is run by the same partners as Cañon Lodge, & is also on land that forms part of the Gondwana Reserve. It is further north, signposted about 17km off the C12 at near Holoog (a large dot on the map, but a tiny settlement), along the C37.

If the name is a little off-putting, think of this as a comfortable roadside inn & you'll be near the mark. Accommodation is set at the back, around a quiet, cactus-planted courtyard. Comfortable rooms with en-suite bathrooms show the hand of a thoughtful designer, with décor picking out the rich reds & creams of the surrounding landscape. The campsite at the back has space for 6 pitches, & there is a swimming pool for guests' use.

Many visitors are drawn here as if to an oasis by the reliable fuel station, & find themselves staying for a drink on the front terrace, or something to eat in the restaurant, which is adorned with old farm implements & related artefacts. The à-la-carte menu features light lunches in the N$20–45 range, or several more substantial dishes, including game. Activities are as for Cañon Lodge, above.
N$495/700 sgl/dbl, B&B. Camping N$40 pp, plus N$60 per site.

🏠 **Cañon Mountain Camp** Contact as for Cañon Lodge, above. This simple converted farmhouse within driving distance of the lip of the canyon is a further offshoot of Cañon Lodge. Visitors coming here should book in at the reception for Cañon Lodge, from where they will be directed the 4km to the camp. All meals & activities are shared with the lodge.

Accommodation is ideal for small groups or families who are self-catering. Basic but comfortable rooms are set around an enclosed courtyard, with en-suite bathrooms, a communal kitchen & a large braai area overlooking the hills. There are plans under consideration to convert a small water reservoir into a swimming pool, but for now this remains a secluded spot with very few mod cons (there's no electricity), offering the opportunity to

experience at first hand the peace of this unspoilt environment.
N$245 pp.

🏠 **Cañon Village** (42 rooms) Contact as for Cañon Lodge, above. At the foot of the surrounding mountains, the 'village' is mainly used for groups, who stay in thatched, semi-detached cottages of stone, with en-suite facilities. Original Namibian artwork painted on the walls of both the rooms & the large restaurant, built around the rocks, gives a glimpse of the history of the area. Meals are served buffet style; there's also a bar & swimming pool.
N$245 pp.

Canyon Nature Park (☏ 063 683005; f 063 693006; m 084 327 6760 e book@canyonnaturepark.com; www.canyonnaturepark.com) The 600km² Canyon Nature Park is divided over the east and west sides of the Fish River, including a 32km stretch of the Fish River Canyon, as well as 12km of the adjacent Löwen River Canyon. The park incorporates a range of accommodation: Fish River Guest Farm, Grande View Lodge and the Koelkrans Campsite. Both the guest farm and the lodge are accessible by 2WD, but visitors to the campsite in the canyon will need a 4x4.

One of the major attractions of a stay here is the possibility to hike in the canyon without some of the restrictions that apply inside the national park's conservation area further south. Hiking remains restricted to April–September, since temperatures in the canyon soar in the summer months, but visitors may spend anything from one to five days hiking without a guide, from N$504.35 pp, making this an attractive option for those with less time to spare. Hikers will still need to be fully equipped, with sufficient food and water for the duration of their hike.

🏠 **Fish River Guest Farm** (6 rooms) On the east side of the Fish River Canyon, the guest farm caters exclusively for families with a low to medium budget on self-catering holidays. To get there, take the C12 for about 33km south of Naute Dam, then turn west & continue for a further 23km.

Accommodation is in the original farmhouse, where there are 3 bathrooms shared between the rooms, with all linen provided. The kitchen is fully equipped & there's a large northwest-facing veranda.
Self-catering N$223.83 pp.

🏕 **Koelkrans Campsite** (6 huts) Deep on the floor of the canyon, the campsite has self-catering, wooden huts with twin beds, but here no linen is provided.
Camping N$80.60 pp, plus N$150 per vehicle.

🏠 **Grande View Lodge** (6 chalets) Rather more upmarket are the chalets at Grande View, which were being upgraded in early 2007. It is the only lodge on the western rim of Fish River Canyon & is accessed by driving past Seeheim on the B4 towards Lüderitz. After 30km turn left onto the D463 & continue along this for 85km until you see a signboard which reads 'Canyon Nature Park'. Turn left here & continue for 5km on the farm road until you see 2 farmhouses, where you will be directed to the reception. The lodge is located a further 14km from the reception. Set on the rim of the canyon, the living/dining area of this small lodge has stunning views over the canyon from its veranda, making it a great spot for sundowners. Photographers should note that the lodge is east-facing so the potential for good sunset shots is excellent. Rock-&-thatch chalets have en-suite showers & they, too, have spectacular views from their individual verandas.

There are 2hr walking trails along the rim, as well as guided walks & nature drives. There are also longer, guided, fully serviced & catered hikes in the 120km privately owned section of the canyon over 1–5 days.
N$1,513.04–2,521.74 pp sharing, FB & activities.

Within the conservation area
Ai-Ais Hot Springs Ai-Ais is best reached from Keetmanshoop by driving south on the main B1, and then turning west onto the C10. (Try to avoid this in the late afternoon, as the sun is directly in your face.)

Alternatively, from Lüderitz, reach Seeheim on the B4 and take the gravel C12 south. Then turn right onto the D601 towards Hobas, left along the D324, and right onto the C10. Coming from the south, you can turn left off the B1 onto the D316 – though this road is quieter and perhaps less well graded than the C10.

However you reach it, the final few kilometres of the C10 spirals down, cut into the rock layers of the canyon's side, until it reaches the bed of the Fish River. It's a marvellous road, though steep in parts, with some sharp corners – so drive carefully. You can arrive at any time, so do not fear being locked out if you are late.

🏠 **Ai-Ais Restcamp** (bungalows, flats, camping) 🐾 063 262045; f 063 262047/8; reservations 🐾 061 2857200; f 061 224900; e reservations@ nwr.com.na; www.nwr.com.na. Open all year & recently renovated, this large restcamp sits at the bottom of the canyon, at the end of the C10 road. This is towards the southern end of the conservation area, & is the finishing point for the canyon's hiking trail.

Ai-Ais means 'burning water' in the local Nama language, a reference to the hot, sulphurous springs which well up here, the original reason for the siting of the restcamp. It's very much a little spa, with a large, naturally hot, outdoor pool & private hot tubs as well as the usual restcamp facilities that give it the air of a holiday camp.

There's a choice of simple, clean restcamp accommodation: luxury flats (2 beds), flats (4 beds) & bungalows (4 beds). All have a fridge, kettle & hotplate for self-catering, & bedding & towels are provided. The flats also have en-suite shower &

toilet, whilst the huts or 'bungalows' share their ablutions ('tatty' as one recent visitor described them) with the campers. The luxury flats have a bath as well as a shower, plus AC. A word of warning – having booked your accommodation in advance, it's worth rechecking before you arrive. Some travellers have been caught out when changes have been made without notification.

The restcamp has a basic shop, post box & fuel station, as well as a restaurant that serves b/fast 07.00–08.30, lunch 12.00–13.30 & dinner 18.00–20.30. These may be à la carte, but they are still like school dinners.

Entrance to the hot tubs is N$15 per adult, inc children over 10, except where costs are included with your accommodation. The more active might bring tennis racquets, to play on the courts here, or wander off on a walk up the canyon – which is beautiful.

Bungalow N$550; flat N$600; camping N$50 per site plus N$30/15 adult/child. Park fees extra.

Hobas

🏕 **Hobas Campsite** 🐾/f 063 266028; reservations 🐾 061 285 7200; f 061 224900; e reservations@ nwr.com.na; www.nwr.com.na. Within the conservation area, & run by the NWR, Hobas is a busy campsite near the main viewpoint of the canyon. The sites are spread out under shady, willowy trees & there are thatched sunshades for extra shelter during the intense midday sun, as well as tables & chairs for picnics, & a small swimming pool.

As the only convenient base in the area for overland groups, this site gets many large trucks stopping here – so can become festive at times. Competition for the quieter sites is high. Beside the gate is the park warden's station & office, where you can buy a few curios & refreshments. Those just coming to see the canyon must stop here to pay their park entry fees.

Camping N$50 per site plus N$20/10 adult/child (max 8 people), exc park fees.

VISITING THE CONSERVATION AREA (*Entry N$80 per adult per day, plus N$10 per vehicle; under 16s free. Fees are payable by all visitors on entry to Ai-Ais & at Hobas campsite, & are in addition to any fees charged for accommodation*) In 1969 the area around the Fish River Canyon was proclaimed a conservation area, which made sense. The land was as poor in potential for agriculture as it is rich in potential for tourism, and this was a way of protecting the area from uncontrolled development. The 345,000ha conservation area now encompasses Ai-Ais and Hobas, whilst all the private lodges are outside.

Flora and fauna Driving around you will probably see few larger animals, though there are many if you look hard. These include herds of Hartmann's mountain zebra, small groups of kudu and the smaller klipspringer antelope, which are usually seen in pairs. Baboon make no secret of their presence if around, whilst dassies (alias rock rabbits) are common but leopard, though certainly present, are very rarely seen. It's not unusual to drive for a few hours, and see no mammals at all.

Birds, too, are around but often not obvious. This isn't a centre for birdwatching, as only about 60 species are thought to live here, but look out for the majestic black eagle, as well as the rock kestrel and rock pigeon, and especially for the localised yellow-rumped eremomela which occur near Ai-Ais. Karoo bustards and ostrich are the highlights of the open plains above the canyon itself. Vegetation is sparse. Both on the top and on the canyon's slopes, the larger species are mostly *Euphorbias*, with the odd quivertree. However, parts of the canyon's base where there is water are quite lush – like the Sulphur Springs and Ai-Ais areas. There you can expect camelthorn, wild tamarisk and ebony trees, amongst others.

What to see and do Once in the area, a day is enough to see the canyon properly, unless you've arranged (in advance) to do the hike. Do note that, with the exception of those booked on the five-day hike (see below), no visitors are allowed to descend into the canyon from the lip at any time of year.

Start the morning by driving past Hobas to the **Main Viewpoint**. This is *the* classic view of Hell's Bend, featured in most of the photographs – and probably the only view that you'll see if you're on a bus tour. A 3km track leads off to the right, to the **Hiker's Viewpoint**, which lends a different perspective and is worth the wander if it is cool.

Then take the road that leads to the left of the Main Viewpoint. This is a continuation of the D324 which doubles back, to run roughly parallel to the canyon, generally keeping within a few hundred yards. There are several stops for viewpoints along its length, perhaps the best being the **Sulphur Springs Viewpoint** (Palm Springs), which has a picnic table and a stunning view of another tight switchback in the river's course.

This road is little used and graded less, so it's bumpy in parts but suitable for a 2WD car driven slowly and carefully. The scenery is so spectacular that you won't want to rush. If you have a 4x4, you can continue past the Sulphur Springs Viewpoint to the southernmost viewpoint at Eagle's Rock – a further 12km of very rough, stony road, but offering a good view of the canyon further south. Either way, you'll eventually have to retrace your tracks to return on the D324, back past the Hobas gate and south.

Ai-Ais makes a great afternoon stop during the winter (see its opening dates, above), giving you time to relax in a mineral pool, or to take a gentle walk up the canyon, for a taste of what the hikers will experience. Note that permits to visit the conservation area for a day are valid at both the Ai-Ais and Hobas gates.

HIKING THE FISH RIVER CANYON For very fit, experienced and self-sufficient backpackers, the Fish River Canyon is the venue for one of southern Africa's greatest hikes: a chance to follow the river where vehicles never venture, about 90km from Hiker's Point to Ai-Ais. However, numbers are limited to one group per day, which must be pre-arranged with the NWR in Windhoek months in advance, so you need to work out your logistics carefully long before you get here.

One company that specialises in hiking the canyon is Trail Hopper (\ *061 264521;* f *061 264389;* e *hiking@mweb.com.na; www.trailhopper.com*).

Regulations Hiking trips are allowed from from 1 May to 15 September, and the NWR insists on the group being 3–30 people for safety, with no children under the age of 12. Hikers need to bring a medical certificate, which has been issued within 40 days of the hike and is signed by their doctor, stating that they are fit to do the hike.

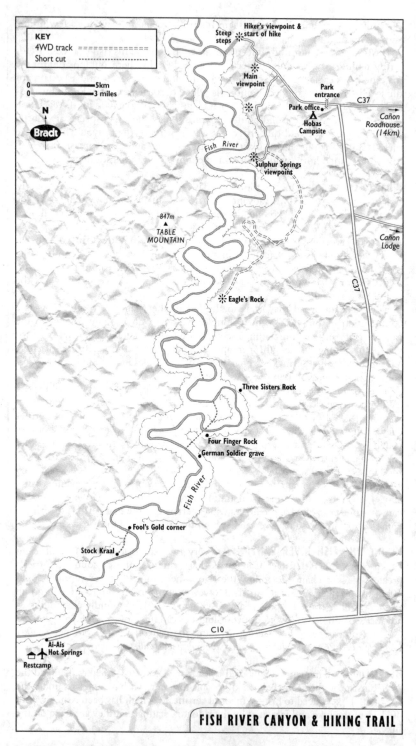

KEY
4WD track
Short cut

0 — 5km
0 — 3 miles

N

Bradt

Steep steps
Hiker's viewpoint & start of hike

Main viewpoint

Park entrance

C37

Cañon Roadhouse (14km)

Park office

Hobas Campsite

Fish River

Sulphur Springs viewpoint

Cañon Lodge

C37

847m
TABLE MOUNTAIN

Eagle's Rock

Three Sisters Rock

Four Finger Rock

German Soldier grave

Fish River

Fool's Gold corner

Stock Kraal

C10

Ai-Ais Hot Springs
Restcamp

FISH RIVER CANYON & HIKING TRAIL

The hike costs N$100 per person, paid for in advance at the NWR in Windhoek, and hikers are responsible for all their own food, equipment, safety and transport to/from the canyon. Hikers must stay at least one night in the national park, either at Hobas Campsite or at Ai-Ais Restcamp.

Preparations This is a four- or five-day hike covering 80–90km in what can be some of the subcontinent's most extreme temperatures. There's no easy way out once you start; no chance to stop. So this isn't for the faint-hearted, or those without experience of hiking in Africa.

For those who come prepared, it's excellent. Your own large, comfortable backpack with your normal hiking equipment (see pages 108–9) should include: at least a two-litre water bottle, with some method of purifying water; a sleeping roll and bag, though a tent is not needed; and food and cooking utensils for at least six days (wood for fires is generally available on the second half of the hike). Also, each group should have at least one comprehensive medical kit, as help may be days away if there is an accident. A light rainproof jacket is also a good idea, in the unlikely event of a shower.

Finally, make sure that you've a good map. One rough route-plan with pretty colour pictures and lots of advice is usually available at Hobas, though it is best when used in conjunction with a more 'serious' version from the Surveyor General's office in Windhoek (see page 122).

Transport If you're driving yourself in, leave your vehicle near the start of the hike at Hobas, since there is transport available from Ai-Ais back to the start point of the hike at a cost of N$120 pp. If you are hitchhiking, remember that your arrival date will be unpredictable, and you might miss your start date.

The hike The descent into the canyon is steep in parts, taking 45–90 minutes. Chains are provided on the more difficult sections. The first day is taxing, with stretches of loose river-sand between areas of large boulders. It can be slow going, and the trail stays mostly on the eastern side of the river. After 14km there is an 'emergency exit' up to the Sulphur (Palm) Springs Viewpoint, but most people eventually reach the area around Sulphur Springs and overnight there, 16km into the walk. The springs themselves are fast-flowing, hot (57°C), and apparently rich in fluorides, chlorides and sulphates.

It gradually gets easier after Sulphur Springs, traversing fewer stretches of boulders, and more sand and rounded river-stones. The river zigzags sharply, so most hikers cut the corners and get their feet wet. There are several more significant shortcuts, and an 'emergency exit' at 70km. Finally, 90km from the start (80km if you cut corners) you arrive at Ai-Ais.

Trail etiquette The correct trail etiquette here is the same as sensible rules for responsible hiking anywhere in the bush (see pages 110–13). However, as groups cover the same trail regularly here, these guidelines are all the more vital. In particular:

- There are no 'official' fireplaces; use existing ones if possible. Use only dead wood for fires, and bring a stove as there's little wood at the start of the trail.
- Leave no litter in the canyon – even fruit peel will look unsightly.
- Use only biodegradable soap, and wash away from the main river from which people will be drinking.
- Never feed animals; baboons would be a problem here if fed.
- There are no toilets, so burn all toilet paper and bury it with the excrement, in a shallow hole far from the water.

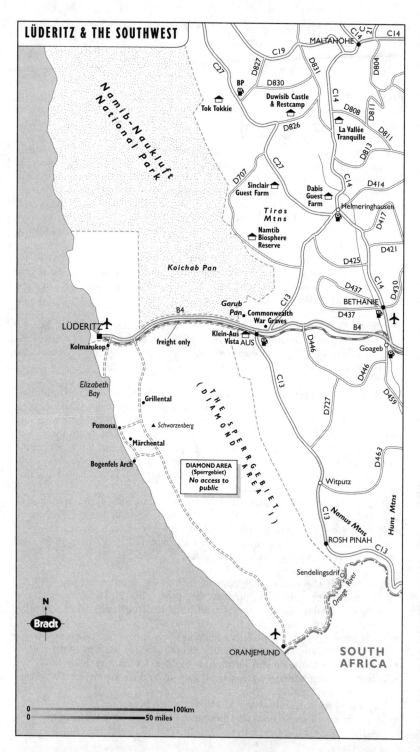

LÜDERITZ & THE SOUTHWEST

MALTAHÖHE

C14

C14/21

C14

C19

D827

D831

D804

C27

D830

BP

Duwisib Castle
& Restcamp

D808

D811

Tok Tokkie

C14

La Vallée
Tranquille

D813

D826

C27

D707

Sinclair
Guest Farm

Dabis
Guest Farm

D414

Namib-Naukluft
National Park

Tiras
Mtns

Helmeringhausen

D417

Namtib
Biosphere
Reserve

D421

D425

Koichab Pan

E15

D437

C14

D430

BETHANIE

Garub
Pan

Commonwealth
War Graves

D437

B4

B4

LÜDERITZ

Klein-Aus
Vista AUS

Goageb

Kolmanskop

freight only

D446

D446

Elizabeth
Bay

C13

D727

D459

Grillental

(THE SPERRGEBIET)

Pomona

▲ Schwarzenberg

Märchental

Bogenfels Arch

DIAMOND AREA
(Sperrgebiet)
No access to
public

D463

Witputz

C13

Namus Mtns

Huns Mtns

ROSH PINAH

C13

Sendelingsdrif

Orange River

N

Bradt

ORANJEMUND

SOUTH
AFRICA

0 ————————— 100km
0 ————————— 50 miles

11

Lüderitz and the Southwest

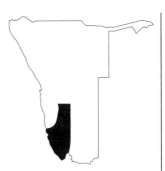

Though the European colonisation of Namibia started in this southwestern corner, this remains perhaps the country's least-known area for visitors. At the end of a long road, Lüderitz is now being rediscovered, with its wonderful turn-of-the-20th-century architecture, desolate beaches, and position as the springboard for trips into the forbidden area, the *Sperrgebiet*.

But there is more than Lüderitz in this area. Early historical sites from the 1900s are dotted throughout the region – and though places to stay are often far apart, most of the hotels and guest farms are excellent value. Best of all are the amazing landscapes. Rugged mountains and flowing desert sands make the empty roads spectacular – with the D707, the southern sections of the C13, and even the main B4 across the Koichab Pan ranking amongst the country's more dramatic drives.

THE ROADS TO LÜDERITZ

FROM KEETMANSHOOP As you drive east from Keetmanshoop to Lüderitz, the main B4 road is now all tarred. After about 44km the C12 turns off left to the Fish River Canyon. A kilometre or so afterwards the B4 crosses the Fish River itself, which meanders down a broad, shallow, vegetated valley with few hints of the amazing canyon to the south.

To the north of the road are some spectacular flat-topped hills, capped by hard dolorite which erodes slowly. One of these has been named Kaiserkrone, the 'Kaiser's crown', as it is an unusual conical shape capped by a symmetrical dolorite crown.

There are several small towns along this road. Most can supply fuel and essentials, but none is comparable in size to Lüderitz or Keetmanshoop, so few visitors stop at any for long. There's also a café about halfway between Goageb and Aus. The main towns are outlined below.

Seeheim About 45km from Keetmanshoop on the B4, Seeheim has accommodation that offers straightforward access along the C12 to the Fish River Canyon, passing Naute Dam on the way:

Seeheim Hotel (22 rooms, camping) \/f 063 250503; e seeheim@iway.na. On the main B4, the Seeheim Hotel is something of a one-stop shop, since it also offers fuel, & a shop selling souvenirs, bread & soft drinks. Its accommodation, all in one building, is divided between luxury rooms, which have en-suite bathrooms & ceiling fans, & standard rooms with shared facilities. There is also a dining room with à-la-carte menu & a separate bar. Outside, there is a swimming pool, while around the hotel are some marked hiking trails, & horseriding is available by arrangement.
Luxury N$450/380 sgl/pp sharing, standard N$180 pp sharing, all B&B. Camping N$60 pp.

Goageb The tiny community of Goageb, with fewer than 20 telephones, lies 106km west of Keetmanshoop. It has a fuel station at the **Konkiep Motel** (\ 063

283566l; f *063 283107*), but it's not the most attractive of places. The region's only railway station is at Goageb, which could increase its importance when or if passenger trains run through here again, but the Starline bus service no longer stops here.

A convenient place to stop is the **Kuibis Restaurant**, shop and roadside café, 100km west of Goageb, serving light meals all day.

Bethanie About 30km north of Goageb, Bethanie (also spelt Bethanien) is a larger town and centre for local administration. The main road into the small town is the tarred C14, just to the east of Goageb, but if you're coming from Lüderitz turn off onto the D435 about 20km further west. There is no longer any public transport here.

The town is dominated by the apparently modern Lutheran church, which was actually one of the first churches in Namibia. Originally built in 1859, it was restored by American evangelists in 1998. Rather more in keeping with the surroundings are several shops (including the gloriously named Pick a Dilly), a post office, an agency for the **Standard Bank**, a take-away restaurant, two **fuel stations** (not 24 hours) and a hotel:

Bethanie Hotel (10 rooms, camping) Keetmanshoop St; \ 063 283013; f 063 283071. One of the country's oldest hotels, the Bethanie was built around 1880, & remains dark & old-fashioned. Nevertheless, the owner is helpful, & there's a bar, snooker room & dining room. Rooms are off a courtyard at the back. Dbls are en suite, but sgls share a (clean) outside toilet block with the campsite. Four of the rooms have AC. *N$300/490 sgl/dbl, B&B; camping N$25 pp.*

For those heading north, there's a restcamp on the C14, 35km from Bethanie:

Å Konkiep Lapa Restcamp (9 cabins, camping) \ 063 283151; f 063 283087; e betuit@iway.na. Self-catering 2-bed cabins & a separate campsite share ablution facilities here. There's a bar & lapa, as well as an inside braai. Wood & water are available, but otherwise you'll need to bring everything with you. *Cabin N$200; camping N$60 per pitch, plus N$30 pp.*

Aus About 211km west of Keetmanshoop a slip-road turns left off the B4 to Aus, notable for its unpredictable weather and its history as a POW camp. Some 500m from the main road there's a **police post** (\ 063 258005) on the left, and further on a **fuel station** stands in the heart of this small hillside town. Just after turning off the B4, you'll find a new museum with a tourist information centre, which should encourage more visitors to stop and discover something about an area that is all too often ignored.

Aus's weather can be extreme, very cold in winter and hot in the summer. It is also unpredictable – which stems from its proximity to the Cape – although the winter rain, and its associated flora, is more pronounced in the area around Rosh Pinah. (The Cape has a different weather pattern from anywhere else in southern Africa, with winter rainfall from May to September, and gloriously warm, *dry* summer weather from November to February.)

Sometimes Aus's weather will follow a typically Namibian pattern; at others it will have the Cape's weather, with showers in winter, and occasionally even snow. If heavy or prolonged, this rain can cause a sudden flush of sprouting plants and blooms, rather like the 'flower season' in Namaqualand, south of the border. Many unusual plants have been catalogued here, including a rather magnificent species of bulb whose flowers form a large globe, the size of a football. When these seed, the globe breaks off and rolls about like tumbleweed. Endemic to this small area is the yellow-flowered Aus daisy, *Arctotis fastiosa*, which grows only within a 30km radius of the town (a slightly more orange sub-species is found at Rosh Pinah). In winter, the yellow *kuibi* or butter flower, *Papia capensis*, brightens up the plains at the foot of the mountains, interspersed with the blue sporry, *Felicia namaquana*, and the bright purple fig bush. Higher up, the mountain butterflower holds sway, the western slopes are scented by wild rosemary, and the Bushman's candle is to be found – although here it is yellow or, rarely, white, unlike its bushier pink cousin in the desert to the west.

When the German colonial troops surrendered to the South African forces in 1915, a camp for the prisoners of war was set up a few kilometres outside what is now Aus. At one point 1,552 German POWs were held here by 600 guards. It seems that the German prisoners worked hard to make their conditions more comfortable by manufacturing bricks, building houses and stoves, and cultivating gardens. They eventually even sold bricks to their South African guards. The camp, now marked by a monument 4km from town, closed shortly after the end of the war. Sadly, little remains of the buildings bar a few ruined huts. On a hill 1.3km to the east of town, however, there is a small cemetery maintained by the Commonwealth War Graves Commission. Here lie 61 prisoners of war, and a further 60 members of the garrison, most of them victims of a flu epidemic in 1918. If you're driving up here, keep to the right-hand track.

Getting there Nowadays, visitors to Aus have little choice but to arrive by car. A railway runs through the town, but it has been closed for some time, and although work is nearly complete on reopening it, there are at present no plans to run passenger trains on the line. The Starline bus that used to run through to Keetmanshoop from Lüderitz has been discontinued.

Where to stay and eat

Klein-Aus Vista (24 rooms, 9 chalets, hikers' cabin, campsite) 063 258116; f 063 258021; e ausvista@namibhorses.com; www.namibhorses.com, www.gondwana-desert-collection.com. Nestled against the Aus Mountains, 1,400m above sea level, Klein-Aus Vista is 3km west of Aus to the south of the main B4. The family-run business is managed by three brothers, Piet, Johann & Willem, who grew up on the farm, went away, & eventually returned to build up Klein-Aus Vista. They amalgamated 5 farms to form the privately owned 51,000ha Gondwana Sperrgebiet Rand Park, a landscape defined by granite outcrops & mountains, dry riverbeds scattered with rocks & sweeping desert plains. After winter rain from Jul to Sep the landscape explodes into an expansive carpet of yellow & violet flowers. To the north, the park borders the Namib Naukluft Park, home of the Namib desert horses.

Set against this backdrop, accommodation is diverse, catering for pretty well every sector of the market. All guests are welcomed at the reception of the **Desert Horse Inn**, where there are 20 new, comfortable and stylish rooms, tastefully decorated, with en-suite bathrooms, small lounge and veranda with ceiling fans, and facilities for making tea or coffee. There are also the 4 original rooms, close to the main reception, which are also decorated in a stylish fashion. Here, too, are a wooden deck and bar, and the restaurant where an excellent 3-course dinner is served, with a reasonable selection of wines. Also on offer are water and fruit juice bottled on the farm.

Those seeking to enjoy the solitude and beauty of the mountains may be better served by the chalets at **Eagle's Nest**, some 7km from the reception inn. Built around gigantic granite boulders, each to their own design, these all have en-suite facilities and lack for nothing, from a fireplace to a kitchenette and a private veranda. Visitors can arrange take-away barbecue packs or breakfast platters, or eat in the main restaurant.

Small groups can take advantage of the **hikers' cabin** at *Geister Schlucht*, or 'Ghost Gully', named after a group of diamond thieves who were shot by detectives trying to escape in a Hudson Terraplane in 1934, & are said to return at full moon looking for their lost treasure. Inside, bunks & sgl beds are arranged to accommodate up to 20 self-catering visitors, with a kitchen/bar & living area. Finally, there is a 10-pitch **campsite** with spotless ablution blocks.

11

Hiking is a major attraction here, with a number of waymarked trails, varying from 1–5hr circular walks. Though the terrain is rugged, the trails are predominantly on an even level, & there are occasional springs & pools for cooling off. Alternatively, there is plenty of scope for striking out on your own to seek out wild flowers or choose a vantage point to watch the sunset. Visitors also have the opportunity to go with a highly knowledgeable guide on tours in both parks: including excursions to see the famous desert horses and the Koichab dune sea. Trips range from sunset drives (from N$120–195 pp), through half-day trips (from N$280 pp, min 3 people), to full-day tours (N$670 pp, min 3).

This is a super spot to spend a day or three unwinding during a long trip, & highly recommended. *Room N$460/790 sgl/dbl, B&B. Chalet N$795/1,190 sgl/dbl. Hikers' cabin N$95–125 pp, according to group size. Camping N$60 pp. B/fast N$45, dinner N$130.*

🏠 **Bahnhof Hotel** (13 rooms) ☎ 063 258091; 📱 081 235 6737; f 063 258092; e bahnhof-hotel-aus@iway.na; www.hotel-aus.com. This once old-fashioned hotel in the centre of Aus has recently come under new management & been given a complete facelift. Gone are the old, dingy rooms, their place taken by modern twins with en-suite showers, one with wheelchair access. À-la-carte meals with freshly baked bread are available to guests & non-residents alike — & since the manager used to be the chef at the Burning Shore in Walvis Bay, you can expect standards to be high — while those on the move can order lunch packs. A new wooden deck & beer garden make a pleasant place to eat, or to while away an hour or so with a cool drink. *From N$395/365 sgl/pp sharing, B&B.*

🏠 **Namib Garage** (7 rooms, camping) ☎/f 063 258029; e namibaus@mweb.com.na. Self-catering rooms here, one with an en-suite bathroom, are simple & clean, ideal for longer stays. The campsite with 7 pitches is enclosed by a wall. Accommodation enquiries should be made at the garage in Aus, which is open 07.00 to 10.00, & which also has a well-stocked shop & a small restaurant with bar. *N$180 B&B, N$150 pp self catering; camping N$40 pp, plus N$20 for power.*

Garub Pan At the foot of the Aus Mountains, about 20km west of Aus, a sign 'feral horses' points north off the road. Follow the track for just 1.5km and you find Garub Pan, an artificial waterhole which sustains the desert horses and is popular with the local gemsbok as well.

There is a display about their origins, which is largely faded and illegible, and a shaded wooden observation hide – though staying in the car will give almost as good a view.

KOICHAB PAN TO LÜDERITZ Driving west from Garub, you enter the flat, gravel plains of the huge Koichab Pan, ringed by mountains in the distance. It's a vast and spectacular place where you'll be able to see any oncoming traffic on the straight road for perhaps 20km before you pass it.

About 52km from Aus, almost halfway to Lüderitz, is a lay-by containing a picnic table in the shade, and half a dozen well-watered trees. Don't miss the chance to stop here, as it must make one of the most bizarre and solitary picnic sites on the continent.

Finally, as you draw much nearer to Lüderitz, the last 20km or so of the road cross a coastal dune-belt of marching barchan dunes – which are constantly being blown across the road from south to north. Ever-present bulldozers are constantly clearing these, but sometimes you will still encounter low ramps of sand on the tar. Drive very slowly for this last section, as hitting even a small mound of sand can easily wreck a vehicle's suspension.

FROM AI-AIS OR NOORDOEWER VIA ROSH PINAH Noordoewer (see pages 201–2) is one of the main access points into Namibia from South Africa. But while most drivers head north on the fast B1 towards Keetmanshoop, there is a second road, the C13, that travels northwest, running more or less parallel to the country's southern border until it meets the Orange River, just south of the Ai-Ais and Fish River Canyon national parks.

For those coming from Ai-Ais, it is well worth considering taking the southerly route to Lüderitz, which eventually joins up with the C13 along the Orange River, and on to Aus via Rosh Pinah. Not for those in a hurry, it nevertheless affords some superb scenery to the south of the mountains, with fascinating plantlife, including many succulents and endemics. Note that, as there are no settlements along here, and very little traffic comes this way, you should take more than the usual 'emergency rations' of food and water.

Some 10km after leaving Ai-Ais on the C10, there is a turning to the right on the D316. Though a minor road, this is in good order, leading across open farmland, down to a small river and then uphill on its way – eventually – to join the main B1. If Lüderitz is your goal, though, look out for a sandy track on the right, a short way up the hill, signposted simply 'Rosh Pinah 4x4' (✪ 28°09.775'S, 17°35.752'E). The signpost is slightly misleading, for when it's dry one of the tracks in this direction is passable, with care, for 2WD vehicles.

From here, the track winds back down through apparently barren terrain towards a dry riverbed, backed by mountains (✪ 28°09.409'S, 17°31.338'E). Here, the white monotone of the sand is broken by low-lying bushes and, after the rain, flowering succulents which carpet the valley in a deep red, enlivened by splashes of bright yellow stonecrop. Some 19km from the D316, the track splits (✪ 28°12.651'S, 17°26.292'E). Those with a 4x4 can take their pick, but if you have

THE DESERT HORSES

On the edge of the Koichab Pan, around the Garub Pan, perhaps the world's only desert-dwelling horses are thriving. In 1996 there were about 134 horses, and '97 was a good year for them with at least ten new foals born; a sharp drop to just 89 animals in 1999 has since been redressed, with the current number standing at around 150. On average, the numbers fluctuate between 90 and 300 at any one time.

Their origins have fuelled considerable controversy over the years. Some considered that they were descended from farm animals that had escaped, or horses that the German Schutztruppe abandoned at the start of World War I. Others, that they came from Duwisib Castle, near Maltahöhe. By October 1908 Captain Von Wolf, Duwisib's owner, had assembled a herd of about 33 animals, namely '2 imported stallions, 17 imported mares, 8 Afrikaner mares, 6 year-old fillies'. He was a fanatical horseman, and by November 1909 he had expanded this collection to '72 horses. Mares: 15 Australians, 23 others, 9 thoroughbreds. Rest: Afrikaners and foals. 2 imported thoroughbred stallions'. Von Wolf left Duwisib in 1914 and was later killed at the battle of the Somme. Yet there were reports of wild horses near Garub in the 1920s, ten years before Von Wolf's farm manager reported the loss of any horses.

New research conducted by biologist Telané Greyling in 2005, with the support of the Ministry for the Environment and Tourism, as well as Klein-Aus Vista and the Gondwana Desert Collection, suggests that the herd was drawn together from all of these sources, as well as those of the South African Army. Rather more important, though, has been to draw up a plan for the future of horses that are neither domestic animals nor natural game. As a result of Greyling's research, a number of goals were agreed, including raising awareness among the public, and to improve opportunities for tourism (and thus help to resource measures to preserve the horses). Pass them in March, surrounded by a wavy sea of fine green grass, and their situation seems idyllic. But see them on the same desolate gravel plains on an October afternoon, and you'll appreciate their remarkable survival.

11

a 2WD vehicle it's important that you take the left fork, through the gate, which continues on slightly higher land until it joins up with the C13 on the Orange River (✪ 28°19.650'S, 17°23.268'E). The 4x4 trail more or less follows the line of the river, coming out on the same road (✪ 28°16.430'S, 12°22.097'E), just half a kilometre closer to Rosh Pinah.

As it twists and turns along the country's southern border, the C13 narrows and widens according to the proximity of mountains and river to either side. At times the vista opens out across the river, offering some excellent picnic spots and opportunities for birdwatching – particularly as it crosses the Fish River (✪ 28°5.606'S, 17°10.306'E) – only to be restricted again as the road hugs close to the mountains to the north. Goats may be in their element, but drivers should take particular care along this stretch, for the road is unpredictable: many of the turns are sharp and hidden inclines may be unexpectedly steep. Eventually, the Orange River is left behind as the road heads northwest through desolate hills towards Rosh Pinah, along the border of the Sperrgebiet.

Along the Orange River Forming the border between Namibia and South Africa, the Orange River tends to be overlooked by visitors. However, with South Africa's wild Richtersveld National Park (now amalgamated with Ai-Ais National Park as one of the first 'Peace Parks' in the region) on its southern side, and very little access to its northern banks, it makes a perfect wilderness destination.

The flora in this area of the Namib is particularly unusual, because its proximity to the Cape leads it to receive some winter rainfall. This seems to promote the growth of succulents, including various *Lithops* and *Mesembryanthemum* species, several of which are endemic to this area. Visit in July, August or September and you may find whole areas in bloom, like Namaqualand just over the border to the south.

There are some fascinating larger plants here too, including *Aloe pillansii*, a close relative of the quivertree, which grows to 6–7m in the shape of a candelabra, and the rare, protected *Pachypodium namaquanum*, or half-man, a curious succulent which grows to 2m tall with a great girth. Its head always faces north.

Canoeing Several companies run canoeing trips along the Orange River, most of which are based out of Cape Town. These are generally geared towards South African visitors, and work well for those driving across the border who want to stop for a few days' canoeing.

Unlike the Victoria Falls, this isn't a white-water experience at all, and neither is it a game experience, though you may catch glimpses of game as you paddle. Rather it is a gentle trip through a stunningly beautiful wilderness area, notable for its scenery and lack of people.

What to take The arrangements with each canoeing company are different, but most will supply two-person Mohawk canoes, paddles, lifejackets, all meals and cool boxes for your own drinks. They will also have watertight containers to keep limited luggage dry.

You must bring your sleeping bag, personal toiletries (preferably biodegradable), a set of clothes for the river and one for when you're away from the water. A hat, long cotton trousers and long-sleeved cotton blouse/shirt, as well as a bathing costume, are fine for the river, plus trainers and warm tracksuit (the temperatures can drop!) for wearing off the river. Many ask you to bring your own drinks (soft, alcoholic and bottled water). Note that glass bottles are not allowed down the river, and so you'll need to decant liquids before you start.

Some companies advise that you will also need your own knife, fork, spoon, mug, plate, torch, toilet paper and sleeping mat. Visitors sometimes take small tents and even folding chairs along, and often you'll be requested to bring large, strong plastic bin liners. The better companies, like Felix Unite, have stocks of all this kit available to hire for their trips.

Rafting companies The southern Cape, around Cape Town, is the base for most of these trips, and companies to contact include:

Felix Unite ☎ +27 21 404 1830; f +27 21 448 4915; e info@felixunite.com; www.felixunite.com. The most experienced & probably the largest of the companies currently running this river. A 4-day trip costs from N$2,115 pp, inc meals.

Aquatrails 4 Constantia Rd, Wynberg 7800, Cape Town, South Africa; ☎/f +27 21 782 7982; e info@aquatrails.co.za; www.aquatrails.co.za
Intrapid Rafting ☎ +27 21 461 4918; f +27 21 465 3161; e raftsa@iafrica.com; www.raftsa.co.za

If you need further information on rafting companies, then contact Captour, the Cape's tourist information centre (☎ +27 21 418 5214).

Where to stay There are a couple of places to stay in Noordoewer itself (see pages 201–2). Otherwise, you'll be looking at camping en route. Even in winter this is can be an attractive option where the canyon walls provide shelter from the extremes of winter temperature. A couple of good campsites are in the area:

Å **Bo Plaas** PO Box 32, Noordoewer; telephone connected via Radio 251 in Walvis Bay on ☎ 064 203581; e jansenkobus@yahoo.com. Between the Gamkab and Fish rivers (✪ 28°8.378'S, 17°11.775'E), Bo Plaas lies in a tranquil setting at the foot of the hills near the Huns Mountains, right on the Orange River. It's an attractive, rustic site, with space for up to 40 people. Aside from wood and water, you will need to bring everything with

you. Guests may use the pool, but the river is a far more appealing prospect for swimming, also offering opportunities for canoeing trips to Fish River. Horseriding is available on request. N$30 pp.
Å **Namuskluft** ☎ 063 274134; f 063 274277. This lies some 14km east of the C13, about 1km before it reaches Rosh Pinah. It offers a swimming pool, walking trails, 4x4 trips and even a bar.

Rosh Pinah About 165km south of Aus, and a similar distance from Ai-Ais (171km) or Noordoewer (154km), the mining town of Rosh Pinah lies in a very remote corner of Namibia, almost on the eastern border of the Sperrgebiet.

A deposit of copper was discovered just south of here by a Prussian Jew, Mose Eli Kahan, who had fled Europe to escape persecution. By the 1920s this was being worked, but was abandoned when the price slumped in the 1930s. Thirty years later, in 1968, Kahan found a zinc deposit in the mountains, which he named Rosh Pinah. Though he died soon afterwards, his son eventually joined forces with the large South African mining company Iscor to develop it.

Production began in 1969, and by the end of the century the mine was producing around 72,000 tonnes of zinc per year, as well as a lead concentrate, and also a little silver. A more recent discovery of better-quality zinc has led to the development of the nearby Scorpion mine, which opened in 2003 at a cost of U$54 million, representing the largest investment in Namibia since independence in 1990. Designed to extract up to 150,000 tonnes of high-grade zinc per year over a 15-year period, the mine currently accounts for around 4% of the country's gross national product, employing around 600 people.

As part of related improvements to the region's infrastructure, the road between Rosh Pinah and Aus is being upgraded to tar; by 2006, an 80km stretch out of Rosh Pinah had been finished, with completion of the work imminent. Even before this, the drive from Ai-Ais to Aus could be undertaken in around six hours or so; once the road is tarred right through, the journey time will be cut considerably. In addition to work on the roads, work to repair and improve the railway from Aus to Lüderitz is expected to be completed during 2007, although only freight trains will run on the newly opened line.

Few visitors pass through Rosh Pinah so there is little in the way of tourist accommodation, though if you've friends at the mine you may be able to use the company's guesthouse. There has, though, been a considerable investment in services in the town since the opening of the Scorpion mine, with branches of the First National and Standard banks, a couple of supermarkets, a fuel station and a post office. It's also worth noting that there is mobile phone coverage in the town itself – something of a rarity in this predominantly desert environment.

LÜDERITZ

Trapped between the desiccating sands of the Namib and the freezing waters of the South Atlantic's Benguela current, Lüderitz is a fascinating old German town, full of character. It is usually sleepy and laid-back, with relaxed locals who often have time to talk. (Witness the number of public phones, which seem to be everywhere.) Around the centre of town, houses are painted in improbable pastel shades, which makes Lüderitz feel like a delightful toy town at times.

The air here is tangibly clean, even on the foggiest of mornings. Local Namibians say that Lüderitz can have all four seasons in a day, as the weather can change in hours from bright, hot and sunny, to strong winds, to dark, cold and foggy – and then back to sunshine again. This variation, together with a cold sea and the prevailing southwest wind, rule out Lüderitz as a beach destination, though brave souls still take brief dips from the beach near the Nest Hotel or round on the peninsula.

In the evenings, there are a few lively bars, and a handful of quiet restaurants, notable for their seafood. But the entertainment here pales in comparison with Swakopmund. Because of its location, Lüderitz is not somewhere to 'drop in on' as you need to make a special journey to come here – but it's worth visiting for its architecture, its peninsula, and to see a part of Namibia which seems almost unaware of the outside world. Try to avoid Sundays, though, when almost everything closes down, and the town is empty.

Tourism is having an impact here, but only gradually. Several new hotels have been opened in the last few years, and more guesthouses have opened their doors. Lüderitz's prosperity is likely to be increasingly based on tourism, with a trendy waterfront development near the harbour the most recent innovation. Over the next year or two, there are plans to develop the area alongside the old power station overlooking the sea near the Nest Hotel. Rumours abound as to the eventual use of this site, but luxury flats are almost certain to feature in the equation. Whether or not the town gets the sports centre that the locals would like may well be a matter of economics.

In recent years there has been considerable debate over the impact on Lüderitz of the Kudu gas field in the South Atlantic. In the end, however, the decision was taken to base operations for the US$800 million project in Oranjemund, leaving Lüderitz unaffected. Of greater relevance to Lüderitz, however, is the use of the harbour as the export base for the Scorpion zinc mine near Rosh Pinah, which has brought considerable new business into the town.

Meanwhile, the only thing that seems to disturb the peace is a siren sounded at noon during the week, to remind the townspeople of the time! (The same siren sounded intermittently means that there's a fire somewhere.)

HISTORY Stone Age tools and artefacts found in the region confirm that Khoisan people knew the area centuries before any Europeans arrived. The first recorded visit by a European was that of Bartholomeu Dias, the great Portuguese explorer, who sheltered here in 1487. He returned the following year and erected a limestone cross at the spot now known as Diaz Point, naming the place Angra Pequena, or 'Little Bay'.

Passing mariners recognised it as one of the best natural harbours on the southwest coast of Africa – even if the land around the harbour was desolate, forbidding, and totally lacking in fresh water. The Dutch East India Company sent an emissary to start trading with Nama groups in the region. This failed. In 1793 the area was annexed by the Dutch authorities in the Cape ... who proceeded to do nothing with it.

By the mid-1800s, whalers, sealers, fishermen and guano collectors were exploiting the area's rich marine life and there are reports of hundreds of ships around the harbour area. By 1862 some had set up shore bases here.

In March 1883 a German trader, Adolf Lüderitz, with help from Heinrich Vogelsang, a merchant from the Cape, bought a small ship, the *Tilly*, and surreptitiously set sail northwards from the Cape. They arrived at Angra Pequena on 10 April, landed their supplies, and Vogelsang set off to Bethanie in the interior. By 1 May Vogelsang had bought the bay (and 8km around it) for Lüderitz from Nama Kaptein Josef Frederiks for £100 and 200 rifles.

On 12 May the German flag was hoisted in Angra Pequena, and in August Vogelsang returned to Kaptain Josef, buying a 32km-wide coastal belt from the Orange River to the 26th degree of latitude south for a further £100 and 60 rifles. He named the area Lüderitzland.

Whilst Vogelsang cultivated a business selling guns throughout the region, Lüderitz returned to the Cape in September to find his land rights challenged. Negotiations ensued, by which time Germany was waking up to the scramble for Africa, and sent a gunboat, the *Nautilus*, to what they called Lüderitz Bay. By August 1884 the British had agreed that Germany could found its first colony here – their first foothold which led to the eventual annexation of South West Africa.

Lüderitz himself made little money out of the venture, and disappeared a few years later while out prospecting. The town grew slowly, and was an important supply base for the German Schutztruppe during the war with the Nama people in 1904–07. The construction of a railway line to Keetmanshoop, between 1906 and 1908, promised more trade, but was overshadowed by the diamond boom that began as the railway was finished (see *The diamond boom*, page 233).

From then the town exploded as the centre of supplies and operations of the diamond-mining company, CDM. Gradually the town's fishing industries developed, and an important export trade of rock lobster was established. However, the CDM headquarters moved to Oranjemund in 1943, precipitating the start of the town's slow decline. What does remain, though, is the significant diamond-diving industry (see page 221), and the diamond company NAMDEB continues to have a considerable stake in the town.

Only in the last few years, through tourism and fishing, has Lüderitz's economy started to look up again. Ironically tourism has been helped by the lack of development between the 1940s and the '90s – which preserved many of the beautiful buildings of the early 1900s.

GETTING THERE Most visitors drive to Lüderitz, between visiting the Namib-Naukluft National Park and the Fish River Canyon. Because the town is out on a limb, the drive takes time. Although the town is bisected by a railway, passenger trains have not run for several years, but recent work on the track means that zinc from the Scorpion mine near Rosh Pinah will soon be transported from Aus to Lüderitz by rail. If you choose to visit the area, allow yourself a minimum of two nights to appreciate it, and to see its surrounds properly.

By car See *The Roads to Lüderitz* (pages 211–18) for comments on the whole journey, but note that for the last 20km there is a 60km/h speed limit. This is because the fast tarmac road cuts through a field of shifting barchan dunes, which constantly march across it. Go slowly. Even a small pile of sand is hard when hit at speed.

By air Lüderitz has one flight per day, except Saturday, to Windhoek via Walvis Bay (N\$2,760 from Windhoek; N\$1,900 from Walvis Bay). The airstrip is about 9km east of the town, opposite Kolmanskop.

By bus/hitchhiking There are currently no bus services linking Lüderitz with the rest of Namibia, increasing the town's isolation. (TransNamib's Starline bus service, which used to connect Lüderitz with Keetmanshoop, has recently been discontinued.) It is, though, perfectly possible to take a combi taxi between the township in Lüderitz (The Location) and Keetmanshoop (N\$100) or Windhoek's Katutura (N\$160). Ask a local taxi driver to direct you to the appropriate stop. Lüderitz Safaris and Tours (see page 225) is a booking agent for Intercape Mainliner, so you can plan onward journeys here.

Fortunately, compared with many of Namibia's attractions, Lüderitz is relatively easy to reach by hitching. The tar road from Keetmanshoop has a steady trickle of traffic along it, and intrepid hitchhikers have even made it from Walvis Bay along the C14 via Sesriem – though taking food and water with you is essential on this route.

By sea There are no regular passenger boats calling at Lüderitz, but the town is a port of call for a number of cruise ships, usually between January and March.

GETTING AROUND If you don't have your own car, there are two options – hire a car or use the service of one of the town's tour operators (see page 225). Transport from the airport or to Kolmanskop with one of the tour operators costs N\$80 for two people, and a further N\$40 for each additional passenger, plus 15% VAT.

Car hire Three of the big car-hire companies have offices in Lüderitz:

Avis ☎ 063 203968; m 081 124 1827; f 063 203549

Budget BP Depot, Main Rd; ☎/f 063 202777

Imperial Cnr Bismarck & Bahnhof sts; ☎ 063 202728

WHERE TO STAY Lüderitz has several hotels varying from the upmarket Nest and rather less corporate Zum Sperrgebiet to several more personal establishments. A proliferation of bed and breakfast-type guesthouses in recent years reflects the increase in visitors to the town, which also offers a backpackers' lodge and a windswept campsite (complete with super lighthouse). It is best to book most of them in advance, as the town's rooms quickly fill up during the busier times of year (see *When to go*, pages 47–8).

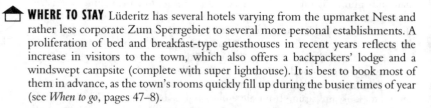

Nest Hotel (73 rooms) 820 Diaz St; ☎ 063 204000; f 063 204001; e reservations@ nesthotel.com; www.nesthotel.com. Set on its own right on the sea to the southwest of town, with its own beach, the Nest is Lüderitz's largest hotel, & reputedly cost N\$30 million to build. Rooms are built around a sheltered central courtyard enclosing a good-size swimming pool, & each has a sea view. Facilities are as you would expect from a

4-star hotel all rooms have en-suite shower or bath, twin or double beds, TV, phone, AC/central heating, coffee/tea-making facilities & hairdryer. Three are adapted for paraplegics. Public rooms feature a rather small bar set off a considerably larger reception area, & a good waterfront restaurant, as well as an oyster bar. There's also a sauna with a sea view, a children's play area, & a 'sundowner' bar that is open only to hotel

The wealth of southwestern Namibia may have been built on diamonds from the Sperrgebiet, but today the greatest proportion of the diamonds found in the area around Lüderitz are mined from under the sea rather than in the Sperrgebiet itself. These alluvial diamonds are found all along the Orange River and at its mouth, but over the years many have been swept farther north by the Benguela Current, with significant deposits now to be found in the seas around Lüderitz harbour.

The leading company in this field is Namibian Minerals Corporation (NAMCO), which has been operational since 1994. Following the company's estimates that around 2.6 million carats of diamonds were to be found in these waters, large-scale operations went live in 1998, with some 650,000 carats now produced each year. Boats put out to sea regularly from the harbour in Lüderitz. On the larger diamond boats, robotic machines trawl in waters up to 150m deep, digging a trench in the sea bed then sucking up the material from depths of 10–16m, up to 25m, ready for processing on board. While the first bags collected contain little except sand, beneath this layer is gravel; it is among the gravel that diamonds are most likely to be found. NAMDEB, too, has considerable resources devoted to this sector within an area that extends 200km out into the Atlantic.

Smaller boats are owned and operated under licence to NAMDEB by diamond divers. Each boat is allocated a specific area, not more than 5km from the coast, in which to search. Theirs is a dangerous job, in unforgiving conditions, but the potential rewards are high: in 1999, 60,000 carats of diamonds were collected in this way.

When the boats return to port, the sacks are taken by officials from NAMDEB to their processing plant, where the contents are classified. All boats, including any personal luggage on board, are thoroughly checked and inspected for any gravel that may have been overlooked before they are declared 'clean'.

residents — perhaps a casualty of the town's fabled cool breezes! The recent addition of an internet café is a useful extra. Outside is a guarded parking area.
Low season (Dec–Mar, Jun) N$600/884 sgl/pp sharing; high season N$750/1,105 sgl/pp sharing, B&B.

⌂ **Sea-View Hotel Zum Sperrgebiet** (22 twin rooms, 2 flats) Cnr Woermann & Stettiner streets; ✆ 063 203411/2/9; f 063 203414; e sperrgebiet@proteahotels.com.na; www.proteahotels.com.na. A recent addition to the South African Protea Hotels group, this modern hotel is still managed by former owner, Ingrid Morgans. Compact, smart & very comfortable, it sits slightly out of the centre of town. Each of the small rooms is well designed, with TV, coffee/tea maker, hairdryer, en-suite facilities that include a good shower (some also have baths), & a small balcony with a view over either the harbour or the courtyard.

The efficient-looking restaurant sits beside a small (but spectacular) indoor swimming pool, surrounded by banana trees & shaded glass walls,

overlooking the harbour in the distance. A sauna & garden are tucked away, out of view.
N$593/945/1,267/1,605 sgl/dbl/trpl/family, B&B.

⌂ **Bay View Hotel** (29 rooms) Diaz St; ✆ 063 202288; m 081 128 0780; f 063 202402; e bayview@ldz.namib.com; www.namibweb.com/bayview.htm. On the corner of Bismarck & Diaz streets, opposite the museum, the Bay View is clean, comfortable & friendly. If you're looking for a hotel with a feel for the old town, the Bay View is the best there is. Despite being one of the town's larger hotels, it still feels small, perhaps because the rooms are built around a courtyard & swimming pool.

Each twin-bedded room has a TV & direct-dial phone. There is off-street parking at the back, and internet access for guests and non-residents alike. A small, bright restaurant with adjoining bar serves breakfast, lunch, & dinner to allcomers.
N$369/639/739 sgl/dbl/trpl, B&B.

⌂ **Kapps Hotel** (14 rooms) Bay Rd; ✆ 063 202345; f 063 203555; e pmk@mweb.com.na. The Kapps is Lüderitz's oldest hotel, built in 1907 & once owned by the Lüderitz family. Modern fabrics liven up the

en-suite rooms, each with TV, phone, & tea-making facilities. These are set around a brick-lined courtyard at the back. Breakfast & à-la-carte dinner are served in the hotel's Rumours Grill (see page 225), which also has a sports bar & beer garden.
N$285/225 sgl/pp sharing; family N$550.

🏠 **Haus Sandrose** (1 room, 1 flat, 1 hse) 15 Bismarck St; ☎ 063 202630; m 081 241 5544; f 063 202365; e haussandrose@iway.na. Walk-in guests only; no advance bookings. Christine & Erich Looser's centrally located accommodation is guaranteed to make visitors feel individual. Three entirely distinct styles mark out their 3 units, from the roomy Grosse Bucht self-catering house that sleeps up to 5, through the 2-bed Bogenfels flat with shower & toilet across a small private courtyard, to the colourful dbl room. Anin bed linen adorns each of the rooms, which also have their own cooking facilities (the bedroom has just an egg boiler, kettle & toaster) & individual private seating areas in the garden. There is also guarded street parking in front of the Sandrose gift shop.
N$350/200 sgl/pp sharing. B/fast N$50.

🏠 **Zur Waterkant** (4 rooms, 2 flats) Bremer St; ☎/f 063 203145; e zur-waterkant@raubkatzen.de; www.raubkatzen.de. Marlene & Hartmut Halbich's homely B&B offers comfortable accommodation, though if Hartmut is not in, you'll find a smattering of German is helpful. En-suite rooms are simply furnished with dbl beds, & each has a small, sea-facing balcony. There are also two self-catering flats. Dinner is available on request.
N342/470 sgl/dbl, B&B. Self-catering N$230 pp.

🏠 **Hansa Haus Guesthouse** (4 rooms) Mabel St; ☎/f 063 203581; m 081 129 9311; f 063 202605; e mcloud@africaonline.com.na. Right at the top of Mabel St, this imposing blue house was built in 1909 with a commanding view of the town. It was opened as a guesthouse in 2001, focusing exclusively on self-catering guests. High-ceilinged dbl rooms with high ceilings are attractively furnished & have basic cooking facilities (stove, fridge, microwave, kettle, cutlery & cooking utensils), with tea, coffee, sugar & biscuits provided; braai facilities are available, too. Guests share 2 bathrooms, with either shower or bath, & there's a separate TV lounge.
From N$195/380 sgl/dbl. No b/fast available.

🏠 **Hartmann Mansions** (20 rooms) Bismarck St; ☎ 063 203684; f 063 203863; e jjsports@iway.na. Catering for the budget market, Hartmann's offers a range of basic accommodation, from a 10-bed dorm to 5 singles, a family room, and 2 en-suite doubles. Furniture comes into the essentials category: bed,

dressing table and wardrobe, but there's a dining room with TV, and rather surprisingly also a photocopying service. If you don't fancy eating out, there's a take-away service in the building.
N$160/220/250 sgl/dbl/dorm/family. En-suite double is N$250, dorm bed N$79, all B&B.

🏠 **Kratzplatz** (10 rooms) 5 Nachtigal St; ☎/f 063 202458, m 081 129 2458; e kratzmr@iway.na; www.kratzplatz.com. This friendly & comfortable B&B run by Manfred & Monica Kratz stands on the continuation of Bay Rd after it crosses the railway line. It's painted bright red, so you can't miss it! The main building, a converted church, features whitewashed, high-ceiling rooms, all of which are now en suite. Most rooms have TV, & the style & furnishings are modern & simple: this is a pleasant place, with secure parking. A word of caution, though: the adjacent Barrels restaurant can get pretty lively, so if you need your sleep, it's probably best to avoid staying at the weekend.
N$310/430/600/730 sgl/dbl/trp/family, B&B.

🏠 **Obelix Village Guesthouse** (15 rooms) ☎ 063 203456; f 063 203457; m 081 128 3667; e obelixvillage@iway.na; www.obelixvillage.com. This relative newcomer to Lüderitz has double & family rooms set in a long, low block under thatch. Comfortable & spacious, all are en suite, with simple décor & traditional furnishings. By contrast, the central lapa has a more rustic feel. Guests may use the braai facilities, & safe inside parking makes for a stress-free stay.
N$325/490/620 sgl/dbl/family.

🏠 **Krabbenhöft und Lampe** (2 flats, 5 rooms) 25 Bismarck St; ☎ 063 202466 (after hours 202674); m 081 129 2025; f 063 202549; e info@klguesthouse.com; www.klguesthouse.com. This imposing place at the top of the town houses some unexpected guest accommodation. Constructed in 1880, the building used to be home to a carpet-weaving factory but is now simply a shop. Upstairs, however, the large, spotless, if rather stark rooms retain many architectural features, with scarcely a nod in the direction of modernity. Two flats on the first floor are fully self-catering, while one flight further up ('Oberdeck') are 5 twin-bedded rooms with shared bathrooms, toilets & kitchen facilities, as well as TV & phone. It's certainly distinctive, & represents good value for money.
Oberdeck N$145/249 sgl/dbl, or N$1,099 for the whole floor; 2-bed flat N$379, 6-bed flat N$829.

🏠 **Backpackers Lodge** (3 rooms, 14 dorm beds, camping) 7 Schinz St, opposite Nature Conservation office; ☎ 063 202000; e luderitzbackpackers@

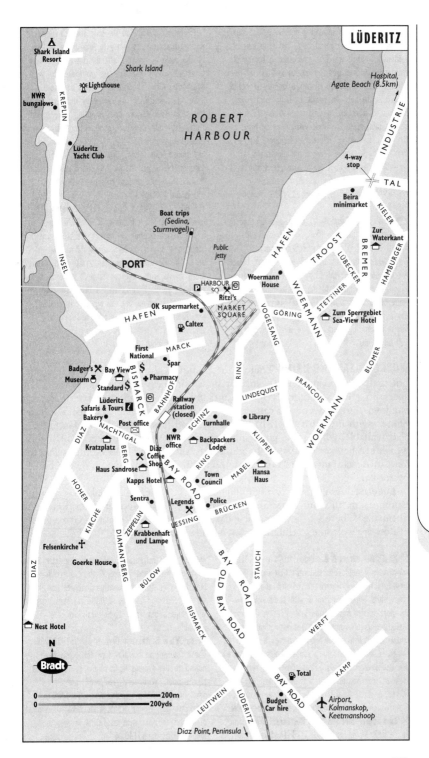

LÜDERITZ

Shark Island Resort

Shark Island

Lighthouse

NWR bungalows

KREPLIN

Lüderitz Yacht Club

Hospital, Agate Beach (8.5km)

ROBERT HARBOUR

INDUSTRIE

4-way stop

TAL

Beira minimarket

KIELER

TROOST

Zur Waterkant

BREMER

HAMBURGER

Boat trips (Sedina, Sturmvogel)

Public jetty

INSEL

PORT

HAFEN

LÜBECKER

STETTINER

WOERMANN

Woermann House

Zum Sperrgebiet Sea-View Hotel

BLOMER

HARBOUR SQ

Ritzi's

MARKET SQUARE

VOGELSANG

GÖRING

OK supermarket

Caltex

HAFEN

First National

MARCK

Spar

RING

LINDEQUIST

FRANCOIS

Badger's

Bay View

BISMARCK

Pharmacy

Museum

Standard

Lüderitz Safaris & Tours

Bakery

Post office

BAHNHOF

Railway station (closed)

SCHINZ

Turnhalle

Library

WOERMANN

DIAZ

NACHTIGAL

NWR office

Backpackers Lodge

KLIPPEN

Kratzplatz

BERG

Diaz Coffee Shop

RING

MABEL

Hansa Haus

Haus Sandrose

Kapps Hotel

Town Council

BAY ROAD

Sentra

HOHER

Legends

Police

BRÜCKEN

STAUCH

KIRCHE

ZEPPELIN

LESSING

DIAMANTBERG

Krabbenhaft und Lampe

Felsenkirche

Goerke House

BÜLOW

BAY OLD BAY ROAD

Nest Hotel

N

Bradt

BISMARCK

WERFT

KAMP

0 ——— 200m
0 ——— 200yds

BAY ROAD

Total

Budget Car hire

LEUTWEIN

LÜDERITZ

Airport, Kolmanskop, Keetmanshoop

Diaz Point, Peninsula

hotmail.com. With an increasing number of backpackers finding Lüderitz, this central lodge had something of a monopoly when it was first established. It has simple twin rooms with shared facilities, as well as dormitories, an equipped kitchen, a laundry service & a yard at the back for braais. Its large main room has lots of space and is used for watching TV & playing table tennis — albeit surrounded by beds, as the room doubles as an overflow dormitory for overland truck groups. There is an informative noticeboard at the front & the manager is also a mine of useful information about the area.
N$189/230 dbl/family; dorm bed N$75, camping N$45 pp.

🏠 **Shark Island Campsite** (3 bungalows, lighthouse, 20 campsites) Book via NWR, ☏ 061 2857200; f 061 224900; e reservations@nwr.com.na; www.nwr.com.na. Along Hafen & Insel streets, beside the harbour & past the Caltex refinery, lies Shark Island, which is linked to the mainland by a causeway & a road. Here Lüderitz's only campsite has a superb location, with power & braai facilities, but it is amazingly windy; make sure your tent is well anchored.

If there's nobody on the gate then campers can just pitch their tents — try to find a site sheltered by the rocks — and the attendants will come over to collect money. The sites are overlooked by a lighthouse, with 2 bedrooms, kitchen, bathroom & living area, which can be rented by small groups — this must be Lüderitz's most imposing place to stay. The nearby bungalows are good value, & are warmer than the campsites!
Lighthouse N$850, bungalow (sleep 6) N$450, camping N$50 per site plus N$20/10 per adult/child (max 8 people). Standard entry fee N$40 pp.

🏠 **Island Cottage** (2 cottages) ☏ 063 203626; m 081 292 2984; f 063 204113; e retha.c@mweb.com.na. Shark Island is a windlashed spot for a pair of self-catering cottages, but these 2 are brand new & very modern, so should at least stand up to the elements better than a tent. Each caters for 4 guests, with either a dbl or 2 sgl beds, & a couch. As you'd expect, there's a shower, kitchen, TV, phone & braai area, but the big plus is a superb west-facing view out to sea from an upstairs veranda.
N$320 per room.

✕ **WHERE TO EAT AND DRINK** There's not an endless choice of cuisine in Lüderitz, but seafood (and particularly lobster in season, best ordered in advance) is a speciality – it is what most visitors want, and what most places serve. If seafood is above your budget (you can expect to pay upwards of N$110 for a seafood platter, with more for crayfish) then steaks and more usual Namibian fare are also available, while some good smaller take-aways serve burgers and bar food which can be excellent value. In addition to those listed below, there's also the Pelican Restaurant at the Nest Hotel, with its panoramic views, or the hotel's oyster bar.

Lüderitz doesn't major on nightlife, but locals congregate at the bars adjacent to Rumours or the Butcher's Shop & Grill, or at the German club above the Turnhalle. There's a bowling alley (*kegelbahn*), next to Rumours Grill, where visitors are welcome to club nights on Monday and Thursday.

✕ **Ritzi's Restaurant & Bar** Hafen St; ☏ 063 202818; www.ritzisrestaurant.com. Lüderitz's best eatery has moved to the new waterfront complex, above the coffee shop. Smart, modern & with good views over the port, it also has outside seating. As you'd expect, the menu majors on seafood, but with plenty of innovation. If fish is not for you, there's a good choice of alternatives, inc a range of pizzas, & there are also several specials. Prices come as a very pleasant surprise, including a seafood platter at N$110, & the wine list is unbelievably good value. *Open lunch & dinner except Sun; booking advisable.*

✕ **Zum Sperrgebiet Sea-View Restaurant** Woermann St; ☏ 063 31 3411; f 063 31 3414. Like many

modern hotel restaurants, this lacks character, but is stylish, with good service, & there are ceiling fans for when (if?) the weather becomes hot. It serves good food at around N$80 for steaks served with chips and veggies. Light meals are also available.

✕ **Bay View Restaurant** Diaz St; ☏ 063 202288. The restaurant at the Bay View Hotel has been moved to the ground floor, in the courtyard next to the pool. With very good food, and an adjoining bar, it's a popular venue. For dinner, expect to pay around N$65, while a blow-out meal of oysters to start, with crayfish & dessert to follow, might be N$140.

✗ Barrels 5 Nachtigal St; ☎ 063 202458. The lively restaurant at Kratzplatz is popular with the backpacking fraternity and beyond, with occasional live music. Among a wide-ranging menu that includes pizza & light meals, the fish & chips is reputed to be excellent.

✗ Butcher's Shop & Grill Cnr Bay Rd & Lessing St; ☎ 063 203110. Opposite the police station, this informal but comfortable restaurant, which was formerly Legends, has its own bar alongside. Friendly staff serve the normal seafood & steak fare, as well as burgers & pizzas, & there are vegetarian options too – all in generous portions at around N$40–90. *Open daily, lunch & dinner; happy hour Sat 20.00–21.00.*

✗ Rumours Grill Bay Rd; ☎ 063 202345. The broad-ranging menu of the restaurant at Kapps Hotel features everything from burgers & steaks to seafood. Rumours is popular locally, but the restaurant surroundings aren't particularly edifying, & crayfish at

N$135 is pretty expensive by these standards. There's a separate, lively sports bar with large TV. *Open 18.00–late; sports bar serves bar lunches.*

☕ Diaz Coffee Shop Cnr Bismarck St & Nachtigal Rd; ☎ 063 203147. This well-positioned & relaxed café is a good place to take the chill off a Lüderitz morning, with snacks & cakes, as well as light meals. It's open on Sundays, too, which is an added bonus. *Open Mon–Sat 08.00–17.00, Sun 09.00–13.00.*

Seabreeze Coffee Shop On the harbour front, this simple café serves light meals, coffee & cake. *Open Mon–Sat all day, Sun mornings only.*

✗ Badger's Bistro 3 Diaz St; ☎ 063 204010. Badger's nowadays is simply a take-away, with an adjacent bar. *Open Mon–Fri 09.00–midnight, Sat 09.00–14.00 & 17.00–midnight.*

✗ Captain Macarena ☎ 063 203958. Serves fish & chips to take away from its premises in the modern Harbour Square development. *Open Mon all day, Sat until 12.00.*

OTHER PRACTICALITIES As you'd expect, most of the major Namibian banks have branches in Luderitz: Standard, First National and Nedbank are all on Bismarck Street. **In an emergency**, the police are reached on ☎ 063 10111, whilst the ambulance and hospital are on ☎ 063 202446, and the fire service on ☎ 063 202255. There's a pharmacy (☎ *063 202806*) on Bismarck Street, next to the First National Bank. The town's **newspaper**, *Buchter News*, is edited by groups of British or Dutch volunteers who each spend a year working on the paper, with sponsorship from major businesses.

Tour operators If you merely need advice about enjoying yourself, there are several companies who might be able to help. Note that trips into the Sperrgebiet (except to Agate Bay and Kolmanskop) must be booked at least five working days in advance. You will need to provide names, passport numbers and nationalities for all who want to take part in order to get the right permits. The **NWR** office is housed in the old post office building, dating back to 1907, on Schinz Street (☎ *063 202752;* f *063 2203213;* e *reservations@nwr.com.na; www.nwr.com.na*).

Lüderitz Safaris & Tours Bismarck St; ☎ 063 202719; f 063 202863; ludsaf@africaonline.com.na. Run by Marion Schelkle, this is a convenient & very efficient tour operator that also doubles as the tourist information office & is the booking agent for Intercape Mainliner. They can help with bookings in Lüderitz, or further afield, & can issue permits for Kolmanskop. They are also agents for both tours of Kolkmanskop & the *Sedina & Sturmvogel* boat trips, & run a range of day excursions to ensure that the visitor can make the most of a limited stay in the town. Marion also organises trips around southern Namibia. A large selection of Namibian books & crafts is on sale in the office here, which is open daily.

Ghost Town Tours Goerke House, 1 Diamantberg St;

☎/f 063 204031, e kolmans@iafrica.com.na; www.ghosttowntours.com. The company that administers Kolmanskop also runs trips there (see pages 231–2) and issues permits for self-drive visitors (min 8 people). A longer trip incorporating Elizabeth Bay and Kolmanskop costs N$315 pp, while the 'Elizabeth Bay Special', for 4–8 people, takes in both the above, including lunch at Kolmanskop, followed by a visit to Diaz Point and a guided tour of Lüderitz itself, for a total of N$630 pp. Tours leave daily at 08.30, returning at around 16.30.

Coastways Tours Hafen St; ☎ 063 202002; m 081 122 9336; f 063 202003; e lewiscwt@iway.na. Coastways started up with self-drive 4x4 trips to Saddle Hill & Spencer Bay to the north of Lüderitz, in the Namib-Naukluft Park, but in 2002, the company was granted the concession to take trips to Pomona & Bogenfels in the Sperrgebiet. For details, see page 232.

Shopping Lüderitz has three main supermarkets – of which the **Spar**, on the corner of Bahnhof and Moltke streets, and **OK Grocer**, on Hafen Street opposite the main harbour, are probably the best. Passing the harbour on the left, the **Beira minimarket** is a few blocks away and has, as its name suggests, a Portuguese bias. There's also a Portuguese supermarket at the southern end of Bismarck Street.

On the practical side, there's a branch of Cymot on Nachtigal Street (✆ 063 203856), handy in case you need any camping equipment before heading north into the Namib-Naukluft.

The new harbour development, the Waterfront, provides a number of small shops catering for visitors, with curios, postcards and jewellery available alongside the more usual hair salons and food shops. Also well worth a visit are the craft shop that is part of Haus Sandrose on Bismarck Street, and that at Lüderitz Safaris and Tours further down the same street.

Communications In addition to internet facilities at the post office, on the corner of Nachtigal and Bismarck streets, and at the Bay View Hotel, there's a new internet café on the Waterfront.

WHAT TO SEE AND DO Even visitors with a limited attention span find enough to occupy themselves around Lüderitz for a day, whilst those who enjoy a more leisurely pace will take three or four to see the area's main attractions. Every other year, at the end of August, a two-day German Festival (Luka Karneval) takes place in Lüderitz and at Kolmanskop; the next is in 2007.

For the visitor, the focus of the town is the new harbourfront development. With a small tower that affords a good overview of the town, and a public jetty, it is a pleasant place to while away an hour or so watching the boats in the harbour. There is also a good seafood restaurant, a café, and public toilets (with a nominal charge).

Shark Island This erstwhile island is now joined to the mainland by a causeway, and most people visit only if they're staying here – at the campsite, the new self-catering houses or the lighthouse (see page 224). The windswept attractions of the place have obviously caught on, though, with several modern houses now in evidence.

Felsenkirche (*Open Mon–Sat for just one hour in the afternoon: 17.00 in summer, or 16.00 in winter; donations welcome*) If you approach the town from the sea, this small, rather stark Lutheran church is clearly visible. Located on a hill close to the Goerke Haus, it was built in 1912 and has some interesting stained-glass windows.

Museum (*Open Mon–Fri 15.30–17.00; open Sat 09.00–11.00 by arrangement only. N$10 pp*) Opposite the Bay View, on Diaz Street, this small museum (✆ 063 202532) has exhibits on the diamond-mining industry, including fake diamonds, an egg collection, a good section on the Bushmen, a variety of small exhibits on other indigenous cultures, and assorted cases of local flora and fauna.

Goerke Haus (*Open Mon–Fri 14.00–16.00, Sat 16.00–17.00, closed public holidays. Entry N$16 pp*) High up on Diamantberg, at the end of Zeppelin Street, Goerke House is the beautiful cream building with a blue roof that is built into the rocks above the level of the road. (Note that the house has recently been repainted;

references to the 'blue house' refer to this.) It is the town's best-preserved historical building, visible from around town, and if you visit nothing else in Lüderitz, make sure you see this.

Hans Goerke was born in Germany in 1874 and arrived in German South West Africa with the Schutztruppe in 1904. In 1907 he became provisions inspector for the German forces – just before diamonds were discovered near Kolmanskop. By the end of 1909 he had resigned from the army and was making a fortune in the diamond rush, which enabled him to have this house built between October 1909 and September 1910. It was then valued at 70,000 Deutschmarks (£3,500/US$5,250). One of Lüderitz's so-called 'diamond palaces', it is thought to have been designed by a German architect, Otto Ertl. Although it was built during the art nouveau period (*Jugendstil* in German), 1890–1920, and has many relevant features, it isn't typical of that style.

Goerke left Namibia for Germany in 1912. In 1920 the house was bought by Consolidated Diamond Mines (CDM), the forerunner of the present-day NAMDEB Diamond Corporation (which is now a partnership between South Africa's huge De Beers and the Namibian government). In 1944 they sold it back to the government of South West Africa for £2,404 (US$3,606), and the house became the residence of the local magistrate, and hence known as the Drostdy.

In 1981 the magistrate was recalled to Keetmanshoop – Lüderitz just didn't have enough crime – and the CDM repurchased the house and restored it for use as a VIP guesthouse.

There is an informative small leaflet about the house. Get one from the curator before you look around if possible. It notes some of the interesting art nouveau details to look out for, including:

- The flamingo motifs used on the stained-glass windows. The side profile of the flamingos' necks is a wavy form typical of the art nouveau style.
- The decorative detail on either side of the hat and coat stand in the hall, resembling Egyptian papyrus bells. Early art nouveau took inspiration from the shapes of plants.
- The mix of artistic styles, which is typical of art nouveau: Roman arches over the stairwell, supported by an Egyptian lotus column, capped by a Grecian Doric capital.
- The posts at the foot of the stairs resembling dentilled Gothic spires.

Other interesting features of the house include:

- The carpets and curtains which, although new, are typical of the period around 1910.
- The light fittings, some of which are original, as seen in the old photographs on display, are classic examples of the art nouveau style.
- The stunning pine flooring which is original, though during Goerke's time it was covered in patterned linoleum, a little of which remains in the study.
- The original stained-glass windows at the entrance and on the stairs.
- The friezes on the walls which have been restored, and the kitchens and bathrooms which have been modernised so that guests of NAMDEB can stay here.

Moves are afoot to have the house's original furniture sent back from South Africa, where it was taken years ago. However, the current furniture, although not original, is beautiful, from the piano with ivory keys to marble-topped dressing tables in the bedrooms and oak furniture around the lounge. Don't miss it.

11

Diamantberg Behind Goerke House, Diamantberg is the highest land around town. With a pair of stout shoes you can easily scramble up for a good view of the town and harbour beyond. Standing in the cool sea breeze, under desert sun, much about the landscape seems extreme. There is little vegetation to soften the parched land, whilst the sea beyond seems cold and uninviting. However, as if to compensate, the town's people have painted many of their buildings in soft pastel shades. Quaintly shaped wooden buildings, just a few storeys high and painted baby-blue, pink and green, all give Lüderitz the air of a pleasant, gentle town.

EXCURSIONS FROM LÜDERITZ

If you have your own transport then Lüderitz peninsula, Agate Beach and Kolmanskop are well worth visiting. To see some of the area to the south of Lüderitz, in the Sperrgebiet – the restricted diamond area – you must join an organised tour. There is also an excellent boat trip from the harbour.

BOAT TRIPS Weather permitting, the small schooner, *Sedina*, leaves the harbour at around 08.00 (departure times vary depending on the season) for a 2½-hour trip (N$240 pp) – under sail if you're lucky – around Diaz Point to Halifax Island in search of African penguins, seals and the endemic heavyside dolphin. While visitors are almost guaranteed to see these creatures, keep your eyes open and you'll spot plenty of birds as well, from scoters and various species of cormorant to oystercatchers and flamingos. The boat's skipper, Gunther, has sailed these waters for years, and is only too happy to share his considerable knowledge of marine wildlife.

Boat trips can also be taken further afield to the whaling station at Sturmvogel Bucht. Allow around four hours for this, at a cost of N$290 pp.

Both trips may be booked through Lüderitz Safaris & Tours or Ghost Town Tours (see page 225). Oliver Morgans (e *morgans@iafrica.com.na*) will also take visitors out on his boat, the *Hannah*, both for trips around the bay or to go out fishing.

LÜDERITZ PENINSULA To the southwest of the town lies the Lüderitz peninsula, surrounded by sea on three sides yet a rocky desert within. Here, the lower slopes are dotted with a surprising variety of salt-tolerant succulent plants. In winter, if there's been some good rain, many of these are in flower, affording scope for hours of plant spotting. Around the coast there are some rocky beaches and some sandy ones; all are worth exploring if you have a car.

Note that whilst the roads here are fine for 2WD cars, don't be tempted to follow tracks across soft sand made by local 4x4 enthusiasts, or you'll need their help to pull your vehicle out.

To reach the peninsula, simply follow Bismarck Street into Lüderitz Street, keeping the railway line on your left. If you'd prefer a tour, this can be arranged through Lüderitz Safaris & Tours (see page 225), from N$225 per hour.

The most interesting parts of the peninsula are:

Radford Bay This is reached shortly after leaving the town, and is often home to a flock of flamingos.

Second Lagoon Also a popular spot with visiting flamingos, and sometimes the odd stranded motorist. Continuing to the right –

Griffith Bay Excellent views of the town across the cold, misty sea, plus a few crystal-clear rocks pools to dabble in. It is named after an American officer who sheltered here and was then killed during the American Civil War.

Angra Club Believe it or not, there really is a golf course here, its nine holes played exclusively on sand. Although it's open to the public, locals advise visitors to go with someone who knows the course.

Sturmvogel Bucht The whaling station here can be visited from the *Sturmvogel* (see *Boat trips*, above).

Diaz Point Reached by a short wooden bridge is a granite cross, a replica of the one erected by Bartholomeu Dias, the first European explorer to enter the bay. He sheltered here in the late 14th century, referring to the bay as Angra Pequena, or 'Little Bay'. There are often seals sunning themselves on the rocks here. Just south of Diaz Point is a grave bearing a stark reminder: 'George Pond of London, died here of hunger and thirst 1906'. Talk of establishing a campsite and café here in the future is nearer to reality, with the imminent opening of some new self-catering houses. There are also plans for a small shop and bicycle rentals.

Halifax Island The large African penguin colony here can be viewed with a good pair of binoculars from the cliffs and beaches on the western side of Guano Bay, or – closer up – from the deck of the *Sedina* – see above.

Guano Bay Another good place to spot flamingos, either from land or from the *Sedina*.

Essy Bay A number of very rocky little bays, each with a place for a braai. All are linked by a network of good sand roads. The beach to the south side has a toilet block.

Eberlanz Höhle A cave cut deeply into the rock, about ten minutes' walk from the road; there's a path marked over the rocks. The small visitors' book in the cave was filled up some time in 2000!

Kleiner Fjord A small sandy beach with deep water and lots of kelp, so unsuitable for swimming.

Grosse Bucht A wide sandy beach with dark sand, long stranded pieces of kelp, plenty of kelp flies, and several turn-off points for stopping. The sand is dotted with mounds of salt-tolerant succulent plants in beautiful greens and reds, and the bay is perfect for accomplished windsurfers (strong winds). There are toilets here as well.

THE SPERRGEBIET: DIAMOND AREA NO 1 The Sperrgebiet, or 'forbidden zone', was first declared in 1908. Then mining was confined to within a few kilometres of the coast, whilst a coastal belt 100km wide was declared 'out of bounds' as a precaution to prevent unauthorised people from reaching the diamond fields.

At the height of restrictions there were two diamond areas: No 1 from the Orange River to 26°S, and No 2 from 26°S northwards to the Kuiseb, incorporating most of the Namibia's great dune-sea. Now these areas have shrunk, leaving only parts of No 1 as forbidden. This may not be for much longer, though, for discussions are currently under way to have the whole of this area, as far south as Oranjemund, designated as a national park. At present, the focus is on the type of activities that could be permitted in a region with such highly sensitive ecosystems, and the infrastructure that would be needed to support any development of this nature.

In the meantime, security here remains tight. Signs by the roadside threatening fines or imprisonment for just entering these areas are serious.

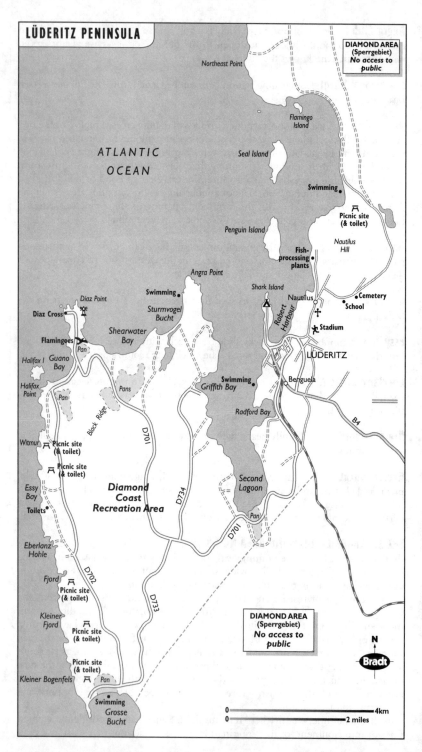

LÜDERITZ PENINSULA

DIAMOND AREA
(Sperrgebiet)
*No access to
public*

Northeast Point

ATLANTIC
OCEAN

*Flamingo
Island*

Seal Island

Swimming

Picnic site
(& toilet)

*Nautilus
Hill*

Penguin Island

**Fish-
processing
plants**

Angra Point

Shark Island

Swimming

*Sturmvogel
Bucht*

Nautilus

Cemetery

Diaz Point

Diaz Cross

*Shearwater
Bay*

Robert
Harbour

School

†

Stadium

Flamingoes

Pan

LÜDERITZ

Halifax I *Guano
Bay*

Swimming
Griffith Bay

Benguela

*Halifax
Point*

Pan

Pans

Radford Bay

B4

Witmur Picnic site
(& toilet)

Black Ridge

D701

Picnic site
(& toilet)

*Essy
Bay*

Toilets

Pan

*Diamond
Coast
Recreation Area*

D734

*Second
Lagoon*

Pan

*Eberlanz
Hohle*

Fjord Picnic site
(& toilet)

D702

D733

*Kleiner
Fjord* Picnic site
(& toilet)

Picnic site
(& toilet)

DIAMOND AREA
(Sperrgebiet)
*No access to
public*

N

Kleiner Bogenfels Pan

Swimming
*Grosse
Bucht*

Bradt

0 ————————— 4km
0 ————————— 2 miles

Getting there and permits If you wish to visit Elizabeth Bay or Bogenfels then you must give your full names, passport or ID number, and nationality to the relevant tour operator (see page 225) at least five working days before the trip, as it takes NAMDEB that long to issue a permit for you. Therefore trips must be booked well in advance. Note that visitors may not take anything out of the area, including rock samples – take note all amateur geologists. Vehicles coming from the Sperrgebiet are subject to random searches by NAMDEB officials.

Increasing tourism is encouraging increased access, and several attractions within the Sperrgebiet are now easily visited:

Agate Beach This windswept beach is a 5km drive north of Lüderitz, alongside fenced-off areas of the Sperrgebiet that add to the air of desolation, particularly in winter. To get there, follow the signs out of Luderitz along the coast road from the corner of Tal and Hamburger streets. When you turn inland at the last signpost, turn immediately right (by the NAMDEB sign), then just keep going. En route, a pond to the side of the road attracts small numbers of flamingos and other waterbirds, while nearby the odd springbok or oryx takes advantage of a patch of green around the water-treatment plant. The beach stretches a long way and is fun for beachcombers. The almost-black sand is sprinkled with fragments of shining mica – and the occasional agate. The occurrence of agates depends on the winds and the swell: sometimes you will find nothing, at others – especially at low tide – you can pick up a handful in a few hours. The beach's braai spots make it a popular place at weekends, and swimming, too is an (albeit chilly) option.

Kolmanskop (*Open daily 07.00–13.00; longer with photographic pass. Entry N$40 with pre-bought ticket only; see 'Getting there' below*) This ghost town, once the principal town of the local diamond industry, was abandoned over 45 years ago and now gives a fascinating insight into the area's great diamond boom. A few of the buildings, including the imposing concert hall, have been restored, but many are left exactly as they were deserted, and now the surrounding dunes are gradually burying them. What a spectacular place this would be for a large party.

In a room adjacent to the concert hall, there is a simple café-style restaurant (*open Mon–Sat 09.00–14.00*). Do make time to look at the photographs that adorn the walls, from early mining pictures to some chilling reminders of the far-reaching effects of Nazi Germany.

Almost a century since diamonds were first discovered here, it's now possible to buy diamonds in the newly opened 'Diamond Room'. In addition to the sale of diamonds, with prices upwards from N$500, there's a display charting the history of the diamond boom and the people with whom it is inextricably linked.

Getting there Kolmanskop is just beside the main B4 road, 9km east of Lüderitz. You need to buy a permit (N$40) in advance from Lüderitz Safaris & Tours or Ghost Town Tours in Lüderitz (see page 225); permits cannot be bought at Kolmanskop, and without one, you will be turned away. Guided tours, included in the cost of the permit, start at the museum in Kolmanskop at 09.30 or 11.00, Monday to Saturday, and take 40 minutes. On Sunday and most public holidays tours are at 10.00 only. Alternatively, buy a photographer's pass for N$125, which includes a guided tour, but allows you to park outside the gate and visit at any time of day (sunrise to sunset), for as long as you like, giving the chance to absorb the eerie atmosphere without other visitors. For the best photographs, set off with your camera to catch photos at first light, taking a snack breakfast to eat before one of the guided tours (or try out the café on site).

11

Elizabeth Bay This south-facing bay, 40km south of Lüderitz, has a band of diamond-bearing coarse grits and sands measuring about 3km by 5km. It was mined from 1911 to 1948, and then reopened in about 1991, with a projected minimum lifespan of ten years.

Getting there Guided tours run by Ghost Town Tours (see page 225) pass into the Sperrgebiet through the Kolmanskop gate, and from there to Elizabeth Bay. The scenery on the way is mostly flat gravel plains, with some dunes as you approach the coast. This is a chance to see the working diamond mine, albeit from a distance. Trips for between four and eight people run Monday–Friday from 08.30 to about 13.00, costing N$315 per person, including a light snack. No children under 14 are permitted.

Pomona/Bogenfels A day trip into the Sperrgebiet as far as Bogenfels covers some 265km on mostly good gravel roads, passing through areas of considerable historical, geological and botanical interest.

Where it has been untouched by diamond mining, much of the environment is pristine, but many of the diamond areas have been ravaged by the industry, leaving behind expanses of bare rock devoid of sand and without a hint of vegetation. The road passes through areas of shining dolomite rock, its colours varying in the sun from blue or pink to pure white. In the occasional winter, if there has been some rain, areas of the Sperrgebiet are alight with colour from numerous plants, many of them seen only once every ten years or so, taking advantage of nature's brief bounty. Here, in amongst grey scrubby plants, are the soft green of new grasses, the bright pink Bushman's candle, and the milk bush, favoured by oryx; here too are the so-called 'window' plants, whose leaf tips feature tiny windows that allow light through to the main plant buried below, so that photosynthesis can take place inside the plant.

Pomona itself once housed over a thousand people, of whom some 300–400 were German, and the rest black Namibian workers, these latter living in huts that accommodated up to 50 people. While the black workers were on fixed-term contracts, whole families of Germans lived here, with their own school, church, hotel and even a bowling alley. Water was brought in by narrow-gauge railway from Grillen Tal, several kilometres away, where the crumbling ruins of the main pump station can still be explored.

In the early years, a claim could be bought for 60 Deutschmarks, rising to a staggering 6,000DM by 1917–18. Diamonds were not mined, but were sifted by hand with great trommel sieves, their rusting frames now good only for photographers.

The third mining town in the area was at Bogenfels, where a small desalination plant is still to be seen right on the beach. The main attraction for visitors, though, is the spectacular rock arch that stands about 55m high beside the sea. Despite its inaccessibility, photographs have made it one of the south's better-known landmarks.

Getting there Guided tours (currently run by Coastways Tours, see page 225) take a whole day to reach Bogenfels, in the Sperrgebiet, visiting the ghost town of Pomona and the Idatel or Märchental ('fairytale') valley, famous for the diamonds that were collected in the moonlight here. Trips depart at 09.00 and return at around 16.30, and include lunch at Pomona. Costs are N$850 per person, based on a minimum of four people, and are subject to changes in entry fees that may be imposed by NAMDEB.

Oranjemund This is a prosperous mining town in the far southwest corner of Namibia, where the headquarters of NAMDEB are based. It is a closed town,

Kolmanskop, or 'Kolman's hill', was originally a small hill named after a delivery rider, Kolman, who used to rest his horses there.

In April 1908, Zacharias Lewala was working nearby when he picked a rough diamond from the ground. He took this to his German foreman, August Stauch, who posted a claim to the area, and then got the backing of several of the railway's directors to start prospecting. Stauch exhibited some of his finds in June 1908, prompting an immediate response: virtually everybody who could rushed into the desert to look for diamonds. Famously, in some places they could be picked up by the handful in the moonlight.

T V Bulpin (see *Appendix 3*) records the story of one resident, Dr Scheibe, going prospecting:

> While he plotted his position on a map, he told his servants to look for diamonds. One of them simply went down on his knees, filled both hands with diamonds, and even stuffed some into his mouth. Dr Scheibe stared at the scene in amazement, repeating over and over again, '*Ein märchen, ein märchen*' (A fairytale, a fairytale).

This first large deposit at Kolmanskop lay in the gravel of a dry riverbed, so soon a mine and a boomtown developed there. Deposits were found all over the coastal region, all around Lüderitz. Quickly, in September 1908, the German colonial government proclaimed a Sperrgebiet – a forbidden zone – to restrict further prospecting, and to license what was already happening.

Between 1908 and the start of World War I over 5 million carats of diamonds were found, but the war disrupted production badly. At the end of it Sir Ernest Oppenheimer obtained options on many of the German mining companies for South Africa's huge Anglo American Corporation, joining ten of them into Consolidated Diamond Mines (CDM) of South West Africa. In 1922–23 CDM obtained exclusive diamond rights for 50 years over a coastal belt 95km wide, stretching 350km north of the Orange River, from the new South African administrators of South West Africa. These were later extended to the year 2010. This allowed CDM to control the country's diamond production until independence, and NAMDEB to do so now.

Meanwhile many small towns like Kolmanskop were flush with money. It had a butcher's, a baker's and a general shop; a large theatre, community hall and school; factories for furniture, ice, lemonade and soda water; a hospital with the region's first X-ray machine; comfortable staff quarters, elaborate homes for the managers – and a seawater pool fed by water pumped from 35km away. Yet Kolmanskop was fortunate: it was next to the main railway line. Often deposits were less accessible, far from water or transport – and many such early mines still lie half-buried in the Namib.

where NAMDEB own all the property – hence regular Air Namibia flights linking the town with Windhoek. Without an invitation from a resident, and the permission of NAMDEB, you cannot enter it. Even then, those leaving the mining area have to pass strict X-ray checks, which search for hidden diamonds. Living conditions there are reported (by NAMDEB!) to be very good; many of the workers come here from northern Namibia and are on lucrative 'six-months-on, six-months-off' contracts. However, even here the diamond deposits are gradually being exhausted, and within 20 years operations are likely to be scaled down.

Yet as supplies of one form of natural wealth diminish, another is set to make its mark: gas. The discovery of the Kudu gas fields off the coast of Oranjemund has excited considerable discussion as to just how far this new resource can go in addressing Namibia's energy needs, currently supplied in part from South Africa. Development of the field, estimated to cost some US$800 million, will be operated by a consortium with the resultant electricity sold to NamPower and the South African Eskom. It is anticipated that supply will go live towards the end of 2009.

NORTH OF THE B4

HELMERINGHAUSEN Despite being a large dot on the map, this is just a farm that has grown into a village, in the middle of some very scenic roads. Just to the north are flat plains with little hills of balancing rocks – rather like the cairns found on Scottish mountains, only somewhat bigger.

Heading southwest on the C13 towards Lüderitz the road winds down and opens out into an immense valley – a huge plain lined by mountains with a clear escarpment on the east, and a more ragged array to the west. It is most spectacular, especially at sunset.

In Helmeringhausen itself there is a shop for basics, and a small agricultural museum displaying tools and machinery from around the turn of the century (get the key from the hotel: it's free for residents!). Also there is a vital fuel station (*open daily 07.00–19.00 Mon–Sat*), and the all-important hotel:

Where to stay

Helmeringhausen Hotel (22 rooms) ⟍/f 063 283307; e info@helmeringhausen.com; www.helmeringhausen.com. This super little place, started in 1938, is a classic example of a well-maintained local hotel. Located right next to the museum, it has been expanded considerably in recent years, but continues to offer simple yet attractive rooms with twin beds, pristine bed nets, & en-suite facilities. There is safe parking at the back (though it's difficult to imagine a crime problem here), & a few tables & chairs around a small pool with a braai area.

Lunch & a set 3-course dinner are available in the hotel's restaurant, & even those passing through could stop for afternoon tea & a snack. The welcoming owners have plastered their bar wall with various currencies, underneath which is an excellent range of spirits. For those winter evenings, there's a separate lounge with its own fireplace and even a piano, while for the more energetic hikes or farm drives can be arranged.
N$453.02/380 sgl/pp sharing, B&B. Dinner N$109.25.

Nearby guest farms There are three excellent small guest farms around here. Dabis and Sinclair make natural overnight stops when driving between the Fish River Canyon and the Sesriem area, whilst Namtib is also a candidate if you are travelling between Lüderitz and Sesriem. There's also the simpler Farm Tiras just off the C13. Note that roads further west in this area, the C13, D707, D407 and D826, often run between mountains and the dunes of the Namib-Naukluft Park – and can be particularly spectacular.

Sinclair Guest Farm (6 rooms) ⟍ 061 226979; f 061 226999; e logufa@mweb.com.na; www.natron.net/tour/sinclair. Situated on the D407, about 59km northwest of Helmeringhausen, Sinclair's farmhouse is signposted clearly and is 3km from the road. All around are rolling hills, whose valleys are dotted with the odd camelthorn tree.

Inside Sinclair is a shady, green oasis, with palms & a variety of fruit trees from pomegranate to orange, grapefruit, lemon & mandarin. Looking

onto these are various shady verandas outside with tables, chairs & places to relax. It is a restful environment, good value & perfect for a short stop.

The rooms here are simple & carpeted, & all have en-suite facilities including showers (one also has a bath). If you're stopping for one night, then arrive for tea before 16.00, & spend a few hours wandering over to see the old copper mine, & perhaps up a nearby hill for sunset. If staying for two then join a farm drive, or walk around a little further – perhaps guided by the farm dogs.

Sinclair is still run by Gunther & Hannelore Hoffmann as a working farm, though recent droughts have left it increasingly reliant on guests for income. Fortunately, it has good food & a pleasant, relaxed atmosphere, so is often full.
N$700/620 sgl/pp sharing, DBB.

🏠 **Dabis Guest Farm** (7 rooms) ☎ 063 626820. Reservations ☎ 061 232300; f 061 249937; e photographer@mweb.com.na. Dabis has been owned by the Gaugler family for 3 generations, since 1926. Currently run by Jo & Heidi Gaugler, it will shortly be taken over by their twin sons, Jurg and Stefan. It is just a few kilometres north of Helmeringhausen, about 7km off the main C14 down a track with some steep dips, & has achieved an effective balance between welcoming visitors & operating as a farm.

Accommodation is in comfortable twin-bed rooms with en-suite shower (one has a bath instead) & toilet. Outside, guests benefit from a swimming pool & tennis court (racquets available). One of the main attractions of staying here, however, is learning about the farm. Most guests arrive by 15.00, have tea at 16.00, and then go out on a farm drive with Jo for an hour or two. Jo will explain his techniques in depth, complete with information on the area's climate over the last four decades. Dabis now farms mainly sheep for lamb production – karakul & a cross breed – using advanced rotation techniques to survive on the meagre rainfall. Although the main emphasis is on farming, there are a number of bat-eared foxes to be seen if you are lucky. The Gaugler family are more than happy to share their farm with guests, & their knowledge can considerably enrich your stay.
N$882/1,392/2,088 sgl/dbl/trpl inc DBB, & evening farm drive on arrival.

🏠 **Namtib Biosphere Reserve**, incorporating **Namtib Desert Lodge** (5 rooms) and **Little Hunter's Rest** (5 campsite pitches) ☎/f 063 683055; e reservations@namtib.com; www.namtib.com. Don't be put off by the name – this is not a scientific project, but a welcoming lodge with a personal feel, run on ecological lines by the Theile family. It lies 12km east of the scenic D707 road, which runs between the Namib's dunes on the west and the jagged Tiras Mountains on the east. Namtib Desert

Lodge is clearly signposted about 76km south of the D407 junction, or 47km north of the C13.

The lodge nestles in an isolated valley surrounded by mountains, overlooking the edge of the desert plain. Its rooms are unusually designed, comfortable & clean: simple farm-style bungalows with twin or dbl beds are separated from a private bathroom (with shower, toilet & washbasin) by a small open-air square, where many visitors choose to sleep in the heat of the summer. Electricity, a recent addition to the farm, is provided in the rooms by generator, & lights are battery powered, but for guests who have come to appreciate the simplicity at Namtib, candles are still in the rooms. A newly built lounge & dining area provides guests with room to relax in front of the fire after a hike in the mountains or a nature drive. Home-cooked 3-course meals are served *en famille* in a separate dining room.

About 2.5km from the lodge is a separate campsite, overlooking the plains & the desert. Pitches are widely spread under camelthorn trees, and there's a central ablution block. Provisions such as firewood & meat are available; alternatively, campers may have dinner at the lodge, space permitting.

This is a working farm, with cattle, sheep & game, & visitors are welcome to go out on 3hr guided nature drives to gain a deeper insight into life at the edge of the desert. The Theiles aim to make a living from the land, whilst regenerating what they can of its natural flora & fauna. Oryx & springbok roam the plains and the the evasive kudu is just one of the inhabitants of the gorges & mountains. Certainly there are some inquisitive mongooses around, not to mention bat-eared fox, aardwolf & porcupine, while hidden in the surrounding hills are leopard, cheetah & lynx. It all adds up to a good en-route stopover, or a place to spend several days relaxing.
N$478 pp sharing, B&B. Dinner N$100. Nature drive N$75 pp.

🏠 **Farm Tiras** PO Box 35, Helmeringhausen; ☎ 063 683048. Just off the main C13, Farm Tiras is run by Klaus Peter & Anita Koch. Accommodation ranges from a smart bungalow on the farm itself, to a one-room chalet with balcony & good views, & a campsite, both across the road. Visitors may drive themselves around the farm.
N$710/630 sgl/pp sharing; camping N$95; hut N$150–210; self-catering guesthouse N$1,150 (6 people).

The area around Namtib has been loosely designated by a group of local farmers as the Tiras Berge Conservancy. Various types of accommodation are available

11

through members of the group, from basic campsites like Weissenborn (❧ *0638 6522*) to more upmarket establishments such as Landsberg (❧ *063 683050*). Here Wilfried Izko has five guestrooms at N$569 per person for dinner, bed and breakfast, and takes visitors on drives across his 75,000ha farm. Be warned, though, that publicity material showing the P409 through the mountains is misleading – this is a private track, and visitors who are not staying overnight may well meet with a hostile reception.

MALTAHÖHE

This small town is an important crossroads, as it is linked by a tar road to the main north–south B1 artery, but it is too far from the desert to be a major centre for visitors in its own right.

Maltahöhe's most interesting attraction is virtually unknown. About 30km north of here, on the farm Sandfeld, is a fascinating valley which, when the rains are good, fills with water to a depth of about 30cm. This doesn't happen every year, but when it does – normally between mid-February and mid-March – the shallow lake quickly becomes covered in a spectacular bloom of red, pink and white lilies, *Crinum crinum paludosum*. These last about a week, and are said to be endemic to the valley, which is known as the 'lily-veld'.

The town itself has a few shops and garages, a post office, Standard and First National banks, and a useful information office at the Maltahöhe Hotel associated with the Namib Pappot Safari Company, who run trips around Sesriem from the hotel. There are two accommodation options in town.

WHERE TO STAY

⌂ **Maltahöhe Hotel** (27 rooms, 18 bed dorm, camping) PO Box 20, Maltahöhe; ❧ 063 293013; f 063 293133. Under new management, the Maltahöhe Hotel has undergone some fairly significant refurbishment. The veranda has been glassed in & the predominantly German clientele now sit at tables adorned with fresh flowers & sip filter coffee. There is a well-stocked bar, an à-la-carte restaurant serving lunch & dinner, a pool at the rear & a small internet café. The en-suite dbl & family rooms are clean & cool: tiled floors, good walk-in showers, & fans. There is also an 18-bed dormitory across the road for backpackers & budget travellers, & alongside this are 4 camp pitches. Whilst the facilities of this hotel are far superior & distinctly more reliable than those at the town's other accommodation option, it is a very serious place & perhaps

lacking in some of the atmosphere found further down the road. However, it's worth popping in for a drink if only to study the large old map mounted in the bar: it shows the allocation of Namibia's farmland.
N$290/460 sgl/dbl, B&B. Dorm bed N$60.

⌂ **Oa Hera** ❧ 063 293028; f 063 293508; e oaheraa@iway.na; web: www.oaheraart.com. Run by the son of the owners of La Vallée Tranquille, Oa Hera, meaning 'that which is sought after', is primarily a warehouse-style art gallery & small craft centre with an affiliated café, the Red Stone restaurant. There were a few basic rooms under construction when we last visited. Located at the end of town, the whole complex is open daily 08.00–17.00, & arrangements can be made on arrival. There is a standard (slow) internet connection available for N$12.50 per 15 mins.

Nearby guest farms There are several guest farms and restcamps in the area, including:

⌂ **Farm Duwisib Restcamp** (4 rooms, 3 bungalows) PO Box 21, Maltahöhe; ❧/f 063 293344. Adjacent to the west side of Duwisib Castle is a small private restcamp, on the D826. Meals can be arranged in advance, & there's a basic farm store here.

N$410 pp, HB.
⌂ **La Vallée Tranquille** (8 rooms) ❧/f 063 293508; e valleet@iway.na; www.lavalleetranquille.com. The French ownership of this small farmhouse some 60km south of Maltahöhe on the C14 is clear from

the décor of the en-suite bedrooms, set in 2 separate buildings, & of the restaurant, bar & comfortable lounge. Recently constructed self-catering units with braais broaden the appeal of the lodge, which also has its own shop selling fresh produce & homemade bread. The owners offer hiking, birdwatching, ostrich feeding & other activities on the farm, & there's a small pool for cooling off. Wheelchair access to the lodge is an added bonus. N$460 pp sharing, DBB.

✕ WHERE TO EAT

✕ **Red Stone Restaurant** Part of the Oa Hera complex (above). This is a funky restaurant, semi-circular in design. Vibrant orange poles support its welcome hessian shade, while succulent plants in terracotta pots, unusual sculptures & brightly painted concrete tables & benches rest on the gravel floor. It's a cool, pleasant place to rest & have a bite to eat. The menu is simple but good. Fish & chips N$45, toasted sandwiches N$16, soup N$25 or cake & ice cream for N$14.

DUWISIB CASTLE (*Open daily 08.00–13.00, 14.00–17.00; entrance N$30/15 adult/child*) Standing solidly amidst the rolling hills 72km southwest of Maltahöhe, beside the D826, the sandstone fortress of Duwisib Castle is another of those anachronisms in which Namibia seems to specialise. Look from a distance and you won't believe it: a small, square castle with fortified battlements and high turrets in the middle of the African bush.

The castle itself is built around an open central quadrangle, where there is now a small lawn and fountain, shaded by a couple of beautiful jacaranda trees. Its rooms are sparsely furnished, though there are some excellent original pieces dating back to around the turn of the 20th century, and interesting paintings and prints on the walls – many equestrian in theme.

Above the entrance hall is a steep set of stairs (easily missed) up to a small gallery overlooking the entrance, and there is also a cellar, which now seems to be a storeroom.

You can park around the back, where you'll find a café selling drinks and snacks – including homemade apple pie – and a shady garden.

History The castle's history has been documented in an excellent booklet by Dr N Mossolow (see *Appendix 3*), available at the castle. It details how Hansheinrich von Wolf was born in 1873 into a military family in Saxony and served with the Royal Saxon Artillery near Dresden. He came to South West Africa as a captain in the Schutztruppe, when he volunteered after the outbreak of the Herero War. He was decorated in 1905, and returned to Germany where he married Miss Jayta Humphrey in 1907.

Later that year he and his wife returned to German South West Africa, and over the next few years bought up farming land in the area. By October 1908 he had '33 horses, 68 head of large stock and 35 head of small stock' on his farm, and two wells. An 'extravagant residence of undressed stone, with 22 rooms and a cellar' had reached 2m above its foundations. He bought up more farmland, up to 50,000ha, and by 1909 the castle was complete, with furnishings and paintings imported from Germany.

Von Wolf proceeded to enlarge the area under his control by buying more land. A fanatical horseman and breeder of horses, he spent much time and energy developing his stable. (See *The desert horses*, page 215.)

In 1914 he set off with his wife to England, to purchase another thoroughbred stallion, but on the way war broke out. The ship diverted to South America, where they were briefly interned before he arranged a secretive passage back to Europe. Eventually they arrived back in Germany where Von Wolf reported for duty as an officer. On 4 September 1916 he was killed at the battle of the Somme.

11

⚤ Where to stay

⚤ Duwisib Campsite ⤡/f 066 385303; reservations ⤢ 061 236975/6/7; f 061 224900; e reservations@nwr.com.na; www.nwr.com.na. This friendly NWR site has 10 pleasant camp pitches (no 3 is a favourite, under a great tree) which should be reserved in advance in Windhoek. Ablutions have been retiled.

N$50 per site plus N$20/10 per adult/child (max 8 people).

12

The Namib-Naukluft National Park

People have different reactions when they encounter a desert for the first time. A few find it threatening, too arid and empty, so they rush from city to city, through the desert, to avoid spending any time there at all. Some try hard to like it for those same reasons, but ultimately find little which holds their attention. Finally there are those who stop and give the place their time, delighting in the stillness, strange beauty and sheer uniqueness of the environment. The desert's changing patterns and subtly adapted life forms fascinate them, drawing them back time after time.

Covering almost 50,000km², the Namib-Naukluft National Park (*entry N$80 pp, under 16s free, plus N$10 per vehicle*) is one of the largest national parks in Africa, protecting one of the oldest deserts on earth, South America's Atacama Desert being the other contender for this title. The Namib's scenery is stunning, and its wildlife fascinating; you just need to make the time to stop and observe it.

The sections in this chapter run roughly south to north. Note that the NamibRand, Sesriem, the Naukluft and Solitaire are very close together.

HISTORY

The park has grown gradually to its present size. In 1907 the area between the Kuiseb and Swakop rivers was proclaimed as 'Game Reserve No 3'. Later it was augmented by the addition of Sandwich Harbour in 1941.

In 1956 the Kuiseb Canyon and Swakop River Valley were added, along with the Welwitschia Plains, and in 1968 the park was renamed the Namib Desert Park. In 1979 a large area of what was the protected 'Diamond Area No 2' was added, including Sesriem and Sossusvlei, and the park was officially joined to the Naukluft Park, creating the Namib-Naukluft National Park.

Most recently, in 1986, the rest of 'Diamond Area No 2' was added, taking the park's southern boundary as far south as the main road to Lüderitz, and increasing its area to its present size of 49,768km² – larger than Switzerland, or about the same as Maryland and New Jersey combined.

FLORA AND FAUNA

Though the Naukluft's wildlife is discussed separately, the flora and fauna elsewhere in the Namib-Naukluft are similar, dependent more on the landscape than on precise location. (Dr Mary Seely's book, *The Namib*, is a superb and simple guide to this area, widely available in Windhoek and Swakopmund. See *Appendix 3*, page 489.) The four basic types of environment found here, and some of their highlights are:

SAND-DUNES Dunes are everybody's idea of a desert, and generally thought of as being bare and lifeless. Whilst this is not inaccurate for many deserts, the Namib is sufficiently old for endemic species to have evolved.

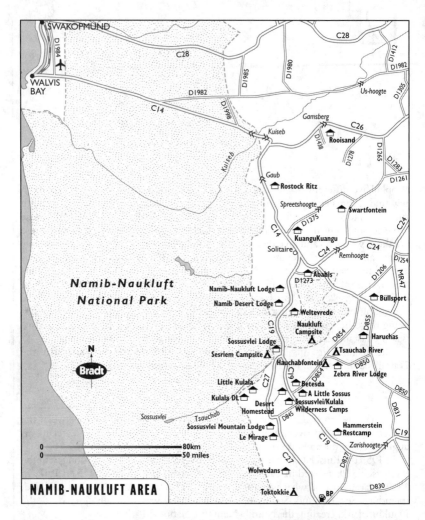

NAMIB-NAUKLUFT AREA

Various grasses grow on some of the more stable dunes, but most of the vegetable matter comes from windblown detritus. This collects at the bottom of the dunes, to be eaten by fish-moths (silver-fish), crickets and the many tenebrionid beetles – or *tok tokkies*, as they are known – near the base of the food chain. Particular tenebrionid species occur in specific environments, with those in the coastal fog belt adapting ingeniously to harness the available moisture.

These then provide food for spiders, geckos, lizards and chameleons which, in turn, fall prey to sidewinder snakes. Rare Grant's golden moles eat any small beetles or larvae that they can catch, and birds are mobile enough to move in and out of the dunes in search of the smaller animals. The dune lark is endemic to this region, and is seldom found outside the dune areas.

RIVER VALLEYS AND PANS The river valleys that run through the Namib are linear oases. Though dry on the surface, their permanent underground water sustains trees and bushes, like the camelthorn, *Acacia erioloba,* and nara melon, *Acanthosicyos horrida,* found in the middle of the great dune-sea at Sossusvlei.

Other common river-valley trees include the anaboom, *Acacia albida*; shepherd's tree, *Boscia albitrunca,* easily identified by its white trunk; the wild green-hair tree, *Parkinsonia africana*, and the marvellously weeping false ebony, *Euclea pseudebenus*.

The lush vegetation found in these valleys makes them a favourite for numerous insects and birds, as well as larger mammals like gemsbok, kudu and springbok. These are the most likely areas to find nocturnal cats from leopard to caracal, especially where the rivers cut through mountains rather than dunes.

GRAVEL PLAINS Throughout the desert, and especially north of the Kuiseb River, the Namib has many expansive, flat plains of rock and stone. These come alive during the rains, when they will quickly be covered with tall thin grass and creeping yellow flowers, attracting herds of gemsbok, springbok and even Hartmann's mountain zebra. During drier times there are fewer large mammals around, but still at night black-backed jackal, aardwolf and the occasional aardvark forage for termites, while bat-eared and Cape foxes scavenge for insects, reptiles, and anything else edible.

Spotted hyena and even the rare brown hyena are sometimes recorded here. Both leave distinctive white droppings, but only the sociable spotted hyenas make such eerie, mournful calls.

Resident larger birds include ostrich, secretary birds, Rüppell's korhaan and Ludwig's bustard, while enthusiastic 'twitchers' will seek the pale, apparently insignificant Gray's lark (amongst other larks), which is endemic to the gravel plains of the Namib.

INSELBERGS AND MOUNTAIN OUTCROPS Throughout the Namib there are mountains, often of granite or limestone. Some, like many between Sesriem and Sossusvlei, have become submerged beneath the great dune-sea. Others, especially north of the Kuiseb River, jut up through the flat desert floor like giant worm casts on a well-kept lawn. These isolated mountains surrounded by gravel plains are inselbergs (from the German for 'island-mountain') – and they have their own flora and fauna. *Euphorbia, Acacia, Commiphora, Zygophyllum* and *Aloe* species are common, whilst the succulent *Lithops* (often called living rocks, for their pebble-like shape) occur here, though less frequently.

Many inselbergs are high enough to collect moisture from morning fogs, which sustain succulents and aloes, and with them whole communities of invertebrates. Temporary pools in crevices can be particularly interesting, and there's a whole microcosm of small water creatures that lay drought-resistant eggs. These survive years of desiccation, to hatch when the pools do finally fill.

Being open land these make perfect perches for raptors – and lappet-faced vultures, greater kestrels and red-necked falcons are typical of this environment. Also watch for sandgrouse, which congregate at water around dusk and dawn, and other well-camouflaged foraging birds.

NAMIBRAND NATURE RESERVE

Covering about 2,100km², an area equivalent to about half the size of Belgium, the NamibRand Nature Reserve is one of the largest private reserves in Africa. Lying south of Sesriem, it borders onto the main Namib-Naukluft National Park in the west, a boundary of about 100km, and in the east its extent is generally defined by the Nubib Mountains.

There are a wide variety of different desert landscapes and environments within this, from huge red sand-dunes to vegetated inter-dune valleys, sand and gravel plains, and some particularly imposing mountains. It's a spectacular area of desert.

There are several ways to visit this, all utilising small lodges and camps as bases for expert-led guided trips. If you want a detailed look at the central Namib, with guides who understand it, this is an excellent complement to a day or two of driving yourself around Sesriem and Sossusvlei.

HISTORY Before becoming a nature reserve, this was a number of separate farms formed in the 1950s to eke out an existence farming in the desert. Several severe drought years in the 1980s demonstrated that farming domestic stock here just wasn't viable. There were allegations of farmers opening their fences to game from the Namib-Naukluft National Park, only to kill the animals for their meat once they left the park.

Game was the only option, and this survived well on the farm Gorrasis, owned by Albi Brückner (a businessman, rather than a farmer, who'd bought the farm for its landscapes).

In 1988 Brückner bought out two neighbouring farms, Die Duine and Stellarine, and gradually the reserve was broadened from that base. Now various shareholders have contributed money to the reserve, and different operators hold 'concession' areas which they utilise for tourism.

FLORA AND FAUNA The NamibRand's flora and fauna are the same as that in the western areas of the Namib-Naukluft. However, there are also red hartebeest, which aren't usually found in the national park, and blesbok which have been introduced from South Africa.

WHERE TO STAY/WHAT TO SEE AND DO What you see and do here depends entirely on where you stay, as many of the camps in the concession have a different emphasis.

Wolwedans 061 230616; f 061 220102; e info@wolwedans.com.na; www.wolwedans.com. Wolwedans now comprises 4 separate accommodation choices, each a considerable distance from the other across the reserve. While all cater for the top end of the market, they have a range of styles to suit different visitors. The turning to the main farmhouse, west off the C27, is about 32km to the north of the junction of the D827 & C27 (27km past the BP petrol station). Coming from the north, it is 50km south of the C27/D845 junction. If you are approaching from Sesriem, that's about 40km south of the first NamibRand signboard south of Sesriem on the C27. The camp has its own airstrip as well. Once on the 'drive' to Wolwedans, ignore the small house on the left & continue about 20km from the gate to the Wolwedans farmhouse, from where transfers into the various camps are arranged. Beware of turning off this track, as you may become stuck in the sand.

Particularly special to Wolwedans is the possibility of arranging a wedding, from a religious service to a civil ceremony.

Wolwedans Dune Camp (6 tents) Wolwedans Dune Camp has been the flagship operation in the reserve since it opened. The whole camp is built on wooden decks, raised above the sand. Each dome tent (about 3.5m square) has twin beds and solar-powered lights. Behind each is its own private hot shower & toilet, & in front is a veranda. There's a central open dining area & sun deck. Activities usually consist of afternoon & whole-day drives, including a picnic lunch, into the reserve with a professional guide & guided walks. Scenic flights to the Diamond Coast & Sossusvlei can be arranged. There is an open kitchen (the standard of food is excellent) which allows you to chat to your chef while your meal is being prepared.

This lodge is more suited to the adventurous traveller with the charm of the camp being its quiet atmosphere and old-style feel. *N$2,590/1850 sgl/dbl, inc FB and activities. Min stay 2 nights. Closed 1 Dec–Feb 28.*

Wolwedans Dune Lodge (9 chalets, 1 suite) Originally opened in 1998, Wolwedans Dune Lodge is run with all the courtesy & attention to detail of a country house, with an atmosphere of relaxed gentility. More luxurious than the Dune Camp, & sited atop one of the red dunes, it was destroyed by a fire in 2002, but has since risen from the ashes to return to its former glory. Accommodation consists of purpose-built wooden chalets, each built on stilts with its own secluded veranda & en-suite shower & toilet. The real coup is the bedrooms. Solid wooden twin beds, draped with nets that give all the allure of a dreamy 4-poster, face directly east through a canvas 'wall' that, when rolled up, affords unparalleled stargazing & a front-row view of sunrise over the mountains.

Simple walkways over the dunes lead to the hub of the camp, where a comfortable bar with leather armchairs, a separate library & 2 lounges all share that same view. There are also 2 dining rooms where meals are taken at individual tables or around a large table, depending on individual preference. Dinner is a relatively formal affair, with some of the best food to be had in Namibia, & good wines to match from their own chilled wine cellar. And after dinner, what better than to while away the evening around the campfire on the deck? This is a place to relax, unwind & get a real feel for the surroundings. Guided activities follow the same pattern as those of the camp, usually returning in time for a civilised afternoon tea, or perhaps a leisurely dip in the pool before lounging on the surrounding deck.
N$3,990/2,850 sgl/dbl, inc FB and activities.
⌂ **Wolwedans Private Camp** (1 suite) Tucked away in a secluded valley, the Private Camp caters for just 4 guests in a single suite: ideal for honeymooners or anyone seeking the ultimate in privacy. It has 2 spacious bedrooms with verandas & en-suite bathrooms, while an adjoining *sala* with a day bed makes an inspired place for children to sleep, sharing a bathroom with their parents. The camp boasts its own lounge, dining area, library & a fully equipped kitchen. But forget the washing up — all this comes with a dedicated chef & housekeeper, so total relaxation is the order of the day.
N$3,850 pp (2-4 guests), inc FB, all activities and private drives. Min stay 2 nights.
⌂ **Aanster Boulders Camp** (4 chalets) Set between large granite boulders 40km south of the base camp, this latest addition to the collection is scheduled to open in 2007. The rooms will be constructed from canvas and wood.
N$3,990/2,850 sgl/pp sharing, inc FB and activities. Open Easter–Oct.

⌂ **Sossusvlei Mountain Lodge** (10 chalets)
☎ +27 11 809 4300; f +27 11 809 4400;
e information@ccafrica.com; www.ccafrica.co.za, www.ccafrica.com. Windhoek office ☎ 061 236276;

e wdh@afroventures.com. In the north of the NamibRand Reserve, about 32km south of Sesriem and 6km from the D826, Sossusvlei Mountain Lodge is one of the most stylish modern lodge in Namibia.

Spacious chalets, made largely of stone & glass, are built into the rocks overlooking a desert plain. Their graceful interiors use a mix of bright chrome & earthy, desert colours; these personal cocoons have minibars, CD systems & AC. Most of their glass walls slide or fold away to open up the room to the desert, & at night an electric skylight can slide back above your bed allowing you to stargaze. Serious astronomers will also appreciate the large, computer-controlled telescope that's on hand.

The main lodge is similarly luxurious, with AC (on despite the windows all being open during our last visit); there's a satellite TV, email & internet connection if you need them. The food is excellent; the wine cellar impressive — & there's a slightly surreal pool outside. Activities focus on Sossusvlei trips, although quad-biking excursions over nearby dunes are an unusual, & fun, addition to the normal walking & driving trips.
N$3850 pp, inc FB and activities, high season, based on 3-night stay.
⌂ **Le Mirage Desert Lodge & Spa** (25 luxury rooms)
☎ 063 293293, 061 375300; f 063 293230;
e res@leadinglodges.com,
lemirage@leadinglodges.com; www.leadinglodges.com. Forget hazy images in the desert heat: Le Mirage is a collection of sizeable buildings merging little with the desert surroundings. It's a curious fusion of a grand Arthurian castle — cathedral-style windows, trefoil turrets, monogrammed linen — & a Moroccan *riad*, with inner courtyards, antique chests & sapphire-blue mosaic bathrooms. The accommodation is divided between 2 buildings: the older being smaller (6 rooms) & characterised by its cool, galleried courtyard, complete with gushing waterfall & cascading bougainvillea; the newer was completed in August 2004, housing the remaining rooms. Rooms in both locations are spacious & tastefully furnished with antiques & good quality, modern amenities: AC, safe, minibar & coffee/tea station. Stone walls, sand-blasted room dividers, high, beamed ceilings & 4-poster beds add to the interior of grandeur. In the new building each room boasts a small balcony, & 2 of the rooms have access to 'star decks' where guests can sleep under the night sky on top of the turret. At ground level, there is a decadent spa offering all types of massage, including Thai & Indian, in 6 treatment rooms; an outdoor

pool; & a colonial style, open-sided bar & lounge. The last of the buildings contains the restaurant & wine cellar. Here, heavy wooden tables are interspersed with gas patio heaters, as the central atrium can make this a chilly dining option. *N$3,000/2,500 sgl/pp sharing, inc FB and activities.*

🏠 **TokTokkie Trails** ⊻/f 066 385230; reservations Safari Unlimited; ☎ 061 264521; e toktokki@iway.na. New owners Thomas & Kirsten took over Toktokkie Trails in 2006. The place is 11km west of the D827, its turning is signposted 400m or so north of the C27/D827 junction.

As the name suggests, this is the place for walking trails, for which you'll need to allow 2 nights, arriving on the first day no later than midday. Walking is leisurely, concentrating on the flora & fauna, & their adaptations to the desert, and typically covering no further than 10km in a day. It's not a route march (they go at the pace of the slowest) & you need carry only your camera, binoculars & water.

While visitors can be provided with a tent, most spend the night sleeping out in the desert, under the stars. Any luggage that you need will be driven out to the overnight stop for you, & then collected in the morning. It's magical.

The desert landscape around here is a spectacular mix of wide plains, mountains, the odd tall sand-dune & many smaller vegetated ones. It's great country for walking, dotted with marvellously knurled old camelthorn trees. *N$1,200 pp sharing, inc FB and guided activities.*

Driver's note The D826, C27 and D707 are amongst the most scenic routes in the country. Sand-dunes line the west of these roads, and mountains overlook the east – spectacular stuff. However, they do tend to be quite slow-going, and the gravel is sometimes not as good or as wide as the faster C19 or C14 routes, so allow plenty of time for your journey (an average of about 50km/h is realistic).

Surprisingly, there is a fairly reliable **fuel station** on the D826, 5km to the north of the junction of the D827 and D826. They also sell cold drinks, if you ask.

NAUKLUFT MOUNTAINS

An hour's drive northeast of Sesriem, the main escarpment juts out into the desert forming a range known as the Naukluft Mountains. In 1968 these were protected within the Naukluft Mountain Zebra Park – to conserve a rare breeding population of Hartmann's mountain zebra. Shortly afterwards, land was bought to the west of the mountains and added to the park, forming a corridor linking these mountains into the Namib National Park. This allowed gemsbok, zebra and other game to migrate between the two, and in 1979 the parks were formally combined into the Namib-Naukluft National Park.

GEOLOGY The uniqueness of the area stems from its geology as much as its geographical position. Separated from the rest of the highlands by steep, spectacular cliffs, the Naukluft Mountains form a plateau. Underneath this, to a height of about 1,100m, is mostly granite. Above this base are alternating layers of dolomites and shales, with extensive deposits of dark limestone, rising to about 1,995m. Over the millennia, rainwater has gradually cut into this massif, dissolving the rock and forming steep *kloofs*, or ravines, and a network of watercourses and reservoirs – many of which are subterranean. The name *Naukluft*, which means 'narrow ravine', is apt for the landscape.

Where these waters surface, in the deeper valleys, there are crystal-clear springs and pools – ideal for cooling dips. Often these are decorated by impressive formations of smooth tufa – limestone that has been re-deposited by the water over waterfalls.

FLORA AND FAUNA Receiving occasional heavy rainstorms in summer that feed its network of springs and streams in its deeper kloofs, the Naukluft supports a surprisingly varied flora and fauna.

The high plateau and mountainsides tend to be rocky with poor, if any, soil. Here are distinctive *Euphorbia*, *Acacia*, *Commiphora* and *Aloe* plants (including quivertrees – which are found in a dense stand in Quivertree Gorge). Most are low, slow-growing species, adapted to conserving water during the dry season. The variations of slope and situation result in many different niches suiting a wide variety of different species.

Down in the deeper kloofs, where there are permanent springs, the vegetation is totally different, with many more lush, broad-leaf species. Wild, cluster and sycamore figs are particularly prevalent, whilst you should also be able to spot camelthorn, buffalo thorn, shepherd's and wild olive trees.

The Naukluft has many animals, including large mammals, though all are elusive and difficult to spot. Hartmann's mountain zebra, gemsbok, kudu and klipspringer are occasionally seen fleeing over the horizon (usually in the far distance). Steenbok and the odd sunbathing dassie are equally common, and springbok, warthog and ostrich occur, but are more often found on the plains around the mountains. The mountains should be a classic place for leopard, and the smaller cats – as there are many small mammals found here – though these are almost never seen.

Over 200 species of birds have been recorded here, and a useful annotated checklist is available from the park office. The Naukluft are at the southern limit of the range of many species of the northern Namib – Rüppell's parrot, rosy-faced lovebirds and Monteiro's all occur here, as do species typical of the south like the Karoo robin and chat. In the wetter kloofs, watch for species that you wouldn't find in the drier parts of the park, like the water-loving hamerkop, brubru and even African black ducks. Raptors are usually seen soaring above. Black eagles, lanner falcons, augur buzzards and pale chanting goshawks are common.

GETTING THERE The national park's entrance is on the D854, about 10km southwest of the C14, which links Solitaire and Maltahöhe. Approaching from Windhoek, pass Büllsport and take the D854 towards Sesriem.

Alternatively, Büllsport Guest Farm owns a section of the Naukluft Mountains, accessible from the farm without going into the national park, and Ababis borders onto the mountains.

WHERE TO STAY The options are to camp at the basic national park's site, or to use one of these guest farms as a base. The mountains are also within a few hours' drive from most of the lodges in the Solitaire and Sesriem areas.

Büllsport Guest Farm (8 rooms, inc family room) P Bag 1003, Maltahöhe; 063 693371/693363; f 063 693372/293365; e info@buellsport.com; www.natron.net/tour/buellspt. About 230km from Windhoek (3 hrs' drive), Büllsport has its own dot on the normal tourist board map of Namibia – which is puzzling. Apart from the farm's shop & garage (for punctures, fuel & small repairs), there's just the guest farm here. (NB: The petrol station here has been closed, the result of new regulations which made it uneconomic to upgrade the facility.)

Run by Johanna & Ernst Sauber, this is one of the best traditional guest farms in the country, attracting a wide range of nationalities to stay. You can expect good food (often braais in the evening),

a comfortable (though not luxurious) twin room with en-suite shower & toilet, & a warm welcome. There is an indoor dining area as well as tables under a large camelthorn tree on the gravel terrace outside, & whilst the motel-style accommodation overlooks the neat car park, the lovely swimming pool has picturesque views of the surrounding mountains. Indeed, many visitors use this as a base for visiting the Naukluft Mountains, as Büllsport owns a section of them. You can walk up them for a long day hike, or Ernst will drive you up in a 4x4 for an afternoon stroll on the top of the plateau, or to the Quivertree Gorge, from where it's about 2½ hrs' hike down to the farm. Within a short drive of the farmhouse there's an old German Schutztruppe post,

& a few hours' walk from that is a large natural rock arch — which they call the 'Bogenfels of the Naukluft', after the original in the Sperrgebiet. Johanna also offers short horseriding trails into the mountains, with even inexperienced riders welcome. These cost around N$132.25 pp/hour. For two or more experienced riders, she can arrange a 2-day trail, including meals & an overnight bushcamp in the Naukluft. Alternatively, the farm is just under 2 hrs' drive (115km) from Sesriem, so it makes a practical base for day trips there, if closer accommodation is full. 4x4 excursions to Sossusvlei are available by arrangement. The long-establshed nature of this guest farm means it has a good supply of tourist information leaflets & books. *N$664/990/1,310 sgl/dbl/trpl, DBB.*

🏠 **Zebra River Lodge** (7 rooms) ☎ 063 693265; f 063 693266; e marianne.rob@zebrariver.com; www.zebrariver.com. Run by Rob & Marianne Field, Zebra River has established itself as one of the friendliest, most welcoming places in Namibia. It is situated in its own canyon in the Tsaris (aka Zaris) Mountains, reached by turning south from the D850 (between the D854 & the D855). Note that their driveway is several kilometres long, & crosses a sand river which, in exceptional years, flows across the road.

The guest rooms lead off a wide veranda around the plunge-pool, with a green garden around. All have en-suite shower & toilet, & plenty of space — apart from the 'honeymoon' suite which has a large stand-alone bath, a huge king-sized bed, & even more space.

Marianne's cooking is superb (she has now trained local women to cook in the same way, too), & the atmosphere is very relaxed & unpretentious. Usually everyone sits around the large table for dinner, with both wine & conversation often lasting late into the evening, although guest numbers & individual preferences are taken into consideration.

ZRL can be used as a base for driving yourself to Sesriem or the Naukluft, but don't ignore the lodge's own area. There are several clear trails around the canyons, varying in both length & degree of difficulty, & 2 of them leading up to freshwater springs. Whilst they are only a day's hiking away, you can arrange to walk part of the way & have Rob or August drive you the rest. There were resident black eagles & rosy-faced lovebirds in the canyon on the author's last visit, & a day spent hiking here was a perfect introduction to the challenging hiking in the Naukluft.

As an alternative to hiking, consider a full-day 4x4 trip to Sossusvlei with Rob or the resident guide, taking in the Dead Vlei, Sesriem Canyon & a picnic lunch (N$900 pp; min 2 people). They should be booked in advance, when you make a reservation. *N$700/1,200 sgl/dbl, FB.*

▲ **Tsauchab River Camp** (4 bungalows, camping) ☎ 063 293416; reservations ☎ 061 226979; f 061 226999; e tsauchab@iafrica.com.na, logufa@mweb.com.na; www.natron.net/tsauchab/index.html. For 8 years, Johan & Nicky Steyn have been offering a very warm welcome & well-priced accommodation at their fun & highly original camps. The entrance is on the D850, very close to the junction with the D854. They operate 12 different campsites, varying in size from 2–50 guest capacities, as well as 3 en-suite twin-bed bungalows at Tsabi-Tsabi (with 12v power, water & BBQ), & the Eagle Hide Out with its 5 permanent tents & a solid room for families & small groups. The sites are all very different in feel & facilities & are spread across this huge farm. Walking in the wild fig forest (detailed trail maps available), tackling the 4x4 drives, chilling out in the springs & water pools, & taking time to admire Johan's inspired, home-made metal sculptures that line the entrance are all great pastimes. There is not a formal restaurant menu but Nicky will do any meals on request, from picnic lunches to tasty braais, or there's a wide selection of fresh food & cold drinks available in the farm shop. *N$580/480 sgl/pp sharing, B&B; camping N$80 plus N$60 pp.*

▲ **Naukluft View** (camping) Contact via Tsauchab River Camp (see above). Owned by Johan of Tsauchab River, Naukluft View is a stunning campsite, but is currently only available to pre-booked groups & overland trips (check with Johan if you're travelling off-season though). Set in the river valley in a grove of shady Cape False Ebony trees, there are sites for pitching tents as well as 6 permanent tents on raised decks. The site takes a maximum of 20 people on an exclusive-use basis. The stone ablution blocks are immaculate with terracotta tiles & white sanitaryware. 24hr hot water is available by gas, & lanterns light the raked gravel paths by night. There are two short walking trails, including one Sunset Viewpoint which ends at a firepit surrounded by canvas-covered sofas: perfect for a relaxing G&T or chilled beer. *N$80 per site, plus N$60/40 per adult/child. Tented camp N$195/145 sgl/pp sharing.*

▲ **Hauchabfontein Camping** (camping) ☎/f 063 293433; m 081 2334436; e infodesk@

hauchabfontein.com; www.hauchabfontein.com. Part of Immo & Irmi Foerster's farm, this neat, scenic camping site lies beside the Tsauchab riverbed & close to a lovely quivertree forest. It's located on the D854, between the D850 & C19, about 5km west of the Naukluft View, 59km from Sesriem & 44kn from Naukluft. Facilites are clean & reliable with a stone-built showers & toilets, & acacia-shaded pitches. Occasionally fresh fruit & vegetables are available from the farm, as are trips to the nearby natural springs. *N$85 camping.*

🏠 **Betesda Lodge & Camping** (22 rooms; 14 campsites) 🕿 063 693253; f 063 693252; e betesda@iway.na; www.betesda.iway.na. Created by Tony & Leny Rust in 1998, Betesda is a Christian retreat at the junction of the C19 and D854 which has opened its doors to wider tourism; as you'd expect, it's a calm, friendly place. There are 18 twin & 4 family rooms built in a sgl line, with a long, shaded veranda running along one side & small private terraces along the other. The room interiors are cool & clean with crazy-paving-style stone floors, apricot walls, pine furniture & en-suite bathrooms with large tiled showers. There is a mosi net, free-standing fan & solar heating in each room. Family rooms here are huge with a $^{1}/_{2}$-height partition wall separating the dbl & 2 sgl beds. The main stone & thatch building is very lodge-like, with a wide check-in area, lounge furniture made from disused cartwheels, & a huge dining area with large leaded patio doors & a long buffet counter. There is a lovely stone pool area with shaded loungers & a stepped-down rectangular boma with fixed tables, chairs & a built-in BBQ & bar. The campsite is set a little distance away & has 14 pitches around a large tree, 5 showers & toilets with electric lights, a fire pit & running water. Wood can be bought at the lodge, or campers can eat in the restaurant with advance bookings. *N$570/715 sgl/pp sharing, DBB. Camping N$65 pp; dinner N$110 pp.*

🏠 **Ababis Guest Farm** (4 dbl rooms, 1 family room) 🕿 063 683080; f 063 683079; e info@ababis-gaestefarm.de; www.ababis-gaestefarm.de. Ababis stands on the west side of the C14, opposite the junction with the D1261, on the north side of the Naukluft Mountains. It has been a guest farm since 1993, & is quite traditional in character, though it has changed hands recently & is now owned by Kathrin & Uwe Schulze Neuhoff. The farm has some cattle & a few ostriches, as well as areas devoted purely to wildlife including gemsbok, springbok, blesbok, ostrich, occasional zebra, a few kudu, &

some bat-eared foxes. On the edge of the Naukluft, it is a good base for long hikes, while there's also a gentle walking trail around the farm which takes a few hours, down to a (usually) dry river.

A 4x4 drive on to the Naukluft Plateau, lasting about 8 hours, a morning or afternoon trip into Sossusvlei, or a 1/2-day drive encompassing local Bushman paintings, a spring and a small 'kokerboom forest' in the hills are all options for those not driving themselves. Trips costs about N$2,127.50 per vehicle (up to 4 people). *N$643/495 sgl/pp sharing, DBB.*

🏠 **Hammerstein Lodge & Camp** (5 bungalows, 52 rooms) 🕿 063 693111; f 063 693112; e hammerst@hammerstein.com.na; www.hammerstein.com.na. Situated on the C19, the turn-off north to Hammerstein has a clear signpost between the D854 (which goes past the Naukluft Mountains), & the D827. This is a well-established private restcamp catering predominantly (90%) to large, German groups. It has 52 en-suite, twin rooms in staggered rows, & 5 self-catering bungalows with 2–4 beds in each. Room interiors are clean but slightly musty, & feature pine furniture & knitted throws. Each has an outside bench overlooking the wide gravel pathway, or there's a more pleasant grassy area beside the pool where white wrought-iron furniture is shaded by lovely camelthorn trees. Buffet meals are served in either the cavernous restaurant or at a long banqueting table, & there's a bar, complete with wall-mounted animal skins, for after-dinner drinks. There is some game kept here: 2 caracal, 2 cheetah & a leopard in unimpressive 1ha enclosures, as well as a mini-reserve with oryx, kudu, giraffe & hartebeest. *2-bed bungalow N$391, 4-bed N$552. Rooms N$350 pp sharing, B&B. Camping N$40 pp.*

🏠 **Haruchas Guest Farm** (6 rooms) 🕿 063 293399; f 061 251682; e haruchas@natron.net; www.natron.net/tour/haruchas/index.htm. Situated on the bumpy D855, between Büllsport and the D850, Haruchas is a typical farm (it covers 200km²!) set high up on the Tsaris Mountains. The farm buildings themselves sit in an established oasis of palms, eucalyptus & flowering shrubs. Wolfgang & Milena Sauber, who between them speak German, Afrikaans, English, Czech & Italian, run Haruchas.

The 1907 outhouse has been converted into a family unit with 2 twin rooms, each with their own entrance, and a shared en-suite. They have simple pine furniture, clean patterned bedding & lovely thick walls to ensure good insulation. The 4 other rooms are much newer, & found in neat, purpose-

built, semi-detatched buildings beside the swimming pool. Painted white with cheerful, red doors & borders around the windows, the rooms are uniformly spacious & clean, with verandas, en-suite toilet & bath (with shower attachment) & pine furniture. Communal meals are served in the main house, where you're also free to relax in the lounge, or peruse the impressive wall of curios. There are a couple of hiking trails which you can take from the farm, detailed in books in the rooms, & this would make a good writer's or artist's retreat. Take time while you're here to see the old charcoal cold room.
Sgl N$475, N$395 pp sharing, HB.

⋏ Naukluft Campsite (camping) About 10km southwest of Büllsport, on the D854, is the ornate entrance to the Naukluft section of the Namib-Naukluft National Park. Through the gates, a road winds up northwest into the Naukluft for about 12km before the NWR's campsite.

The site has no bungalows, but 8 beautifully situated camping spots, surrounded by mountains & trees. Only water, firewood & toilets/showers are provided, so bring all your supplies. It can get busy, so it's wise to book in advance at the NWR in Windhoek.
N$50 per site plus N$20/10 pp adult/ child (up to 8 people). Max stay 3 nights when busy.

WHAT TO SEE AND DO Animals are seldom seen in this mountainous area, so hiking is the main activity here. A recent addition is the 4x4 off-road driving trail, which takes two days and is aimed at local enthusiasts testing their vehicles to the limits.

Hiking Naukluft has two circular day hikes, the Waterkloof and Olive trails. Both can be started from the campsite, and don't need booking ahead, or any special equipment. That said, at least a day's water, snacks and a medical kit should be taken along, as rescue would be difficult if there was an accident. Walkers should be fit and acclimatised, and strong hiking boots are essential, as the terrain is very rocky.

There is also one long eight-day Naukluft Trail, rated as one of Africa's toughest hikes. Like the others, this is unguided, but simple diagrammatic maps are available from the park warden's office.

Waterkloof Trail The Waterkloof is 17km long and starts near the campsite. It takes six or seven hours to walk comfortably, and is marked by yellow-painted footprints on the rocks. At first the trail follows the Naukluft River upstream, through some beautiful gorges, and in the early months of the year you'll often find pools here, complete with tadpoles and frogs.

After a gentle two hours you reach a painted rock marking the last water point (though bring water, don't rely on this), beyond which the canyon opens out. After about two hours more there's a marked halfway point, from where a steep climb leads you to the trail's highest point: a 600m peak with fine views all around.

From there the trail winds down through a stand of *Euphorbia* into a large valley, to follow the course of the (usually dry) river. It cuts off several of the bends, and keeps left to avoid some steep shelves, which form waterfalls in the rainy season. In this area some large cairns mark the route of the old German cannon road, which also follows the river valley for a while, before climbing steeply up to the main southern ridge of the plateau. Below those waterfalls, you meet the Naukluft River, and turn left to follow the trail for a few kilometres back to camp.

Olive Trail This starts about 4km from the park office – clearly signposted off the track from the entrance gate. You can walk here, or drive and park in a small parking area.

The Olive Trail is 10km long and takes about four hours to complete. From the parking area it gradually climbs to the top of a small plateau, before descending through a series of river valleys and gorges (using chains in places), to meet a rough 4x4 track which leads back to the parking area.

Naukluft Trail (*Open 1 March to third Friday in October. Walks start every Tue, Thu & Sat for the first 3 weeks of each month. Book in advance at the NWR in Windhoek. Group limit 3–12 people. N$100 pp, inc space at Hiker's Haven for nights before & after trail, exc park fees, paid separately*) This 120km trail starts from the park office, where there's a bunkhouse known as Hiker's Haven. Hikers can use this on their first and last nights. Initially it follows the (usually dry) Naukluft River south for a while, as it flows out of the mountains, before climbing up to the edge of the escarpment, with excellent views to the left over the plains. The Putte shelter is reached about 14km (6 hours) after starting.

On the second day the route covers 15km (6 hours), crossing a rolling plateau to the Bergpos junction, before dropping down the narrow Ubusis Kloof to reach Ubusis Hut. Day three starts by retracing your steps to Bergpos, and turning left across the plateau to Alderhost shelter (12km, taking 6 hours).

On day four the trail is level, before dropping down to a shelter at Tsams Ost for the evening – 17km later (6 hours). There's a rough 4x4 track from here down and west to the main C19, and hikers doing only a four-day trip can be collected here.

Day five is steep and then undulating, though it levels out towards the end where it follows a tributary of the Die Valle River, to reach the Die Valle shelter about 17km (6 hours) later. Day six is a tough one, climbing up a narrow gorge to reach a high point called Quartz Valley, before dropping down the Arbeid Adelt Valley to the Tufa shelter, 16km and about six hours later.

On day seven the trail climbs steeply, using chains in places, back up to the plateau and some excellent views, to reach Kapokvlakte shelter after 14km (5 hours). Finally, on the last day, the trail descends gradually, then steeply, to meet the Waterkloof Trail and follow the Naukluft River back to camp. Energetic hikers could combine the last two days into a 30km walk which would take about 11 hours to complete. An early start from Tufa shelter is essential, and if there are less than five hours of daylight, then you should stop at Kapokvlakte shelter.

4x4 trail (*Open all year, weather permitting. Book in advance at the NWR in Windhoek. Groups of 1–4 vehicles, with max 4 people per vehicle. N$220 per vehicle, exc park fees, which are paid separately*) This is a 73km two-day trail for those with a 4x4 and the experience to use it properly. After the first 28km there is an overnight camp, where four stone-walled, partially open, A-frame shelters have built-in bunk beds. There are toilets here, water, a solar-heated shower and a braai area. Bring your own firewood, camping kit and supplies.

SESRIEM AREA AND SOSSUSVLEI

When people speak of visiting the Namib Desert, this is often where they mean. The classic desert scenery around Sesriem and Sossusvlei is the stuff that postcards are made of – enormous apricot dunes with gracefully curving ridges, invariably pictured in the sharp light of dawn with a photogenic gemsbok or feathery acacia adjacent.

Sesriem and Sossusvlei lie on the Tsauchab River, one of two large rivers (the other being the Tsondab, further north) which flow westward into the great dune-field of the central Namib, but never reach the ocean. Both end by forming flat white pans dotted with green trees, surrounded by spectacular dunes – islands of life within a sea of sand.

GETTING THERE Sesriem is clearly signposted 12km southwest along the C27 from its junction with the C19. The best, easiest and cheapest way to see the area is with your own car – so the vast majority of visitors drive. There is no public transport,

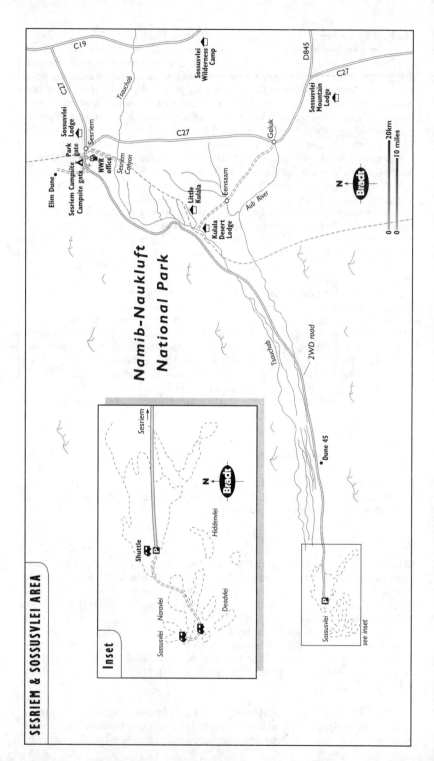

SESRIEM & SOSSUSVLEI AREA

Namib-Naukluft
National Park

Inset

and whilst hitching is possible it is difficult, as there are many possible routes here. (This also makes it easier to get away than to arrive.)

If you don't have your own transport, you have several choices. Various tour groups run trips to Sossusvlei from both Windhoek and Swakopmund (see *Tour operators*, pages 125–6 and 283–4). Alternatively, there's a private shuttle bus that links Namib-Naukluft Lodge with Windhoek and Swakopmund (see page 105). This lodge runs day trips into Sesriem and Sossusvlei which cost about N$550 per person. The third option is to fly in by light aircraft with one of the pleasure flight companies (see pages 300–1). These drop visitors at either Sossusvlei Lodge or Wolwedans, from which there are guided tours around the area – though neither is a cheap option.

Best routes The **quickest** route from Windhoek is normally south on the B1, then west on the C47 just after Rehoboth to Rietoog, right onto the D1206 to Büllsport (where the guest farm makes a good overnight stop if you're just off a plane). Then continue on the D854, almost in the shadow of the Naukluft Mountains, right onto the C19 and then left for 12km to Sesriem. This takes about 4½ hours.

The **most spectacular** route from Windhoek is via the C26, followed by the steep Spreetshoogte Pass on the D1275 – which could easily be a six-hour drive. Swartfontein Lodge is the obvious stopover en route.

Approaching **from Keetmanshoop**, taking the main tar road to Maltahöhe is best, followed by the obvious C19, whilst **from Lüderitz**, Sesriem is really too far for comfort in one day. A stopover would be wise. This approach does allow you to take the D707 and the C27, which can both be slow going, but are certainly amongst the most spectacular roads in the subcontinent – with desert sands to their west, and mountain ranges on the east.

From Swakopmund, it is quickest to drive south to Walvis Bay and then take the C14, via the Kuiseb River's canyon. Allow at least four hours for this – more if you want to drive at a leisurely pace and stop for a picnic.

Rainy season access For a few days each year, rain causes rivers to wash across certain roads – making them difficult, or impossible, to cross. (See advice on crossing rivers, page 95.)

The D854 is often badly affected, having three or more rivers flowing across it, fed by rains that fall on the Naukluft Mountains. The third of these, nearest Sesriem, usually seems the deepest – though this does depend on where the rain falls in the mountains.

Similarly, the Tsauchab River (which flows through Sesriem Canyon, and on to Sossusvlei) crosses the C19 between its junctions with the D854 and C27. It also crosses the C27 south of Sesriem (but north of the turn-off to Kulala). Both these river crossings look very wide, but are usually shallow and can be crossed with care in a normal 2WD.

If you anticipate problems, then approaching from Maltahöhe, on the C19, is probably the safest route – though it's a long way around from Windhoek. It is vital to ask reliable local advice before you set off.

WHERE TO STAY If you want to stay very close to Sesriem, your choices have been limited to the campsite by the park gates, or to the neighbouring Sossusvlei Lodge, but the new Sossus Dune Lodge should help somewhat. Alternatively, you can broaden your choice and stay at one of the nearby lodges. None of these is cheap, but if you're prepared to travel 35km, then the Desert Homestead is probably the least expensive. Realistically, though, anywhere in the Naukluft, Solitaire or even northern NamibRand also makes a practical base for visits to the Sossusvlei area, provided that you don't insist on being at Sesriem for sunrise. In fact, as tourism to this corner of the desert increases, brighter visitors are starting to move away from the busy Sesriem and Sossusvlei area, to find superb desert experiences in the private areas of desert that lie to the north and south – like Wolwedans. For the present, however, this remains an area where you must book well in advance to have any hope of finding good accommodation when you arrive.

⚑ Sesriem Campsite (20 pitches, overflow field) ➘ 063 293245; f 063 293244; central reservations ➘ 061 285 7200; f 061 224 900; e reservations@nwr.com.na; www.nwr.com.na. In 1989, Sesriem campsite had just 10 pitches, and was the only place in the area. Each was shaded by an old camelthorn tree, which boasted a tap sprouting beside its trunk, & was protected by a low, circular wall. It was stunning. Times have changed. Now there are 20 pitches, an overflow field (on the left) which is often busy, & 2 ablution blocks, which can be none too clean. But it's still a marvellous place to camp, especially if you get one of the original pitches, on the edge of the campground. Fuel & wood are normally available at the NWR office, as are a few simple foodstuffs — though it's better to bring food with you. The neighbouring Sossusvlei Lodge welcomes campers to dinner, provided they book a table before midday, & don't become rowdy.

To guarantee camping space, especially in the high season, you should book at the NWR in Windhoek before arriving, although it's always worth checking on arrival to see if there's a space available. Gates into the park from the campsite open at 04.30, half an hour earlier than the main gates.

N$100 per pitch plus N$50/25 pp adult/child, plus park fees (N$80 pp & N$10 per vehicle).

⌂ Sossus Dune Lodge ➘ 061 285 7200; f 061 224900; e reservations@nwr.com.na; www.nwr.com.na. In July 2007, the NWR is set to open the first lodge inside the park, with pairs of rondavel-style chalets in wood, canvas and thatch. For the first time, visitors will have access to Sossusvlei before sunrise, and will stay in the park after sunset. *N$2,300/1,800 sgl/pp sharing, inc DBB & park fees. Sunset/nature drives N$400 pp.*

⌂ Sossusvlei Lodge (45 tents) ➘ 063 693223; f 063 693231; reservations ➘ +27 21 9304564; f +27 21 9304574; e reservations@ sossusvleilodge.com; www.sossusvleilodge.com. Immediately on the right of the national park entrance at Sesriem, Sossusvlei Lodge has the most convenient possible location for anyone wanting to drive to Sossusvlei at first light, or leave the park as late in the day as possible. When built it caused quite a stir: a large lodge so close to the restcamp

& park, but now it is accepted as part of the scenery, into which it blends surprisingly well. Flooding during the heavy rains of 2006 caused serious damage to the lodge, & it has since been totally refurbished.

Its construction is an innovative mix of materials & colours: concrete, ironwork, canvas & leather; reds, apricots, greens & whites. The twin 'tents' are elaborate, permanent constructions; each has an en-suite shower, toilet & basin built as part of the solid base, which supports the canvas walls of the bedrooms. Inside is luxurious & spacious, with adjoining large sgl beds, bedside tables, lamps, easy chairs, a dressing table, etc — so banish any thoughts of camping when you read of 'tents' here.

The bar is popular with campers as well as guests, & the restaurant is good, serving help-yourself breakfasts & light, modern, à-la-carte lunches. Dinner is buffet-style, with various meats (often including unusual game) cooked to order. The swimming pool faces the desert & feels sublime after a dusty day in the dunes.

The lodge has a 10-inch, computer-controlled, light refraction telescope. This can be linked to a PC, to pinpoint any one of 281,000 objects in the night sky, including such southern-hemisphere 'specials' as Omega Centaurus & the Jewel Box, & even be programmed to track (or 'slew') them. The sky at Sesriem is clear for about 300 days per year, & there is virtually no pollution. Ask at reception if anyone is available to work the telescope for you; if not, climb the central water tower to see the stars at their best. (Clouds or rain are a cause for celebration here; don't expect sympathy if you can't see any stars.)

The atmosphere is that of a hotel, as you will be left to organise yourself, though morning & afternoon trips are available into the park using the nearby Namib-Pappot Safari Company.

Sossusvlei Lodge is not cheap, but is very comfortable & perfect for early starts into the Sossusvlei area of the national park.

Low season N$1,564/2,083 sgl/dbl; high season N$1,670/2,226 sgl/dbl, all DBB.

⌂ Desert Camp (20 safari tents) Contact via Sossusvlei Lodge, above; e reservations@ desertcamp.com; www.desertcamp.com. For self-catering visitors, Sossusvlei Lodge has introduced the new

Desert Camp, some 4km from the lodge. Here, somewhat unusual safari tents of light-brown canvas have exterior wooden pole frames on a deep red base, blending into the surrounding desert scenery with views across to the mountains. Inside, each of these has twin beds, en-suite bathroom, and granite tiled floors. The surprise is on the outside, where a compact lock-up kitchen compartment, complete with 2-plate stove, fridge/freezer, utensils & washing facilities sits to one side of the porch, fronted by a picnic table. Each tent also has its own BBQ and a shaded parking spot. For groups a central boma with self-catering facilities is available on request, with a fully stocked and serviced bar. There's also a small pool. N$735/495 sgl/dbl pp sharing, B&B.

🏠 **Kulala Desert Lodge** (17 rooms) ✆ 061 274500; m 081 124 3066; f 061 239455; e info@ nts.com.na; www.wilderness-safaris.com. Opened in 1996, Kulala is signposted off the C27 some 15km south of Sesriem (but north of the junction with the D845), & is then about 14km from the road. Overlooking the national park from the southern banks of the Tsauchab River, Kulala is easily the closest lodge to Sossusvlei. However, if you are self-driving, access to the vlei remains limited to the C27, & the park entrance at Sesriem, thus the Sesriem campsite & Sossusvlei Lodge are effectively a shorter drive from the vlei.

Inside, Kulala's ethnic décor owes much to André & Coralee Louw – designers of Villa Verdi, in Windhoek – whilst inspiration for its cool clay construction was drawn from North African designs. Green directors' chairs sit at heavy wooden tables, an apricot cushioned area encourages relaxation, rich mahogany-leather sofas surround a blazing fire, free-standing iron candelabra & cheerful African music all add to the cosy charm of the place. A wraparound deck provides lovely views across the dunes, whilst a small, kidney-shaped pool & shaded loungers are welcome relief from the midday heat.

The chalets, or kulalas, are large tents built on wooden platforms overlooking the riverbed, topped with thatched roofs. Each incorporates an en-suite clay adobe bathroom, complete with shower & toilet. Gnarled & polished wood furniture is lovely, circus-tent-style mosi-nets are fun & the colourful appliqué bedcovers are both unusual & tasteful. There are 16 twin and 1 dbl rooms, with 2 pairs being adjoining units for families. Outdoors enthusiasts can request a night under the stars & have their mattresses placed on the solid roof of the room's rear – a fun option, though chilly in winter.

Sandwiched between the national park to the

northwest, & the private NamibRand Nature Reserve to the south, Kulala has 32,000ha of its own land on which it operates balloon safaris & nature drives. The balloon safaris, organised by Eric & Nancy Hesemans, who started Namibia's first ballooning at Mwisho, begin at first light, before the heat of the sun stirs powerful thermals over the desert. They end some 60–90 minutes later with a champagne breakfast served wherever you land. In between, you float serenely above a rolling vision of mountains, plains & iridescent sand-dunes, observing the silent dawn as it rises over one of the earth's most beautiful landscapes. It's a truly wondrous experience & well worth the cost.

Morning drives into Sossusvlei with the lodge's own guides are easily arranged & include drinks & entrance fees. These use the lodge's private access to the national park, which is significantly closer than driving round to the main entrance gate. Shorter evening drives (about 16.00–19.00), take a closer look at some of the smaller fauna & flora in the desert & include sundowner drinks & a spotlit night drive on the way back. Alternatively, many guests drive themselves around the area using Kulala as merely a stylish base. N$2,295–3,040 pp sharing, inc FB, activities & local drinks. N$1,185–1,680 pp sharing DBB. N$860–1,450 sgl supplement.

🏠 **Little Kulala** (11 kulalas) Contact as Kulala Desert Lodge above. Rebuilt in 2006, Little Kulala is unlike any other property in Namibia: a stunning, uber-chic, modernist take on a safari lodge. It's striking interior design is characterised by bleached timber decks, striking achitectural objets d'art & textured fabrics in muted desert tones.

There are 11 kulalas (meaning 'to sleep' in the Oshiwambo language), inc 1 family room which sleeps 4. The rooms are light, bright & airy, with 2 sides being entirely glassed to ensure maximum views across the dunes. Shaggy rugs, felt pebble cushions, fabulous beds & candles aplenty make them a great place to retreat to, whilst the large private deck, curved wicker loungers & plunge pool make the space beyond the room equally appealing. Bathrooms are en-suite with an indoor power-shower & an equally lovely, pebble-strewn outdoor shower. All rooms have AC, fully stocked fridge, tea/coffee station & a digital safe. Roof-top 'skybeds' (waterproof covered duvet & mattress) can also be arranged for romantic stargazing, but be aware of the cold night air when electing this option.

The central dining area offers excellent cuisine under dramatic makuti thatch; there are suspended swinging chairs on the deck for casual daydreaming; a library & wine cellar for connoisseurs; a pool for a cooling dip & a friendly bar for fireside drinks at the end of the evening. Early morning guided game drives to the dunes use the reserve's private access, & local walks, sunset drives & ballooning can be arranged. *N$3,750–4,505 sgl/pp sharing, inc FB, activities & local drinks.*

🏠 **Sossusvlei Wilderness Camp** (9 twin rooms) ☏ 061 274500; f 061 239455. For other contact details, see Kulala Desert Lodge above. Sossusvlei Wilderness Camp opened in 1998, catering to upmarket fly-in safaris using its own landing strip. For those driving, it is about 30km from Sesriem on the 7,000ha farm named Witwater. Its entrance is on the west of the C19, just north of its junction with the D845.

Set into a low kopje, around which desert plains fade into mountains & distant dunes, the camp has 9 thatched guestrooms, which have been built from rock & timber. The whitewashed interiors, built-in furniture, crisp linens & concertina windows make the rooms light & airy, & each has an en-suite bathroom with shower & its own private wooden deck & small plunge pool overlooking the waterhole & with a westward orientation for catching picture-perfect sunsets.. There's a central lounge, dining room & bar that is linked to the tents & telescope boma, by raised stone & wooden walkways. If cost is no object, then this camp is excellent & one of the most stylish in the area. *N$2,600–3,515 pp sharing, inc FB & guided activities. Sgl supplement N$1,450.*

🏠 **Kulala Wilderness Camp** (10 rooms) Contact as for Kulala Desert Lodge, above. On the same property as its sister lodge above, Sossusvlei Wilderness Camp, Kulala Wilderness Camp is a delightful, relaxed retreat, which hugs the rock escarpment. Rooms here are walk-in, Meru canvas tents with a thatched roof & stone en-suite bathrooms at the rear. Most of the rooms have twin beds (room 8 is a trpl), and 2 have an interconnecting platform, making them ideal for families or travelling friends. Interiors are fresh & appealing: white bedding with jade woollen throws, olive-green batik cushions, carved wooden chairs, camelthorn-pod light-pulls & natural sisal rugs. Even the en-suite bathroom has been thoughtfully designed with a large glass window placed opposite the toilet for scenic mountain views. The rooms are all raised on decks & each tent has a wooden door onto its own private area; you can even have a bed made up on the roof. The main area is elevated to give commanding views of the surrounding dunes &

mountains, & consists of a thatched dining room complete with sizeable banqueting table, a lounge (with great reference books), bar & a sunken swimming pool in the deck. *N$2,295–3,040 pp sharing, inc FB & guided activities. Sgl supplement N$1,450.*

🏠 **A Little Sossus Lodge** (16 rooms) Reservations ☏ 061 226979; m 081 127 9920; f 061 226999; e logufa@mweb.com.na; www.littlesossus.com.na. Formerly the Desert Homestead (the previous managers taking the established name when they set up their own nearby property), A Little Sossus Lodge is now owned & run by Nico & Norma Grobler. There are 4 semi-circular, family rooms (sleeping 4), which are found in cleverly converted old water tanks, 11 cottage-style twin rooms, & a dbl. The rooms are reasonably spaced out & all have their own adjoining carport. Interiors are cool and bright, with carefully fanned towels, hessian ceilings, sisal rugs, polished wood furniture & large en-suite shower. The dbl room has a particularly lovely view from the bed, & all the cottages overlook the waterhole with sweeping views of the distant Nubib Mountains. The main lodge area offers outside dining on the veranda, a curved bar, small pool area, email & camera charging (no sockets in the rooms), Sundowner trips can be arranged at N$150 pp (max 4 people) & Nico will escort 4x4 trips on request. *N$665/1,252/1,573/1,875 sgl/dbl/trpl/family, B&B. Dinner N$145, lunch pack N$65.*

🔺 **Sossusvlei Campsite** (7 pitches) Contact via A Little Sossus Lodge (see above). Less than 8km from A Little Sossus Lodge, this campsite opened in July 2006, having been built by the same owners. There are 7 pitches on concrete bases with tin roofs overhead & stone/pole walls. Each has its own 'en-suite' bathroom (shower, hot & cold water & flush toilet), sinks, hosepipe, washing line, & a large table with integral braai. One of the pitches is designed to take a roof tent; the others have an adjoining, shaded car port. The highest site, Hilltop, has the best views of the surrounding mountains. There is a reception area at the entrance which has a small lounge & basic shop. When we visited the construction vehicles had sadly made a shocking mess of the approach drive, & had created countless tyre gullies in the process. *N$50 per site plus N$50 pp (max 7 people).*

🏠 **The Desert Homestead & Horse Trails** (20 bungalows) ☏ 061 246788, 063 683103; f 061 243079; e info@deserthomestead-namibia.com; www.deserthomestead-namibia.com. On the C19, 3km northwest of the D854 junction, the new Desert

Homestead sits in a wide grassy valley, sheltered by the Nubib, Tsaris & Naukluft mountains. It has sensational views shared by both the elevated central area & the sweeping curve of well-spaced bungalows. The large terrace, between the thatched entrance & the rock garden & crystal-clear swimming pool, is an idyllic spot for lunch or sundowners. Thatched, whitewashed pole bungalows are set below the main area & make for excellent retreats in the midday sun. The interiors are simple but stylish with elegant dark wood furniture, crisp white linen, a few pieces of interesting objet d'art, a long shower room, & a pleasing lack of general clutter. Ceiling fans keep the rooms cool by day & thick fur blankets do the opposite in winter. Outside a pair of directors' chairs on the concrete terrace make a great spot for solitary reading or simply admiring the view.

Horseriding, for both beginners & experienced riders, is a core activity here with well trained horses used for trips lasting from 1 hr to overnight trips available; the sunrise (N$500) & sunset (N$300) rides come particularly well recommended. *N$700/1,150 sgl/dbl, B&B.*

△ **Footloose** (camping). Also on the C19, Footloose camping has a few places to pitch tents behind a lush, walled farmhouse. An attractive rockery filled with desert succulents & a series of circular bird baths greet visitors here, along with an off-beat teapot-filled tree and neat wrought-iron garden furniture. Camping is possible only when the owner is present, & facilities will likely prove adequate if you time your stay right. Look out for the hiker logo on the main road to find this place. *Camping N$50.*

WHAT TO SEE AND DO Sesriem is the gateway to this part of the park, and the hub of the area. This has the NWR office, where everybody stops to buy their entry permits and fill up with fuel and supplies of cold drinks. From here a short road leads left to Sesriem Canyon, and another heads straight on, through a second gate, towards Elim Dune, Sesriem's small airfield, and Sossusvlei.

Ballooning Namib Sky Adventure Safaris (✆ *063 683188;* m *081 304 2205;* f *063 683189;* e *info@namibsky.com; www.namibsky.com*) run early morning ballooning trips over the desert – which are expensive but superb. You start from Sossusvlei Lodge, Kulala or Mwisho, before dawn, and are driven to a take-off site, which varies with the winds and conditions – though if it's too windy, the flight may be cancelled.

The crew gradually unfurl the balloon, and inflate it with propane burners. When ready, everybody climbs into the basket, and it is inflated to take off. Gradually, the balloon sails higher over the surrounding dunes and mountains. Floating at wind speed is travelling in still air – with only the occasional burst of gas interrupting the silence. It's an eerie experience, and an excellent platform for landscape photography.

Beneath the balloon a support vehicle follows as best it can, carrying a table, chairs and full supplies for a champagne breakfast – which is set up wherever the balloon lands. Eventually, everything is loaded onto the support vehicle and its trailer, and guests are returned to where they started, usually a little before midday.

Though a morning's ballooning costs N$2,750 per passenger, it is such an unusual and exhilarating experience that it is not only highly recommended, but also (arguably) quite good value.

Sesriem Canyon About 4km from Sesriem, following the signs left as you enter the gates, is Sesriem Canyon. This is a narrow fissure in the sandstone, 30m deep in places, carved by the Tsauchab River. It was used by the early settlers, who drew water from it by knotting together six lengths of hide rope (called *riems*). Hence it became known as *ses riems.*

For some of the year, the river's bed is marked by pools of blissfully cool water, reached via an easy path of steps cut into the rock. It's a place to swim and relax – perfect for the heat of the day. At other times, though, the water can be almost stagnant and definitely not a place to bathe. It's also worth following the watercourse 500m upriver from the steps, where you'll find it before it descends into the canyon – another great place to bathe at times.

Beware of flash floods in the canyon itself. Heavy rain in the Naukluft Mountains occasionally causes these, trapping and drowning visitors.

Elim Dune
As you drive towards Sossusvlei, Elim Dune is about 5km from Sesriem. The turning off to the right is shortly after the entrance into the park, leading to a shady parking spot. It is the nearest sand-dune to Sesriem, and if you arrive late in the afternoon, then you may, like me, mistake it for a mountain.

From the parking spot you can climb it, though this takes longer than you might expect – allow at least an hour to get to the top. The views over plains towards the Naukluft Mountains on the east, and dune-crests to the west, are remarkable. It is especially worth the long climb at sunset, and conveniently close to the gates at Sesriem.

Sossusvlei area
(*Open 05.00–21.00; admission N$80 per adult, under 16s free, N$10 per car*) To protect the area, entry permits for Sossusvlei are limited. In theory, only a certain number of vehicles are allowed to start along the road during each of three periods in each day. The first is from sunrise, the second in the middle of the day, and the third in the afternoon. Until now, the number of visitors arriving has rarely exceeded the quota, but this may change as the area receives more visitors.

The road from Sesriem to Sossusvlei
After paying for your permit at the gate, continue southwest past Sesriem, along a road that is tarred through to the parking area. Although it was resurfaced during 2006, it's important to drive carefully: the 60km stretch takes a lot of traffic and in the searing heat the condition can deteriorate rapidly.

The road is soon confined into a corridor, huge dunes on either side. Gradually, this narrows, becoming a few kilometres wide. This unique parting of the southern Namib's great sand-sea has probably been maintained over the millennia by the action of the Tsauchab River and the wind.

About 24km after leaving Sesriem, you cross the Tsauchab River. Although this seldom flows, note the green camelthorn, *Acacia erioloba*, which thrives here, clearly indicating permanent underground water.

Continuing westwards, the present course of the river is easy to spot parallel with the road. Look around for the many dead acacia trees that mark old courses of the river, now dried up. Some of these have been dated at over 500 years old.

Along this final stretch of road are a few side-tracks leading to the feet of some of the dunes, numbered according to their distance along the road from the office. Dune 45, on the south side, is particularly photogenic. About 36km after crossing the Tsauchab, this road ends at the parking area, which is currently free of charge.

Parking
Here low sand-dunes apparently form a final barrier to the progress of the river or the road. There is a large group of acacias, which shade a couple of picnic tables. Nearby are a few toilets of dubious cleanliness.

Nowadays, this is as far as you can drive yourself. To reach Sossusvlei, you must either walk or take the shuttle bus. Alternatively, if you are staying at a nearby lodge and taking one of their guided excursions, the guide will usually be able to drive into the old 4x4 parking area.

The first pan is only about 500m over the sandbar, though it'll take an hour or more to cover the 5km to the farthest pan, Sossusvlei itself. Shuttle 4x4s are run by Hobas Shuttle and Tours from 08.00 until 16.00. The return trip costs N$80 per person or N$50 one way. The driver will collect you from Sossusvlei or Dead Vlei at a pre-arranged time – if you don't want to be rushed, allow around two or three hours. Most visitors choose a leisurely walk into the pan when it's relatively cool, returning by bus as the heat intensifies.

Hidden Vlei On the left of the parking area, you'll see signs to Hidden Vlei – which is reached by climbing over the dunes. As at Dead Vlei, here you'll find old, dead acacia trees, which were deprived of water when the river changed course, but still stand to tell the tale.

Dead Vlei Like Hidden Vlei, but perhaps more accessible, Dead Vlei is an old pan with merely the skeletons of trees left – some over 500 years old. Many consider it to be more starkly beautiful than Sossusvlei.

From the parking area, walk over the sandbar following the track that will lead you into the large main pan. Keep over to the left-hand side, and you'll soon find the old parking area for Dead Vlei, your start point for the 500m hike over the dunes into Dead Vlei.

Sossusvlei and Nara Vlei After about 4–5km the track bends round to the right, and ends in front of Sossusvlei. This is as far as the pans extend. Beyond here, only tall sand-dunes separate you from the Atlantic Ocean.

Most years, the ground here is a flat silvery-white pan of fine mud that has dried into a crazy-paving pattern. Upon this are huge sand mounds collected by nara bushes, and periodic feathery camelthorn trees drooping gracefully. All around the sinuous shapes of the Namib's (and some claim the world's) largest sand-dunes stretch up to 300m high. It's a stunning, surreal environment.

Perhaps once every decade, Namibia receives really torrential rain. Storms deluge the Naukluft's ravines and the Tsauchab sweeps out towards the Atlantic in a flash flood, surging into the desert and pausing only briefly to fill its canyon.

Floods so powerful are rare, and Sossusvlei can fill overnight. Though the Tsauchab will subside quickly, the vlei remains full. Miraculous lilies emerge to bloom, and the bright yellow devil thorn flowers (*Tribulus* species) carpet the water's edge. Surreal scenes reflect in the lake, as dragonflies hover above its polished surface. Birds arrive and luxuriant growth flourishes, making the most of this ephemeral treat.

These waters recede from most of the pan rapidly, concentrating in Sossusvlei, where they can remain for months. While they are there, the area's birdlife changes radically, as waterbirds and waders will often arrive, along with opportunist insectivores. Meanwhile, less than a kilometre east, over a dune, the main pan is as dry as dust, and looks as if it hasn't seen water in decades.

SOLITAIRE AREA

North of the Sesriem area, the C19 leads into the equally beautiful C13 road, often with dunes on one side and mountains on the other. These are the main routes from Sesriem to Swakopmund, so are relatively busy (typically a few cars per hour).

SOLITAIRE Solitaire is a large dot on the NWR's map, but a small place. It is just a few buildings, run by the helpful, if idiosyncratic, Moose; but it is so atmospheric, so typical of a middle-of-nowhere stop in the desert, that it's been the location for several film and advert scenes.

There is a fuel station here that is pretty reliable, and it is still the best place for miles to have punctures mended. The Solitaire General Dealer behind the garage opens all hours, selling quite a wide range of supplies (the best around, though that's no great praise). Buy anything here from superb fresh bread and apple crumble baked on the premises, to ostrich egg necklaces, kudu leather shoes, cold beer, firewood and basic medicines. Most people stop for a drink and a snack either here or at the neighbouring Café Van Der Lee (*open 12.00–15.00*), which serves a selection of sausages and chips for N\$26.

Where to stay

Around Solitaire are several good places to stay while visiting the desert, several of them frequented by group trips. Many of these establishments can be used as bases from which to explore the Sesriem area, whilst those further north have spectacular mountainous scenery of their own worth seeing, and are useful stopovers on the way to/from Sesriem.

Solitaire Country Lodge (25 rooms, camping) ℡ 061 240375, 061 374750; f 061 256598; e reservations@ncl.com.na; www.namibialodges.com. Immediately next to the bustling petrol station & general store, behind a pole fence neatly planted with aloes & cacti, Solitaire Country Lodge opened in June 2002. It is part of the Namibia Country Lodges group that includes Twyfelfontein near Damaraland. The bedrooms & glass-fronted restaurant bound a lush central quad of grass & a large swimming pool, making this a pleasant outpost. The single-storey buildings are painted apricot & have flat roofs & a wide, inward-looking veranda area which continues around the quad. Off this walkway are 23 twin rooms & 2 large family rooms with a dbl bed and 2 sofa beds. All are very clean & spacious with free-standing fans, wrought-iron beds, clean linen (albeit in gaudy animal-print patterns) & en-suite, tiled shower rooms (hot water available all day). Meals are served at set times (breakfast 07.00–09.00, dinner 19.00–21.00), or visit the neighbouring café. There is quite an amount of noise from the on-site generator (lights on 18.00–22.00), petrol station traffic & nearby airstrip. Camping can also be arranged here & there's an ablution block, tap for fresh water & braai facilities behind the lodge. Two walking trails are signposted from the lodge: 8km Sunset Hill & 3.8km Viewers Nest Trail.
N\$370/260 sgl/pp sharing, B&B. Camping N\$55. Dinner N\$120.

Solitaire Guest Farm (6 rooms) ℡/f 062 682033; f 062 682034; e solf@iway.na; www.solitaireguestfarm.com. Situated just 500m east of the fuel station at Solitaire on the C14, this small 5,000ha guest farm has en-suite dbl rooms, a self-catering house, a campsite & a swimming pool. Walking, hiking & game drives ensure that the visitor can see something of the area, returning to

the option of farm-cooked meals.
N\$350 pp sharing, B&B; self-catering house N\$450; camping N\$50 pp.

Namib-Naukluft Lodge (16 rooms) African Extravaganza; ℡ 061 372106; f 061 215356; e afex@afex.com.na; www.natron.net/afex. On the C19, south of Solitaire & just 17km from the Namib Desert Lodge, the Namib-Naukluft Lodge is outwardly rather uninspiring, despite being designed by a well-known Namibian architect. Inside, though, it is plush, with 'normal' rooms; if these, rather than trendy tents, appeal, perhaps this is the place for you.

Its modern rooms are built in line. Through sliding glass doors, leading onto a veranda, they face a huge desert plain. Each has adjacent twin beds, en-suite toilet & (powerful) shower. By reception are a large lounge bar & a dining room, though meals are often eaten on the veranda facing the desert.

Behind the lodge, in the shade of a large kopje, is a braai area for moonlit dining, while at the far end of the row of rooms is a small (popular) swimming pool & a shaded area for relaxing. If you don't have a car while you're here, you can take short walks on the lodge's own land, & reserve a seat on their daily 4x4 trips into Sossusvlei (N\$550 pp).

The lodge is owned by African Extravaganza, & is linked by a shuttle service to/from Windhoek & Swakopmund (see page 105). This departs from both towns at 14.00 (13.00 Jun–Sep), arriving at the lodge just before sunset.
N\$900/750 sgl/pp sharing, DBB.

Weltevrede Guest Farm (12 bungalows, camping) ℡ 063 683073; f 063 683074; e aswarts@ mweb.com.na; www.weltevredeguestfarm.com. Signposted off the east side of the C14, Weltevrede is about a 47km drive from Sesriem & just south of Namib Desert Lodge, 37km from Solitaire. It opened in 1994 with 5 purpose-built bungalows & has recently added two additional family rooms (1 dbl & 2 sgl beds each). Located next to the farm's main

buildings, these are motel-style, simple structures with a reasonable good-size private terrace & parking. They are sparsely furnished with an open iron wardrobe, carved table, ethnic fabric on the beds & curtains & plastic hyacinths in pots, but are clean & spacious. There are en-suite bathrooms whose signs read 'Namibia is a dry country — please adapt!', & include an efficient glass shower unit. There's a large thatched dining area, accessed over a small bridge beside the papyrus-filled pond, where meals are served, & an honesty bar operates. Weltevrede also has two pitches for tents, under shady trees, which have water but no electricity (in the bungalows, electricity is on 19.00—22.00 but this is due to become 24hr in 2007). Campers have use of showers, flush toilets & a fire pit (wood can be bought here), & are best booked in advance. For campers or farm guests, there's a 'reservoir' (a round tank used for water storage) nearby that can be used for swimming. This is very much more a working farm than a lodge for visitors.
N$420/480 sgl/pp sharing, DBB. Camping N$50 pp.

🏠 **Namib Desert Lodge** (60 rooms) ☎ 061 230066; f 061 251863; www.gondwana-desert-collection.com. Namib Desert Lodge sits at the foot of a red sandstone cliff, the 'fossilised' dunes of the protomorphic Namib. It is set within the private Gondwana Namib Park, a 10,000ha reserve which incorporates a range of these petrified dunes, & is frequented by oryx, springbok & ostrich. With its location just 60km north of Sesriem, & a mere 5km from the main C19, the lodge is a good starting point for an excursion to Sossusvlei. Set among trees & palms are 60 en-suite rooms (including 2 family rooms), a restaurant & 2 swimming pools, fronted by an illuminated waterhole, while beyond this visitors may take drives through the park to experience the magnificent scenery. The rooms are neat & functional if a little uninspired & the large central dining area has several long tables to accommodate the many bus groups that stay here. The main area is decorated with attractive murals, cow-skin rugs & a raised, hexagonal fireplace.

Despite the 2 Total petrol pumps at the entrance to the lodge drive, there has been no fuel here for a significant time &, with new petrol regulations being enforced in 2008, the pumps are unlikely to reopen.
N$455/365 sgl/pp sharing, B&B.

🏠 **Rooisand Desert Ranch & Holiday Club** (9 rooms, camping) ☎ 062 572119, 061 253542; f 061 259247; e lifestyle@rooisand.com; www.rooisand.com. Rooisand is situated at the foot

of the Gamsberg Pass on the C26 — about 30km from the junction of the C14 & C26. Once a traditional guest farm, it has been reinvented with a focus on activities. Now, in addition to hiking & drives in the mountains, there's a fitness suite & sauna, a large swimming pool, & even a floodlit tennis court. Of course, activities don't stop in the evening — that's when the pool table & darts come into their own, or the opportunity to stargaze using the farm's telescope arises. Added interest comes from Bushman paintings to be seen on various rocks around Rooisand, as well as an old Schutztruppe camp, & a quarry that occasionally throws up some interesting semi-precious stones. More mundanely, both dbl & sgl rooms have AC, minibar & cordless phone.
N$960/840, sgl/pp sharing, DBB. Camping N$72 pp.

🏠 **Swartfontein Mountain & Desert Guest Lodge** (8 rooms) ☎/f 062 572004/572044; e info@ swartfontein.com; reservations ☎ 061 226979; f 061 226999; e logufa@mweb.com.na; www.natron.net/tour/logufa. Run by Silvia & Roberto Scarafia, Swartfontein Lodge is at the top of the steep Spreetshoogte Pass, off the D1261, north of the D1274, & south of the D1275. It is conveniently located about midway on a scenic route between Windhoek & Sesriem (C26–D1265–C24, then along the D1275).

The elegant farmhouse has Italian furnishings, the odd antique painting, comfortable sofas & an interesting collection of Africana. A curio shop is to be added shortly.

A small lodge with Italian owners, its new, well-kept guest rooms are in a separate wing with good en-suite facilities. Living rooms & dining room are very comfortable, & the food is excellent, with homemade bread, pasta & ice cream. What is more, the vistas from the nearby Spreetshoogte Pass, particularly at sunrise & sunset, are spectacular.

Swartfontein, in the Namib Spreetshoogte Nature Reserve, covers about 81km² of rolling mountains, with game & no domestic stock. They offer early morning birding walks, day & night game drives & private flights (if booked in advance). If you're staying for a while then they will also arrange trips to the Naukluft Mountains & even to Sossusvlei. This excellent lodge deserves to be better known.
N$600/525 sgl/pp sharing, DBB.

🏠 **Rostock Ritz** (22 'igloos') ☎/f 064 69400; reservations ☎ 061 257467; f 061 257469; e info@rostock-ritz-desert-lodge.com; www.rostock-ritz-desert-lodge.com. Run by Kücki, of Kücki's in Swakopmund, this unusual lodge is about 5km off the C14, a few mins' drive south of the C26. Low, stone-built individual 'igloos' with en-suite facilities are designed to keep cool. Each sleeps 2 people, & has magnificent view of the surrounding desert. Two units are suitable for wheelchairs. Outside, the infinity pool has its own commanding views.

Day visitors are welcome to take advantage of the lodge's à-la-carte restaurant, which is a good spot to break for lunch on a long drive (open 12.00–15.00). Attractions include a range of hiking trails, from the easy to moderately difficult routes leading through dunes, canyons & mountains, with overnight treks a possibility. Camel rides are also on offer, while for the less energetic there are dune drives & scenic flights. *N$862.19/682.56 sgl/pp sharing, B&B. Lunch from N$66, dinner N$150.*

🏠 **KuanguKuangu** e filanciu@kuangukuangu.com; www.kuangukuangu.com. For those seeking the ultimate in privacy, this could be the answer: a hideaway cabin built of natural materials (with kitchen & bathroom, hot water, electricity & — for those who simply can't escape — mobile-phone coverage) for just 2 people in an isolated setting to the northeast of Solitaire. The answer to every romantic city-dweller's dream lies on a farm owned by Willem & Hannetjie about 3km off the D1275; coming from Rehoboth, take the C24 to Nauchas, turn right on to the D1275, then about 20km beyond the Spreetshoogte Pass you'll reach a sign on the left saying 'Barchan Dune'. Follow this to the farm. If total solitude palls, help is at hand: meals or a braai pack are available at the farm, & a farm drive can also be organised. *€90 dbl; b/fast €7, dinner €23; braai pack, farm drive €13 (rates in euro).*

THE PARK'S NORTHERN SECTION

Between the normally dry beds of the Swakop and Kuiseb rivers, the desert is largely rock and stone. Though the area has few classic desert scenes of shifting dunes, the landscapes are still striking and certainly no less memorable. They range from the deeply incised canyons of the Swakop River Valley to the open plains around Ganab, flat and featureless but for the occasional isolated inselberg.

WHEN TO VISIT The best time to visit this section of the park is towards the end of the rains, when the vegetation is at its best and, if you are lucky, you'll find scattered herds of gemsbok, springbok and zebra. During this time the best sites to go to are the more open ones, like Ganab, on the plains.

For the rest of the year it is still spectacular, but you'll find fewer animals around. Then perhaps it's better to visit Homeb, or one of the inselbergs, as the flora and fauna there remain a little more constant than those on the plains – not shrivelling up so much in the dryness of winter.

GETTING ORGANISED To venture off the main roads in this area (that is anywhere *except* the C14, C28, D1982 and D198), you need a permit (*N$40 per adult, plus N$10 per vehicle; under 16s free*), easily obtained from the NWR in Windhoek or the park office at Sesriem. These permits allow you to venture onto the park's smaller roads and to camp in any of the area's sites for an additional fee. Most of the roads are navigable by 2WD, with only a few around Gemsbokwater and Groot Tinkas classed as 4x4. Even these are probably negotiable with a high-clearance 2WD and a skilled driver, though you'd be waiting a very long time indeed for anyone to pass by if you became stuck.

Few of the maps of Namibia show these roads clearly, with the notable exception of the Globetrotter map, published by New Holland in London.

▲ WHERE TO CAMP

Namib-Naukluft campsites (☏ *063 293245;* f *063 293244; reservations* ☏ *061 285 7200;* f *061 224900;* e *reservations@nwr.com.na; www.nwr.com.na; N$50 per site plus N$20/10 adult/child, exc park fees*) Basic campsites are situated at Kuiseb Bridge,

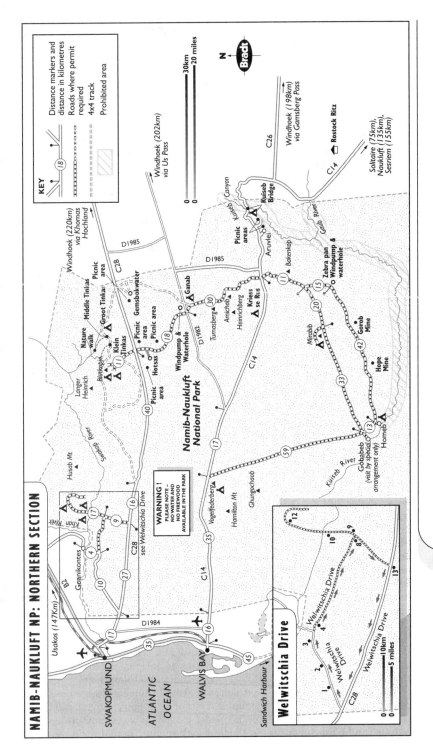

NAMIB-NAUKLUFT NP: NORTHERN SECTION

KEY

⊙⑧ Distance markers and distance in kilometres

▥▥▥ Roads where permit required

---- 4x4 track

░░░ Prohibited area

Bradt

N

30km
20 miles

Usakos (147km)

SWAKOPMUND

ATLANTIC OCEAN

WALVIS BAY

Sandwich Harbour

Khan River

Goanikontes

Husab Mt

Swakop River

Langer Heinrich

Blutkoppie

Klein Tinkas

Middle Tinkas

Groot Tinkas

Nature walk

Picnic area

Picnic area

Hotsas

Gemsbokwater

Picnic area

Windpump & Waterhole

Ganab

Tumasberg

Anichab

Henrichberg

Kriess se Rus

Windhoek (202km) via Us Pass

Windhoek (220km) via Khomas Hochland

D1985

C28

D1982

D1985

Namib-Naukluft National Park

WARNING!
PLEASE NOTE –
NO WATER AND
NO FIREWOOD
AVAILABLE IN THE PARK

see Welwitschia Drive

Vogelfederberg

Hamilton Mt

Ghungochoab

C14

C28

D1984

Kuiseb River

Gobabeb (visit by special arrangement only)

Homeb

Mirabib

Gorob Mine

Hope Mine

Zebra pan Windpump & waterhole

Bokenkop

Aruvlei

Picnic areas

Kuiseb Canyon

Kuiseb Bridge

Gaub River

C26

C14

Windhoek (198km) via Gamsberg Pass

Rostock Ritz

Solitaire (75km), Naukluft (135km), Sesriem (155km)

Welwitschia Drive

10km
5 miles

Welwitschia Drive

C28

12

Homeb, Mirabib, Tinkas, Kriess-se-Rus, Vogelfederberg, Bloedkoppie, Ganab and Welwitschia. They have no facilities to speak of, except for communal ablution facilities, but there is plenty of variety for you to choose from. To spend a night or two camping here – which is the only way to do this part of the desert justice – you must be fully independent in terms of fuel, food, water and firewood.

Ⓧ Bloedkoppie (or Blutkopje) Literally 'blood hill', for its colour in the red light of sunset, this large, smooth granite inselberg rises out of the Tinkas Flats, near the Swakop River. It can provide some challenging scrambles if the heat has not drained your energies. Be careful not to approach any birds' nests, as some of the raptors in the park are very sensitive to disturbances. They may even abandon them if you go too close. Look out for the temporary pools after the rains, filled with life.

Ⓧ Ganab Immediately next to a dry watercourse, which winds like a thin green snake through the middle of a large gravel plain, this open site has a wind-powered water pump nearby. Around March, if the rains have been good, then it can be an excellent spot for herds of springbok and gemsbok – and you can see for miles.

Ⓧ Groot Tinkas Hidden away in a valley amidst a maze of small kopjes, there is a small dam with sheer walls of rock and some fairly challenging rough driving too. Look out for frogs in the pool, and turn over a few stones to find scorpions and their harmless mimics, pseudo-scorpions.

Ⓧ Homeb This excellent site is in the Kuiseb River Valley where the perennial vegetation includes camelthorn (*Acacia erioloba*), false ebony (*Euclea pseudebenus*), wild tamarisk (*Tamarix usneoides*), and several species of wild fig. The Kuiseb forms the northern boundary of the great southern dune-field, so observe the dunes on the south side of the river as they creep northwards. Soon you realise that it's only the periodic floods of the river which prevent the park to the north from being covered in shifting sands. The site is adjacent to a small village.

Homeb's well-placed location leaves you with the opportunity to cross the riverbed and climb amongst the dunes, as well as to explore the river

valley itself. The proximity of three different environments is why Namibia's Desert Research Centre is located at Gobabeb, on the Kuiseb to the west of Homeb.

Ⓧ Kriess-se-Rus Again found in a dry riverbed, Kriess-se-Rus lies just below a bank of exposed schist – with the layers of rock clearly seen, providing an interesting contrast to the flat calcrete plains nearby. Around you'll find quivertrees (*Aloe dichotoma*), many camelthorns, and some *Euphorbia* and *Commiphora* bushes.

Ⓧ Kuiseb Bridge Just off the main C14 route, west of the Gamsberg Pass, the river is said to have less underground water stored here than further down its course, though it is more prone to flash floods. This can be very bare during the dry season, but is really pleasant after the rains. Make it your lunchtime picnic stop if you are travelling between the Swakopmund and Sesriem areas (take your rubbish away with you).

Ⓧ Mirabib Yet another great grey inselberg, but one that is even quieter than the others. It has great views from the top. Around it, where any rainwater runs off, are small trees and bushes. There are always a few lizards to be found around here, and even the odd snake.

Ⓧ Swakop River Being also beacon number 10 on the Welwitschia Drive (see below) means that this beautiful dry riverbed can get rather busy at times with day trippers from Swakopmund.

Ⓧ Vogelfederberg This rounded granite outcrop is the closest of the sites to the ocean, and as such it gets more moisture from the fog than the others. Its gentle shape helps form a number of fascinating temporary pools. Polaroid glasses will help you to see past the reflections and into these pools; if you've a pair, take them.

WELWITSCHIA DRIVE In the northern corner of the Namib-Naukluft National Park, the Welwitschia Drive is perhaps best treated as a half-day excursion from Swakopmund. Don't forget to get a permit first, and note that the condition of the road is pretty poor, so think carefully before taking a 2WD along here.

This is a route through the desert along which are 13 numbered stone beacons at points of particular interest. It culminates at one of the country's largest, and hence oldest, welwitschia plants (see page 334, and take a look at www.plantzafrica.com, a website run by the South African Biodiversity Institute). To find the drive, leave

Swakopmund on the B2 towards Windhoek, then turn right shortly onto the C28. Follow this road for around 16km when you'll come to a junction with the D1991. Turn left here for the start of the circuit (see map, page 261). You'll need to allow about four hours so that you can stop at each place and explore.

An excellent, detailed booklet – well worth getting – is available from the NWR to cover this route. However, as it is often difficult to obtain, here's a brief outline of the different points of interest at the beacons:

1 **Lichen field** Look carefully at the ground to see these small 'plants', which are in fact the result of a symbiotic relationship (ie: a mutually beneficial relationship between two organisms, each depending on the other for its survival) between an alga, producing food by photosynthesis, and a fungus, providing a physical structure. If you look closely, you'll see many different types of lichen. Some are thought to be hundreds of years old, and all are exceedingly fragile and vulnerable.

2 **Drought-resistant bushes** Two types of bush found all over the Namib are the dollar bush, so called because its leaves are the size of a dollar coin, and the ink bush. Both can survive without rain for years. Despite the sign here, there are few drought-resistant bushes to be seen!

3 **Tracks of ox-wagons** Although made decades ago, these are still visible here, showing clearly the damage that can so easily be done to the lichen fields by driving over them.

4 **The moonscape** This is an unusual and spectacular view, usually called the moonscape, looking over a landscape formed by the valleys of the Swakop River. It is best seen in the slanting light of early morning or late afternoon.

5 **More lichen fields** These remarkable plants can extract all their moisture requirements from the air. To simulate the dramatic effect of a morning fog, simply sprinkle a little water on one and watch carefully for a few minutes.

6 This is another impressive view of the endless moonscape.

7 **Old South African camp** This is the site of an old military camp, occupied for just a few days during World War I.

8 Turn left at this marker to visit the next few beacons.

9 **A dolorite dyke** These dark strips of rock, which are a common feature of this part of the Namib, were formed when molten lava welled up through cracks in the existing grey granite. After cooling it formed dark, hard bands of rock which resisted erosion more than the granite – and thus has formed the spine of many ridges in the area.

10 **The Swakop River Valley** Picnicking in the riverbed, with a profusion of tall trees around, you might find it difficult to believe that you are in a desert. It could be said that you're not – after all, this rich vegetation is not made up of desert-adapted species. It includes wild tamarisk (*Tamarix usurious*), and anaboom (*Acacia albida*), better known for its occurrence in the humid Zambezi Valley almost 1,000 miles east – sustained by underground water percolating through the sands beneath your feet.

11 **Welwitschia Flats** This barren, open expanse of gravel and sand is home to the Namib's most celebrated plant, the endemic *Welwitschia mirabilis*. These plants are found only in the Namib, and at just a few locations which suit their highly adapted biology.

12 **The big welwitschia** This beacon marks the end of the trail, and one of the largest *Welwitschia mirabilis* known – estimated at over 1,500 years old. Visitors are asked not to walk inside the ring of stones placed here to protect the plant.

13 **Old mine workings** On the way back to Swakopmund, continue straight past beacon 8, without turning right. Where the road joins route C28 to Swakopmund, marked by this final beacon, is one of the desert's old mine workings. In the 1950s iron ore was mined by hand here. Now it is just another reminder of the park's chequered past.

13

Swakopmund and Walvis Bay Area

Flying low over Namibia's coastline is probably the best way to get a sense of perspective about it. You see how it divides the South Atlantic Ocean from the baking desert. Both seem harsh and unforgiving.

Clinging to the boundary, often under a blanket of morning fog, are Swakopmund and Walvis Bay. Politically, Walvis Bay has always been vital. It has the only deepwater harbour between Lüderitz and Angola. Historically, Swakopmund is probably the more interesting, with old German architecture to rival that in Lüderitz.

Most visitors stay in Swakopmund, which tends to be the livelier of the two, though birdwatchers may prefer Walvis Bay. Both have a good choice of small hotels and restaurants, making them obvious stops when driving between the Namib-Naukluft Park and the Skeleton Coast or Damaraland.

HISTORY

In 1884, the whole of present-day Namibia was declared a protectorate of Germany – except the region's only large natural harbour, Walvis Bay, which remained under British control. Thus, in order to develop their interests in the area, the German authorities decided to make their own harbour on the northern banks of the Swakop River, and beacons were planted in 1892 to mark the spot, where the Mole is today (see page 284).

Following this, the German authorities made several (largely unsuccessful) attempts to develop landing facilities. A quay was built, although it subsequently silted up, followed by a wooden, and later an iron, jetty. Finally in 1915, when Germany's control of the country was surrendered to South Africa, all maritime trade reverted to Walvis Bay.

During the South African administration of Namibia, before Independence, there was a deliberate policy of developing no other ports to compete with Walvis Bay – as South Africa anticipated keeping hold of the Walvis Bay enclave, even if it was forced into giving most of Namibia independence.

As planned, South Africa kept the Walvis Bay enclave as part of the Cape Colony even after Namibian independence in 1990, though it agreed to a joint administration in 1992, and finally relented in February 1994, when Walvis Bay officially became part of Namibia.

SWAKOPMUND

Considered by most Namibians to be the country's only real holiday resort, this old German town spreads from the mouth of the Swakop River out into the surrounding desert plain. Climatically more temperate than the interior, the palm-lined streets, immaculate old buildings and well-kept gardens give Swakop (as the

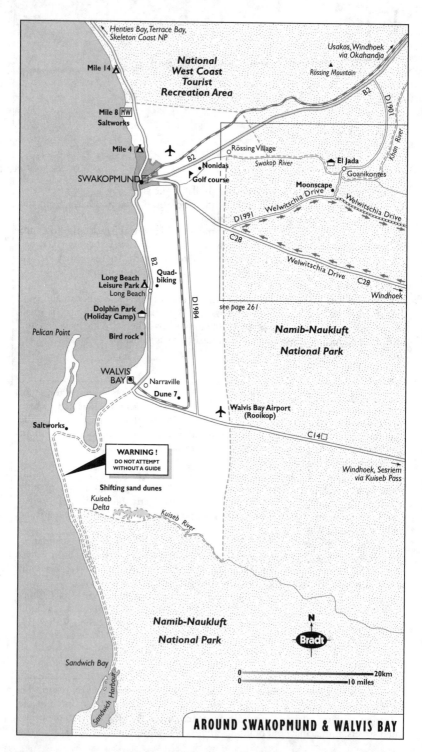

Henties Bay, Terrace Bay, Skeleton Coast NP

Usakos, Windhoek via Okahandja

Rössing Mountain

National West Coast Tourist Recreation Area

Mile 14

Mile 8 MW Saltworks

Mile 4

SWAKOPMUND

B2

D1901

Khan River

Rössing Village

Nonidas

Golf course

Swakop River

El Jada

Goanikontes

Moonscape

Welwitschia Drive

Welwitschia Drive

D1991

C28

Welwitschia Drive

C28

Windhoek

see page 261

Namib-Naukluft National Park

B2

Long Beach Leisure Park

Quad-biking

Long Beach

Dolphin Park (Holiday Camp)

Pelican Point

Bird rock

WALVIS BAY

Narraville

Dune 7

D1984

Saltworks

Walvis Bay Airport (Rooikop)

C14

Windhoek, Sesriem via Kuiseb Pass

WARNING!
DO NOT ATTEMPT WITHOUT A GUIDE

Shifting sand dunes

Kuiseb Delta

Kuiseb River

Namib-Naukluft National Park

Sandwich Bay

Sandwich Harbour

N

Bradt

0 _____ 20km
0 _____ 10 miles

AROUND SWAKOPMUND & WALVIS BAY

locals call it) a unique atmosphere, and make it a pleasant oasis in which to spend a few days.

Unlike much of Namibia, Swakopmund is used to tourists, and has a wide choice of places to stay and eat, and many things to do. The town has also established a name for itself as a centre for adventure travel, and attracting adventurous visitors seeking 'adrenalin' trips, with numerous new and highly original options, from free-fall parachuting to dune-bike riding and sandboarding. This is still too small to change the town's character, but is enough to ensure that you'll never be bored. On the other hand, visit on a Monday during one of the quieter months, and you could be forgiven for thinking that the town had partially closed down!

To a certain extent, Swakopmund is a victim of its own success, with more and more people seeking to buy property on the coast, which in turn has created pressure on its infrastructure. Whilst the increasing diversity of shops is for some a positive result, it also means that you'll have to book a table at the town's most popular restaurants, even out of season. Rather more importantly, there is now enormous pressure on the already over-stretched water supply, which is currently piped in from elsewhere in Namibia. Talk of building a desalination plant so that the town can be self-sufficient has been going on for years, but costs would be high, both for the construction and for the resulting water, and as yet no decisions have been taken.

ORIENTATION Viewed from above the Atlantic, Swakopmund has a simple layout. One tar road, Sam Nujoma Avenue (the B2), enters the town from the interior; another heads off left, northwards, to Henties Bay (C34). A third crosses the mouth of the Swakop, southwards towards Walvis Bay. Where they meet is the centre of town, a raised area about four blocks from the Promenade – the palm-lined road that skirts the seashore.

Most of the hotels are near the compact centre, as are the shops and restaurants, so it's an easy town to walk around. In recent years, though, an explosion of development has hit this small resort, obliterating sea views almost overnight in the scramble to build ever closer to the shore. Whereas once the campsite at 'Mile 4' was quite literally four miles from Swakopmund, today the town's suburban sprawl has crept up to meet it. While this has had little impact on the centre of town in itself, it has certainly changed the picture from above.

Street name changes A number of street name changes have recently been introduced in Swakopmund, replacing the familiar German names with others to honour local and national dignitaries. Inevitably, many of the former names are still used, as follows:

Anton Lubowski Avenue	*was*	Lazarett Street
Daniel Tjongarero Avenue	*was*	Post Street
Hendrik Witbooi	*was*	Roon Street
Libertina Amathila Avenue	*was*	Brücken Street
Moses Garoëb Street	*was*	Nordring/Sudring
Nathaniel Maxuilili Street	*was*	Breite Street
Rakotova	*was*	Knobloch
Sam Nujoma Avenue	*was*	Kaiser Wilhelm Street
Theo-Ben Gurirab Avenue	*was*	Bahnhof Street
Tobias Hainyeko Street	*was*	Moltke Street
Welwitschia	*was*	Schlacter

There are yet more changes in the pipeline, with roads to be affected including the Strand, Fischreier and First Street, but final decisions have yet to be taken on these.

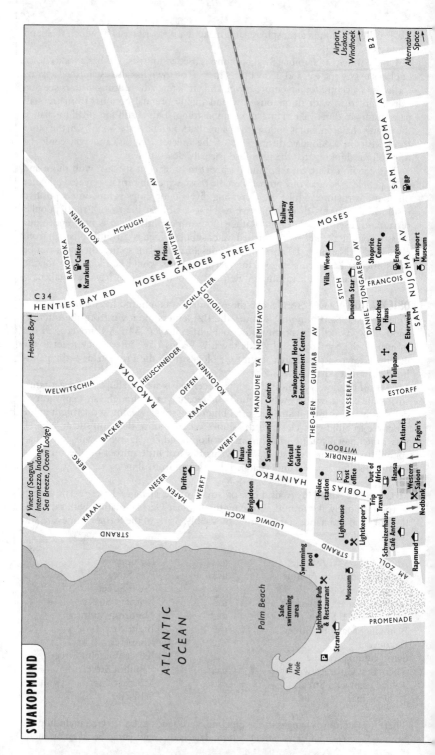

SWAKOPMUND

ATLANTIC OCEAN

Palm Beach

The Mole

PROMENADE

Safe swimming area

Lighthouse Pub & Restaurant

Museum

Strand

Lighthouse

Lightkeeper's

Swimming pool

Brigadoon

Drifters

Haus Garnison

Swakopmund Spar Centre

Kristall Galerie

Police station

Post office

Out of Africa

Hansa

Trip Travel

Schweizerhaus, Café Anton

Western Saloon

Nedbank

Rapmund

Il Tulipano

Atlanta

Fagin's

Eberwein

Deutsches Haus

Dunedin Star

Villa Wiese

Shoprite Centre

Engen

Transport Museum

BP

Swakopmund Hotel & Entertainment Centre

Railway station

Old Prison

Caltex

Karakulia

Henties Bay

C34

HENTIES BAY RD

MOSES GAROEB STREET

RAKOTOKA

KOLONNEN

MCHUGH

AV

CHAMUTENYA

SCHLACTER

HIDIPO

HEUSCHNEIDER

WELWITSCHIA

BÄCKER

BERG

KRAAL

NESER

HAFEN

WERFT

LUDWIG KOCH

STRAND

OFFEN

KOLONNEN

KRAAL

WERFT

HAINYEKO

MANDUME YA NDEMUFAYO

GURIRAB AV

THEO-BEN

WASSERFALL

HENDRIK WITBOOI

TOBIAS

AM ZOLL

ESTORFF

STICH

DANIEL TJONGARERO AV

FRANCOIS

SAM NUJOMA AV

SAM NUJOMA AV

MOSES

B 2

Airport, Usakos, Windhoek

Alternative Space

Vineta (Seagull, Intermezzo, Indongo, Sea Breeze, Ocean Lodge)

268

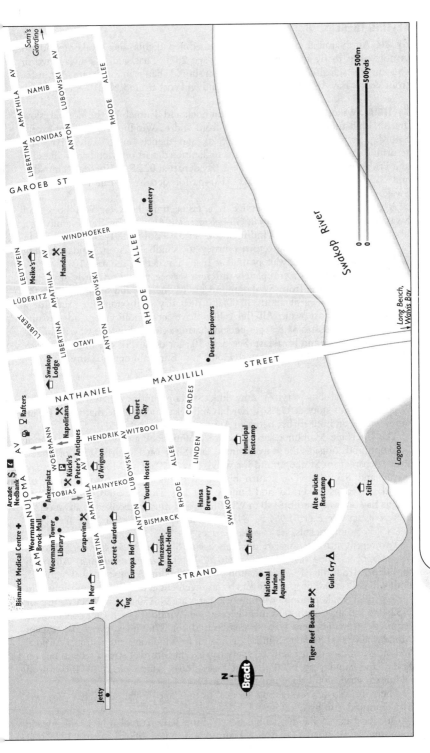

Sam's
Giardino →

AMATHILA AV

NAMIB

LIBERTINA NONIDAS

ANTON LUBOWSKI AV

RHODE ALLEE

GAROEB ST

Cemetery

WINDHOEKER

LEUTWEIN

Meike's

Mandarin

LÜDERITZ

AMATHILA AV

LÜBBERT

LIBERTINA

OTAVI

ANTON LUBOWSKI AV

RHODE ALLEE

Desert Explorers

Swakop
Lodge

NATHANIEL

MAXUILILI   STREET

Rafters

Napolitana

CORDES

Desert Sky

HENDRIK WITBOOI AV

Kücki's

Peter's Antiques

WOERMANN AV

d'Avignon

Municipal
Restcamp

Ankerplatz

TOBIAS

LINDEN

Arcade

Nedbank

NUJOMA

Woermann Brock Mall

SAM

Woermann Tower

Library

Grapevine

LIBERTINA AMATHILA AV

HAINYEKO

ANTON LUBOWSKI AV

Youth Hostel

Bismarck Medical Centre

A la Mer

Secret Garden

Europa Hof

Prinzessin-
Ruprecht-Heim

BISMARCK

Hansa
Brewery

RHODE ALLEE

SWAKOP

Alte Brücke
Restcamp

Stiltz

Adler

STRAND

National
Marine
Aquarium

Gulls Cry

Tug

Tiger Reef Beach Bar

Jetty

N

Bradt

Swakop River

Long Beach,
Walvis Bay

Lagoon

500m
500yds

0
0

GETTING THERE

By air Air Namibia currently has no scheduled flights into Swakopmund, so visitors need to fly to Walvis Bay (see page 287). That said, it's always worth checking the schedules in case the situation should change in the future. A transfer from Walvis Bay Airport into Swakopmund will cost around N$210 per person.

By train Swakopmund is linked to Windhoek and Tsumeb by the normal, slow TransNamib train services. These run from and to Windhoek every day except Saturday, arriving Swakopmund at 05.20, and thence on to Walvis Bay, and returning to Windhoek at 20.45. Trains to Tsumeb depart on Monday, Wednesday and Friday at 18.00, and those to Walvis Bay depart at 02.35 on Tuesday, Thursday, and Saturday. See *Chapter 6*, pages 101–3, for details, or call the station in Swakopmund (*064 463538*).

A recent addition to the service is a faster train between Windhoek and Swakopmund, called the *Omugulu Gwombashe Star*. Also run by TransNamib it's a luxury train that leaves Windhoek on Friday only at 14.00, arriving in Swakopmund at 20.30; the return journey to Windhoek is on Sunday, leaving Walvis Bay at 13.00, and Swakopmund at 13.49. For details, see page 101.

The *Desert Express* is a completely different service, aimed primarily at visitors on holiday. It departs from Swakopmund on Wednesday and Saturday at 15.00, arriving in Windhoek at about 10.00 the next day, with stops en route for a sundowner or short walk. All the cabins have air conditioning and en-suite facilities. Tickets cost N$1,850 per person sharing a twin cabin, one way, including excursions, dinner and breakfast. See page 103 for details, or call in at the *Desert Express* office in the Swakopmund Hotel and Entertainment Centre (f *064 400372*).

By bus Several bus services now link Swakopmund with Walvis Bay and Windhoek, with stops at Usakos, Karibib and Okahandja. Note that times for all buses will be an hour earlier between April and October.

The Intercape Mainliner service between Windhoek and Walvis Bay stops at Swakopmund, outside the now-defunct Talk Shop on Hendrik Witbooi Street. Buses depart from Swakopmund for Walvis Bay at 10.40 on Monday, Wednesday, Friday and Saturday. The return bus to Windhoek leaves Swakopmund on Monday, Wednesday, Friday and Sunday at 12.15. Tickets cost around N$30 to Walvis Bay one way, and N$140 to Windhoek, and must be booked in advance. To book, contact Intercape (*061 227847; www.intercape.co.za*) or Sure Ritz Travel (see below). For more details, see *Chapter 6*, pages 104–5.

Two recent introductions are the Welwitschia Shuttle (*064 405105/2721*) and Townhoppers (*064 407223;* m *081 210 3062;* e *townhoppers@iway.na*). Although they depart from the BP service station on Sam Nujoma Avenue in Swakopmund, both will collect and drop passengers by arrangement at hotels and guesthouses in the centre of Swakopmund or Windhoek. Fares are N$150 to Windhoek centre, or N$280 to the airport (this last includes a stop in Windhoek with later collection as required). Townhoppers leave Swakopmund for Windhoek every day except Monday at 08.00 (10.00 on Sunday), going on to Windhoek International Airport. Welwitschia buses depart at 07.00 every day except Saturday, with a second bus on Friday and Sunday at 14.00. Return buses leave Windhoek at 14.00, with an additional service on Friday and Sunday at 19.00.

There is also a weekly bus service from Cape Town to Walvis Bay, via Swakopmund, run by Ekonolux. For details, see page 287.

One local agency handles all bus tickets: **Sure Ritz Travel** at Nedbank Arcade (opposite the Brauhaus) (10 Tobias Hainyeko St; *064 405151;* m *081 122 7264;*

f 064 405131; **e** *dunjaw.ritzswp@galileosa.co.za*). Note that they charge a ticket-handling fee of N$25 per person.

By car For comments on the choice of roads from Swakopmund to Windhoek, see *Chapter 9*'s section *From Windhoek to the coast*, page 161. If you're taking the C28 or C26 then also see comments on the northern section of the Namib-Naukluft National Park, pages 260–4. The long coastal road to the north is covered in the *Chapter 14, The Skeleton Coast*.

GETTING AROUND Swakopmund's centre is so small that most visitors walk around it, though obviously you'll need a car to get out of the centre. Alternatively, the **Cycle Clinic** (*10 Hendrik Witbooi St;* ⤵ *064 402530*), between the Hansa Hotel and Sam Nujoma Avenue, hires out bicycles for N$20 per hour, or N$100 a day. These range from mountain bikes to touring models, and come complete with (compulsory) cycle helmets. A deposit of N$200 is required.

If you're hiring a car on arrival, then all of the local **car-hire** companies will meet you at Walvis Bay Airport (there are currently no direct flights into Swakopmund). Contact details are:

Avis Swakopmund Hotel & Entertainment Centre; ⤵ 064 402527; **f** 064 405881; www.avis.co.za
Budget Woermann Brock Centre, Tobias Hainyeko St; ⤵ 064 463380; **f** 064 463284; www.budget.co.uk
Crossroads Car Hire ⤵ 064 403666/777. 4x4 specialist.
Hertz 16 Libertina Amathila Av; ⤵ 064 461826; **f** 064 461854

Into Namibia 1 Tobias Hainyeko St; ⤵ 064 464157; **f** 064 464158
Namib 4x4 Sam Nujoma Av; ⤵ 064 404100; m 081 124 2504; **f** 064 405277; pager: 405544
Odyssey Car Hire Sam Nujoma Av & Hendrik Witbooi St; ⤵ 064 400871; **f** 064 403571
Triple Three Rentals Sam Nujoma Av; ⤵ 064 403190; m 081 127 3331, 081 127 8878; **f** 064 403191; **e** oliver@iafrica.com.na; www.333.com.na

A word of warning for drivers It is not advisable to drive between Swakopmund and Walvis Bay late in the evening. Although the distance is short and the road good, it tends to be used as a race track by drink-drivers, and there are frequent accidents.

If you'd rather not drive yourself, there's a recently opened **taxi** service, Taxi Krauss (m *081 298 8886*).

WHERE TO STAY When thinking about visiting Swakopmund, note that from about mid-December to mid-January, the whole population of Windhoek seems to decamp to the relative cool of Swakopmund for their 'summer break'. This means that the hotels and guesthouses are fully booked, and the town is filled with bursting. Reservations are essential. At other times, Swakopmund is not so frantic, though the better (and better-value) hotels usually need reserving before you arrive. As the town is well used to families, many establishments offer a special rate for children, so it's well worth asking.

Because of Swakopmund's cooling morning fogs, and the moderating maritime influence on its temperatures, air conditioning is seldom needed here and few of the hotels provide it, though several do have heating. For the same reason, camping on the large, open sites by the sea can be very cold and uncomfortable, while the cheaper bed and breakfasts and guesthouses are very reasonably priced. So even if you're camping for most of your trip, this may be a good place to treat yourself to a bed for the night. Below, the various establishments are divided, by atmosphere, into hotels, pensions and bed and breakfasts, backpackers' lodges, restcamps and camping.

13

Hotels The large Hotel and Entertainment Centre is Swakopmund's only international-standard hotel, though if you're in search of any local flavour then look elsewhere. You'll find various basic, budget places, many small hotels full of character, and a few gems.

Swakopmund Hotel & Entertainment Centre (90 rooms, inc 1 paraplegic) 2 Theo-Ben Gurirab Av; 064 410 5200; f 064 410 5360–2; e swakopmund@legacyhotels; www.legacyhotels.co.za. Built from the shell of Swakopmund's old railway station, this leisure complex is now owned by Legacy Hotels, & includes the Mermaid Casino, a gym, a hair salon & a reflexologist. Avis car hire is also situated here.

Entering the huge lobby &, passing reception, you emerge into a central grassy quadrangle, dominated by a pool. This is surrounded by palm trees & easy chairs, & surmounted by fountains. Overlooking the courtyard are brightly furnished & well-equipped rooms, which come with a tea/coffee maker, phone, Mnet TV, minibar/fridge, AC, wireless internet connectivity, & a safe deposit box as standard. The box may come in useful for your winnings at the casino, which has some 177 slot machines & 10 gaming tables. Fortunately, as this is often busy, it is a few hundred yards away — the hotel is having more success attracting local clientele than high-rolling foreign gamblers. Close by is an 18-hole golf course.

The centre has 2 restaurants, Platform One & the Station Grill (open 18.30–22.00). The former offers a varied menu while the latter specialises in seafood — the seafood treasure chest (N$180) being a firm favourite. A special Sun lunch is good value at N$55. At other times, you can expect grills at N$55, or fish at N$40–70 (seafood platter for 2, N$340).
N$990/1,580 sgl/dbl, B&B.

Hansa Hotel (58 rooms) 3 Hendrik Witbooi St; 064 414200; f 064 414299; e reservations@ hausahotel.com.na; www.hansahotel.com.na. The Hansa is privately owned, & probably the best hotel in Swakopmund. It is fairly large, though has an intimate residents' lounge & bar, with fireplace for the winter, & a terrace area for light lunches (about N$55), as well as an award-winning restaurant (see pages 278–9).

Its rooms are a good size with solid furnishings, & feel old but well maintained & cared for. They are heated (there's no AC, nor need for it), & have direct-dial phones, safes, & TVs with CNN, Mnet & local stations. The garden rooms at the back have small fridges, & a few have disabled facilities & ramps for easier access. Eight of the rooms have balconies overlooking the garden. The Hansa's management is sharp, & the service here good.
N$880/1,250/2,150 sgl/dbl/suite, all B&B.

Hotel Schweizerhaus (24 rooms) 1 Bismarck St; 064 400331–3; f 064 405850; e schweizerhaus@mweb.com.na; www.schweizerhaus.net. Above the genteel Café Anton, the Schweizerhaus has character & perhaps the best location of any of Swakopmund's hotels — overlooking the ocean & yet near to town. Its rooms are simple & German in style, with en-suite toilet, bath & shower, TV & direct-dial phone. Most also have a balcony, including all of the luxury rooms which face the sea. Others overlook a courtyard at the back, home to free-flying parrots & various tropical birds.

The café (see page 280) opens for extensive breakfasts & stays open until the mid evening, The staff are normally very friendly, & there's a night porter on duty should you arrive late, making the Schweizerhaus a good-value hotel option.
N$450–650/650–880 sgl/dbl, B&B.

Strand Hotel (45 rooms) Beach Front; 064 400315; f 064 404942; central reservations 064 405161; e centralres.nsh@olfitra.com.na; www.namibsunhotels.com.na. Beside the Mole (see page 284) & the ocean, the Strand — now part of the Namib Sun Hotels group — is a large & ostentatious hotel, & the only one in Swakopmund so close to the sea. Its rooms all have Mnet TV, direct-dial phone, tea/coffee makers, ceiling fans, & baths with overhead showers. The larger ones have couches that will take two children, & interconnect as family rooms. Half face the sea, & half of those have balconies.

Downstairs is a lounge & bar, & the Commodore Room, where breakfast is served. The adjacent Ocean Basket restaurant provides a varied menu which can be eaten on the terrace overlooking the Mole. Outside, the cheap-&-cheerful Strand Café is a busy open-air café serving burgers & snacks under parasols, & ice creams to those on the beach alongside.
High season (Nov–Jan, Jul–Oct) N$670–725/ 885–940/1,145 sgl/dbl/suite; low season N$635–690/840–895/1,085 sgl/dbl/suite; all B&B.

Europa Hof Hotel (35 rooms) 39 Bismarck St (cnr Anton Lubowski Av); ✆ 064 405898/405061/405061; f 064 402391; e nicole@europahof.com.na; www.europahof.com. Built in the striking *fachwerk* style of German architecture – best described as 'Bavarian Tudor' – the Europa Hof is a solid, imposing place. Its rooms are comfortable & carpeted, & furnished in quite an old, heavy style. All have twin beds, en-suite toilets & showers or baths, TV with Mnet, & direct-dial phone.

Behind the hotel is a large central courtyard, used both for parking & open-air dining, under palm trees, at the hotel's restaurant (which closes at 22.00 on weekdays, & 21.30 at weekends). The menu follows traditional German lines, focusing on game & fish; there is also a children's menu. The Europa Hof is one of Swakopmund's more traditional, German-style hotels. N$508.70/763.04/864.78 sgl/dbl/trpl, B&B.

Atlanta Hotel (14 rooms) 6 Hendrik Witbooi St; ✆ 064 402360; f 064 405649; e atlantah@africaonline.com.na; www.atlantahotel.com.na. Between Sam Nujoma Av & Daniel Tjongarero Av, the Atlanta Hotel is perhaps most noted for Fagin's Bar beneath it. It's simple & very central, with all its rooms having en-suite bathrooms, direct-dial phones & TVs. There's also secure off-street parking. If you're looking for somewhere inexpensive & central, perfect for forays into Swakopmund's nightlife, perhaps this is the place. N$400/550 sgl/dbl, 2–6-bed N$225 pp sharing, all B&B.

Hotel Eberwein (17 rooms) Sam Nujoma Av (cnr Otavi St); ✆ 064 414450; f 064 414451; e eberwein@iafrica.com.na; www.eberwein.com.na. This former family house close to the centre of town was transformed into a privately owned hotel in December 1999. Its 16 dbl rooms & 1 sgl all have en-suite shower, TV, minibar, phone & underfloor heating. They are clean & bright, with pastel pink a dominant theme, though some are Victorian in style. It is German in character, efficiently run & with friendly staff. Although the restaurant does not normally serve evening meals, these can be arranged in advance for groups of more than 10 people. N$590/860/990 sgl/dbl/trpl; Victorian room N$670/990/1,050, all B&B.

Rossmund Lodge See *Golf*, page 286.

Lodges, pensions and B&Bs If you don't need the facilities of a larger hotel, then several of these smaller pensions and B&Bs, recently joined by The Stiltz, are both delightful and very good value. Almost all are within walking distance of the town centre, but those that are particularly central are listed first, followed by others that, being situated in more residential areas of town, are often quieter.

Close to the centre

Hotel Adler (13 rooms, 1 studio) 3 Strand; ✆ 064 405045–7; f 064 404206; e adler@iafrica.com.na; www.natron.net/tour/adler/hoteld.htm. Opposite the aquarium, & just 50m from the sea, Hotel Adler is a modern, stylish pension designed with space, taste & good facilities. All the well-appointed rooms are slightly different, but expect en-suite toilet & shower, remote-control satellite TV, phone, clock/radio & hairdryer. Luxury rooms are slightly larger, with safe, a bath & shower, & a fridge, while the private studio has its own balcony with sea view.

Breakfast is taken in a simple dining area, or outside in the attractive courtyard, while above is a rooftop sun-terrace. There's also a bar & lounge in the reception area. Parking is secure, & garages may be rented for N$50 per day.

A highlight is the heated indoor pool, & a sauna (booked on a private basis for N$50 pp), plus a couple of exercise machines. Massages are available from N$50. Standard N$525/725 sgl/dbl, luxury N$560/845, studio 640/950, all sgl/dbl; family N$1,126, all B&B, exc bed levy.

A La Mer (28 rooms) 4 Libertina Amathila Av; ✆ 064 404130; f 064 404170; e alamer@iway.na; www.pension-a-la-mer.com. Formerly Dig By See, this has been the site of a hotel for years. Situated near the promenade, its rooms are basic but all have a bath, shower & TV, & the restaurant downstairs serves b/fast. Lunchpacks are also available for N$30. Outside is secure parking. N$245.70/386.10/456.30 sgl/dbl/trpl, B&B.

Hotel-Pension d'Avignon (10 rooms) 25 Libertina Amathila Av; ✆ 064 405821; f 064 405542; e hotel.davignon@iafrica.com.na; www.natron.net/tour/davignon. This small, central pension focuses on German visitors but is perfectly welcoming of others. Rooms are clean if unremarkable, with en-suite showers. There's a small pool at the back, & a TV lounge with tea & coffee. N$250/395/520/580 sgl/dbl/trpl/family, B&B.

⌂ **Brigadoon** (7 cottages, 1 flat) 16 Ludwig Koch St; ☎ 064 406064; e brigadoon@iway.na; www.wheretostay.co.za/brigadoon. Quite close to the town centre, near the swimming pool & the Entertainment Centre, Brigadoon is run by the welcoming Bruce & Bubble Burns – of Scottish descent, if you haven't guessed. Its Victorian-style cottages, individually furnished with traditional wooden chests & wardrobes, are fronted by small gardens. Each cottage has a shower/toilet, a fully equipped kitchen & TV, & is serviced daily (laundry service is possible). There is secure parking, too, for extra peace of mind. With its emphasis on privacy & a central location, this makes an excellent place to stay. A recent addition is a self-contained, 2-bedroom flat in a new building across the road, just 50m from the beach & with sea views as an added bonus.
N$425/555 sgl/dbl, B&B; flat N$1,300.

⌂ **Deutsches Haus** (20 rooms) 13 Lüderitz St; ☎ 064 404896; f 064 404861; e deuhaus@ iway.na; www.deutsches-haus-swakopmund.com. This privately run hotel is in a quiet part of town & includes a sauna & a solar-heated swimming pool. The rooms are simply decorated but all have phone, TV & en-suite bathroom or shower. The small but functional dining room is open for lunch & dinner every day. Staff are polite & efficient.
N$390/585 sgl/dbl, B&B.

⌂ **Haus Garnison** (11 rooms) 4 Garnison St; ☎/f 064 403340; m 081 124 3340; e garni@ iafrica.com.na; www.natron.net/garnison. Inland from Brigadoon, and north of the centre, Garnison is on the right of the main road towards Henties Bay, offering dbl & family rooms. Each of these has a fridge, TV & phone, & garage facilities are available.
N$270/470, sgl/dbl, family rooms at dbl rate plus N$50 for children 2–6, or N75 for 7–12s, all B&B.

⌂ **Meike's Guesthouse** (4 rooms) 23 Windhoeker St; ☎ 064 405863; f 064 405862; e meike@ africaonline.com.na; www.natron.net/meikesguesthouse/. This bright, modern guesthouse is about 5 mins' walk from the centre of town. You can be guaranteed a warm welcome from Meike, who used to run Ababis Guest Farm in the Naukluft Mountains, but has since opened up her family home for the use of guests.

The rooms are simple & tastefully decorated, all with en-suite shower, TV, fridge & a small terrace in front. One room comprises a family unit of 3 beds. This is very much a personal B&B run on traditional lines.
N$260 pp, B&B.

⌂ **Pension Prinzessin-Ruprecht-Heim** (23 rooms) 15 Anton Lubowski Av; ☎ 064 412540; f 064 412541; e reservation@prinzrupp.com.na, info@prinzrupp.com.na; www.prinzrupp.com.na. Just west of Bismarck St, this was originally a German military hospital, built in 1901, & tends to appeal to an older clientele. The oldest of its buildings, at the front, has enormous rooms with high ceilings, accessed via wide old doors; most of these rooms have showers & toilets en suite. Newer rooms at the back are smaller, with a bath/shower instead of just a shower, & lack the character of the older rooms.

In the pension's centre is a large courtyard, dotted with palm trees & places to sit. You may have to seek out the manager here by going around the right-hand side of the pension when you arrive.
N$250/225–245 sgl/dbl; small sgl room (sharing bathroom) only N$150, all B&B.

⌂ **Pension Rapmund** (25 rooms, family room) 6–8 Bismarck St; ☎ 064 402035; f 064 404524; e rapmund@iafrica.com.na. Standing beside the Schweizerhaus (Café Anton) on Bismarck St, overlooking the promenade, the old-style Rapmund has recently had all its rooms refurbished. All are clean & simple, with en-suite facilities, & 4 overlook the sea. A family room has its own kitchenette. There's also an excellent small art gallery, a showcase for Namibian artists. Friendly, central & relatively cheap, the Rapmund offers very good value for money.
Sgl N$245–280, dbl N$409.50, trpl N$444.60–468, B&B. Family room N$491.40–549.90. No credit cards.

⌂ **Secret Garden Guesthouse** (8 rooms) 36 Bismarck St; ☎/f 064 404037; e sgg@iway.na; http://natron.net/tour/secretgarden. Just 500m from the beach, & close to the centre of town, this attractive, terracotta-painted guesthouse is just opposite the Europa Hof. En-suite rooms – 6 dbls & 2 suites – look over the palm-shaded garden courtyard that gives the guesthouse its name. Modern & well appointed, with soft blue furnishings, each has tiled or wooden flooring, coffee/tea facilities, hairdryer, fruit basket & underfloor heating in the bathroom. Suites have a kitchenette, 4 beds, TV & AC. In addition to a spacious lounge with DSTV, there's a breakfast room with honesty bar, an attractive jacuzzi in the garden, &, for self-catering guests, a kitchen & barbecue. Secure parking is available, as well as lock-up garages (N$35 per night). Transfers to & from the airport & station are offered free of charge.

N$396.80/264.50 sgl/pp sharing; 3rd person sharing N$193.40; suite N$305.20–406.95 pp sharing, all B&B. Surcharge for 1-night stay.

⌂ **The Stiltz** (9 rooms); ✆ 064 400771; f 064 400711; e info@the stiltz.in.na; www.thestiltz.in.na. In an entirely new departure for Swakopmund, The Stiltz combines a great location at the edge of town, within easy reach of restaurants & shops, with a flair for design, resulting in a place that defies conventional categorisation. Accommodation consists of a series of rustic wooden chalets, built (as the name suggests) high on stilts, & linked by wooden walkways. Zany colours adorn the insides,

North and east of town

⌂ **Beach Lodge** (16 rooms) Stint St; ✆ 064 400933; f 064 400934; e beach@iafrica.com.na; www.natron.net/tour/belo/main/html. The architects have excelled themselves here! Each room forms part of a boat-shaped building that occupies a stunning site right on the beach. Located 5km from town, Beach Lodge is just beyond Sea Breeze (see below). Continue past Sea Breeze & follow the road to the yellow house, then turn left into Rosequartz St, left into Plover St & left again into Stint St.

Light, airy & stylish, rooms all have en-suite shower &/or bath, with sliding doors onto a patio or a private balcony area, TV & direct-dial phone. The breakfast room follows the nautical theme with large porthole windows looking out to sea, & African music plays softly in the background. The atmosphere is one of shipshape efficiency rather than personal care, so it's well suited to those seeking absolute privacy & relaxation. *N$595/680/880/1,060 sgl/dbl/trpl/qudpl, B&B.*

⌂ **Guesthouse Indongo** (6 rooms) 12 Moses Garoëb St; ✆ 064 414750; f 064 414769; e guesthouse@proteawalvis.com.na; www.proteahotels.com/indongo. This somewhat surprising addition to the Protea Hotels group is a converted family house on a quiet residential road. To get there, take the road north along the seafront, turn right at the roundabout along Moses Garoëb St, & the guesthouse is on the left before the bend.

Each of the carpeted rooms, with their sunny yellow walls & sea-themed fabrics, has en-suite shower, phone, TV, kettle & fridge. Some have access to a small garden area, whilst the family room looks out to sea across the rooftops. Public areas feature a spacious lounge with leather chairs, a sun room with wide-screen TV, & a breakfast area with a hint of a sea view in the corner. Outside, a sundeck is to be built alongside a braai area.

accentuating the days when the sun shines, & compensating for those when the sea is shrouded in mist. Views from the chalet balconies vary — some look out over the dunes, some out to sea, & others over the Swakop River bed or the lagoon at its mouth. Typically, each has twin beds or a large dbl, en-suite bathroom, a minibar, heating, & one or two idiosyncratic design features that serve to accentuate the individuality of the place. B/fast is served in a large purpose-built chalet set on its own with panoramic views. It's definitely a place to linger. *N$1,020–1,220, according to layout & view, B&B; family chalet (4 people) N$1,734.*

Standard N$640.96/742.70, executive N$895.30/997, family N$691.82/793.57, all sgl/dbl, B&B.

⌂ **Intermezzo** (7 rooms) 9 Dolphin St; ✆ 064 464114; m 081 129 8297; f 064 407099; e intermezzo@iway.na; http://swakop.com/intermezzo. About 20 mins' walk from the town centre, or 2 mins by car, this ultra-modern pension has recently been taken over but remains friendly & welcoming. To get here, follow the Strand north from town, go over the roundabout, & take the second on the right.

Echoing marble floors in passages & bathrooms are offset by carpet in some rooms, with mature plants softening the overall effect. Simple en-suite rooms feature white bedding & light wooden furniture; facilities include TV, phone, & kettle with coffee/tea, while some also have a small balcony. There are also big family rooms with 2 beds & a seating area. There's a guest lounge with TV, but for a sea view you'll need to adjourn to the light, airy, breakfast area. *N$320/490 sgl/dbl, B&B.*

⌂ **Sam's Giardino** (12 rooms) 89 Anton Lubowski Av, Kramersdorf; ✆ 064 403210; f 064 403500; e samsart@iafrica.com.na: www.giardino.com.na. This charming Swiss-run B&B on the outskirts of Swakopmund is in a quiet residential area, just 10–15 mins' walk to the centre of town. The emphasis here is very much on individual attention. High-ceiling rooms are simple & airy, with pine-clad ceilings & furniture to match, plus en-suite shower, phone & hairdryer. There is also a deluxe suite, with bath & shower & views over the dunes as well as the garden. In July 2007, a further 3 first-floor rooms facing the dunes will open on the adjacent plot; these will have their own music lounge, & integral garages beneath. Almost all the other rooms overlook the well-kept garden that gives the pension its name. It is here that Sam Eggar's canine aide-de-camp, formally known as Mr Einstein, holds court with his new partner, posing regally for photographers on the bridge over the fishpond. There is secure parking & a security guard on duty at night.

Indoors, expect candles & Wagner for breakfast, with real Swiss muesli & the warmth of an open fire to offset Swakopmund's famed morning mists. There are books aplenty, & a TV lounge with a selection of natural history videos. In the evenings, Sam will lay on a 5-course meal (N$135 pp) with the help of local staff whom he has trained in European cuisine & service; the small restaurant is soon to be expanded to seat 24 diners. But his real passion is for wine. Ask to take part in a wine tasting & you'll find yourself surrounded by South African wines of every style in a small, purpose-built *enoteca*, or 'wine restaurant'. With a growing selection of 150 reds & 50 whites on offer, there's plenty of choice — & the relaxed atmosphere that makes wine tasting so pleasurable. And to round off the occasion, ask Sam about his cigars. This is a highly individual pension that would appeal to anyone seeking an oasis of calm & relaxation. *N$640/840 sgl/dbl, all inc Swiss b/fast.*

⌂ **Sea Breeze** (5 rooms, 4 self-catering flats) 48 Turmalin St; ☎ 064 463348; f 064 463349; e seabre@bigfoot.com; www.seabreeze.com.na. Overlooking the beach, this immaculate pension reflects the pride of its Italian owners, Oscar Malaman & Giancarlo Ladurini. To get here, follow the beach road north towards Veneta along the Strand. The road becomes First Av, then eventually Fischreier; turn left into Turmalin St, & Sea Breeze is on the left by the beach. It's about 4.5km from the centre of town, which represents a 30-min stroll along the beach, or a N$10 taxi ride. Sadly, the recent construction of a few properties on the beach has partially obscured its sea views.

Individual rooms are simple & tastefully decorated, with en-suite shower &/or bath. The permutations here are seemingly endless, so it's well worth checking what's available. Some of the rooms still have sea views; others are in the owners' house next door, with softer décor & a shaded patio area overlooking the garden. Flats have a bedroom, lounge/kitchenette with TV, bathroom & balcony over the beach; some have up to 5 beds, & 2 have

heating. The family room has no view, but 4 beds & a kitchenette. There's even a honeymoon suite with 1½ bathrooms & sea view.

Outside, there is secure parking, & garage spaces for up to 5 vehicles at no extra charge; there is also a nightwatchman.
N$400/580 sgl/dbl, B&B; family (4 people) N$770, without b/fast. English b/fast N$50 pp.

⌂ **Seagull B&B** (5 rooms) 60 Strand St North, Swakopmund; ☎ 064 405278; f 064 407141; e sea@iafrica.com.na; www.seagullbandb.com.na, www.namibia1on1.com. Very much a home from home, this rather idiosyncratic guesthouse just a few mins' walk from the town centre is run by Cumbrian-born owner, Keith. It's easy to find — just follow the Strand north out of Swakopmund & it's the first B&B accommodation you come to on the right.

The aim here is quite straightforward: every guest has different needs, & Keith aims to cater for them all. From the grandeur of a king-sized bed, with opulent décor to match, to English country chintz, & primary colours for the kids, each room is totally individual. Smaller, economy rooms have 2 or 4 beds; another has its own garden shared with three tortoises. Each, however, has an en-suite shower &/or hip bath, & most have a private entrance onto a central courtyard area. 24hr security adds to the sense of privacy. Keith is a fount of knowledge about what's on where, having travelled the length & breadth of Namibia, & can arrange pretty well anything. Free transfers from Swakopmund Airport or station, & Walvis Bay.
Sgl N$195–380, dbl N$280–380; b/fast N$20–30. Sgl night surcharge N$25 per room.

⌂ **The (Alternative) Space** (4 rooms) 67 Anton Lubowski Av (cnr Alfons Weber St); ☎ 064 402713; m 081 300 9352; e nam00352@mweb.com.na. The Space is found by following Anton Lubowski Av beyond Aukas, about 15 mins' walk due east of the centre of town. Having started life as an 'off-the-wall' backpackers' lodge, The Space now classes itself as a B&B. The rooms are simple & clean with en-suite shower & toilet, & guests can also use the kitchen. The atmosphere remains as relaxed as ever, though, with music, a bar & access to a wide-ranging music collection, & Frenus & family are still pretty offbeat.
N$285/385 sgl/dbl, B&B. Children under 6 free.

Backpackers' lodges

With good transport connections, and an exploding line in adventure sports, Swakopmund has taken advantage of its reputation as Namibia's backpacking capital. However, a wide choice of bed and breakfasts and cheap hotels means few dedicated backpackers' places, a situation not helped by the municipality's strict rules on licensing. Those currently around include:

🏠 **Desert Sky** (10 dorm beds, 5 dbl rooms, 1 family room, camping) 35 Anton Lubowski Av; ☎ 064 402339; m 081 248 7771; e dsbackpackers@swakop.com; www.swakop.com/dsb. Opened in 2001, this centrally located backpackers' hostel not far from the beach is one of the most popular venues in town, & it is easy to see why. It's welcoming & helpful, the atmosphere is friendly, & facilities are good. In addition to clean, cheerful dormitories & private rooms, there is a fully equipped kitchen, storage lockers, safe, plus central coffee & tea area, TV lounge, bar & a small balcony. A laundry service is available. Outside is safe parking & a grassed area for tents. If you're after action, this is also a pretty good place to come for advice.
Dorm bed N$70, room N$200/300 dbl/family, camping N$60 pp.

🏠 **Swakop Lodge** (27 twin rooms, 81 dorm beds) Nathaniel Maxuilili Av; ☎ 064 402039; f 064 405016; e bookings@swakoplodge.com; www.swakoplodge.com. In the centre of town, on the corner of Nathaniel Maxuilili Av & Woermann St, this once run-down hotel (previously the Gruner Kranz) has had a big facelift, now firmly catering for the younger market. If the entrance remains basic, the deep terracotta walls of the rest of the place are far more welcoming. On the main site, relatively spacious dbl or twin rooms are bright & colourful, with en-suite facilities & wooden floors, plus TV & safe. Three dormitories have 7 beds each, with a further 8 dorm rooms in the annexe just up the street, where there's also a kitchen for guests' use. Although rooms can be quite hot, fans are available on request. Two bars, one open at midday, the second 17.30–02.00, attract plenty of custom, with the latter particularly busy at weekends. There's also a small upstairs deck with tables & chairs. The Cape to Cairo restaurant (see page 279) forms part of the hotel, but is under separate management. Secure parking & laundry service. Internet N$10 for 30 mins. *N$280/380 sgl/dbl, regardless of room size, dorm bed N$90 pp. B/fast extra.*

🏠 **Villa Wiese** (32 dorm beds, 10 dbl rooms) cnr Theo-Ben Gurirab Av & Windhoeker St; ☎/f 064 407105; e villawiese@compuscan.co.za; www.villawiese.com. This colourful old building on the outskirts of town is named after the German who built it in 1905. Now owned by Tinkie & Johan, the place was completely renovated in 2002 to give a roomy & friendly backpackers' lodge with plenty of atmosphere. Facilities include a self-catering kitchen, large upstairs bar area open until 23.00, & a safe for valuables. Each dormitory has 8 beds on two levels, & its own shower & separate toilet, while dbl rooms are all en suite. Outside there's a BBQ in a pleasant courtyard, & secure parking. If you don't have a vehicle, just ring ahead; collections from the town centre are free of charge.
Dorm bed N$85, rooms N$240/285/368 sgl/dbl/trpl, all B&B.

🏠 **Dunedin Star** (24 rooms) 50 Daniel Tjongerero St (cnr Windhoeker St); ☎/f 064 403437; e villawiese@compuscan.co.za; www.dunedinstar.com. Opened in 2005, this new budget option under the same ownership as Villa Wiese is just 5 mins' walk from the centre of town. Modern en-suite sgl, dbl & trpl rooms are simple, no-frills affairs, catering mainly for groups. Given the main-road location, it's fortunate that most rooms are at the back, so reasonably quiet, & that there's secure parking. *N$240/285/368 sgl/dbl/trpl, B&B. Laundry N$45 per bag.*

🏠 **Youth Hostel** (60 beds, camping) Anton Lubowski Av; ☎ 064 404164; f 064 405373. Situated diagonally opposite the Europa Hof, the government-run youth hostel occupies a grand old barracks building. Recent refurbishment has brought tiled bathrooms & floors, & landscaped grounds with tables under umbrella shade, though it remains somewhat austere. It is limited to travellers aged 15–30, who are housed in simple, en-suite rooms with fridge, or separate male & female dormitories. No food is served. Office open Mon–Fri 07.00–13.00 & 14.00–18.00, Sat 07.00–13.00 & 15.00–17.00, Sun/holidays 07.00–13.00. *Dbl N$80 per room, dorms N$20 pp under 18, N$30 over 18, camping N$15 pp.*

🏠 **Drifter's Inn** 6 Werft St (cnr Mittel); www.drifters@mweb.com.na. When visited in 2006, plans were in hand to demolish the centrally located Drifter's Inn & to rebuild with 20 rooms, catering for the B&B market.

Restcamps If you want your own self-catering facilities then you'll have a choice of three restcamps around Swakopmund, all very different. See also those that are south of here, around Walvis Bay, pages 291–2.

⌂ **Alte Brücke Restcamp** (23 chalets, 24 camping pitches) Strand; ☏ 064 404918; f 064 400153; e accomod@africaonline.com.na; www.altebrucke.com. At the southern end of the Strand, by the Swakop River's mouth, Alte Brücke has been open since around 1992 – an upmarket version of the nearby municipal restcamp, which is also surrounded by a vicious electric fence.

The chalets here are all large, the majority with 2 bedrooms (2 beds in each) & a bed-settee, which will take 2 small children. Thus they could sleep a family in each. Each has a bath/shower room, a separate toilet, & a large open-plan lounge/kitchen with Mnet TV, telephone, linen & towels.

The kitchen has cutlery, crockery & glassware, ironing board, iron, toaster, kettle, microwave, electric stove, fridge/freezer & a separate minibar – making these into comprehensively equipped little holiday homes.

There is also a spacious grassy camping area (max 6 people per site) with private facilities, including electricity & braai area.
N$395/275 sgl/pp sharing; 3–4 adults sharing N$255–225 pp. Children 2–16 sharing N$100 each. Camping N$200 (1–2 persons); additional N$50 for 3 or more people (under 12s N$30).

⌂ **El Jada Restcamp** (5 rooms, 1 flat) ☏/f 064 400348; reservations e info@namibweb.com; www.langstrand.com/eljada.htm. About 12km from Swakopmund, on the D1901 (just south of the B2), El Jada is beside the Swakop River & the northern boundary of the Namib-Naukluft National Park. Its plain, en-suite rooms have a b/fast bar with kettle, toaster & fridge, & there's also a 5-person flat with its own kitchen. Other guests have the use of a self-

catering kitchen & braai area. The place is quiet & quite isolated, despite its proximity to Swakopmund, with birdwatching along the Swakop River Valley an attraction, and horse- or camel-riding nearby. There's also a swimming pool.
N$219/299/360 sgl/dbl/trpl; flat N$599.

⌂ **Swakopmund Municipal Restcamp** (200 chalets) ☏ 064 402807/8; f 064 404212; e restcamp@swkmun.com; www.swakopmund-restcamp.com. On the north side of the road that crosses the Swakop River to Walvis Bay, this huge old restcamp is quite an institution. Within a large electric fence lie some 200 chalets & bungalows, all packed closely together. These vary from tiny fishermen's cabins, whose cramped beds in minute rooms have changed little in the last decade, to luxury VIP flats with modern décor & bright pastel colours. Each chalet has a phone.

There's a rolling programme of modernising the restcamp, which at present supplies linen but not towels. The flats are fine & simple, with the luxury flats being larger, but otherwise similar. The A-frame chalets have a much more interesting design, & their wooden construction is warmer in the winter than the others – though all the beds in these are sgls. All are good value, provided you don't mind getting lost in the maze of other identical chalets while you search for your own. When arriving, note that the office is open Mon–Fri 07.30–16.00 & Sat/Sun 07.30–11.00. The camp has its own restaurant serving b/fast, lunch & dinner from 09.00; it also incorporates a pizza place.
Working out the costs for these is an art, but in general the following applies: 2-bed N$153–193; 4-bed N$292; 'A' frame to VIP resthouses N$419–571. Key deposit N$150–300.

Camping

⋏ **Gull's Cry** (40 pitches, max 6 people per site) The Strand; m 081 214 6854, 081 280 8768; e seagulls@iway.na. Swakopmund's campsite has a prime position close to the sea at the southern end of town, near the aquarium, & boasts a bird lagoon with over 60 different species. The spacious site offers a rather rustic setting, with simple washing & toilet facilities. It is protected by a discreet electric

fence & has 24hr surveillance, ensuring the safety of visitors. On the minus side, the adjacent Tiger Reef beach bar opens from 18.00 to late, and can be quite noisy in season, with cars traversing the site to get to the bar & restaurant.
High/low season N$120/80 per site plus N$20 pp; electricity N$30 per visit.

✖ WHERE TO EAT AND DRINK

Restaurants Almost all of Swakopmund's hotels, and many of the pensions, have their own restaurants. Those listed here are for the most part independent, with one or two notable exceptions. Unless stated, all are open for both lunch and dinner.

✖ **Hansa Hotel** 3 Hendrik Witbooi St, Swakopmund; ☏ 064 414200. The Hansa Hotel (see page 272)

has an award-winning European restaurant serving stylish, elaborate & quite heavy cuisine – using lots of sauces – in quite formal surroundings. It majors on seafood, though has a good range of steaks & 1 or 2 vegetarian dishes. There is also a children's menu. Its selection of South African wines is impressive, with bottles averaging around N$80–100 each, from some good vineyards. *Mains N$55–90.*

✕ The Tug The Strand; \/f 064 402356; e tug@iafrica.com.na. Without doubt the most interesting place to eat in Swakopmund, The Tug is just that – an old tug raised up above the seafront next to the old jetty. Inside, the tabletops have been individually painted by different artists, & below is a very arty gift/curio shop. The terrace is a great place to watch the surf as the sun goes down. The menu is amongst the best in town & majors on seafood, in a style that's lighter & less traditional than the restaurants of the Hansa or Strand. The wines here are undistinguished & a little expensive, but the place is always full & bookings are essential. It's open every evening, but at weekends only for lunch. *Mains from N$60.*

✕ Grapevine 42 Libertina Amathila Av; \ 064 404760. Swakopmund's newest 'don't miss' restaurant has an unprepossessing entrance, but inside, relaxed surroundings are balanced by unobtrusive professionalism. A well-chosen menu is matched by the wine 'list' – in the form of a wall of around 200 bottles from which to select, under the guidance of owner Jürgen Baas (from the Homestead in Windhoek), with many wines available for tasting. Prices remain accessible. *Open for dinner Mon–Sat 18.00–21.30, lunch Tue–Sat 11.00–15.00.*

✕ Kücki's 22 Tobias Hainyeko St; \ 064 402407; m 081 128 2407; e kuecki@mweb.com.na. One of the best places in town, Kücki's has a lively atmosphere & serves very good food. It is German in character, though there are always visitors around. Kücki's shellfish is excellent, & its service is friendly. Tables are situated both on the ground floor & on a surrounding balcony area beneath huge pelican mobiles. Do book in advance, as it's often full. *Mains N$50–80.*

✕ Cape to Cairo Nathaniel Maxuilili St; \ 064 463160. The restaurant next to Swakop Lodge serves traditional African food from an assortment of countries, with a Western twist. Weekly specials add additional flair to its imaginative menu, with plenty for vegetarians. Good value, friendly service, & popular well beyond the backpacker market. *Open daily 17.30–23.00.*

✕ Dunes Hendrik Witbooi St. Formerly the Blue Whale, this was in the throes of change when last visited. The author would welcome any feedback on the new restaurant.

✕ Napolitana 33 Nathaniel Maxuilili St; \ 064 402773. On the corner across from Swakop Lodge, this Italian restaurant serves a variety of traditional pasta dishes and pizza, for around N$45–60, as well as the more usual steaks. *Open Mon–Thu 17.00–21.45, Fri–Sun 18.00–21.45; lunch Fri–Sun only, 11.30–13.45.*

✕ Erich's Restaurant 21 Daniel Tjongarero Av; \ 064 405141. The name hasn't changed, but the management & décor have at this well-established, centrally located restaurant. The enlarged Erich's now boasts a bar & restaurant in a softer setting, but has retained its good, traditional-style service. Regarded as *the* place for well-presented fish in Swakopmund (*seafood platter N$142.50*), it has a generally innovative menu, with a good selection of vegetarian dishes. *Closed Sun.*

✕ De Kelder Klimas Shopping Arcade, 10 Tobias Hainyeko St; \ 064 402433. In a very uninspiring setting, hidden at the back of a concrete shopping arcade, De Kelder serves some of the best food around, including interesting options such as *boboti*, some innovative vegetarian options, and a range of pasta dishes at around N$36. The atmosphere is almost traditional Afrikaans, quite formal but with no frills. *Open Mon–Sat 18.30–22.00.*

✕ Tiffany Café Libertina Amathila Av; \ 064 463655. Despite the name, & the cottage-garden décor, this is actually a fully fledged German restaurant, with separate bar. Tiffany's specialises in fresh fish, including a fish fondue. *Closed Mon.*

✕ Il Tulipano 37 Daniel Tjongarero Av (corner Otavi St); \ 064 400 0122. This newish Italian restaurant sits on the site of a backpackers' lodge, but has been extensively refurbished, its dark red exterior being hard to miss. *Open from 18.00 (lunch served on Sun); closed Tue.*

✕ Zur Weinmaus Theo-Ben Gurirab Av; \ 064 400098. Just along the road from the Schweizerhaus, this German restaurant with its small, dark bar is open evenings only 18.00–21.30, with a limited menu. *Mains N$42–72. Closed Mon.*

✕ Brauhaus Nedbank Arcade, Sam Nujoma Av; \ 064 402214. Tucked away in the centre of town, this easy-going restaurant is very popular for both lunch & dinner. Although it's reputed to serve good seafood, the meat here is generally a better bet. *Mains N$40–80.*

✕ Western Saloon 8 Tobias Hainyeko St; \ 064 405395. Lively & popular, this small, crowded restaurant is not a place for a quiet evening *à deux*. The menu majors on steaks, fish & game at around N$75 a throw – and the pizzas are reported to be excellent.

✗ **Pizzeria** 8 Tobias Hainyeko St; ✆ 064 403925. Next to the Western Saloon, & open evenings only, the relaxed Pizzeria serves pizzas to eat in or take away.

✗ **Lighthouse Pub & Restaurant** Pool Terrace, Main Beach; ✆ 064 400894. Good for sundowners overlooking the sea, the large restaurant here adjoins an equally large bar. You can eat outside on the wooden terrace with magnificent sea views, or there are tables inside for cooler periods. You can pay from as little as N$25 to N$300 for the much-vaunted seafood platter. Charcoal grills & burgers are also available. *Pub open all day; restaurant 11.00–22.00.*

✗ **Mandarin Garden Chinese** 27 Libertina Amathila Av; ✆ 064 461461; m 081 284 8000. The relatively limited menu, by Chinese standards, has prices at around N$50, including rice or noodles. Take-away service available.

Cafés and lights meals

🖵 **Café Anton** (at the Schweizerhaus Hotel) 1 Bismarck St; ✆ 064 402419. Overlooking the Mole and the ocean, the café opens for extensive breakfasts, & stays open until the mid evening – though it's really more of a place for morning coffee or afternoon tea. There are tables outside, under the palm trees, & a small curio market just below. Inside the atmosphere is genteel – perfect for reading a book or relaxing, with an excellent range of cakes & pastries, & very good coffee.

🖵 **Gelateria Bella Italia** ✆ 064 404454. If it's coffee & an ice cream that you're after, look no further. Come here, too, for pastries & the Italian deli. *Open Mon–Fri 08.00–18.00, Sun 14.00–18.00.*

✗ **Lightkeeper's Cottage** Ducks & chickens share the lawns of this excellent café where lunch is taken outside under umbrellas overlooking the sea. Not to be confused with the Lighthouse pub by the beach, it's located on the hill behind, & serves a great range of salads & sandwiches, as well as breakfasts, with the emphasis on healthy eating – including homemade bread & some innovative fillings. Picnic baskets can be prepared on request (N$150 for 2 people, inc wine).

🖵 **Out of Africa Café** Daniel Tongarero Av, near Hansa Hotel; ✆ 064 404752. According to one reader, this serves the best coffee in Swakopmund.

✗ **Pandora's Box** Sam Nujoma Av; ✆ 064 403545. This small gift shop in the attractive new Ankerplatz centre off Sam Nujoma Av also serves snacks & light meals, including potato pancakes every Fri from 12.00. Seating is inside or on a shaded terrace. *Open 09.00–18.00 (17.00 in winter); Sat to 13.00.*

✗ **Papa's Pizza** Shoprite Centre, Sam Nujoma Av; ✆ 064 404747. Well off the beaten track, Papa's is Swiss owned, simple & friendly, with good pizzas as well as salads & burgers. There's a take-away & delivery service as well. *Open from 09.00; closed Mon.*

🖵 **Shepherd's Garden** The café/tea garden outside the Snake Park & Transport Museum is a pleasant spot for a coffee or light meal during the day.

✗ **Swakop Butchery & Bistro** Sam Nujoma Av. Daily specials in the café alongside Swakopmund's centrally located butcher include dishes such as venison curry & rice – strictly for meat eaters!

🖵 **Café Treffpunkt** Sam Nujoma Av; ✆ 064 461782. Opposite the Nedbank, this bakery & cake shop is also open at lunchtimes for sandwiches & light meals; it has a good selection of ice creams, too.

Fast food Next to the ubiquitous **KFC** on Hendrik Witbooi Street, there's the rather less corporate **Beryl's** which is frequented by local office workers. There's also a Wimpy and Debonairs Pizza at the Swakopmund Spar Centre, and the Pizza Box at the municipal restcamp. (If it's pizza you're after, a couple of the pizza restaurants above also offer take-aways.)

ENTERTAINMENT AND NIGHTLIFE Swakopmund has surprisingly lively nightlife, especially in the summer holiday season, although many travellers just have a few drinks in their hotel bar before retiring to bed. Then, around Christmas and New Year, many of Windhoek's more affluent residents arrive at their cool seaside cottages, intent on fishing by day and partying by night. If you're just looking for somewhere for a sundowner, try the bar at The Tug, or The Lighthouse. The 'in' places for evenings out change with the tides, so ask around for what's in fashion – currently Rafters and Plush top the list.

☆ **Rafters Action Pub** 18 Tobias Hainyeko St; ☎ 064 404171. Next to the First National Bank, on the corner of Woermann St, Rafters is a lively venue, popular with tour groups. Open 16.00 till late.

☆ **Fagin's Bar** 6 Hendrik Witbooi St, ☎ 064 402360. A favourite watering hole for travellers & locals alike, Fagin's doesn't serve food, but it is a firm fixture on the itinerary of most overlanders. With a friendly, cosmopolitan atmosphere, the bar's main nights are Thu, Fri & Sat, when it stays open until around 02.00; like the rest of town, it can be very, very quiet on Sun & Mon.

☆ **O'Kelly's Pub** Hendrik Witbooi St, near the post office. Next to Fagin's, & downstairs in the basement, this poorly signposted bar has no food but a good dance floor. Many of Fagin's customers move here when it closes, as O'Kelly's stays open after 02.00.

☆ **Swakop Lodge** The upstairs bar stays open until 02.00 & gets busy at weekends.

☆ **Plush** 33 Nathaniel Maxuilili St. A rather unexpected newcomer to Swakopmund, this cocktail bar opens daily at 17.00, with half-price cocktails on offer 18.00–19.00.

☆ **Club Oxygen** Junction of Louis Botha & Henties Bay roads, as you head north out of Swakopmund. Out of the centre of town, this is one where you'd be well advised to go by taxi or with someone who knows the area.

Cinema and concerts There's a cinema in the Nedbank Mall off Sam Nujoma Avenue, with tickets at approximately N$25 before 19.00, or N$30 in the evening. In the foyer is a small café (☎ 064 402743; open Mon–Sat 07.00–17.00) where lunchtime specials cost from N$25.

If you're in Swakopmund over a holiday weekend, you may be lucky enough to get an impromptu concert from local schoolchildren in one of the shopping areas such as Ankerplatz. For a musical evening, check to see if there's anything happening at the **Hotel and Entertainments Centre** (page 272), or at one of the other two venues which regularly present concerts: the local **Namib Primary School** (☎ 064 405028; f 064 405029) and **Haus der Jugend – Deutsche Evangelisches Luthern Gemeinde** (☎ 064 402874).

SHOPPING Swakopmund's compact shopping centre offers plenty of choice, both for practical items and for souvenirs and curios.

Food and drink The Swakopmund Spar Centre (*cnr Tobias Hainyeko & Mandume ya Ndemufayo streets*) is the town's most recent shopping complex, with a large Spar supermarket and a range of other shops offering everything from mobile phones to shoes. On the main B2 road out of Swakopmund, at its intersection with Windhoeker Street, is the Shoprite Arcade, which houses a First National Bank cash machine, a good pizzeria (Papa's Pizza; see page 280) and Shoprite supermarket. More central are the **Model supermarket** (*Sam Nujoma Av, opposite the tourist information office*) and the **WB supermarket** (*Woermann Brock Mall on Sam Nujoma Av, near Bismarck St*). Rather less corporate are the Swakop Butchery on Sam Nujoma Avenue, which has a bistro alongside where you can try out some of their meats, and the Blue Olive delicatessen on Libertina Amathila Avenue.

Clothes and equipment For **camping** equipment, **car spares** and **cycling** gear, try Cymot (*43 Sam Nujoma Av;* ☎ *064 400318; www.cymot.com.na*) or Time Out (*32 Nathaniel Maxuilili St;* ☎ *064 405920; f 064 405921; e timeout@iafrica.com.na*), who also have **angling** gear and fresh bait. Another option for fishing tackle is Tide Out fishing (*Nathaniel Maxuilili St;* ☎ *064 405920*), which also sells camping gas. There is a Land Rover Parts Centre on Theo-Ben Gurirab Avenue (☎ *064 403713; f 064 403717*).

Safari clothes and equipment – including wide-brimmed hats – may be obtained from Namib Safari Shop in Nedbank Arcade (☎ *064 463214*), or

Safariland at 21 Sam Nujoma Avenue (☏ *064 462387*), which is also open 10.00–12.00 on Sunday mornings.

For **photographic equipment**, your best bet is the efficient Photo Studio Behrens (7 *Tobias Hainyeko St;* ☏ *064 404711*), who will also carry out minor camera repairs. They stock a range of binoculars, too, and the increasingly difficult-to-find Fuji Velvia slide film. Processing and digital printing are available both from here, and from Photographic Enterprises (*Nedbank Mall, Sam Nujoma Av,* ☏ *064 405872*).

Books and music

Die Muschel 10 Hendrik Witbooi St; ☏ 064 402784. A good selection of books & fine art.
Swakopmund Buchhandlung Sam Nujoma Av, next to Nedbank. Reasonable selection of English-language books on Namibia, & some novels too.

CNA Hendrik Witbooi St, next to Namib i. A branch of the South African chain; more mainstream than Swakopmund Buchhandlung.
Young Ones 32 Sam Nujoma Av; ☏ 064 405795. African music specialist.

Arts, crafts and souvenirs

Swakopmund is filled with commercial **art galleries** and **curio shops**, particularly in the centre of town around Nedbank Arcade, off Sam Nujoma Avenue, and in the attractive new Ankerplatz further down the road near the sea. Some of the best of these include the Hobby Horse Art Gallery (☏ *064 402875*) in Nedbank Arcade, which specialises in Namibian (as against African) art, and in the same complex, African Curiotique (☏ *064 461 062*) and Okaporo Curio Shop (☏ *064 405795; open daily*). Nearby is Die Muschel (see above), next to the Cycle Clinic, and in Ankerplatz are Bushman's Paradise and Sunset Arts & Crafts. There is also a curio market around the lighthouse area in front of the Schweizerhaus Hotel, with a good range of crafts on sale.

For **leather** goods, try Leder Chic in Nedbank Arcade, or Deon Sibold (☏ *064 464182*), who specialise in kudu and seal boots and shoes, or African Leather Creations (7 *Moses Garoëb St;* ☏ *064 402633*). The latter, previously Swakopmund Tannery, has recently moved to a more central location, though note that tanning is no longer carried out on the premises.

A few rather more original places are worth taking a look at:

African Kirikara Art Ankerplatz, Sam Nujoma Av; ☏ 064 463146; m 081 124 5268; e Claudia@ kirikara.com; www.kirikara.com. This is a first-class place to look for hand-woven rugs, made on the owner's farm. It also has a range of crafts & gemstones. Open Mon–Fri 09.00–13.00, 14.30–17.30, Sat 09.00–13.00, 16.00–18.00, Sun 10.00–12.00.
Casa Anin Nedbank Arcade; ☏ 064 405910. Beautifully crafted bed linen & tableware sold here comes from the Anin project near Uhlenhorst (see pages 190–1).
Engelhard Design 55 Sam Nujoma Av; ☏ 064 404606; e engel@mweb.com.na. To the east of the centre, this modern shop & gallery features contemporary Namibian art & jewellery, with exhibitions changing every 6 weeks or so.

Karakulia 2 Rakotoka St; ☏ 064 461415; f 064 461041; e info@karakulia.com.na; www.karakulia.com.na. Karakulia has a shop in Nedbank Arcade, off Sam Nujoma Av, but its workshop is just off the main road as you head north from Swakopmund, opposite the junction of Tobias Hainyeko & Moses Garoëb streets. It's a very long walk, so transport would be useful! Here you can watch the whole art of spinning & weaving karakul wool into carpets & wall-hangings, as well as buy the finished products. You can even have designs made to order, & then reliably shipped home for you. Karakulia has grown considerably since its inception in 1979, & now has around 50 employees, who also benefit from a programme of adult education.

Semi-precious stones are much in evidence in this part of Namibia, but two places stand out:

Kristall Galerie (see *What to see*, page 286).
Stonetique 27 Libertina Amathila Av; ✆ 064

405403. Open Mon–Sat 09.00–13.00, Mon–Fri
15.00–18.00.

Antiques For antique books and old African artefacts, **Peter's Antiques** (*24 Tobias Hainyeko St, PO Box 920, Swakopmund;* ✆f *064 405624; open Mon–Fri 09.00–13.00, 15.00–18.00, Sat 09.00–13.00, 17.00–18.00, Sun 17.00–18.00*) is perhaps the best shop in Africa, with a most comprehensive and eclectic collection. Peter is a small, intense Namibian of German origin. He started the shop around 25 years ago as an extension of his hobby, and since then his collection, his reputation, and the shop have gradually grown. Now he has a network of collectors all over sub-Saharan Africa, who buy and ship old African artefacts to Swakopmund. (Purchasers should carefully consider the ethics of such a collection before even considering buying.) He also sells some new, cheaper arts and crafts that are produced specifically for tourists.

The shop is now quite large, and densely packed with all sorts of things. The smells of wood, skins and dyes that go to make the pieces pervade the place, making it instantly fascinating and slightly revolting. As well as tribal artefacts, Peter's has an extensive collection of antique books, many in German, concerned with Namibia's history. In recent years he has been involved with commissioning and distributing facsimile reprints of old books and maps, reproducing these manuscripts for future generations.

OTHER PRACTICALITIES

Emergency and health The police are reached on ✆ 064 10111, whilst the ambulance and hospital are on ✆ 064 412200, the fire service is on ✆ 064 402411/ 205544/405613(a/h)/404230(a/h), and if you need any sea rescue services then call ✆ 064 404213 or the police – which is also the emergency number to use if you can't get through anywhere else. For less serious illness, there's the Bismarck Medical Centre (*17 Sam Nujoma Av,* ✆ *064 405894*), which has a pharmacy that's also open at weekends (*Sat 09.00–12.00, 17.00–19.00, Sun 10.00–11.00, 17.00–18.00*).

The most central of the town's pharmacies is Swakopmund Apotheke, just down from Namib i (*Sam Nujoma Av;* ✆ *064 402825, or 463610 after hours*). On the opposite corner is Dolphin Pharmacy (✆ *064 400772*).

Banks There are plenty of banks in the centre of town, many with ATMs. These include the Nedbank on Sam Nujoma Avenue, close to the tourist information office.

Fuel and vehicle repair There are plenty of 24-hour **fuel stations** around town. Garages for **vehicle repairs** include Kwik-Fit Exhaust Systems (*18th Rd;* ✆ *064 202409*), Autowagen Repairs (*271 Theo-Ben Gurirab St;* ✆ *064 206949*) and Hans Kriess Motors (*8th St;* ✆ *064 202653;* f *064 206748*), who specialise in VW and Audi models, but will also repair others.

Tourist information and travel agents If you want to organise your return flights home, or a trip around the rest of Namibia, then useful addresses include:

Air Namibia Sam Nujoma Av; ✆ 064 405123. This is a useful office for re-confirming onward flights & other airline business.
Henckert Tourist Centre Cnr Sam Nujoma Av & Nathaniel Maxuilili Av

Ministry of Environment & Tourism Cnr Sam Nujoma Av & Bismarck St; ✆ 064 402172. This is where you can obtain permits for entry to national parks & make reservations for accommodation, inc campsites in the parks.

Namib i Cnr Sam Nujoma Av & Hendrik Witbooi St; \/f 064 404827/403129; e namibi@iway.na; www.namibi.org.na. The tourist information bureau in the centre of town has an extensive selection of pamphlets & information on Namibia, with a special emphasis on the local area – don't miss it. *Open* Oct–Mar Mon–Fri 08.30–13.00, 14.00–17.30, Sat/Sun 09.00–13.00; Apr–Sep Mon–Fri 08.00–13.00, 14.00–17.00, Sat/Sun 09.00–13.00. **Palmwag Lodge & Travel Shop** See page 298. Linked to Palmwag Lodge in Damaraland.

For details of local tour operators, see *Activities*, pages 298–301.

Communications

The **post office** is on the corner of Garnison and Daniel Tjongarero streets. It's open Monday–Friday 08.30–16.00, Saturday until 12.00.

There are a few **internet cafés** in town, as well as facilities in many backpackers' hostels and pensions. Expect to pay around N$12 for half an hour.

Compucare 12 Hendrik Witbooi St (near Namib i); \ 064 463775; f 064 461063; e comp@mweb.com.na. *Open Mon–Sat 08.00–19.00.*
Swakopmund i-café Woermann Brock Mall, Sam Nujoma Av; \ 064 464021; e swakopicafe@swakop.com; www.swakop.com/icafe. Small coffee shop. *Open Mon–Thu 07.15–22.00, Fri/Sat 07.15–22.00, Sun 10.00–22.00.*

If you're after a local SIM card for your mobile, or indeed the whole handset, try Coastal Cellular in Swakopmund Spar Centre (\ *064 405936;* m *081 128 3283*).

WHAT TO SEE AND DO

Unlike most Namibian towns, there's plenty to do in Swakopmund. Below are a few attractions in town, but see also *Around the towns,* from pages 298–301, for ideas in the areas surrounding Swakopmund and Walvis Bay.

The Mole

If you only have a little time to spare, then wander down to the Mole, by the Strand Hotel. This was to be a harbour wall when first built, but the ocean currents continually shifted the sandbanks and effectively blocked the harbour before it was even completed. A similar 'longshore drift' effect can be seen all along the coast, at inlets like Sandwich Harbour. Partially because of this sandbank's protection, the beach by the Mole is pleasant (though watch out for jellyfish) and safe to swim from, if small and surprisingly busy at times.

Historical buildings

As you might expect, Swakopmund is full of amazing old German architecture in perfect condition, some of the buildings now housing museums, art galleries or libraries. Pre-eminent among these is the beautiful Woermannhaus Building, in the centre of town just off Sam Nujoma Avenue, dating from 1894. Also of note are the old railway station, completed in 1901 and now the home of Swakopmund Hotel and Entertainment Centre, and the old prison, on Moses Garoeb Street as it heads north out of town.

Guided walking tours of the individual buildings can be arranged in English with Karene (m *081 124 3329;* e *bunker@iway.na; N$100 pp*) or in German with Frau Angelika Flamm-Schneeweiss (*Sam Cohen Library;* \ *064 402695*). For a more general overview, contact Heinz Heuschneider at Namib Tours (\ *064 404072, or see page 302*), who runs a one-hour tour of the town by car (N$150 pp), or Charly's Desert Tours (\ *064 404341*).

Alternatively, the handout from the municipality itself, or the short book entitled *Swakopmund – A Chronicle of the Town's People, Places and Progress*, available at the museum, both give descriptions and brief histories for some of the buildings.

For an overview of the town and its setting, you could do worse than climb the 93 steps up the **Woermann Tower** just behind the Ankerplatz complex on Sam Nujoma, near Bismarck Street. The key is held at African Kirikara, with tickets available from the Jetty shop in Ankerplatz. *Adults N$10, under 16s N$5, under 10s free.*

Museums, galleries and libraries
Opening times given here are the official times, but aside from the Swakopmund Museum itself, you can expect a rather more erratic service than is indicated.

Swakopmund Museum (✆/f *064 402695;* e *museum@mweb.com.na. Open daily 10.00–13.00, 14.00–17.00, inc holidays. Adults N$18, children N$5, students N12*) Situated in the old customs building, next to the municipal swimming pool, by the Strand Hotel, the main Swakopmund Museum was founded by Dr Alfons Weber in 1951. It now has exhibits on life in the Namib Desert and the South Atlantic, huge collections of insects and birds' eggs, an excellent section on rocks and minerals, and lots of information on the colonial German history in the region. There's also a recreation of what old doctors' and dentists' surgeries must have been like. Frightening stuff.

In the museum's new wing, the 'People of Namibia' exhibition covers Namibia's indigenous cultures, while the Rössing room depicts the process of uranium mining (with tours on offer to Rössing mine). The museum also encompasses the Sam Cohen Library, the Transport Museum and the Snake Park.

Sam Cohen Library (*Open Mon–Fri 09.00–13.00, 15.00–17.00, Sat 10.00–12.30; admission free*) Next to the Transport Museum, the impressive collection of Africana books at the Sam Cohen Library contains about 8,000 volumes, encompassing most of the literature on Swakopmund, and a huge archive of newspapers from 1898 to the present day (some in German, some in English). There's also a collection of old photographs and maps.

Swakopmund Transport Museum (*Cnr Sam Nujoma Av & Windhoeker St, opposite the Engen garage. Open daily from 10.00; admission free*) The restored Otavi Bahnhof was once the west-coast terminal of the narrow-gauge railway line, which linked Swakopmund to a copper mine at Tsumeb. A fire a few years ago destroyed some of the exhibits, and it's now looking rather run down, but this is where the photographic history of the building, the railway, the Mole and even aviation in the area is housed, with some of the old machinery kept in the grounds. Occasionally there is craftwork on sale outside the museum, but this is by no means a regular occurrence.

Living Desert Snake Park (✆ *064 405100;* m *081 128 5100. Open Mon–Fri 08.30–17.00, Sat 08.30–13.00; admission N$12, under 12s N$10*) Next door to the Transport Museum, the Snake Park boasts more than 25 types of Namibian snakes, lizards, chameleons, scorpions and other creatures, which is enough to satisfy even the most inquisitive child – or adult. The animals are kept under glass in two small rooms, where snake feeding takes place on Saturdays from 10.00 to 12.30. Outside, a pleasant open-air café is set in gardens that incorporate plants from the Namib.

National Marine Aquarium (✆ *064 410 1000; www.namibweb.com/aquarium.htm. Open Tue–Sun & public holidays 10.00–16.00; admission N$30 adults, N$15 children, students & pensioners*) This relatively new aquarium at the southern end of town is worth a visit for its impressive displays of local marine life. It has a total of about 20 tanks, including a huge main tank containing 320m³ of water, and is crossed by an underwater walkway. Coastal angling species dominate, with plenty of kob, blacktail, steenbras, spotted grunters, sharks, skates and rays. Feeding time is at

13

15.00 daily, and on Tuesday, Saturday and Sunday the larger fish are hand-fed by divers – an excellent time to visit.

Kristall Galerie (☏ *064 406080;* e *gems@kristallgalerie.com; www.kristallgalerie.com. Open 0.900–17.00*) This ultra-modern building on the corner of Garnison Street and Theo-Ben Gurirab Avenue houses what is claimed to be the largest-known crystal cluster in the world, estimated to be around 520 million years old. Displays include a scratch pit where visitors can search for semi-precious stones, a replica of the original Otjua tourmaline mine, and a craft area. There's a shop, of course, with semi-precious stones available in many guises, and a café area with videos about crystals. It's well worth a visit by anyone fascinated by geology.

Woermannhaus Art Gallery (☏ *064 402473. Open Mon–Fri 10.00–12.00, 15.00–17.00, Sat 10.00–12.00*) Declared a national monument in 1971, Woermannhaus is home to the town's art gallery, but it's the building itself that is the real draw.

Sporting facilities
Swimming Opposite the main museum, by the Strand, there's an indoor Olympic-size swimming pool (entry N$6). Saunas (N$48 per hour) must be booked at least an hour in advance. Masochists shouldn't miss the opportunity to use these, then run straight into the cold surf on the nearby beach by the Mole. Swimming elsewhere in the sea is generally not safe, for rip tides are common, so it's important to seek local advice.

Golf About 8km west of Swakopmund, on the main B2 road from Windhoek, Rossmund golf course (☏/f *064 405644;* e *rossmund@iafrica.com.na*) is set on the northern banks of the Swakop River, backed by the dunes. The 18-hole, par 72 course is open to day members, who occasionally find themselves playing alongside the local springboks. The club has its own restaurant overlooking the greens, and a 22-room lodge, Rossmund Lodge (☏/f *064 414600;* f *064 414649;* e *roslodge@mweb.com.na; www.swakoresorts.com*), with its own swimming pool.

For Walvis Bay golf club, see page 296.

WALVIS BAY

Walvis Bay seems larger and more spaced out than Swakopmund, though also quieter and slightly lacking in character. Perhaps Afrikaans was the dominant influence here, whereas German was clearly the driving force in shaping Swakopmund's architecture and style.

Most visitors still stay in Swakopmund, where they eat and relax, and venture down to Walvis Bay to go birdwatching, as there are a number of sites attracting huge flocks of seabirds and migrant waders, including the famous flamingos and pelicans. Even if you haven't much time, the drive on the Trans-Kalahari Highway between the two towns is an excursion in itself, for here is nature at its most elemental, as white rollers from the sea crash right into the sand-dunes from the Namib Desert.

Although a small-town feel still prevails, Walvis Bay has changed fast in recent years, reflecting the town's expanding population and its increasing popularity with visitors keen to stay near the lagoon. Alongside lots of new development, both industrial and commercial, several new hotels, restaurants and bed and breakfasts have sprung up.

HISTORY From 1990 until 1994 the port of Walvis Bay, and the enclave that surrounds it, remained part of South Africa – despite being surrounded by the newly independent country of Namibia. However, at midnight on 28 February 1994 the South African flag was taken down, and five minutes later the Namibian flag was raised here. This transferred the enclave to Namibian control and ended a point of contention between the two countries. Walvis Bay is strategically important as the coast's only deepwater port, and ceding control of it to Windhoek was a very significant step for South African politicians to make.

GETTING THERE

By air Air Namibia has regular flights between Walvis Bay and both Windhoek (N$1,160) and Lüderitz (N$1,900), but there are currently no scheduled flights to Swakopmund. The airport is located 11km to the east of town on the northern edge of the desert. A shuttle from the airport into the centre of Walvis Bay can be pre-booked through the tourist information office in Swakopmund for around N$165 per person.

By train Walvis Bay is linked to Windhoek and Tsumeb, via Swakopmund, by the normal, slow train services. These run to and from Windhoek every day except Saturday, arriving Walvis Bay at 07.15 and departing at 19.00. Trains to Tsumeb depart on Monday, Wednesday and Friday at 16.15. See *Chapter 6,* pages 101–3, for details, or call TransNamib in Walvis Bay (\ *064 208505*). For details of the *Omugulu Gwombashe Star,* a faster weekly train run on a Friday between Walvis Bay and Windhoek, see page 101.

By bus Intercape Mainliner run a good service linking Windhoek and Walvis Bay, which stops outside the Hickory Creek Spur restaurant on Theo-Ben Gurirab Street, close to 12th Road. This arrives from Windhoek at 11.15 on Monday, Wednesday, Friday and Saturday, and returns Monday, Wednesday, Friday and Sunday at 11.30. Tickets cost around N$30 to Swakopmund, and N$150 to Windhoek, and must be booked in advance.

There is also a weekly bus service between Cape Town and Walvis Bay, via Swakopmund. Run by Ekonolux (\ *061 258961;* e *ekonolux@iway.na; www.ekonolux.com; fares N$525 sgl, N$795 return*), trips in both directions depart on Sunday, Wednesday and Friday. Buses leave the Ekonolux office at 76 Theo-Ben Gurirab Street in Walvis Bay at 12.00 (an hour earlier in winter), arriving in Swakopmund at the Spar shopping complex at 12.30, and in Cape Town at 13.30 the following day. The return trip leaves Cape Town at 09.30, arriving in Swakopmund at around 11.30, and Walvis Bay at 12.00.

For reservations, contact Ekonolux direct, or one of their agents (you'll need to go to their office in person) – and see *Chapter 6,* pages 104–5 for more details:

Ultra Travel 161 Nangolo Mbumba Dr, Walvis Bay; \ 064 207997; m 081 129 7997; e ultra@galileosa.co.za; www.ultratravel.net

Sure Ritz Travel Swakopmund (see pages 270–1). **Trip Travel** Swakopmund; \ 064 404031

ORIENTATION Without Swakopmund's beautiful architecture or its buzz, Walvis Bay seems to have no real focus or centre for visitors. However, if you're a keen birdwatcher you'll probably base yourself here just for the lagoon.

Walvis Bay was built for its harbour, and its streets number from there: 1st Street is nearest the harbour, parallel to the sea, and 16th Street is furthest from it. Similarly its roads are perpendicular to the harbour, starting with 1st Road in the south and continuing to 18th Road in the north.

These somewhat unexciting thoroughfares form a grid that is the city, and are easily navigable. Or at least would have been easily navigable if the planners had

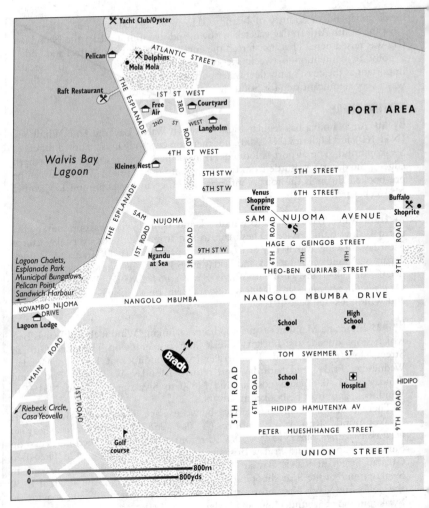

had a little imagination. Instead they stuck zealously to numerical names and, where roads were split, they coined names like 3rd Street North, 3rd Street West and 3rd Street East for completely separate roads. So, whilst most things are easily found, if you see north, south, east or west in a street name, consult a map immediately.

Street name changes Over the last few years, various street names in Walvis Bay have been changed. Although in theory these are all now in place, many people still refer to the original names, so the following may be useful:

Sam Nujoma Avenue	was	7th Street
Hage G Geingob Street	was	8th Street
Theo-Ben Gurirab Street	was	9th Street
Nangolo Mbumba Drive	was	10th Street
Tom Swemmer Street	was	12th Street
Hidipo Hamutenya Avenue	was	13th & 14th streets

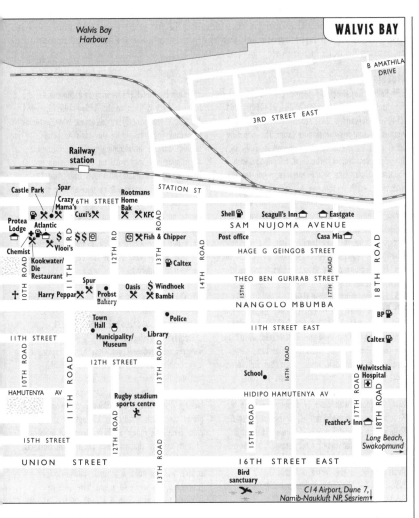

Peter Mueshihange Street	was	15th Street
Nathaniel Maxuilili Avenue	was	Kuiseb Street
Ben Amathila Drive	was	Oceana Street

GETTING AROUND Most visitors to Walvis Bay have their own transport, as the city's quite spread out and there's little in the way of local public transport. If you've no vehicle then walking is usually pleasant, and hitching is occasionally successful, even in town.

If you're hiring a car on arrival, or dropping one here, then try:

Avis Walvis Bay Airport; ☎ 064 207527; f 064 209150; www.avis.co.za

Budget Walvis Bay Airport; ☎ 064 204624; after hours m 081 128 6900; f 064 202931; e nam.wb@budget.co.za

WHERE TO STAY Walvis Bay doesn't have the variety of places to stay, or to eat, found in Swakopmund, although the opening of the Pelican Bay Hotel near the lagoon has widened the options considerably. There is also the odd gem, and if you're looking for large, family self-catering units for a longer stay, then something here may be perfect for you.

Hotels

🏠 **Pelican Bay Hotel** (47 rooms, 2 suites, 1 room for disabled) The Esplanade; ☎ 064 214000; f 064 214040; reservations: 061 213231; e info@united-hospitality.com; www.proteahotels.com. This imposing hotel right by the lagoon was opened in 2003 by President Sam Nujoma. The light, lofty lobby, with fountains either side of the entrance, reinforces the architect's vision of sun, sea & sand. All the rooms are sea facing, furnished using a light lime-washed wood. All have en-suite bathroom/showers with AC, TV, phone & coffee-making facilities; some are interconnecting, to make family suites. The elegant blue-themed Aquarius restaurant looks out across the bay. The Neptune coffee shop provides light snacks throughout the day.
N$795/489 sgl/pp sharing, B&B.

🏠 **Protea Lodge** (58 rooms) Cnr Sam Nujoma Av & 10th Rd; ☎ 064 213700; f 064 213701; e info@proteawalvis.com.na; www.proteahotels.com. Owned by the large Protea chain, the Protea has been significantly enlarged in recent years, but still caters more to business people than tourists. Its rooms follow the standard Protea formula: modern, carpeted twin-bed rooms with Mnet TV, facilities to make tea & coffee, direct-dial phones, AC, & en-suite toilet & bath with a powerful overhead shower. There is a wheelchair-adapted room, a restaurant, & a lounge. In short, this is an efficient & comfortable if rather soulless hotel, in the centre of Walvis Bay.
N$502/668/615–720, sgl/dbl/superior (more space), B&B.

🏠 **Atlantic Hotel** (20+ rooms) Sam Nujoma Av; ☎ 064 202811; f 064 205063; e reservations@atlantichotel.com.na; www.atlantichotel.com.na. The centrally located Atlantic changed hands in July 2005, & was undergoing a complete renovation when visited a year later, though its focus is likely to remain on the business market. Gone is the dark, dingy entrance of old; in its place, a light, newly tiled entrance hall leads through to the whitewashed restaurant with light-wood furnishings; there's also a separate bar area. Rooms are being enlarged throughout to feature a large oval bath & shower, ceiling fans, tiled floors & 1 new bed. Outside, the courtyard will soon be shaded by bougainvillea.
N$250/356 sgl/dbl, B&B, but increasing when refurbishment complete.

🏠 **Casa Mia Hotel** (23 rooms) Sam Nujoma Av, between 17th & 18th roads; ☎ 064 205975; f 064 206596; e casancor@iafrica.com.na; www.casa-mia-hotel.com. The entrance of this old-style hotel remains dark & unwelcoming, but a refurbishment programme has brightened up the rooms no end, & facilities are reasonable. All rooms have Mnet TV, phone, tea/coffee maker, & en-suite shower or bath. The adjacent restaurant has rested on a good reputation for years, but don't come here expecting any trendy modern cuisine. There's also a rather dingy bar (open 12.30–14.00, 19.00–21.00). Despite the changes, the Casa Mia is still rather expensive for what it's offering.
From N$380 pp, B&B.

🏠 **The Courtyard** (11 twin, 3 family suites, 4 sgl rooms) 16 3rd Rd (cnr 2nd St), PO Box 3493, Walvis Bay; ☎ 064 206252; f 064 207271; e courtyard@iafrica.com.na; www.thecourtyardhotel.com. Close to the Esplanade in a residential road, just a few blocks from the harbour, The Courtyard has recently been refurbished & now has a large & lively bar area with braai facilites inside & out. Everything is set around two grassy courtyards, shaded by a couple of sturdy palm trees. The rooms all have direct-dial telephone, TV with satellite channels, & a radio/alarm clock, as well as a microwave, coffee machine, kettle, a little cutlery, washing bowl, & a small minibar/fridge (stocked if you wish). All rooms have en-suite facilities, some with bath & shower, others just with bath. The furniture is sturdy & stylish, but kept to a minimum. There is secure parking. It is certainly one of the better places in Walvis Bay, good value for money & very near to the Raft restaurant – though it is a distance from the nightlife of Swakopmund.
N$400/450/500 sgl/dbl/family (2–3 people), B&B.

🏠 **Langholm Hotel** (13 rooms, 1 suite) 24 2nd St West; ☎ 064 209230/1/2; m 081 129 9230; f 064 209430; e desk@langholmhotel; www.langholmhotel.com. This friendly, green-&-white-painted small hotel, owned by the welcoming Nic Adams, is very near to the lagoon. Dbl & twin rooms all have en-suite bathrooms, direct-dial phones & TVs. One is a self-catering suite, big enough for 5 people. There's a relaxing lounge with a bar (open every evening until 22.00), the ceiling of which is festooned with a huge assortment of hats left by

visitors, but don't sleep in so late that you miss the extensive b/fast. A 3-course meal with a choice of main dishes (N$100) can be ordered.
N$450/510/620 sgl/dbl/suite (2 people), B&B.

⌂ **Ngandu at Sea** (23 rooms, 3 flats) Cnr 1st Rd & Theo-Ben Gurirab St West; ☏ 064 207327/8; f 064 207350; e theart@mweb.com.na. Although owner Oswald Theart is normally in residence at Ngandu Safari Lodge in Rundu, he views the 'new Ngandu' as his seaside home. Just a stone's throw from the lagoon, it takes as its theme the coastal location, with colourful murals & paintings by local artists.

A range of rooms — dbl, twin, sgl & family, each has en-suite shower, & some have views of the lagoon. Dbl rooms have TV with 3 channels, phone, tea/coffee-making facilities, fridge & fan. Several rooms are also self-catering. A further 3 self-catering flats are a short walk from the main building.

In the large, angular dining area it's difficult to shake off the sense of being in a café, although lunch & dinner are served here, & there's a bar area & pool table as well. Outside are a tea garden & BBQ, while on the lagoon there are canoes for the use of guests. Run with Germanic efficiency, & with conference facilities for up to 40, this is a place that would suit business people as well as holidaymakers.
N$300/400 sgl/dbl, B&B.

Pensions, B&Bs and restcamps

⌂ **Lagoon Lodge** (8 rooms) 88 Nangolo Mbumba Dr; ☏ 064 200850; m 081 129 7953; f 064 200851; e french@lagoonlodge.com.na; www.lagoonlodge.com.na. This distinctive yellow building decked with flowers is owned & run by a French couple, Helen & Wilfred Meiller, & is a must for bird lovers: it is situated right opposite the lagoon with daily entertainment provided by flocks of flamingos & other waterbirds. Eagle-eyed returning visitors may notice the change of road number. The lodge hasn't moved, but the numbers were changed to ensure that the president's house, should he buy a property at the other end of the road, would be number 1!

Wilfred's skills as a woodturner are evident in the individually decorated rooms, each with a different theme — if you're into the seaside, then a large mural of Walvis Bay may suit your style. And if birds are your passion, ask for their bird room. All are en suite, with TV, phone, & a balcony or terrace facing the lagoon. Facilities also include a small swimming pool in the secluded rear garden.
N$590/940/1,020 sgl/dbl family room (2 children max), B&B.

⌂ **Kleines Nest** (6 rooms) 36 Esplanade; ☏ 064 203203; f 064 206907; e kleinnest@iway.na; www.natron.net/tour/kleines-nest/. This small, modern pension that shares its premises with the owners' engineering firm has an enviable location opposite the lagoon. Upstairs, away from the functional office-style entrance, all is light and airy. Four well-appointed rooms, each with its own balcony, have en-suite shower, TV, fridge/minibar & a small kitchenette area. Minimalist design is offset by pine & cane furnishings, with all rooms looking out over the water. A further 2 budget rooms at the back are en suite, but have no view, & just a kettle. Johann & Melani van den Berg offer guests the use of bicycles, a windsurfer & a canoe, & there's even a quad bike available for a small fee. The aromatheraphy massages may be the perfect antidote to all that exercise.
N$300–400/400–550 sgl/dbl, B&B.

⌂ **Free Air Guesthouse** (10 rooms) Cnr Esplanade & 2nd St West; ☏ 064 202247; m 081 127 8847; f 064 203412; e free-air@iway.na; www.free-air.net. In a prime position opposite the lagoon, & near the Raft restaurant, this relaxed, modern guesthouse takes its name from its sports centre. Here, kitesurfing & windsurfing are on offer, including equipment rental & lessons (from N$300 per hour; see *Watersports* page 301).

Neutral colours dominate the rooms, which feature en-suite shower or bath, kettle & safe. Those at the front have a view over the lagoon, & TV. The b/fast room upstairs looks over the lagoon, while downstairs an informal bar/dining area doubles as a pizza place, with its own stone oven. Flexible dining is the order of the day, with braais & pizzas the norm. Secure parking outside is secure parking.
N$470/510 sgl/dbl top floor; N$400/480 sgl/dbl ground floor without view.

⌂ **Casa Yeovella** (7 rooms) 16 Mandume Ndemufayo Circle, Meersig; \/f 064 200502; m 081 242 6713; e yeovella@namibnet.com. Rather hidden away to the left before the lagoon, Casa Yeovella has a range of sgl & dbl rooms, some of which would be suitable for families — particularly as they can provide prams, camp cots, high chairs & other equipment. En-suite rooms are kitted out like home, too, with a microwave, fridge, kettle, crockery, cutlery, iron & hairdryer — as well as a TV. This is a good-value option for those on a tight budget.
N$200/300 sgl/dbl; 15-45% discount for longer stays. B/fast N$25 pp.

🏠 **Feather's Inn Guesthouse** (10 rooms) 61 18th Rd; 📞 064 209799; 📱 081 252 3245; 📠 064 209737; 📧 feathers@iway.net. En-suite rooms in this rather genteel but friendly guesthouse have TV, fan, fridge & kettle.
N$240/300 sgl/dbl. B/fast N$20–30 pp; other meals on request.

🏠 **Seagull Inn** (9 rooms) 215 Sam Nujoma Av; 📞 064 202775; 📠 064 202455. Despite the uninviting entrance, it's clear that the owner, Andreas, has put some work into upgrading the Seagull, with modern, light, en-suite rooms with TV. It's good value, so perhaps worth checking out once renovation is complete sometime in 2007. And note that it's not to be confused with the excellent B&B of the same name in Swakopmund.
N$160/260 sgl/dbl (older rooms N$220 dbl). B/fast N$20 pp.

🏠 **Esplanade Park Municipal Bungalows** (27 bungalows) Esplanade; 📞 064 206145; 📠 064 215510; 📧 info@wbresorts.com.na; www.wbresorts.com.na. Situated past 8th Rd on the left, on the way south towards Sandwich Harbour, this is a complex of quite smart, well-equipped bungalows facing the lagoon. Each of the 1- and 2-bedroom bungalows, sleeping 3 or 5 people respectively, has its own living room, inside toilet & separate bathroom, & a proper kitchen with stove, fridge/freezer, kettle, toaster, cutlery, crockery, & glasses. They also have outside braais & a private garage. Bedding is provided, but towels & soap are not. Good-value accommodation, though it feels like a restcamp & is not at all cosy. Office open Mon–Fri 08.00–13.00, 15.00–19.00, weekend 08.00–13.00, 15.00–18.00.
3-bed bungalow N$275, 5-bed N$392, inc bed levy.

🏠 **Lagoon Chalets** (28 chalets, 7 rooms) Hage G Geingob St, Meersig; 📞 064 217900; 📠 064 207469; 📱 081 128 7151; 📧 lagoonch@mweb.com.na; www.lagoonchalets.com.na. Two types of chalet are on offer here: the first has only 1 separate bedroom, but can sleep 6 people throughout; the better chalets are a similar size but with 2 separate bedrooms; some have an additional loft bedroom. All are fully furnished & equipped, designed for self-catering families on long-stay trips. En-suite dbl rooms above the restaurant are modern & functional, if rather institutional, with no door to the bathroom. There is secure parking, & garage facilities are available.
1-bedroom chalet N$330, 2-bedroom N$350, 2-storey N$380, dbl room N$200, caravan N$150–170.

At Long Beach (Langstrand)

Some 10km before Walvis Bay, on the road from Swakopmund, is the area known as Long Beach, or Langstrand. Once scarcely more than a handful of houses, Long Beach has recently become the focus of property developers, with houses of all styles joining up the once-isolated resorts that flank the beach. While it remains very quiet out of season, with only you and the sea to share the area, expect the whole atmosphere to go up a few notches in the main holiday periods, especially around Christmas and New Year. Fortunately, with the development have come a couple of places to eat, with a choice of the sophistication of The Burning Shore or the more down-to-earth cuisine of the restaurants at Long Beach Leisure Park.

🏠 **The Burning Shore** (7 rooms, 5 suites) 152 4th St, Long Beach; 📞 064 207568; 📠 064 209836; 📧 burningshore@mweb.com.na; www.burningshore.na. The exterior of this beachfront lodge, now combined with Restless Waves, gives no hint of the luxurious interior beyond the gate. But step inside & the atmosphere is one of discretion & taste. All the rooms & suites are beautifully decorated. En-suite bathrooms all have shower & bath (& one has its own jacuzzi), & most have an uninterrupted sea view.

Downstairs, the 2 lounges ooze colonial-style elegance, overlooking an expanse of lawn & beyond to the sandy beach. The lodge also has a reputedly excellent restaurant (see opposite).

Standard N$990/495; luxury N$1,290/645; suite N$1,990/995, all sgl/pp sharing, all B&B.

🏠 **Dolphin Park** (20 bungalows) 📞 064 204343; 📠 064 215510; 📧 info@wbresorts.com.na; www.wbresorts.com.na. About 10km out of Walvis Bay, beside the road to Swakopmund and close to Long Beach, this purpose-built resort, with self-catering bungalows that look like railway carriages, is reminiscent of the UK's Butlins chain of resorts. It lies in the desert, by the sea, on the edge of Long Beach, dominated by a large waterslide leading into a swimming pool. The atmosphere here is one of a holiday camp, aiming for families with children. Used mainly by Namibians & South Africans, it is very busy during the summer school holidays, but can be almost deserted during the quieter seasons. Bedding is provided, but bring your own towels. *From N$280 per 2-person bungalow to N$702 for 3-bedroom VIP chalet.*

🏠 **Levo Chalets** (3 chalets) Long Beach; 📠 064 207555; e levo@iway.na; www.levotours.com. Substantial self-catering chalets on 2 storeys are just a few mins' walk from the beach. Each has 3 dbl rooms sleeping up to 6 people, a fully equipped kitchen, balcony with sea view, satellite TV & a lock-up garage, so are ideal for longer stays. No meals are available. *From N$255/357(sgl/dbl) to N$662 (6 people).*

🏠 **Long Beach Leisure Park** (120 camping sites, 1 chalet) 📞 064 215500; f 064 215510; e info@wbresorts.com.na; www.wbresorts.com.na. Predominantly a campsite with static caravans & spaces for both caravans & tents, Long Beach is an established resort. There is also a beachfront chalet sleeping 6 people.

The on-site restaurants & bar, open to non-residents as well, are a popular focus for holidaymakers. Of these, the African Grill & Seafood restaurant offers a couple of set menus at N$95 & N$120 pp respectively. An à-la-carte menu features a mix of dishes, some with an African twist, & there's a menu for 'kids and kids at heart', including the likes of spare ribs & calamari & chips at around N$30 (restaurant open Wed–Sun 11.00–15.00 & 18.00–23.00; bar terrace 10.00 to late). There's also Little Antonio's Pizzeria (064 220970, open 10.00–22.00).

Camping N$80 per site plus N$23 pp; chalet N$397–702 (4–6 people).

🏠 **Longbeach Lodge** (14 rooms) Longbeach Circle; 📞 064 218820; f 064 218855; e longbeachlodge@iway.na; www.africa-adventure.co.za. In a prime beachfront location, this pleasant lodge was opened in 2000. With its terracotta tiles & ochre-patterned fabrics, it reflects the warmth & setting of the surrounding desert. A large lounge/(honesty)bar overlooks the beach, with its own veranda. Upstairs, dbl or twin en-suite rooms each have an all-important sea-view balcony, but otherwise they vary: some have bath, some just a shower, & a few have both. TV, fridge, coffee machine & direct-dial phone are all standard. There's a small pool & braai area for guests' use, & meals are available on request. *N$396.78/508.78 sgl/dbl, B&B.*

✗ **WHERE TO EAT** The number of restaurants and cafés in Walvis Bay has burgeoned in recent years. While it's to the Raft that most first-time and regular visitors are drawn initially, it's also worth checking out some of the smaller or less well-known establishments. Most of the hotels and guesthouses also have their own restaurants, including the new Pelican Hotel, whose Aquarius Restaurant overlooks the bay.

Restaurants

✗ **Raft** Esplanade; 📞 064 204877; f 064 202220. Owned by the team that also owns the Tug in Swakopmund (see page 279), this even more adventurous construction is a raft built on stilts in the middle of Walvis Bay lagoon, near the new Pelican Hotel. It is very good, but relatively expensive, with the same menu at lunch & dinner. If the house *steenbras* speciality is on the menu when you visit, it's strongly recommended, & vegetarian options are well worth trying, too. Alternatively try the 'light bites' menu in the bar, including fish & chips for N$39. At lunchtime, bring your binoculars & ask for a window table – the opportunities for birdwatching here are such that you may just forget about your meal. Later on, the bar – which is open daily from 11.00 – is a great place to watch the sun sink into the waves, & is still the most stylish place in town. *Mains N$50–80 (with crayfish from N$240). Open 12.00–15.00, dinner 18.00–22.00; closed Sun low season.*

✗ **Buffalo Action Pub & Restaurant** Sam Nujoma Av. At the junction with Theo-Ben Gurirab St, this heavily wooded & dimly lit sports bar is open all day. Of note is the big buffalo rump steak at around N$90.

✗ **The Burning Shore** 152 4th St, Long Beach; 📞 064 207568. The new-look Burning Shore also has an excellent restaurant overlooking Long Beach. Oysters & crayfish are its specialities, served in sophisticated surroundings. *Mains N$50–140.*

✗ **Castle Park** Sam Nujoma Av, nr Nangola Mbumba St; 📞 064 207148. This relatively new sports bar is open all day (restaurant 12.00–15.00; 18.00–22.00). The menu focuses primarily on grilled game at N$50–85.

✗ **Crazy Mama's** 133 Sam Nujoma Av, between 10th & 11th roads; 📞 064 207364. Opposite the Atlantic Hotel, Crazy Mama's has an enthusiastic fan club of locals & travellers. It serves what some claim are the best pizza & pasta dishes in Namibia, & does a

13

reasonable line in seafood, too. It's also good value at around N$100 for a 2-course meal with a beer or a glass of wine. It's second only to the Raft, but much lighter and less serious. *Mains N$45–65.*

✗ **Harry Peppar** Cnr Nangolo Mbumba Av & 11th Rd; ☎ 064 203131/209977. An unexpected but very good pizza restaurant with cosy décor & wooden furnishing, where every pizza is a flat N$43. *Open daily, 11.00 till late; free delivery.*

✗ **Hickory Creek Spur** Theo-Ben Gurirab St, close to 12th Rd; ☎ 064 207990/1. This lively upstairs chain outlet serves good American burgers, steaks, & a host of side orders together with a good salad bar & children's menu. *Mains N$50–76. Open daily 11.00–23.00 except Sat, open 09.00.*

✗ **Lagoon Restaurant** 8th Rd West; ☎ 064 209412. On the same site as Lagoon Chalets, but privately run, the Lagoon restaurant is open for breakfast, lunch & dinner. More pub than restaurant, it is

rather drab inside, with dark, rustic décor. Upstairs, the bar stays open 'till the last man falls'. In addition to pool tables & gambling machines, there is occasional live music.

✗ **Oyster Restaurant** 36 Atlantic St; ☎ 064 203676. The restaurant that's adjacent to Walvis Bay Yacht Club serves a varied seafood menu that comes with a good recommendation. Though the venue is more traditional than the Raft, it's a great place for sundowners overlooking the sea, with its own veranda & lawns leading down to the beach. Candlelit dinners are sometimes served on the beach. *Mains from N$50; seafood platter for 2 will set you back N$225. Open daily 10.00–24.00.*

✗ **Die Restaurant** 10th Rd, nr cnr with Sam Nujoma Av; ☎ 064 220036. Light & airy but quite formal in style, this serves everything from breakfast to pizza & more substantial dishes, with lunchtime specials. *Open daily 07.30–22.00.*

Cafés, lights meals and take-aways

✗ **Cuxi's** Sam Nujoma Av; ☎ 206208. This air-conditioned coffee shop opposite the Computerland internet café has daily homemade specials, plus sandwiches, burgers & ice creams. *Open Mon–Fri 07.00–19.00, weekends 07.00–14.00.*

☕ **Dolphins** Cnr Esplanade/Atlantic St; ☎ 064 205454. Close to the yacht club, in the same building as Mola Mola, this busy, friendly 'coffee shoppe' serves breakfast, cakes, sandwiches & light meals. *Open Tue–Fri 07.00–16.00, Sat–Mon 07.00–14.00.*

✗ **Kookwater** 10th Rd. Serving breakfast, salads & light meals, this informal, fan-cooled place with wooden tables & African-influenced décor is just off Sam Nujoma Av, near the Protea Hotel. Popular with local workers at lunchtime. *Open Mon–Fri 07.00–18.00, Sat/Sun to 15.00.*

☕ **Oasis Café** Cnr Nangolo Mbumba Dr & Tom Swemmer St; ☎ 064 205629. Opposite the town hall, this is a cheerful spot to stop for breakfast, burgers & toasted sandwiches. *Open Mon–Fri 07.00–19.00, Sat to 15.00, Sun to 14.00.*

☕ **Probst Bakery & Café** 148 Theo-Ben Gurirab St (near 12th Rd); ☎ 064 202744. This popular café & bakery with seating inside & out has a reasonably priced menu for breakfast & lunch, as well as being a good place for snacks & take-away fare. *Breakfast N$4.50–10.50; set lunches N$20–25. Open 06.15–18.00.*

☕ **Rootmans Home Bak** Sam Nujoma Av; ☎ 207916. A simple place serving breakfast, cakes & pastries, set lunches (around N$23), & soft drinks. *Open Mon–Fri 07.00–17.00, Sat 07.00–13.00.*

☕ **Steve's Steakhouse & Take-away** 89 Theo-Ben Gurirab St; ☎ 064 205384. A surprisingly varied menu, from pies to T-bone steak. *Closed Sun.*

✗ **Vlooi's Nest** Hage G Geingob St; ☎ 064 220157. A spacious venue with pine furniture & a broad menu, this friendly new restaurant is run by its eponymous owner. Choose from daily lunch specials, good grills, & their popular salads, & eat inside or out under umbrella shade. *Open Mon–Fri 07.00–18.00, Sat 08.00–14.00.*

NIGHTLIFE AND ENTERTAINMENT Like Swakopmund, Walvis Bay usually has several **nightclubs** which operate all year. More spring up during the peak holiday period for the local market around December/January. These can be great fun, but go in and out of fashion swiftly – probably rendering obsolete anything written here. Ask local advice as to what's good, and take care if you're thinking of a club in one of the townships. Currently, locals tend to gravitate towards the Raft, the Yacht Club or Crazy Mama's for a night out, perhaps starting the evening with a drink at Champs Pub – and returning there or to Cantina's later on.

♀ **Champs Pub** 120 6th St; ☎ 064 209884. A sports bar that's popular both early evening and post-dinner, Champs also has a small dance floor.
Cantina Walvis Bay's best disco is in the industrial area, and is open into the small hours.
☆ **The Plaza** Above the old Plaza Cinema on Nangola Mbumba St, this late-night club is in quite a rough area, though it's racially very mixed. Open daily from midnight onwards, though Fri & Sat are best.

Club 9-5 This is in Naraville township, so less racially mixed, but it's still fairly safe & hassle-free – though do go with a local guide if possible, or by taxi.

Aside from these, it may be worth checking out the bars at the Lagoon Restaurant or the Casa Mia Hotel. Along Sam Nujoma Avenue, numerous seedy gambling houses feature banks of slot machines and little else.

The only **concert venues** in Walvis Bay are the Municipal Hall (*Nangola Mbumba St;* ☎ *064 205981*) and the sports complex. Any touring show will perform either here or at one of Swakopmund's main venues (see page 281).

SHOPPING With your own car, you are close enough to drive easily to Swakopmund, where the choice of shops is usually greater. However, there are a number of shops and services within Walvis itself.

Food and provisions There's plenty of choice for food and provisions, with the most central being Shoprite on Sam Nujoma Avenue, the OK Grocer (formerly the Portuguese Market Garden) further up the road, and the nearby Spar, or Model on Hage G Geingob Street.

Equipment For **camping equipment**, car spares and cycling gear, try Cymot (*136 Hage G Geingob St;* ☎ *064 202241; f 064 205745; www.cymot.com.na*). **Anglers** will appreciate Anglers Kiosk behind Caltex petrol station (*166 Theo-Ben Gurirab St;* ☎ *064 206373*).

For **photographic** needs try Photo Krause (*141 Sam Nujoma Av,* ☎ *064 203015; f 064 206439*). They have film and some camera equipment, and can print digital images as well as processing print film.

Souvenirs On the main street, Sam Nujoma Avenue, there are a couple of shops catering for the tourist market. **Desert Jeweller & Curios** has an upmarket range of gifts and souvenirs, including woodcarvings, while if modern art is more your style, take a look at **Die Galerie** on the opposite side of the road.

In recent years, various **curio sellers** have taken to setting up their wares on the Esplanade close to the Raft and the Pelican Hotel.

OTHER PRACTICALITIES

Emergency and health Although there's a state hospital in Walvis Bay (☎ *064 216300*), visitors in need of treatment would be better advised to contact the private Welwitschia Hospital (☎ *064 218911*), which brought Namibia to worldwide attention following the birth of Angelina Jolie and Brad Pitt's baby in 2006. Should you need a pharmacy, try Walvis Bay Pharmacy (*Sam Nujoma Av;* ☎ *064 202271*) or the ABC Chemist at the Welwitschia Centre (☎ *064 202271*).

In an emergency, the police are reached on ☎ 064 10111, the fire service on ☎ 064 203117, and the ambulance on ☎ 064 209832. If you need any sea rescue services then call ☎ 064 203202/203581 or contact the police – which is also the emergency number to use if you can't get through anywhere else.

Tourist information For tourist information, you'll have to go to the municipality offices on Nangolo Mbumba Drive (☎ *064 201 3111*), or – far more usefully – to

Namib i in Swakopmund (see page 284). The town's once-efficient tourist office has sadly been closed.

Communications
Internet cafés

Computerland 144 Sam Nujoma Av; ℡ 064 205667; www.namibnet.com. N$10 for ½ hr. *Open Mon–Fri 08.00–17.00.*

Dreamworld Creations Sam Nujoma Av; ℡ 064 209306. N$15 for ½ hr.

WHAT TO SEE AND DO Most of the town's activities centre around the **lagoon**. There are some superb birdwatching opportunities both here and in the surrounding area (see pages 304–6), and a couple of highly recommended kayak trips in the lagoon and out to Pelican Point (see page 298). Boat trips from the yacht club take visitors out to see dolphins in the lagoon and beyond (see pages 296–7). Alternatively, you can also drive out towards Pelican Point around the lagoon, past the saltworks: a desolate track lined with salt ponds that have been reclaimed from the sea, inhabited only by seabirds and just the occasional brown hyena.

Off the water, options are more limited. At the office of the Municipality of Walvis Bay, where local people make their water and electricity payments, the walls are covered in an intricate **bas-relief** of wooden carvings, showing, amongst other things, the mating dance of flamingos, desert life, sea life and human fishing. Impressive, and all done by the local artist Peter Downing. Otherwise, there is little to see in the town itself, although the small museum (*open Mon–Fri 09.00–12.30, 15.00–16.30*) next to the Civic Centre has a collection that includes photographs and maps.

At the edge of town, bordering the industrial area, it's possible to visit a **diamond factory**. Mars Investment Holdings (℡ *064 217200;* m *081 127 3717;* f *064 217212;* e *mars@marsdiamonds.com*) offers guided tours daily, albeit by arrangement only, at 09.00 (not Sunday), 11.00, 14.00 and 16.00. Tours cover the history of diamonds, where they're found, diamond mining and diamond cutting – and there's also a shop that sells diamonds and jewellery straight from the factory.

There is a 9-hole **golf course** on the left of 18th Street before the lagoon. For details of fees for visitors, contact them on m 081 271 6950.

Boat trips
There are a few companies running excellent boat trips from the harbour around the lagoon and out to Pelican Point and Bird Island, with catamaran trips a recent introduction to the opportunities on offer. Trips usually start from the yacht club at around 08.30, and vary from short cruises in the lagoon to longer cruises round the harbour and out to Pelican Point, or birdwatching trips further out to sea. Many operators include elaborate snacks that may include oysters or a seafood platter, with sparkling wine. Typically, a half-day trip to see dolphins will cost around N$350–390 per person, with lagoon cruises slightly cheaper.

In October and November, whales frequent these waters, with possible sightings of humpback, southern right, Minke and even killer whales, while from then until April there is the chance of seeing the leatherback turtle. Dolphins – both the bottlenose and the endemic Benguela (heavysides) – are present all year round, as are Cape fur seals, which may often cavort around the boats.

For details of fishing trips, see page 301.

Boat operators

Aquanaut Tours ℡ 064 405969; m 081 128 0374; e info@aquanauttours.com; www.aquanauttours.com. Offer 3–4hr trips to view dolphins, seals & birdlife, or a lagoon cruise. Fishing from the shore (N$800 pp) or by boat (from N$690 pp), with a minimum of 3 people.

WALVIS BAY LAGOON: A BLEAK FUTURE

Walvis Bay lagoon dates back some 5,000 years, making it the oldest lagoon on the Namibian coast. A safe haven for over 150,000 birds, it also acts as a feeding station for a further 200,000 shorebirds and terns on their bi-annual migration to and from the Arctic. Up to 90% of all South African flamingos spend the winter here, while 70% of the world's chestnut-banded plovers depend on the lagoon for their survival.

Pressure on the lagoon in recent years has built up from a number of areas: construction of housing to the southeast, salt pans to the south and west, and a road dyke to the east and south. All these factors have served to reduce flooding, which would naturally keep up the water levels. Added to this is the knock-on effect of the diversion of the Kuiseb River in 1967, since when the dunes have effectively 'marched round' and headed straight for Walvis Bay. The sand blown from the desert contributes significantly to the silting up of the lagoon.

The saltworks that surround the edge of the lagoon in Walvis Bay are South African owned; salt is exported raw from Namibia, then processed in South Africa for industrial use (as against that from Swakopmund which is for human consumption). The salt pans in Walvis Bay are entirely manmade, with the company now owning as far as Pelican Point. As salt extraction increases, it is forecast that the entrance to the lagoon will eventually close up and the lagoon itself will dry up. Initiatives to re-establish the natural flow of water include the construction of culverts under the road leading to the saltworks.

On the basis of current estimates, the lagoon is likely to disappear completely within just five to ten years. The Coastal Environmental Trust of Namibia (\ 064 205057; m 081 269 3280; f 064 200728; e cetn@iafrica.com.na; www.nnf.org.na/CETN/index.htm) is working hard to protect the lagoon, which since June 1995 has been a wetland of international importance under the Ramsar Convention. Protection of the lagoon is also part of the Walvis Bay Local Agenda 21 Project, based at the municipality.

Catamaran Charters 12th Rd (next to Probst Bakery); \/f 064 200798; m 081 129 5393; e seawold@iway.na; www.namibiancharters.com. A ½-day sail aboard the 15m catamaran *Silverwind* to view the marine life & birds of Walvis Bay makes a winning combination, with plenty of space on deck to enjoy the boat trip in itself.

Laramon Tours \/f 064 402359; m 081 124 0635; 081 128 0635; e laramontours@mail.na. Half-day dolphin & sightseeing cruises by motorised catamaran. Most trips operate from Walvis Bay, but in good weather they depart from Swakopmund.

Levo \/f 064 207555; e levo@iway.na; www.levotours.com. Ottmar & Merrilyn started up Levo seal & dolphin cruises from Walvis Bay in 1990. Trips in ski-boats depart from the Tanker Jetty & last about 4 hrs, covering around 50km in that time. They also offer fishing trips: boat fishing costs on average from N$700 pp (min 4 people).

Mola Mola Cnr Esplanade & Atlantic St; \ 064 205511; m 081 127 2522; f 064 207593;

e mmsaf@mweb.com.na; www.mola-namibia.com. The well-respected Mola Mola organises 4hr bird- and dolphin-watching cruises, as well as 4x4 trips to Sandwich Harbour (min 2 people). Highly recommended fishing trips cost N$750 pp.

Pelican Tours \ 064 207644; m 081 124 5123; e pelican@iway.na; www.namplaces.com/pelicantours. Offer dolphin & seal cruises, as well as trips to Sandwich Harbour, desert tours & an unusual 'combo' which combines a dolphin cruise with a half day at Sandwich Harbour (N$1,050 pp).

Sunrise Tours & Safaris 8 Hendrik Witbooi St, Swakopmund; \/f 064 404561; e sunrisetours@iafrica.com.na; www.sunrisetours.com.na. Boat trips, fishing excursions & desert tours.

Sun Sail Namibia \/f 061 232008; m 081 124 5045; e fun@mweb.com.na; www.sailnamibia.com. Offer 3–4hr cruises aboard the catamaran *Fairweather I* setting off from the yacht club. Sunset cruises are also available. Sunset cruise N$300/200 adult/child.

Kayak trips Jeanne Meintjes runs Eco Marine Kayak Tours (\f *064 203144;* e *emkayak@iway.na; www.emkayak.iway.na*). There is a choice of two guided excursions. The first takes birdwatchers onto the lagoon for two hours (N$200 pp), while the second involves a Land Rover trip to Pelican Point, where visitors kayak around Pelican Point and out to the seal colonies (N$380 for a 5hr trip). Trips are run in the mornings only, when winds are light and the sea is generally calm.

AROUND THE TOWNS

Because the towns of Swakopmund and Walvis Bay are just 30km apart (about 25 minutes' drive, on a super tar road), this section covers attractions in the areas outside both of the towns. For boat trips and kayaking around Walvis Bay, however, see pages 296–8.

ACTIVITIES Swakopmund has become a lively centre for adventure-sports, attracting those in search of action and extra adrenalin. It is already a stop on the route of the overland companies, which supply a constant flow of people in search of thrills.

Many of the adventure companies are specialists in a particular field, so are listed under that activity, but for information under one roof try:

NamibFun At the Swakopmund tourist office; \ 064 463921; f 064 463917; e namibfun@mweb.com.na; www.namibfun.na.

Desert Explorers Adventure Centre Nathaniel Maxuilili St; \ 064 406096; f 064 405038; e desertex@iafrica.com.na. This is the booking office for the Desert Explorers quad-bike trips. It also acts as agent for most, but not all, of Swakopmund's small

adventure operators, with activities like dune-boarding, skydiving, kayaking, abseiling, etc.

Palmwag Lodge & Travel Shop 14A Sam Nujoma Av; \ 064 404459; m 081 269 7271; www.palmwag.com.na/swakopmund.htm. An efficient one-stop shop that acts as agent for many of Swakopmund's adventure operators.

Action in the dunes New activities in the dunes are constantly being dreamed up to add to the existing range, and others dropped as they prove less of a draw. Some, such as quadbiking and sandboarding, may be combined in one trip. Current options include:

Sandboarding in the dunes was pioneered by Alter-Action, which is still the major player. They've been joined by the more expensive Dune 7, which specialises in stand-up boarding (also known as dune-boarding), and ferries its customers up the dunes by quad bike. Typically, trips leave from Swakopmund in the morning, collecting you from your accommodation. Alter-Action participants are supplied with a large flat piece of masonite/hardboard, plus safety hats, elbow guards and gloves. The idea is to push off the top of a dune, and lie on the board as it slides down. Speeds easily reach 70km/h or more, though first you'll do a few training rides on lower dunes, where you won't go much faster than 40km/h. Finally, they take you to a couple of the larger dunes, for longer, faster runs, before lunch in the desert, and the return drive to Swakopmund. As a spin-off from sandboarding, offered by both operators, stand-up boarding, also known as dune-boarding, uses a modified snowboard. Participants stand up on a small surfboard, which shoots down the side of dunes – rather like skiing, only on sand. It may have more finesse, and certainly requires more skill. Trips cost about N$275 per person lying down, or N$365–440 for stand-up boarding.

Quad-biking involves riding four-wheel motorcycles through the dunes, and is organised by a number of companies, of which the best known is Desert Explorers.

DESERTS – BY DEFINITION

'Desert' is an arbitrary term whose meaning is widely disputed, even amongst experts. Some refer to Noy-Meir's definition of a 'water-controlled ecosystem with infrequent, discrete and largely unpredictable water inputs'. Others are quantitative, defining a desert as receiving an average of less than 100mm of rain per annum. In practice, any arid habitat can be called a desert – and the Namib is certainly very arid.

Antarctica has close to zero precipitation, and most of the water there is frozen, so, strictly speaking, the whole continent is a desert. However the normal usage of 'desert' refers to dry places which are also hot. These cover 5% of the land on Earth, and are to be found in two neat rings around the globe, straddling the lines of the tropics of Capricorn and Cancer.

The uniform distribution of deserts is due to the pattern of sunlight landing on the planet. Sunlight intensity is highest at the Equator, which is directly underneath the sun for most of the year. With all this light energy, water evaporates more vigorously at this latitude. As the water rises in the atmosphere, it condenses and falls onto the equatorial rainforests. The dry air remaining in the upper atmosphere journeys away from the Equator towards the tropics. Here it descends to ground level, waterless. What water there is at ground level is then picked up and exported by low-altitude winds travelling back towards the Equator to complete the cycle – hence the desert.

This desiccating climate creates a habitat that challenges life. Levels of solar radiation are enormous; air temperatures can soar during the day and, without insulating cloud cover, plunge below freezing at night; the ground is almost too hot to touch; strong winds are common and, where there is sand, sandstorms scour the land. Worst of all, water becomes a luxury. Since all living things are built from water-packed cells, there could hardly be a more uninhabitable environment on Earth. It is a credit to evolution that deserts are often inhabited by a wealth of organisms with sophisticated adaptations to survive in these conditions.

With a wide variety of fascinating species and unique adaptations, the Namib's community of animals and plants may not be as obviously appealing as those on Africa's grasslands, but it is equally impressive to the informed and observant visitor.

Trips cost around N$400 per person for two hours, although longer and shorter trips are available as well, departing through the day. Manual, semi-automatic and automatic bikes are available. Helmets, goggles and gloves are provided.

If you're setting off on your own, consider the harmful effect on the environment (see box, page 300). Note that bikes are not allowed into the Namib-Naukluft National Park.

Adventure operators in the dunes

Alter-Action Ltd \/f 064 402737; m 081 128 2737; e alteraxn@iafrica.com.na; www.alter-action.com. The original sandboarding company.
Dare Devil Adventures \ 064 209532/400858/401183/400180; m 081 127 5701/127 6005/129 0010/128 4492; e daredev@iway.na. Based opposite Long Beach, between Swakopmund & Walvis Bay.
Desert Explorers See page 298.
Dune 7 Sandboarding \/f 064 220881; m 081 127 7636; e dawayner@hotmail.com; www.duneseven.com

Kuiseb Delta Adventures \ 064 202550; m 081 128 2580; e fanie@kuisebonline.com. www.kuisebonline.com. Historian tour & adrenalin dune run.
Namib Quad Rentals m 081 129 5794/204 3143; e longbeachlodge@iway.na. Quad-biking.
Outback Orange \ 064 400968, m 081 129 2877/128 1778; e outbackorange@yahoo.com. They offer a free video of your trip.
Swakop Sandboarding \ 064 461118; m 081 271 6838; e hata-angu@mail.na

Many companies in the Swakopmund area have taken advantage of the unique environment to bring adventure sports to the area. Quad-biking, sandboarding, sand-skiing and other such activities are growing in popularity, but their proliferation could have serious consequences for the sand-dunes and other desert areas on which they depend.

While most operators take this issue seriously, confining their sports to a specific area and spelling out to participants the harm that can be caused by thoughtless manoeuvres, individuals may not be so careful. Even then, sandboarding and sand-skiing have a weight-to-surface relationship that is unlikely to cause significant damage. Sadly, though, serious harm is being caused by individuals on privately owned bikes setting off across the dunes and gravel plains without any understanding of the nature of the area.

Broadly, the low-impact part of the dunes is the area on the top, with the greatest potential for danger to the habitat being on the lee side. Since most of the life in the dunes is found in the top 10cm, a thoughtless biker can cause untold damage in just a few seconds of 'fun'. Beyond the dunes, slow-growing lichens form an integral part of the region's ecology, but they are extremely fragile. Trample them underfoot, or ride over them, and they are unlikely to survive, depriving many forms of wildlife of food and even shelter. And then there is the Damara tern. The gravel plains of the Namib Desert are the nesting area of this endemic bird, one of the rarest terns in the world, yet – with a quick twist of the handlebars – a nest can be crushed in seconds.

Action in the air With clear air and a starkly beautiful coastline, Swakopmund is a natural space to learn to fly or even skydive. Ground Rush Adventures run tandem **skydives** for novices in conjunction with Swakopmund Skydiving Club at the local airport. After a basic safety chat and a scenic flight over Swakopmund and the surrounding area, you are strapped to an experienced instructor to throw yourselves out of a plane at 10,000ft. Your free-fall lasts for about half a minute before, hopefully, your parachute opens and there's a further five-minute 'canopy ride' before landing outside the clubhouse. The cost is NS$1,500 per jump; for safety reasons, participants may be limited to those over 16, and within a weight range of 105–220kg.

For a more leisurely aerial experience, African Adventure Balloons organise champagne breakfast **flights** over the desert (N$1,740/2,340 pp, 1/2 hr/1 hr). The breathtakingly early 05.00 pick-up time is offset by flights over areas such as Rössing Mountain, Spitzkoppe, the moon landscape and the Naukluft Mountains. With the same operator, the more intrepid can try their hand at **parasailing** over the dunes (N$500 pp) or, if it's an adrenalin rush you're after, the 1,100m **flying fox** at Rössing Mountain for N$700 per person; trips include a 4x4 journey to the top through spectacular mountain scenery.

Scenic flights can also be organised through a number of operators, including Pleasure Flights & Safaris, Atlantic Aviation, Wings over Africa or Desert Explorers (page 298) to a number of places, including Sossusvlei (2 hrs 20 mins) and the Skeleton Coast (3½ hrs). Prices with Pleasure Flights are currently N$1,450 and N$1,870 per person respectively, based on five people sharing, but note that the cost of fuel is linked to the US dollar, so prices can fluctuate in line with exchange rates. It's worth booking in advance, since that gives companies the chance to fill flights, thus keeping the costs down to those quoted here.

Flight operators

African Adventure Balloons ✆/f 064 403455;
m 081 242 9481; e flylo@iway.na;
www.swakop.com/balloons

Atlantic Aviation 5 Hendrik Witbooi St; ✆ 064
404749; f 064 405832; e info@flyinnamibia.com;
www.flyinnamibia.com

Bush Bird ✆ 064 404071; m 081 250 7171;
e bushbird@iway.na

Desert Explorers See page 298.

Ground Rush Adventures m 081 124 5167;
e freefall@iafrica.com.na; www.skydiveswakop.com.na

Pleasure Flights & Safaris ✆/f 064 404500;
e redbaron@iafrica.com.na;
www.pleasureflights.com.na

Wings over Africa ✆ 064 403720; f 064 403920;
m 081 246 3606; e wings@mail.na

Riding Okakambe Trails (✆ *064 402799*; f *064 405258*; e *okakambe@iway.na*) have well-trained **horses** available for both novices and experienced riders to take accompanied rides into the moon landscape and the Swakop River Valley. At N$290 per person for 1½ hours, based on two people, it's not cheap, and a single rider will pay N$400. Riding hats are available. There's also bed and breakfast accommodation at the farm, and the potential for overnight horse and hiking trails. To find the farm, take the B2 from Swakopmund for about 12km, then turn right onto the D1901, and follow the road for 1.7km.

Alternatively, for a more Arabian experience, short (15-min or so) **camel-riding** excursions in the desert are available between 14.00 and 17.00 each afternoon from the same location, with Arab-style attire for hire (✆ *064 400363*).

Action at sea

Boat trips/Kayaking For details of these trips, run from Walvis Bay, see pages 296–8.

Fishing Fishing has long been popular all along this coastline with South African visitors. Although fishing is good all year round, the best times are October to April. The turn of the year is particularly popular, with many anglers arriving in search of big-game fish such as copper sharks and other similar species, which can weigh as much as 180kg. Other species that may be caught include kabeljou, steenbras, barber, galjoen and garrick.

The area is good for crayfish, too, though the catch may be limited to a maximum of seven per person, or 14 per vehicle. Permits are required for all types of fishing.

Several local tour operators specialise in fishing, either from the beach or by boat, but watch out for operators who may be less environmentally aware. Established outfits include Levo, who also have bottom and deep-sea fishing, Mola Mola and Aquanaut (see pages 296–7 for contact details). Expect boat fishing to cost from around N$700 pp, and fishing from the shore from N$800 pp, depending on numbers.

Watersports Walvis Bay is the place to head for to try out watersports that include kitesurfing and windsurfing. Free Air (see page 291) offers equipment rental and lessons (from N$300 per hour). Tuition is mainly one-to-one, and is tailored according to the individual client, and taking the weather into consideration.

In recent years, surfing has been gaining in popularity on the stretch between Long Beach and Walvis Bay, but there is currently no formal outfit operating here.

EXCURSIONS BEYOND THE TOWNS

Tour operators Several tour operators and guides specialise in land-based local excursions. Almost all operators will visit the Namib Desert, but the experience you get will depend very much on your guide. Several operators also run tours of the towns, as well as speciality excursions, focusing for example on gems, or up the

13

coast to the seal colony at Cape Cross (see page 314). There's also one company (Swakopmund Township Tours) taking visitors into the townships – a new departure for Swakopmund. Prices vary according to the type of terrain, the destination, the number of people and the individual operator, but you can expect to pay around N$300–450 each for a half-day trip, or N$450–650 each for a full day. Operators include the following:

African Eagle ☎ 064 403866; m 081 127 5705; f 064 403833; e daytours@iway.na

Charly's Desert Tours ☎ 064 404341; f 064 404821; e info@charlysdeserttours.com; www.charlysdeserttours.com. One of Swakopmund's longest-running operators, established in 1966. Half-day trips include sightseeing tours of Swakopmund & Walvis Bay, plus trips into the desert & to Cape Cross; full days go further into the desert or down to the Kuiseb Delta.

Desert Adventure Safaris ☎ 064 403274; f 064 403469; e info@dastours.com.na; www.das.com.na. Full- & half-day excursions around Swakopmund & to Cape Cross, Spitzkoppe or the Namib Desert, plus longer trips & into Damaraland and Kaokoland.

Kallisto Tours & Services ☎/f 064 402473; m 081 269 5630; e hdgothje@iway.na; www.natron.net/kallisto-tours. A full range of town tours, excursions & longer trips, as well as transfers.

Living Desert Adventures ☎/f 064 405070; m 081 127 5070; e nature@iafrica.com.na. A highly respected company offering 4–5hr trips into the desert. Also include Sandwich Harbour, Cape Cross & the option of tailor-made tours.

NamibFun Cnr Sam Nujoma Av & Hendrik Witbooi; ☎ 064 463921; e namibfun@iway.na; www.namibfun.com.na

Namib Tours ☎/f 064 404072; m 081 128 6111. A range of tours, from a 1½hr tour of Swakopmund trip to desert tours, visits to Rössing Mountain & day trips to Cape Cross & Spitzkoppe.

Pelican Tours See page 297.

Swakop Tour Company Daniel Tjongarero St; ☎ 064 404088; m 081 124 2906; e proverb@mweb.com.na. This well-recommended company, run by Georg Erb, offers set tours for small groups, & are of particular appeal for geologists & botanists. These include a 5hr klipspringer tour into the desert, & a shorter 'dunes of the Namib' tour around

sunset, as well as a 2–3hr desert walk. Customised itineraries can be arranged focusing on individual interests.

Swakopmund Township Tours m 081 124 6111; f 064 462721; e hata_angu@hotmail.com. Also known as Hata Angu ('Let's get to know each other') Cultural Tours, this new company has set out to 'bridge the gap' between visitors & the local community by offering cultural trips into the township of Mondesa & the Democratic Resettlement Community (DRC). Tours depart at 11.00 & 16.00, & last up to 4 hrs. N$300 pp, inc light meal.

Tommy's Tours & Safaris ☎/f 064 461038; m 081 128 1038; e tommystours@yahoo.com. Tommy Collard's tours cover almost every aspect of this area, including a 4–5hr trip through the dunes, as well as town tours, & trips to Sandwich Harbour, the Namib Desert & Cape Cross.

Turnstone Tours ☎ 064 403123; f 064 403290; e turn@iafrica.com.na; www.turnstone-tours.com. If you're interested in a really informative day in the desert with a first-rate guide who is also excellent company, try Bruno Nebe at Turnstone Tours. You might pay a bit more than you will for a normal tour, but you often get the Land Rover & Bruno to yourselves. Turnstone's trips come with a delicious picnic hamper full of food & drink (instead of just a lunch pack) & visit destinations like Sandwich Harbour & the Namib Desert (half-day tours are also available for a minimum of 4 people at N$490 per head), as well as others on request. For those with more time, there are short camping tours into Damaraland, the Erongo Mountains & the Namib Desert, as well as from Bruno's own farm, Mundulea, to the east of Etosha. Day trips cost N$880 pp (inc VAT, lunch, soft drinks & park permits), with a minimum of 2 people – a bargain for one of Namibia's best guides.

Welwitschia Drive
In the northern corner of the Namib-Naukluft National Park, an afternoon's excursion from Swakopmund or Walvis Bay, the Welwitschia Drive is a route through the desert with numbered beacons at points of interest, culminating in one of the country's oldest welwitschia plants.

Permits for the park must be bought beforehand from the Ministry of Environment and Tourism (MET) in Swakopmund (*cnr Sam Nujoma Av &*

Bismarck St; ☏ *064 402172; N$40 pp, & N$10 per vehicle*). See *Chapter 12,* pages 262–4, for a full description of the route.

Part of the Welwitschia Drive is the 'moon landscape', or 'moonscape' – a rolling, barren area of rocky desert formed by the valleys around the course of the Swakop River. It's a spectacular sight, often spoken of, and best viewed by the slanting light of mid morning or late afternoon.

Dune 7 Past the Bird Sanctuary, just off the C14 on the way to the airport and Sesriem, this is one of the highest dunes in the area and has a small picnic site near its base, amongst a few shady palms. It's a popular spot for both energetic dune-climbers and sundowners.

Other desert tours While many local companies offer half-day or even full-day tours covering a relatively well-beaten trail that includes the Welwitschia Drive, a really attractive alternative is to discover less well-known areas of the desert in the company of a specialist, such as Turnstone Tours. One such trip might take you inland near the old railway, then over rolling dune fields towards the moonscape, from where you can see Rössing Mountain in the distance. Down below, mining claims have been staked out here and there on the gravel plains. While most of the material mined is granite, many other minerals are to be found, including small quantities of yellowish-green uranium oxide, or purpurite; this is the raw material that is processed into yellowcake, and eventually refined into plutonium and other substances. Look out, too, for the cellophane-like hornblend, or the pinky-orange of titanium.

There's a lot more to this apparently barren plain than minerals, though. Individual welwitschia plants and quivertrees form an integral part of the landscape, as do the tiny stone plants, *Lithops karasmontana,* that may be encountered hidden beneath an outcrop of quartz. Lichens cling to the rocks, small holes tell of hairy-footed gerbils, where day geckos scurry past. Across the plain is the linear oasis of Goanikontes on the Khan River. Built by the Germans, Goanikontes was originally used as a staging post for horsecarts from Swakopmund, since food for horses and cattle could be grown. Here, and along the huge plain of the Swakop River, numerous plants can be identified clinging to life in this harsh landscape, and klipspringers eke out a precarious existence along the rocks.

Rössing mine Rössing is remarkable, particularly if you're interested in engineering, mining or geology. It's an enormous, open-cast uranium mine. For children (especially the sort that never grow up) there are the biggest lorries in the world and some enormous vehicles.

The open-cast mine is awesome, so deep that the same vehicles working at the bottom of the pit look like Dinky toys. You certainly get an alternative view of the desert, and the viewpoints Rössing has set up (with information plaques) provide interesting photo opportunities. There's a video charting the mines and the uranium production process, with the requisite emphasis on safety, and a tour of the whole site.

Visiting Rössing is probably the sort of thing that I would have done when I was a child, on holiday with my family, to fill in a rainy day. Then I'd look back on it, and be glad that I'd done it. It certainly appeals to those already interested, but many will feel only too glad to leave this kind of suspect industrial 'development' behind them in Europe. Trips leave from outside Café Anton on Bismarck Street in Swakopmund on the first and third Fridays of each month (*N$25/15 adult/child*). Reservations should be made at Swakopmund Museum.

BIRDWATCHING AND OTHER WILDLIFE There is some excellent birdlife in the vicinity. Just take a walk on the southwest side of Walvis Bay, around the lagoon. The flock of feeding flamingos and pelicans that I often find there usually allows me to get much closer than others that I come across in the area. Birdwatchers might also want to stop at one of the guano platforms in the sea between Walvis and Swakopmund.

Bird sanctuary If you follow an extension of 18th Road (the C14 towards Sesriem and the airport) inland from Walvis Bay and over the roundabout, heading for Dune 7, then on your right you will shortly see a series of freshwater pools, albeit often close to dried up. Sit here with binoculars for a few minutes and you'll often be able to spot some of the pelicans, flamingos, avocets, and assorted waders that attract birdwatchers to flock to Walvis Bay. Enthusiasts may wish to check what's here as well as scanning the main lagoon itself.

Swakop River Delta Here small tidal lagoons surrounded by reeds are very good for birding. Expect whimbrels, curlews, the odd flamingo and pelican, white-breasted cormorants, Cape cormorants, black-winged stilts, avocets, and more.

The remains of the old railway bridge lie here, washed down in 1934 when the Swakop River performed its flood-of-the-century stunt. On the pillars there are often crowned and bank cormorants, while along the riverbed, between the tamarisk trees, kestrels swoop around catching mice.

The local Wildlife Society has laid out a pleasant, well-marked 4km trail starting next to the cemetery. This takes you downstream into the river mouth, and back to the beach. Walkers should beware of quad-bikes that move pretty fast through this area.

Kuiseb Delta This fascinating area is criss-crossed by a labyrinth of tracks in which even experienced guides sometimes get lost. Various unmarked archaeological sites dot the area, where pottery shards, beads, shell middens and stone tools can be seen. The wildlife found here includes springbok, ostrich, jackal and brown hyena, and many birds including the endemic dune lark.

Look out for the nara bushes, *Acanthosicyos horrida* – their spiky green (and hence photosynthesising) stems have allowed them to dispense with leaves completely. This is an advantage given the propensity of leaves to lose water. Naras are perhaps not truly desert plants for their roots go down many metres to reach underground water, which they need in order to survive. From February to April and August to September the local Topnaar people harvest nara melons here.

The whole area is accessible only by 4x4 and you'll only appreciate it with a good guide. To approach on your own, take the Esplanade by the lagoon southwest from Walvis Bay, and after about 4km ignore the sign to Paaltjies (where the road divides) and keep left. The tracks then splits and you take the left fork marked Rooibank via Wortels.

Sandwich Harbour This small area about 45km south of Walvis Bay contains a large saltwater lagoon, extensive tidal mudflats, and a band of reed-lined pools fed by freshwater springs – which together form one of the most important refuges for birdlife in southern Africa. Typically you'll find about 30 species of birds at Sandwich at any given time. It offers food and shelter to countless thousands of migrants every year and some of the most spectacular scenery in the country – for those visitors lucky enough to see it. Where else can you walk alone along a pelican-covered beach while pink flamingos glide above the sand-dunes?

Of the world's half-dozen or so species of flamingo, two are found within southern Africa: the greater, *Phoenicopterus ruber*, and the lesser, *Phoenicopterus minor*. Both species have wide distributions – from southern Africa north into East Africa and the Red Sea – and are highly nomadic in their habits.

Flamingos are usually found wading in large areas of shallow saline water, where they filter-feed by holding their specially adapted beaks upside down in the water. The lesser flamingo will walk or swim while swinging its head from side to side, mainly taking blue-green algae from the surface of the water. The larger greater flamingo will hold its head submerged while filtering out small organisms (detritus and algae), even stirring the mud with its feet to help the process. Both species are gregarious; flocks can number millions of birds, although hundreds are more common.

Only occasionally do flamingos breed in southern Africa, choosing Etosha Pan or perhaps Botswana's Makgadikgadi Pans. When the conditions are right (usually March to June, following heavy rains) both species build low mud cones in the water and lay one or (rarely) two eggs in a small hollow on the top. These are then incubated by both parents for about a month until they hatch, and after a further week the young birds flock together and start to forage with their parents. Some ten weeks later the young can fly and fend for themselves.

During their first few months, the young are very susceptible to the shallow water drying out. In 1969, a rescue operation was mounted when Etosha Pan dried out. Thousands of chicks were moved to nearby Fischer's Pan, which was still covered in water.

The best way to tell the two species apart is by their beaks: that of the greater flamingo is almost white, whilst the lesser flamingo has a uniformly dark beak. Looking from further away, the body of the greater flamingo appears white, whilst that of the lesser looks smaller and more pink.

Namibia's best places for flamingos are usually the lagoons at Walvis Bay and Sandwich Harbour – unless you hear that Etosha or Nyae Nyae are full of water. Then, by the time you arrive, the flamingos will probably have beaten you there.

Regulations and warning Getting to Sandwich Harbour requires a high-clearance 4x4 and an experienced driver. As several vehicles have been lost to the sea in recent years, many of the area's guides have stopped coming here. Despite this difficulty of accessing it, Sandwich Harbour is still the best place for birding in the area. So don't believe convenient rumours that it's silted up, or devoid of birdlife. It isn't – it's superb. That said, very occasionally there may be problems with access as a result of fog or flooding, which can lead even the experts to cancel or curtail a trip.

The most experienced operator doing proper trips here regularly is Bruno Nebe, of Turnstone Tours (N$880 pp; see page 302), who runs full-day trips for a minimum of two people. These are best booked far in advance, and are highly recommended. Other operators include Mola-Mola Tours and Pelican Tours (both charging N$950 pp, based on a minimum of two people; see page 297), and Living Desert Adventures (page 302) Trips with all operators include lunch and soft drinks.

The reluctance of most guides to come here should be a warning to you: even experienced desert drivers get stuck here regularly if they don't know the place, so it's dangerous to go without a local expert. If you do try to drive yourself, then check the fine print of your vehicle's insurance and buy an NWR permit in advance from the NWR office in Swakopmund, or the Omega or other filling stations in Walvis Bay. These cost N$40 per adult, and N$10 for the vehicle.

Getting there Take the Esplanade by the lagoon southwest out of Walvis Bay. After about 4km ignore the sign to Paaltjies (where the road divides) and keep to your left. The tracks then splits and you take the right fork, ignoring the road marked Rooibank via Wortels. Cross the salt flats and continue until you reach a fence which marks the boundary of the Namib-Naukluft National Park. Turn right and drive along the fence towards the beach, crossing into the park where the fence stops. You'll be turned away if you don't have a permit.

From this checkpoint it's about 20km of sandy terrain to Sandwich Harbour. You can drive all the way on the beach if you wish, following in the tyre tracks of the fishermen, although the going can get rough. Beware: if the tide is high and catches you, expect serious problems.

It's better to take an immediate left after passing the control post, and follow these tracks. After some 200m, they turn parallel to the sea and are considerably firmer than the ones on the beach. Leaving these tracks to cross the apparently dry pans, where there are none, is foolhardy.

What to see and do Once you reach the bird sanctuary, vehicles must be left and you have to proceed on foot. The northern part consists of a number of almost enclosed reed-lined pools at the top of the beach, which back directly onto huge dunes. These are fed partly by the sea via narrow channels which fill at high tide, and partly with fresh water which seeps from a subterranean watercourse under the dunes and enables reeds (albeit salt-tolerant ones) to grow. These in turn provide food and nesting sites for a number of the resident waterbirds found here. On my last visit I managed to spot dabchicks, moorhens, shelducks, common and marsh sandpipers, several species of tern (Caspian, swift, white-winged and whiskered all visit) and even avocets and African spoonbills – as well as the pelicans and flamingos.

As you continue along the beach, the 'harbour' itself comes into view. During the early 18th century it was used by whalers for its deep, sheltered anchorage and ready supply of fresh water. Subsequently a small station was established there to trade in seal pelts, fish and guano. Later, in the early part of the 20th century, it was used as a source of guano but, after the mouth of the harbour silted up, this ground to a halt in 1947, leaving only a few bits of rusting machinery to be seen today.

It's worth climbing up one of the dunes, as from there you can see the deep lagoon, protected from the ocean's pounding by a sand spit, and the extensive mudflats to the south – which are often covered by the tide.

This is definitely a trip to make a whole day of, so, when you start walking from your vehicle, bring some windproof clothes and a little to eat and drink, as well as your binoculars, camera and lots of film. Even if you're not an avid ornithologist, the scenery is so spectacular that you're bound to take endless photos.

14

The Skeleton Coast

By the end of the 17th century, the long stretch of coast north of Swakopmund had attracted the attention of the Dutch East India Company. They sent several exploratory missions, but after finding only barren shores and impenetrable fogs, their journeys ceased. Later, in the 19th century, British and American whalers operated out of Lüderitz, but they gave this northern coast a wide berth – it was gaining a formidable reputation.

Today, driving north from Swakopmund, it's easy to see how this coast earned its names of the Coast of Skulls or the Skeleton Coast. Treacherous fogs and strong currents forced many ships onto the uncharted sandbanks that shift underwater like the desert's sands. Even if the sailors survived the shipwreck, their problems had only just begun. The coast here is but a barren line between an icy, pounding ocean and the stark desert interior. The present road (C34) runs more or less parallel to the ocean, and often feels like a drive along an enormous beach – with the sea on one side, and the sand continuing forever on the other.

For the first 250km or so, from Swakopmund to about Torra Bay, there are almost no dunes. This is desert of gravel and rock. Then, around Torra Bay, the northern dune-sea of the Namib starts, with an increasingly wide belt of coastal dunes stretching north to the Kunene River. But nowhere are these as tall, or continuous, as the Namib's great southern dune-sea, south of the Kuiseb River.

At first sight it all seems very barren, but watch the amazing wildlife documentaries made by the famous film-makers of the Skeleton Coast, Des and Jen Bartlett, to realise that some of the most remarkable wildlife on earth has evolved here. Better still, drive yourself up the coast road, through this fascinating stretch of the world's oldest desert. You won't see a fraction of the action that they have filmed, but with careful observation you will spot plenty to captivate you.

FLORA AND FAUNA

SAND-RIVERS A shipwrecked sailor's only hope on this coast would have been to find one of the desert's linear oases – sand-rivers that wind through the desert to reach the coast. The Omaruru, the Ugab, the Huab, the Koichab, the Uniab and the Hoanib are the main ones. They are few and far between. Each starts in the highlands, far inland, and, although normally dry, they flood briefly in years of good rains. For most of the time their waters filter westwards to the sea through their sandy beds. Shrubs and trees thrive, supporting whole ecosystems: green ribbons which snake across seemingly lifeless plains.

Even in the driest times, if an impervious layer of rock forces the water to surface, then the river will flow overland for a few hundred metres, only to vanish into the sand again as swiftly as it appeared. Such watering places are rare, but of vital importance to the inhabitants of the area. They have allowed isolated groups of Himba people to stay in these parts, while also sustaining the famous desert

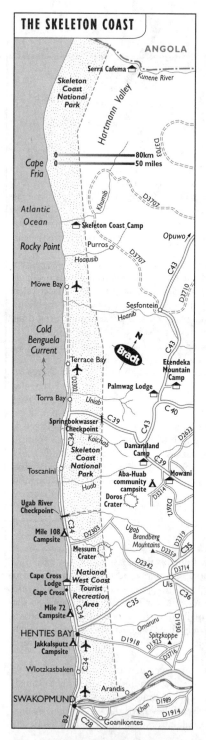

THE SKELETON COAST

ANGOLA

Serra Cafema

Skeleton Coast National Park

Kunene River

Hartmann Valley

D3703

Cape Fria

0 ————— 80km
0 ————— 50 miles

Atlantic Ocean

Khumib

D3707

Rocky Point

Skeleton Coast Camp

Purros

Opuwo

Hoarusib

D3707

Möwe Bay

C43

Sesfontein

D3710

Hoanib

Cold Benguela Current

Bradt

N

Terrace Bay

C43

Etendeka Mountain Camp

D3002

Palmwag Lodge

Torra Bay

Uniab

C40

C39

Springbokwasser Checkpoint

C34

Koichab

C43

D2633

Skeleton Coast National Park

Damaraland Camp

C39

Mowani

Toscanini

Aba-Huab community campsite

Huab

Doros Crater

D3214

D2612

Ugab River Checkpoint

C34

Ugab

D2303

Brandberg Mountains

D2319

Mile 108 Campsite

D2359

C35

Messum Crater

D2342

D3714

National West Coast Tourist Recreation Area

Uis

C36

Cape Cross Lodge

Cape Cross

C35

Mile 72 Campsite

C34

Omaruru

D1930

HENTIES BAY

D1918

Spitzkoppe

D1925

D3716

Jakkalsputz Campsite

C34

B2

Wlotzkasbaken

SWAKOPMUND

Arandis

D1989

B2

C28

Khan

D1914

Goanikontes

populations of elephant and black rhino.

In many of these river valleys there are thriving populations of gemsbok, kudu, springbok, steenbok, jackals, genets and small wild cats. The shy and secretive brown hyena is common, though seldom seen. Giraffe and zebra are scarce residents, and even lion or cheetah will sometimes appear, using the sand-rivers as alleys for hunting forays. Lion used to penetrate the desert right to the coast to prey on seals. Although it is many years since the last such coastal lion was seen, rising game populations in the interior are encouraging a greater population of lion in the region, so perhaps we'll see individuals on the beaches again before too long.

BESIDE THE SEA Outside the river valleys, the scenery changes dramatically, with an outstanding variety of colours and forms. The gravel plains – in all hues of brown and red – are bases for occasional coloured mountains, and belts of shifting barchan sand-dunes.

Yet despite their barren appearance, even the flattest of the gravel plains here are full of life. Immediately next to the sea, high levels of humidity sustain highly specialised vegetation, succulents like lithops, and the famous lichens – which are, in fact, not plants at all but a symbiotic partnership of algae and fungi, the fungi providing the physical structure, while the algae photosynthesise to produce the food. They use the moisture in humid air, without needing either rain or even fog. That said, frequent coastal fogs and relatively undisturbed plains account for their conspicuous success here.

In some places lichens carpet the gravel desert, in places surrounded by protective fencing. Take a close look at one of these gardens of lichen, and you'll find many different species, varying in colour from bright reds and oranges, through vivid greens to darker browns, greys and black. Most cling to the rocks or the crust of the gypsum soil, but a few species stand up like the skeletons of small leafless bushes, and one species,

Xanthomaculina convoluta, is even windblown, a minute version of the tumbleweed famous in old Western films.

All come alive, looking their best, early on damp, foggy mornings. Sections appear like green fields of wispy vegetation. But if you pass on a hot, dry afternoon, they will seem less interesting. Then stop and leave your car. Walk to the edge of a field with a bottle of water, pour a little onto a small patch of lichens, and stay to watch. Within just a few minutes you'll see them brighten and unfurl.

Less obvious is their age: lichens grow exceedingly slowly. Once disturbed, they take decades and even centuries to regenerate. On some lichen fields you will see vehicle tracks. These are sometimes 40 or 50 years old – and still the lichens briefly crushed by one set of wheels have not re-grown. This is one of the main reasons why you should *never* drive off the roads on the Skeleton Coast.

FURTHER INLAND East of the coastal strip, between about 30 and 60km inland, the nights are very cold, and many mornings are cool and foggy. However, after about midday the temperatures rocket and the humidity disappears. This is the harshest of the Namib's climatic zones, but even here an ecosystem has evolved, relying on occasional early morning fogs for moisture.

This is home to various scorpions, lizards and tenebrionid beetles, living from windblown detritus and vegetation including dune-creating dollar bushes, *Zygophyllum stapffii*, and perhaps the Namib's most fascinating plant, the remarkable *Welwitschia mirabilis*.

NATIONAL WEST COAST RECREATIONAL AREA

The coast is divided into three areas. North of Swakopmund up to the Ugab River, covering about 200km of coast, is the National West Coast (Tourist) Recreational Area. No permits are needed to drive through here and there are a few small towns and several campsites for fishing parties.

GETTING THERE It is even more vital here than in the rest of Namibia: you need a vehicle to see this part of the Skeleton Coast. Hitchhiking is not restricted, but with bitterly cold mornings and desiccating afternoons it won't be pleasant – heat exhaustion would be a real danger. A few tour companies in Swakopmund run excursions to Cape Cross, about 120km or 1½ hours' drive from Swakopmund (see page 302), which stop at one of the lichen fields, and some of the more obvious sites of interest on the way.

By far the best method is to drive yourself, equipped with plenty of water and a picnic lunch, and stop where and when you wish to explore. Set off north as early as possible, catching the southern sections of the road in the fog, and pre-book to stay at Terrace Bay for the night. The drive alone will take about five hours, though most people stop to explore and have refreshments, and so make a whole day of it.

Until the C35 turn-off, just north of Henties Bay, the main C34 is what is known locally as a salt road. Made of salt, gypsum and gravel compacted hard over the years, it has no loose surface, so is almost as solid and safe as tar. You can drive faster on this than you would on normal gravel, though it sometimes twists around and gets bumpy – so there's no leeway for a lack of concentration. Beyond the turn-off, the road reverts to the more normal gravel.

SWAKOPMUND TO HENTIES BAY

The sea ponds About 7km north of Swakopmund lie a number of large, shallow ponds. These are mostly natural ponds used for salt production by the Salt Company. Some are filled with seawater, which is then left to evaporate, whilst others are used for farming oysters. Sometimes you'll see one coloured bright red or green by algae, or pink by a flock of feeding flamingos!

Nobody lives here, but workers from Swakopmund manage the site. Both the salt and the oysters are sold within Namibia, and most restaurants in Swakopmund will offer you both.

Wlotzkasbaken This small settlement, about 31km north of Swakopmund, looks like a colony on the moon. Its houses spread out along the desert coast, each overshadowed by its own long-legged water tower (which rely on tankers driving the water from inland). It was named after Paul Wlotzke, a keen Swakopmund fisherman who first built a hut here, and guided visitors to this rich area for fishing.

Like the ghost towns near Lüderitz, nobody lives here permanently. Wlotzkasbaken is simply a collection of holiday homes, used mainly by those Namibians who love sea fishing and come here for their annual summer breaks around December and January.

East of here are a few apparently barren hills and boulders. Get out of the car to take a closer look, and you'll find many small plants and shrubs there. The Namib's fogs are densest (and so deliver the more moisture) at higher elevations, so even these relatively small hills catch much more water from the fog than the flat plains.

Amongst the boulders are also small land snails, beetles and small vertebrates. These include what is thought to be the world's only lizard that actually mimics an invertebrate for protection. The juveniles of the *Eremias lugubris* species have the same coloration and style of movement as a beetle known locally as the 'oogpister' – which protects itself like a skunk by expelling a foul-smelling liquid.

⚠ Where to stay Government-owned campsites are positioned regularly along this coastline, used mainly in the high season by families and those on fishing trips. Typically, pitches are spread along the beach at intervals of 100m or so, each with toilets and running water. Central ablution blocks are perfectly adequate, with showers at N$3 pp, and water available at N$0.5 per litre. You can expect these to be totally empty except for high summer, when plenty of Namibians and South Africans descend for the holidays. During Namibian school holidays, in December and January, there is usually also a basic shop – though this is hard to believe if you pass in the quiet season. Each campsite also has a freezer available for campers to freeze the day's catch. Bookings should be made in advance via the NWR in Windhoek (see page 124), but out of season it's possible just to turn up.

⚠ Mile 14 Campsite This is the first coastal campsite north of Swakopmund, & is particularly popular with families. It is massive, stretching some 3–4km along the beach, with sites marked by wooden pegs. *N$50 per site, up to 8 people, plus N$20/10 per extra adult/child; showers N$3; water (litre) N$0.50.*

⚠ Jakkalsputz Campsite This is about 9km south of Henties Bay, and similar to Mile 14 – small plots of desert beside the beach, with pitches marked off as campsites. *Rates as for Mile 14, above.*

HENTIES BAY About 76km from Swakopmund, this windswept town is set immediately above the shore and around one stream (normally just sandy) of the Omaruru River. A surge in property development in recent years reflects the town's popularity with Namibians, who flock here during their annual holidays in December and January to escape the interior's heat and to go fishing. Perhaps the pair who erected the town's gallows in 1978 – as an appeal to residents to keep the place clean – are winning the battle.

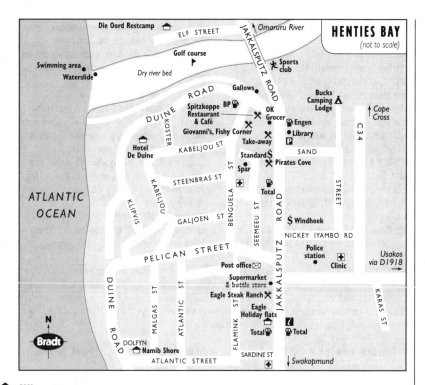

Die Oord Restcamp
ELF STREET
Omaruru River
HENTIES BAY
(not to scale)

JAKKALSPUTZ ROAD

Golf course
Sports club

Swimming area
Waterslide
Dry river bed

DUINE ROAD
Gallows
Bucks Camping Lodge
Cape Cross

KOSTER
Spitzkoppe Restaurant & Café
BP
OK Grocer
Engen
Library

Giovanni's, Fishy Corner
Take-away

KABELJOU ST

Hotel De Duine

Standard
Spar
Pirates Cove

SAND STREET

KABELJOU
STEENBRAS ST

ATLANTIC OCEAN

KLIPVIS
GALJOEN ST
BENGUELA ST
SEEMEEU ST
Total
JAKKALSPUTZ ROAD
Windhoek

NICKEY IYAMBO RD

PELICAN STREET
Police station
Clinic
Usakos via D1918

Post office
Supermarket & bottle store
Eagle Steak Ranch
Eagle Holiday flats

DUINE ROAD
MALGAS ST
ATLANTIC ST
FLAMINK ST
Total
Total

KARAS ST

N
Bradt
DOLFYN
Namib Shore
SARDINE ST
Swakopmund
ATLANTIC STREET

Where to stay

🏠 **Hotel De Duine** (20 rooms) 34 Duine Rd;
☎ 064 500001; f 064 500724; e deduine@
ncl.com.na; www.namibialodges.com. This reliable
hotel is owned by Namibia Country Lodges, & is
across the road from a steep beach & the ocean.
Its staff are friendly & helpful, & if you stay a
while will go out of their way to help you
organise fishing trips – especially if you don't
arrive in their busy season.

Rooms are comfortable, with direct-dial phones &
en-suite bathrooms. The restaurant is à la carte,
simple but good. Some claim that Henties Bay has
the world's best crayfish, so perhaps this is the place
to try them out. If you are just passing through &
want a break, you'll find b/fast served about
8.00–10.00, lunch 12.30–14.00 & dinner (N$120)
usually 19.00–21.00.
N$390/275 sgl/dbl pp sharing, B&B.

🏠 **Die Oord Restcamp** (15 chalets) PO Box 82, Rob
St, Henties Bay; ☎ 064 500239; f 064 500239. This
small, pleasant restcamp has fully equipped chalets
for 3–6 people. Don't expect luxury, but if you want
a place to sleep then this is fine.
*3-bed bungalow N$160, 5-bed N$240, 6-bed
N$300, all plus tax.*

🏠 **Eagle Holiday Flats** (2 chalets, 13 rooms) 175
Jakkalsputz Rd; ☎ 064 500032; f 064 500299;
e eaglesc@iafrica.com.na; www.eagleholiday.com. Basic
twin rooms & simple self-catering chalets, each with 2
bedrooms, are conveniently situated on the main road
alongside all other things 'Eagle': a bottle store,
restaurant & supermarket. Considered to be very good
value, its rooms have en-suite facilities; flats are clean,
cool & a little Spartan. The kitchens have microwaves,
toasters & even a second freezer specifically for fish.
Each has a TV, & bathroom with a shower.
Chalets N$120 pp, backpackers N$60 pp, plus tax.

🏠 **Byseewah Lodge** (9 rooms) Aus St; ☎ 064
501111; f 064 501177; e fishermanslodge@iway.na;
www.fishermanslodge.com.na. The bright yellow
building that is Byseewah (formerly Fisherman's)
Lodge lies just 200m from the beach. Public rooms &
3 of the bedrooms are accessible by wheelchair.
Popular with anglers, & with a strong nautical theme,
it has a large lounge, bar & restaurant area, with
meals available by arrangement. Dbl/twin rooms are
all en suite, with minibar, TV & phone; there's also
an attractive family room. Outside, a sheltered garden
overlooks the sea, & secure parking is available.
Deep-sea fishing, guided rock & surf angling, &

dolphin- & seal-viewing trips can all be organised, along with other shore-based activities.
N$285/400 pp sharing/sgl, inc b/fast; bed levy extra.

⌂ **Haus Estnic** (3 rooms) 1417 Omatako St; ☏ 064 500992; e hausestnic@yahoo.com; www.hentiesbay.com. This small, German-owned B&B offers well-appointed dbl rooms around a small courtyard with braai facilities. Each en-suite room has a fridge, hairdryer, kettle & cafetière. *N$200/300 sgl/dbl, B&B.*

⌂ **H&H Accommodation** (1 room, self-catering flat) 1616 Spitzkoppe St; ☏ 064 500908; e h+htrenckner@africaonline.com.na. *N$180 pp B&B; flat N$380 (max 3 people); all plus tax.*

⌂ **Namib Shore Guesthouse** (4 rooms) Dolfyn St; ☏/f 064 500182; m 081 127 5663, 081 293

9234; e namshore@iway.na; www.namshore.iway.na. This simple guesthouse has secure and quiet accommodation in dbl rooms, within walking distance of the beach. Also on offer are fishing trips from the shore, and desert tours. *N$200/380 sgl/dbl B&B. Lunchpack N$35.*

⌂ **Bucks Camping Lodge** (camping, 3 chalets) PO Box 519, Henties Bay; ☏/f 064 501039. Conveniently located for the town's shop, restaurants & pubs, as well as the golf course & tennis courts, this campsite with 24hr security offers 45 pitches, each with its own shower, toilet, washing-up facilities & power points. There are also 1-bedroom chalets, each sleeping 4 people. *Camping N$130/150 per pitch (max 4 people), extra person N$20/30, Feb–Nov/Dec–Jan; chalet N$95 pp, plus refundable N$100 key deposit.*

✕ **Where to eat** Close to the supermarket and petrol stations are a number of simple restaurants. It's also possible to get take-away pizzas at the Total garage. For really fresh fruit and vegetables, visit the Tulongeni Community Garden Project, which is set in a dry riverbed of the Omaruru; to get there, drive north through the town over the golf course, then turn immediately right.

✕ **Eagle Steak Ranch** ☏ 064 500574. Next door to Eagle supermarket, this is a good bet for grills, fish & seafood, with chef's specials at N$36. *Open 08.00–01.00.*

✕ **Pirates Cove** ☏ 064 500960. A sports bar serving steak & 'divine' pizza.

✕ **Spitzkoppe Pub & Restaurant** Behind the bank; ☏ 064 500394

✕ **Fishy Corner** By the Spar supermarket; ☏ 064 601059

☕ **Giovanni's Coffee Shop** ☏ 081 127 5663

Other practicalities Do fill up with fuel in Henties Bay if you're heading north or east. Fuel stations are rare in either direction, but there are several here, including one on the main road that slightly bypasses town, and two in the town itself.

Henties Bay has some reasonable supermarkets, a couple of bottle stores, and a few general shops. Some are centred on the Eagle Complex (location of the holiday flats), in the middle of town, but carry on up the road and bear left, and you'll come to a Spar supermarket, a couple of restaurants, and the fuel stations. There's also a bank, with ATM. Angling equipment is available in many places, including the Spar supermarket.

Should you need a doctor, there's the Benguela Health Centre in the Spar complex, which also has a pharmacy (☏ 064 500599).

Tour operators
Rock & Surf Angling m 081 240 3219
Henties Angling Tours m 081 251 1489

West & Skeleton Coast Angling Tours ☏ 064 500066; e anglingc@het.namib.com

What to see and do Though most visitors will simply refuel here before leaving as quickly as they arrived, the truly excellent **tourist information office** based at the Total fuel station (☏ 064 501143; e info@hentiesbay.com; www.hentiesbay.com; open Mon–Fri 08.00–13.00, 14.00–17.00) is doing its utmost to persuade them otherwise. There are plenty of helpful leaflets and maps here, and staff who really know the area well.

If you'd like to join the locals **fishing**, you'll need a permit (N$14 per month) from one of the tour operators such as West & Skeleton Coast (see above). Sought-after fish include galjeon (blackfish), kabeljou (carp), steenbras and stompneus, as well as the now-scarce dassie, or – when the waters are very warm – shad.

While keen fishermen delight in the pronunciation of their catches, ardent **golfers** can have a game at the Henties Bay Golf Course (*064 500393*). This resides in a section of the original Omaruru Delta, just near to De Duine Hotel, and doesn't suffer from a shortage of sandy bunkers. If you're more into racquet sports, there's **tennis** (*064 500168*) for N$10 per person per day, or **squash** courts at the De Duine Hotel.

Non-fishing visitors might also like to take a short wander up the Omaruru's course (see below), while fit, acclimatised hikers can choose from two circular but unmarked **hiking trails** taking in some of the desert scenery around the town. The 20km Omaruru River Walking Trail takes you north along the coast, then inland along the riverbed, returning to the centre of town; the Jakkalsputz Walking Trail is slightly shorter at 18km, and runs south along the coast to Jakkalsputz Campsite, returning on a parallel track just inland.

The tourist board also has route maps with GPS co-ordinates for a series of **4x4 trails** from the town, costing N$25 each, including a short route description. The routes vary in length from 246km to 312km, and take in some of the region's most spectacular scenery, including the Maruru and Ugab rivers, and Messum Crater. Rather nearer to Henties Bay, about 30km along the C35 to Uis, the **Omdel Dam** on the Omaruru River attracts numerous bird species when it's holding water, and makes a good picnic spot.

NORTH FROM HENTIES BAY Two roads break away from the main coastal road near Henties Bay. The D1918 heads almost due east for about 121km, passing within 30km of Spitzkoppe (see page 329) before joining the main tarred B2 about 23km west of Usakos. The more popular C35 heads northeast across an amazingly flat, barren plain: certainly one of the country's most desolate roads. This is the way to Uis Mine, Khorixas, and southern Damaraland, unless you are planning to stop for the night somewhere like Terrace Bay.

Ignoring both these right turns, and continuing northwest along the C35 coast road, you soon reach…

⚑ Mile 72 Campsite Book via the NWR in Windhoek; see page 124. Yet another desolate row of ablution blocks — unless you're here in the summer. For general details, see page 310. N$50 per site, for up to 8 people, plus N$20/10 per extra adult/child; shower N$3; water (litre) N$0.50.

The Omaruru River Driving north past Henties Bay, note all the vegetated depressions (indicating watercourses) that you pass through, spread out along 10–15km around the town. These are all part of the Omaruru River Delta. Because of the high rainfall in its catchment area, in the mountains around Omaruru, this flows regularly and the sandy riverbed usually supports quite a luxurious growth of vegetation.

The vegetation includes a variety of desert flora, native to the Namib's many riverbeds, as well as some exotics like wild tobacco (*Nicotiana glauca*), jimson weed (*Datura stramonium*) and the castor oil plant (*Ricinus communis*). These are found from here northwards, in many of the other river valleys also; Dr Mary Seely, in her excellent book *The Namib* (see *Appendix 3*), suggests that the seeds for the first such plants might have been imported with fodder for horses during the South African War. As they are hardy plants, eaten by few animals, they have been very successful.

Gemstones With so little precipitation, even unobservant visitors notice that the basic geology of the Namib often lies right on its surface, just waiting to be discovered. Don't miss the chance to stop somewhere on the C34 or C35 around here. Wander a few hundred metres from it, and do some gem hunting. Even if you're not an expert, you will find some beautiful crystals.

It was while staying at Mile 72 in 1972 that a Namibian mineralogist, Sid Peters (owner of the House of Gems in Windhoek, see pages 147–8), went hunting for minerals. He found several aquamarines and then a long light-blue crystal that he couldn't identify. Eventually the Smithsonian Institute in Washington DC confirmed that this was jeremejebite, a very rare, hard mineral containing boron, first discovered in its white form over 80 years ago in Siberia.

CAPE CROSS SEAL RESERVE (*Open daily 10.00–1700. Admission N$20 per adult, N$2 per child, plus N$20 per car; no motorcycles*) Here, in 1485, the Portuguese captain and navigator Diego Cão landed. He was the first European of his time to reach this far south down the coast of Africa, and to mark the achievement he erected a stone cross on the bleak headland, inscribed in Latin and Portuguese with:

> Since the creation of the world 6684 years have passed and since the birth of Christ 1484 years and so the illustrious Don John has ordered this pillar to be erected here by Diego Cão, his knight.

Diego Cão died for his daring, and was buried on a rock outcrop nearby, which they called Serra Parda. His cross remained in place until the 1890s, when it was taken to the Oceanographical Museum in Berlin, and in 1974 the whole area was landscaped and a replica cross erected, which stands there today.

David Coulson, in his book *Namib* (see *Appendix 3*), relates that an old slate was found half-buried in the sand around here, with a message dated 1860 reading:

> I am proceeding to a river sixty miles north, and should anyone find this and follow me, God will help him.

It is not known who wrote the message, or what became of them.

All along the Namibian coast there are seal colonies, though the one at Cape Cross is one of the easiest to access. It is a colony of the Cape fur seal, *Arctocephalus pusillus pusillus*, numbers up to 100,000 animals, and is occupied all year round.

At any time of year, the amazing sight of tens of thousands of heads bobbing on land and in the water is matched only by the overpowering stench of the colony that greets you. The noise, too, is unexpected – a positive cacophony of sound that resembles an entire farmyard of animals at full volume.

Where to stay

🏠 **Cape Cross Lodge** (20 rooms) ☎ 064 694012; f 064 694013; e info@capecross.org; e bookings@capecross.com; www.capecross.org. Opened in 2001, just 4km from the seal colony, this lodge is a beacon for visitors to this area, with accommodation that puts Cape Cross firmly on the map. This is where the desert meets the sea, & the large, airy rooms of this well-appointed lodge reflect the vast open spaces all around.

En-suite rooms are modern & spacious, with 8 rooms at the front having panoramic views out to sea from individual balconies. Other rooms are behind the main lodge, but still have a sea view from their verandas. There is a real sense of taste here, with solid, limed-wood furniture, stone floors & soft blue-&-white décor that complement the nautical setting. Two of the rooms are linked by an adjoining door, making a family suite possible.

Downstairs is a huge lounge & dining area with a central BBQ & a bar at one end. The restaurant is open to day visitors as well as residents, with both snacks & main meals available. In the evenings,

In mid- to late October the large males, or bulls, arrive, their massive body weight of around 360kg far exceeding that of the 75kg females. They stake their territorial claims and try to defend them from other males. Shortly afterwards, in late November or early December, each of the pregnant females gives birth to a single pup. These will remain in and around the colony, and continue suckling for the next ten or eleven months.

Shortly after giving birth, the females mate with the males who control their harems, and the cycle continues, with the pups born about a year later. When the females have all given birth, and mated, most of the males will leave to break their fast and replenish the enormous amounts of body fat burned while defending their territories. In the last few months of the year, the scene can be quite disturbing, with many pups squashed by the weighty adults, or killed by the area's resident populations of jackal and brown hyena.

though, the place is open only to residents, with occasional candlelit dinners on the beach, & a good selection of wines on offer. There is also a rather quirky wine cellar & a cosy dining area if you're seeking more privacy. Lunch for residents is N$85 pp, & should be pre-booked.

Aside from the seal colony itself, visitors here are attracted by the sheer beauty of the setting. Just to sit on the outside terrace & watch baby seals cavorting in the waves can occupy half the afternoon, though for the more energetic there are plenty of walks & opportunities for birdwatching. There are as yet no formal facilities for watersports, so those planning to kayak, or to discover 'some of the best surfing in Namibia', should bring their own equipment & discuss plans with the staff, some of whom are enthusiasts themselves. A word of warning: don't even think of swimming without taking local advice; the water is cold, currents are very strong & riptides can be extremely dangerous. Traditionally, fishing has been the main attraction for visitors to the area; advance notice is required for fishing trips, which cost N$1,000 pp (min 2 people). Tours can also be arranged to visit the Messum Crater (about N$600 pp, min 3 people, 5 hrs), taking in Cape Cross, the lichen fields & other local attractions. Shorter excursions are on offer to Cape Cross Seal Reserve.

Seafront balcony N$850/650 sgl/pp sharing, courtyard sea view N$750/650 sgl/pp sharing, DBB.

Å Mile 108 Book via the NWR in Windhoek; see page 124. Could this be even more desolate than Mile 72? Again, in season Mile 108 has a useful fuel station & a small kiosk. For general details, see page 310. *N$50 per site, for up to 8 people, plus N$20/10 per extra adult/child; shower N$3; water (litre) N$0.50.*

WRECK OF THE *WINSTON* Just before the entrance to the Skeleton Coast Park is a signpost west to the first of the coast's wrecks: the *Winston*, a fishing boat that grounded here in 1970.

Note Beware of driving on the saltpans here (or anywhere else on this coast), as they can be very treacherous.

SKELETON COAST PARK

Entrance N$80 per adult (under 16 free), plus N$10 per car

From the Ugab to the Kunene, the Skeleton Coast Park and Wilderness Areas protect about one-third of the country's coastline. The southern half of this, the Skeleton Coast Park, is easily accessible to anyone with a car and some forward planning. It's a fascinating area and, surprisingly, is often omitted from scheduled tours and safaris. This is a shame, though it does mean that from July to September – when some of the rest of the country is busy with overseas visitors – this is still a blissfully quiet area.

GETTING THERE Because the climate here is harsh, and the area quite remote, the Ministry of Environment and Tourism have fairly strict regulations about entry permits – which must be followed.

If you are just passing through, then you can buy your entry permit at either gate: the Ugab River gate on the C34, or the Springbokwasser gate on the D3245. You *must* reach your gate of entry before 15.00 to be allowed into the park – otherwise you will simply be turned away.

If you plan to stay at either Torra or Terrace Bay, then you must have a booking confirmation slip, issued by the main NWR office in Windhoek (see page 124). You cannot just turn up at the gate, or one of the camps, to see if they have any space. You *must* pre-book these camps in Windhoek. In that case, if you arrive from Swakopmund along the C34, you must pass the Ugab River no later than 15.00. Similarly, if coming from Damaraland, on the D3245, you must pass the Springbokwasser gate by 17.00.

In the Skeleton Coast Park, the road is mostly just normal gravel, so keep your speed below 80km/h to be safe.

THE UGAB RIVER Its catchment area stretches as far as Otavi, so the Ugab is a long and important river for the Namib. It flows at least once most years, and you drive across its bed just after the gate into the park. Although much of the visible vegetation is the exotic wild tobacco, *Nicotiana glauca*, there are still some stunted acacia trees and other indigenous plants, like the nara bushes, *Acanthosicyos horridus*, with their (almost leafless) spiky green stems, and improbably large melons.

Shortly after passing the Ugab, look east to see the view becoming more majestic, as the escarpment looms into view above the mirages, which play on the gravel plains. Near the mouth of the Ugab is the wreck of the *Girdleness*, though it is difficult to see.

Ugab River hiking trails For keen, self-sufficient hikers there is a two-night, three-day hiking trail, guided by one of the Nature Conservation rangers, which explores the Ugab River in much more depth. Trails run throughout the cooler months, from April to October, starting on the second and fourth Tuesdays of each month, and ending on the Thursday afternoon. Most people camp at Mile 108 (see above) for the previous night.

The trail covers a total of about 50km, reaching as far inland as the foothills of the escarpment where there are some natural springs. Groups are limited to between six and eight people, and the guiding costs N$200 per person. You need to bring a sturdy rucksack with all your own camping equipment and food, and make a booking for the trail with the Nature Conservation office in Windhoek as far in advance as possible (ideally 18 months or so). Then all the participants will need a medical certificate of fitness issued a maximum of 40 days before the hike commences. Having gone to all this trouble, you won't regret it – participants confirm that it is fascinating.

WRECK OF THE *SOUTH WEST SEA* Near the road, just north of the Ugab River, this is clearly signposted and very easy to visit. It is one of the coast's most convenient wrecks (for the visitors, not the sailors), so if you're looking for a picnic stop, it is ideal. The ship itself was a small vessel that ran aground in 1976.

Imagining the Skeleton Coast, most people think that it's littered with dozens of picturesque wrecks – but that's really no longer the case. Shipwrecks do gradually disintegrate. They're pounded by the waves, corroded by the salt water, and eventually what's left of them washes out to sea or vanishes into the sands. Further, modern navigation techniques, using accurate charts and most recently GPS receivers, have greatly reduced the accident rate on this coast. Thus whilst a few decades ago the coast probably was littered with wrecks, now they're few and far between – so take advantage to wander down to this one while you can!

THE HUAB RIVER North of the Ugab, the next river crossed is the important Huab River. This rises in the escarpment around Kamanjab, and is one of the coast's most important corridors for desert-adapted elephants and rhinos – though you're most unlikely to see either so far from the mountains.

Immediately north of the river, if you look to the east of the road, you can see the beginnings of barchan dunes standing on the gravel plains. Here sand is blowing out of the bed of the Huab, and actually forming a dune-field (see page 35 for the origins of barchan dunes).

It's much easier to spot the rusting hulk of an old oil rig, c1960, with a turn-off to a small parking area adjacent. This was originally part of a grand scheme to extract oil from the coast, organised by Ben du Preez, which ran up huge debts before his banks foreclosed. Amy Schoeman's superb coffee-table book, *The Skeleton Coast* (see *Appendix 3*), relates this story in detail. As a postscript, she notes that some of Terrace Bay was originally built by du Preez as his base.

Now the old framework provides a perfect breeding spot for Cape cormorants, so be careful not to disturb the birds by getting out of your car between around September and March.

TOSCANINI For such a significant dot on the map, this minute outpost will seem a great disappointment, especially if you miss it! Despite sounding like another campsite, it is in fact the site of a disused old diamond mine. More rusting hulks and decaying buildings.

Elsewhere this kind of dereliction would be bulldozed, landscaped and erased in the name of conserving the scenery, but here it's preserved for posterity, and the visiting seabirds.

THE KOICHAB RIVER Squeezed between the larger Huab and Uniab rivers, the Koichab (not to be confused with the Koichab Pan near Lüderitz) has quite a small catchment area and floods relatively rarely. Thus it seems more of a depression than a major riverbed. For fishing visitors, the Koichab is the southern boundary of the Torra Bay fishing area.

Meanwhile south of this river, but north of Toscanini, you do pass the wrecks of the *Atlantic Pride*, the *Luanda* (1969) and the *Montrose* (1973), though they're not easy to spot, and often the road is far enough from the sea for what's left of these wrecks to be obscured.

Jonathan Hughes

Many of the Namib's species can only survive at all if they either escape or retreat from the extremes. An 'escape' is an extended period of absence from the desert community, such as a suspension of the life cycle, aestivation (the desert equivalent of hibernation) or by actually migrating out of the desert.

Many of the Namib's plants stop their life cycle for particularly harsh periods, leaving behind dormant seeds able to withstand temperatures of up to 100°C and remain viable for years. Growth is eventually triggered by a threshold amount of rainfall, leading to the phenomenon of the 'desert bloom', where a carpet of flowers covers the ground. These plants, called ephemerals, must then complete their life cycles in a matter of days before the water disappears. A blooming desert obviously requires its pollinators, so various insect species also conduct ephemeral life cycles, switching them on and off as rainfall dictates.

On the great plains of the Namib, a different community waits for rain in any slight depression. When it arrives, and the depression fills, an explosion of activity occurs and pond life comes to the desert. Algae, shrimps and tadpoles fill the ponds for their short lives, employing rapid development techniques to swiftly mature to adulthood.

Large-scale migrations are not common in the Namib, but springbok do trek between arid regions, following any rain, and the Namib's largest mammal, the gemsbok, also moves in a predictable pattern. They move into the Namib's dune-sea after rainfall, looking for the ephemeral grasses. When these vanish, they travel to the dry Kuiseb River bed to compete with the resident baboons for acacia pods and water. Here they excavate waterholes, which they maintain from year to year.

TORRA BAY Shortly before Torra Bay, the D3245 splits off from the main coastal C34 and heads east, leaving the park (39km later) at the Springbokwasser gate and proceeding into Damaraland. This beautiful road passes the distinctive Sugar Loaf Hill on the right and some large welwitschia colonies, which spread either side of the road, before gradually climbing into the foothills of the Kaokoveld. Watch the vegetation change quite quickly on this route, as the road passes through ecosystems that are increasingly less arid, before finally entering Damaraland's distinctive mountains dominated by huge *Euphorbia damarana* bushes.

Just north of this C34/D3245 junction is a section of road standing in the path of barchan dunes that march *across* it. Stop here to take a close look at how these dunes gradually move, grain by grain, in the prevailing southwest wind. Then turn your attention to the build-up of detritus on the leeward side of the dunes, and you may be lucky enough to spot some of the area's residents. Look carefully for the famous white beetles, *Onymacris bicolor*, which are endemic to the area and have been the subject of much study. White beetles are very uncommon, and here it is thought they have evolved their colouration to keep cool, enabling them to forage for longer in the heat.

Many of the plants on this gravel plain around the barchan dunes build up their own small sand-dunes. The dollar bushes, *Zygophyllum stapffii*, with their succulent dollar-shaped leaves, and the coastal ganna, *Salsola aphylla*, are obvious examples. Big enough to act as small windbreaks, these bushes tend to collect windblown sand. These small mounds of sand, being raised a little off the desert's floor, tend to have more fog condense on them than the surrounding ground. Thus the plant gets a little more moisture. You will normally see a few beetles also, which survive on the detritus that collects, and add their own faeces to fertilise the plant.

Just inland from Torra Bay is a fascinating area of grey-white rocks, sculpted into interesting curves by the wind and the sand-grains.

Where to stay

Torra Bay Campsite Book via the NWR in Windhoek (see page 124). The campsite at Torra Bay will be another disappointment unless you arrive in December or January, when this coastal site opens for the summer. It has 10 ablution blocks, a shop & a filling station. The small, square pitches are marked out by rows of stone. Expect a plethora of fishing parties, & a charge for taking a shower or buying water.
N$50 per site, up to 8 people; N$20 per extra adult/child. Open 1 Dec–31 Jan only.

THE UNIAB RIVER Perhaps the most accessible river for the passing visitor is the Uniab River Valley, between Torra Bay and Terrace Bay. If you stop in only one river for a good look around, stop here in the Uniab. Not only is it quite scenic, but its headwaters come from around the huge Palmwag concession, home to many of the region's larger mammals. So the Uniab offers your best chance of spotting the park's scarce bigger game.

In ancient times, the river formed a wide delta by the sea, but that has been raised up, and cut into by about five different channels of water. When the river floods now, the water comes down the fourth channel reached from the south, though the old channels still support much vegetation.

At one point while crossing the delta, there's a sign to a waterfall about 1.5km west of the road. Here a gentle trickle of water (supplemented by an occasional rainy-season torrent) has eroded a narrow canyon into the sandstone and calcrete layers of the riverbed, before trickling to the sea. If you go down as far as the beach, then look out for the wreck of the *Atlantic*, which grounded here in 1977.

All throughout this delta you'll find dense thickets of reeds and sedges and small streams flowing over the ground towards the sea. Sometimes these will attract large numbers of birds – plovers, turnstones and various sandpipers are very common. Palaearctic migrants make up the bulk of the species.

As well as the waterfall walk, there's a shorter walk to a small hide overlooking an open stretch of water that attracts birds. Keep quiet while you are walking and you should also manage to spot at least some springbok, gemsbok and jackal, which are all common here.

Elephant, lion and cheetah have also been spotted here, but very rarely. Slightly elusive are the brown hyena, whose presence can be confirmed by the existence of their distinctive white droppings (coloured white, as they will crunch and eat bones). Their local name, *strandwolf*, is an indication that they are often to be seen scavenging on the beaches for carrion (especially near seal colonies). Whilst these animals look fearsome with powerful forequarters and a thick, shaggy coat, they are solitary scavengers posing no danger to walkers unless cornered or deliberately harassed.

TERRACE BAY Terrace Bay makes an excellent short stop between Swakopmund and Damaraland, and offers the opportunity for you to get to know the desert better.

Where to stay

Terrace Bay Campsite (bungalows) Book via the NWR in Windhoek (see page 124). About 287km from Henties Bay, the restcamp at Terrace Bay is the furthest north that visitors can drive on the coast. It's a real outpost, appearing just a few kilometres after a sign points off to Dekka Bay. It was built originally for a mining venture, & inherited by the government when that failed. Now there's nothing here apart from the small camp for visitors, run by the NWR, & its staff accommodation. I

Jonathan Hughes

A 'retreat' is a short term escape, typically a matter of hours. This has a serious disadvantage: it results in what ecologists call a 'time crunch', where time for foraging and social activity is greatly reduced. It follows that retreating animals must be very efficient at foraging.

Most species retreat to some extent. The Namib's beetles, reptiles, birds and mammals disappear into burrows and nests during the hottest periods of the day. One of the most visible is the social weaver bird, which builds enormous communal nests which insulate the birds during cold nights, and provide a handy retreat during the heat of the day.

In order to extend the time spent on the surface, and minimise this time crunch, one Namib resident, the sand-diving lizard, has developed the remarkable behaviour of 'dancing' on the surface. By lifting its legs at intervals, (never all at once!), it manages to reduce its body temperature and stay out for a few extra minutes of activity.

Although some form of escape or retreat is practical for most animal species, plants do not have the same luxury. They cannot move quickly and therefore have to become tolerant.

---

normally recommend visitors who don't fish to stay here for no longer than one night.

Fishermen come here all year, & even the ex-president, Sam Nujoma, often took his holidays here. His phalanx of bodyguards used to make fun company for the unsuspecting visitors he met there, though in later years it seems he booked the whole place for himself & his entourage.

Terrace Bay's facilities are mostly old & basic, but all the bungalows have a fridge, a shower & a toilet. Bedding & towels are provided. Though not luxurious, the accommodation is adequate & Terrace Bay feels so isolated & remote that it can be a lot of fun for a day or two.

All your meals are provided while staying here, but there is also a small food shop by the office stocking alcohol, basic frozen braai meats & a few basic supplies, & a vital fuel station/garage. Before you dine, take a look at the big shed behind the

office. On it you'll see (& smell) hundreds of cormorants which roost there every night – attracted by the warmth from the generator within. Check with the staff, but it may also be worth returning around 22.00 as a brown hyena is said to often stroll by then, looking for hapless cormorants that have fallen from the roof. Check also by the waterfront, where the day's catch is gutted.

If your time allows, one of the staff members might be persuaded to take you fishing. A typical trip would take from 14.00 to 17.00. Note that because the staff at Terrace Bay are government employees, they are forbidden from charging for such fishing expeditions, but do appreciate a reasonable 'tip' for their time and help.

Basic 2-bed bungalows N$800/N$1,200 sgl/dbl,DBB, inc use of freezer space; presidential suite (sleeps 8) N$3,000 – complete with TV and hi-fi!

MÖWE BAY Around 80km north of Terrace Bay, this is the administrative centre of the Wilderness Area, and is not open to visitors. This acts as a base for the few researchers who are allowed to work here.

SKELETON COAST WILDERNESS AREA

To understand the current situation in the Wilderness Area, you need to know the recent history of the park, as well as some politics.

HISTORY The Skeleton Coast Park was initially part of the Etosha National Park, proclaimed in 1906. Then in 1967, South Africa's Odendal Commission cut it down to 25% of its original size, making in the process several 'homelands' for the existing communities. Included amongst these were parts of what is now known as Damaraland and Kaokoland, and also the Skeleton Coast.

During the late 1950s and '60s permission was granted to private companies, including one called Sarusas Mining Corporation, for mining and fishing rights on the Skeleton Coast. During the late 1960s, they assembled a project team to build a brand-new harbour at Cape Frio. They did all the research and got backing from investors, but at the last moment the South African government pulled the plug on the project. After all, a new Namibian port would reduce the stranglehold that Walvis Bay had on the country – and that had historically belonged to South Africa even before it took over the administration of German South West Africa (Namibia).

The Sarusas Mining Corporation were not happy and took the case to court. Instrumental in this was the young lawyer on their team, Louw Schoemann. As part of the out-of-court settlement, the South African government agreed to allow the area to be re-proclaimed as a national park – and hence the Skeleton Coast was proclaimed as a park in 1971.

However, during the course of all this research, Louw had fallen in love with the amazing scenery and solitude of the area. He had already started to bring friends up to the area for short exploratory safaris. As word spread of these trips, he started taking paying passengers there as well.

In order to preserve part of the area in totally pristine condition, the northern part was designated as a 'wilderness area' – to be conserved and remain largely untouched. Strictly controlled rights to bring tourists into one part of this area were given to just one operator. Rules were laid down to minimise the operator's impact, including a complete ban on any permanent structures, a maximum number of visitors per year, and the stipulation that *all* rubbish must be removed (no easy task) and that visitors must be flown in.

Louw won the tender for this concession, giving him the sole right to operate in one section of the wilderness area. So he started to put his new company, Skeleton Coast Fly-in Safaris, on a more commercial footing. The logistics of such a remote operation were difficult and it remained a small and very exclusive operation. Its camps took a maximum of 12 visitors, with much of the travel by light aircraft. The whole operation was 'minimum impact' by any standard. Louw was one of the first operators to support the pioneering Community Game Guard schemes in Namibia (see page 44), and he maintained a very ecologically sensitive approach long before it was fashionable.

I travelled to the coast with Louw in 1990. It was spellbinding; one of the most fascinating four days that I've spent anywhere. Partly this was the area's magic, but much was down to the enthusiasm of Louw, and the sheer professionalism of his operation.

Gradually, Skeleton Coast Fly-in Safaris had become a textbook example of an environmentally friendly operation, as well as one of the best safari operations in Africa. Louw's wife, Amy, added to this with the stunning photographs in her book, *The Skeleton Coast*. The latest edition of this (see *Appendix 3*) is still the definitive work on the area. His sons, André and Bertus, joined as pilot/guides, making it a family operation. In many ways, Louw's operation put the area, and even the country, on the map as a top-class destination for visitors. Fly-in safaris to the Skeleton Coast had become one of Africa's ultimate trips – and largely due to Louw's passion for the area.

POLITICS SINCE 1992 In 1992, the new government put the concession for the Skeleton Coast Wilderness Area up for tender, to maximise its revenue from the area. No local operator in Namibia bid against Louw; it was clear that he was operating an excellent, efficient safari operation in a very difficult area – and such was the operation's reputation, no local company would even try to bid against them. However, a competing bid was entered by a German company, Olympia Reisen, which has extensive political connections in Namibia and Germany. They offered significantly more money, and won the concession.

Local operators were uniformly aghast, and Louw, somewhat inevitably given his legal background, started legal proceedings to challenge the bid. Tragically, the stress of the situation took its toll and he died of a heart attack before the case was heard. Although his challenge succeeded, the decision was overturned by the cabinet, and Olympia Reisen was awarded the concession for an unprecedented ten years.

The monthly 'rent' for the concession that Skeleton Coast Safaris used to pay was abolished. In its place, Olympia Reisen paid the government N$1,000 for every visitor taken into the concession. However, with no 'rent' and no minimum number of visitors, the government's income from the area dropped drastically. By the mid 1990s it was becoming clear that Olympia Reisen was never going to make a commercial success of safaris to the area. Finally, in 1999, Wilderness Safaris – a major player in southern Africa with a good reputation for sensitive development and responsible operations – made a deal with Olympia Reisen to take control of tourism in the area. They ripped down the poor structures that Olympia Reisen had erected, removed from the area truckloads of accumulated rubbish, and set about a series of ecological impact assessments prior to opening a totally new Skeleton Coast Camp in April 2000. They also took control of all the ecological monitoring in the area, ultimately providing a base for a number of wildlife researchers who now have projects in the area. When the tender came up for review in 2003, Wilderness retained the concession.

Meanwhile, after losing the rights to use the Skeleton Coast Wilderness area in 1992, the Schoeman family continued to operate their own fly-in safaris. They did this using remote areas of the Skeleton Coast just south of the wilderness area, and parts of the western Kaokoveld and Damaraland just east of the park's boundary. Although these are slightly different areas of the coast and its hinterland, their style and guiding skills remained as strong as ever – and their trips remained superb. On several occasions I've spoken with travellers whom I've sent on these trips who have been full of praise and described them as 'life-changing experiences'.

FLY-IN SAFARIS: THE TWO OPTIONS Thus the visitor looking to see this remarkable area has two choices. Both are fairly costly and packed full of activities, but they're very different in style. Both rank amongst the best trips on the subcontinent.

The only caveat to this eulogy is that whilst this region appears harsh and 'in your face', it actually offers some of Africa's most subtle attractions. Endless savanna covered with wildebeest is enthralling; gravel plains dotted with *Welwitschia* may seem less so. Most appreciate leopards, but the lichens' appeal is less obvious. Hence in some ways both of these trips are better suited to visitors who have been on safari to Africa before. Often it seems that the trips are praised most highly by the most experienced safari-goers. Much of the credit here is due to the calibre of the guides: the area's subtle attractions require top guiding skills to bring them to life – and both operations have this.

Skeleton Coast Fly-in Safaris *(PO Box 2195, Windhoek;* ✆ *061 224248;* f *061 225713;* e *info@skeletoncoastsafaris.com; www.skeletoncoastsafaris.com)* Visitors imagine that the original fly-in safaris to the Skeleton Coast went only into the narrow concession area, by the ocean's edge. But they are wrong. Even in 1990, when I first visited with Louw Schoeman, we spent much time outside the concession – in the adjacent Kaokoveld, for example, and visiting Purros and the Kunene – as well as time in it. Thus although being excluded from the concession in 1992 was a blow, they were able to adapt their trips to use similar, adjacent areas and offer trips which were just as good, if not better, than the original ones. The flying and guiding ability of the Schoemans is such that they could organise a fly-in safari to an industrial wasteland … and end up making it one of the most fascinating places you've ever been.

Skeleton Coast Safaris use light aircraft (typically six-seater Cessnas) like most safaris use Land Rovers; exploring areas from the sky, flying low-level over dune-fields, and periodically turning back for better views. So there's a lot of flying in small aircraft – generally short 30–40-minute hops which most people find fascinating. Currently they concentrate on four main trips, Safaris A, B, C and D respectively, though these are really just variations around the main theme of their most popular trip.

Trips operate all year, and normally require a minimum of two people to confirm a safari on any given date. As with most upmarket options in Africa, you

14

SURVIVING IN THE NAMIB: ANIMAL ADAPTATIONS

Jonathan Hughes

Water, the ultimate limitation of the desert, is of key importance to the Namib's animals. Without exception, all of the animal species here tolerate extreme levels of desiccation, and some employ interesting techniques. The male namaqua sandgrouse travels miles to find water each day. When successful, he paddles in it, allowing his breast feathers to absorb water like a sponge. Laden with this cargo he travels back to the nest to feed the thirsty young and his partner. Springboks and gemsbok have kidneys that are so efficient at absorbing water that a pellet form of urine is produced.

The African ground squirrel faces away from the sun at all times, and uses its tail as a parasol while it forages. Perhaps most peculiar to the Namib are the dune beetles, which inhabit the crests of the desert's taller sand-dunes. They are early risers when there is fog about, and sit motionless for hours in order to allow it to condense on their bodies. Periodically they perform a spectacular dance to move the precious water along their bodies and into their mouths.

should find it slightly cheaper to book this through an overseas tour operator who specialises in the region.

Safari A (*4 days/3 nights; US$3,995 pp, inc all meals, drinks & activities*) This starts at 10.00 at Eros Airport in Windhoek, before flying west over the escarpment to Conception Bay, south of Sandwich Harbour, and north to refuel at Swakopmund. It stops again at Cape Cross, for lunch and a visit to the seal colony, before flying north and inland to the first of their three main camps, **Kuidas Camp**. This is in the Huab River Valley, west of Damaraland Camp and east of the park's boundary. It's positioned in a dry, rocky landscape that's typical of western Damaraland, and there are some rock engravings within walking distance of the camp. Like all these camps, Kuidas has small but comfortable igloo tents containing twin beds separated by a bedside table, an en-suite bucket shower, and a chemical loo (so you don't need to go outside of your tent to use the toilet at night). There's also one main flush toilet in the camp. Kuidas Camp is the base for the next morning's exploration of the Huab River Valley and huge gravel plains dotted with *Welwitschia mirabilis*.

After lunch you'll hop to Terrace Bay for a short Land Rover trip to explore the beach and nearby roaring dunes (one of the highlights of the trip for me; totally surreal), before flying out to **Purros Camp**, in the heart of the Kaokoveld near the Himba community at Purros (see page 356). Camp is under a broken canopy of camelthorns (*Acacia erioloba*) and makalani palms (*Hyphaene petersiana*), near the (invariably dry) Hoarusib River. From here the early morning is spent exploring the river valley, which has a thriving population of desert-adapted elephants, amongst other game, and visiting some of the local Himba people.

Continuing up the coast there are the remains of the Kaiu Maru shipwreck to be seen before the northwestern corner of Namibia is reached: the mouth of the Kunene River. Further inland, east of the dunes (which cover most of the park in this northern area), you'll land at the north end of Hartmann's Valley. The afternoon is spent exploring this beautiful and very remote area, before finally reaching the last camp, **Kunene Camp**, which overlooks the river at the north end of Hartmann's Valley (see page 357). The last morning of the trip is usually spent on a boat trip on the Kunene, before lunch and a long scenic flight to arrive back at Eros Airport, in Windhoek, in the late afternoon.

Safari B (*4 days/3 nights; US$4,275 pp, inc all meals, drinks & activities*) This starts earlier, and includes a stop at Sesriem, a drive into Sossusvlei, and a scenic flight over the vlei before flying on to Conception Bay, and continuing with the normal plan for Safari A.

Safari C (*4 days/4 nights; US$4,695 pp, inc all meals, drinks & activities*) Starts off like Safari B, but then after Kunene Camp includes a final night beside Etosha National Park, at one of the lodges on the eastern side, and time spent exploring the park by private 4x4.

Safari D (*6 days/5 nights; US$5,935 pp, inc all meals, drinks & activities*) Starts off at 07.00, with a flight to Sesriem and a trip into Sossusvlei, before flying on to Wolwedans Dune Lodge (see pages 242–3), your base for two nights. An afternoon exploring the NamibRand Reserve is followed the next day by a flying day trip south, to Lüderitz, for a 4x4 excursion into the Sperrgebiet, ending up at Elizabeth Bay (see page 232). This has big advantages over doing the same excursion on your own from Lüderitz, as you'll have one of Skeleton Coast's excellent guides with you, who will bring this amazing area to life. After your second night at Wolwedans, this trip continues as Safari A.

Wilderness Safaris: Skeleton Coast Camp (*PO Box 6850, Windhoek;* ↘ *061 274500;* f *061 239455; www.wilderness-safaris.com*) With just 12 beds, the Skeleton Coast Camp is one of the flagships of Wilderness Safaris in the subcontinent. Note that they normally prefer travellers to make arrangements through a good overseas tour operator (see pages 52–4) in their own country, rather than directly with them in Namibia.

Trips Trips lasting four nights and five days usually start on a Saturday morning from Eros Airport, and return on Wednesday afternoon. Flights up to the camp, and back, are usually in a comfortable twin-engine 13-seater 'caravan' (a type that's increasingly common in southern Africa). From July to November, these trips cost US$4,525/5,175 per person sharing/single, and include all meals, drinks and activities; the rest of the year, they are between US$3,675/4,325 pp sharing/single and US$4,045/4,695 pp sharing/single. A shorter trip, lasting three nights and four days, usually starts on a Wednesday morning and costs US$4,015/4,535 pp sharing/single in high season, and between US$3,480/4,000 pp sharing/single during the rest of the year. Opt for the longer trip if funds allow – you'll still leave feeling that you've only scratched the surface – or consider combining a trip here with Serra Cafema Camp (see pages 356–7), on the northern edge of Hartmann's Valley, northeast of the Skeleton Coast Camp.

🛖 **Skeleton Coast Camp (6 tented rooms)** In contrast to the Schoemanns' operation, this one fairly luxurious camp is the base for your safari here which usually lasts 3, 4 or 7 days.

The camp itself stands in a sheltered corner of the Hoarusib River. All of the tented rooms are raised on wooden decks, & have en-suite bathrooms with flush toilets, a hand basin & a hot shower. These substantial rooms are very comfortable, complete with fans & 12v lighting systems – although given the cold nights, it's the thick duvets & warm comfy beds that often prove more essential.

Artistic arrangements of local materials, & welcome hot-water bottles that magically appear in your bed, help make the rooms a real pleasure.

The main dining area is also raised up, & includes a dining room & comfy lounge/bar area, surrounded by plenty of glass which, when there's no fog around, allows good views of the desert. After-dinner drinks, & sometimes dinner, are often taken around a campfire outside, under an old leadwood tree. The food, as you'd expect, is of a high standard.

The sights While you'll have dinner, sleep and have breakfast at camp, you'll usually spend each of your days out on a whole-day 4x4 safari exploring some of the area's many attractions. These can be long days, but are always varied – and punctuated by stops for regular drinks and picnics. Although the area has some specific 'sights' to see, these are almost incidental in comparison with simply experiencing the solitude and singular beauty of the area. Visiting this whole region is about experiencing a variety of beautiful landscapes, each with its own fragile ecosystem, existing side by side. While on safari, you'll frequently stop to study the plants and smaller animals, or perhaps to capture landscapes on film. A few of the better-known places in the area include:

Rocky Point is a rocky pinnacle that juts out from a long, open stretch of sand, and in times past was an important landmark on the coast for passing ships. Now it's a good spot for a little gentle surf fishing, birdwatching, or simply watching the odd Cape fur seal crawl out onto the rocks for some sun.

Cape Frio is another, smaller rocky outcrop on the coast, but this one is home to a colony of up to 20,000 Cape fur seals. With patience and care, you can approach close enough to get a good portrait photograph whilst still not disturbing them.

Keep an eye out for jackals, and if you watch for prints in the sand you'll usually find brown hyena have also been here.

Strandloper rock circles are found in several places on the coast. Probably made by Khoisan people, some of these are simply circles, the remains of shelters used by hunter-gatherers who lived near the shore (Strandlopers). Others are more elaborate, covering larger areas and laid out in lines, and it's speculated that perhaps they were hunting blinds – which suggests that the area had a denser population of game in relatively recent (in geological terms) times.

Lichen fields and welwitschia plants are widespread on gravel plains throughout the Namib. However, here they are at their most extensive and usually in pristine condition. In several places there are clearly visible vehicle tracks which have left a lasting impression on the lichens. These can be precisely dated by historical records. They're the subject of much scientific interest, including a project by an Oxford University researcher who is based at the camp.

The clay castles of the Hoarusib Canyon are tall structures made of soft sand which line the sides of the steep canyon, resembling some of the ancient Egyptian temples. When I first visited the area many years ago, our driving on the dry river's sand here was instantly halted by a patch of quicksand.

The beaches Throughout the coast's misty, desolate beaches there is always something of interest to take a closer look at, or to photograph. Ghost crabs scuttle amongst the flotsam and jetsam of the centuries, while rare Damara terns fly overhead.

The Roaring Dunes are one of the most amazing experiences on the coast. If you slide down one of the steep lee sides, these large sand-dunes make an amazing and unexpected loud noise which reverberates through the whole dune. It really has to be felt to be believed, and gets even louder when you slide a whole vehicle down the dune! One theory links the 'roar' with electrostatic discharges between the individual grains of sand when they are caused to rub against each other. Why some dunes 'roar' and others don't remains a mystery – but there are other roaring dunes: some in the Namib south of the Hoanib River, and in Witsand Nature Reserve in South Africa's northern Cape.

Himba village One of the camp's first guides, the excellent Chris Baccus, worked with the Himba communities for years before helping to set up and start off the Skeleton Coast Camp. Now the camp's guides will take visitors (who approach with some cultural sensitivity) to one of the area's Himba villages, and introduce them to the people there. As with all such meetings, it can be a fascinating and humbling experience. Also, importantly, the villages are deriving a good income from these visits, both directly and by making and selling traditional crafts.

15

The Kaokoveld

The Kaokoveld is one of Africa's last wildernesses. Namibia's least inhabited area, it stretches from the coastal desert plain and rises slowly into a wild and rugged landscape. Here slow-growing trees cling to rocky mountains, whilst wild grass seeds wait dormant on the dust plains for showers of rain.

Because of the low population in the northern parts of the Kaokoveld, and the spectacularly successful Community Game Guard scheme (see *Chapter 3*, page 44), there are thriving populations of game here, living beyond the boundaries of any national park. This is one of the last refuges for the black rhino, which still survive (and thrive) here by ranging wide, and knowing where the seasonal plants grow.

It is also home to the famous desert elephants. Some naturalists have cited their apparently long legs, and proven ability to withstand drought, as evidence that they are actually a sub-species of the African elephant. Though this is not now thought to be the case, these remarkable animals are certainly adept at surviving in the driest of areas, using their amazing knowledge of the few water sources that do exist.

Historically the Kaokoveld has been split into two areas: Damaraland in the south, and Kaokoland in the north. Though the area is all now officially known as the Kunene region, this book has retained the old names as they are still widely in use. Further, this chapter subdivides Damaraland because, for the visitor, its north is very different from its south.

Southern Damaraland's most interesting places are easily accessible in your own 2WD vehicle. It is an area to explore for yourself, based at one of the camps or lodges. Its main attractions are the mountains of Spitzkoppe and Brandberg, the wealth of Bushman rock art at Twyfelfontein, the Petrified Forest, and various rock formations.

Northern Damaraland attracts people to its scenery, landscapes and populations of game – and is best visited by driving yourself to one of the four huge private concession areas: Hobatere, Palmwag, Etendeka and the Damaraland Camp. From there you can join the guided 4x4 trips run by these lodges, which is the best way to appreciate the area.

Kaokoland is different. North of Sesfontein, there are no lodges and few campsites. This is the land of the Himba (see *Chapter 2*, page 23), a traditional, pastoral people, relying upon herds of drought-resistant cattle for their livelihood. Their villages are situated by springs that gush out from dry riverbeds. Kaokoland's remote 'roads' need high-clearance 4x4 vehicles and are dangerous for the unprepared. The best way to visit is by air, or using one of the more experienced local operators who know the area and understand the dangers. To visit independently you need your own expedition: two or more equipped 4x4s, with experienced drivers and enough fuel and supplies for a week or more. This isn't a place for the casual or inexperienced visitor.

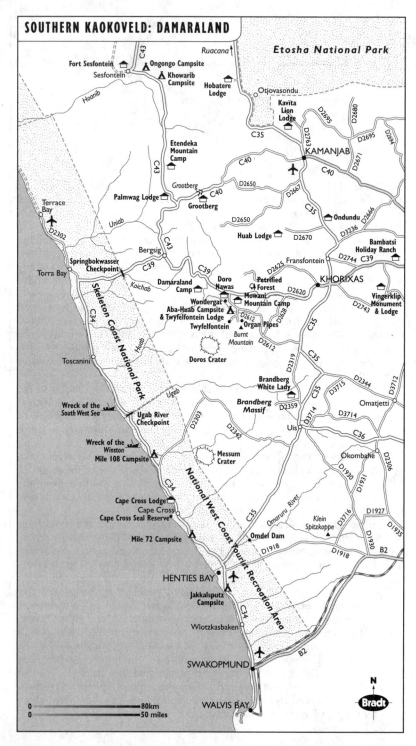

SOUTHERN KAOKOVELD: DAMARALAND

Ruacana

Etosha National Park

C43

Fort Sesfontein
Sesfontein
Ongongo Campsite
Khowarib Campsite
Hobatere Lodge
Otjovasondu

Hoanib

Kavita Lion Lodge

D2695
D2680
D2694

C35
D2763
D2671

Etendeka Mountain Camp
C40
KAMANJAB
C40
D2695

C43

Grootberg
C40
D2650
D2667
C35
D3694

Palmwag Lodge
C40
Grootberg
D2650
C35
Ondundu
D2666
D3236

Terrace Bay

D2302

Uniab

Huab Lodge
D2670
Bambatsi Holiday Ranch

Bergsig
C43

D2625
Fransfontein
D2744
C39

Springbokwasser Checkpoint
C39
C39
Doro Nawas
Petrified Forest
KHORIXAS

Torra Bay
Koichab
Damaraland Camp
D2620

Skeleton Coast National Park
Wondergat
Aba-Huab Campsite & Twyfelfontein Lodge
Twyfelfontein
Mowani Mountain Camp
D2612
Organ Pipes
D2628
Vingerklip Monument & Lodge
D2743

Huab

Burnt Mountain
D2612
C35

Doros Crater
D2319

Toscanini

Brandberg White Lady
C35
D3715
D2344
D3712

Ugab

Brandberg Massif
D2359
Omatjetti
D3714

Wreck of the South West Sea
Ugab River Checkpoint
D2203
Uis
D3714
C36

Wreck of the Winston
Mile 108 Campsite
D2342
Messum Crater
Okombahe
D1930
D1931
D2306

C34

National West Coast Tourist Recreation Area

Cape Cross Lodge
Cape Cross
Cape Cross Seal Reserve
C35
Omaruru River
Klein Spitzkoppe
D3716
D1927
D1935

Mile 72 Campsite
Omdel Dam
D1918
D1930
B2

HENTIES BAY

Jakkalsputz Campsite
C34

Wlotzkasbaken

B2

SWAKOPMUND

N

Bradt

0   80km
0   50 miles

WALVIS BAY

With several very accessible attractions, this is an easy area to visit yourself. Because of the region's sparse population, it's wise to travel here with at least basic supplies of food and water, and if you come fully equipped to camp and fend for yourself, then you will be more flexible in visiting the area's great mountains: Brandberg and Spitzkoppe.

If you see local people hitching, bear in mind that there is no public transport here. In such a rural area, Namibians will stop to help if there is a hope of cramming a further person into their car. Seeing foreign tourists pass by with a half-empty vehicle will leave behind very negative feelings. (Although, as anywhere, single women drivers might justifiably pause for thought before offering lifts.)

SPITZKOPPE At the far southern end of the Kaokoveld lies a small cluster of mountains, rising from the flat gravel plains that make up the desert floor. These include Spitzkoppe, Klein Spitzkoppe and the Pondok Mountains. Of these the highest is Spitzkoppe which towers 600m above the surrounding plains: a demanding technical climb. Its resemblance to the famous Swiss mountain earned it the name of the Matterhorn of Africa, while the extreme conditions found on its faces ensured that it remained unclimbed until 1946.

There's a small entrance fee (*N$45.50/22 per adult/child per night, plus between N$5–10 per vehicle*), payable at the entrance, where semi-precious stones are on sale.

Getting there Spitzkoppe is reached on the D3716. Approaching from Henties Bay take the D1918 westwards for 103km, then turn left onto the D3716. Coming from Usakos, take the Henties Bay turn-off after 23km on the B2 and follow it for about 18km before taking a right turn onto the D3716. From Uis Mine, leave on the C36 to Omaruru, but turn right onto the D1930 after only 1km. From there it's about 75km to the right turn onto the D3716.

Where to stay

Spitzkoppe Rest Camp www.nacobta.com.na. The local community runs a basic, very quiet campsite with pitches dotted around at the foot of the rocks, as well as simple bungalows with bedding. At the entrance to the site is an ablution block where you can also purchase beer & soft drinks, a few provisions such as firewood at N$10, a few souvenirs, & (prebooked only) basic hot meals. In spite of this, several campers have reported that you should take all your own water. All proceeds go back into the local community, so this is well worth supporting.
Camping N$35 pp; bungalow N$100 pp, B&B. Vehicle N$20. B/fast N$20, dinner N$30.

What to see and do Aside from being yet another spectacular place to camp, Spitzkoppe's lower slopes provide some difficult scrambles. At the extreme eastern end of this group of hills is a verdant valley known as Bushman's Paradise, which you can reach with the help of a fixed steel cable. Sadly the rock paintings under the overhang have been vandalised (even here!) and little is left of them, but the valley is still worth a visit. If you have an hour to spare, then an alternative descent is to continue to follow the gully out of the valley – though this route is not an easy option.

Because of their height and proximity to the ocean, these mountains receive more fog and precipitation than most, much of which runs off their smooth granite sides to form small pools. These are ideal places to search for the shrimps and invertebrates, which have adapted to the environment's extremes by laying drought-resistant eggs.

15

UIS Once known as Uis Mine, this small town was almost an extension of the tin mine which dominated it. Sadly this closed, and much of the town's population left as a result. Those who remained are fighting to survive, with tourism an important source of income.

The smart tourist information office at the eastern entrance to the village comes courtesy of a government grant. Display panels about the mine and local rock art are genuinely interesting, even if information of a practical nature is in rather short supply. More rewarding is a cool drink and a snack at Vicky's Coffee Shop next door.

Uis has a useful fuel station (*open daily 05.00–21.00*) opposite the Brandberg Restcamp. Next door to the restcamp, the Brandberg supermarket (*open Mon–Fri 08.00–17.00, Sat & Sun 08.30–13.00*) sells basic foodstuffs.

Where to stay and eat
Perhaps reflecting the importance of tourism to the area – although some could argue that the reality is rather less rosy – Uis and the surrounding area is almost awash with places to stay. Most are targeted at a similar market, with three, confusingly, capitalising on the appeal of the White Lady (see below).

Brandberg Restcamp (5 flats, 4 rooms, camping) PO Box 35, Uis; \/f 064 504038; e brandberg@ africaonline.com.na; www.brandbergrestcamp.com. The longest-established restcamp in the area, the Brandberg was reopened in August 2005 under the management of the enthusiastic, if somewhat eccentric, Basil Calitz. It's an unusual, no-frills complex, arranged round a 25m swimming pool, overlooked by a large restaurant which spills out onto a shaded poolside terrace with bench tables. Breakfast (N$25), light lunches (N$50) and 3-course dinners (N$100), with the occasional braai, are open to non-residents, as is the Old Prospectors Pub – complete with dartboard. In addition to standard twin rooms, there are 2-bedroom flats each with 2 bathrooms, a living area & a kitchen. There's also a campsite (with electric points & ablution block), a full-size snooker table, table tennis, a badminton court – & a shop selling gemstones.

Basil's enthusiasm for the region & its geology makes him a fascinating guide. Sundowner tours – often to the old Uis tin mine – are included in the rates, while other trips include desert elephant tracking (from May onwards), 360° around the Brandberg & an excursion to Spitspkoppe. Geological tours of 1–2 days with a qualified geologist need to be organised well in advance. All trips require 2 people min. N$235/410 sgl/dbl inc b/fast, self-catering N$700 per flat (max 4), camping N$50 pp.

Lizenstein Guesthouse (8 rooms) 15 4th Av; \ 064 504052; f 064 504005; e lizen@iway.na. The only place to stay in Uis itself with a view of the Brandberg Mountains, Lizenstein is a personally run guesthouse on the edge of town. To get there, take the road between Montes Usti & the White Lady restaurant, and follow it round to the left; Lizenstein is at the end on the left. Indigenous trees & shrubs, including *Cyphostemma curori*, *Aloe dichitoma* & *Acacia pseudebonis*, dominate the garden, while a small pool attracts a good number of birds. En-suite rooms vary in style from cool & modern to more traditional; some are in the main house, others off the garden. Dinner – a home-cooked 3-course buffet – is available by arrangement. N$250 pp B&B; dinner N$100.

Montes Usti Restaurant & Guesthouse (5 rooms) Cnr Uis & Sports streets; \/f 064 504219; m 081 257 1307. On the corner diagonally opposite the fuel station, Montes Usti (named after the *Acacia montes-usti*, which is endemic to the Brandberg area) was opened in 2006 by Wilna De Klerk, whose sister owns the White Lady B&B. It's primarily a restaurant – barn-like in design, with whitewashed walls, serving b/fast, light lunches & steaks in the evening; a separate bar & take-away service are in hand, & Wilna has ambitious plans for a beer garden. Very simple sgl & family rooms are off the restaurant; all are en suite, with AC. N$250/300 sgl/dbl; b/fast N$25.

White Lady B&B & Camping (12 rooms, camping) \ 064 504102; m 081 128 0876; e whitelady@ iway.na; http://whitelady.webz-i.com. Clearly signposted from the entrance to the town, this is the original White Lady guesthouse, restored in mid 2006 by its Namibian-born owner, Analene Van Dyk. Tile-floored rooms with high, thatched roofs & ceiling fans/AC are designed to keep cool; each has metal-framed dbl or twin beds, a fridge, & coffee machine.

The discovery of tin deposits in the Uis area was made early in the 20th century, but it was not until 1924 that even small-scale extraction was carried out. This continued for over three decades, until the end of the 1950s, when the South African state-owned company, ISCOR, set out to realise the commercial potential of the mine.

Full-scale production started in the early 1960s. This was an open-cast mine, for several years the world's largest hard-rock tin-mining operation. Materials were transported from the pits by truck and the waste dumped in huge white heaps, which continue to dominate the town. Some 84,000 tonnes of tin were extracted over the years, much of it low-grade ore. This, however, was expensive to process, and by 1990 the business was rapidly losing money. The cost of production, together with a downward spiral in the market price of tin, finally led to closure of the mine in 1990. Around 2,000 jobs were lost, and the small town that had grown up to support the workers was left destitute.

Alongside is a grassy area & pool, with breakfast served in the poolside lapa. The shaded campsite is spotlessly clean with neatly separated pitches around its own small pool, with space for a fire & separate braai area.
N$280/500 sgl/dbl; camping N$45 pp.

⌂ **White Lady Restaurant & Guesthouse** (5 rooms, camping) Cnr Sports & Uis streets; ⌕/f 064

504120; m 081 231 2306; e dina@iway.na. Next to Brandberg Restcamp, this White Lady was being refurbished in 2006, and offers very simple twin & trpl rooms with AC. A campsite was also in preparation. The bar & large à-la-carte restaurant open 07.30–late, serving basic grills & light snacks.
N$180/350 sgl/dbl, B&B; camping N$90 per site.

What to do Although most visitors to Uis are en route to somewhere else, the village still has two strong draws. For most people, the nearby Brandberg Mountains (see pages 331–4), now a national monument in recognition of the importance of the wealth of Bushman art secreted among its rocks, are the greatest attraction. Rather less obvious, though, are the mines themselves. There are no organised tours as such, but Basil Calitz at Brandberg Restcamp regularly takes visitors up in the evening for a sundowner. With its air of desolation and stunning scenery, the place would make a great film set. Should you visit alone, don't attempt to swim in – or drink – the water, however tempting. Its mineral content makes it toxic, and the depth, as well as the near impossibility of access, makes it unsafe for swimming.

For those interested in geology, Uis and the surrounding area is something of a Mecca, with even the shortest walk in the hills likely to throw up something of interest. It's straightforward enough to set out on foot from the village, but for guided tours contact Basil at Brandberg Restcamp (see above).

BRANDBERG Measuring about 30km by 23km at its base, and 2,573m at its highest point, this ravine-split massif of granite – Namibia's highest mountain – totally dominates the surrounding desert plains. Designated a national monument in 1951, and now under consideration for World Heritage Site status, the mountains contain one of the world's richest galleries of rock art, dating from 1,000 to 6,000 years ago. Of these, the most famous – and fortunately for visitors among the most accessible – is the White Lady.

Getting there Though you cannot miss seeing it while driving in the vicinity, getting to Brandberg without driving over the fragile lichen plains needs thought.

Its eastern side, around the Tsisab Ravine, is easily reached in an ordinary car via the D2359, which turns west off the C35 about 14km after Uis on the way to Khorixas. This is the location of a ranger post where guides are on hand to take visitors into the hills, and it is from this point that visitors can see the White Lady (*Witvrou* in Afrikaans), the famous rock painting.

Those with 4x4 vehicles can also use the extensive network of rough tracks which turn towards the massif from the north, west and south, off the D2342, starting some 14km southwest of Uis Mine on the Henties Bay road.

If you are heading out to the coast, then the D2342 and D2303 are passable in a 2WD. The second is in better repair than the first, as it gets much less traffic. The D2342 is often used by small-scale miners, and it has patches of bad corrugations with sharp turns, though the spectacular scenery and profusion of welwitschia plants make it worth the journey. Note that the most northerly 5km of the D2303, where it approaches the Ugab River, is in very poor shape and should not be attempted. If taking either road, phone ahead to your destination so that someone expects you, and will know where to look for you if you don't arrive.

Where to stay In addition to several places to stay in nearby Uis (see page 330), there are a couple of campsites in the Ugab Valley, close to the mountains, and one (White Lady!) lodge:

Å Ugab Campsite Signposted 10km to the right off the D2359.

Å Ugab Wilderness Camping Signposted after 14km on same track as Brandberg White Lady Lodge.

Brandberg White Lady Lodge (23 rooms, 5 tents, camping) ☎ 064 684004; f 064 684006; e ugab@iway.na; www.brandbergwllodge.com. Beautifully situated at the foot of the mountains, this new lodge was opened in 2003. It's a joint venture between the Tsiseb Conservancy & the owners, who come from Henties Bay, with staff drawn from the local community. Its central garden with small pond is overlooked by a terrace with chairs & tables, shaded by passion fruit & an Angolan bean climber. Behind lie a thatched, brick-built dining area, separate bar & lounge with squashy sofas, all furnished in dark wood. B/fast,

lunch & dinner are available at N$45, N$55 & N$75 respectively. There's a range of accommodation, all some way from the hub, so very quiet. Two blocks of rather small, twin-bed rooms are pleasantly furnished & decorated in ochres & browns, with rush ceiling & en-suite shower; without a fan, though, they could get very hot in summer. Set further out, & very well spaced across a huge site, rather shabby dome tents with 2 beds & open-air bathroom on a stone platform are adequate, if overpriced. Self-camping under camelthorn shade is a better bet – each pitch has its own BBQ, water tap & rubbish bin, & ablution blocks are simple but clean. Overlanders have a separate site & their own ablutions & bar.
Rooms N$290/400 sgl/dbl inc b/fast, tent N$290 dbl, camping N$45 pp & N$20 for vehicle.

What to see and do Two attractions are drawing increasing numbers of visitors: the area's rock art, and the opportunities for climbing in the mountains. Walking alone into the mountains is no longer permitted, so you'll need to take a guide from the Dâureb Mountain Guide Centre at the end of the D2359, to the eastern side of the mountains. A third option, a one-hour balloon flight over the mountains, can be arranged through African Balloon Safaris (*reservations* e *info@namibweb.com; from N$1,750 pp, based on 3–5 participants; min age 12*). Trips depart from the tourist information centre in Uis, where participants gather half an hour before sunrise.

Rock paintings This area has been occupied by Bushmen for several thousands of years and still holds a wealth of their artefacts and rock paintings, of which only a fraction have been studied in detail, and some are undoubtedly still to be found. The richest section for art has so far been the Tsisab Ravine, on the northeastern

The figure of the 'white lady' stands about 40cm tall, and is central to a large frieze which apparently depicts some sort of procession – in which one or two of the figures have animal features. In her right hand is a flower, or perhaps an ostrich egg-cup, whilst in her left she holds a bow and some arrows. Unlike the other figures, this has been painted white from below the chest. The colouration and form of the figure are reminiscent of some early Mediterranean styles and, together with points gleaned from a more detailed analysis of the pictures, this led early scholars to credit the painters as having links with Europe. Among the site's first visitors was the Abbé Henri Breuil, a world authority on rock art who studied these paintings and others nearby in the late 1940s, and subsequently published four classic volumes entitled *The Rock Paintings of Southern Africa* (see *Appendix 3*). He concluded that the lady had elements of ancient Mediterranean origin.

More recent scholars consider that the people represented are indigenous, with no European links, and they regard the white lady as being a boy, covered with white clay while undergoing an initiation ceremony. Yet others suggest that the painting is of a medicine man. Whichever school of thought you prefer, the white lady is well signposted and – though somewhat faded – worth the 40-minute walk needed to reach it.

If you wish to get more out of the rock art, then Breuil's books cannot be recommended too highly – though as beautifully illustrated antique Africana they are difficult to find, and expensive to buy.

More accessible, but well worth a visit, is the exhibition on rock paintings at the Alte Feste and State Museum in Windhoek.

---

side of the massif. Here one painting in particular has been the subject of much scientific debate, ever since its discovery by the outside world in 1918: the famous White Lady of Brandberg (see box above).

Further up the Tsisab Ravine there are many other sites, including the friezes within the Girls' School, Pyramid and Ostrich shelters.

Guided walks to see the paintings (*1½ hrs White Lady N$25 pp, 2 hrs highlights N$30; 3 hrs archaeology or geology N$35*) initially follow the riverbed, taking in some of the area's flora and fauna on the way including the tall endemic Brandberg acacia, *Acacia monti-usti*, with its red trunk, and the khoris or mustard bush, *Salpatma persica*. Families of dassies make their homes among the rocks, while colourful lizards dart in and out of the shrubby vegetation. The walk to the White Lady is relatively flat and not particularly challenging, with just a few rocky areas and a short climb at the end, but even in the early morning the heat is intense, so go prepared with a hat and plenty of water. The site itself is fenced, and to prevent further damage flash photography is not permitted.

Climbing With the highest point in Namibia and some good technical routes in a very demanding environment, the massif attracts serious mountaineers as well as those in search of a few days' interesting scrambling. It's very important to remember to take adequate safety precautions though, as the temperatures can be extreme and the mountain is very isolated. Unless you are used to such conditions, stick to short trips in the early morning or late afternoon, and take a long siesta out of the scorching midday heat.

To organise a guide, contact the Dâureb Mountain Guide Centre, where a three-day trip up the mountain's highest peak, Konigstein, costs N$200 per person per day. You'll need to be fully self-sufficient with tents, sleeping bags and all food

Welwitschia, perhaps Namibia's most famous species of plant, are usually found growing in groups on the harsh gravel plains of the central Namib and western Kaokoveld. Each plant has only two, long, shredded leaves and is separated from the other welwitschia plants by some distance. They appear as a tangle of foliage (some green, but mostly desiccated grey) which emerges from a stubby wooden base.

They were first described in the West by Friedrich Welwitsch, an Austrian botanist who found them in 1859. Since then scientists have been fascinated by welwitschia, earning the plant the scientific name of *mirabilis* – Latin for marvellous!

Research suggest that welwitschia can live for over 1,000 years and are members of the conifer family (some sources still class them with the succulents). Though their leaves can spread for several metres across and their roots over a metre down, it is still a mystery how they obtain water. One theory suggests that dew condenses on the leaves, and then drips to be absorbed by fine roots near the surface of the ground.

Welwitschia rely on the wind to distribute their seeds, but young plants are rare. They germinate only when the conditions are perfect, in years of exceptional rain. I was shown one on the Skeleton Coast that was eight years old. It was minute: consisting of just two seedling leaves and no more than two centimetres tall.

Their ability to thrive in such a harsh environment is amazing, and their adaptations are still being studied. There has even been a recent suggestion that the older welwitschia plants may change the chemical constitution of the soil around them, making it harder for young plants to establish themselves nearby and compete for water and space.

supplies and drinks. Serious climbers should seek advice from Windhoek Mountain Club (\ *061 241829*) well before they arrive.

TWO CRATERS In the remote west of southern Damaraland, these two craters are close to accessible areas, and yet themselves very remote. The only practical way to get in here is with a guide who knows the area – as for safety's sake you need back-up in case of problems.

Messum Crater Southwest of Brandberg, straddling the boundary of the West Coast Recreational Area, Messum Crater is an amphitheatre of desert where once there was an ancient volcano, over 22km across. Now two concentric circles of mountains ring the gravel plains here.

Messum is named after Captain W Messum, who explored the coast of southwest Africa from the sea, around 1846–48, venturing as far inland as Brandberg – which at that time he modestly named after himself. Only later did it become known as Brandberg.

Doros Crater Just south of Twyfelfontein, northwest of Brandberg, is the Doros Crater (or Doros Craters, as it is sometimes called). A permit from the NWR, and a full 4x4 expedition, is needed to get into this remote concession area in southern Damaraland. The geology's interesting here, and there's evidence of early human habitation.

KHORIXAS Khorixas used to be the administrative capital of the old 'homeland' of Damaraland. Now it is less important – and certainly isn't excessively tidy or even pretty – but it is conveniently placed for the visitor between Swakopmund and

Etosha. Because of this, and its accessibility by tarred road from the east, it makes a good base for visiting southern Damaraland's attractions. On a practical note, the town has a reliable Total fuel station, with an ATM, and several shops. Nevertheless, you can expect a hefty level of hassle here, so if you do stop, keep a careful eye on your belongings, and be prepared to be firm if anyone attempts to persuade you to purchase a craft – such as a key ring with your name on – that you don't want. On weekdays there's a craft shop opposite the fuel station, close to iGowati Lodge, where a sign proclaims 'Crafts for Conservation' (*open Mon–Fri 08.00–17.00*).

Where to stay There are several accommodation options both in and around Khorixas, all with their advantages.

iGowati Lodge (20 rooms, camping) PO Box 104, Khorixas; ☎ 067 331592; f 067 331594. Right in the centre of Khorixas, opposite the fuel station, iGowati Lodge is something of a peaceful oasis, with its well-kept grounds & cool fountains, & makes a good overnight or lunch stop. Opened in 2002, it is efficient & pleasantly run, with a comfortable restaurant that is open all day, as well as a bar, a pool, & a curio shop. Simple, clean, en-suite rooms run in a curved thatched block overlooking a central lawn. Each has twin beds, or a dbl bed with twin loft room. Camping is at the back, with power & braai facilities. *N$379.50/317.50 pp B&B high/low season (low Dec–May); camping N$45 pp. Lunch N$60, dinner N$95.*

Khorixas Lodge (38 bungalows) Reservations ☎ 061 2857200; f 061 224900. In a convenient position, just 1km to the west of town along the D625, this restcamp has been here for years & is now managed by Namibia Wildlife Resorts. The camp is quite large, & the bungalows come as standard, semi-luxury or luxury although none is luxurious. (If 4 plan to share 1 bungalow, then it's worth going for 'luxury'.) Expect clean towels & linen to be supplied, & each bungalow to have an en-suite shower/toilet, but the place has seen better days. The restcamp has a large swimming pool, a relaxed, almost café-style, small restaurant with an à-la-carte menu, & a shop in reception selling the basics. It's clean & unpretentious. *Standard N$280//475 sgl/dbl, luxury (max 4) N$470/750 sgl/dbl, all B&B.*

Around Khorixas Lodges here are listed broadly from east to west, starting closest to Khorixas.

Bambatsi Holiday Ranch (8 chalets) PO Box 120, Outjo; ☎/f 067 313897; f 067 313331; e bambatsi@iway.na; bambatsi@natron.net. On the C39 about 58km east of Khorixas, & 75km from Outjo, Bambatsi is situated 5km up a bumpy track on a plateau overlooking mopane woodlands. Bambatsi is a guest farm, not a restcamp, offering 'German hospitality'. Each of the recently refurbished chalets has an en-suite shower & toilet, with a private terrace at the back overlooking the plains. Meals are served on a broad terrace, & facilities include a large swimming pool. Owner-manager Rudi Zahn has two tamed cheetah, Shaka & Shiri, which he found as orphaned puppies in 1996. *N$675/600 sgl/pp sharing, inc dinner, BB.*

Vingerklip Lodge (24 bungalows) Reservations ☎/f 061 255344; e vingerkl@mweb.com.na; www.vingerklip.com.na. Just 1km from the Vingerklip itself, on the D2743 southeast of Khorixas, this lodge has been designed to take advantage of the scenery.

From the top, a thatched seating area with 360° views leads down through a bewildering series of terraces, where pools, a jacuzzi, bars, a braai area & sunloungers share the equally breathtaking views, many of them overlooking the lodge's waterholes.

Despite the name, Vingerklip is more hotel than lodge. Its small bungalows are spread out in pairs along an adjacent hillside. Each has twin or dbl beds & en-suite facilities, with a safe & private terrace; well appointed but not luxurious. Their strongest point is a stunning view. The main lounge–dining area is large, & the food is buffet-style, so don't leave dinner too late, or you may find little left. On the hilltop opposite the lodge, a café/bar was under construction in 2006, with unbeatable views across the plains in all directions. Although this is an award-winning lodge, it seemed when last visited that standards had slipped, though it's to be hoped that this will be rectified soon. Nevertheless, Vingerklip remains a good overnight stop, with some excellent waymarked & guided walks in the immediate area. It's also possible to organise a range of day trips, including a sundowner drive (N$50 pp).

N$864.45/742.40 sgl/pp sharing, DBB. Lunch N$60–85.

🏠 **Francolino Fly-ins** (4 rooms) 📞 067 697041; 📠 067 697042; 📧 francolino-flyins@iway.na; www.francolinoflyins.com. Set up around 2001, & run by Francesca Mattei & Wolfgang Rapp, Francolino is an established operation that has recently constructed a few intriguing rooms for guests, most of whom come to take advantage of the opportunities for ballooning, micro-lighting & scenic flights in light aircraft ranging from 2–5-seaters. These *epondoks* – Ovambo for 'rooms' – are airy, igloo-shaped constructions built of granite set among the kopjes with stunning views across the surrounding plains. Each has a private veranda roofed by tree branches, beds that can be set up outside for sleeping under the stars (the area doesn't suffer from mosquitoes) & a rustic outdoor shower, loo & basin. Meals are served in a cool central room decorated with Francesca's hallmark metalwork sculptures, or on a wide terrace that shares the views, & there's a small pool tucked among the rocks.

Francolino, named after the 'reluctant but very good fliers' that populate the riverbed, is signposted from the D2612 at Rag Rock, very close to Mowani, & about 4km from Aba-Huab Campsite. Since the owners also take the flights, pre-booking is essential. *N$750 pp DBB. Ballooning N$2,650 for about 1hr, inc champagne b/fast on landing; microlight N$1,100 pp for about 1 hr; scenic flights from N$1,700 pp per hr (max 3 passengers) in Cessna 2900. Closed June. Booking essential.*

🏠 **Mowani Mountain Camp** (12 Meru-style tents, honeymoon suite) 📞 067 697008; 📠 067 697009; reservations 📞 061 232009; 📠 061 222574; 📧 mowani@visionsofafrica.com.na; www.mowani.com. Well signposted on the D2612, about 6km south of its junction with the D3214, the once-independent Mowani is now owned by Visions of Africa. The rounded, thatched domes of Mowani's main buildings, with views over the surrounding countryside, give the impression of a grand African village, whilst blending beautifully with the granite boulders that surround them.

Away from these, & dotted around the surrounding kopje, 12 large tents of varying standards are raised up on platforms, 4 of them sharing the views. Athough all are fairly stylish, with dbl or twin beds, & en-suite showers & toilets, some

were in need of a facelift when visited in 2006. By contrast, the honeymoon suite is truly special, combining the best of African colonial design with a high standard of 21st-century luxury, including lounge area with DSTV, in/outdoor bath & shower, & its own private pool set into the rocks.

Activities include nature drives & excursions to the local attractions around Twyfelfontein although, like Twyfelfontein Country Lodge, many people use this as a base for driving themselves around the area. Mowani is far from cheap, but you do – in parts – get a lot of good design for your money! *Std tent N$1,855/2,330, view tent N$2,070/2,545, suite N$3,590/4,065, all pp sharing/sgl, FB. Nature/elephant drive N$420 pp. Open all year.*

⛺ **Aba-Huab Community Campsite** c/o Elias Aro Xoagub, PO Box 131, Twyfelfontein via Khorixas; 📞 067 697981/2. This was the first of several camps in Damaraland to be set up with the help of Namibia's Save the Rhino Trust, & run by local people. Aba-Huab camp is now effectively owned & managed by the entrepreneurial Elias, & is well signposted about 11km before Twyfelfontein, on the D3254. It stands beside a (usually) dry riverbed, & provides campers with solar-heated showers & toilets (albeit in just one block), a communal fire pit, shady pitches & a bar for cool drinks. Note that there's just one waterpipe for the whole site. As an alternative to camping, there are simple A-frame shelters for sleeping which raise you off the ground – though you need at least a sleeping bag, & preferably a foam mattress. Heading towards Twyfelfontein, the main camp is on the right. However, if you don't mind walking a little to the toilets, then you can camp on the left – the 'exclusive' site on the other side of the track – which is much quieter. Note that you can't easily book this in advance, but they'll always have camping space. *Camping N$50 pp, A-frame N$300/500 sgl/dbl, plus N$10 per vehicle.*

🏠 **Twyfelfontein Country Lodge** (56 rooms, 1 VIP room) 📞 061 374759; 📠 061 256598; 📧 twyelfontein@ncl.com.na; www.namibialodges.com. Owned by Namibia Country Lodges, this well-staffed 3-star lodge was opened in July 2000. Set in a rock-strewn valley near the Aba-Huab River, 10km from the world-renowned rock art site of Twyfelfontein along the D3214, the lodge boasts its own 2,000-year-old rock engravings at the entrance. The thatched rooms are built in blocks of 8, with 4 that will convert into family units; all feel quite small inside – in contrast to the completely over-the-top VIP suite. Expect twin beds, a fan, a shower

& flush toilet, & fairly traditional, even heavy, décor with dark wood & African-print fabrics. All rooms have AC but only until 22.00, when the generator shuts down. A very large thatched open-plan central area, built in 2 tiers with open sides, backs onto a rocky hillside. This has a dining room & bar upstairs, with toilets, offices & a curio shop below. It all overlooks a good-size, curved swimming pool.

Walks can be arranged from here, as can nature drives (in quite large, truck-like 4x4s) down the Huab River in search of elephants & other wildlife. Bicycles are available for guests' use, a pleasant way to spend an hour or so in the cool of the evening or early morning. There's an airstrip at the lodge, & scenic flights are possible in high season (May–Nov). That said, most people will use this simply as a base to drive themselves around the area, or as a stopover that's conveniently close to Twyfelfontein. *N$1005/705 sgl/pp sharing, B&B. Lunch N$107, dinner N$135. Open all year.*

🏠 **Camp Xaragu** (10 chalets, 7 tents, camping) PO Box 86280, Eros, Windhoek; ☎ 061 256770; ℱ 061 256813. Just 2km from the C39 turn-off, between the turnings to Twyfelfontein & Doro Nawas, you can't miss the giant-sized model meerkat at the entrance of this slightly ramshackle camp. Up the drive, model & farm animals jostle for position, too, with cattle, goats & springbok in evidence, though the chained baboon (said to have been rescued) isn't appealing. En-suite chalets have twin or dbl beds; tents are simple – this is definitely not 'luxury', but the staff are friendly. Activities include game drives & horseriding (N$100 per hr; no experience necessary). *Chalets N$320/430, tents N$210/340, all pp sharing/sgl, B&B. Camping N$60 pp. Dinner N$100.*

🏠 **Doro Nawas** (16 chalets) Contact via Wilderness Safaris; ☎ 061 274500; ℱ 061 239455; e info@ nts.com.na; www.wilderness-safaris.com. Brooding on the crest of a low hill, like a dark Moorish castle, Doro Nawas has 360° panoramic views of the Damaraland Plains. Opened in July 2005, it sits between the Etendeka Mountains in the north & Twyfelfontein in the south, & is one of the most recent additions to the Wilderness Safaris stable.

Guest chalets are huge, individually spaced around the foot of the hill, their soft thatch merging into the surrounding landscape. A moody darkness prevails in the natural stone walls, dark wood for the roof & heavy, stone-effect bedhead, though the cave-like effect is lightened slightly by sliding doors leading out to a wide, totally secluded veranda looking across to the distant hills. A roomy ablutions area incorporates 2 washbasins, separate toilet, & inside & outside showers, all adding to the sense of space.

Up in the castle, the dining room-cum-bar dominates the whole of one side, while stairs lead up to an open-air rooftop area that lends itself to sundowners or taking in the majesty of the stars. There's a pool with a view, too, ensuring that you're never divorced from the beauty of the location. Attentive & well-trained staff set out to ensure that your visit is enjoyable – even on the rare occasions when activities are on hold & lashing rain serves to intensify the brooding atmosphere.

A highlight of a visit here is the opportunity to see desert elephants, which are regularly spotted quite close to the lodge in the afternoons, either in the riverbeds or near Twyfelfontein. Other trips include visits to Twyfelfontein, the organ pipes & Burnt Mountain, although many guests drive themselves to these attractions. Guided walks in the early morning or afternoon are included in the rates. *N$2,290 pp FB; N$855 pp B&B.*

What to see and do There's a lot to see and do in southern Damaraland, and virtually all of it is easily accessible with your own vehicle.

Vingerklip (*Open 09.00–17.00, N$4 pp, free to lodge guests*) For years now the Vingerklip, or 'rock finger', has been a well-known landmark in this area, some 61km to the east of Khorixas. Around it are flat-topped mountains, reminiscent of Monument Valley (in Arizona), which are so typical of much of Damaraland. They are the remains of an ancient lava flow which has largely now been eroded way.

Amidst this beautiful scenery, Vingerklip is a striking pinnacle of rock, a natural obelisk balancing vertically on its own. It's an impressive sight, and similar to the (now collapsed) Finger of God near Asab.

Twyfelfontein rock art (*Entrance N$30/10 per adult/child, N$10 per vehicle; local guide (compulsory) N$20 pp; small extra tips are greatly appreciated*) Twyfelfontein was named 'doubtful spring' by the first European farmer to occupy the land – a reference to the failings of a perennial spring of water which wells up near the base of the valley.

Formerly the valley was known as Uri-Ais, and seems to have been occupied for thousands of years. Then its spring, on the desert's margins, would have attracted huge herds of game from the sparse plains around, making this uninviting valley an excellent base for early hunters.

This probably explains why the slopes of Twyfelfontein, amid flat-topped mountains typical of Damaraland, conceal one of the continent's greatest concentrations of rock art. This is not obvious when you first arrive. They seem like any other hillsides strewn with rocks. But the boulders that litter these slopes are dotted with thousands of paintings and ancient engravings, only a fraction of which have been recorded.

Amongst African rock art sites, Twyfelfontein is unusual in having both engravings and paintings. Many are of animals and their spoor, or geometric motifs – which have been suggested as maps to water sources. Why they were made, nobody knows. Perhaps they were part of the people's spiritual ceremonies, perhaps it was an ancient nursery to teach their children, or perhaps they were simply doodling.

Even with a knowledgeable local guide, you need several hours to start to discover the area's treasures. Begin early and beware of the midday heat. Take some water up with you, also stout shoes and a hat!

Getting there To reach the valley, which is well signposted, take the C39 for 73km west from Khorixas, then left onto the D3254 for 15km, then right for about 11km (ignoring a left fork after 6km) on the D3214.

Organ Pipes Retracing your tracks from Twyfelfontein, take the left fork which you ignored earlier (see directions above), onto the D3254. After about 3km there's a small gorge to your left, and above it a flat area used for parking. Leave your vehicle and take one of the paths down where you'll find hundreds of tall angular columns of dolorite in a most unusual formation. These were thought to have formed about 120 million years ago when the dolorite shrank as it cooled, forming these marvellous angular columns up to 5m high in the process.

Burnt Mountain Continuing just past the Organ Pipes, on the D3254, you'll see what is known locally as the 'Burnt Mountain'. Seen in the midday sun this can be a real disappointment, but when the red-orange shales catch the early morning or late afternoon light, the mountainside glows with a startling rainbow of colours, as if it's on fire.

Petrified Forest (*Entrance N$25 pp, inc guide, plus N$10 per vehicle*) Signposted beside the C39, about 42km west of Khorixas, lie a number of petrified trees on a bed of sandstone. Some are partially buried, whilst others lie completely exposed because the sandstone surrounding them has eroded away. It is thought that they were carried here as logs by a river, some 250 million years ago, and became stranded on a sandbank. Subsequently sand was deposited around them, creating ideal conditions for the cells of the wood to be replaced by silica, and thus become petrified.

Now there is a small office here with good crafts for sale, a car park, and demarcated paths around the site. The helpful guides will show you some of the highlights of the forest in about an hour

Wondergat From the Petrified Forest to Wondergat it's about 30km along the C39 before the clearly signposted turn-off to the left. Follow this road until a track heads west. After about 500m this comes to a huge hole in the ground – thought to be the remnants of a subterranean cave whose roof collapsed long ago. There are no signposts or safety barriers, so be careful near the edge.

Ballooning, microlighting and scenic flights

Francolino Fly-ins 🝑 067 697041; f 067 697042; e francolino-flyins@iway.na; www.francolinoflyins.com. Wolfgang Rapp & Francesca

Mattei have run ballooning, micro-lighting & scenic flights since around 2001. For details & prices, see page 336.

NORTHERN DAMARALAND

THE CONCESSION AREAS North of the Huab River lie a number of large areas known as concession areas, which are set aside for tourism. These are chunks of land that the government has allocated to one operator, who has the sole use of the land for tourism purposes. Local people can live and even keep animals within some of these tourism concessions, but development is limited.

Currently four such concessions are being used by operators to give visitors an insight into the area's ecosystems: Palmwag, Etendeka, Damaraland Camp and Hobatere Lodge. Each is different, but all require time to do them justice. These aren't places that you can drop into for a day and expect to fully appreciate, and a visit to any is best arranged in advance. (Huab Lodge's private reserve isn't technically a concession area, but is similar in style and so included here.)

LANDSCAPES AND VEGETATION Approaching from the coast, along the D3245, is perhaps the most interesting way to enter this area. After the flat coast, you soon find the gravel plains dotted first with inselbergs, then with low chains of weathered hills. The land begins to rise rapidly: you are coming onto the escarpment, around 50km from the coast, which is the edge of one of the largest sheets of ancient lava in the world. Sheets of molten lava poured over the land here in successive layers, about 300 million years ago. Now these Etendeka lavas dominate the scenery, with huge flat-topped mountains of a characteristic red-brown-purplish colour.

The rainfall here is still low, and the sparse covering of grasses is dotted with large *Euphorbia damarana* bushes. These grow into spiky, round clumps, perhaps 3m in diameter and over 1m tall, and are endemic to this region. Break a stem to reveal poisonous milky-white latex, which protects the bushes from most herbivores, except black rhino and kudu, which are both said to eat them. (A tale is told of a group of local people who roasted meat over a fire of dead *Euphorbia* stems – only to die as a result.)

If you could continue as a bird, flying northeast towards Etosha, then the land below you would become progressively less dry. Flying over the Hobatere area, you'd notice that the higher rainfall promotes richer vegetation. In the northern areas of that concession you would see an undulating patchwork of mopane scrub and open grassy plains, dotted with various trees, including the distinctive flat-topped umbrella thorn, *Acacia tortilis*. You would have left the desert.

FAUNA Generally the amount of game increases as the vegetation becomes more lush in the east. In the mountains around Palmwag, Etendeka and Damaraland Camp, there are resident steenbok, baboon, kudu, porcupine and the occasional klipspringer and warthog, joined by wide-ranging herds of Hartmann's mountain zebra, gemsbok and springbok. Equally nomadic but less common are the giraffe and desert-adapted elephant.

An enduring memory from here is the sight of a herd of giraffe. We watched them for almost an hour, as they skittishly grazed their way across a rocky hillside beside the main C34 (D3706) road. Their height seemed so out of place in the landscape of rocks and low trees.

Black rhino are present throughout the region, but spend most of their days sleeping under shady bushes, and so are rarely seen, even by those who live here. (Both Etendeka and Palmwag occasionally run strenuous rhino-tracking trips, the former more on foot, the latter making more use of vehicles. These expensive but fascinating trips are specially arranged on request.)

Leopard occur, and both cheetah and lion have been seen – but it is thought that only small numbers of big cats are left in the region, and they range over huge areas in search of suitable prey.

The birdlife is interesting, as several of the Kaokoveld's ten endemic species are found here. Perhaps the most obvious, and certainly the most vocal, are Rüppell's korhaan – whose early morning duets will wake the soundest sleeper. The ground-feeding Monteiro's hornbill is another endemic, though not to be confused with the local red-billed hornbills. There is also an endemic chat, the Herero chat, which occurs along with its more common cousins, the ant-eating tractrac and familiar chats. Though not endemic, black eagles are often seen around the rockier hillsides: surely one of Africa's most majestic raptors.

Looking further east, to Hobatere and Huab, there is more vegetation, making a classic environment for big game animals. These areas can support more game, and it shows. Elephants are certainly more common, and more easily spotted. The

FRANZ AND THE SILVER OTTER

From an article by the author in Wanderlust, February 1998

'I applied for a job as guide, but I was good at entertaining guests – and so trained for the bar. But I still want to be a guide, so I've built a small water-bowl near my tent. I watch the birds, and learn to identify them from a book.'

Franz Coetzee's bird-bowl seemed a long way from the Savoy, where a waiter filled our glasses as we listened for the British Guild of Travel Writers' Silver Otter award to be announced. I wondered if all this pomp would make any difference to Damaraland Camp, or Franz's rural community there that ekes out its living on the fringes of the Namib Desert.

The trip to London had certainly affected Franz, who had seldom stopped smiling. Until now, his longest journey had been as a child, when his parents' community had been displaced from South Africa and trekked into Namibia. They settled in the arid, semi-desert region of Damaraland. 'It was good that we came to Damaraland,' he assured me. Despite entering an area already occupied with Damara people, 'We mixed with those people, and we accept each other.' So Franz and his family stayed on, when most returned to South Africa, two years ago. 'We won our land back, but my parents wanted to stay in Namibia. I don't know anything more. So I stayed also.'

After finishing school, he searched for a job. 'I went to town, with no luck. To Walvis Bay, as my sister was there. There is a really big problem with jobs – unemployment. I decided to go back to Damaraland to concentrate on farming.'

Hence, like most of his community, Franz lived by tending cattle, sheep and goats. Damaraland may be spectacularly beautiful, but its land is poor for farming. Rocky hills and minimal rainfall mean a difficult life. There is game around, and sometimes he would hunt springbok, or even zebra, kudu or oryx. Occasionally he would glimpse the area's desert-adapted black rhinos – but elephants were a different story. 'They visited the water-points during the night and our vegetable gardens on the farm. I remember once, a month before the harvest, a lot of elephants came, damaging the farm. The dogs barked, and we became nervous. We just ... stood. You can do nothing to an elephant. You can't even desert-adapted species seen to the west are joined in Hobatere by eland, black-faced impala and Damara dik-dik – both of the latter are sub-species endemic to the region. Similarly, the variety of birds becomes wider as you move east, with species that occur in Etosha often overlapping into Hobatere.

WHERE TO STAY Although each of the concessions is totally different, Damaraland Camp, Palmwag and Etendeka occupy broadly similar environments, as do Hobatere and Huab Lodge. The lodges listed below follow a rough clockwise circle.

Damaraland Camp (10 Meru tents) Contact via Wilderness Safaris; ☎ 061 247500; f 061 239455; e info@wilderness.com.na, info@nts.com.na, www.wilderness-safaris.com. Damaraland Camp was originally modelled on Etendeka (see page 344), & initially they seemed very similar. It was another remote tented camp on a rocky hill, nestling amidst the stunning red-purple mountain scenery that is typical of the Etendeka lava flows. Its tents – all fully refurbished in April 2006 – have always been a little more luxurious than Etendeka's, as each had a flush toilet & shower en suite from the start. Now there's both a family room & a dbl room, as well as the original twins, all under canvas with solar powered lights & a stone porch. However, Damaraland Camp has always had a much stronger community involvement, & that's what shines out when you visit.

Physically, the camp is about 13km west of the D2620 road (despite the 11km on the signpost!), just north of the point where the Huab River crosses the road, next to a smallholding. It's not a

chase him away. You just clap your hands, but stay out of the way.' Though rare, these desert elephants meant nothing to Franz when compared with his vegetables.

Then things started to change. A government survey visited farms, explaining how they could benefit directly from the wildlife and tourism. Eventually the 70 households in Franz's community established themselves as custodians of the land, forming the Ward 11 Residents' Association – with its own constitution and membership. They then sought investors, and after two years of tortuous negotiations, involving the whole community, they settled on an agreement with Wilderness Safaris, who would build Damaraland Camp, and train local people to run it. The community gets the jobs, and 10% of the profits. Eventually, ownership of the camp will revert to the community.

Franz is enthusiastic about the benefits, but he recognises that the next challenge is to decide how to use the increasing revenues. 'Farms which have had windmills damaged [by elephants seeking water] will be the first to get help. And there are other problems – predators like jackal catch goats and sheep.'

Gradually attitudes to wildlife have changed. Now Franz tells stories about elephants over breakfast, before guests go out on safari. The community knows how to deal with them, and nobody kills wild animals to eat – they're worth more alive, as attractions.

Almost two years since it started, Damaraland Camp is now one of the most popular camps in Namibia. Except for two managers from Wilderness, all the staff are from the community – and next year two will start training to replace the existing managers. Franz explained that his work of 'entertaining guests' meant 'telling them about yourself – visitors usually want to know about our traditions'. With a ready smile, and a disarming line in chat, it's clear why he was perfect for this.

Later that evening, the winner was announced: the city of Dubrovnik, for its restoration work. Damaraland Camp was highly commended, followed by Madikwe Game Reserve, in South Africa, which had a similar approach to conservation.

Franz's smile never wavered – clearly the award would make no difference to that. But why was this project so special? Surely all camps should be run like this?

camp that you can just drop into; your stay must be arranged in advance. Although an experienced driver going slowly could negotiate the drive in a normal 2WD vehicle that's not overloaded, a rendezvous is normally arranged just off the main D2620, where cars are left under the watchful eyes of a local family. Then you'll be taken to the camp by 4x4. Check the rendezvous time when you book.

The area around the camp is dry & hence vegetation is sparse – even *Euphorbia damarana* is not present to any great extent except along the riverbed. However, there are some good examples of *welwitschia* nearby, on the way to the Huab Valley. This river valley makes a good venue for expeditions in search of desert elephant, & other game, so many drives head in that direction. Activities are based on walks & drives, with the emphasis on the driving – usually into the Huab River Valley in search of wildlife, where elephants are fairly frequently seen.

Damaraland Camp's own brand of community involvement is especially interesting, meriting a high commendation from the British Guild of Travel Writers (see box, pages 340–1), & numerous subsequent accolades. These aside, this is one of Namibia's best camps, and it is also owned & now largely run by the local community. Visitors often return commenting on just how positive & happy the atmosphere is, so it is well worth stopping for 2–3 nights (just 1 night is too short).
Jan–Jun N$2,310 pp sharing, Jul–Nov N$3,030 pp sharing, inc all meals, game drives & walks; N$1,450 sgl supplement.

Palmwag Concession

The huge Palmwag (pronounced 'Palumvag') concession (*day fee N$30 pp, plus N$70 per vehicle; overnight N$70 pp*) lies to the north of the junction of the C34 (D3706) and the D2620, immediately after the veterinary fence. To the west, it stretches as far as the Skeleton Coast. On the eastern side of the C34 is the Etendeka concession. Experienced 4x4 enthusiasts, who are used to the terrain, and have good navigational skills (and preferably a GPS), can buy a day permit to drive around the Palmwag concession. However, for most visitors this is not practical. (One trainee guide based at Palmwag got lost in his vehicle, became disoriented, and was found severely dehydrated in the Skeleton Coast Park. It is a difficult area.) The best way to see the area is still to leave your car at the lodge (see below) and take one of the guided game drives. The area's ecosystem is too fragile to withstand the impact of many vehicles, and the animals are still wary of people. They have enough problems without being frightened from waterholes by tourists seeking pictures.

Just before the fence is a small shop, poorly stocked, though still the best in the area, and a welcome place for a cold drink or a packet of crisps. It's open daily 08.00–22.00, but there may be no-one there at meal times. Fuel is available from the station next to the veterinary fence from 07.00 to 19.00 every day. Everybody seems to fill up here (but remember that payment for fuel is accepted only in cash). This is also the location of the airstrip.

🏠 **Palmwag Lodge** (13 bungalows, 2 family units, 5 Meru tents, camping) Contact via Palmwag Travel Shop, PO Box 339, Swakopmund; 📞 064 404459; 📠 064 404664; ℮ reservations@palmwag.com.na; www.palmwag.com.na. The lodge is beautifully situated on the edge of the concession, 500m after the veterinary fence on the left, & next to a palm-lined tributary of the Uniab River. This often flows over-ground and, as water is very scarce in this area, its presence regularly draws elephants close to camp.

Palmwag is the oldest lodge in the area. Until 2002 it was run by Desert Adventure Safaris (DAS), a Namibian company based in Swakopmund. Since then it has seen an ongoing programme of change, although it remains slightly offbeat. Something of a crossroads for travellers in the area, it attracts all sorts, from South African families camping to shady mineral prospectors, & from upmarket visitors on fly-in safaris to local game guards back from the bush, who are staying at the adjacent base of the excellent Save the Rhino Trust (see page 343). The resultant holiday atmosphere indicates that most people are here to relax & unwind.

The range of accommodation reflects the range of guests. At the centre of the camp, simple thatched, reed bungalows, one of them a family unit, have en-suite facilities; all are clean, bright & functional, but not overly large or luxurious. Nearby is the Uniab restaurant, where guests can enjoy a buffet dinner (N$120) overlooking the hills. Set further away, large en-suite twin-bed tents, all raised on decking, overlook the reedbeds & palm trees of the Uniab River. Electricity is supplied from a generator for most of the day, with battery powered lights at night.

On the other side of the lodge are 9 campsites, with a small swimming pool nearby, surrounded by lawns; there's also a pool bar, open for meals all day. Be aware that camping is limited to 6 groups, so if it's busy those who haven't booked will be turned away.

Guided game drives at 07.00 & 16.30, taking around 3 hrs, cost N$300 pp (max 6 people). Short self-guided walks on marked trails are also possible. *Bungalow N$1,040/745 sgl/pp sharing; Meru tent N$1,425/1,020, all DBB. Camping N$80 pp. Game drive N$300 pp; day trips from N$880 pp. Concession fees extra. Open all year.*

🏠 **Palmwag Rhino Camp** (8 twin-bed tents) Contact via Wilderness Safaris; 061 274500; f 061 239455; e info@wilderness.com.na, info@nts.com.na, www. wilderness-safaris.com. This small, tented camp stands in the Palmwag Concession & usually takes a maximum of just 12 guests. Although the tents are large, walk-in Meru-style, & each has an en-suite flush toilet & simple bucket shower (hot water available on request, by the bucket!), the camp's location can be fairly easily moved.

Activities will major on rhino-tracking excursions — usually with one of the Save the Rhino Trust team guiding the party. These usually involve driving around while tracking from the vehicle, & then following a set of tracks on foot when an animal is located. It's an excellent option if you are moderately fit & want to do some serious rhino-tracking.

However, note that the dangers inherent in approaching big game at close quarters can be thrown into sharp contrast on rhino-tracking trips. No trip to Africa (or indeed anywhere) can be guaranteed as totally safe, and this is no different. If you don't follow your guide's instructions precisely, then you're quite likely to have 1,000kg of nimble-footed, sharp-horned rhino heading at you very rapidly. These activities are not for the faint-hearted, so don't book in here unless you fully accept that you may be placing yourself far out of your comfort zone — and potentially in some danger. *N$2,270 pp sharing Jan–Jun, N$3,000 pp sharing Jul–Nov, inc all meals, game drives & rhino-tracking; N$1,450 sgl supplement. Pre-booking essential.*

SAVE THE RHINO TRUST

This excellent local charity (*PO Box 2159, Swakopmund;* 064 403829; e *srt@rhino-trust.org.na; www.rhino-trust.org.na*), founded by the late Blythe and Rudi Loutit, grew out of the slaughter of the region's wildlife that was taking place in the early 1980s. As the rhino numbers shrank to near extinction, Blythe and Rudi started a pressure group to stop the indiscriminate hunting in the area. (This was mainly perpetrated by military staff of the South African Defence Force who were shooting black rhino and elephant from vehicles and even helicopters.)

Once the worst of the hunting was stopped, SRT continued and pioneered conservation and protection in the area, even employing convicted poachers as game scouts. Who would know better the habits of rhino, and the tricks of the hunters? Eventually, they were able to reverse the extermination of the rhino from the communal areas of the Kaokoveld – a process that's has been enthusiastically supported by the chiefs and headmen, as well as the neighbouring farming community. In many ways it's work like this so long ago that laid the foundations for the successful community conservation programmes that now operate in the region.

Working with the government and many local communities has gradually brought more benefits to these communities, through revenues generated by tourism, as well as providing security for the rhino. SRT continues to operate many daily rhino patrols, monitoring and protecting the rhino. These include patrols from Palmwag Lodge (*2–3 people N$1,680 pp per day; 4–10 people N$2,403 pp per day*) and Palmwag Rhino Camp, which guests can join. The income from these trips funds some of the trust's patrols and rhino-monitoring programmes.

15

There are a few designated **campsites** in the vicinity that are signposted from the entrance to the concession, but which have not been visited by the author:

▲ **Elephant Song Campsite** 120km from the entrance, on the southern bank of the Hoanib River, within the concession area.

▲ **Mbakondja River Campsite** 51km from the entrance, outside the concession area.

▲ **Khowarib Campsite** 73km from the entrance, also outside the concession area (see page 346)

North and east of Palmwag

⌂ **Etendeka Mountain Camp** (10 twin-bed tents) ☎ 061 226979; f 061 226999; e logufa@ mweb.com.na; www.natron.net/tour/etendeka. Etendeka is an excellent tented camp about 18km east of Palmwag, on the open, rolling Etendeka lava plains. It is owned and run by Dennis Liebenberg, who takes a no-frills approach to giving his guests a real experience of the Kaokoveld.

Numbers are limited to 16 guests, accommodated in large tents. Each of the walk-in tents is provided with 2 beds, linen, towels, washbasin, a bush shower with hot & cold water, a flush toilet & electric light. Etendeka doesn't aim at luxury; but what it does, it does very well. The main dining & bar area are under canvas, and meals are a social occasion when everybody, including Dennis & the guides, normally eat together around the fire (it gets very chilly in winter), upon which much of the food is cooked. Such bush-cooking has been refined to an art form, so the cuisine from the embers is impressive.

Activities — guided walks & scenic & game drives — are all included, & tailored to guests' interests & abilities. After an early breakfast, a normal day might include a 2–4hr walk, lunch, a few hours to relax, & perhaps a long afternoon game drive, incorporating a short hike onto one of the area's mountains for a sundown drink. If you're fit & active, then this is a great place to come walking.

The concession's game includes good populations of Hartmann's mountain zebra, oryx & springbok, as well as occasional giraffe & desert-adapted elephant, & very occasionally black rhino. The striking *Euphorbia damarana* are the predominant shrubs all around this area, & Etendeka's guides are excellent on their plants & birds, as well as animal identification.

Etendeka is remote & you cannot 'drop in' as you can at Palmwag. It must be booked in advance. Visitors normally drive themselves to a rendezvous by the veterinary fence (normally 16.00 in summer, 15.30 in winter — but check when you book), where Etendeka has covered parking places. From there the camp's 4x4 will transfer them to the camp.

It is especially good to note that Etendeka is closely involved with the region's Community Game Guard scheme, & that it gives a proportion of its revenue to the local communities, so that they benefit from the income generated by visitors, & have an incentive to help preserve Kaokoveld's wild game.

N$1,850/1,450 sgl/pp sharing, FB, inc full bar, transfer to camp, guided nature walk & scenic drive. Closed Jan. Pre-booking essential.

⌂ **Grootberg Lodge** (11 chalets) ☎ 067 687043; f 067 687044; e lodge@grootberg.com; www.grootberg-lodge.com; reservations ☎ 061 246788; f 061 243079; e reservations@ grootberg.com; www.grootberg.com. Perched at the top of the Grootberg Pass, between Palmwag & Kamanjab, this new lodge was opened in the /Khoadi//Hoas Conservancy in July 2005. Under the watchful management of Dominic (ex-Wilderness Safaris) & Simonetta, hailing respectively from South Africa & Italy, local staff will be trained to run the lodge, with the aim of running it themselves within 10 years.

To get there, simply follow the C40 from Palmwag towards Kamanjab; the lodge is at the very top of the Grootberg Pass, at a commanding 1,645m. Unless you have a good 4x4, & are very confident in your driving ability, don't attempt the steep, narrow track up to the lodge. Just park at the bottom & the warden will arrange for you to be collected.

The lodge's primary attraction is its stunning location, with views from on high sweeping south down the valley towards the Brandberg Mountains. The buildings, clad in the local 'lava' stone, are whitewashed inside, with an uncluttered décor that is both cool & relaxing — think comfy, neutral sofas with casual throws, classic wooden tables & chairs in the dining area, classy photographs on the walls, & a small range of well-chosen books. Outside, a wide veranda with tables & umbrellas makes the most of the view, though the vertiginous drop would make this a less-than-relaxing place for parents with young children.

Each of the twin or dbl chalets faces south, with sliding doors leading to en-suite bedrooms whose handmade furniture is of unpolished pine. Power is supplied from a generator.

In addition to guided walks & game drives, guests can take a ¹/₂-day elephant tracking, or a ¹/₂-day rhino tracking. There are also plans for horseriding safaris for all abilities in the valley, to include an overnight camp.

N$945/1,470 sgl/dbl, DBB. Activities (min 2 people): game drive N$250/350 (pm/am), guided walk N$150, rhino tracking N$900, elephant tracking N$600.

🏠 **Hobatere Lodge** (12 rooms, treehouse, camping) ☎ 061 237294; e reservations@exclusive.com.na, www.exclusive.com.na. About 80km north of Kamanjab, Hobatere is easily found on the banks of the small Otjivasondu River. To get there, take the main C35 road northwest from Kamanjab towards Ruacana. After about 65km, just past the entrance to western Etosha, Hobatere is signposted to the left through imposing gates. A clear bush road then leads through several riverbeds for about 16km before reaching the lodge. A 2WD is usually fine for this but, if attempting the road during the rains, ring the lodge as you pass through Kamanjab – so that they know of your arrival, & will search for you in those riverbeds if you get stuck.

Steve & Louise Braine have run Hobatere for 16 years now. Accommodation is in comfortable twin-bedded, thatched brick cottages – 6 in one block, & 6 individually spaced – each with en-suite shower & toilet (the internal doors are decorative, not functional, so you will be on intimate terms with your companion). These are set in plenty of space, spread around the main lodge allowing you a feeling of independence: to join in if you wish to, or just to relax if you don't. For complete privacy, there's also a treehouse in an old leadwood tree about 5km from the lodge, overlooking a waterhole.

In the lodge's main building there is a bar, lounge & separate dining area, where good food is served from the house menu. Guests dine separately, as at a restaurant, rather than automatically joining in on one big table with the hosts. For cooling afternoon dips there's a clear pool, which was recently fortified to be elephant-proof, after a baby elephant fell in & its mother smashed up the whole area in her frantic (and eventually successful) attempts to help it out. Approximately 300m from the lodge there is a hide overlooking a waterhole, which is especially interesting in the dry season.

Hobatere's game is established & relaxed & its standard of guiding is good (with Steve himself being a birder of note). It is normal to book here on an FB basis, & then pay the lodge for your activities (game drive N$175 pp, night drive N$205 pp; walk N$155 pp). An added attraction is the terrarium: a thatched, open-sided snake park where a guide will show you anything from puff adders to twig snakes, all collected by Steve within a 500km radius of the lodge – and all housed safely under glass.

N$877.57/812 sgl/pp sharing high season (Mar, May, Jul–Nov), FB; MasterCard, Visa & American Express accepted. Open all year.

⛺ **Hobatere Campsite** (6 pitches) Reservations via Hobatere, above. For those wishing to camp, there's a separate campsite about 45 mins' drive from the lodge. Each of the pitches has its own toilet, basin & braai area, & there are 6 hot showers in a communal block. The site overlooks its own waterhole. The campsite turn-off is approximately 100m from the Otjovasando turning on the western side of the road, then a further 1.5km from the main road. Activities at the lodge must be booked in advance, & are subject to availablility.

Camping N$60 pp.

🏠 **Huab Lodge** (8 bungalows) ☎ 067 687058; f 067 687059; e info@huab.com; www.huablodge.com; reservations ☎ 061 224712; f 061 224217; e reservations@resdes.com.na. Though frequently listed as a guest farm near Kamanjab, or even Outjo, Huab is a private concession area in spirit. It is owned & run by Jan & Suzi van de Reep, who have worked in tourism in Namibia for years. Together with friends, they bought up a number of adjacent farms in a hilly area, around the headwaters of the Huab River. Although this land was of significance as a refuge for some of the Huab River's desert-adapted elephants, farmers had fenced the land, & didn't enjoy the elephants' feeding forays onto their farms, causing much tension for both men & beasts. Now that the fences are down, antelope have returned, the ecosystem has reverted to its natural state, & elephants are being seen around the lodge more. This is a textbook demonstration of how tourism can be used to finance conservation initiatives, & is a compelling argument for encouraging ecotourism to Namibia.

The lodge is situated on the banks of the Huab (beware: if the rivers are in flood, reaching here can be difficult). It is along the D2670, well signposted from the C35 between Kamanjab & Khorixas. The approach road is some 30km long, with 4 farm gates, & becomes increasingly scenic, so don't expect a quick arrival.

Huab has been voted Namibia's best lodge every year since 1994, & you can see why: classic thatch-on-brick design, tasteful décor, a little landscaping, & lots of quality. Light, spacious bungalows, with a wide frontage & private veranda, all have two queen-sized beds & separate en-suite rooms for the toilet, & shower. Electricity & hot water are mostly solar. Solid, handmade Rhodesian teak furniture reflects the strong sense of family that emanates through the place, while soft furnishings are made up at the lodge from locally designed fabrics, which are also on sale in the curio shop.

The guiding is top class. Jan is renowned as founder of Etosha Fly-in Safaris, & one of the country's best guides, so even if there's no game around (and that's unusual now that the animals have repopulated the land), you'll still find the drives & walks fascinating, or plenty to spot from the bird hide. Similarly, Huab's hospitality is excellent, with meals served for everyone together — relaxed, social occasions in a thatched central hub where it's easy to feel completely at home. For total relaxation, you can bathe away the day's aches under thatch in natural hot springs, alongside a cooler tub for contrast, or treat yourself to a session of shiatsu therapy (the only extra cost, at N$300/hr).

All this comes at a price, but I've yet to hear a visitor say that it was poor value — & it costs a fraction of the price that similar quality commands in the rest of Africa.
N$1,640 pp, inc all meals, wine, game drives & walks. Open all year. Pre-booking essential. Transfers from Windhoek by arrangement.

WARMQUELLE About 87km north of Palmwag Lodge, on the way to Sesfontein, lies Warmquelle, a small settlement situated on the site of a spring. In the early years of the 20th century the spring was used in an irrigation project, for which an aqueduct was constructed. Now only a few parts of the old aqueduct remain, together with a small Damara settlement and quite a large school.

Near here there are two locally run and very simple campsites, both just off the C34. Khowarib and Ongongo were set up with the help of the Save the Rhino Trust and the Endangered Wildlife Society, and both aim to channel most of their income back into their local communities.

⚊ Where to stay

⚊ **Khowarib Camp** (7 huts, camping)
e office@nacobta.com.na; www.nacobta.com.na. The turn-off for the Khowarib campsite is signposted about 75km north of Palmwag, 25km south of Sesfontein, on the C34. The track to the camp is suitable for 2WD vehicles & runs for about 3km east from the main road along the Khowarib Gorge.

The campsite sits on the banks of the Khowarib River & consists of very basic huts, built by the local villagers using local materials to traditional designs. Some are rounded & mud-clad, Himba-style, & others are thatched. There are also 5 pitches for tents. Bucket showers & bush toilets are provided &, with notice, simple local meals can be arranged.

The local community runs the camp. Guides can sometimes be arranged for walks around the area. (Note that a Save the Rhino base camp, sited just next to this visitor's camp, has long been one of the bases for their camel-mounted anti-poaching patrols around the region.)
Camping N$40 pp.

⚊ **Ongongo Campsite** e office@nacobta.com.na; www.nacobta.com.na. About 11km further along the C34 is the turn-off northeast for the Ongongo campsite. To reach this, turn at Warmquelle & watch for the signs (if there are any left). You will follow a water pipeline for about 6km, heading roughly northwards. The road is rough & very rocky in parts, sandy in others, & at one point you cross the dry bed of the river, before turning right to reach the site's office hut. A 2WD will usually just make it — depending on its ground clearance.

The main attraction here is the Ongongo waterfall, where a deep, clear pool is sheltered by an overhang of rock. Few resist the temptation to strip off & swim here, which isn't surprising given the temperature. The Ongongo community now administers the camp & several shaded huts are available to camp under, but bring all your food & equipment as nothing else is available.
Day visit N$20 pp; camping N$40 pp.

SESFONTEIN Sesfontein was named after the 'six springs' that surface nearby. It stands in the Hoanib Valley and marks the northern edge of Damaraland. The road from Palmwag, the C34 (D3706), makes an interesting drive in a normal 2WD vehicle, and passes through a narrow gap in the mountains just before this small town. North of town, the going gets much tougher.

Sesfontein is a dusty but photogenic spot, set between mountains in the Hoanib Valley. The local vegetation is dominated by umbrella thorns (*Acacia tortilis*), the adaptable mopane (*Colophospermum mopane*, recognised by its butterfly-shaped leaves), and the beautiful, feathery real fan palms (*Hyphaene petersiana*). You will often be offered the 'vegetable ivory' seeds of these palms, carved into various designs, as souvenirs by the local people – which are highly recommended, as often the sellers are the carvers, and it is far less destructive than buying wood carvings.

In the earlier part of this century, the German administrators made Sesfontein into an important military outpost. They wanted to control movement of stock around the country, after the severe rinderpest epidemic in 1896. So in 1901 they built a fort here, complete with running water and extensive gardens to grow their own supplies. However, by the start of World War I this had been abandoned, and it is only in the last few years that this has been renovated into a picturesque new lodge.

Sesfontein still feels like an outpost in many ways, despite being an important centre for the local people, who live by farming goats and the occasional field of maize. The efficiency of the foraging goats is witnessed by the lack of vegetation lower than the trees, and hence the clouds of fine dust which often hang in the valley's air.

Sesfontein offers the adventurous an interesting view of a real town, not sanitised by the colonial designs of townships. It is spread out, and very relaxed. If you're staying here, then try to rise early to watch the village come to life. On most days the national anthem will drift across the cool air, beautifully sung by the school within earshot of the fort. Watch as the farmers drive their cattle to water, and smartly dressed workers head for town.

In the afternoon there are always a few people about, and there's no better way to watch village life than sitting with a cold drink on the steps of one of the shops – though you may attract a crowd of playful children. If you are just passing through then you'll find the supplies in these shops useful, and there is a convenient petrol station here. There is little other fuel available between Sesfontein and the Kunene, except at Opuwo.

Where to stay If you've passed the Khowarib and Ongongo campsites, mentioned above, then Fort Sesfontein is the area's only other place to stay.

Fort Sesfontein (13 rooms, camping) ☎ 065 275534/5; f 065 275533; e fort.sesfontein@ mweb.com.na; www.fort-sesfontein.com. Opened in 1995, Fort Sesfontein is one of the most original & imaginative places to appear since independence. The fort has been rebuilt more or less to its old plans, set around a lush central courtyard full of palm trees & fountains. The rooms are spacious & rustically decorated, with en-suite facilities & fans — which are as essential as the swimming pool: Sesfontein can get very hot. The old officers' mess is now a large bar/lounge with sitting & dining areas, & there's also a poolside bar, where meals are available from around N$85. Given its remote location, the standards of food & service in the lodge are superb. The rather dusty campsite has some very basic chalets (without mosquito protection) as well as individual tent pitches.

Electricity is from a generator, which runs for most of the day, but if you need a TV, or contact with the outside world, then you are in the wrong place: there is no direct phone or fax here. The difficult radio-telephone, via Walvis Bay, is the swiftest way to communicate in an emergency.

15

If you don't have your own 4x4 then the lodge can organise full-day (N$500 pp, min 4 people) or half-day (N$300 pp, min 4 people) tours to local Himba villages, with a guide. A full-day tour down the Hoanib River Valley also costs N$500 pp, and includes lunch. If you haven't got a vehicle at all, then there is a 2km landing strip at Sesfontein, from which the lodge will collect you.
N$800/620 sgl/pp sharing, B&B. Camping N$65 pp, chalets N$85 pp. Dinner N$150, lunchpack N$70.

What to see and do Aside from relaxing in town, to explore further into Kaokoland is difficult (see below). For most people, the best way to see the area is on an organised trip: either one pre-arranged with a specialist before you arrive, or a day trip arranged by Fort Sesfontein.

KAOKOLAND

This vast tract of land is Namibia at its most enticing – and yet most inhospitable. Kaokoland appeals to the adventurer and explorer in us, keeping quiet about the dangers involved. On the eastern side, hilly tracks become mudslides as they get washed away by the rains, whilst the baking desert in the west affords no comfort for those who get stranded. Even dry riverbeds hide soft traps of deep sand, whilst the few which seem damp and hard may turn to quicksand within metres. Having struggled to free a Land Rover with just one wheel stuck in quicksand, it is easy to believe tales of vehicles vanishing within an hour.

One road on the eastern side was particularly memorable for me – it started favourably as a good gravel track. After 20km, it had deteriorated into a series of rocky ruts, shaking us to our bones and forcing us to slow down to 10km/h. After a while, when we'd come too far to think of returning, the track descended into a sandy riverbed, strewn with boulders and enclosed by walls of rock. The only way was for passengers to walk and guide the driver, watching as the tyres lurched from boulder to boulder.

Hours later we emerged – onto another difficult track. Gradually it flattened and the driving eased: we were happy to be travelling faster. Then the pace was interrupted. Streams crossed the road. Someone would wade across to check the depth, and then the 4x4 would swiftly follow, its momentum carrying it across the muddy bed. The third stream stopped us: more than thigh-high, fast flowing – a river in flood. We slept dry in our tents, thankful that the floods hadn't reached that first rocky riverbed while we were there.

In recent years, several of the roads in the vicinity have been improved, making the region more accessible to independent drivers. Where roads are now designated as C roads on the map supplied by the tourist board, these are generally safe enough in the dry season; the D roads, though, are another matter. Nevertheless, you should ideally still have a two-vehicle 4x4 expedition, all your supplies, an experienced navigator, detailed maps and good local advice on routes. Even then you'll probably get lost a few times. This is not a trip to undertake lightly: if things go wrong you will be hundreds of kilometres from help, and days from a hospital.

If you can get an expedition together, then in contrast to Damaraland's regulated concession areas, you'll find that Kaokoland has yet to adopt any formal system of control, and you are free to travel where you can. However, this freedom is causing lasting damage to the area. The Kaokoveld's drier areas, especially to the west, have a very fragile ecosystem: simply driving a vehicle off the tracks and 'across country' can cause permanent damage – killing plants and animals, and leaving marks that last for centuries. Vehicle trails made 40 years ago can still be seen, as the crushed plants and lichens haven't yet recovered. So you must be responsible and treat the environment with care – and never drive off the tracks.

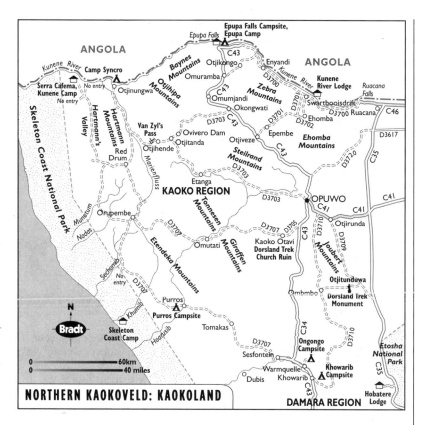

In addition to one or two upmarket lodges, there are several demarcated campsites, some run directly by the community, and others by Kaokohimba Safaris (see page 350). All cater for self-sufficient expeditions in 4x4s, and travellers are urged to support them. Where there is no such provision, you can choose your own site, provided that you obtain permission from the head of the local village, and show due respect to the area's inhabitants (see *Where you can camp*, pages 107–8). Here, more than anywhere else, there is a need to be responsible.

HOW TO VISIT KAOKOLAND Because Kaokoland is remote, the few camps here tend to be either very basic or very organised. The basic ones are a couple of simple campsites, often run by the local communities with the backing of one of the conservation/development organisations. The organised camps are a few expensive camps, most linked with small, specialist, fly-in operators. Following upgrades to some of the roads, it is possible to drive north to Epupa Falls, but touring the area independently is not an option.

Specialist Kaokoland operators When planning a visit to this area, you should consider who is taking you, rather than exactly where you're staying. Choose the most knowledgeable operator with whom you feel comfortable, and then go with them.

Kaokoland is rugged and remote. Trusting your arrangements to anyone who does not know it intimately is foolish. Don't visit here accompanied by someone who runs general trips all over the country. Instead choose one of the specialists who concentrate on this area. Finally, do satisfy yourself that your operator values the fragility of the area and its culture. Amongst other things, consider:

- How (if at all) your operator ensures that the local people benefit from your visit. Do they charge an automatic bed-night levy which is then paid into local community funds?
- How sensitive the operator is to the local cultures. Do their staff speak the local languages?
- Whether they use local people for staff, creating local employment prospects.

Such operations may use their own fixed camps, or mobile camps, which can be moved when necessary. This is the most comfortable way to see Kaokoland, and also the best way. You need a good guide here. Amongst many that run occasional trips, two excellent specialists stand out:

Kaokohimba Safaris \/f 061 222378;
e kaokohim@mweb.com.na;
www.natron.net/tour/kaoko/himbae.htm. Kaokohimba Safaris started up in 1989 & are certainly a contender for the area's best operation. Until recently, they organised tours in this area, conducted in person by the company's founder, Koos Verwey. Now the emphasis is changing towards activities such as hiking, for which self-catering huts are available. They are also involved in positive local community projects, & you probably won't find anyone who knows this area better. In fact, Koos is often said to care more for the Himba people than he does for the difficult guests on his safaris.

Kaokohimba's base is their Camp Syncro (see pages 357–8), at the northern end of the Marienfluss, east of the Hartmann Mountains. Their trips are active, though not necessarily strenuous. If you want to sit back passively & just watch, these are not for you. A new departure is a 14-day Epupa–Marienfluss hike, covering a distance of 180km. For details, contact Koos direct. The company will also be covering southwest Angola from 2008.

Skeleton Coast Fly-in Safaris \ 061 224248; f 061 225713; e scs@iway.na, www.skeletoncoastsafaris.com. See pages 323–4 for further information. Though you might not immediately associate the experts on the Skeleton Coast with the Kaokoveld, most of a trip to the Skeleton Coast is, in fact, spent just inland in the Kaokoveld. They normally visit the Purros area, and the region around the Kunene River, at the north end of the Hartmann's Mountains. The experience offered by Skeleton Coast Safaris is just as much about the Kaokoveld as it is about the coast – and that's how these trips have always been. Their founder, the late Louw Schoeman, was also an early supporter of the Auxiliary Game Guard scheme (now called the Community Game Guard scheme) that has done so much good in the region. Their eco-credentials are amongst the best in the business, and it remains a superb operation.

Also worth considering in this region are another local specialist, **Kunene Tours and Safaris**, run by Caesar Zandberg (e *zandberg@iafrica.com.na*), and the more general operator **Namibia Tours and Safaris** (☏ *064 406038;* f *064 406036;* e *aas@aas.com.na; www.namibia-tours-safaris.com*).

OPUWO This rough-and-ready frontier town is the hub of Kaokoland. It has shops, a good bakery, several garages, a large school, and even a short stretch of tarred road in the centre of town, despite being over 100km from the nearest other tar (south of Kamanjab, or east of Ruacana).

Getting there Opuwo is 54km of mediocre gravel from the main Kamanjab–Ruacana road and greets you with large, irrigated maize fields on the right, and probably a couple of stray cattle in front. Soon the dry, dusty town appears, sprawling over a low hillside with no apparent centre: its buildings are functional rather than attractive, and the outskirts fade into groups of round Himba huts.

Where to stay There's little accommodation in Opuwo, as most visitors just drive through on their way into Kaokoland, or back towards Etosha. This is a shame, but hardly surprising. While the town is the Himba 'capital', it does not provide the photographic opportunities to match the visitor's image of 'primitive tribespeople', and it isn't an attractive place in its own right; the proliferation of bars tells its own tale.

If you do stop here, then ignore the ill-informed advice of guidebooks that mention asking for help from the town's missions. They have more pressing calls from local people, and little time for scrounging travellers. Instead head for:

🏠 **Opuwo Country Hotel** (40 rooms, camping) ☏ 061 240375; f 061 256598; e opuwo@ ncl.com.na; www.namibialodges.com. Situated on a hilltop overlooking the valleys & mountains, this new hotel was officially opened in August 2005 by Namibia Country Lodges, & is an ideal base from

which to explore the area, albeit with no indication of the region's culture. There's an impressive main building with dining area, curio shop, wine cellar, bar & swimming pool, & guests can choose from 'luxury' or standard rooms.
N$695/495sgl/pp sharing; 'luxury' N$1,005/705 sgl/pp sharing, all B&B; camping N$75. Dinner N$135.

⌂ **Ohakane Lodge** (10 rooms) ⌇ 065 273031; f 067 273025; e ohakane@iway.na. This small lodge, named after the local word for 'wild dog', opened in 1995 & is well signposted just after the Shell fuel station. Its rooms all have AC & en-suite facilities, & there's even a swimming pool outside. Lunch & dinner are served, & there's a small selection of curios for sale. Unfortunately, the proximity to a local bar ensures loud music 24/7.

N$420/391 sgl/pp sharing, exc b/fast. Lunch N$60; dinner N$120.

⛺ **Kunene Village Restcamp** (2 bungalows, camping) ⌇ 065 273043; e office@nacobta.com.na; www.nacobta.com.na. This community-run campsite is well signposted about 2km west of Opuwo, on the road to Etanga (D3703). Its stone bungalows have twin beds (though no linen), & there are a number of grassy campsites, though reports suggest that it's not terribly well maintained. There's also an ablution block with flush toilets & showers. The bar here, of stone construction with carved-out windows, is a good place to share a cool drink with both locals & other travellers.
Camping N$50 pp; bungalows N$120/180 sgl/twin. Firewood N$10 per bundle.

Getting organised Turn right for the town's main attraction, the fuel station. As recently as 1990 there were no proper fuel supplies, just a few private entrepreneurs who sold it from drums on the back of pick-up trucks for twice the normal price. Now it is available at the 24-hour BP station, which helps with logistics, being the only fuel north of Sesfontein and west of Ruacana. However, beware of depending upon it, as this station can (and does) run out.

While waiting to fill up, or taking a stroll, look around – there is a fascinating mix of people, including the traditional rural Himba, who come into town to trade or buy supplies, with their decorated goatskin dress and ochre-stained skins. Strong, powerful faces speak clearly of people who have yet to trade their own culture for what little is being offered to them here. As with any frontier post, the place abounds with shady local traders. These mix with occasional businessmen, and the eccentric characters who emerge from the bush to replenish supplies, and then disappear again with equal speed. More open – and very annoying – are the very persistent youngsters who will try to sell you key rings with your name carved on them.

The BP garage sells cool drinks, and the adjacent bakery has excellent fresh bread, rolls and tasty-looking cakes, not to mention good pasties and sausage rolls. For more supplies go to OK Grocer, which is next to the BP garage. It's fairly well stocked with cold drinks, ice, wine and beer, as well as fresh fruit and vegetables on Fridays and Saturdays, and some basic hardware. The store also has its own bakery, a good butcher, and even a simple coffee shop. Branches of Bank Windhoek and First National Bank both have ATMs and foreign exchange bureaux, making Opuwo more traveller-friendly than in previous years. And the internet café near OK should ease any communications problems while in the area.

EPUPA FALLS Though visitors go to Kaokoland more for the whole experience than any individual sight, Epupa is one of its highlights.

About 145km west of Ruacana, the Kunene River is already threading its way through the Baynes Mountains, en route to the Atlantic. It winds between arid hills and wild, rough-looking mountains on both sides. Angola lies to its north, Namibia to its south: both look identical. As it meanders east, a thin strip of verdant palm-forest lines its path. Photogenic, feathery fronds of green Makalani palms extend for perhaps only 30m from the river itself. Further from the water than that, the land reverts to its parched, dry state: the preserve of the Kaokoveld's semi-desert flora and fauna.

Here at Epupa the river widens to accommodate a few small islands, before plunging into a geological fault. This is 35m deep in places and, as the river is sizeable, it makes a lot of noise and some spray. The Epupa Falls don't compare to Victoria Falls in scale, but they are all the more beautiful for occurring in such an arid region. Add to the scene a phalanx of watchful baobabs, many balancing improbably on precarious rocks above the chasms, or standing forlornly on the small islands in the stream. It's a magical spot.

Flora and fauna Epupa's flora and fauna are representative of the ecosystem found in the palm-forest which lines the river for most of its length.

Hippos have been exterminated from this section of the river, though crocodiles are still common (bathing is safe only immediately beside the falls) and small mammals are common in the palm-forest. There are few large wild mammals commonly seen around here, although spotted impala and kudu are resident.

Ornithologists will find a fascinating variety of birds, including the inevitable fish eagles, various bee-eaters, kingfishers ranging from the giant to the tiny malachite kingfisher, louries, bulbuls and hornbills, as well as rollers (purple, lilac breasted and European), golden and lesser masked weavers, scarlet-breasted sunbirds, and perhaps the odd, lost, great white eagret. The rare rufus-tailed palm thrush also occurs in this riverine palm-forest, which is typical of its highly restricted habitat; they are resident at Epupa Camp.

Easier to see, though, is a breeding colony of rosy-faced lovebirds, living amongst the trees in a nearby valley, and the fearless pair of paradise flycatchers that were nesting at eye level just above my tent.

Other attractions Gemologists should seek out the same valley as the lovebirds, but keep their eyes on the ground for the rose quartz crystals that abound. You may also find the chipped stone implements of past inhabitants.

Sunrise bathes the nearby hills in clear red light, and this is a good time to explore. The hills have an uneven surface of loose rock so wear a stout pair of shoes and watch out for snakes. Temperatures are cold at first, but it warms up very rapidly so take water, a sunhat and suncream. As with exploring anywhere near this border, seek local advice. Some areas were mined during the liberation struggle, and injuries still occur, albeit not in the last ten years or so.

Because Epupa is situated in a traditional Himba area, you may get the opportunity to visit a typical local family. Go with a guide who speaks the local language, and try to learn a few words yourself – *Perivi* ('Hello, how are you?) and *Okuhepa* ('Thank you') make a good start. Make sure, too, that the village receives some real benefit from your visit. Buying craftwork made by the villagers is one very good way of doing this, but simply taking along some mealie-meal would also be a positive gesture. With patience, your interpreter should help you to glimpse a little of their lifestyle.

Of all the Namibians that you encounter, the Himba require some of the greatest cultural sensitivity. Their culture is adapting to centuries of changes within a matter of years. Until the late 1980s there were people living in the area who relied entirely on a hunter-gatherer existence, using only stone implements – a reminder of how remote this area was until very recently.

Where to stay

Epupa Camp (9 safari tents) ☎ 061 232740; f 061 249876; e epupa@mweb.com.na; www.epupa.com.na. On the palm-fringed banks of the Kunene, 700m east of the main falls, Epupa Camp features safari-style tents with en-suite shower &

toilet, lights powered by a generator or batteries, & mosquito-netted doors & windows. Seven of the tents face the river, as do the dining area & swimming pool.

Activities include nature walks around the local

THE CONTROVERSY For several years the Namibian and Angolan governments have been co-operating in studies to build a hydro-electric dam across the Kunene. Two sites have been mooted: one in the Baynes Mountains, and one at Epupa, although this latter is no longer under consideration. Advocates of the scheme have pointed to Namibia's rising power consumption, and the apparent 'waste' of the Kunene's huge potential. They also cite the project as a source of work in the northern Kaokoveld – an area that lacks virtually any formal employment opportunities.

Critics regard this as a 'prestige project' for the government, which is both superfluous and damaging. They claim that its power will be expensive and unnecessary, and that it will do immense damage to the Kunene's ecosystems and the culture of the Himba people who live near the river. Cynics suggest that part of the SWAPO government's enthusiasm for the project is due to the work that it would generate for migrant workers from outside the Kaokoveld. Most would come from the densely populated areas to the east, the Owambo heartlands, which are SWAPO's constituency. They also observe that the Himba generally did not side with SWAPO during the liberation struggle, and suggest that the government is now trying to marginalise them and destroy their traditional lands and culture.

Despite Namibia's constitution, ex-president Sam Nujoma has been reported as becoming exasperated by the extended opposition to the project, which he seemed to believe is fermented by foreign groups rather than local people. The debate continues.

Several organisations have helped the Himba communities to put their point forward, and campaign against the dam. These include, in Namibia, the non-profit law firm Legal Assistance Centre (LAC) and, abroad, the London-based Survival (*6 Charterhouse Bldgs, London EC1M 7ET;* \ *020 7687 8700;* f *020 7687 8701;* e *info@survival-international.org; www.survival-international.org*). Survival works to support tribal peoples. It stands for their right to decide their own future and helps them protect their lives, lands and human rights.

THE FEASIBILITY STUDY To dispel the controversy over the project, a full feasibility study was commissioned by the government for the Epupa Dam project, but nobody was surprised when, at the start of 1998, the official report backed the dam, claiming that its few negative impacts would be greatly outweighed by the positive ones. However, a panel of international experts swiftly discredited this feasibility report. These included internationally renowned specialists in ecology, water management, economics, alternative energy and Namibian law. They scrutinised it at the request of several non-governmental organisations, including the California-based International Rivers Network (IRN: *www.irn.org/programs/epupa*). These independent experts concluded that the report was 'riddled with incorrect conclusions, false assumptions and missing data so that it cannot be used as a basis for a well-informed decision on the project'.

area & guided visits to a local Himba village, as well as ¹/₂-day rafting trips on the Kunene. The camp works closely with the local community & makes much of its 'sound ecological policy'. In the last year, the road to Epupa has been upgraded, but a 4x4 is still recommended. The easiest route is from Opuwo via Okongwati (about 200km). Note there is no help on this route if an emergency occurs. As with anywhere in this area, it is advisable to be in a party of at least 2 4x4s with

experienced drivers, & to take particular care during the rainy season.
N$1,260/850 sgl/pp sharing, DBB.
N$1,640/1,230.00 sgl/pp sharing, fully inclusive, except rafting (N$300 pp).
Å **Epupa Falls Campsite** \ 065 695 1065. Epupa has become such a Mecca for visitors to the Kaokoveld that people camped here long before a site existed. Eventually the community set up a couple of sites next to the falls to benefit from

THE VIEW OF THE HIMBA PEOPLE Most Himba people don't want a dam. In February 1998, 26 out of the 32 traditional leaders in the Kunene Region submitted a detailed document to the government noting 11 major objections to the proposed site at Epupa:

- **Loss of land** The dam would inundate about 190km² on the Namibian side of the river, including 110 permanent dwellings.
- **Loss of riverine resources** The narrow palm-forest beside the river is a vital source of food for both people and livestock.
- **Loss of gardens** Many of the Himba people cultivate small gardens on the alluvial soils.
- **Disappearance of wildlife** Without the river much wildlife would be lost.
- **Inundation of ancestral gravesites** These are very important in Himba culture in defining to whom the land belongs.
- **Barrier effect of the dam** Himba communities live on both sides of the river, and regularly cross it. A large dam would make this difficult or impossible.
- **Health threats** A large lake would introduce more malaria and bilharzia, and the influx of a mobile labour force would probably bring with it carriers of HIV infection, and other sexually transmitted diseases.
- **Overcrowding** The dam would require about 1,000 workers, and a construction town would probably have a population of about 5,000. When the dam is finished the area would go 'from boom to bust'.
- **Increased crime** The influx of construction workers would probably increase the crime rate, which is currently very low.
- **Loss of control** The Himba people fear the loss of their lands to outsiders.
- **Loss of ecotourism potential** Without the dam, Epupa could be a major attraction for tourists, which would benefit the local community.

THE CURRENT SITUATION With the discovery of the Kudu gas fields near Oranjemund, at least some of Namibia's energy requirements look set to be met from an entirely different source. Nevertheless, a further source of power is required, and a dam on the Kunene remains on the agenda, despite government recognition that climate change will inevitably have an impact on hydro-electric projects. Discussions are now under way between the Namibian and Angolan governments as to the preferred siting for the dam, which now focuses on an alternative site, Baynes. This lies some 40km downstream of Epupa Falls, and was originally considered to be too small, but with the potential for a lower environmental impact than the Epupa site, it is now back in the frame. While the cultural impacts of the Baynes site are considerably lower than those of the Epupa site, many problems remain. It is anticipated that a feasibility report on the project will be completed some time in 2008.

these visitors, & in order to protect the fragile palm-forest from being ruined by visitors in search of virgin camping sites. Today these rustic sites are operated by Kaokohimba (see page 350), with a local manager, Amos. One is next to the falls; the second is a short distance upstream, near some hot springs in the middle of the river (though the combination of fast-flowing water & the presence of crocodiles makes it impossible to reach them). Expect spotlessly clean flush toilets & hot showers

behind reed screens. Campers can often buy vegetables & even a few crafts from the local villagers, & there's also a small shop on site. *N$50 pp.*

🏠 **Kunene River Lodge** (11 chalets/bungalows, camping) ☎ 065 274300; 🖷 065 274301; ✉ info@kuneneriverlodge.com; www.kuneneriverlodge.com. Near Swartbooisdrift, about 50km west of Ruacana, on the D3700, this privately run lodge has rustic chalets & more upmarket bungalows, all of them en suite. Nearby, grassy, tree-shaded camping sites with clean ablutions, flush toilets & hot water are set along the Kunene River. There is also a pleasant bar & restaurant overlooking the river.

Among the activities available are whitewater rafting, quadbiking, canoeing & fishing.

N$400/600 sgl/dbl; camping N$75 pp.

THE WESTERN VALLEYS

THE WESTERN VALLEYS In the west, Hartmann's Valley and the Marienfluss are often visited by the Kaokoveld's specialists. Both valleys run north–south, bounded in the north by the Kunene, which flows all year. The main approach road is along the D3707, a 4x4 track heading northwest from Sesfontein.

Some 100km from Sesfontein, you'll come to the village of Purros, where there's a community campsite that's well worth visiting:

 Purros Campsite also known as **Ngatutunge Pamue Campsite** (6 pitches) Reservations ✆ 061 255977; f 061 222647; e office@nacobta.com.na; www.nacobta.com.na. The community-run Ngatutunge Pamue, meaning 'We build together', is about 100km northwest of Sesfontein, 2km north of Purros, on the D3707. The approach road has deep patches of sand, so drive with care. The pitches are on the wooded bank of the Hoarusib River, with flush toilets (though recent reports suggest that these are now long drops) surrounded by reeds There are also (cold) showers & fireplace (no grid) with tap & bin. Nearby is a section of the river that is normally forced over-ground by a rock barrier.

A major purpose of the camp is to provide employment for the local Himba from Purros village, so you are strongly encouraged to hire guides for your own game drives & to take guided walks looking for plants used in traditional medicine, as well as escorted trips to Himba villages. Costs are very reasonable, & this is an effective way to put some money directly into the local economy. Around Purros it is usually possible to visit Himba villages on foot, which is a more leisurely & satisfying way to meet these pastoral people, allowing plenty of time for an exchange of views & questions through your guide. After all, how would you like it if a group of strangers drove up to your house, came in & took pictures of your family & then departed within 5 or 10 mins? So do greet the villagers, & spend time talking with them, & learning a little of how they live. Many now are helped by the income made from selling jewellery, or guiding visitors around their local area – they deserve your support.

Note that elephants occur frequently in the area & around the campsite & should not be harassed in any way; they are dangerous & unpredictable animals, & have killed people.

N$40 pp camping. Firewood N$15 per bundle – but use sparingly as it's in very short supply.

Hartmann's Valley

Hartmann's Valley As you enter the valley, there is a small sign covered with weatherworn glass. It stresses the ecologically important things you must do, and includes a diagram of how to turn a vehicle around to minimise damage to the environment. Take time to read it and remember.

Hartmann's Valley itself is very arid, though its weather can vary dramatically. As well as searing heat, the valley receives sea mists, which creep up from the coast, making it an eerie place to visit.

It is 70km from end to end, a minimum of 2½ hours' drive one way, and the condition of the track along it varies. In the south, the road starts by crossing a number of steep-sided river valleys. It soon changes to compacted corrugated sand, which shakes your vehicle violently. Finally, this becomes soft before high dunes prevent you reaching the Kunene by vehicle. Despite the harsh conditions, it is very beautiful. Drive through at sunrise if possible; then it's cooler than later and shows off the surrounding hills at their finest.

Where to stay There are two private camps at the end of the valley:

Serra Cafema Camp (8 tents) Contact via Wilderness Safaris; ✆ 061 274500; f 061 239455; e info@nts.com.na; www.wilderness-safaris.com. This exclusive camp on the edge of the Kunene was rebuilt in 2003 on the foundations of a much simpler camp, with the aim of giving visitors a relaxed environment after the harshness of the Skeleton Coast. Nestled in a narrow fringe of riverine vegetation, its tented chalets, shaded under thatch, are constructed on elevated wooden decks by the river. Soft lighting & natural wood aplenty are offset by cream-coloured fabrics. Comforts abound, with each of the chalets having an overhead fan, indoor & outdoor shower, & twin beds (there's 1 dbl, & 2 rooms join to make a family suite). A veranda looks over the river, with a hammock to while away the hours & catch any natural breeze.

This is the place to explore the farthest reaches of the Kunene River, home to springbok, ostrich & oryx – but very few people. Visitors can walk in the mountains & along the river valley, take guided quad-bike excursions into the dunes, or discover the secrets of the river by boat. Fishing, too, is on the agenda, making this a camp that appeals to a range of guests. Because of the difficult logistics of getting here, though, & the high comfort levels of the camp itself, it's not a cheap place to stay. *N$3,400–4,500 pp per night, depending on time of year.*

🏠 **Kunene Camp** Run by Skeleton Coast Safaris, this very small & simple camp is usually used for a final night as part of their fly-in trips to the Skeleton Coast & the Kaokoveld. See pages 323–4 and 350–1 for more details on this operation, & note that this is always pre-booked as part of a fly-in trip. They cannot accept people who try to just drop in.

The Marienfluss

The next valley inland from Hartmann's is the Marienfluss. If you are driving, this is reached via Red Drum – a crossroads marked by a red oil can. There is a fairly new-looking Himba settlement at Red Drum.

The Marienfluss has more soft sand and is greener than Hartmann's Valley. It is covered with light scrub and the odd tree marks an underground river. A most noticeable feature of the Marienfluss is its 'fairy circles', although they are also found, to a lesser extent, in Hartmann's Valley. These are circular patches without any vegetation. Studies by Professors G Theron and E Moll, from the universities of Pretoria and Cape Town, put forward three possible theories for their origin.

One theory suggests that *Euphorbia* bushes once grew here. It's thought that when they died, they may have left poisonous chemicals in the soil, which prohibit grass from growing. Another idea is that tropical termites may be blown into the Pro-Namib during wet cycles, starting colonies that kill the grasses. During the dry cycles, these die off leaving the bare circles that we see. A third theory suggests that there are 'hardpans' in these patches. That is, layers of soil through which water cannot penetrate, making plant life impossible. Of course, one other common explanation is that they were, indeed, made by fairies.

🏠 **Where to stay** At the northern end of the Marienfluss, there is a public and also a private campsite. Both are set on the banks of the Kunene mainly under the shade of camelthorn trees, *Acacia erioloba*.

On the track that goes past these camps there is a sign saying 'no photographs'. (The logic of this isn't obvious, except for the proximity of the Angolan border.) After a further 3km the road divides into three. The left fork goes to an excellent viewing point, over some rapids in the river. The centre and right turns are both blocked. If you walk up the middle track, you'll find a small beach on the Kunene. The right track leads off to some trees, which may have been a campsite once.

In the morning and evening you'll see many Himba people going about their business, often with their cattle. There is also some wildlife around, including springbok, ostrich, bat-eared fox, bustards, korhanns, and many other birds.

🏠 **Camp Syncro** (4 houses) ☎ 065 685021; e koos.cunene@iway.na; www.natron.net/tour/camp-syncro/. This small, simple camp run by Kaokohimba Safaris (see page 350) occupies a lovely spot overlooking the Kunene, from the end of the Marienfluss. Its simple thatched houses, constructed with stones from the river, stand in the shade of ana trees. Each has water for drinking & twin beds. Two showers & flush toilets are shared between the houses, & from 2008 these will be en suite. There's also a kitchen, so the camp works well for self-catering guests as well. Most important, of course, is that you come to explore the area with Koos, & to meet the local people.

N$1,045/945 sgl/pp sharing, FB.

⋏ Okarohombo Campsite e office@nacobta.com.na; www.nacobta.com.na. On the banks of the Kunene, at the northern end of the Marienfluss, is a simple signposted campsite under ana trees, run by the local Himba community (who speak little English). Facilities at the 5 pitches are limited to a few flush toilets & fireplaces. Cold showers are sometimes available but could be washed away as the camp is at floodwater level. As this is one of the more remote areas where Himba people live, it is less commercialised than other places, & is a good location to experience their lifestyle. Like most community campsites, this is worth your support.

N$30 pp camping.

16

Etosha National Park

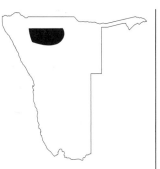

Translated as the 'Place of Mirages', 'Land of Dry Water' or the 'Great White Place', Etosha is an apparently endless pan of silvery-white sand, upon which dust-devils play and mirages blur the horizon. As a game park, it excels during the dry season when huge herds of animals can be seen amidst some of the most startling and photogenic scenery in Africa.

The roads are all navigable in a normal 2WD car, and the park was designed for visitors to drive themselves around. If you insist on guided trips then look to one of the private lodges just outside the park or, better, to the concession areas in Damaraland. Etosha is a park to explore by yourself. Put a few drinks, a camera, lots of film and a pair of binoculars in your own car and go for a slow drive, stopping at the waterholes – it's amazing.

There are three restcamps within the park, and several lodges outside its boundaries, and yet the park is never busy in comparison with equally good reserves elsewhere in Africa.

BACKGROUND INFORMATION

HISTORY Europeans first knew Etosha in the early 1850s when Charles Andersson and Francis Galton visited it. They recorded their early impressions:

> ... we traversed an immense hollow, called Etosha, covered with saline encrustations, and having wooded and well-defined borders. Such places are in Africa designated 'salt pans' ... In some rainy seasons, the Ovambo informed us, the locality was flooded and had all the appearance of a lake; but now it was quite dry, and the soil strongly impregnated with salt. Indeed, close in shore, the commodity was to be had of a very pure quality.

They were amongst the first explorers and traders who relentlessly hunted the area's huge herds of game. In 1876 an American trader, McKiernan, came through the area and wrote of a visit to Etosha:

> All the menageries in the world turned loose would not compare to the sight that I saw that day.

The slaughter became worse as time progressed and more Europeans came until, in 1907, Dr F von Lindequist, the Governor of German South West Africa (as Namibia was then), proclaimed three reserves. These covered all of the current park, and most of Kaokoland – between the Kunene and Hoarusib rivers. The aim was to stem the rapid depletion of the animals in the area, and protect all of the land through which the seasonal migrations passed. It was an excellent plan for conserving the wildlife – though perhaps not so perfect for the people who lived in these areas.

This protected area remained largely intact until the 1950s and '60s. Then, just as a nature conservation unit and several tourist camps were set up, the reserves were redefined and Etosha shrank to its present size.

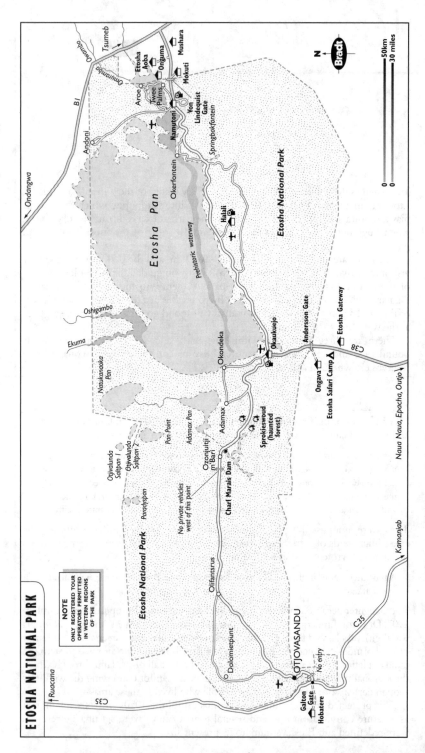

ETOSHA NATIONAL PARK

NOTE
ONLY REGISTERED TOUR
OPERATORS PERMITTED
IN WESTERN REGIONS
OF THE PARK

Ruacana

C35

Ondangwa

Omuramba

Omuramba

B1

Tsumeb

Etosha
Aoba
Onjuma
Mushara
Mokuti

Aroe
Twee
Palms
Namutoni
Von
Lindequist
Gate
Springbokfontein

Andoni

Okerfontein

Halali

Etosha Pan

Prehistoric waterway

Etosha National Park

Oshigambo

Ekuma

Natukanooka
Pan

Okondeka

Okaukuejo

Andersson Gate

Etosha Gateway

C38

Ongava
Etosha Safari Camp

Ojivalunda
Saltpan I
Ojivalunda
Saltpan 2

Pan Point

Adamax Pan

Paradyspan

Adamax

Ozonjuitji
m'Bari

No private vehicles
west of this point

Charl Marais Dam

Sprokieswoud
(haunted
forest)

Etosha National Park

Olifantsrus

Dolomietpunt

OTJOVASANDU

No entry

C35

Kamanjab

Naua Naua, Epacha, Outjo

Galton
Gate
Hobatere

N

Bradt

50km
30 miles

360

GEOGRAPHY, LANDSCAPE AND FLORA The defining feature of the national park is the huge Etosha Pan, which appears to be the remnant of a large inland lake that was fed by rivers from the north and east. One of these was probably the Kunene, which flowed southeast from the Angolan highlands and into the pan. However, some 12 million years ago continental uplift changed the slope of the land and the course of these tributaries. The Kunene now flows west from the Ruacana Falls and into the Atlantic. Thus deprived, the lake slowly vanished in the scorching sun, leaving behind only a salty residue. Few plants can grow on this and so erosion by the wind is easy, allowing the pan to be gradually hollowed out.

The pan has probably changed little over time. It is roughly 110km from east to west and 60km from north to south, covering an area of 6,133km² (around a quarter of the park's surface) with flat, silvery sand and shimmering heat. If the rains to the north and east have been good, then the pan will hold water for a few months at the start of the year, thanks mainly to the Ekuma River and Omuramba Owambo. Only very rarely does it fill completely.

In the rest of the park, beyond the sides of the pan, the terrain is generally flat with a variety of habitats ranging from mopane woodland to wide, open, virtually treeless plains. In the east of the park, around Namutoni, the attractive makalani palms, *Hyphaene ventricosa*, are found, often in picturesque groups around waterholes. The small, round fruit of these palms, a favourite food of elephants, is sometimes called vegetable ivory because of its hard white kernel. In the west, one of the more unusual areas is the Haunted Forest, *Sprokieswoud* in Afrikaans, where the contorted forms of strange moringa trees, *Moringa ovalifolia*, form a weird woodland scene.

Etosha is so special because of the concentration of waterholes that occur around the southern edges of the pan. As the dry season progresses, these increasingly draw the game. In fact, the best way to watch animals in Etosha is often just to sit in your vehicle by a waterhole and wait.

Three types of spring create these waterholes, which differ in both appearance and geology:

Contact springs These occur in situations where two adjacent layers of rock have very different permeabilities. There are many to be seen just on the edge of the pan. Here the water-bearing calcrete comes to an end and the water flows out onto the surface because the underlying layers of clay are impermeable. Okerfontein is the best example of this type of spring, which is generally weak in water supply.

Water-level springs These are found in hollows where the surface of the ground actually cuts below the level of the water table, often in large depressions in the limestone formations. They are inevitably dependent on the level of the water table, and hence vary greatly from year to year. Typical of this type are Ngobib, Groot Okevi and Klein Okevi.

Artesian springs Formed when pressure from overlying rocks forces water up to the surface from deeper aquifers (water-bearing rocks), here they normally occur on limestone hillocks, forming deep pools, which will often have clumps of reeds in their centre. These springs are usually very reliable and include Namutoni, Klein Namutoni, Chudob and Aus.

MAMMALS The game and birds found here are typical of the savanna plains of southern Africa, but include several species endemic to this western side of the continent, adjacent to the Namib Desert.

The more common herbivores include elephant, giraffe, eland, blue wildebeest, kudu, gemsbok, springbok, impala, steenbok and zebra. The most numerous of these are the springbok which can often be seen in herds numbering thousands, spread out over the most barren of plains. These finely marked antelope have a marvellous habit of pronking, either (it appears) for fun or to avoid predators. It has been suggested that pronking is intended to put predators off in the first place by showing the animal's strength and stamina; the weakest pronkers are the ones predators are seen to go for. The early explorer Andersson described these elegant leaps:

> This animal bounds without an effort to a height of 10 or 12 feet at one spring,
> clearing from 12 to 14 feet of ground. It appears to soar, to be suspended for a
> moment in the air, then, touching the ground, to make another dart, or another
> flight, aloft, without the aid of wings, by the elastic springiness of its legs.

Elephant are very common, though digging for water below the sand wears down their tusks and so big tuskers are very rare. Often large family groups are seen trooping down to waterholes to drink, wallow and bathe. The park's population has been under scientific scrutiny for the infrasonic noises (below the range of human hearing) which they make. It is thought that groups communicate over long distances in this way.

Among the rarer species, black rhino continue to thrive here, and the floodlit waterholes at Okaukuejo and Halali provide two of the continent's best chances to observe this aggressive and secretive species. On one visit here, I watched as a herd of 20 or so elephants, silently drinking in the cool of the night, were frightened away from the water, and kept at bay, by the arrival of a single black rhino. It returned several times in the space of an hour or so, each time causing the larger elephants to flee, before settling down to enjoy a drink from the pool on its own.

In recent years, about a dozen white rhino have been introduced. Your best chance of seeing these is in the east of the park, around Aus, Springbokfontein, Batia or Okerfontein, either early or late in the day.

Black-faced impala are restricted to Namibia and southern Angola, occurring here as well as in parts of the Kaokoveld. With only isolated populations, numbering under a thousand or so, they are one of the rarest animals in the region. The Damara dik-dik is the park's smallest antelope. Endemic to Namibia, it is common here in areas of dense bush.

Roan antelope and red hartebeest occur all over the subcontinent, though they are common nowhere. This is definitely one of the better parks in which to look for roan, especially in the mopane areas around Aus and Olifantsbad.

All of the larger felines are found here, with good numbers of lion, leopard, cheetah and caracal. The lion tend to prey mainly upon zebra and wildebeest, whilst the cheetah rely largely upon springbok. The seldom-seen leopard take a varied diet, including antelope and small mammals, whilst the equally elusive caracal go for similar but smaller prey.

There have been several attempts to introduce wild dog here, but so far no success. The usual problem has been that the dogs don't know to avoid lion, which have subsequently killed them for no apparent reason.

Also found in the park are both spotted and brown hyenas, together with silver jackal (or cape fox), and the more common black-backed jackal – many of which can be seen in the late evening, skulking around the camps in search of scraps of food.

BIRDS For ornithologists, some 340 species of birds have been recorded, including many uncommon members of the hawk and vulture families.

Amongst the birds of prey, bateleur, martial, tawny and Wahlberg's eagles are fairly common, as are black-breasted and brown snake eagles. Pale chanting goshawks are more often seen than the similar Gabar or the smaller little banded goshawk. The list of harriers, falcons and kestrels occurring here is even longer, and worthy of a special mention are the very common rock kestrels, which are everywhere, and the unusual red-necked and particularly cute pygmy falcons, which are less readily seen. The impressive peregrine falcon and Montagu's harrier are two of the rarer summer migrants.

Lappet-faced and white-backed vultures are common here, outnumbering the odd pair of white-headed or hooded vultures. Palmnut vultures are occasionally seen in the east of the park.

The number of large birds stalking around the plains can strike visitors as unusual: invariably during the day you will see groups of ostriches or pairs of secretary birds. Equally, it is easy to drive within metres of many kori bustards and black korhaans, which will just sit by the roadside and watch the vehicles pass.

Blue cranes, both beautiful and endangered, are common here in the wet season. Etosha is worth visiting in January and February for them alone. Other specialities of the park include violet wood hoopoe, white-tailed shrike, bare-cheeked and black-faced babblers, short-toed rock thrush, and a pale race of the pink-bellied lark.

PRACTICAL INFORMATION

To see Etosha you need to drive around the park *(entry N$80 pp (under 16s free), plus N$10 per vehicle. Get entry permit at gate, but pay fees at the first restcamp you come to. Speed limit 60km/h).* There is no way to walk within it, or to fly just above it. If you do not have your own vehicle then you must either hire one, or book an organised trip.

Hiring your own vehicle is best done in Windhoek. See *Driving in Namibia,* pages 87–91. However, if you are travelling through, and hiring a car just for Etosha, then consider doing so from Tsumeb. This is normally best organised in advance, through a tour operator (pages 52–4) or the car-hire companies in Windhoek (see page 91), some of which will let you pick up and drop-off cars at Mokuti or Ongava.

Organised trips to the park emanate from the private lodges around the park. See *Accommodation near Etosha* (pages 368–72) for ideas about what is possible from each. Other than these, many operators organise guided trips around Namibia, including a few days in Etosha, often staying in the national park's accommodation. However, you only need to see one air-conditioned 75-seater coach driving through the park to convince you that this is not the best way to visit either Etosha or Namibia. Most have their bases in Windhoek; see pages 155–7 for details.

WHEN TO VISIT To decide when to visit, think about the weather, consider the number of other visitors around, and work out if your main reason for coming is to see the animals or the birds.

Weather Etosha's weather is typical of Namibia, so see *Chapter 3*'s section on *Weather*, pages 33–5, for a general overview. At the beginning of the year, it's hot and fairly damp with average temperatures around 27°C and cloud cover for some of the time. If the rains have been good, then the pan will have some standing water in it.

The clouds gradually disperse as the rains cease, around March–April. Many of Etosha's plants are bright green during this time but, with some cloud cover, the park's stark beauty isn't at its most photogenic.

From April to July the park dries out, and nights become cooler. Nights in August are normally above freezing, and by the end of September they are warm

16

again. October is hot, and it gets hotter as the month progresses, but the humidity remains very low.

Even the game seems to await the coming of the rains in late November, or perhaps December. When these do arrive, the tropical downpours last only for a few hours each afternoon, but they clear the air, revive the vegetation, and give everything a new lease of life.

Photography From a photographic point of view, Etosha can be stunning in any month. A personal favourite is late April to June, when the vegetation is green, yet the skies are clear blue and there's little dust in the rain-washed air.

Other visitors Etosha is never crowded. Compared with the hordes of tourists that fill Kruger or the game parks of east Africa, Etosha always seems deserted, even when its lodges and restcamps are full. It becomes busier around Easter and from late July to September. Then advanced bookings are *essential*; you may not even get a camping site without a prior reservation. The accommodation inside the park during August can be full as early as the end of April.

The dates of the South African school holidays seem to be less relevant than they used to be, as Namibia is no longer the only foreign country where South African passport holders are welcomed. However, ideally try to avoid Namibian school holidays. February to mid-April, late May to July, and November are probably the quietest months.

Game-viewing Etosha's dry season is certainly the best time to see big game. Then, as the small bush pools dry up and the green vegetation shrivels, the animals move closer to the springs on the pan's edge. Before the game fences were erected (these now surround the park completely) many of the larger animals would have migrated between Etosha and the Kaokoveld – returning here during the dry season to the region's best permanent waterholes. Now most are forced to stay within the park and only bull elephants commonly break out of their confines to cause problems for the surrounding farmers.

Hence the months between July and late October are ideal for game. Though the idea of sitting in a car at 40°C may seem unpleasant, October is the best month for game and the heat is very dry. Park under a shady tree and be grateful that the humidity is so low.

During and after the rains, you won't see much game, partly because the lush vegetation hides the animals, and partly because most of them will have moved away from the waterholes (where most of the roads are) and gone deeper into the bush. However, often the animals you will see will have young, as food (animal or vegetable) is at its most plentiful then.

Birdwatching The start of the rainy season witnesses the arrival of the summer migrants and, if the rains have been good, the aquatic species that come for the water in the pan itself. In exceptional years thousands of flamingos will come to breed, building their nests on the eastern side of the main Etosha Pan, or in Fischer's Pan. This is an amazing spectacle (see box on *Flamingos*, page 305). However, bear in mind that Etosha's ordinary feathered residents can be seen more easily during the dry season, when there is less vegetation to hide them.

GETTING THERE AND AROUND All of Etosha's roads are accessible with a normal 2WD vehicle, and an excellent map of the park is available from the restcamps. A more colourful 'Honeyguide' publication also has a few pages of colour sketches of most of the common birds and animals. Both are normally for sale at a reasonable price in the restcamp shops, and the maps are also available from the restcamps' fuel stations.

By road You can enter the park via either the Von Lindequist Gate, near Namutoni, which is 106km from Tsumeb, or the Andersson Gate, south of Okaukuejo, 120km from Outjo. There is a road through to the western end of the park, and a gate on the park boundary. Until the long-planned fourth camp, Otjovasandu, opens, this whole region is closed to private visitors.

Entry permits to the park are issued at both gates. Then you must proceed to the nearest camp office and settle the costs of your accommodation and permits. Accommodation costs include entrance fees to the park, so the only extra that you will have to pay if you are staying overnight is the charge for the entry of your vehicle (N$10 for most small vehicles).

If you are just visiting the park for the day, then you will have to pay 'day visitor' park fees of N$80 per person per day, plus N$10 for the car. If you go out of the park for lunch, then strictly you should pay two park entry fees, but this rule *might* be relaxed if you politely tell the gatekeeper that you intend to return later in the day.

The gates open around sunrise and close about 20 minutes before sunset. For the precise times on any given day, see the notice next to the entry gates of each camp. Driving through the park in the dark is not allowed, and the gates do close on time. Neither hitchhiking nor bicycles (push or motor) are allowed in the park.

By air Air Namibia runs daily scheduled flights to Katima Mulilo (N$1,931), and twice daily to Ondangwa (N$1,181 per leg). There are also three flights a week between Windhoek and Victoria Falls via Maun.

Both Mokuti Lodge and Ongava have good airstrips, though flights are not currently scheduled.

Organised tour Etosha was designed for visitors to drive themselves around. The roads are good; a normal 2WD car is fine for all of them. The landscapes are generally open, as the vegetation is sparse, so you don't need eyes like a hawk to spot most of the larger animals. Thus very few people use organised tours to visit the park. However, if you really don't want to drive yourself around, then the main alternatives are either one of the lodges just outside the gates (see pages 368–72) or:

Etosha Fly-in Safaris 447 5th Av, Tsumeb; 067 220574; f 067 220832; e info@etosha.com; www.etosha.com. Based in Tsumeb, Etosha Fly-in Safaris is probably the only operator specialising in guided trips throughout the park & the Caprivi. A day trip to Etosha from the eastern gate costs from N$4,190 (up to 5 passengers), in a VW Combi minibus. As the company name suggests, they offer fly-in safaris around the country, including Etosha & the Caprivi, but can also do land-based safaris by VW Combi throughout Namibia & the Caprivi, with an emphasis on nature, wildlife & birding.

Etosha Game Viewers 064 402799; m 081 124 6344; f 064 405258; www.etoshagameviewers.com. This is the company used by some of the lodges close to the park gates.

WHERE TO STAY

Restcamps inside Etosha There are three national park restcamps inside Etosha, all of them very similar – offering good simple facilities at reasonable prices.

Aim to spend a minimum of two nights at any camp you visit. Remember that, with a speed limit of 60km/h, it will take you at least two hours to drive between Namutoni and Halali, or Halali and Okaukuejo.

The reception office at each restcamp opens from dawn to dusk, and there you pay for your stay, as well as any park fees due. Don't forget to pay *all* your park fees before you try to leave the park. You can't pay them at the gate.

16

Facilities Each camp has a range of accommodation, including bungalows and a campsite (see below). Each also has a fuel station (*open 06.30–12.00 & 15.00–18.00*), but don't run it too close; diesel wasn't available at Halali when we last visited), a restaurant, swimming pool and shop. The camp shop (*open 07.30–09.30, 11.30–14.00 & 17.00–20.00*) usually sells a remarkable assortment of foodstuffs: frozen meat, sausages and firewood (with braais in mind), as well as tinned and packet foods and often bread, eggs, and cheese. Beer, lots of cold drinks, and a limited selection of wine (but no wine can be sold on a Sunday) are also found here. Take your own cooking equipment.

Aside from food, there is also the usual mix of tourist needs from curios, T-shirts, print film (occasionally slide, but nothing too unusual) and wildlife books to postcards and even stamps; shops at Namutoni and Okaukuejo seem to have a little more stock than the one at Halali. You can normally buy phonecards at the shop for the nearby payphone. Okaukuejo also has an internet café (*open daily 08.00–21.00*).

Bookings Booking accommodation in advance at the NWR (e *reservations@ mweb.com.na; www.nwr.com.na*) in Windhoek (page 124) is wise, but you need to be organised and stick to your itinerary. The alternative is to plan on camping, whilst hoping for spaces or cancellations in the chalets and bungalows. For this you'll need to ask at the camp office just before it closes at sunset. This is often successful outside the main holiday months, but you need a tent in case it is not.

Note that during the main holiday seasons, around Easter and August, even Etosha's campsites are fully booked in advance. If you haven't a reservation, you must stay outside the park and drive in for day trips.

Accommodation: styles and costs All the camps have roughly similar rooms and bungalows – see the NWR's current *Accommodation Guide for Tourists* for the fine details of the facilities at each.

Almost all the rooms have private toilet and baths or showers, a fridge and a kettle. Towels and bed linen are always supplied. Most have air conditioning, and the VIP units even have cutlery and utensils. Bungalows also have hotplates and kitchen facilities, whilst rooms (which used to be called 'bus quarters') generally do not. All are normally clean and well kept, though functional rather than luxurious.

Accommodation prices vary slightly between camps. A camping pitch at around N$240 for up to eight people and two vehicles makes camping cheap for large parties.

🏠 **Okaukuejo Restcamp** (90 bungalows, 26 tent pitches) PO Box 36, Okaukuejo; ☎ 067 229800; f 067 229852. This was the first restcamp to open, & is the administrative hub of the park & the centre of the Etosha Ecological Institute. It occupies a level, grassy site situated at the western end of the pan, about 120km north of Outjo.

One big attraction of this camp is that it overlooks a permanent waterhole which is floodlit at night, giving you a chance to see some of the shy, nocturnal wildlife. The animals that come appear oblivious to the noises from the camp, not noticing the bright lights or the people sitting on benches just behind the low stone wall. The light doesn't penetrate into the dark surrounding bush, but it illuminates the waterhole like a stage – focusing all attention on the animals that come to drink. During the dry season you would be unlucky not to spot something of interest by just sitting here for a few hours in the evening, so bring a couple of drinks, binoculars, & some warm clothes to settle down & watch. You are virtually guaranteed to see elephant & jackal, while lion & black rhino are very regular visitors. The main annoyance is noise from the bungalows beside the waterhole, or from the many people sitting around.

Accommodation is in well-spaced luxury & standard bungalows. The campsite pitches have BBQ facilities & power points, but no grass & little shade. Good food (it's a buffet in season) is served at reasonable prices in the modern restaurant, which has AC. Sweets & drinks are available from the kiosk by the large circular swimming pools.

Okaukuejo's shop is well stocked, while opposite reception is the park's only post office (open Mon–Fri 08.30–13.00 and 14.00–16.30, Sat 08.00–11.00), as well as a tourist information office & a self-contained curio shop. Nearby, a small round tower can be climbed, by a spiral staircase inside, for a good view of the surrounding area. The differences between the homes of the Bushman, HImba & Nshembo can be seen through full-size huts that have been erected in the grounds. Okaukuejo also has a small museum in the main reception area.

'Luxury' 4-bed bungalow N$1,000, 'standard' 2–3-bedroom bungalow N$490, basic 2-bedroom bungalow N$390, camping pitch N$240.

⌂ **Halali Restcamp** (62 bungalows, 40 tent pitches) P Bag 2016, Tsumeb; ☏ 067 229400; ☏ 067 229413. The newest of the camps, opened in 1967, Halali stands between the others, 75km from Namutoni, 70km from Okaukuejo. It is just to the northwest of the landmark Tweekoppies, & there's a small dolomite kopje within the camp's boundary, accessible on a short self-guided trail signposted as 'Tsumasa'.

Halali is the smallest, & usually the quietest, of the 3 camps. In 1992 an artificial waterhole, the Moringa waterhole, was built on its boundary, & can be viewed from a natural rock seating area a few hundred metres beyond the campsite. This regularly attracts elephant, black rhino & other game. It isn't as busy as Okaukuejo's waterhole, but it is set apart from the camp, so has fewer disturbances & a more natural ambience.

The shop & restaurant at Halali are either side of the office & reception, on the right as you enter the camp. Meals are served buffet style in season, or

à la carte for the rest of the year. The kiosk is behind the restaurant, by the pool. Halali is probably the best of the restcamps in the park — perhaps because it's relatively quiet — with a good pool & a campsite with plenty of shade.

'Luxury' 4-bed bungalow N$980, simple 4-bed bungalow N$500–570, basic 2-bed room N$435, camping pitch N$235 (with electricity).

⌂ **Namutoni Restcamp** (72 bungalows, 25 tent pitches) P Bag 2015, Tsumeb; ☏ 067 229300; ☏ 067 229306. Situated on the eastern edge of the pan, Namutoni is based around a beautiful old 'Beau Geste' type fort, in an area dotted with graceful makalani palms, Hyphaene petersiana. It originally dates back to a German police post, built here before the turn of the 20th century. Later it was used as an army base & then for English prisoners during World War I, before being restored to its present state in 1957. Perhaps as a reminder of its military past, sunrise & sunset are heralded by a bugle call from the watchtower in the fort's northeastern corner — onto which you can climb for a better view of the park in the setting sun. Some of the rooms within the fort itself share facilities & are not air conditioned, but the newer rooms have en-suite shower, toilet & bath, and usually AC. The campsite is well shaded, with grassy pitches, but it's quite small so feels crowded when overland groups appear. Namutoni's office & reception are on the right beyond the fuel station, as you enter camp. Its shop (open 07.00–19.30 in summer) and restaurant are a few mins' walk — if driving then continue past the office & turn right.

A bonus for those staying at Namutoni is that game drives can be organised to restricted waterholes. The morning drive starts an hr before the gates open; the evening one ends an hr after they close; each costs N$205 pp, inc b/fast or finger meal. Basic 2-bed room N$320–490, 4-bedroom flat or chalet N$540–590, 'luxury' 4-bedroom flat N$675–1,060, camping N$240 per pitch (max 8 people).

✗ **WHERE TO EAT** Each restcamp has a restaurant where most visitors eat at least one of their meals. In recent years these have been privatised, introducing buffet meals rather than silver-service à-la-carte menus, at least during the main season. However, they have all carefully retained some of the old feeling of school dining halls.

Breakfast is normally served 07.00–08.30, lunch 12.00–14.00 and dinner 19.00–21.00, though if you arrive after 08.00, 13.30 or 20.30 respectively, the staff may refuse to serve you. In any case, buffet meals mean that it is *much* wiser to arrive earlier rather than later if you want a good choice of hot food.

Expect dinner to cost about N$110 for three courses. It's not haute cuisine, but is varied, good value, and generally has a reasonable choice of vegetables.

Outside of the prescribed meal times, there's normally a kiosk that sells drinks and snacks. These open between meals, 08.30–12.00 and 13.30–18.00. After dinner, the bar normally stays open until about 21.30.

Otjovasandu For many years there has been a small base for the park's wardens and researchers at Otjovasandu, in the far western end of the park. Around there the land is hilly with much bush: very pretty but with few obvious centres for the game to congregate. At present, only organised groups, led by a licensed Namibian tour operator, are allowed into this area, and then only to transit between the western gate near Hobatere and Okaukuejo. The government is said to be seeking suitable bids to establish a camp for private safaris here – so in the next few years it is likely that something will open. When it does it would be best to combine it with a stay further east, where the more prolific areas of game occur.

 Accommodation near Etosha Several private lodges are clustered around each of Etosha's entrance gates. Notable among these are Mokuti, Onguma, Etosha Aoba and Mushara on the eastern side, near Namutoni, with Ongava and Etosha Gateway (formerly Toshari Inn) south of Okaukuejo. Other options lie with 30–45 minutes' drive of the gates in each direction. Hobatere is adjacent to the park's western boundary, but operates as a self-contained concession area, rather than an adjunct to Etosha.

All usually cost more than the public camps, but their facilities are generally more modern and comfortable. Some have their own vehicles and guides. However, all vehicles in the park are subject to the park's strict opening and closing times. None is allowed off the roads while inside Etosha. Places listed below start with those closest to the park gates. For additional accommodation south of Etosha, but within easy distance of the national park, see *Chapter 17, North-Central Namibia*, pages 392–3.

South of Etosha

⌂ **Ongava Lodge, Little Ongava, Ongava Tented Camp**
📞 061 274500; 📠 061 239455; 📧 info@ nts.com.na; www.wilderness-safaris.com. Down a long drive just by Etosha's Andersson gate, Ongava (managed by Wilderness Safaris) consists of 3 discrete camps operating on its own private game reserve of 30,000ha, abutting Etosha's southern side. For costly but quick transfers, you can use small aircraft, operated by Sefofane Air Charters.

The environment & wildlife are similar to those near Okaukuejo, although without the huge saltpan its scenery it is less spectacular. Nevertheless, Ongava offers a greater choice of activities than is possible in the national park. The reserve has over 20 lions & in excess of 3,500 head of game, & is one of the few remaining places in Africa where visitors have a fairly reliable chance of encountering both black & white rhino. Don't try to walk without a guide.

Activities at each of the camps are conducted independently. They feature escorted walks/drives on Ongava's own reserve, & longer game drives into the national park. In summer there is normally a long (around 5hr) activity in the morning. This is followed

by lunch & time at leisure before dinner, after which there is a night drive. In winter the morning activities are shorter, about 3–4 hrs long, & lunch is normally followed by a late-afternoon game drive which often continues after dark by floodlight.

⌂ **Ongava Lodge** (12 chalets) This is the original focus of the reserve, set on a hill 10km from the entrance gate &, in 2006, undergoing significant refurbishment. Centred around a 3-level thatched boma that covers the lounge, bar & restaurant (serving excellent food), it overlooks 2 waterholes from a well-designed viewing area. There's plenty of space for relaxing & a swimming pool to cool off. The original thatched, stone-built chalets stand on the hillside, each surrounded by eco-friendly vegetation with a view over the reserve from its own enlarged wooden deck, with comfy chairs. Rooms are large & luxurious, with AC, twin queen-sized beds, 24hr mains electricity, fridge, a kettle with tea/coffee, & lots of other mod cons. En-suite bathrooms have showers inside & out, as well as twin basins & a toilet. Lower down the hill, but still with a commanding view (& steep steps!), 2 chalets already boast the new specification, with the added bonus of complete privacy. At the entrance, a large curio shop also stocks camera film & safari clothes. N$2,600 (Jan–Jun), N$3,590 (Jul–Nov) pp sharing, inc all meals & activities. Sgl supplement N$1,450.

🏠 **Little Ongava** (3 luxury suites) An exclusive hideaway, set on the crest of the hill above Ongava Lodge. It operates as an entirely self-contained camp, with dedicated & exceptionally well-trained staff. Wooden walkways link the chalets, with spectacular views across the reserve, views that are shared by the central living area, & accentuated by an eternity pool on the veranda. And if that's not enough, contemplation of the view from a gazebo with its own day bed is another option.

The individual chalets boast all the mod cons of a 5-star establishment but manage to combine style with comfort & — crucially — a strong sense of place. A series of sliding doors separate the bedroom from a huge bathroom, & further sliding doors lead outside. All is tastefully furnished, with solid wood & neutral colours bringing an intimacy that is all too often lacking in similar upmarket establishments. N$4,495 (Jan–Jun), N$6,495 (Jul–Nov) pp sharing, inc all meals and activities. Sgl supplement N$1,900

🏠 **Ongava Tented Camp** (6 tents) Meru-style tents, under thatch shadings, form the basis of this small, relaxed camp, located some 10km north of Ongava Lodge. The tents, erected on solid slate bases, have twin beds, chairs & mosquito nets, plus an en-suite bathroom with star-lit shower, & a wooden veranda. There's also a family unit with 4 beds. Meals are taken as a group in the central boma area, which overlooks a waterhole, with a pool alongside. N$2,430 (Jan–Jun), N$3,145 (Jul–Nov) pp sharing, inc all meals & activities. Sgl supplement N$1,450.

🏠 **Etosha Safari Camp** (22 tents) \/f 061 245847; e res@etosha-safari.com; www.etosha-safari.com.. Right by the C38, & just 9km south of Etosha, this rather ramshackle self-catering camp was opened in early 2005. From the bar/restaurant close to the road, it leads uphill to a series of tented bungalows, with en-suite facilities at the side, or twin dome tents with shared ablutions. There's also a campsite, with no power points, a swimming pool, braai area & internet access. Lunch & buffet dinner (N$100) require several hrs' notice. Popular with groups, this is a functional site offering good value, particularly for small groups of campers, and easy access to Etosha. Bungalow/tent N$370/180 pp sharing. Camping N$40 pp. Lunch N$50, dinner N$100.

🏠 **Etosha Gateway Lodge** aka **Toshari Lodge** (17 rooms, camping) \ 067 333440; f 067 333444; m 081 124 2567, 081 129 2567; e toshari@ namibnet.com; www.etoshagateway-toshari.com. About 71km north of Outjo, & 27km from the Andersson Gate, the erstwhile Toshari was taken over in 2005. A programme of renovation has started with the garden; for now, the place is more of a restcamp than a lodge, but welcoming, & good for groups: a pleasant & affordable alternative to Okaukuejo.

Spacious, en-suite rooms, built in blocks, are all alike, with carpets, 2 dbl beds, table fans, & mosquito-proof netting at the windows. Clean, comfortable & functional. There's also a shaded grassy campsite with power & braai area. Nearby, a large above-ground water-reservoir has been converted into a pool. Three waymarked trails of 1–2.5km lead to a small waterhole in the bush, which attracts the odd steenbok, kudu, warthog or porcupine. Game drives into the park (max 10) cost N$600. N$450–390 sgl/pp sharing, B&B; family (max 5) N$980. Camping N$50 pp. Open all year, except few weeks in Jan.

🏠 **Naua Naua Lodge** (8 rooms) \ 067 687100; f 067 687101; e info@nauanaua.com; www.nauanaua.com; reservations \/f 061 252299. About a 45-min drive from Etosha, Naua Naua was opened in 1998. To get there from the C38, take the D2695 to the west opposite Etosha Gateway Lodge, follow this for 6km, then turn south down a signposted 12km track which leads through 3 gates; if it's wet, be sure to phone ahead as the road may not be passable. The central area, under deep thatch, overlooks a good pool & a floodlit waterhole. In addition to game drives & a 2hr walking trail, the lodge has a cheetah project set up in collaboration with the American Cheetah Conservation Foundation, with feeding sessions a regular attraction for guests. € 97/€ 117 pp sharing, inc b/fast, afternoon coffee, cheetah feeding & sundowner (rates in euro). Dinner N$160.

🏠 **Epacha Game Lodge & Spa** (18 chalets) \ 067 697047; f 067 697050; e epacha@ leadinglodges.com; www.epacha.com. The private Epacha reserve covers 21,000ha of the Ondundozonondadana Valley, & is home to 2 exclusive camps owned by Leading Lodges of Africa. The reserve is stocked with game that includes 21 species of antelope, as well as black rhino. Aside from day & night game drives, & guided walks, guests can take part in quad-biking, horseriding & clay-pigeon shooting. The entrance to the reserve is situated 27km along the D2695, beyond Naua Naua Lodge. Both Epacha & its sister camp, Eagle Tented Lodge, are set on a gentle slope in surrounding bush.

At Epacha Game Lodge, the emphasis is on luxury, with colonial-style solid-wood furniture, large en-suite bathrooms & open-air showers, private balconies & all the trappings of a smart hotel. Within the rather grand central area are several lounges overlooking a waterhole, while guests seeking more than the environment alone can seek out the cigar lounge, library or billiard room, or cool off in the pool. For further indulgence, there's a health spa with sauna, jacuzzi, steam room & splash pool, as well as a range of treatments. *N$1,760/1,480 sgl/pp sharing, DBB; N$3,000/2,500 FB.*

🏠 **Eagle Tented Lodge & Spa** (8 walk-in tents) ✆ 067 697047; f 067 697050; e eagle@leadinglodges.com; www.eagletentedlodge.com. Also on

the Epacha reserve (see above), Eagle Tented Lodge is by any standards luxurious. Here, though, accommodation is in en-suite safari-style tents, each built on a 4m-high wooden platform with glazed wooden doors leading out to its own private balcony & splash pool. If it feels like upmarket camping, with paraffin-style lamps by the beds, that's the way it's been carefully designed, for there's no lack of creature comforts. On this site the main building is constructed of rustic-looking stone, carefully designed to incorporate a restaurant, where tables are laid with flowers, sparkling glasses & starched napiery, a bar & a wine cellar, while outside a pool with its own bar fits seamlessty into the whole. Even the boma is surrounded by stone columns & immaculate lawns. To complete the picture, a health spa offers pedicure, manicure, massage & a yoga centre to ease away the troubles of the day. *N$1,100/850 sgl/pp sharing, DBB; N$1,720/1,320 FB.*

West of Etosha

🏠 **Hobatere Lodge** (12 rooms, treehouse, camping) ✆ 067 237294; e reservations@exclusive.com.na; www.exclusive.com.na. This long-established private concession area is about 80km northwest of Kamanjab, reached by taking the main C35 road towards Ruacana. Its imposing gates are just past the entrance to western Etosha. The guides at

Hobatere sometimes run trips in the western part of Etosha, which is closed to the general public, although Hobatere is too far west to organise trips into the most interesting areas of the park around the pan. See *The Kaokoveld*, page 345, for a comprehensive description.

East of Etosha

🏠 **Mokuti Lodge** ✆ 067 229084; f 067 229091; e mokuti.reservation@olfitra.com.na; www.namibsunhotels.com.na/mokutilodge. Situated on the C38, 25km west of the B1, Mokuti is set in its own small reserve, immediately next to Etosha's Von Lindequist Gate. This is the flagship of the Namib Sun Hotel group, with helpful staff & a number of awards for its excellent facilities. More hotel than lodge, it's traditional in design, yet spread out & with up-to-date facilities. Mokuti's reserve has no very dangerous game, & is safe to wander around. A couple of short hiking trails are clearly marked, though it is equally easy to spot wandering antelope from the poolside; more elusive on the trails are the snakes that can be seen in the hotel's reptile park. Look out for the bontebok, which are not indigenous, but come from the Cape. The lodge has conference facilities & a comfortable bar. A gift shop has the usual nature books, T-shirts, postcards & stamps. Most of the twin rooms, with their AC, high thatched ceilings & en-suite facilities, are dotted across the lawns. A few

more luxurious units boast dbl beds & separate lounges. There are also several 'family units' (2 adults + 3 children), which are cheaper if you are travelling with children; & 2 twin & 2 luxury units for disabled people.

Most people who stay here have their own cars (the hotel has useful fuel pumps for diesel & unleaded petrol), & drive themselves around eastern Etosha. However, Mokuti does run game drives into Etosha with its own vehicles & guides (N$290 pp per drive), leaving at 07.30 winter time & 07:00 summer time for 4hrs, & at 15.00 until sunset. *High season (Jul–Oct) N$850/1,190/1,300/1,470 sgl/dbl/family/luxury; low N$765/1,065/1,170/1,320 sgl/dbl/family/luxury, all inc b/fast.*

🏠 **Onguma Game Ranch** ✆ 061 232009; f 061 222574; e onguma@visionsofafrica.com.na; www.ongumanamibia.com. Right next to Etosha's eastern gate, & sharing its boundary on Fischer Pan Reserve, Onguma is the newest of the lodges around Etosha; it was opened in 2005 on the site of an old hunting lodge. The easy drive along its 9km approach road is through a private reserve, which feels like eastern Etosha, with its mix of pans, woodland & open plains. Game found here includes lion, leopard, rhino & elephant, as well as the widely seen impala, oryx, wildebeest & springbok; some 300 species of bird have been spotted.

When visited in 2006, Onguma comprised 3 separate accommodation options, with a fourth — the exclusive Plains Camp — under construction:

⌂ Onguma Bush Camp (6 dbl, 1 family) This fully fenced camp is Onguma's budget option, geared to families, but decidedly utilitarian in feel. In the original farmhouse, next to reception, the family suite is plain, almost Spartan, with two pairs of twin beds, metal-framed windows, a ceiling fan & a computer desk; the only enlivening feature is the bathroom with its zebra-cartoon tiles. Individual rondavels close by have more of the same, but are at least interesting in their own right. The current large pool & central lapa, set among tree-shaded grass, were scheduled for renovation in late 2006 to give a smaller pool, reorientated lapa & 3 more rondavels. *N$395/645 pp sharing/sgl. Lunch/dinner N$115, or à la carte.*

⌂ Onguma Campsite (6 pitches) Alongside the Bush Camp, & also fully fenced, lies Onguma's campsite. Campers can use the facilities at the Bush Camp (meals require advance reservation); otherwise, with the exception of water & firewood, they'll need to bring all their own supplies. *N$60 pp.*

⌂ Onguma Tented Camp (7 luxury tents) Some 2km further on, Onguma's Tented Camp reinvents the term 'tents', even by southern Africa's luxury standards; it is difficult to believe that this & the Bush Camp are under the same ownership.

Ultra modern & minimalistic, this is most definitely not for the traditionalist; think style, think chic, & you'll be closer to the mark. From the tall, brushed-steel Chinese lanterns at the entrance to lime-washed giraffes by the door, the camp has something of the atmosphere of an art gallery rather than a bush lodge. In the central area, creamy canvas held aloft by solid light wood poles hints at a circus tent, but here with light & air aplenty. A backdrop of stone-clad walls & a cement floor are balanced by squashy sofas, unusual beaded armchairs, & director-style chairs featuring luminous-green dyed hides. Skin rugs complete the picture. In the corner, a tiny infinity pool suggests a design feature rather than somewhere to cool off. To the front, a floodlit waterhole that is overlooked from all

sides is set among indigenous vegetation; fortunately, no attempt has been made to beautify the bush.

The big-top effect continues to each of the rooms, where more skin rugs soften the chrome, stone & cement of the fixtures & fittings — & visitors lack for nothing (except AC), including an intercom system for safety, & sliding doors to a private deck where comfy chairs afford a great view of the waterhole. When visited, game drives (included in the rates in the private reserve) were shared with the other camps on the reserve, but a dedicated vehicle for the Tented Camp was on order. *N$1,350/1,800 pp sharing/sgl, DBB. Lunch N$90. Game drives N$420 pp (full day N$650). No children under 12.*

⌂ Etosha Aoba Lodge (10 bungalows) ✆ 067 229106; f 067 229107; e info@etosha-aoba-lodge.com; www.etosha-aoba-lodge.com. Leased until the end of 2006 by Mushara Lodge, Etosha Aoba was poised to be taken over by Onguma when visited. The lodge lies 30 mins' drive from Etosha's Von Lindequist entrance gate on the C38: the first 10km along the C38 to the entrance is followed by a twisting 10km drive, through a dense area of woodlands dominated by tamboti, terminalia & leadwood trees. This is all part of a 7,000ha reserve which boasts lion, kudu, zebra, wildebeest & giraffe. Thatched bungalows are well designed with plenty of natural light. A large patio window, which interchanges with a gauze screen, opens from a small veranda with a couple of chairs. Inside are twin beds covered by a mosquito net, beneath a ceiling fan. There's a tiled bathroom with toilet & shower — all spotless. The main oval lodge consists of a large thatched area with bar & tables for breakfast & dinner, & a small office that doubles as a curio shop. Close by is a large pool surrounded by sun-loungers for the foolhardy. There's also a waymarked botanical trail. Game drives have been run in conjunction with Etosha Game Viewers, & there's a sundowner drive to Fischer's Pan, but most guests drive themselves into the park from here. Etosha Aoba lacks the camaraderie of an all-inclusive lodge, but it's comfortable, pleasantly run, & with good food, making an excellent base for driving around eastern Etosha. *N$900/1,390 sgl/dbl B&B. 3-course set dinner N$150. No children under 13.*

⌂ Mushara Lodge (15 rooms, 2 villas) ✆ 067 229106; f 067 229107; e mushara@iafrica.com.na; www.musharalodge.com. Located 8km from the eastern entrance of the national park, Mushara is close to a private airstrip, just 500m from the main road. Despite the name, its style is more that of a hotel, albeit one with a high standard of service & attention to detail.

A cavernous entrance leads through to a split-level bar & smart lounge where ostrich-egg chandeliers, zebra hides & solid wood are complemented by modern, comfortable chairs & metal tables arranged into intimate seating areas. Outside, more seating surrounds a large pool surrounded by lawns.

Top-of-the-range accommodation is in luxury villas, whose thatched roofs contrast with the glass & monochrome décor of their beautifully kitted-out interiors, each with all the accoutrements you could possibly wish, & a mini patio & square pool that would grace Chelsea Flower Show. More reasonably priced but still very attractive rooms are built in pairs in spacious terracotta-painted bungalows. Each is slightly different, but all are decorated in neutral colours, airy & light, with a porch overlooking the pool. Expect AC, all-round mosquito nets, an en-suite bath or shower, fridge, hairdryer & phone. Nature walks & regular game drives are available to guests through Etosha Game Viewers.
Villas N$3,328.70/2,320 sgl/pp sharing DBB; rooms N$940/1,580/2,300 sgl/dbl/trpl B&B. Dinner N$150.

Sachsenheim Guest Farm (14 chalets, camping) ☎ 067 230011; f 067 230072; e sachse@iway.na. Off the B1, 3km north of the C38 turning towards Namutoni, & across the railway line, Sachsenheim is an old-style game farm (accepting hunting & photographic clients) turned restcamp. German-owned, with a wide range of accommodation options, it brings to mind a model village, with its neat individual chalets, small central campsite under trees, & even a garden centre. Although its rooms — most en suite - are nicely appointed with fridge, kettle, ceiling fan & mosquito nets, and it's spotlessly clean, Sachsenheim really comes into its own only when Namutoni Restcamp is full; it doesn't compare to other lodges in the area.
From N$275.40 pp sharing, B&B. Camping N$51.75 pp, N$111.50 per vehicle. Dinner N$109.50.

WHAT TO SEE AND DO If you are staying at one of the private lodges then you may have the choice of walking trips on their land. That aside, most visitors come to Etosha to explore the park for themselves by car.

Organising your own safari
The best times for spotting animals are in the early morning and the late afternoon, when they are at their most active. So, if you can, leave your camp as the gates open at sunrise, for a few hours' drive before breakfast. Before you leave, check the book of recent sightings in the park office, as animals are creatures of habit. This record may help you to choose the best areas to visit for that particular day.

Use the middle of the day for either travelling or relaxing back at camp. Dedicated enthusiasts may park beside one of the more remote waterholes. Excellent sightings are occasionally reported in the midday heat – though photographs taken in the glare of day are disappointing.

Finally, check when the gate to your camp closes, and then leave for a late afternoon drive. Aim to spend the last few hours before sunset at one of the waterholes near your restcamp, or the entrance gate if you're staying outside the park. Leave this in time for a leisurely drive back.

Most of the roads in Etosha are made of calcrete and gravel, which gives a good driving surface, without tar's unnatural appearance, although they can be slippery when wet. Be warned that most of the park's accidents occur near sunset, as people try to dash back to camp before the gates close.

The waterholes
The excellent map of Etosha available at the park shows the roads open to visitors, and the names of the waterholes. Obviously the game seen at each varies enormously. One day you can sit for hours watching huge herds; the next day the same place will be deserted. However, some waterholes are usually better, or at least more photogenic, than others. Here are a few brief personal notes on some of the main ones:

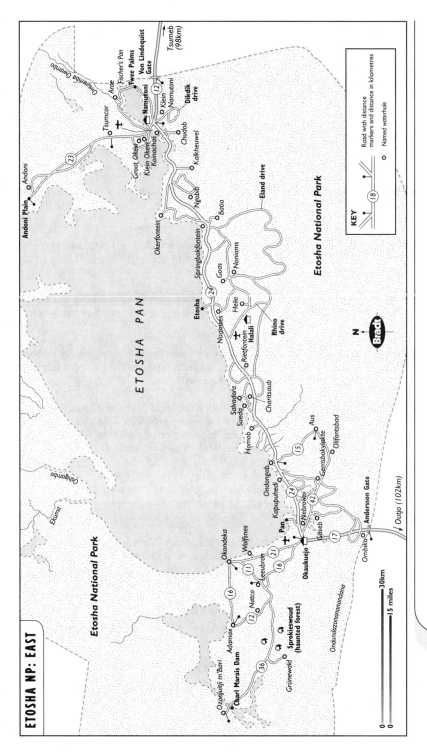

ETOSHA NP: EAST

KEY

Road with distance markers and distance in kilometres

○ Named waterhole

N

Bradt

0 ____ 30km
0 ____ 15 miles

Etosha National Park

Etosha National Park

ETOSHA PAN

Tsumeb (98km)

Von Lindequist Gate

Twee Palms

Fischer's Pan

Aroe

Namutoni

Klein Namutoni

Dikdik drive

(12)

Chudob

Kalkheuwel

Koinachas

Klein Okevi

Groot Okevi

Tsumcor

Andoni Plain ○ Andoni

(23)

Okerfontein

Ngobib

Springbokfontein

Batia

Eland drive

Etosha

(24)

Goas

Noniams

Helio

Naaptes

Rietfontein

Halali

Rhino drive

Salvadora

Charitsaub

Sueda

Homob

Aus

Ondongab

Olifantsbad

Gemsbokvlakte

(15)

Kapupuhedi

(24)

(42)

Nebrowni

Goseb

Pan

Okandeka

Wolfsnes

(11)

(21)

Leeubron

(16)

Okaukuejo

(17)

Ombika ○

Andersson Gate

Outjo (102km)

Natco

(16)

(12)

Adamax

Sprokieswoud (haunted forest)

Grünewald

(36)

Charl Marais Dam

Ozonjuitji m'Bari

Onduindozonanandana

Ekuma

Oshigambo

Omuramba Owambo

Etosha National Park **PRACTICAL INFORMATION**

16

373

Adamax A dry waterhole in acacia thickets, notable more for adjacent social weaver nests than for its game.

Andoni As far north as you can go, through some elephant-damaged mopane woodlands, this isolated spot is a manmade waterhole in the middle of an open vlei. I've never seen much game up here.

Aus A natural water-level spring here is supplemented by a solar pump, in the middle of woodlands of stunted mopane. As you look from the parking area, the sun rises directly over the pan. It is said to be a good, busy spot for animals – though I've never had much luck here.

Batia Away from the side of the pan, near Springbokfontein, the road to Batia is often better than the waterhole itself, which is a very flat and almost marsh-like collection of reeds with puddles dotted over a large area.

Charitsaub Away from the pan, Charitsaub is in the middle of a huge area of grassy plains. It has a small spring below, and close to, the parking area. Likely game includes zebra, wildebeest and springbok.

Chudop An excellent artesian waterhole, which usually hosts good concentrations of game. There's lots of open space around the water, and I've spent many hours here on several occasions. Don't miss it.

Etosha Just north of Halali, this is not a waterhole, but a most spectacular lookout place. There's a short drive across the pan, joining a circle where you can stop and admire the flatness. It is often closed when wet.

Fischer's Pan The road from Namutoni skirts the edges of this small pan, and when there's standing water in the pan it is *the* area for waterbirds. Take care of the road across the pan, between Aroe and Twee Palms, which often floods. When dry there will be fewer around, though the palm trees remain picturesque.

Gemsbokvlakte In the middle of a grassy plain, dotted with the odd stand of *Acacia*, *Combretum* and mopane bushveld, this permanent (with a solar-powered pump) waterhole attracts plains game species like springbok, gemsbok, zebra, giraffe and ostrich.

Goas This is a large, flat, natural waterhole and cars can view it from several sides, which is good as there's often a lot of game here. Elephants drinking here can be spectacular, and it is big enough to attract a constant buzz of bird activity.

Groot Okevi The parking area is a super vantage point, overlooking the waterhole which is about 25m away. There is some thick bush around the water. This is a known haunt of black rhino and conveniently close to Namutoni.

Helio A small, flat manmade waterhole near Halali, just a few hundred metres from one of the kopjes. Its position is marked incorrectly on the national park map, and I've rarely seen any game there.

Homob A small spring in a deep depression, quite far from the viewing area. Just a few springbok and oryx were present when last visited. There is also a long-drop toilet here; bring your own toilet paper.

above **Damaraland landscape with black rhinoceros** (CM) page 327

right **Black rhinoceros** *Diceros bicornis* (AZ) page 482

above **Leopard**
Panthera pardus,
Okonjima
(CM) page 471

centre **Bat-eared fox**
Otocyon megalotis,
Etosha NP
(AZ) page 473

below **Black-backed jackals**
Canis mesomelas,
Etosha NP
(AZ) page 473

above left **Brown hyena** *Hyaena brunnea,* **Skeleton Coast NP** (CM) page 474

above right **African wild dog** *Lycaon pictus,* **northern Kalahari** (CM) page 472

below **Spotted hyena** *Crocuta crocuta,* **Etosha NP** (CM) page 474

above   **Desert-adapted elephants** *Loxodonta africana* **fording an ephemeral river, Damaraland** (AZ) page 481

below   **Red hartebeest** *Alcelaphus buselaphus* (AZ) page 477

top **Zebra** *Equus burchelli,*
Etosha Pan
(CM) page 483

above left **Southern giraffe**
Giraffa camelopardalis
(CM) page 483

above right **Male black-faced**
impala *Aepyceros*
melampus petersi,
Etosha NP
(AZ) page 479

right **Springbok** *Antidorcas*
marsupilis, **Etosha**
(CM) page 479

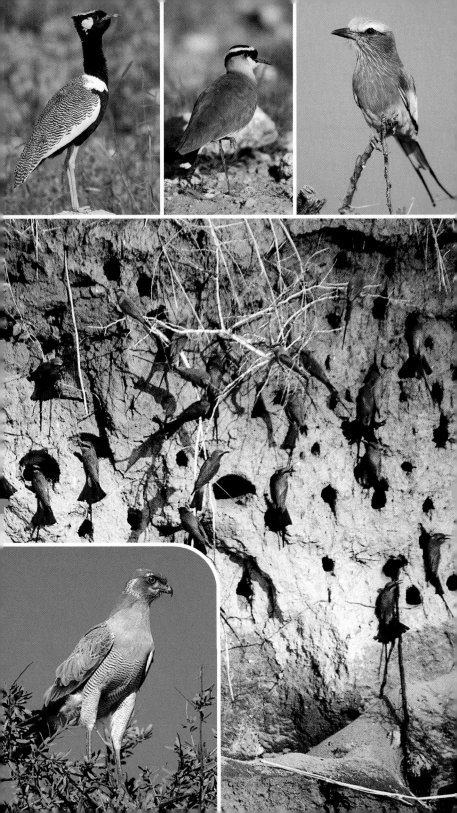

top   **Cape fur seals**
Arctocephalus pusillus pusillus,
Cape Cross
(CM) page 314

above left   **Flap-necked chameleon**
Chamaeleo dilepsis (TH)

above right   **Peringuey's adder**
Bitis peringueyi,
endemic to Namib Desert (AZ)

left   **Meerkats**
Suricata suricatta
(CM) page 485

Kalkheuwel A super waterhole which often has lots of game. There's a permanently filled water trough, and usually also a good pan, which is close to the car park.

Kapupuhedi On the edge of the pan, with the parking area above it, this is often dry.

Koinachas A very picturesque artesian spring, perhaps 100m in diameter, with a large thicket of reeds in the centre. It's an excellent birding spot, but seldom seems crowded with game.

Nebrowni A small waterhole on the edge of a side channel to the main pan. This is just 200m from the main road, but often omitted from maps. With bush to one side, and grassy plains to the other, it can attract a wide variety of game, though is often deserted.

Noniams Though it's convenient for Halali, I've never had much luck seeing any game here.

Nuamses A very deep water-level spring with a large clump of tall reeds in the centre. Quite photogenic with lots of rocks around – though the foreground is obscured by a lip of rock in front of the waterhole. Not known for its prolific game.

Okerfontein Right on the edge of the pan. The viewpoint is slightly elevated, and the nearer parts of the water are hidden from view by a lip of rocks.

Okondeka This waterhole often attracts large numbers of wildebeest, zebra, oryx, springbok and ostrich. On the edge of the pan, Okondeka often has streams of game arriving and leaving it, which stretch for miles across the surrounding grasslands. The water is a little far from the car-parking area for close-up photos, but shots taken from the road just before the parking area, with vistas of the main pan in the background, can be spectacular.

Olifantsbad Literally 'elephant's bath', this is another natural water-level spring helped by a solar pump – making two good waterholes in a large arena for wildlife. It is notable for elephant, kudu, red hartebeest and black-faced impala.

Ombika Despite its proximity to the Andersson Gate, Ombika shouldn't be underestimated as it is often a busy waterhole. Unfortunately for photographers, this water-level spring is far from the viewing area, inside a deep natural rock cavern, allowing even zebra to almost disappear from view when drinking.

Ondongab Like Kapupuhedi, this is on the edge of the pan but recently dry. Its view is spectacular.

Ozonjuitji m'Bari A small waterhole filled by a solar pump. This is the furthest point west that private visitors are allowed to drive themselves. Flat, grassy plains surround it, and the game varies greatly. Sometimes it is deserted, and on other occasions you'll find one of the park's largest gatherings of gemsbok. In the dry season, likely sights include ostrich, wildebeest, zebra, springbok, perhaps the odd giraffe and lots of dancing dust-devils in the background. (One correspondent recently spotted a black rhino here during the day.)

Pan On the edge of the pan, the waterhole is not obvious, and there is often little game. This road becomes a mess of sludge in the wet season.

Rietfontein A large, busy water-level spring, with quite a large area of reeds in the water, surrounded by much open ground. There's a wide parking area with plenty of space, and at the waterhole giraffe, zebra and springbok were drinking when last visited.

Salvadora On the edge of the pan, Salvadora attracts columns of zebra, wildebeest and springbok. The viewpoint is higher than the spring, and close to it – so is perfect for photographs, with the main pan stretching off forever behind it.

Springbokfontein Shallow collection of reeds to one side of the road, which often has little game at it. However, look to your right as you drive to nearby Batia, as there is often game at a spring there.

Sueda Away from the pan, and just west of Salvadora and Charitsaub, Sueda has a large area of reeds, and rock-like clay outcrops, around a spring on the edge of the pan. Again, parking is above the level of the spring.

Wolfnes A location where you can appreciate the vast expanse of the pan. Just switch your motor off, and listen to the silence.

17

North-Central Namibia

While Etosha is the main attraction in the north of Namibia, the region south of it has much of interest. Large farms dominate these hilly, well-watered highlands, and many have forsaken cattle in favour of game, to become guest farms that welcome tourists. Okonjima Guest Farm has been one of the first of these, and is a major draw for visitors. Many of the others are less famous, but they still offer visitors insights into a farmer's view of the land, and opportunities to relax. On the eastern side of this area, the Waterberg Plateau is superb, though more for its hiking trails and scenery, and feeling of wilderness, than for its game-viewing.

OMARURU

On the tarred C33, about 60km north of Karibib, Omaruru is a green and picturesque town astride the (usually dry) river of the same name, in a gently hilly area. Many of the farms around it have turned to tourism, which is on the increase, so there is no shortage of lodges or guest farms in the area. The town is also acquiring something of a reputation for the creative arts, with many artists settling here to work.

GETTING THERE

By train TransNamib sleeper trains connect Otjiwarongo with Windhoek and Walvis Bay on Monday, Wednesday and Friday in each direction, stopping at Omaruru. Trains depart from Omaruru for Otjiwarongo at 02.10 and 00.20; to Windhoek at 22.00; and to Walvis Bay at 20.40.

The faster new *Omugulu Gwombashe Star*, which leaves Windhoek on a Friday, returning from Ondangwa on a Sunday, also calls at Omaruru. Tickets between Windhoek and Omaruru cost N$68 one way.

For details, see *Chapter 6*, page 101.

WHERE TO STAY

Central Hotel (13 rooms) Wilhelm Zeraua Rd; ℡ 064 570030; f 064 571100; e central@omaruru.na. On the main street north of the river, this small, traditional hotel has modern rooms set in line in a whitewashed block, softened by thatch. It also has a pool, a restaurant, & secure parking. *N$260/380 sgl/dbl, B&B.*

Omaruru Kleines Nest (2 bungalows, camping) 55 Wilhelm Zeraua Rd; ℡ 064 203203; f 064 206907; e kleinnest@iway.na; www.natron.net/omaruru-kleinesnest. Close to the centre of town, but in a quiet spot on the river, this new property is under the same ownership as

Kleines Nest in Walvis Bay. The wooden bungalows are geared to self-catering guests, so in addition to sleeping for 4 people & an en-suite bathroom, each has a fully equipped kitchen, & its own veranda. There's plenty of tree shade for these & the campsite, & a shared pool. *N$150 pp sharing; camping N$50 pp.*

Little Bush Rest (2 rooms) 8 Franke St; ℡ 064 570436; e omw-bush@iway.na. Owner Martina Baumann has opened this tiny B&B just next to the Franke Tower. Its rooms are en suite, & there's a pool, braai area & shaded parking. *N$160/220 sgl/dbl, B&B.*

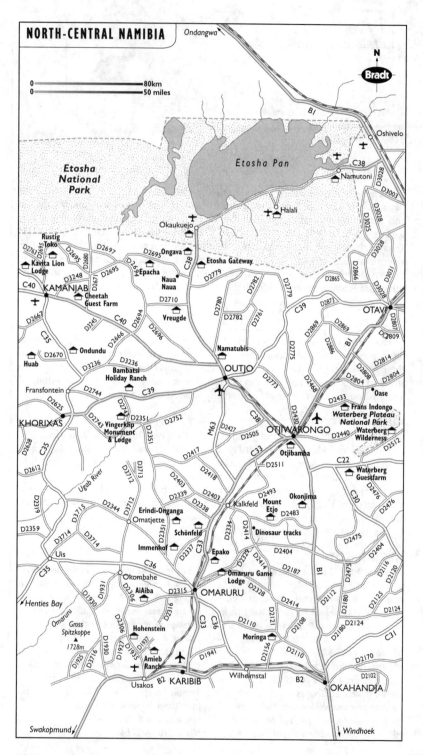

Ondangwa

N

Bradt

0   80km
0   50 miles

B1

Oshivelo

Etosha Pan

C38

Namutoni

D3003

*Etosha
National
Park*

D3028

D3025

Halali

D3028

Okaukuejo

D3028

Rustig
Toko

D2763 D2695

D2695 D2697

D2695 Ongava

D3031

D2865

Kavita Lion
Lodge

D2667 D2695

D2695 D2694 Epacha

C38

Etosha Gateway

D2779

D2782

D2779

D2866

D3028

C40 KAMANJAB

D3248

Naua
Naua

D2779

D2780

D2782

D2761

C39

D2873

OTAVI

D2807

Cheetah
Guest Farm

C40

D2694

D2696

D2710

D2782

D2775

D2869

D2869

B1

D2809

D2245

D2666

Vreugde

D2869

D2886

D2814

D2667

C35

Ondundu

Namatubis

D2808

D2804

Huab

D2670

D3236

D3236

Bambatsi
Holiday Ranch

OUTJO

D2773

D2468

D2804

D2433

Oase

Fransfontein

D2625

D2744

C39

C38

D2430

Frans Indongo
Waterberg Plateau
National Park

KHORIXAS

D2743 D2741

D2351

D2752

M63

D2427

OTJIWARONGO

Waterberg
Wilderness

D2628

C35

Vingerklip
Monument
& Lodge

D2351

D2505

C33

Otjibamba

D2440

D2512

D2612

Ugab River

D3712

D3713

D2417

D2511

C22

Waterberg
Guestfarm

D2319

D2359

D3715

D3714

D2344

D3714

D7122

D2403

D2403

D2418

Kalkfeld

D2493

Mount
Etjo

Okonjima

C30

D2476

D2476

Erindi-Onganga

D2339

D2338

D2483

D2475

Omatjette

Uis

D2351

Schönfeld

D2334

Dinosaur tracks

D2404

D2475

D2404

C35

C36

Immenhof

D2337

Epako

D2329 D2414

D2187

D2116

D2120

Okombahe

D2306

AiAiba

D2315

Omaruru Game
Lodge

D2328

D2414

B1

D2112

D2125

D2124

Henties Bay

D1930

D2316

OMARURU

D2121

D2108

D2180

D2124

Omaruru

*Gross
Spitzkoppe*
▲
1728m

D3306

Hohenstein

C36

C33

Moringa

D2110

C31

D1930

D1927 D1935

D1927

D2156

D2110

D2170

D1925 D3716

Amieb
Ranch

D1941

D2102

Usakos

B2 KARIBIB

Wilhelmstal

B2

OKAHANDJA

Swakopmund

Windhoek

Nearby lodges and guest farms

AiAiba (20 rooms) ✆ 064 570330; f 064 570557; e info@aiaiba.com; www.aiaiba.com. Self-styled 'the Rock-painting lodge', AiAiba is under the same ownership as Okapuka Ranch, north of Windhoek. It is situated about 45km west of Omaruru, just off the D2315, & within the Erongo Mountain Nature Conservancy. Nestling in the shelter of giant granite boulders, each of its attractive thatched bungalows houses 2 en-suite rooms, their cool tiled floors offset by solid rustic furniture & neutral fabrics. The matching central building, its open beams giving it the feeling of a large barn, overlooks a small pool flanked by palms. Guided walks, 4x4 drives to visit rock paintings, & a 6hr picnic tour are the main draws.
N$764/1,069 sgl/dbl, B&B, inc lion-feeding tour. Dinner N$$125.

Omaruru Restcamp (23 rooms, camping) Wilhelm Zeraua Rd; ✆ 064 570516; f 064 571017; e jdg@iway.na. The municipal restcamp just on the north side of town has rondavels, chalets & bungalows, each with AC & TV. The campsite has power & DSTV points, hot water & 24hr security surveillance, as well as a new swimming pool. Meals can be ordered at the sports bar.
N$356/456/515 dbl/trpl/qudpl, B&B. Camping N$60 pp.

Omaruru Game Lodge (20 bungalows, of which 5 self-catering) ✆ 064 570044; f 064 570134; e omlodge@iafrica.com.na; www.omaruru-game-lodge.com. Just north of Omaruru, about 15km along the D2329, Omaruru Game Lodge is owned by a Swiss architect, which explains the impressive design of its bungalows. All are beautifully built of stone, with thatched roofs that reach almost to the ground, AC, heating, & en-suite showers & toilets. Some are designated 'superior', which simply means they are bigger.

The lounge/bar/dining area is equally impressive, & overlooks a dam on one side of the lodge's 'small game park' (150ha in size), which is regularly visited by game, including giraffe, hartebeest, wildebeest, eland, sable & roan antelope to name but a few. This fenced-off small reserve is separate from the lodge's 'large game park' which covers a more respectable 3,500ha, & is home to the same range of antelope plus 4 elephants.

The paths around the camp, the lounge/dining area & the figure-of-eight pool all wind amongst well-watered lawns under beautiful apple-ring acacias, *Acacia albida* — which the elephants would relish if only they could get to them. Walk at night,

when the paths are lit, & it's hard to escape the feeling that this is Africa at its neatest & tidiest, but not its wildest.

The lodge also has 5 self-catering bungalows set a few hundred metres from the rest. These are more basic, each with a useful kitchenette (but with no cutlery, crockery or pans) & an outside fireplace. They share a separate swimming pool.
Standard N$$720/1,120 sgl/dbl; superior N$900/1,300, all sgl/dbl, DBB. Self-catering chalet N$215 per adult sharing.

Epako Game Lodge (23 rooms) ✆ 064 570551; f 064 570553; e epako@iafrica.com.na; www.epako.com. Some 23km north of Omaruru, just off the main C33, Epako is one of Namibia's more luxurious game lodges & occupies about 110km² of the Omaruru River Valley. It has a wide variety of game, including white rhino, several elephant, giraffe, eland, kudu, oryx, blesbok, waterbuck, ostrich, blue & black wildebeest, Hartmann's mountain & Burchell's plains zebra, black-faced & common impala, & many other buck, several of which are not native to the area. Leopard & cheetah also occur, but there are no lion. Visitors can watch cheetah & caracal being fed, take game drives on the reserve, or tackle a 7km guided hiking trail into the mountains. More mundanely, there's a swimming pool, tennis court & table tennis.

Epako's accommodation is plush. The rooms have the style & quality of very good hotel rooms, with air conditioners that double as heaters in the cooler months, & heavy teak furniture made from railway sleepers. Their facilities include a minibar, phone, & bath as well as separate shower. In the main building is an upmarket curio shop, a bar (with satellite TV) that is opened when needed, & the real focus of the lodge: the restaurant. Food is taken seriously here. The elegant restaurant has glass sides that overlook the river & a busy waterhole below. Its food is excellent, so expect extensive choices for b/fast & 4-course dinners of quality cuisine with a French influence.
N$1,150/767 sgl pp sharing, DBB, N$1,275/892 sgl/pp sharing, FB. Game drive N$200 pp.

Erongo Wilderness Lodge (10 tents) ✆ 061 239199; f 061 243971; e info@erongowilderness.com; www.erongowilderness.com. Travelling from Omaruru, take the C33 south for 2km & turn right onto the D2315. You'll soon enter an area of many kopjes — huge piles of rounded rocks which make up hills that look like piles of giant pebbles. These are the Erongo Mountains, &

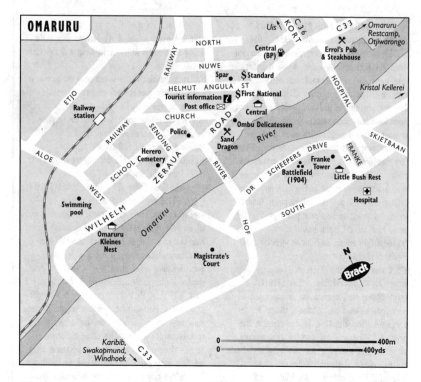

OMARURU

Uis — C36 KORT — C33 — Omaruru
Restcamp,
Otjiwarongo

NORTH

Central (BP)

Errol's Pub & Steakhouse

NUWE

Spar

Standard

HELMUT ANGULA ST

HOSPITAL

Kristal Kellerei

Tourist information
Post office

First National

Railway
station

Central

CHURCH

Ombu Delicatessen

Police

Sand
Dragon

River

SKIETBAAN

Herero
Cemetery

DR I SCHEEPERS DRIVE

FRANKE ST

Battlefield
(1904)

Franke
Tower

Little Bush Rest

Swimming
pool

River

SOUTH

Hospital

Omaruru
Kleines
Nest

Omaruru

HOF

Magistrate's
Court

N

Bradt

Karibib,
Swakopmund,
Windhoek — C33

0 — 400m
0 — 400yds

10km from the junction you'll find the lodge on the south side of the road. Unless you have a 4x4 & are confident using it, leave your vehicle at the bottom & you & your luggage will be transferred to the lodge.

The lodge forms part of the Erongo Mountain Nature Conservancy, a 200,000ha area encompassing both farms & lodges over which fences have been taken down & which aims to protect the area. Accommodation is in thatched, Meru-style tents that have been built high on wooden stilts among the foothills. The rustic feel is deliberate, but with a minibar, kettle, fan & toiletries, guests won't be depriving themselves of mod cons. Various wooden walkways & paths connect these to the main lounge & dining room area, which has a large veranda overlooking a stunning vista of the mountains. Nearby a small swimming pool has been built into the rocks.

It's a lovely spot to spend a few days, but Erongo's real attraction is as a base for walking in the hills. Guides are on hand for both short walks in the late afternoon (usually to the top of the nearby kopje for a G&T while the sun sets), & longer walks from the lodge, on the flat, or around the base of the hills, or on steeper routes where

short scrambles may be needed. For those wishing to set out unaccompanied, there are 4 marked walking trails of 1½–4½ hrs. Even so, a GPS would be useful – it's easy to get disoriented or lost in these hills. The rough rock generally grips rubber soles well.

Pause for a while wherever you are & you'll realise that there's game around, from leopards & klipspringers to dassies & brightly coloured rock agamas, but you'll have to look for it. And for birders, this is also a good spot to see Harlaub's francolin.
N$1,250/1,050 sgl/pp sharing, inc DBB, afternoon tea & guided walks.

Erindi-Onganga Guest Farm (5 rooms) f 067 290112; e fnolte@iway.na; www.natron.net/erindi-onganga (in German). This traditional, working guest farm with a German atmosphere is about 64km from Omaruru. To reach it take the C36 towards Uis for about 6km before branching right onto the D2344 towards Omatjette. Follow this for about 25km before turning right onto the D2351 towards Epupa (note this Epupa is closer than the one on the River Kunene!). After about 25km Erindi-Onganga is signposted off to the right, about 6km along a farm road.

Accommodation is carpeted throughout, & rooms are clean, with en-suite facilities. The main farmhouse has a dining room (where traditional farm-cooked meals are served), a lounge area with large fire for cool evenings, & even a sauna. Outside there is a swimming pool, some marked hiking trails & the working farm which most visitors come to see. *N$420 pp sharing, FB, inc farm drives for guests staying 2 or more nights.*

🏠 **Omandumba Farm** (camping) 📞 064 571086; fax; 064 570845; e omandumba@iway.na. Situated 38km from Omaruru on the D2315, Omandumba is the basis for walking trails in the Erongo Mountains, with opportunities to see the area's rock paintings & engravings. The farm's campsite has its own kitchen. *Camping N$75 pp.*

🏠 **Hohenstein Lodge** (10 rooms) 📞 064 530900; f 064 430931; e hohenstein@iway.na;

www.hohensteinlodge.de. Reservations 📞 064 224712/250725; f 064 224217; e hohenstein@Reservation-Destination.com. To the southwest of the Erongo Mountains, Hohenstein is about 25km north of Usakos on the D1935. It's a community venture, set on the edge of Damaraland within the Erongo Mountain Nature Conservancy, & with panoramic views. The lodge has been carefully built to take advantage of the views from both the bungalows & the central area, where dinner is taken inside or out on the veranda, overlooking a waterhole. Simply decorated rooms have twin beds with bright animal-print covers.

Visitors may opt from a guided walk to the Boulder Forest, a 2hr horse-and-cart ride along the valley, nature drives, or a sundowner drive to see Bushman & Damara paintings. *N$775/525 sgl/pp sharing, B&B, inc sundowner drive. Lunch N$65, dinner N$120.*

✗ **WHERE TO EAT** In addition to the hotel and lodge restaurants, there are the following options:

✗ **Sand Dragon** 94 Wilhelm Zeraua Rd; 📞/f 064 570707. The American-Indian influence on this well-recommended restaurant's décor reflects the original owner's origins. A wide-ranging menu includes steaks, burgers & a Fri pizza night. There's also a 5-course meal including a film (the restaurant doubles as Omaruru's cinema!).

✗ **Kristall Kellerei** 📞 064 570083; f 064 570593;

e winery@omaruru.na.. At the region's only vineyard offering wine-tasting, and the only manufacturer of Namibian brandy, they serve an excellent lunch of cold meats and cheeses, but you'll need to book ahead. *Open Mon–Fri 09.00–18.00, Sat 09.00–13.00.*

Ombu Delicatessen 65 Wilhelm Zeraua St; 📞 064 570119

GETTING ORGANISED There is a First National Bank, a Standard Bank, and a post office, all on the main Wilhelm Zeraua Road, as well as several garages. For **food and provisions**, there's both a Spar supermarket (complete with thatched porch!) on Helmut Angula Street, and the OMBU delicatessen at 615 Wilhelm Zeraua Road. Next to the post office is a good **Namib i** tourist office and curio shop, and there are a couple of other craft shops worth visiting.

In an emergency, the police are reached on 📞 064 10111, the ambulance and hospital on 📞 064 570037/570051, and the fire brigade on 📞 064 570028/570046.

WHAT TO SEE AND DO The town's main attraction is **Franke Tower**, a monument to Captain Victor Franke who is said to have heroically relieved the garrison here, after they were besieged by the Herero in 1904. The achievement earned him Germany's highest military honour and this monument built by grateful German settlers in 1908. It's normally locked, but to climb up it ask at your hotel to see if they have a set of keys.

Mineralogists shouldn't miss dropping in to see Karen and Christopher Johnston, who have a fascinating selection of very specialist local minerals which they even send abroad on a mail-order basis. Contact them first at PO Box 636, Omaruru; 📞/f 064 570707; e autumn@sanddragon.com.na.

You can also visit the **Kristall Kellerei** (see above) for a tour of their cellars and vineyards and an insight into the making of the local wine, or visit one of the local artists by appointment – the tourist information office has a list.

Originally a staging post on the railway from Tsumeb to Swakopmund, this small town is conveniently situated at a crossroads for both the railway and the road network, in an area dominated by commercial cattle ranching. Though pleasant enough, with a small market that makes an enjoyable place to wander and a mix of people that includes many Herero women in traditional dress, Otjiwarongo has few intrinsic attractions, and most visitors just pass through.

GETTING THERE

By bus The Intercape Mainliner service linking Windhoek with Victoria Falls drops into Otjiwarongo, stopping at BP Express on Hage G Geingob Street. Going northbound, it stops at 20.25 on Monday, Wednesday and Friday. Heading south it stops at 10.00 on Sunday, and 03.40 on Monday, Thursday and Saturday. One-way fares are around N$150 to Windhoek, and N$430 to Victoria Falls. See *Chapter 6*, pages 104–5, for more details.

By train While rail buffs will be interested to know that the narrow-gauge steam locomotive played an important part in the history of the town, today's train service is more mundane.

As far as regular passenger trains are concerned, Otjiwarongo is now the end of the line. Trains depart for Walvis Bay on Monday, Wednesday and Friday at 17.15 and for Windhoek at 18.15. The return trips, on the same days, are at 03.15 and 05.00 respectively.

However, a recent introduction to the service is a weekly fast train, the *Omugulu Gwombashe Star*. It leaves Windhoek on Friday, stopping at Otjiwarongo en route for Ondangwa, with the return train leaving Ondangwa on Sunday. Tickets between Windhoek and Otjiwarongo cost N$68 one way.

For details, see *Chapter 6*, page 101.

Hitching Hitching from central Otjiwarongo is difficult. First start walking out in the direction you want to go, and then hitch from there.

WHERE TO STAY

Most visitors in the area stay at one of the guest farms, and even business people find Otjibamba Lodge so close to town that it can be treated as a hotel. However, actually in town are:

Bush Pillow 47 Sonn Rd; 067 303 885; f 067 301264; e artworks@iafrica.com.na. This good, trendy small guesthouse is reached from the Windhoek road by turning left into Sonn Rd at the first Caltex fuel station; Bush Pillow is on the corner of Sonn Rd & Hoog St. It has safe parking & a pleasant garden (with pool) behind secure walls, where there's also space to have a braai. The rooms, each named after a famous (or infamous!) elephant, are clean & bright, with en-suite bathrooms & satellite TV; many also have fun artistic touches. The communal areas include a bright b/fast/lunch area, a new dining area where award-winning meals are served, & a well-stocked bar. There's a satellite TV in the lounge, & both laundry & internet facilities are available.

Day trips to the Cheetah Conservation Foundation, 40km away, are a highlight (N$500 pp, inc lunch); those just staying overnight can instead opt for the Whale Rock sundowner (N$95 pp).
N$270/390 sgl/dbl, B&B. Dinner N$125.

C'est Si Bon Hotel (22 rooms) Swembad Rd; 067 301240/304915; f 067 303208; e sibon@iafrica.com.na; www.namibweb.com/sibon.htm. Driving from Windhoek, you'll enter town on the main Hage G Geingob St. Take a left turn between the church & the BP fuel station, & follow the signs to the hotel.

C'est Si Bon is one of a growing breed of medium-sized hotels/lodges in Namibia that are situated in the provincial towns & aim to cater for small groups that stop over for the night. This means

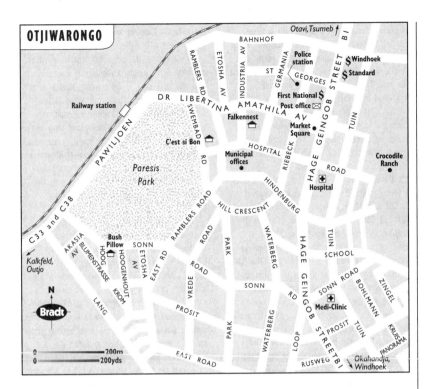

OTJIWARONGO

that it's a thoroughly efficient, & comfortable place, though it lacks some of the individuality (& idiosyncrasies) of the smaller establishments. That said, it's certainly the best place in town to stay & eat.

Its thatched rooms are spread around the edges of a large lawn. Each is adequate but not huge, with twin beds, a TV, tea/coffee facilities, & an en-suite toilet, shower & washbasin. Some also have AC. N$450/690/520 sgl/dbl/trpl, B&B.

⌂ **Falkennest** (10 rooms) 21 Industrial Av; ☎/f 067 302616 e otjbb@iafrica.com.na;

www.natron.net/tour/falkennest. To find this small B&B, follow Dr Libertina Amathila Av west from where it crosses Hage G Geingob St at the market square. Three blocks later, take a left onto Industrial Av, & number 21 is shortly on your left. Within, Karin Falk runs a small-scale operation with bedrooms that are clean, pleasant & have en-suite toilets & showers. There is also a pool & safe off-street parking. N$190/330/450 sgl/dbl/trpl, B&B.

⌂ **NEARBY GUEST FARMS** There are several guest farms in the area. Otjibamba makes an excellent stopover, fairly close to the town. Okonjima is well known for its excellent work with big cats, and Mount Etjo has much good publicity material, though seems to appeal more to Afrikaans-speaking visitors than those who rely on English. Waterberg is close, but deserves a separate section to itself, following this one.

⌂ **Otjibamba Lodge** (20 rooms) ☎ 067 303133; f 067 304561; e bamba@iway.na. Situated just 1km off the main B1, a few kilometres south of Otjiwarongo, Otjibamba has become a popular overnight stop for visitors, including coach parties, on their way from Windhoek to Etosha. It's more like a modern hotel set in the country than a guest

farm, with a large, comfortable lounge & dining room, & similar-style restaurant. There's a well-stocked curio shop & a pool outside.

Otjibamba's rooms are purpose-built bungalows, set out in rows separated by lawns. They are like hotel rooms in style, & quite close together. Each has the same 2 dbl beds, carpets, & medium-size

383

en-suite bathroom, with separate bath & shower cubicles. Efficient but anonymous, although if you've been forced to be sociable at lots of guest farms, then a dinner from room service may be just what you need. The rooms overlook a waterhole frequented by a variety of game.

The lodge stands in its own small game park, stocked with giraffe, black & blue wildebeest, red hartebeest, blesbok, gemsbok, kudu, eland, nyala, springbok, impala, zebra, ostrich & waterbuck. N$495/360 sgl/pp sharing, B&B.

⌂ **Okonjima Lodge** (10 rooms, 8 chalets, 3 tents, 2 luxury rooms, 2 suites, Omboroko Campsite) ☎ 067 687032–4; emergency m 081 142 1195, 081 128 9801; f 067 687051; e okonjima@ iway.na; www.okonjima.com. Set in 220km² of rolling hills, Okonjima is best reached from the B1, about 130km north of Okahandja (47km south of Otjiwarongo). Take the private road that is clearly signposted 'Okonjima 24km', & follow the signs to the lodge.

Run by the Hanssen family, this relaxed place has, over the years, been one of Namibia's most popular & successful guest farms – now a lodge. Much of its appeal has been because this is the base for the work of the Africat Foundation (see box), and thus visitors are virtually guaranteed to get close to some of the big cats. That said, its levels of hospitality have always been well above the norm, & the team here are very professional. (They are particularly adept in dealing with film crews & the media – hence their exposure in the media is second to none in southern Africa.)

All the camps here operate independently, with their own dining facilities. Meals, served plated or buffet style, are consistently good, with quality wines at appropriate prices. **Main Camp** is the old guest farm, familiar to visitors who have been coming here since the early 1990s. This has 10 comfortable dbl rooms, built around a central lawn, & 3 twin-bedded tents which are a very short walk away. All have en-suite facilities. The 8 thatched chalets at the newer **Bush Camp** are both more luxurious & more spacious, with a dbl bed & a sgl sofa bed. Each has canvas panels at the front that roll down at night, and its own birdbath within view. More recently, 2 exclusive options have been added: **Okonjima Villa** is 10km from Main Camp, & has 2 luxury rooms & 2 luxury suites, while the **Bush Suite**, 3.5km from Main Camp (500m from Bush Camp), has 2 luxury rooms. Both provide guests with a private chef, game-drive vehicle & guide. At the other end of the scale, but still exclusive (& with hot showers & flush toilets!), is

the **Omboroko Campsite**, where a minimum of 4 guests spend 1–2 nights with a guide.

While each of the camps has separate activities, of which there's usually a choice, they essentially offer the same ones. In the morning, after a coffee & some cereal, there's usually the option to head out on the 'Bushman Trail', where you walk with a guide through the bush & s/he explains some of the plants that the Bushmen use, & how they use them; or it's sometimes possible to go tracking cheetah in the private 4,500ha park; or to do a nature drive around the farm, or to go on a nature walk. After that there's usually a substantial late morning brunch, & then siesta time.

The afternoon activities start after tea, when visits are organised to the cheetah project, or there's the possibility of tracking one of the resident leopards from a 4x4, & opportunities to view the natural wildlife within the park, which includes the rocky Etjo sandstone outcrops. Leopard tracking has yielded many superb photographs; if you look closely, many winners of photo competitions have taken their shots at Okonjima! After dinner in the evening, scraps are put out at a floodlit hide to attract the local porcupines & honey badgers; if you can drag yourself away from the bar for an hour's watching & waiting, this can be fun. Okonjima used to allow guests into much closer contact with other animals, & even to touch the cheetahs, but they've now stopped this.

Okonjima is ideal for a 1- or 2-night stop at the end of your trip to Namibia. It's usually best to arrive at around 16.00 (15.00 in winter), which is in time for tea & the various afternoon activities. There's nowhere else quite like it & for some visitors it's a 'must-see'. *Omboroko Campsite N$450 pp, inc FB & activities; Main Camp N$980/630 sgl/pp sharing DBB, N$1,750/1,400 sgl/pp sharing FB; Bush Camp N$1,630/1,280 sgl/pp sharing DBB, N$2,450/2,100 sgl/pp sharing FB; Bush Suite & Villa from N$6,300/N$3,200–4,200 sgl/pp sharing, depending on numbers, inc meals, drinks & activities.*

⌂ **Mount Etjo Safari Lodge** (22 rooms in Main Lodge, 8 rooms in Rhino Lodge, camping) ☎ 067 290173/4; f 067 290172; e mount.etjo@ iafrica.com.na. About 63km south of Otjiwarongo, turn west from the main B1 onto the D2483, & Mount Etjo is 40km of gravel away. This becomes quite an interesting drive, as the road heads towards the huge, flat-topped sandstone massif of Mount Etjo, which is often a deep shade of burgundy. The gravel on the road changes from white to red in the distance, but watch how it

This non-profit organisation (e africat@natron.net; www.africat.org), based out of Okonjima, aims for the long-term conservation of large carnivores in Namibia. They aim to rescue, relocate and even rehabilitate problem big cats, and also to raise awareness of the issues involved. Current conservation projects focus on Namibia's large carnivores, and concentrate on environmental education programmes, trying to preserve habitat, and supporting animal welfare.

Visitors interested in the Africat Foundation generally stay at Okonjima, and learn more about the foundation's work from there. Neither the foundation nor the lodge will usually accept day visitors dropping in.

differs from the deeper soil, made into tall termitaria. Approaching from the west, Mount Etjo is about 28km from Kalkfeld: 14km on the D2414 then another 14km on the D2483.

Mount Etjo Safari Lodge was founded in the early 1970s by Jan Oelofse, now well known in local political circles. (The 'Mount Etjo Declaration' was signed here on the way to political independence in 1989.) Etjo means 'a place of refuge'; the refuge here is offered by the lodge itself. Accommodation in the Main Lodge is luxurious, with king-sized beds & en-suite bathrooms, some with large round bathtubs, private dining & sitting rooms, & private gardens with jacuzzis. Dinners are served in a lapa around a campfire.

There are usually 2 activities per day, & there's no lack of game on the ranch, brought in to attract visitors. If photography is paramount then you can probably get very close to some of the game. *From N$850 pp sharing, DBB. Game drive N$50 pp.*

✖ WHERE TO EAT While most visitors eat at their hotels, there's a good bakery/café on George's Street, and – something of a home from home for British readers – the Eden Tea Rooms on Hage G Geingob Street. Alternatively, you could try the Wimpy, or the Crocodile Ranch (see below).

GETTING ORGANISED There are several fuel stations around town (some open 24 hours), and Standard, First National and the Bank Windhoek are all in the centre. For **food and supplies**, seek out the shops on the main Hage G Geingob and George's streets, including a Spar and Pick 'n' Pay.

In an emergency, the police are reached on ☏ 067 10111, the ambulance on ☏ 067 301014, and the main government hospital on ☏ 067 300900. More useful to visitors is the excellent private hospital, **Medi-clinic Otjiwarongo** (*Sonn Rd;* ☏ *067 303734/177543;* f *067 303542*), which handles serious cases for much of northern Namibia. In the event of illness, this should be your first call. A friend of mine needed some serious emergency surgery here, and on returning to London her private consultant told her that the operation had been performed to the highest standards.

WHAT TO SEE AND DO In Otjiwarongo, a visit to the **Crocodile Ranch** (☏ *067 302121; open Mon–Fri 09.00–16.00, weekend 11.00–14.00; admission N$20*), makes for an interesting hour or so. The ranch has been going for over 17 years, and has established a small export business for crocodile skins, while the meat is sold locally. It is one of just a few captive breeding programmes for the Nile crocodile (*Crocodylus niloticus*) which has been registered with CITES. There's a restaurant on site serving light lunches, which include the likes of crocodile steaks.

Further afield, **Waterberg Plateau** is a destination in its own right. The only attraction suitable for an excursion from Otjiwarongo is:

Dinosaur footprints Several fossilised animal tracks are preserved here, on the farm Otjihaenamaparero, in the area's distinctive Etjo sandstone. All date from

17

about 150–200 million years ago. The most spectacular is a series of prints, about 25m in length, which were made by a large, three-toed, two-legged dinosaur. Just imagine yourself in Jurassic Park.

To get here take the C33 south for over 60km from Otjiwarongo until Kalkfeld is signposted left, onto the D2414. The farm with the unforgettable name (above) is 29km from there, signposted 'Dinosaur's Tracks'. Follow the signs which will take you down the D2467, and then through a farm gate (but note that signs for 'Dinosaur Camp Site' lead to Mount Etjo Safari Lodge, not to Otjihaenamaparero.

Where to stay

Otjihaenamaparero (3 rooms, camping) /f 067 290153; e dinotracks @ mweb.com.na, service-team-dino @ web.de; www.dinosaurstracks.com/home.html. Otjihaenamaparero farm has a campsite, to which owners Adele & Reinhold Strobel added a new, whitewashed guesthouse in 2003. Alongside modern, en-suite rooms, there's a living area with kitchen ideal for self catering – though home-cooked meals are available on request. The original tree-shaded campsite is still there, its 4 pitches each with drinking water & fireplace. Farm drives & guided walking tours can be arranged for guests. N$330/500/650 sgl/dbl/family, B&B; camping N$50 pp. No credit cards.

WATERBERG PLATEAU PARK

(2WD. Entrance N$80 pp, plus N$10 per car; under 16s free. Day visitors must phone ahead on ⬧ 067 305001)

Historically important during the war between the German forces and the Hereros, the plateau was first envisaged as a reserve for eland, Africa's largest species of antelope. In 1972 it was proclaimed a reserve and has since become a sanctuary for several rare animals, including eland and (introduced) white rhino. Now it is becoming renowned for its long guided walking safari.

GEOGRAPHY The park centres on a plateau of compacted Etjo sandstone, some 250m high. This lump of rock, formed about 180–200 million years ago, is the remnant of a much larger plateau that once covered the whole area. It is highly permeable (surface water flows through it like a sieve), but the mudstones below it are impermeable. This results in the emergence of several springs at the base of the southern cliffs.

FLORA AND FAUNA For a fairly small park, there are a large number of different environments. The top of the plateau supports a patchwork of wooded areas (mostly broadleaved deciduous) and open grasslands, while the foothills and flats at the base of the escarpment are dominated by acacia bush, but dotted with evergreen trees and lush undergrowth where the springs well up on the southern side. This diversity gives the park its ability to support a large variety of animals.

Recently, Waterberg has become an integral part of a number of conservation projects, seeing the relocation of several endangered species (including white rhino, roan and sable antelope) in an attempt to start viable breeding herds. These have added to the game already found here, which ranges from giraffe and kudu to leopard, brown hyena, cheetah and (reports claim) wild dog.

The birdlife is no less impressive, with more than 200 species on record. Most memorable are the spectacular black eagles, and Namibia's only breeding colony of Cape vultures. Numbers of these imposing raptors have sharply declined in recent years due to both the changing environment, and the increasing use of farm

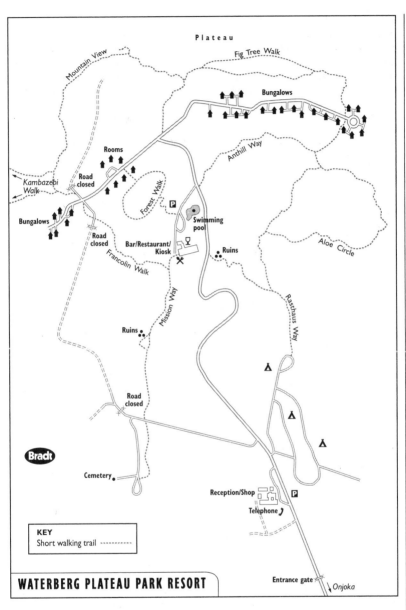

Plateau

Mountain View

Fig Tree Walk

Bungalows

Anthill Way

Rooms

Road closed

Kambazebi Walk

Forest Walk

P

Bungalows

Swimming pool

Road closed

Bar/Restaurant/ Kiosk

Ruins

Aloe Circle

Francolin Walk

Mission Way

Raschaus Way

Ruins

Road closed

Bradt

Cemetery

Reception/Shop

P

Telephone

KEY
Short walking trail ----------

WATERBERG PLATEAU PARK RESORT

Entrance gate

Onjoka

poisons (both intentional poisons, and the chemicals in fertilisers and pesticides). One innovation encourages them to eat at a vulture restaurant (open once a week, on Wednesday morning) where carcasses are prepared and left out for them.

GETTING THERE Waterberg is very clearly signposted, 91km to the east of Otjiwarongo: follow the B1, the C22 and finally the D2512. Note that although the park is accessible in a 2WD, the road from the B1 is very rutted, so allow yourself plenty of time. On the plus side, that gives you a better chance to watch out for wildlife.

WHERE TO STAY

Waterberg Plateau Park Resort Reservations through NWR in Windhoek; ☎ 061 2857200; f 061 224900; e reservations@nwr.com.na; www.nwr.com.na, or at the park office between 08.00 & sunset. The park was made for animals, not visitors, & the restcamp has been operating only since the 1980s. Its amenities are beautifully landscaped over the escarpment's wooded slopes, & include a good restaurant, kiosk, large swimming pool — all quite some way from the campsite.

Accommodation ranges from dbl rooms & 'luxury' dbl bungalows, to 'standard' 2-room bungalows with 4 beds. The grassy campsite is well shaded, with chairs, lights & good ablutions, but watch out for dawn raids from baboons. There's also a fuel station, but note that they don't have diesel.
Room N$500; bungalow N$550/800, luxury/standard; camping N$50 per site, plus N$30/15 pp adult/child (max 8 people).

WHAT TO SEE AND DO This park is unusual in that you can't drive yourself around. Instead you must either hike or take one of the park's organised drives with one of their driver/guides.

Keen walkers will book in advance one of the excellent wilderness trails (see *Hiking* below). But if you haven't done this, then there are some excellent marked trails around the camp area, and even up onto a lookout point on the plateau. These are perfect if you are bored sitting in a vehicle and yearn to stretch your legs.

The park's own organised drives take about three hours; one runs in the morning, and one in the late afternoon. They cost N$260 pp, and are best booked with the park office as soon as you get there. They tour around the plateau in search of game, visiting the permanent waterholes and some of the hides, but are generally disappointing for two reasons. Firstly, the bush is thicker and the game densities appear much lower than, say, Etosha. So although there are good chances of seeing uncommon sable and roan antelope, many visitors find the game disappointing. Secondly, the driver/guides are often very uncommunicative about the wildlife (although if you quiz them, they are knowledgeable). Thus you end up being driven through lots of apparently empty bush, with no illuminating commentary to hold your attention. A final warning from a recent visitor: watch out for your valuables on the game drive.

One possibility for the dedicated is to take the morning trip on to the plateau, get off at one of the hides, and spend the day there game-watching. You need to take some food and water (and perhaps a good book), but can then return to camp with the afternoon drive. Another option is to organise a nature or cultural tour through Stephanus Upani at Waterberg Nature and Culture Safaris (*PO Box 125, Okakarara;* ☎ *067 305001;* m *081 232 4212*). With the guide riding in your vehicle, a typical culture tour will take three to four hours, visiting a traditional Herero village, and perhaps a community centre or school, with the opportunity to try local food.

Hiking This is the way to get the best out of Waterberg. All year round there are nine short trails that you can take around the vicinity of the camp, described in booklets from the office. These are designed to give visitors a flavour of the park, and the panorama from the end of the trail up to Mountain View (*N$50 pp with a guide through the office or Waterberg Nature and Culture Safaris*) is definitely worth the effort that it takes to get there. If you come to Waterberg for the walking, then you won't be disappointed.

During the dry season, from April to November, there are also two hikes organised: an accompanied one in the west of the park, and an unguided alternative in the south. There are no better ways to experience this game park, though reservations must be made months in advance.

You need to bring your own sleeping bag, food and cooking utensils. During both walks you will sleep in stone shelters, provided with simple long-drop toilets and water.

Accompanied trail – Waterberg Wilderness Trail The three-day accompanied 42km hiking trail begins on the second, third and fourth weekends from April to November. It starts at 14.00 on the Thursday and continues until Sunday afternoon, taking one group of between six and eight people, for N$100 each.

The trail starts at Onjoka Gate, the wildlife administration centre, from where the group is driven up onto the plateau. There is no set trail to follow; the warden leading the trail will just guide you across the plateau and go wherever looks interesting. The distance covered will depend on the fitness and particular interests of the group, but 10–15km per day would be typical. This is not an endurance test, but an excellent way to get to know more about the environment with the help of an expert guide.

Unguided trail The four-day unguided 50km trail runs during the same period, starting every Wednesday at 09.00, and returning on Saturday. Only one group of three to ten people is allowed on the trail every week, and it costs N$220 pp.

After a short walk from the restcamp to Mountain View, on the top of the escarpment, the trail begins. From here it is a relatively short 42km. The first night is spent at the Otjozongombe shelter, and the second and third nights at the Otjomapenda shelter, allowing you to make a circular day-walk of about 8km. This all takes place around the spectacular sandstone kopjes on the southern edge of the plateau.

NEARBY LODGES AND GUEST FARMS

Waterberg Wilderness Lodge (9 rooms) Farm Otjosongombe; ☎ 067 687018; f 067 687020; e info@waterberg-wilderness.com; www.waterberg-wilderness.com/wilderness_lodge.htm. The lodge is situated 280 km north of Windhoek: turn off the B1 onto the C22 (28km south of Otjiwarongo), turn left onto the D2512, & drive past the Bernabé de la Bat Camp; at Otjosongombe turn left towards a small gorge in the plateau, & drive for a further 4km. Driving up into the gorge, eventually you reach the lodge in a little green oasis surrounded by cliffs, which mark the edge of the plateau. It's very picturesque.

Here Joachim & Caroline Rust have recently modernised a farm that's long been in their family. They now run this delightful small lodge, with 2 family & 7 dbl rooms. All have en-suite facilities & are spotlessly clean, fairly spacious & designed traditionally though with an eye for touches of stylish minimalism. Expect halogen lights & some of the best showers you'll find anywhere in Namibia. The hosts are German-speaking, but the atmosphere has a very international outlook; Joachim often displays a very English sense of humour. B/fast & lunch are usually buffets, often mixing traditional German fare with other European styles. If you arrive by 15.30 on your first afternoon then you'll be in time for tea & cakes (also included); later dinner is served & everyone eats together. There's a fire for winter evenings, while 2 spring-water pools offer a refreshing dip in the hotter months.

The farm owns part of the Waterberg Plateau itself, as well as some of the flatter farmland around. A stay here includes the option of joining guided hikes onto & around the plateau in the morning or afternoon. These last around 3 hrs & are led by one of the lodge's team. The scenery is stunning, & although getting onto the plateau can be steep at times, walking around the top is relatively flat. You'll see plenty of signs of game although, like walking safaris anywhere, the animals will usually flee before you get too close. Given that both buffalo & rhino live on the plateau, it's wise to keep your wits about you. There's a series of self-guided walking trails, too, with a map provided to identify the plants along the way. Drives on the flat land below the plateau are more productive for game, & the lodge is gradually re-stocking the area, having converted it from a cattle farm to a game area. It's a good place to spot Damara dik-dik, & along with the usual antelope there's also a small group of giraffe here. Finally, there's the option (with a day's notice) of spending half a day visiting a

17

CHEETAH CONSERVATION FOUNDATION (CCF)

The Cheetah Conservation Foundation (*PO Box 1755, Otjiwarongo; \ 067 306225; f 067 306247; e cheeta@iafrica.com.na; www.cheetah.org*) was started by Laurie Marker in 1990 to develop a permanent conservation research centre for cheetah. Today they are based on a 15km² farm northwest of Waterberg Plateau, 44km from Otjiwarongo, Their aim is to 'secure habitats for the long term survival of cheetah and their ecosystem through multi-disciplined and integrated programs of conservation, research and education'.

The foundation has a thriving Visitor and Education Centre (*open daily except Christmas day, 09.00–17.00; N$70/35 adult/child*). To get there, take the B1 north from Otjiwarongo; as you leave the town, the D2440 is on the right, with a brown sign to CCF. Take this road and follow it for about 45 minutes.

Visitors may just turn up during opening hours (last admission 16.30), but if you time your visit for around 14.00 between Monday and Friday, or at noon on Saturday, you should be there for feeding time (though it's as well to phone first to check). It's also possible to watch the cheetahs being exercised, but this is for adults only, and it's important to book in advance; there's also an additional fee. Each morning, at around 07.30, a group of cheetahs is taken out for a run, following a coloured lure that is dragged in front of them around a 'track'.

At all times, you can expect to see some of the orphaned cheetahs living at the centre, and to visit the interactive museum that covers everything from the history of the cheetah to its behaviour and habitat. Conservation issues are prominently covered in the centre, too. There's also a small, well-stocked shop that sells drinks and souvenirs, and the entrance price includes tea or coffee. For those wishing to stay longer, it's possible to take a picnic lunch to eat on the centre's veranda.

The Education Centre houses a museum that provides visitors and students with the opportunity to learn more about the behaviour and biology of the cheetah, and the Namibian ecosystem that supports Africa's most endangered cat species. The excellent graphics and interactive displays in the centre bring the visitor through the history of the cheetah from prehistory to modern times, and explain how their range and numbers have diminished. Other exhibits show where the cheetah fits into the cat species family tree, how the cheetah differs from the 36 other cat species, how the cheetah is adapted for a high speed sprint and its specialised hunting techniques, and finally the cheetah's life cycle from cub to adult. A life-size 'playtree' shows the importance of these trees in a cheetah's territory. The Cheetah Conservation Fund's activities include: radio-tracking research to understand more about cheetah distribution and ecology; bio-medical research to learn more about overall health, diseases and genetic make-up; habitat and ecosystem research; wildlife and livestock management to reduce predator conflicts; and non-lethal predator control methods. CCF also supports extensive environmental education programmes both on site and in schools.

Most visitors to the centre stay for a couple of nights at Waterberg game, or Waterberg Wilderness Trails, and spend half a day visiting the centre from there. There is no accommodation for visitors at the CCF.

local Herero community with a guide.

In short, Waterberg Wilderness is an excellent & good-value spot for a little relaxed walking; it's perfect for a 2- or 3-night stay. *N$960/940 sgl/pp sharing, inc DBB & a guided hike onto the plateau. Afternoon game drives N$60 pp.*

⌂ **Frans Indongo Lodge** (6 rooms, 6 chalets) \ 067 687012; f 067 687014; e info@indongolodge.com; www.indongolodge.com. Relatively new to this area is Frans Indongo Lodge, situated 43km northeast of Otjiwarongo on the D2433. Owned by businessman Dr Frans Indongo, it is designed to reflect his roots as a farmer's son in northern Namibia, with the tall wooden stakes that typically enclose an Ovambo homestead used to separate & define areas of the lodge. It's a very attractive lodge, though note that the reception area has animal heads mounted on the walls & skins on the floor.

Rooms & chalets, some with wheelchair access, are cool & modern in design. All are en suite, with all the extras that you would expect in a good-quality lodge: AC, phone, TV, hairdryer, fridge & kettle. The central area is fronted by a large wooden deck which looks out over the 17,000ha farm. This & an observation tower provide plenty of opportunities for checking out animals at the illuminated waterhole, or birds attracted to the artificial stream..

Guests can take part in game drives on the farm, or a series of three hiking trails, while excursions include visits to the Waterberg Plateau, the Cheetah Farm, the information centre or the Rare & Endangered Species Trust whose focus is the protection of the Cape vulture. *N$600.26/498.52 sgl/pp sharing, B&B. Dinner N$135. Game drive N$110.*

Waterberg Guestfarm (4 rooms, 2 bungalows) 061 253992/7, 253997; f 061 221919; e res@nabozazi.com; www.nabozazi.com. Conveniently situated on the south side of the tarred C22, just a few kilometres east from the main B1, Waterberg Guestfarm has evolved from the earlier Waterberg Game. It's run by the engaging Harry & Hannah Schneider-Waterberg, whose family have owned the 40,000ha farm for nearly 100 years. Now it lies at the centre of the much larger Waterberg Conservancy, which also incorporates the Cheetah Conservation Fund & much of the Waterberg plateau.

The rooms are either in the original farm buildings, which have been converted with care & quality, or in bungalows just 200m from the main house. En-suite rooms are spacious & simply furnished; the 'family unit' consists of linked dbl & twin rooms, each with a small sitting area. Bungalows are built to a traditional Herero design, but with no shortage of modern comforts, including indoor & outdoor showers. Outside is a small splash pool &, beside it, a thatched bar & breakfast area. For cooler days, there's an almost palatial dining room & lounge, which also houses an impressive wine collection.

The main activities here are half-day trips to the Cheetah Conservation Foundation. There are also opportunities for hiking in the mountains behind the farm, which are of a very similar geology & form to the Waterberg. Harry's a good birder, & knows his way around the bush very well, so is a good man to guide you around if he's there. *N$610/525 sgl/pp sharing, B&B.*

Oase Guest Farm (5 rooms) 067 309010; f 067 309011; e oase@natron.net; www.langstrand.com/oase.htm. At the northeastern end of the Waterberg Plateau, on the D2804 about 50km from the B1, Oase offers guests the chance to experience life on a traditional cattle farm, as well as to take guided hikes in the surrounding hills, or a sundowner to finish off the day. Guest rooms are built alongside the farmhouse around a courtyard with a pool. Each is en suite, with a private veranda & views over the farm to the hills. Meals, served *en famille*, are based on farm-grown produce, including beef & game; special diets can be catered for. *N$653/1,278 sgl/dbl, DBB. No credit cards.*

OUTJO

This small ranching town of about 5,000 people is some 65km from Otjiwarongo and 115km south of Etosha's Okaukuejo camp. It stands on a limestone formation in fertile grasslands, dotted with livestock ranches and the odd fruit farm. The name 'Outjo' is variously translated as 'place on the rocks' or 'little hills' – referring to the area's hilly topography. This territory had long belonged to the Herero people when the first Europeans arrived to stay. The adventurer Tom Lambert settled here with his family in 1880, and few others followed until the Schutztruppe established a control post here in 1897. The following year the first 'stand' of town land was officially given out.

In 1901 the town water tower was completed, and is still easily seen today. Development ground to a halt during the Herero war around 1904–5, and again just before independence, but in the last decade or so the town seems to have had a new lease of life.

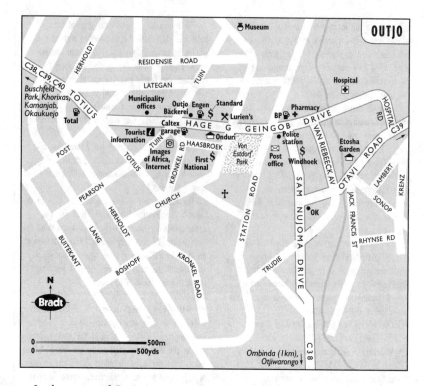

In the centre of Outjo is an open area, like a village green, near which can be found most of the town's facilities, including fuel stations, supermarkets, several curio shops, a couple of cafés and a post office. (The last was memorable for having an old-style public phone as late as 1994, which accepted 10c or 20c pieces and needed cranking into action.) Although the town is something of a backwater, keep an eye out for minor hassle in the form of curio sellers who won't take 'No' for an answer.

Outjo is a useful pit-stop on the way to or from Etosha, Khorixas or the northern Kaokoveld, but not usually a destination in itself; except, perhaps, for the Ugab terraces or the excellent Etosha Garden Hotel.

🏠 WHERE TO STAY

🏠 **Etosha Garden Hotel** (21 rooms) 6 Otavi St;
📞 067 313130; f 067 313419; e egh@
mweb.com.na; www.etosha-garden-hotel.com. The
backstreets of Outjo are the last place that you'd
expect to find a hotel this good, but follow the
signs for a few hundred metres from the centre, &
prepare to be surprised. This was just another basic
hostelry until taken over by an enthusiastic Austrian
couple several years ago. Now it is one of the best
small-town hotels outside Windhoek or Swakopmund.

The rooms are large, normally with twin beds
adjacent to each other, simple wooden furniture, &
rugs scattered on the cool, waxed-concrete or tiled
floors. Each has tea/coffee-making facilities, & a

large bathroom with shower. All overlook an open
courtyard, shaded by jacaranda, palm trees & lush
greenery. There is also a small swimming pool.
Adjacent is an à-la-carte restaurant where you can
enjoy lunch, tea or coffee with apple strudel, or
dinner. The restaurant (mains N$48–78) is well
known for its game specialities. Popular with groups,
this is recommended for a one-night stop, or even
just an extended lunch, on the way to/from Etosha.
N$360/580/720 sgl/dbl/trpl, inc b/fast, exc tourism
levy.

🏠 **Ombinda Country Lodge** (19 chalets, camping)
📞 067 313181; f 067 313478; e discover@
iafrica.com.na; www.discover-africa.com.na. Ombinda

rose from the remnants of Outjo's old municipal restcamp in 1995, & has been thriving ever since. It lies about 1km southeast of town, signposted off the main C38 towards Windhoek.

Chalets are built around a grassy central area with large pool, thatched bar/restaurant with TV & pool tables & al fresco dining area: lunch & dinner are à la carte. The thatched brick chalets have been refurbished with wood cladding; 5 new chalets were

scheduled to open in 2006. Each is clean & well kept with twin or trpl beds & en-suite shower. There's also a small, tree-shaded campsite that's popular with overlanders, tennis courts, & a gold course. Ombinda is clean, safe & secure, ideal for families with children, but its bungalows are close together so this may not be the place to get away from it all.

N$335/550/690 sgl/dbl/trpl, B&B; camping N$50 pp.

Nearby guest farms

⌂ **Buschfeld Park Restcamp** (5 rooms, camping) \/f 067 313665, 313072; e bfeld@mweb.com.na; www.gateway-africa.com/buschfeld. Almost 2km north of Outjo, just across the Storm River on the left, this relaxed restcamp set in 95ha feels more like a small guest farm than a restcamp, & makes a pleasant stopover. Lush grounds with mature citrus trees offset cream-painted buildings with simple but clean rooms, each with twin beds, bathroom, lounge area, fridge & kettle. The sloping campsite has level pitches with power & some shade, & a BBQ area. For entertainment, there's a lovely pool with grassy surrounds, or two self-guided walking trails into the mountains, offering good birding & game such as kudu, Damara dik-dik & duiker.
N$250/460 sgl/dbl, family (3+) N$210 pp sharing, inc b/fast; dinner N$55.

⌂ **Namatubis Guest Farm** (30 chalets) \ 067 313061; e namatubi@iway.na; reservations \ 061 226979; f 061 226999; e logufa@ mweb.com.na; www.natron.net/tour/logufa. Just 15km north of Outjo on the C38, Namatubis is 83km from the gate into Etosha (40 mins' drive). It is only a few hundred metres off the main road, along a palm-lined drive. Hosting guests started as a hobby on the farm for Adri & Freddie Pretorius, and has grown into their main business. Behind an efficient reception area (adorned with work by local artists), the pastel-coloured chalets are lightly built with tin roofs. It's a particularly lush spot: lots of green lawns & colourful plants.

Each en-suite chalet has tiled floors spread with Namibian rugs, twin dbl beds under a fan, tea/coffee maker, & minibar/fridge. Outside is a small pool with sun loungers & a covered dining area. The attractive restaurant (lunch N$40–65) offers good, traditional Namibian cooking, typical of a guest farm, & is open to non-residents. However, Namatubis is a little too big for a guest farm; it feels more like a small hotel. Most visitors are here for just a night, en route to or from Etosha.
N$640/1,060 sgl/dbl, DBB.

⌂ **Vreugde** (4 chalets, 3 rooms) \/f 067 313860; e daniba@vreugde.guestfarm.na, info@vreugde.guetsfarm.na; www.vreugde.guestfarm.na. Since Elsie & Danie Brand opened the 3,400ha family farm to guests in 2001, they have offered a remarkably warm welcome that reflects their name for the farm: *vreugde* means 'joy'. The farm is signposted 9km along the D2710, a turning to the west off the C38 about halfway between Outjo & Etosha's Okaukuejo gate. Accommodation is in traditionally decorated dbl rooms — one en suite, the others used only by families — or in newly built chalets looking over carefully tended lawn & flowerbeds. These are individually decorated in shades of creams & terracotta, with ceiling fans & cool stone floors. Allergy sufferers who struggle with thatch will appreciate the metal roofing of 2 of the rooms, & an en-suite toilet & separate shower room in these rooms is an added bonus. Outside, mature trees provide plenty of shade & attract numerous birds, while in the centre, additional shade is afforded by a lapa that feels like an English summerhouse, albeit thatched & open to the breeze. There is also a new pool to one side, & a braai area. Meals are served around a large table, giving guests the chance to find out about the farm, & drives are also on offer. An added attraction is the couple's pet cheetah, Kambishi, which was brought to the farm from Windhoek as an orphan.

With its location just 40km/1½hr from Etosha, the award-winning Vreugde is a well-recommended place to stop en route from Kaokoland, or for day trips into the national park.
N$475–500/420 pp sharing en-suite/shared facilities, DBB; lunch packs N$40. Transfers & tours by arrangement.

⌂ **Buschberg** (5 rooms) Run by close friends of the Brands at Vreugde, this small guest farm lies 10km further west along the D2710, & on occasion takes the overspill from Vreugde.

For additional accommodation around Etosha's Andersson gate, see *Chapter 16*, pages 368–70.

✕ **WHERE TO EAT** In addition to the restaurants at the hotels, lodges and campsites, Outjo boasts a couple of cafés that would make a good stop; both are on the main Hage G Geingob Drive.

⌨ **Outjo Bäckerei** Directly opposite the Caltex garage on the north side of town. Has eat-in or take-out burgers, some excellent pies & a good range of confectionery & German-style pastries: perfect for a picnic on the road.

⌨ **Koffehuis** ☏ 067 313337. Formerly Lurien's café, this corner venue opposite the green serves b/fast & light meals 07.00–17.00, & is occasionally open in the evening.

GETTING ORGANISED Outjo's a good place to get organised especially for **banks** (*generally open Mon–Fri 08.30–12.45 & 14.00–17.30, Sat 09.00–11.00*): the First National Bank is beside the green, with the Standard Bank (and ATM) almost opposite; the Bank of Windhoek is close to the OK supermarket on Sam Nujoma Drive.

For **fuel** there are the BP station opposite the police station, the Engen garage (with workshop) next to the Standard Bank, and the Total station on the way northwest out of town. All are (in theory) open 24 hours.

There is a helpful **tourist information office** (*open daily 08.00–17.30*) in the Namibia Gemstones shop, on the corner almost opposite the Outjo Bäckerei. The museum and the curio shop opposite the Caltex also have helpful local tourist information.

In an emergency, the police are reached on ☏ 0654 10111, the ambulance on ☏ 0654 313044, and the hospital on ☏ 0654 313250. There's a pharmacy (☏ *0654 313726*) in the centre of town, by the BP garage.

WHAT TO SEE AND DO The town's **museum** (☏ *067 313402; open 10.00–12.00 & 14.00–16.00; admission N$5 pp*) is well worth a visit, with displays of local history and a variety of animal horns, skins and bones, minerals and gemstones. There's also a unique sheep-shearing machine that works with a bicycle chain. If you can't get to it during normal opening hours, it's worth phoning to see if you they will open specially.

Nearby mountains The hills of the Ugab Terrace, near the town, deserve special mention for their unusual shapes. A particularly interesting section can be found about 9km south of the C39, to the west of Outjo, signposted 'Ugab terraces'. There, some of the formations have been likened to castles from the Middle Ages. These are made of conglomerate, and stand on the edge of a plateau that stretches for more than 80km and eventually forms the northern boundary of the Ugab River Valley. Because of differential erosion, only the harder section now remains – often sculptured rather spectacularly.

KAMANJAB

Just to the east of Damaraland, this town's sealed roads and fuel station will come as a relief to those driving south from Kaokoland. However, there are no major attractions here so most people just pass through after stocking up on fuel and cold drinks.

The road from Kamanjab to Ruacana is about 291km of good gravel. Initially it passes through ranch country, and then between the game areas of Hobatere and

Etosha (note the high game fences here). About 8km north of Hobatere's entrance is a checkpoint on the veterinary cordon fence, after which the land reverts to subsistence farms – so watch for domestic animals straying onto the road. From here the bush is bare: only mopane bushes and acacia survive the relentless onslaught of the local goats.

WHERE TO STAY In addition to the following, there's **Kamanjab Rest Camp** south of town offering camping and a pool.

Oase Garni Guest House (8 rooms) PO Box 86, Kamanjab; ☎ 067 330032. This small hotel in the very centre of the town is the only place to stay in Kamanjab itself. Its small rooms are clean & comfortable, with table-top fans & en-suite shower & toilet. There's a lounge area for relaxing, & the owners are friendly & helpful. This is a favourite with local business people, & is fine for tourists

wanting a brief overnight stop. Next door is Debbie's African Kitchen (open Mon–Sat 07.00–09.00, 12.00–14.00 & 19.00–21.00).
N$370/540/720 sgl/dbl/family, B&B.
Oppi Koppi Camping (bungalows, camping) Just 500m from the guesthouse; ☎ 067 330040.
N$200–500 dbl; bungalow N$700; camping N$40 pp.

NEARBY GUEST FARMS There are several guest farms around Kamanjab, especially to the south, and nearby are two large private reserves: **Hobatere** and **Huab**. Though both these are near Kamanjab, in style they are both most similar to the private concession areas of southern Damaraland – so see pages 345 and 345–6 respectively for full descriptions.

Kavita Lion Lodge (8 chalets, cottage) ☎ 067 330224; f 067 330269; e kavita@iway.na; www.kavitalion.com; reservations ☎ 061 224712/250725; e kavita@reservation-destination.com. Signposted from the C35, about 35km north of Kamanjab, Kavita is some 5km east of the road along a track lined with purple-pod terminalia, behind which you may catch the occasional glimpse of springbok, wildebeest or giraffe. It shares a 10km border with Etosha. The lodge is run by Tammy Hoth, who is closely related to the Hanssen family running Okonjima, & her husband Uwe. It clearly aims to emulate Okonjima's success.

Tastefully designed chalets comprise most of the accommodation, some with an upper-storey sitting area, & all with east-facing balcony. Families with children take the 3-room cottage, which is closer to the dining area & pool. All are spacious, clean & well furnished, with plenty of personal touches, like the best guest farms. Carefully prepared meals are served at a central dining table, overlooking attractive gardens with a large pool & a welcoming fire-pit.

Well-planned days for guests involve morning or evening nature/game drives, with time to see how the farm works as well as spot some of the game, plus guided or self-guided birding walks & walking trails; there's a useful bird, mammals & trees checklist available for guests. With notice they can organise day trips & longer safaris into Etosha, the

Kaokoveld or Owamboland. The major attraction, though, is Kavita's lions, the focus of its Afri-Leo Foundation (see box, page 396). The animals – 2 adult males, an adult female & 3 cubs – were rescued from Rundu Zoo when it closed in 1997. Today, they are housed in 2 purpose-built 80ha enclosures, overlooked by a discreet hide which affords both the chance to observe the lions from close quarters, & some great photo opportunities. Chalet N$1,200/895 sgl/pp sharing FB, N$915/610 sgl/pp, family cottage N$880/700 sgl/pp sharing FB, N$700/520 sgl/pp sharing HB, inc activities on the game ranch. Children welcome, but no under 12s on lion activities.

Rustig Toko Lodge & Safaris (12 rooms, camping) ☎ 067 330250; f 067 330265; e info@tokolodge.com; www.tokolodge.com. Run by the delightful Heidi & Jürgen Göthje, Rustig is signposted along the D2763 & D2695, about 19km from the C35 north of Kamanjab; from the road, it's a further 6km to the gate along a reasonably well-maintained track. This is a well-run, traditional lodge, set in attractive gardens on a game farm of some 60km². It isn't for those in search of the glittery or fake, & you'll find no recently arranged attractions to tempt you, but the hospitality is warm & spontaneous, the birding good, & numerous activities are available.

Each of the large, stone-floored rooms – some in the old farmhouse, others built higher up with their own verandas overlooking the plains — has terracotta-painted walls, twin beds with mosquito nets, & a table & chairs; a stone-clad wall screens the en-suite facilities. A veranda runs along the outside of the old farmhouse, & there is a small pool with a good view. A recently built thatched lapa forms an extension to the original farmhouse, with a cool dining & lounge area, & bar. Rustig also has a few good campsites in an area of mopane bush, a little way from the lodge. These are well set up with hot showers, flush toilets & a place to cook, or meals can be arranged at the farmhouse. From here it takes about 2½ hrs across the backroads to the Etosha gate south of Okaukuejo.

Excursions range from game drives around the farm (N$120 pp) to ½-day trips to Peet Albert's Hilltop beyond Kamanjab to see 200,000-year-old Bushman paintings (N$400 pp). Jürgen speaks the Himba language, making him a fascinating guide for a day trip to a Himba village (N$4,000 for 2 people). He also organises a variety of longer trips, inc 2-day trips into western Etosha (around N$8,000 for 4 people), and 3-day trips to Epupa Falls & northern Kaokoveld (around N$12,300 for 4 people). *N$600 pp sharing, DBB; camping N$70 pp.*

🏠 **Ondundu Wilderness Lodge** (4 chalets, 4 tents) ☎ 067 697038; f 067 691039; e ondu@iway.na; www.ondundu.com. Clearly signposted from the C35 between Kamanjab & Khorixas, Ondundu lies 8km east of the road in a heavily wooded setting. Opened in 2001, & run under management, its neat lawns,

small clear pools & 3-storey 'entertainment area' with bar, lounge & dining levels (complete with taped music) come as something of a surprise in this area. Large, stone-clad chalets mask a luxurious interior, with solid furniture, tasteful cream drapes, modern bathrooms & separate dressing room, & screened patio doors; each also has a TV, safe & fan. Walk-in tents, set further away, have simpler accoutrements. Although drives on the 6,330ha estate, with its Bushman paintings & range of game, as well as horseriding, walks, & trips to the Cheetah Farm or a Himba village are on offer, the atmosphere at Ondundu is better suited to those seeking R&R than a real involvement with the region. *Chalet N$1,295/870 pp high/low season, tent N$650/500 pp, all DBB.*

🏠 **Otjitotongwe Cheetah Guest Farm** (6 rooms, camping) ☎ 067 687056; f 067 687057; e cheetahs@iway.na. Clearly named for its main attraction, Cheetah Guest Farm is a working dairy farm about 24km southeast of Kamanjab on the C40. Turn left onto the P2683 & 8km further you will find the reception; the lodge is another 2km from here. Elaborate chalets are faced in local stone, & nearby is a camping area, where overlanders have their own separate sector of the site. There is a bar/dining area for lodge guests, & a separate bar for campers. In the evening, atmospheric paraffin lanterns are used throughout, adding to the impression that this is neither a lodge nor a guest farm, but something between.

To attract visitors, the farm has 5 tame cheetahs, as well as 19 wild ones contained in a 250ha area. Game drives or walks are possible in a small plot containing both cattle & game, including giraffe, oryx, kudu, mountain zebra & some smaller buck. *N$560 pp inc DBB & cheetah tour; camping N$50 pp (it is sometimes possible to arrange meals). Cheetah tour N$100 pp.*

OTHER PRACTICALITIES Kamanjab is a tiny town with a small supermarket, a police station, a mobile Bank of Windhoek (open once a month) and a post office. Notably, there is also a 24-hour fuel station, which is the last certain fuel stop before Ruacana if you're heading north; its shop also sells cold drinks and bread. If you're passing through on a week day, take a look at the Women's Craft Centre, Khâima seni, opposite the fuel station; it was closed when we visited, but looked promising.

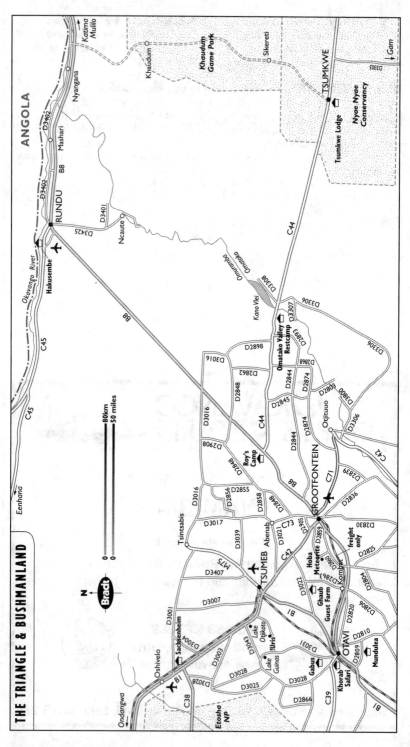

THE TRIANGLE & BUSHMANLAND

18

The Triangle and Bushmanland

The triangle of Otavi, Tsumeb and Grootfontein has long been one of the most prosperous areas of Namibia, rich both minerally and agriculturally. Geologists will find it particularly fascinating because of its interesting underground caverns and the famous Tsumeb mine, whilst the rolling farmland has a lush, well-watered feel that is seldom found south of here.

From the highlands, Hereroland and Bushmanland extend east to the Botswana border, sloping down from the agricultural plains of the central plateau into the endless, gently undulating Kalahari. This 'desert' is very different from the Namib, in landscape and people, although its population density is almost as low. This northeastern corner of the country is time-consuming, and even difficult, to visit, but offers a fascinating wilderness experience for those who are well prepared and make the time to reach it. It's also the home of many groups of San people: a draw for a small, but increasing, number of visitors.

OTAVI

Situated in a fertile farming area, near one of the country's biggest irrigation schemes, this small town has a 24-hour Total service station on the main road that skirts around it. As you turn into the town, Otavi seems small and quiet. Some of the streets are tar, others are gravel. There are two service stations – Circle and Fourways – next to the main road, and a very good Spar supermarket.

Turn right after the Otavi Fruit Store to reach the restcamp (currently closed for refurbishment) and, after that, the municipal offices. You'll find fish and chips at the Fruit Store, and drinks at Ot-Quell Bottle Stall or Mr Liquor World. Alternatively, there's a bar at the Fourways service station where you can stop for a drink and something to eat.

There are branches of Standard, Bank Windhoek and First National banks, and the small post office offers internet facilities, albeit on the slow side.

Near Otavi are several interesting cave systems, though visits to these need to be carefully organised in advance.

GETTING THERE

By train Although the normal passenger train service between Windhoek and Otavi is no longer scheduled, TransNamib has recently introduced a weekly service between Windhoek and Ondangwa that calls at Otavi. Called the *Omugulu Gwombashe Star*, it's a faster service than the normal passenger trains. Trains leave Windhoek every Friday at 17:30, returning from Ondangwa on Sunday at 13:00; a one-way ticket between Windhoek and Otavi costs N$89. For details, see page 101.

By bus Intercape Mainliner's services from Windhoek to Victoria Falls stop at the Total service station in Otavi at 21.40 on Monday, Wednesday and Friday, and in

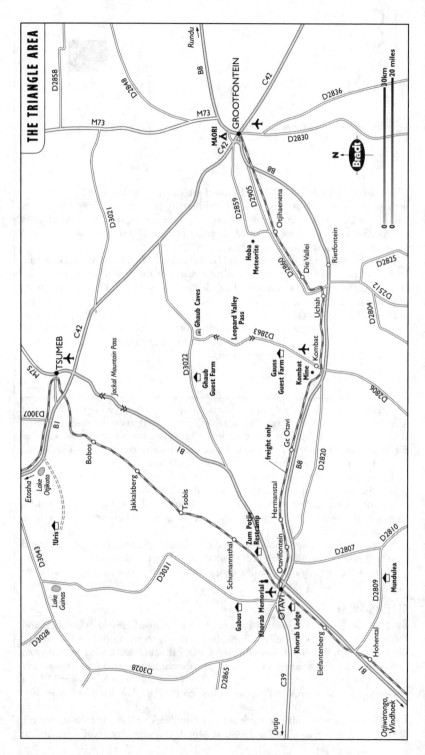

THE TRIANGLE AREA

N

Bradt

30km
20 miles
0
0

the opposite direction at 01.25 on Monday, Thursday and Saturday. The one-way trip costs around N$170 to Windhoek, and N$390 to Victoria Falls. See *Chapter 6*, pages 104–5, for more details.

The small local minibuses (normally VW combis) that link Otavi with Tsumeb and Grootfontein usually stop at the main Fourways Total service station, which is probably the best place from which to hitchhike, too.

WHERE TO STAY

Hotel Otavi & Grasdak Restaurant (10 rooms, 3 chalets) 6 Park St; \/f 067 234334; m 081 127 4913; 081 285 4388. All rooms are en suite with fans & tea/coffee-making facilities. En-suite chalets have AC, with dbl & twin beds. The busy bar seems also to act as reception as well as a restaurant & is a focal point for some of the town in the evening. *Rooms N$120/200 sgl/dbl; chalets N$200/300 sgl/dbl, all B&B.*

Palmenecke Guest House 96 Hertzog Av; \/f 067 234199; e palmenecke@

africaonline.com.na; www.palmenecke.co.za. All rooms have an en-suite bathroom, as well as AC & TV. Guest facilities include a lapa & braai, a bar, swimming pool, & secure parking. *N$195/350 sgl/dbl, B&B.*

Municipality Restcamp The municipality was in the throes of updating their restcamp early in 2007. Prior to that, it had half a dozen well-equipped, but not at all plush, bungalows. Any feedback on the improvements would be welcome.

Around Otavi

Khorab Safari Lodge (10 chalets, camping) \ 067 234352/234522; f 067 234520; e khorab@iafrica.com.na; www.resafrica.net/khorab-lodge. About 3km south of Otavi, Khorab is set back just off the main B1 road to Otjiwarongo. It was built in 1996 & is a beautiful place to stop. The main building has a large, plush bar area, relaxing couches, a small curio shop & a b/fast room, all under high thatched ceilings. At the back, set around green lawns, herbaceous borders & even a small artificial stream, are 10 chalets, 6 of which can be linked if required to make larger family rooms. Each chalet has tiled floors dotted with rugs, twin beds (that can be pushed together for a dbl) & airy thatched ceilings. They are large & well built, using colourful fabrics, with fans & en-suite showers &

toilets – though they do not have phones, or AC. This is a stylish place to stop for a night, but lacks intrinsic reasons to encourage you to stay longer. *From N$535/385 sgl/pp sharing, B&B.*

Zum Potjie Restcamp (5 bungalows, camping) \ 067 234300; f 067 221964; e info@ zumpotjie.com; www.zumpotjie.com. Signposted from the B1 to Tsumeb, 6km north of Otavi, Zum Potjie is 2.5km off the main road. Each of the twin-bed bungalows is clean & simple with a basic, prefabricated design & en-suite shower & toilet. There's a small swimming pool, food is available, laundry can be arranged, & camping is available on request. If you plan to stay, then short guided trips are possible. *N$220–260 pp sharing, B&B; camping N$35 pp.*

Nearby guest farms

Ghaub Guest Farm (10 rooms) \/f 067 240188; e ghaub@iway.na; www.namibsunhotels.com.na. An unlikely part of the large Namib Sun Hotels group, this farm is situated in the Otavi Mountains, in the heart of the Triangle, some 60km east of Otavi. It's on the south side of the D3022, about 3km west of its junction with the D2863.

Ghaub was originally founded as a mission station in 1895. Now a stylish guest farm, it has successfully retained a lot of character, with high ceilings & plenty of space, especially in the rooms, which are clean & well cared for. Each has twin beds & an en-suite bathroom, & a large veranda with impressive views of the surrounding land &

hills; 2 interconnect for families. Tours of the nearby caves are probably easiest to organise from here; other activities include farm drives & walking trails.

The atmosphere at Ghaub is informal & friendly. It's recommended for a few nights if you want somewhere to relax, & perhaps do a little gentle walking – provided that you don't mind a lack of must-see attractions in the vicinity. *N$530/760 sgl/dbl.*

Mundulea (3 walk-in tents) \ 064 403123; f 064 403290; e turn@iafrica.com.na; www.turnstone-tours.com. Biodiversity is the watchword for one of the most intriguing & fulfilling back-to-nature experiences in Namibia's fast-expanding repertoire: Mundulea. A private reserve established at the turn of the 20th century, the farm covers 120km^2 of prime bush & mountain savanna in the ancient Otavi karstveldt. This lime & marble landscape spans dolomite ridges, steep gorges & underground caverns. Deep subterranean water feeds spreading trees & the rich soil provides fertile ground for a huge diversity of animal, bird & plant life.

The farm is surprisingly easy to find. Driving southwest from Otavi, keep to the main B1 for 20km. Just before the railway bridge, turn left onto the D2809 & drive a further 10km on good gravel road. As it bears round to the left, you'll see Mundulea's entrance gate on your right. It will be open if you are expected (booking is essential). Follow the farm road for about 15 minutes to reach the old lime-and-clay farmhouse at the top of the hill.

Here you'll be met by Mundulea's owner, Bruno Nebe, who personally takes guests out for 4-day walking trails across this unforgettable country. The trails were developed to give visitors a chance to get out into the natural environment at the end of a long, round-Namibia journey. Numbers are kept small — maybe 2 or 3 couples — & walks can be gentle rambles or more serious hikes, according to the interests & pace of individual guests. But they always revolve around what occurs naturally, giving a real sense of exploration & minimising disturbance.

Bruno has set out to restore the area to its former importance as the heartland of Namibia's game populations. With everything in its favour in terms of natural habitat, high rainfall & low human impact, Mundulea has made a gradual transition from a heavily fenced cattle ranch to a low-profile but very successful wildlife sanctuary.

There are good numbers of eland, which thrive in the privacy of Mundulea's hills & valleys. Kudu, oryx, hartebeest, wildebeest, duiker, steenbok, dik-dik & warthog are common sights, whereas newly introduced species such as giraffe & zebra are still hard to spot. There are also leopard, cheetah, brown & spotted hyena, as well as delightful rarities like pangolin, aardvark & bushbabies. Soon to be released is a group of indigenous black-faced impala. These were the initial raison d'être for Mundulea, which Bruno envisaged as a safe haven for Namibia's critically endangered endemic game species. Working closely with the Ministry of Environment & Tourism & international researchers, Mundulea was recently entrusted with the safe-keeping of the last of the black rhino sub-species *Bicornis chobiensis*. A breeding programme to keep this bloodline flowing

is in operation, & you'll hear more of this important project during your visit.

For birders, Mundulea has notched up some 230 species, whilst for the more geologically inclined, the reserve offers a fascinating array of rock formations, with the chance to explore caves & caverns first hand. There are fossils dating back to key periods in African palaeontology.

Accommodation, arranged to blend into the natural surroundings, is in rustic tented camps. At the moment these comprise 3 large, walk-in tents, with shared toilets & hot bucket showers. Each tent has proper, comfortable beds, & extensive views. However plans to upgrade accommodation, without spoiling the simplicity of the camps, are under way. The privacy of en-suite bathrooms will be among the improvements.

Excellent meals are prepared on an open fire, & care is taken to provide natural, wholesome food with a stylish twist. The results are delicious: Thai calamari with coconut or pan-fried kudu fillet vie with the traditional braai for supper. A light b/fast before a short morning wander is followed by a hearty brunch & the main walk of the day. Typically this would be to another camp set in contrasting scenery offering a different angle on Mundulea's diverse habitat & wildlife.

Getting acquainted with this place, with Bruno & the project is seriously worthwhile for visitors who want to look a little deeper into Namibia's environmental issues. Mundulea is an ideal 'last stop' on the way back to Windhoek, an opportunity to explore the bush properly, in the company of an outstanding guide. But be warned, guests tend to find themselves drawn back to Mundulea & the ideas it embodies time & time again.

4 days/3 nights N$7,900 pp sharing (4–5 people), N$9,500 pp sharing (2–3 people).

⌂ **!Uris Safari Lodge** (14 rooms) ☎ 067 221818; f 067 220823; e reservations@urissafarilodge.com; www.urissafarilodge.com. Set on a private 17,000ha game reserve, 20km west of Tsumeb, the new !Uris Lodge has a mix of dbl & family rooms laid out in pairs in renovated mine cottages, or *kompongs*. Rooms & central building alike are under steep thatch, complemented by solid furniture that is simple yet comfortable. All rooms are en suite with AC, kettle, hairdryer, safe & phone, while family rooms have an attractive loft area for children 6–12.

There's an attractive swimming pool, & — rather surprisingly — a small chapel that is available for weddings. Walking trails lead visitors in the footsteps of the 19th-century miners, who scoured the

landscape for signs of valuable minerals for export, whilst game drives take in the reserve's wildlife, including eland & kudu.
N$590.09/803.74/1,007.32–1,210.70 sgl/dbl/family, all B&B.

🏠 **Gabus Game Ranch** (7 rooms) ✆ 067 234291; m 081 127 9278; f 067 234290; e kuehl@mweb.com.na; www.natron.net/tour/gabus. Gabus farm has been in the Kuehl family for 4 generations, & is located 10km west of Otavi. To get there, take the C39 towards Outjo for 10km, then turn right onto the D3031 to reach the farm. Its current owners,

Heidi & Heinz Kuehl, have developed it into a comfortable guest farm with well-thought-out accommodation for everyone from couples & honeymooners to families; there's even a sgl room. Guest rooms are individual thatched bungalows with en-suite bath & toilet, & AC. These – & all of the areas open to guests – overlook a waterhole which is the focus of kudu, eland, waterbuck, impala, springbok & hartebeest, among other wildlife. Activities include game drives & guided hikes with Heinz.
N$980 pp, inc DBB & a game drive.

WHAT TO SEE AND DO Otavi doesn't have a wealth of big attractions, unless your passion is caves. In that case, plan to spend quite a lot of time around here, as the area has many systems to explore.

Khorab memorial This marks the spot where the German colonial troops surrendered to the South African forces on 9 July 1915. It is only 3km out of town but exceedingly well signposted.

Gaub caves On the Gaub Farm, 35km northeast of Otavi, there are some caves famous for their stalactites and Bushman paintings. Despite being on private property, these are a national monument so a permit to visit must be obtained from the Windhoek MET before you arrive (see page 125).

They're signposted close to the junction of the D2863 and the D3022, but facilities are minimal and you'll need to inform the landowner that you're going down. After a short walk through the bush, there's a small hole in the ground into which you must squeeze. A lot of powdery sand is around, making this quite difficult, and initially it's a very steep incline to get into the caves. They aren't suitable for a casual visit – there's a locked gate for starters – but if you have a permit then bring a heavy-duty torch (this last is supplied on trips organised through Ghaub Guest Farm).

Aigamas caves Some 33km northwest of Otavi, on a tectonic fault line, this cave system is about 5km long. It has aroused particular interest recently as the home of *Clarius cavernieola*, a species of fish that appears to be endemic to this cave system. These fish, members of the catfish family, are a translucent light pink in colour and totally blind, having evolved for life in the perpetual darkness of these caves. Interestingly, their breeding habits are still unknown and no young fish have ever been found.

To visit the cave, make arrangements at the municipal offices, just to the right of the restcamp. This may take several days.

Uiseb caves More extensive than Gaub, these caves have several different chambers and passages containing some impressive stalactites and stalagmites. With no facilities at all, they are described as 'unspoilt' and arrangements to see them must be made at the municipal offices.

Kombat Kombat is memorable largely for its name. It is just off the main road, about halfway between Otavi and Grootfontein, and known in Namibia for its mine. This accounts for a thriving little centre, where today you'll find Tierkloof Butchery & General Dealers, and a small post office. Turn off here for the Leopard Valley Pass.

18

The attractive town of Tsumeb stands in the north of the central plateau, an area of rich farmland and great mineral wealth. Its wide streets are lined with bougainvillea and jacaranda trees, and in the centre of town is a large, green park, a favourite for the townspeople during their lunch.

Economically the town was dominated by the Tsumeb Corporation which, in the early 1990s, mined a rich ore pipe here for copper, zinc, lead, silver, germanium, cadmium and the variety of unusual crystals for which Tsumeb is world famous. Tsumeb's one pipe has produced about 217 different minerals and gemstones, 40 of which have been found nowhere else on earth. However, in the late 1990s this closed, badly affecting the town. Although the mine has recently been reopened for specimen mining, this isn't on a fraction of the scale of the original operation.

Fortunately, Tsumeb still retains some light industries, and is close enough to Etosha to benefit from a steady flow of tourists. It remains a pleasant place to visit, and doesn't have any of the air of depression that you might expect given the importance of the mine that's now closed.

GETTING THERE Tsumeb is the largest of the Triangle's towns, and once had the best connections. Today, though, although the town has its own airstrip, it is rarely used by visitors, and there are no scheduled flights into the region.

By train Similarly, despite the construction of a new railway line north to Ondangwa, the normal passenger trains no longer run to Tsumeb. However, the recent introduction of a fast weekly service between Windhoek and Ondangwa, the *Omugulu Gwombashe Star*, means that passengers are not entirely stranded. Trains leave Windhoek every Friday at 17.30, returning from Ondangwa on Sunday at 13.00. The fare between Windhoek and Tsumeb is N$89 one way. For details, see page 101.

By bus Intercape Mainliner's services from Windhoek arrive in Tsumeb at the tourism centre on Omeg Allee on Monday, Wednesday and Friday at 21.25. The return journey is on Wednesday, Friday and Sunday, departing from Tsumeb at 00.45.

On Wednesday, Friday and Sunday, buses leave Victoria Falls for Tsumeb at 09.00, arriving at 11.15; they return on the same days, leaving Tsumeb at 21.30, and arriving at 13.00; See *Chapter 6*, pages 104–5, for details. For tickets, contact Tsumeb Tourism Services (*1551 Omeg Allee;* ☎ *067 220728;* f *067 220916*) or Tsumeb Aviation Services (*Jordaan St;* ☎ *067 220520;* f *067 220821*).

For more local transport, keep a lookout for the small minibuses (normally VW combis) that link the Triangle towns. They depart north from the Trek and Caltex, on Hage G Geingob Drive. Southbound local combi buses also stop there.

Hitching Hitching from central Tsumeb is difficult. You must first get yourself to the main junction of the B1 and the C42 (see *By bus* above). If you're going south, then hitch on Omeg Allee, about 500m after leaving town, before the caravan park.

WHERE TO STAY AND EAT Tsumeb has two established hotels, a pension, a restcamp, and a place for backpackers – something for everyone! Most visitors eat in their hotels, with the restaurants at the Makalani and the Minen being the most popular.

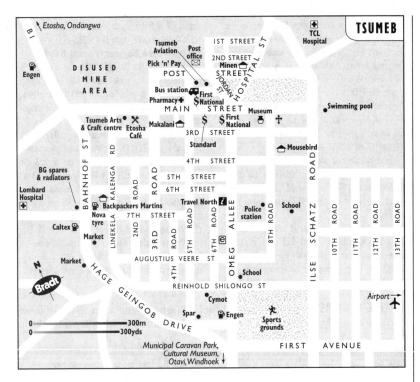

TSUMEB

Etosha, Ondangwa

Bı

Engen

TCL
Hospital

Tsumeb
Aviation

Post
office

1ST STREET

Pick 'n' Pay

2ND STREET

Minen

POST   STREET

DISUSED
MINE
AREA

Bus station

First
National

Pharmacy

MAIN   STREET

Museum

Swimming pool

Tsumeb Arts
& Craft centre

Makalani

Etosha
Café

First
National

JORDAN HOSPITAL ST

3RD   STREET

Standard

4TH   STREET

Mousebird

BG spares
& radiators

Lombard
Hospital

BAHNHOF ST

KALENGA RD

5TH   STREET

6TH   STREET

SCHATZ   ROAD

10TH ROAD

11TH ROAD

12TH ROAD

13TH ROAD

Backpackers

Martins

Travel North

Nova
tyre

7TH   STREET

Police
station

School

Caltex

LINEKELA ST

2ND ROAD

3RD ROAD

5TH ROAD

6TH ROAD

OMEG ALLEE

8TH ROAD

Market

AUGUSTIUS VEERE ST

ILSE

Market

4TH

HAGE GEINGOB DRIVE

REINHOLD SHILONGO ST

School

Cymot

Airport

Spar

Engen

Sports
grounds

0   300m
0   300yds

FIRST   AVENUE

Municipal Caravan Park,
Cultural Museum,
Otavi, Windhoek

Bradt

N

Makalani Hotel (28 rooms) Cnr 4th St & 3rd Rd; ☎ 067 221051; f 067 221575; e makalani@mweb.com.na; www.makalanihotel.com. This smart & efficient hotel, distinctively painted in yellow with green windows, is right in the centre of town. Rooms are comfortable with (firm!) twin beds, direct-dial phones, AC & satellite TV. The restaurant is small & friendly, with a reasonable, if not adventurous à-la-carte menu; alternatively meals may be taken by the pool or in the rustic bar. Other facilities include a private bar, & gambling. *N$386.61/559.57/661.30/712.17 sgl/dbl/trpl/family, B&B.*

Minen Hotel (49 rooms) Post St; ☎ 067 221071/2; f 067 221750; e contact@ minenhotel.com; www.minenhotel.com. In an attractive spot opposite the park, the friendly Minen was fully upgraded in 2005. Its more modern twin rooms are set round a courtyard with a swimming pool & a beautiful lush garden, & the older but refurbished dbl rooms overlook a second courtyard. All have mosquito nets, AC/heating & fan, en-suite toilet & shower or bath, TV & fridge. Rooms are almost out of earshot of the busy bar at the front, which can become quite lively at the

weekends, especially at the end of the month when people are paid.

To the side of the hotel is a pleasant outdoor veranda with umbrella-shaded tables & chairs; a popular spot for lunch or drinks, Inside the more formal restaurant is open during the week 19.00–21.30.
Poolside N$450/ 650 sgl/dbl; garden side N$350/480 sgl/dbl, all B&B.

Travel North Tourism Services (6 rooms) Omeg Allee; ☎ 067 220728; m 081 299 4214; f 067 220916; e travelnn@stu.namib.com. Tsumeb's tourist information office also has a couple of en-suite twin rooms, & a few 4-bed dorms, sharing showers, toilets & a kitchen. Rooms are to the side of the office, & there's always someone to let you in. There's also a coffee shop & a launderette. *N$180/250 sgl/dbl. Dorm bed N$100 pp. B/fast N$40 pp.*

Mousebird Backpackers (4 rooms, 10 dorm beds) 533 4th St; ☎ 067 221777; m 081 272 2650; f 067 221778; e info@mousebird.com; www.mousebird.com. In the centre of town, on the corner of 8th Rd near the museum, the colourful Mousebird is aimed squarely at backpackers, offering safaris around the region, as well as private twin or dbl rooms, dorm accommodation & camping on the lawn. There's a fully equipped kitchen & dining room, with free tea & coffee, & a washing machine. The small bar area is usually busy, & for those who miss their electronic home comforts too much, there is a satellite TV, a collection of videos & a PlayStation in the lounge. Outside, the parking is secure &, if you want to cook for yourselves, you can do so in the braai area. At extra cost there's internet access & a phone/fax.

Trips include 1–2 nights in Etosha (N$1,200/1,700 pp all inc, exc drinks) & day trips to Bushmanland (N$600 pp, or N$1,200 overnight). *Rooms N$175, dorm beds N$75, camping N$50 pp.*

⌂ **Backpackers Martins Africa** (9 rooms, 11 dorm beds) Linekela Kalenga; ☎ 067 220310; f 222964. Somewhat surprisingly, this newly opened backpackers' place was closed for renovation in 2006. We understand that en-suite rooms have a shower, TV & fridge; dorm rooms each have 5 beds. *N$200 dbl en suite, dorm bed N$85–95.*

⌂ **Etosha Café & Biergarten** (5 rooms) Main St; ☎ 067 221207; m 081 127 3855. This pleasant café with a relaxing garden at the back offers light lunches, as well as coffee & cake, until 17.00. It also sells a range of local books & postcards. Basic rooms. *N$110/190 sgl/dbl.*

⌂ **Tsumeb Municipality Caravan Park** ☎ 067 221056; f 067 221464. The tree-shaded municipal campsite lies about halfway between the town & the main road intersection, about 1km from each. It's a flat, grassy site, child friendly & with helpful staff. *Adult/child N$15.30/7.60. Tent N$45.90 per day, caravan N$61.20.*

⌂ **Steinbach Backerei** Main St; ☎ 067 220135. This recommended bakery offers good pizzas, delicious bread, & German & Italian cakes, as well as serving very good cappuccino or espresso. Friendly, helpful service.

GETTING ORGANISED There are several **fuel stations** around town, many of them open 24 hours. Main Street has branches of Standard and First National **banks**.

Tourist information

Travel North Tourism Services Omeg Allee; ☎ 067 220728; m 081 299 4214; f 067 220916; e travelnn@tsumeb.nam.lia.net. Tsumeb's tourist information centre is about 300m from the main traffic lights. They also offer simple accommodation (see *Where to stay*, above). Here you'll find an extensive resource centre of leaflets & information from around the country, & helpful staff. As an efficient local travel agent, they can sort out travel problems, or arrange bookings for elsewhere in Namibia. They are agents for Imperial Car Hire in the north, & representatives for both Air Namibia &

Intercape Mainliner, so can arrange car hire, transfers, & airline & bus tickets. They also organise tours to Etosha (N$500 pp per day, or N$600 pp for 2 days, with overnight camping at Namutoni). At the back of the tourism centre local curios are for sale, & there is an internet café.

Tsumeb Aviation Services Safari Centre Jordan St; ☎ 067 220520; f 067 220821. Despite the name, this is something of a one-stop for everything travel-related, including car hire – this is the local Avis agency.

Internet

Travel North Tourism (see above) N$15 per ¹/₂ hr, or N$25 per hr.

Shopping For **food shopping**, the Pick 'n' Pay supermarket at one end of Post Street (opposite the post office), and Spar in 9th Street, are probably the best places. For those staying longer, the mine has made Tsumeb relatively rich, and its main shopping street is often bustling, with various clothes shops, take-aways and several curio outlets.

Emergency The police are reached on ☎ 067 10111, the ambulance service on ☎ 067 221911/221912/221998. The hospital is on ☎ 067 221082 and the fire service on ☎ 067 221056/221042 (a/h)/221004 (pager). There is also a private hospital serving the mine, ☎ 067 221001, which may be able to help in an emergency. Barry Jacobs Apteek (☎ *067 222190; after hours* ☎ *067 220508*) is the place to call if you're in need of medication.

WHAT TO SEE AND DO

Tsumeb Museum (*Open Mon–Fri 09.00–12.00 & 14.00–18.00, Sat 09.00–12.00; admission N$15 pp*) Facing the park, on Main Street, next to a beautiful Lutheran church, is one of Namibia's best little museums. It has an excellent section on the region's geology and exhibits many of the rare minerals collected from the mine. It also has displays on the German colonial forces, and a small section on the lifestyle of the Bushmen, Ovambo, Herero, Kavango and Himba people. Train buffs will be drawn to the gleaming steam engines outside the museum, as well as to exhibitions covering the construction of the Otavi railway line from Swakopmund to Otavi.

The Khorab Room contains old German weaponry, recovered from Lake Otjikoto, which was dumped there by the retreating German forces in 1915 to prevent the rapidly advancing Union troops from capturing it. Since that time, pieces have been recovered periodically, the most recent being the Sandfontein cannon on display here. Also on display is the uniform of the German Schutztruppe (stormtroopers), along with the photo album of one of them, General von Trotha, which makes fascinating reading if your German is good. Appropriately, the museum is located in a historic German school dating from 1915, now a national monument, but unfortunately for English visitors, many of the exhibits are labelled only in German.

Tsumeb Cultural Village (`\` *067 220787. Open Mon–Fri 08.00–16.00, Sat–Sun & holidays 08.00–13.00; admission N$10 pp*) Facing the park, between the Municipal Caravan Park and the centre of town, is a relatively new building which was constructed with Norwegian funds and modelled on the fort at Namutoni. Open-air displays on most of the country's main ethnic groupings and their traditional housing make for a worthwhile visit. There's also a small curio shop.

Tsumeb Arts and Crafts Centre (TACC) (*18 Main St;* `\f` *067 220257. Open Mon–Fri 08.30–13.00, 14.30–17.00, Sat 08.30–13.00. After-hours visits can sometimes be arranged by phone*) Next to the Etosha Café & Biergarten, the TACC is a charitable trust set up to help develop the skills of Namibian artists and craftspeople. It provides them with a base, training, and some help in marketing their produce – including this shop selling their work at a reasonable price, with no haggling or pressure to buy. It's well worth a visit.

Ombili Foundation (*PO Box 137, Tsumeb;* `\` *067 230050;* e *ombili@namibnet.com; www.ombili.de/html/english.html*) Set up by a group of local farmers, the Ombili Foundation aims to prepare San people for the demands of the 21st century. Aside from being an interesting project in its own right, Bushmen crafts are on sale.

EXCURSIONS AROUND TSUMEB

Lake Otjikoto (*Entry N$12/3 adult/child; campsite N$40 pp; open all year*) About 20km from Tsumeb, signposted just to the west of the B1, this lake (once thought to be bottomless) was formed when the roof of a huge subterranean cave collapsed, leaving an enormous sinkhole with steep sides. Together with Lake Guinas, the lake is home to a highly coloured population of fish: the southern mouthbrooder, *Pseudocrenilabrus philander*. These have attracted much scientific interest for changes in their colour and behaviour as a result of this restricted environment. Now the lake is also home to some *Tilapia guinasana*, which are endemic to Lake Guinas but have been introduced here to aid their conservation.

Sub-aqua enthusiasts regularly dive in the lake's green waters and have recovered much weaponry that was dumped in 1915 by the retreating German

Mining was started in the place now known as Tsumeb well before historical records were kept. Then it's thought that the San, who were known to have settlements at Otjikoto Lake, 24km away, were probably attracted by the hill's green colour, and perhaps mined malachite here. This they probably then traded with Ovambo people who would smelt it to extract the copper. Perhaps the earliest records of this are from the writings of Francis Galton who, in 1851, met both Bushmen and Ovambos transporting copper near Otjikoto.

In 1893, Matthew Rogers came to the Green Hill here for about a year, sinking test mine shafts and concluding that there was a major deposit of copper and lead here, with also quantities of other commodities including gold and silver. Later similar tests in 1893 and 1900 quantified this further; all suggested a very rich area for minerals and ore.

To exploit this deposit, a railway was built in 1905 and 1906, linking Tsumeb with Walvis Bay. By 1907 the mine was producing high-grade copper and lead ores. Despite halting production during the first and second world wars, mining expanded steadily here. By 1947 the mine extended to 576m below the surface, and most of the higher levels of the mine had been exhausted. Further investigations showed the existence of further reserves.

Various changes in ownership of the mine occurred after the wars. By 1966 the mine had produced over nine million tonnes of ore; its reserves were estimated at eight million tonnes. However, in May 1996 mining ceased in some of the deeper levels (which, by then, were around 1,650m below surface) because the cost of pumping out water from these levels had finally outweighed the cost of the ore recovered. This was the beginning of the end. In June one of the main shafts was flooded after its pumps were switched off, and a large strike (July/August 1996) finally stopped mining operations, and the mine closed.

As well as producing huge quantities of ore, Tsumeb was described as 'the greatest crystal-producing mine on earth' for its amazing variety of geological specimens, crystals and minerals. Numerous rare minerals had been found here, some had been completely unique to Tsumeb. Thus, in October 2000, a specialist mining company – Tsumeb Specimen Mining (Pty) Ltd – again started mining the upper levels of the complex. This time they were looking for one-off 'specimens' of minerals, rather than large quantities of ore.

For more information on the mine and its minerals, both past and present, see the excellent www.mineralmining.com. Here you'll also find updates on recent finds, and some very technical information on the mine's geology.

---

forces. Much is now on display in Tsumeb Museum (see page 407), though some is still at the bottom of the lake.

Andersson and Galton passed this way in May 1851, and noted:

> After a day and a half travel, we suddenly found ourselves on the brink of Otjikoto, the most extraordinary chasm it was ever my fortune to see. It is scooped, so to say, out of the solid limestone rock ... The form of Otjikoto is cylindrical; its diameter upwards of four hundred feet, and its depths, as we ascertained by the lead-line, two hundred and fifteen... To about thirty feet of the brink, it is filled with water.

After commenting that the local residents could remember no variation in its height, and musing on where its supply of water came from, Andersson described how he and Galton:

... standing in need of a bath, plunged head-foremost into the profound abyss. The natives were utterly astounded. Before reaching Otjikoto, they had told us, that if a man or beast was so unfortunate as to fall into the pool, he would inevitably perish.

We attributed this to superstitious notions; but the mystery was now explained. The art of swimming was totally unknown in these regions. The water was very cold, and, from its great depth, the temperature is likely to be the same throughout the year.

We swam into the cavern to which the allusion has just been made. The transparency of the water, which was of the deepest sea-green, was remarkable; and the effect produced in the watery mirror by the reflection of the crystallized walls and roof of the cavern, appeared very striking and beautiful ...

Otjikoto contained an abundance of fish, somewhat resembling perch; but those that we caught were not much larger than one's finger. We had several scores of these little creatures for dinner, and very palatable they proved.

The lake has changed little since then, except perhaps for its water level, which has lowered as a reflection of the area's water table. The gradual diminution of the groundwater around here is a threat to the lake's future.

In terms of practicalities, there's a kiosk that sells drinks, curios and woodcarvings from dawn until dusk. There's a small enclosure with eland, ostrich and warthog, as well as an aviary, a croc pool, and a simple restaurant and café. Camping (with power) is available at N$40 pp, though don't expect any frills.

Lake Guinas On a private farm with acess to visitors, 32km west of Tsumeb, Lake Guinas, with its blue waters, is deeper and more attractive than Otjikoto, though there are no facilities at all. To get there, take the B1 towards Ondangwa, turn left onto the D3043, and then left again after 19km onto the D3031. The lake is about 5km along, near the road. It is home to a colourful species of cichlid fish, *Tilapia guinasana*, which is endemic here. In recent years these fish have been introduced into Otjikoto and several reservoirs to safeguard their future.

GROOTFONTEIN

This small, bustling town is found at the northern end of the central plateau, amidst rich farmland. For the visitor, Grootfontein has few intrinsic attractions but is the gateway to both Bushmanland and the Caprivi Strip. If you are heading to either, then resting here or in the environs for a night will allow you to tackle the long drive ahead in the cool of the morning.

There have been incidents of theft from tourist vehicles in the town, so stay on your guard. Typically a gang will approach a vehicle with open windows; some will distract the driver, whilst others steal from the other side of the vehicle. (As far as I know, there has never been any violence reported.)

GETTING THERE

By bus Intercape Mainliner's services between Windhoek and Victoria Falls stop on the main road at Maroela Motors. En route to Victoria Falls, these stop on Monday, Wednesday and Friday at 00.01. Southbound they return on Monday, Thursday and Saturday at 01.55. One-way tickets cost around N$190 to Windhoek, and N$360 to Victoria Falls. See *Chapter 6*, pages 104–5, for details.

Hitching Hitching from Grootfontein is relatively easy with a clear sign, as most traffic passes through town. Alternatively, talk to drivers at the fuel stations.

WHERE TO STAY Grootfontein does not have any really impressive hotels, but several are adequate for brief stops, and there are a few new guesthouses as well.

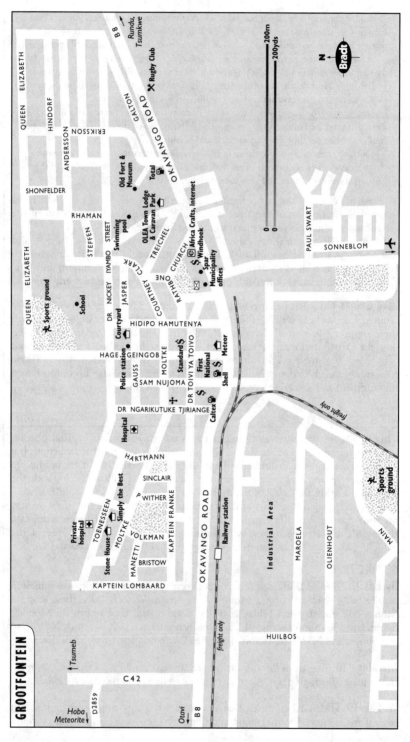

GROOTFONTEIN

⌂ **Meteor Travel Inn** (16 rooms) 33 Okavango Av (cnr Okavango Rd & Kaiser Wilhelm St); ↘ 067 242078/9; f 067 243072; e meteor@iway.na. The Meteor's rooms are laid out around a courtyard at the back. Each has a direct-dial phone, wall-mounted fan, & twin beds. It isn't luxurious, but neither is it at all dingy, as small-town hotels often are. Lunch, dinner & drinks are served in a thatched lapa beneath banana trees. On Friday evenings pizzas are the speciality, from purpose-built brick ovens. *N$270/410 sgl/dbl, B&B, exc bed levy.*

⌂ **OLEA Town Lodge & Caravan Park** (24 rooms, camping) ↘/f 067 243040; e oleatownlodge@nabnet.com. This small camp is close to the centre of town, near the museum. Now privately owned, it has 9 campsites & 4 accommodation blocks, each with 6 en-suite rooms. The mosquitoes are bad in the rainy season &, being so close to town, you should always take precautions to avoid theft. *N$180/280/360/400 sgl/dbl/trpl/4 people; camping N$50 pp, plus N$10 for electricity.*

⌂ **The Courtyard** (5 rooms) 2 Gauss St (top of Hidipo Hamutenya); ↘/f 067 240027; e platinum@iway.na; www.natron.net. The Courtyard was recently taken over by Dirk & Suranda Grundeling. Airy modern en-suite rooms with ceiling fan, fridge, kettle & hairdryer are built around a small courtyard under palms & a sausage tree, while older-style rooms feature the kiaat-wood furniture typical of the Grootfontein region. *N$300/450/500–600 sgl/dbl/family, B&B.*

⌂ **Simply the Best** (5 rooms) 6 Weigel St; ↘ 067 243315. This simple guesthouse under the same ownership as the Rugby Club is just south of the private hospital. It has twin rooms, 1 with private bathroom, & 2 sharing. There's also a 2-room flat. *N$200 pp B&B.*

⌂ **Stone House** (3 rooms) 10 Toenessen St; ↘/f 067 242842; e boet@mweb.com.na. As the name suggests, this small, modern guesthouse on a quiet residential street is clad in stone. Its en-suite rooms have AC, DSTV, minibar & coffee/tea facilities, while outside is a small pool. *N$250/375 sgl/dbl, B&B.*

N$80/120–200 sgl/dbl; camping N$25 pp; electricity N$10; firewood N$10/bundle. B/fast N$15.

Around Grootfontein

⌂ **MAORI Campsite B&B** (4 rondavels, 1 flat, 1 house, camping) ↘/f 067 242351; e farmrestcamp@gmx.de, katpaul@iway.na. Cornelia & Peter Reimann's campsite is signposted from Grootfontein along the B8 towards Rundu; after 2km, turn left onto the D2885 for 1.8km – or take the C42 to Tsumeb for 2km, then turn right onto the D2905. Some 10 pitches with power and BBQ facilities use the same ablution block as simple rondavels, while a flat and 2-bedroom stone house are en suite. The surrounding land, which includes a large citrus orchard & banana plantation, is the domain of various domestic animals, with farm walks on offer to visitors. Birding is also an attraction (a viewing tower will be completed in 2007), as are visits to a local village. Visitors can buy game meat & homemade jam, as well as Bushman jewellery & Kavango crafts.

⌂ **Roy's Camp** (5 rustic chalets, camping) ↘/f 067 240302; e royscamp@iway.na; www.swiftcentre.com. Situated on the main B8 to Rundu, 55km north of Grootfontein & just past the C44 turn-off to Tsumkwe, Roy's is a super little lodge built in an artistic & very rustic style.

It was opened on the established Elandslaagte farm in 1995 by Wimple & Marietjie Otto, whose ancestors were some of the first European settlers in Namibia. The camp is named after Wimple's father, Royal. The owners had originally planned to call it 'Royal Restcamp', but the authorities didn't approve, so they cut it to Roy's Camp.

Bungalows – 1 dbl, & 2 each with 3 or 4 beds – are wonderfully rustic to the point of being quite offbeat, even down to the en-suite showers & private braai area. All are serviced by elecricity although paraffin lamps light the way to your bungalow or campsite. Good home-cooked meals (best arranged in advance) are served in the bar/dining area next to the swimming pool.

15 green, well-watered camp pitches, complete with electricity, braai sites (for which braai packs are available), tree shade, & ablutions with hot & cold water are available to campers; plus a bush kitchen with stove, fridge, etc. All of this is set in 28km² of natural bush, which has been stocked with blue wildebeest, eland, kudu, zebra, duiker, steenbok & warthog. Through this are 2 marked walking trails, of 1.5km & 2.5km respectively, on which many of the trees have been labelled.

Assuming that you're happy with the rustic environment, this is an ideal spot to spend a night en route between the Triangle & the Caprivi. *N$415/355 sgl/pp sharing; 3–4 beds N$300 pp, B&B; camping N$38 pp. Lunch/dinner N$95 pp.*

✗ WHERE TO EAT Grootfontein isn't blessed with much choice for eating out. Most people go to the Meteor, but there's also the new Rugby Club. If you're after something quick, try one of the take-aways at the garages.

✗ Rugby Club m 081 128 9825, 081 127 0074. *Open 09.00–late.*
Serves pub lunches, pizzas & steaks to all comers.

GETTING ORGANISED Grootfontein is a good stop for supplies. There's a Standard, a First National and a Bank of Windhoek, several garages, a tyre centre, and a well-stocked Sentra supermarket, all in the centre of town.

The post office is on the triangle of green just behind the municipal centre, between the main Okavango Road and Rathbone Street.

In an emergency, the police are reached on ☏ 067 10111, the ambulance and hospital on ☏ 067 242141/2, and the fire service on ☏ 067 243101/242321.

Changes of road names Over the last few years, the local council have changed many of Grootfontein's street names, though many of the old names are still found on maps. The main changes are:

Hage G Geingob Street	was	Kaiser Wilhelm Street
Sam Nujoma Drive	was	Goethe Street
Dr Ngarikutuke Tjiriange Street	was	Schiller Street
Hidipo Hamutenya Street	was	Bernhardt Street
Dr Nickey Iyamba Street	was	Upingtonia Street
Dr Toivi Ya Toivo Street	was	Bismarck Street

WHAT TO SEE AND DO There's not much to do in the town itself. The museum is the only real attraction during the day. In the evenings things are even more limited, although the bars at the Meteor Hotel and the Rugby Club are open all week, except Sunday.

Swimming pool The outdoor pool by the restcamp is currently closed. Should it re-open, that's likely to be between October and May.

Old Fort Museum (☏ 067 242456; open Mon–Fri 08.30–12.30 & 14.00–16.30; weekends by arrangement only; admission N$15/5 adult/child) This small, privately run museum is close to the centre of town, near the restcamp. It centres on the original forge of a local blacksmith, featuring a range of tools, and wagon wheels. It also has a large room focusing on the Himba people, with photos and artefacts.

EXCURSIONS FROM GROOTFONTEIN There are a couple of attractions in the area that are accessible only if you have a vehicle, although the second is not currently open.

Hoba Meteorite This famous lump of rock is about 20km west of Grootfontein, clearly signposted from the C42 approach road from Tsumeb. Here, in 1920, the farm's owner discovered the world's heaviest metallic meteorite. It weighs about 50 tonnes, and analysis suggests it is mostly iron (about 80%) and nickel.

It was declared a national monument in 1955 and recently received the protection of a permanent tourist officer because it was suffering badly at the hands of souvenir hunters. The locals became particularly irate when even the UN's Transition Assistance Group (UNTAG) personnel were found to be chipping bits off for souvenirs as they supervised the country's transition to democracy. Now the site is open full time, with a picnic area and a small kiosk selling souvenirs, sweets and soft drinks, and there's an entrance fee of around N$10 pp.

Dragon's Breath cave and lake This cave is claimed to contain the world's largest known underground lake. It is 46km from Grootfontein, just off the C42 to Tsumeb, on the farm Hariseb, owned by Mr Pretorius. Sadly, though, it is not open to visitors.

The lake has crystal clear, drinkable water with a surface area of almost 2ha, and lies beneath a dome-shaped roof of solid rock. The water is about 60m below ground level and to get to it currently requires the use of ropes and caving equipment, with a final vertical abseil descent of 25m from the roof down to the surface of the water. This perhaps explains why it is not open to the public, although it seems likely that it will be developed in the future, when an easier approach can be made.

BUSHMANLAND

To the east of Grootfontein lies the area known as Bushmanland. (This is an old name, but I'll use it here for clarity; it is still what most people call the area.) This almost rectangular region borders on Botswana and stretches 90km from north to south and about 200km from east to west.

Drive east towards Tsumkwe, and you're driving straight into the Kalahari. However, on their first trip here, people are often struck by just how green and vegetated it is, generally in contrast to their mental image of a 'desert'. In fact, the Kalahari isn't a classic desert at all; it's a *fossil* desert. It is an immense sandsheet which was once a desert, but now gets far too much rainfall to be classed as a desert.

Look around you and you'll realise that most of the Kalahari is covered in a thin, mixed bush with a fairly low canopy height, dotted with occasional larger trees. Beneath this is a fairly sparse ground-covering of smaller bushes, grasses and herbs. There are no spectacular sand dunes; you need to return west to the Namib for those!

This is very poor agricultural land, but in the east of the region, especially south of Tsumkwe, there is a sprinkling of seasonal pans. Straddling the border itself are the Aha Hills (see page 425), which rise abruptly from the gently rolling desert. This region, and especially the eastern side of it, is home to a large number of scattered Bushman villages of the Ju/'hoansi !Kung.

The wildlife is a major attraction. During the late dry season, around September and October, game gathers in small herds around the pans. During and after the rains, from January to March, the place comes alive with greenery and water. Birds and noisy bullfrogs abound, and travel becomes even more difficult than usual, as whole areas turn into impassable floodplains. From April the land begins to dry, and during July and August the daytime temperatures are at their most moderate and the nights cold. But whenever you come, don't expect to see vast herds like those in Etosha or you will be disappointed.

The other reason for visiting is to see the Bushman people. The conventional view is that less than a century ago these people's ancestors were a traditional hunter-gatherer society using Stone Age technology. Yet they possessed a knowledge of their environment that we are only just beginning to understand. Tourism is increasingly seen as a vital source of revenue for these people. In placing a high value on traditional skills and knowledge, it is hoped that it will help to stem the erosion of their cultural heritage.

GETTING THERE The C44 road through to Tsumkwe is the main access route into the area. This is long, and continues a further 50km east to the new border post with Botswana at Dobe. From there it's a further 150km (3 hours' drive) of patchy

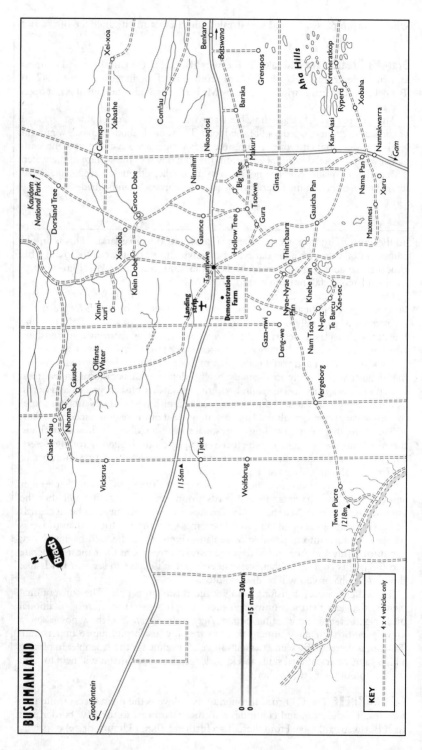

BUSHMANLAND

KEY
========= 4 x 4 vehicles only

gravel road to Nokaneng (a small town on the main tar road which runs down the western side of the Okavango Delta in Botswana).

Tsumkwe feels remote, but it is easily reached from Grootfontein by ordinary 2WD vehicle. From Nokaneng, an experienced driver should be able to get a high-clearance 2WD through to Tsumkwe, but doing this journey in a 4x4 is recommended. Virtually all the other roads in Bushmanland require a sturdy 4x4 and a good guide, or a GPS, or preferably both.

After travelling east from the B8 for about 31km you find a police station on the south side of the road.

Omatako Valley Restcamp is about 88km from the tar, and Tsumkwe about 226km. Around 89km before Tsumkwe, one of the turnings to the right is signposted 'Mangetti Duin', marking the way to one of the best stands of mangetti trees in the area – notable because mangetti nuts are one of the staple foods of the Bushmen.

Otherwise along this road there are a few turnings to villages, but little else. The area is not densely populated, and travellers coming this way should travel with water and some food, as only a handful of vehicles will use the road on any particular day.

One good way to visit is by combining it with a trip through Khaudum National Park, thus making a roundabout journey from Grootfontein to the Caprivi Strip. Alternatively, approaching Bushmanland from the south, via Summerdown, Otjinene and the old Hereroland, would be an interesting and unusual route. Expect the going to get tough.

TSUMKWE Though it is the area's administrative centre, Tsumkwe is little more than a crossroads around which a few houses, shops and businesses have grown up. Apart from the South African Army, it's never had the kind of colonial population, or even sheer number of people, that led to the building of (for example) Tsumeb's carefully planned tree-lined avenues.

It is an essential stop for most travellers in the area though, even if only to get a few cans of cool drinks. It is also the location of the Conservancy Office and of Tsumkwe Lodge, the region's only real lodge for visitors.

Getting organised To visit this area independently you must, as with Kaokoland, be totally self-sufficient and part of a two-vehicle party. The region's centre, Tsumkwe, has basic supplies but *not* fuel. The station referred to in older guidebooks is closed, so the nearest fuel stop is Grootfontein, or at Divundu, as you leave the Bwabwata National Park in the Caprivi. It is essential to set off for this area with supplies and fuel for your complete trip; only water can be relied upon locally.

Before embarking on such a trip, obtain maps from Windhoek and resolve to navigate carefully. Travel in this sandy terrain is very slow. You will stay in second gear for miles, which will double your fuel consumption. Directions can be difficult; if you get them wrong then retracing your steps will take a lot of fuel.

You'll need a minimum of about 100 litres of petrol to get from Tsumkwe to Rundu or Divundu. Because there's none in Tsumkwe, that means at least 150 litres to travel from Grootfontein via Bushmanland and Khaudum to Rundu or Divundu, or vice versa. You'll need more if you plan to do much driving around the area while here. So do plan ahead – arriving in Tsumkwe without enough fuel to get out again is very stupid.

Aside from the lodge, two important places to stop are detailed below

Mi wi a (*PO Box 1073, Grootfontein;* \f *067 244005; ngtsumke@iway.na; www.tsumkwe.com*) 'Mi wi a', which means 'thank you', is a shop run by the Reverend Hendrik van Zyl, the minister of the local Dutch Reform Church

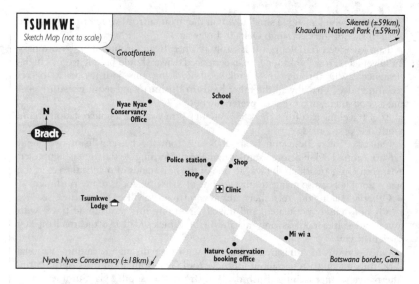

TSUMKWE
Sketch Map (not to scale)

Grootfontein

Sikereti (±59km),
Khaudum National Park (±59km)

School

Nyae Nyae
Conservancy
Office

N

Bradt

Police station   Shop
Shop

Clinic

Tsumkwe
Lodge

Mi wi a

Nyae Nyae Conservancy (±18km)

Nature Conservation
booking office

Botswana border, Gam

Congregation, and his wife, Elize. They sell only Bushman crafts, sourced from Bushman villages throughout the region. Hendrik buys all the authentic curios that the villages want to make and sell, regardless of their commercial value or otherwise. Thus this encourages the full range of traditional skills, and not just the artefacts that are currently in vogue with this year's visitors.

It's a trade that has built up over the last ten years, and virtually all of the region's villages are now involved in regularly supplying crafts for the centre. If the sellers earned cash, then they would have had to walk between 10–50km to Tsumkwe just to buy food. Hence Hendrik takes food out to the villages, and exchanges it for crafts. Given the loss of the large areas used for traditional hunting and gathering, many people are now dependent upon this food source for the more difficult parts of the year. So this scheme provides much needed food relief to many of the poorest villages, and at the same time encourages the people to value their traditional crafts and skills.

It's well worth supporting, not only because it directly benefits the villages, but also because you won't find a larger range of authentic Bushman crafts for sale anywhere. These include axes that also function as adzes, various children's games, bags made from birds' nests woven with wild cotton, hunting bags (containing a dry powder from fungus as kindling), dry grass, flint, wooden sticks, acacia gum, poisons, a 'string bag' made from giraffe tendons (for carrying things home), love bows, witchcraft bows, hunting bows and arrows, necklaces, bracelets and containers for poison pupae. It's fascinating.

So if you're one of the many visitors who see great poverty in Africa, and wring your hands saying: 'What can I do?', now you have an answer. You can come here and buy as much craftwork as you can afford – if you're being honest with yourself, that really is a lot of crafts! – thus appeasing your conscience with a valuable donation, whilst finding endless fascinating curios to give to friends when you return.

Currently, the main problem of this trade is the limitation of current distribution channels for these crafts. Only a few visitors pass through Tsumkwe, and although it's possible to arrange for 'mail order' deliveries overseas, this is not yet happening on a large enough scale. Shame – as it's fascinating stuff which would sell superbly at small craft markets overseas. So if you're reading this from outside Namibia, take a look at their website (*www.tsumkwe.com*). Ignore the religious slant, but think of placing a small order!

Nyae Nyae Conservancy Office (📞 067 244011; *see page 419 for details of the headquarters of Nyae Nyae in Windhoek – though it's not possible to make any reservations through that office*) When travelling east from Grootfontein, this is on the right side of the road, just before you reach the main Tsumkwe crossroads.

Several villages in the Nyae Nyae Conservancy have basic campsites (usually without ablution facilities as yet), and warmly welcome paying visitors. To find out more about them, and what's possible, it's best to stop here at the conservancy office. (If it's closed, then ask for information at Tsumkwe Lodge.) This is also the place to arrange a local guide if you want one – which is highly recommended. If you're planning on just camping in the area for a few days, to explore a little, then a guide can help you get a lot more out of the area – while actively giving a little more back to the local community.

Where to stay On the way east to Tsumkwe there's one community restcamp beside the road, although this is quite limited in scope. If you are not travelling in a self-contained expedition, then Tsumkwe Lodge is the only real option in or near Tsumkwe. Fortunately, it's an excellent option.

🏠 **Omatako Valley Restcamp** (Omatako San Community Project) Reservations 📞 061 255977; f 061 222647; e office.nacobta@iway.na; www.natron.net/nacobta/omatako-valley/main.html. On the way to Tsumkwe, about 88km east of the B8, is a restcamp run by one of the local Bushman communities. Driving into Bushmanland. it is hard to miss, in a dip immediately on the right of the road 13km past the veterinary control.

If you are heading for Tsumkwe then stop here for cool drinks. A small shop sells a good selection of locally made crafts including beads, necklaces, spears, various tools & baskets, all from around N$15.

If you stay, then the community has built a few basic mud-&-thatch rondavels for sleeping in (with your own bedding & mosquito net), & a campsite with a good shower & 1 toilet. There's firewood for sale at N$10, lamps for hire, & sometimes a whole variety of things to do, all arranged & guided by the local people. These include guided village tours (N$25 pp), & bush walks (N$50 pp) for game viewing or birdwatching. The more adventurous can also have bush food cooked & prepared for N$10, or attend a 'traditional magic dance evening' costing N$150 for a small group. However, all of these activities are dependent on which of the villagers are around when you are; so none is at all guaranteed.
Hut N$40 pp, camping N$35 pp.

🏠 **Tsumkwe Lodge** (9 bungalows, camping) 📞 067 244028; f 067 244027; e tsumkwel@iway.na; www.tsumkwel.iway.na. Owned by Arno & Estelle Oosthuysen, this is the area's only lodge, although most of their activities focus on visits to Nhoma village (advance bookings only).

The lodge is well signposted a kilometre or so from the centre of Tsumkwe: just turn right at the crossroads, then right again opposite Nature Conservation. It is the best place to base yourself for exploring the Nyae Nyae Conservancy. At the lodge you'll currently find 5 large wooden bungalows with solid stone floors, & 4 brick-built rooms with solar-powered lights. There are rugs on the floors, & sliding glass or netting (for ventilation) windows, & the bungalows are furnished with chairs, a table & wardrobe, & twin beds surrounded by large mosquito nets. Each has an en-suite bathroom with a powerful shower, a toilet & a washbasin; they are simple but comfortable & very spacious. However, plans to change the accommodation at the lodge into self-catering units are currently in hand. For now, the main building has a relaxed dining room/bar area, but this, too, may go once the self-catering facilities are in place. Adjacent is a small swimming pool.

The lodge is ably run by the lodge's staff who can also arrange a Ju/'hoan–English translator/guide to accompany people to a Bushman village using the visitor's vehicle & paying the appropriate rates for the activities (see page 420) directly to the guide & community.

If you stay at Tsumkwe Lodge before venturing into the bush, then it's a good idea to tell the lodge where you are planning to go, & when you'll be back. Then at least someone will know if you go missing.

The Oosthuysens operate pre-booked tours under the name Namibia Adventure Safaris & Tours: 2–4-day safaris which include drives in the Nyae Nyae area, & the Ju/'hoan cultural experience at Nhoma village with accommodation at the private community-owned tented camp – an experience not to be missed. They have been running trips into this region for years – they know the local people well & have a very sensitive attitude to working with them & introducing tourists. It's fascinating that when visitors go to this village (or in fact any other village) with their own children, the local youngsters will relax & start playing with the young visitors very quickly – integrating far more easily than the adults. So if your children are active & not shy, expect to have difficulty dragging them away from Nhoma when it's time to leave. The Oosthuysens also offer trips to Khaudum National Park with the possibility to overnight in the park in a mobile

camp (Jul–Oct). The cost of day tours to Nhoma village or to the Khaudum National Park, if booked separately from accommodation & departing from the lodge, is N$1,600 per person per day, excluding accommodation. Advance booking is essential.

Note that if you plan to stay at Nhoma Camp, there is no need to go via Tsumkwe Lodge: the turn-off to Nhoma Camp is 41km before you reach Tsumkwe. Before you set off, phone ahead to find out the state of the road & to arrange to be met. *Tsumkwe Lodge N$475/375 sgl/pp sharing accommodation only; or N$675/575 sgl/pp sharing FB. Nhoma Camp N$2,800/2,200 sgl/pp sharing, inc FB & all activities.*

NYAE NYAE CONSERVANCY Stretching east, north and south from Tsumkwe is the new Nyae Nyae Conservancy area. First established in 1988, it is really still in its infancy, and under development, but it is important to realise that now, when you visit Bushmanland, you are within a conservancy where the local people set the rules. Here the communities have won the right to manage their wildlife and tourism as they wish. One possible way forward is that whilst they have always hunted the wildlife here using traditional methods, now they can also derive income from trophy hunting in the area.

Having achieved the funding of a conservancy for the area, the Nyae Nyae Foundation is concentrating on helping to promote the region. As part of this, it has set up a tourism office (see page 417) in Tsumkwe. This should be your first stop in the region. Here you may have to pay entrance or conservancy fees in the future, but currently they are only co-ordinating visitors, helping with information and supplying guides on request. (You should pay any camping fees to the village nearest the campsite.)

The Nyae Nyae Conservancy is in the process of revising their brochure which will include a map and rates for camping and activities with Ju/'hoan (pronounced Zhu-wa) communities (the Ju/'hoansi resorts under the !Kung Bushmen or San people). The conservancy office is on the right-hand side of the road, just before reaching the tarred crossroad if arriving from Grootfontein and should be open during office hours (✆ *067 244011; closed after 17.00, during weekends and on public holidays*). A small conservancy fee of at least N$25 is payable at the office. In return you can expect information and assistance in finding a guide which, due to the low number of tourists in the area, might not be so easy to arrange at short notice. All the villages in the area will welcome tourists, but some of them are more accessible, with cleared campsites underneath baobab trees and where there is a greater likelihood of finding an English-speaking member of the community to act as guide. Some others are very eager to receive tourists and have prepared campsites complete with a water tank such as the one at the Aha Hills site, but because it is far off the main track, they are unlikely to receive many visitors. None of the villages offers organised tourist activities on a daily basis (which makes the experience all the more authentic). Almost all of these villages are accessible only by 4x4 and there are no vehicles for hire in the area, but depending on the season, some can be reached with a 2WD with good clearance.

Where to stay In the past campers have set up their sites randomly in Bushmanland, with no permits necessary. Many left litter behind them and caused problems for the local people and the wildlife. They often used to camp close to

Based just east of Tsumkwe, the Nyae Nyae Farmers Co-operative has been established since 1986 with a charter to support and encourage the Ju/'hoansi of Eastern Otjozondjupa to return to their historical lands known as Nyae Nyae.

Historically, this group of Bushmen has been in a difficult position. The South African Army (SADF) moved into what was Eastern Bushmanland in 1960, to occupy the region as part of its war against SWAPO and the destabilisation of Angola. It formed a battalion of Bushmen to track down guerrilla fighters – using the Bushmen's tracking ability to lethal effect. Many of these people moved to Tsumkwe; whole families were dependent on the SADF.

This social upheaval, with lifestyles changing from nomadic hunter-gathering to dependence on an army wage, led to social problems amongst the people, including crime, alcohol and prostitution. Towards the end of the war, it was decided to improve their quality of life by taking them back to the ground they had come from, a move initiated by the Nyae Nyae Development Foundation and its founder, John Marshall.

So in the late 1980s and early 1990s the Nyae Nyae Farmers Co-operative focused on grass-roots self-help projects, encouraging the Bushmen to start farming, rearing cattle and growing their own food. Boreholes were provided, but few made a success of these projects. The Bushmen are not natural farmers or pastoralists. They seem to have a different approach to survival than most other ethnic groups in Africa.

The Nyae Nyae Development Foundation continues to run various education programmes to train teachers for the five newly built schools in the Nyae Nyae area (lessons are in English and Ju/'hoansi). They also run a workshop for mechanics and some agricultural programmes, but their focus has now changed.

In the last few years a craft programme has been set up, which is trying to improve the quality of the locally made crafts, whilst buying them to sell across the country and often across the world. Locally, this combines with a mobile shop, where people can buy food and other basics.

However, perhaps the most interesting project was initiated by the WWF in 1994. This has aimed to set up a conservancy for sustainable utilisation and management of the wildlife in the eastern area of Bushmanland – which was finally put into place in December 1997. This is being administered by the Nyae Nyae Development Foundation (PO Box 9026, Windhoek; ☎ 061 236327; f 061 225997; e nndfn@iafrica.com.na).

water, frightening the area's already skittish animals, and even go swimming in reservoirs meant for drinking. Visitors were unaware that they were staying in an area used for hunting or gathering, and didn't realise the effect that their presence was having on the wildlife. This 'free camping' has now been banned. Instead, head for one of the (increasing number of) village sites, where you'll find a place to camp for which you pay the nearby community directly.

In the first edition of this book – just nine years ago – I listed three such sites. Now many more villages have simple adjacent sites and welcome visitors. Ask at the Conservancy Office in Tsumkwe and they'll give you a map of these and advise you of their cost, or better still, a local guide.

Guidelines for visiting villages Wherever you camp, you must take great care not to offend local people by your behaviour. It is customary to go first to the village and ask for permission to stay from the traditional leader (n!ore kxao). This is usually one of the older men of the village, who will normally make himself known. Never enter someone's shelter, as this is very rude.

Often the headman will be assisted by someone who speaks Afrikaans or even English, and if he's not around then somebody else will normally come forward to help you. If your Afrikaans is poor, then you may have to rely upon sign language. If you wish to take photographs of the people or place, this is normally fine – provided you ask in advance, and pay for the privilege (see above).

Remember that you are in a wilderness area, where hyena, lion and leopard are not uncommon, so always sleep within a tent. Try not to scare the wildlife, or damage the place in any way. Keep fires to a minimum, and when collecting fuel use only dead wood that is far from any village.

If you wish to buy crafts from the village, then do not try to barter unless specifically asked for things; most people will expect to be paid with money. Similarly, if one of the villagers has been your guide, pay for this with money. Remember that alcohol has been a problem in the past, and do not give any away.

Some local people have been designated as community rangers, with a brief to check on poaching and look out for the wildlife. They may ask what you are doing, and check that you have paid your camping fees.

Water is essential for everybody, and in limited supply for most of the year, so be very careful when using the local waterholes or water pumps. Often there will be someone around who can help you. Never go swimming in a waterhole or reservoir.

Guiding and camping fees Payment to the communities should be fair. Each of the guides will expect between N$150 and N$200 per day plus food if staying out overnight, whether for a full day or a half day. This must be discussed and agreed beforehand. The camping fee is likely to be between N$25 and N$50 per day per person, depending on the village. Usually you will be taken for a bushwalk, for which the hunters usually charge between N$50 and N$75 per hunter. (If you're worried about the hole in your pocket, you can ask that only two accompany you.) It's important to note that people will expect to be paid if you wish to take photos of them. Therefore it's best to offer a lump sum of at least N$350 to include the bushwalk and taking photos in the village rather than to pay each individual for every photo. The same applies to arranging to witness the healing dance: either offer a lump sum of at least N$350, or negotiate a payment of at least N$20 per person taking part.

Cultural sensitivity and language Cultural sensitivity isn't something that a guidebook can teach you, though reading the box on cultural guidelines, in *Chapter 2*, may help. Being sensitive to the results of your actions and attitudes on others is especially important in this area.

The Bushmen are often a humble people, who regard arrogance as a vice. It is normal for them to be self-deprecating amongst themselves, to make sure that everyone is valued and nobody becomes too proud. So the less you are perceived as a loud, arrogant foreigner, the better.

Very few foreigners can pick up much of the local Ju/'hoansi language without living here for a long time. (Readers note that spellings of the same word can vary from text to text, especially on maps.) However, if you want to try to pronounce the words then there are four main clicks to master:

/   is a sucking sound behind the teeth
// is a sucking sound at the side of the mouth, used to urge a horse
!   a popping sound, like a cork coming out of a bottle
≠   a sharper popping sound (this is the hardest).

What to do and what to see Aside from coming here out of a general curiosity about the area's wildlife and culture, one area stands out: the Nyae Nyae Pan. This is a large complex of beautiful salt pans, about 18km south of Tsumkwe. During good rains it fills with water and attracts flamingos to breed, as well as dozens of other waterbirds including avocets, pygmy geese, grebes, various pipers and numerous plovers. Forty-six different species of waterbirds have been recorded here when the pan was full.

Towards the end of the dry season you can normally expect game drinking here, and the regulars include kudu, gemsbok, steenbok, duiker and elephant. Meanwhile black-backed jackals patrol, and the grass grows to 60cm tall around the pan, with a belt of tall trees beyond that.

Cultural activities It's worth being realistic from the outset of your visit here: if you're looking for 'wild Bushmen' clad in loincloths and spending all day making poison arrows or pursuing antelope, you will be disappointed.

The people in this area have been exposed to the modern world, and often mistreated by it, for decades. None now live a traditional hunter-gatherer lifestyle. Walk into any village and its inhabitants are more likely to be dressed in jeans and T-shirts than loincloths, and their water is more likely to be from a solar-powered borehole pump than a sip-well.

However, many of the older people have maintained their traditional skills and crafts, and often their knowledge of the bush and wildlife is simply breathtaking.

Those that I met appeared friendly and interested to show visitors how they live, including how they hunt and gather food in the bush – provided that visitors are polite, and ask permission for what they want to do, and pay the right price.

This kind of experience is difficult to arrange without a local guide who is involved in tourism and speaks both your language and theirs. Without such a guide, you won't get very much out of a visit to a local village. So even if you have your own 4x4 transport, start by dropping into Tsumkwe Lodge or, if it is open, the new conservancy office in Tsumkwe. Ask for a local guide to help you, who can travel around with you. You can pay them directly (see above), and this will open up many possibilities at the villages.

None of the village activities is artificially staged. They are just normal activities that would probably take place anyhow, though their timings are arranged to fit in with your available time. However, because they are not staged, they will take little account of you. As a visitor you will just tag along, watching as the villagers go about their normal activities. All are relaxed. You can stop and ask questions of the guide and of the villagers when you wish. Most of the local villagers are completely used to photographers and unperturbed by being filmed – provided, of course, that you have agreed a fee for this in advance (see above).

Ideally, for a detailed insight, spend a few days with a guide and stay beside just one village. If they are happy about it, see the same people for an evening or two as well as during the days. This way, you get to know the villagers as individuals, not simply members of an ethnic group. Both you and they will learn more from such an encounter, and so enjoy it a lot more. Typical activities might include:

Food collecting/hunting trips These trips normally last about three to four hours in the bush. You'll go out with a guide and some villagers and gather, or hunt, whatever they come across. The Bushmen know their landscape, and its flora and fauna, so well that they'll often stop to show you how this plant can be eaten, or that one produces water, or how another fruits in season.

Even Arno (an expert on the area who runs Tsumkwe Lodge) comments that after years of going out with the Bushmen, they will still often find something new that he's never seen before. It's an ethno-botanist's dream.

Irene Jessop

'I hope someone in the village remembers me from last year.'

'Ja, ja.' Arno, my guide, was certain they would. 'You should have seen the excitement when they shared out the beads you sent. You remembered them: they won't have forgotten you.'

I walked through the circle of yellow, beehive-shaped huts to where the headman was sitting, the only one on a chair, a concession to his age. As he clasped my hand his son, Steve, translated, 'My father says he is very pleased you have come back to see us.' From across the village Javid stared at me briefly and then dashed across to shake my hand. People smiled spontaneously as they recognised me: I didn't know who to say hello to first.

My stay at Nhoma the previous year had been brief. A Ju/'hoan village in remote northeast Namibia, it is one of about 30 villages at the edge of the Nyae Nyae Conservancy. I was persuaded that visitors provided vital revenue to the villagers, but had also read about marginalised people with problems of poverty, unemployment and ill health. I anticipated that a visit would be at best a glum affair, and perhaps even a voyeuristic intrusion on a suffering people. Instead I found fun. Women sat by small fires in front of their huts with tall wooden mortars and pounded protein-rich mangettis that tasted pleasantly nutty, if a little gritty. Some boiled vivid scarlet beans: after the flesh is eaten, the kernel is roasted. Waste nothing: sometimes there is only nothing. While the women prepared food the men made hunting necessities. With his chop-chop, the Bushman's axe, Sao scraped fibres from mother-in-law's-tongue; these are twisted to make rope for a bird trap. Abel cleaned a dried steenbok skin to make a kit bag for the hunt. With great concentration Joseph squeezed the grub of a beetle cocoon to put poison on some arrows. Care is needed, as there is no known antidote and to avoid an accidental scratch it is not put on the tip. Even with all this work going on, it was never quiet: all around was talking and laughter.

The previous year N!hunkxa made ostrich-egg beads, painstakingly filing them to the same size with a stone. These, along with pieces of leather, wood and porcupine quills, were threaded into necklaces and bracelets, all brown and white. But what the women really wanted, they told me, were small glass beads, especially red and yellow ones. A few of them already had brightly coloured glass-bead necklaces and bracelets. Some, mainly the older ones, had bead medallions fixed through their hair so that they hung down onto their foreheads. The beads I had sent had all been used. Not only were the women wearing more necklaces and bracelets than last year, but also rings. Some of the men too wore ornate beaded belts or had circles of beads embroidered on their *shonas*, leather loincloths.

This time I had brought more beads and I was going to learn how to make something.

The hunting tends to be for the smaller animals, and in season the Bushmen set up trap-lines of snares to catch the smaller bucks, which need checking regularly and setting or clearing. Spring-hares are also a favourite quarry, hunted from their burrows using long (typically 5m), flexible poles with a hook on the end.

Don't expect to go tracking eland with bows and arrows in half a day, though do expect to track anything interesting that crosses your path. These trips aren't intended as forced marches, and the pace is generally fairly slow. However, if there's some good food to be had, or promising game to be tracked, then these walks through the bush can last for hours. Bring some water and don't forget your hat.

It's usually best to discuss payment in advance, and agree a cost. However, bear in mind that working with money is relatively new to many of these people, so don't expect any sophisticated bargaining techniques. As a quid pro quo, don't use any

As N!hunkxa unwrapped the beads a dozen or so women stopped work to see what I had brought. We sat on the sand in a circle under the shade of a large tree. Pleasantly warm now; it would soon be too hot to be in the sun. In the middle of the group was a large canvas sheet and we made indentations in it to stop the beads rolling away. N!hunkxa chose an easy style for me to make, two parallel lines which crossed over at intervals. Other women made elaborately decorated coils or wide headbands with zigzag patterns. Steve kept my pattern correct by calling out the numbers and colours of beads, 'Two blue, one red …' Jewellery making was obviously the chance for a good gossip. Though I couldn't understand the words I could absorb the rhythms of the conversation, quick one-line repartee, and long stories with a punchline.

Everyone was generous in praise of my necklace when it was finished. As I tried it on I thought 'When I get home this will always remind me of Nhoma.' This was followed by the realisation that I had brought the beads because the women liked them: it seemed pointless to take them away. Did I really need an object to remind me of that morning? It was better if N!hunkxa had it.

'Steve, please can you tell N!hunkxa that I would like her to have this so that she always remembers me.'

'Gadsha,' (good) several of the women said, knowing this was one of the words I understood. The approval in their expressions too told me that inadvertently or instinctively I had done just the right thing. I was later to find out that in Ju/'hoan society, gift exchange, *xaro*, is important in bonding people together. What is significant is the act of exchanging of gifts, not their value: beadwork is often a preferred offering for exchange.

N!hunkxa disappeared, to return a few moments later with an ostrich-bead necklace with a leather medallion, which she fastened round my neck.

'N!hunkxa would like to give you a name,' Steve said.

'What is it?' I wondered, knowing that visitors are often very accurately if not always flatteringly likened to animals, for example 'Elephant man' for someone with a big nose.

'No, no, you don't understand. She wants to give you her name.'

'Mi-way-ha (thank-you),' I said, sensing that an honour had been conferred, but not quite understanding.

I now know that by taking N!hunkxa's name I had essentially taken on her relationships and obligations. Any customs governing her behaviour towards other Ju/'hoan would apply to me also: thus I would have obligations of care towards those she did. Those who would look after her would look after me too. I had become one of her kin. However, we live so many miles apart that it is difficult to nurture this relationship, to help in difficult times or take pleasure at the good things. So I send beads because I know how much pleasure they give, because beads to me represent the connections made that morning.

such ruses yourself, or try to screw the people into a hard bargain; just aim for a fair price (which you learned when you stopped and asked at the conservancy office!).

Traditional craft demonstrations As part of a half-day trip into the bush, you'll often stop for a while at the village, and there the people can show you how they make their traditional crafts. The Bushmen have a particularly rich tradition of storytelling, and it shows clearly here if they also demonstrate how snares are made and set, and give animated re-enactments of how animals are caught. This would normally be included in a half-day bush trip, above.

Evening singing and dancing In the evenings, you can arrange (in advance, with payment agreed first) to visit a local village, and join an evening of traditional dancing. This probably means driving to just outside a village, where those who want to take part will meet you. They will build a fire, around which the women and children will gradually gather. Eventually those sitting will start the singing and clapping, and men will start dancing around the circle sitting in the firelight. They will often have percussion instruments, like shakers, strapped to their ankles.

The singing is beautiful, essentially African, and it comes as no surprise that everybody becomes engrossed in the rhythm and the dancing. On rare occasions, such concentration amongst the dancers can induce states of trance – the famous 'trance dances' – which are traditionally used as dances to heal, or prevent illness.

As an observer, expect to sit on the ground on the edge of the firelight, outside of the dancers' circle. You will mostly be ignored whilst the villagers have a good time. They will have been asked to dance for your benefit, for which they will be paid, but everything else about the evening is in their control. This is the kind of dancing that they do for themselves, with nothing added and nothing taken away.

Note that they're used to most visitors just sitting and watching whilst they dance. If you want to join in it's often not a problem ... but expect to be the source of a lot of amusement for the resident professionals.

Cultural questions When you see the Bushmen in the Tsumkwe, it's tempting to lament their passing from noble savage to poor, rural underclass: witness the lack of dignified 'traditional' skins and the prevalence of ragged Western clothes, or see the PVC quivers that the occasional hunter now uses for his arrows.

While they clearly need help in the present, part of the problem has been our blinkered view of their past. This view has been propagated by the romantic writings of people like Laurens van der Post and a host of TV documentaries. However, modern ethnographers now challenge many long-cherished beliefs about these 'noble savages'.

Essential reading in this respect is *The Bushman Myth: The Making of a Namibian Underclass*, by Robert J Gordon (see *Appendix 3*). It stands out as an excellent, scholarly attempt to place the Bushmen in an accurate historical context, and to explain and deconstruct many of the myths that we hold about them. In partial summary of some of his themes, he comments about the book:

> The old notion of these people as passive victims of European invasion and Bantu expansion is challenged. Bushmen emerge as one of the many indigenous people operating in a mobile landscape, forming and shifting their political and economic alliances to take advantage of circumstances as they perceived them. Instead of toppling helplessly from foraging to begging, they emerge as hotshot traders in the mercantile world market for ivory and skins. They were brokers between competing forces and hired guns in the game business. Rather than being victims of pastoralists and traders who depleted the game, they appear as one of many willing agents of this commercial depletion. Instead of being ignorant of metals, true men of the Stone Age, who knew nothing of iron, they were fierce defenders of rich copper mines that they worked for export and profit. If this selection has a central theme, it is to show how ignorance of archival sources helped to create the Bushmen image that we, as anthropologists, wanted to have and how knowledge of these sources makes sense of the Bushmen we observe today.

Gordon's book isn't a light or swift read, but it will make you think. See also my comments on the wider context, including the modern media's portrayal of the San, in *Chapter 2*, pages 16–21.

Further information For more information about the area and its people, contact either Arno at Tsumkwe Lodge or the Nyae Nyae Development Foundation (see page 419); both are closely involved with the welfare of the Bushmen.

AHA HILLS Look southeast of Tsumkwe on the maps and you'll find an isolated group of hills straddling the border between Botswana and Namibia: the Aha Hills. Named, it's claimed, after the onomatopoeic call of the barking geckos that are so common in the area, these are remote enough to have a certain mystique about them – like their counterparts in Botswana, the Tsodilo Hills.

However, there the similarity ends. The Aha Hills are much lower and more flattened. Their rock structure is totally different: a series of sharp, angular boulders quite unlike the smooth, solid massifs of Tsodilo. So they are quite tricky to climb, and have no known rock art or convenient natural springs. All of this means that though they're interesting, and worth a visit if you're in the area – they do not have the attraction of Botswana's Tsodilo Hills.

With a guide, the track past !'Obaha village does lead onto the hills, and it's possible to climb up Kremetartkop (which has some lovely baobabs on the top) in an hour or so. The view from the top – across into Botswana and 360° around – is pure Africa.

Do leave at least a whole afternoon for this trip though. I didn't, and ended up driving back to Tsumkwe in the half-light, which wasn't ideal. However, I caught a rare glimpse of a caracal bounding through the long grass in the headlights.

KHAUDUM NATIONAL PARK

(*Minimum 2 4x4 vehicles per party. Entrance N$40 pp per day & N$10 per vehicle*) Situated next to Botswana and immediately north of Bushmanland, Khaudum is a wild, seldom visited area of dry woodland savanna growing on old stabilised Kalahari sand-dunes. These are interspersed with flat, clay pans and the whole area is laced with a life-giving network of *omurambas*.

Omuramba is a Herero word meaning 'vague riverbed', which is used to describe a drainage line that rarely, if ever, actually flows above ground but often gives rise to a number of waterholes along its course. In Khaudum, the omurambas generally lie along east–west lines and ultimately link into the Okavango's river system, flowing underground into the Delta when the rains come. However, during the dry season the flood in the Okavango Delta helps to raise the level of the water-table in these omurambas – ensuring that the waterholes don't dry up, and do attract game into Khaudum. The vegetation here can be thick in comparison with Namibia's drier parks to the west. Zambezi teak and wild syringa dominate the dunes, while acacias and leadwoods are found in the clay pans.

FLORA AND FAUNA The bush in and around Khaudum is quite complex. Different areas have totally different types of vegetation; biologists say that there are nine different 'biotypes' in Bushmanland.

Towards the southern end of the park, and between Tsumkwe and Sikereti, the bush is thick. Umbrella-thorn, leadwood and cluster-leafed terminalia (also known as silver-leaf terminalia) are the dominant vegetation. The dune-crests often have stands of mangetti and marula trees and, although spectacular baobab trees are dotted around the whole region, there is a particularly high density of them in the Chokwe area.

Inside the national park, Khaudum has spectacular forests of teak (especially prevalent in the southeast) and false mopane trees, which form a shady canopy above low-growing herbs and grasses. All over the park, where the dunes are wooded you'll often find open expanses of grassland growing between them.

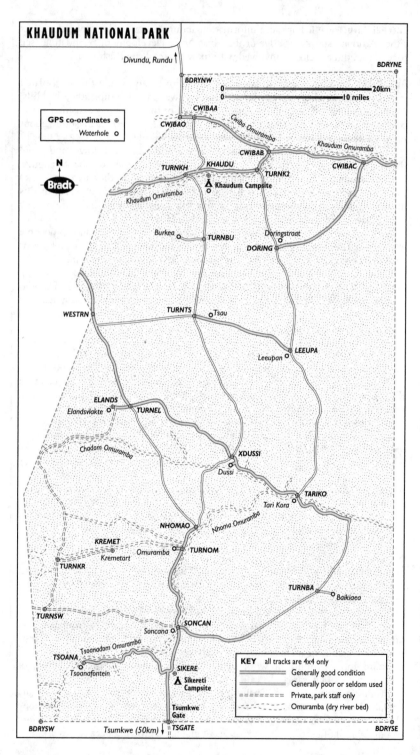

KHAUDUM NATIONAL PARK

Divundu, Rundu ↑

BDRYNE

BDRYNW

CWIBAA

CWIBAO

Cwiba Omuramba

Khaudum Omuramba

0   20km
0   10 miles

GPS co-ordinates ⊕
Waterhole ○

CWIBAB

CWIBAC

N

Bradt

TURNKH   KHAUDU

▲ Khaudum Campsite

TURNK2

Khaudum Omuramba

Burkea ○   TURNBU

Doringstraat

DORING

WESTRN   TURNTS   ○ Tsau

LEEUPA

Leeupan ○

ELANDS

Elandsvlakte ○   TURNEL

Chadom Omuramba

XDUSSI

Dussi ○

TARIKO

Tari Kora ○

NHOMAO   Nhoma Omuramba

KREMET

Omuramba ○   TURNOM

Kremetart

TURNKR

TURNBA

○ Baikiaea

TURNSW

SONCAN

Soncana ○

TSOANA

Tsoanadom Omuramba

Tsoanafontein ○

SIKERE

▲ Sikereti Campsite

Tsumkwe Gate

BDRYSW   TSGATE
Tsumkwe (50km) ↓

BDRYSE

KEY   all tracks are 4x4 only
——— Generally good condition
——— Generally poor or seldom used
===== Private, park staff only
- - - Omuramba (dry river bed)

426

Many omurambas, especially towards the south of the park, have black-cotton soil – which makes them impossible to drive along during the rains, but good and hard during the dry season.

Game-viewing is better here during the dry season, although most of the classic Kalahari game species found here are not strictly dependent on the presence of waterholes. Elephants are a notable exception to this rule, and they usually migrate away from sources of permanent water when it rains.

Though seldom occurring in numbers to rival Etosha's vast herds, there is some good wildlife here and Khaudum has a much wilder feel than any of Namibia's other parks. Its game includes the uncommon tsessebe and roan antelope, the latter noted for their penchant for lots of space, and areas with low densities of other antelope. Most of the subcontinent's usual big game species (excluding rhino and buffalo) are also represented – blue wildebeest, red hartebeest, kudu, oryx, giraffe, steenbok, duiker – as well as smaller animals typical of the Kalahari. In the dry season there are often large herds of elephants that travel from Botswana and this is also one of the few places in Namibia where you can get sightings of wild dog.

Leopard, lion, cheetah, and spotted hyena are the main predators and, though there are good populations of these, they are seldom seen through the dense bush. Khaudum is Namibia's best park for wild dog, which range over vast areas and probably criss-cross the Botswana border. (That said, they are very rarely seen by visitors here, due to the dense bush and relative lack of game-drive loops.)

GETTING ORGANISED Within the reserve, tracks either follow omurambas, or link the dozen or so waterholes together. Even the distinct tracks are slow going, so a good detailed map of the area is invaluable. Try the Surveyor General's office in Windhoek (see page 122) before you arrive. Map number 1820 MUKWE is only a 1:250,000 scale, but it is the best available and worth having – especially when used in conjunction with the one here.

The map with GPS locations is included here by kind courtesy of Estelle Oosthuysen, of Tsumkwe Lodge, who personally mapped it out and noted the GPS co-ordinates in late 2002 (in UTM format – so any translation errors are entirely mine!).

GPS REFERENCES FOR KHAUDUM NATIONAL PARK (OPPOSITE)

BDRYNE	18°22.961'S	21°00.015'E	SONCAN	19°03.211'S	20°43.010'E
BDRYNW	18°23.289'S	20°43.050'E	TARIKO	18°53.661'S	20°52.332'E
BDRYSE	19°09.833'S	21°00.016'E	TSGATE	19°09.903'S	20°42.310'E
BDRYSW	19°09.922'S	20°32.244'E	TSOANA	19°05.648'S	20°35.583'E
CWIBAO	18°26.331'S	20°42.964'E	TURNBA	19°00.440'S	20°53.954'E
CWIBAA	18°26.320'S	20°44.118'E	TURNBU	18°35.032'S	20°44.909'E
CWIBAB	18°28.740'S	20°49.967'E	TURNEL	18°47.192'S	20°39.125'E
CWIBAC	18°29.555'S	20°57.510'E	TURNK2	18°30.143'S	20°49.099'E
DORING	18°35.705'S	20°50.677'E	TURNKH	18°30.479'S	20°43.618'E
ELANDS	18°47.212'S	20°38.052'E	TURNKR	18°57.932'S	20°33.451'E
KHAUDU	18°30.131'S	20°45.253'E	TURNOM	18°57.342'S	20°43.314'E
KHAUNO	18°23.289'S	20°43.050'E	TURNTS	18°40.630'S	20°44.159'E
KREMET	18°57.459'S	20°37.721'E	TURNSW	19°01.720'S	20°32.222'E
LEEUPA	18°43.157'S	20°51.693'E	WESTRN	18°40.484'S	20°36.094'E
NHOMAO	18°55.898'S	20°44.347'E	XDUSSI	18°50.825'S	20°47.092'E
SIKERE	19°06.157'S	20°42.399'E			

Water is available but nothing else, so come self-sufficient in fuel and supplies. Because of the reserve's remote nature, entry is limited to parties with two or more 4x4 vehicles and each needs about 120 litres of fuel simply to get through the park from Tsumkwe to the fuel station at Mukwe, on the Rundu–Bagani road. This doesn't include any diversions while there. You'll need to use 4x4 almost constantly, even in the dry season, making travel slow and heavy on fuel. In the wet, wheel chains might be useful, though black-cotton soil can be totally impassable.

GETTING THERE

From the north Turn off the main road 115km east of Rundu at Katere, where the park is signposted. Then Khaudum camp is about 75km of slow, soft sand away.

From the south Khaudum is easily reached via Tsumkwe and Klein Dobe. Entering Tsumkwe, turn left at the crossroads just beyond the schoolhouse. This rapidly becomes a small track, and splits after about 400m. Take the right fork to Sikereti, which is about 60km from Tsumkwe and 77km south of the camp at Khaudum.

If you have a GPS with you, then Sikereti has co-ordinates 19° 6.318'S, 20° 42.325'E, whilst the crossroads at Tsumkwe is found at 19° 35.514'S, 20° 30.199'E.

WHERE TO STAY In theory, Khaudum National Park has two camps: Sikereti camp in the south, and Khaudum in the north. Each has basic wooden huts with outside facilities, and campsites. In practice, though, both sites are in a state of total disrepair: the huts are falling apart, with no doors, windows or beds, and, whilst there is space to camp, there is no running water. Be aware, too, that neither camp is fenced, so leave nothing outside that can be picked up or eaten, and beware of things that go bump in the night. In an emergency, the park staff at Sikereti and Khaudum may have radios. If you can find them, they can usually help you. A far more attractive alternative would be to organise a trip into the national park through Tsumkwe Lodge (see above).

Should you still be determined to stay at one of the camps, you'll need to make an advance reservation with the NWR in Windhoek, and to arrive with an absolute minimum of three days' food and water. For the sake of completeness:

⋔ Sikereti Restcamp Sikereti stands in a grove of purple-pod terminalia trees, one of several such dense stands in the park.

⋔ Khaudum Restcamp Khaudum stands in a lovely spot on top of a dune, looking out over an omuramba. It is a great spot for sunsets, and there's a waterhole below the camp in the omuramba.

19

Owamboland

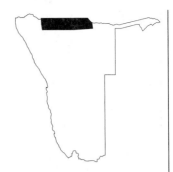

This verdant strip of land between Etosha and the Kunene and Okavango rivers is largely blank on Namibia's normal tourist map. However, it is highly populated and home to the Owambo people, who formed the backbone of SWAPO's support during the struggle for independence. The region was something of a battleground before 1990, and now the map's blank spaces hide a high concentration of rural people practising subsistence farming of maize, sorghum and millet.

Before independence this area was known as Ovamboland, and recently it has been split into four regions: Omusati, Oshana, Ohangwena and Oshikoto. Here, for simplicity, I will refer to the whole area as Owamboland. During the summer Owamboland appears quite unlike the rest of Namibia. It receives over 500mm of rain and supports a thick cover of vegetation and extensive arable farming.

The Owambo people are Namibia's most numerous ethnic group, and since independence and free elections their party, SWAPO, has dominated the government. Much effort is now going into the provision of services here. There are two main arteries through Owamboland: the B1/C46, and the smaller C45. The small towns that line these roads, like trading posts along a Wild West railroad, are growing rapidly.

Alongside the main B1 there is a canal – a vital water supply during the heat of the dry season. Driving by, you pass women carrying water back to their houses, while others wash and children splash around to cool off. Occasionally there are groups meeting in the shade of the trees on the banks, and men fishing in the murky water. Some have just a string tied to the end of a long stick, but others use tall conical traps, perhaps a metre high, made of sticks. The successful will spend their afternoon by the roadside, selling fresh fish from the shade of small stalls.

Always you see people hitching between the rural towns, and the small, tightly packed combi vans, which stop for them: the local bus service. If you are driving and have space, then do offer lifts to people. They will appreciate it, and it's one of the best opportunities you will get to talk to the locals about their home area.

Owamboland has three major towns – Oshakati, Ondangwa and Ruacana – and many smaller ones. With the exception of Ruacana, which was built solely to service the big hydro-electric power station there, the others vary surprisingly little and have a very similar atmosphere.

There is usually a petrol station, a take-away or two, a few basic food shops, a couple of bottle stalls (alias bars) and maybe a beer hall. The fuel is cheaper at the larger 24-hour stations, in the bigger towns, and you can stock up on cold drinks there also. The take-aways and bars trade under some marvellous names: Nowally! Let's Support Bar, Freedom Square Snack Bar, Music Lovers Bar and the Come Together Bar, to name but a few. These can be lively, friendly places to share a beer, but a word of warning: they are not recommended for lone women visitors.

Away from the towns, the land seems to go on forever. There are no mountains or hills or even kopjes – only feathery clumps of palm trees and the odd baobab tree

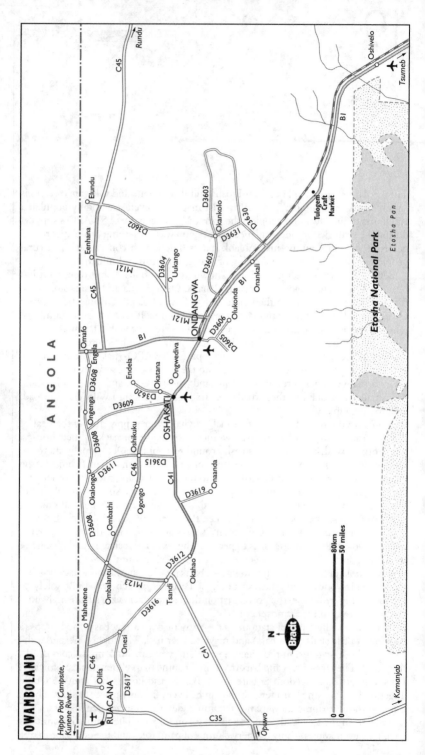

break the even horizon. After a year of good rains, the wide flat fields are full of water, like Far Eastern rice paddies, complete with cattle wading like water buffalo.

Travelling eastwards and slightly south, towards Tsumeb, notice how, as the land becomes drier, the population density decreases, and maize becomes the more dominant crop. Where the land is not cultivated, acacia scrub starts gradually to replace the greener mopane bushes by the roadside. Keep your eyes open for raptors – especially the distinctive bateleur eagles that are common here.

Towards the edge of Owamboland, at Oshivelo (about 150km from Ondangwa and 91km from Tsumeb), you must stop to pass through a veterinary cordon fence. This is just a kilometre north of the bed of the Omuramba Owambo, which feeds into the Etosha pan.

ONDANGWA

This is the first main town you come to in Owamboland if approaching from Tsumeb, and is typical of the region.

GETTING THERE

By air Two Air Namibia flights a day each way, except Saturday, link Ondangwa to Windhoek's Eros Airport. Tickets cost N$2,040 one way.

By road Ondangwa is spread out along the main B1, and you'll find numerous local combi vans, sometimes referred to as taxis, stopping to pick up and drop passengers all along here.

There are at present no long-distance buses plying the route.

By train A new passenger train service between Windhoek and Ondangwa, stopping at Tsumeb and Oshivelo among other stations, has recently been introduced by TransNamib. Called the *Omugulu Gwombashe Star*, it's a faster service than the normal passenger trains. Trains leave Windhoek every Friday at 17.30, returning from Ondangwa on Sunday at 13.00, and a one-way ticket costs N$105. For details, see page 101.

WHERE TO STAY The hotels in the area aim at business people, mostly aid-workers and visiting government employees. They are generally efficient, but don't expect to meet many other tourists.

Pandu Ondangwa (90 rooms) Main St; ☏ 065 241900; f 065 241919; e fom-ondangwa@ proteahotels.com.na; www.proteahotels.com/ondangwa. Now under the Protea Hotels umbrella, this 4-star hotel geared to the business community is typical of business hotels throughout the world. En-suite rooms, which include 2 that are adapted for the disabled, have twin beds, AC & satellite TV, while facilities include a swimming pool, restaurant, bar & free airport transfers.
N$561.74/395 sgl/pp sharing, B&B.
Punyu International Hotel (85 rooms) PO Box 247, Ondangwa; ☏ 065 240556; f 065 240660. One of the oldest hotels in the area, the Punyu is signposted off the main road near Ondangwa, north towards Eenhana. It has a central restaurant & bar

& swimming pool, & each of its rooms has a TV, phone & AC.
N$275/357 sgl/pp sharing, B&B.
Ondangwa Town Lodge (12 rooms) Post Office St; ☏ 065 241715; f 065 241717. Rooms have AC, & there's also a pool & bar.
N$315/207.50 sgl/pp sharing, B&B.
Nakambale Museum & Restcamp (3 huts, cottage, 'tented hut', camping) ☏ 065 245668; f 065 240472; e olukonda.museum@elcin.org.na; www.finland.org.na. Just 10km from Ondangwa, accommodation here is in traditional Owambo huts, 'tented huts' or a missionary's cottage. While these are basic, they prove a point about life here a century ago, & this is reinforced by the availability of traditional Owambo food. There is also a

19

campsite. Local guides are on hand to explain various traditional skills & practices.

Traditional hut N$60 pp; missionary cottage/tented hut N$100 pp; camping N$45 pp.

You could also try the **Fantasia B&B** on Brian Simataa St (↘ *065 240528;* f *065 241014*).

GETTING ORGANISED There are Shell, BP and Engen fuel stations (24-hour), a couple of big supermarkets and even an outdoor market. Try the latter for fresh vegetables, and perhaps a cob of maize to snack on. As a last resort, there is always the aptly named Sorry supermarket.

On Main Road are branches of the Bank of Windhoek, the First National and the Standard banks. Here you'll also find BZ Truck Repairs (↘ *064 241026*). There are also several pharmacies, including the Ondangwa Pharmacy (*off Freedom Square;* ↘ *065 240361*). **In an emergency**, the police are reached on ↘ 065 10111, the ambulance on ↘ 065 240111, and the clinic on ↘ 065 240305.

WHAT TO SEE At Olukonda, on the D3606, about 13km southeast of Ondangwa, are some of the oldest buildings in northern Namibia – a Finnish Mission built here in the late 1870s. (As an aside, Finland seems to have maintained its links with Namibia, forming a significant contingent of the United Nations' UNTAG force, which supervised the country's transition to democracy in 1990.) Here you'll also find the museum restcamp (see above). Towards Tsumeb, you'll find two of the region's small craft markets. The first, the Onankali Omahangu Paper Project, is on the B1, 55km from Ondangwa (↘ *065 286349;* e *onankali@iway.na; open Mon–Thu 09.00–13.00, Mon–Fri 14.00–16.00*). As the name suggests, it specialises in handmade paper and paper products, made from the stalks and leaves of *mahangu* – the millet staple grown throughout the area. Closer to Tsumeb, about 83km from Ondangwa, at the small Tulongeni Craft Market (↘ *064 244095; open Mon–Fri 09.00–16.00*) on the left of the road, you'll find a selection of locally made baskets and pottery.

OSHAKATI

By Namibian standards, this is a large sprawling town, some 40km northwest of Ondangwa, and very similar in character. There are no tourist attractions, but the town acts as the centre for several government departments.

 WHERE TO STAY Oshakati's hotels, as those in Ondangwa, cater mainly for business people, although the choice here is wider.

⌂ **Oshakati Country Hotel** (50 rooms) Robert Mugabe Av; ↘ 065 222380; f 065 222384; e countryhotel@mweb.com.na; www.namibialodges.com; central reservations ↘ 061 374750; f 061 256598. Oshakati Country Hotel was opened in 1999 by Namibia Country Lodges. Its main building has a large thatched structure under which you'll find a substantial public bar, as well as an à-la-carte restaurant & a conference centre that can accommodate 250 people. All rooms have AC, TV, & phone, & there's also a decent swimming pool. *N$625/440 sgl/pp sharing, B&B. Dinner N$107 (set menu) or N$135 (buffet).*

⌂ **Santorini Inn** (29 rooms) Main Rd; ↘/f 065 220457/220506/221803; e info@santorini-inn.com. On the right if arriving from Tsumeb, Santorini Inn has a pool, an à-la-carte restaurant (being renovated with a 'funky African theme' in 2007), a squash court, a sports bar with pool table, & several different types of rooms. All have AC & a phone as well as DSTV. The hotel can offer car hire, a shuttle service, & angling tours. Despite its location, the hotel feels very detached from the town. *N$370–450/230–280 sgl/pp sharing, B&B.*
⌂ **Oshandira Lodge** (16 rooms) ↘ 065 220443/221171; f 065 221189; reservations f 061

244558; e info@namibweb.com; www.namibweb.com/oshandira.htm. Oshandira Lodge is close to the airport, with secure parking, so convenient for business users. Rooms with en-suite bathroom vary in standard, which is reflected in the price, but all have AC, DSTV & a phone. Alongside the swimming pool is a sports bar with large-screen TV, open from 10.00 until the last man leaves. On the other side, the popular restaurant is probably the best place to eat in town, so often gets busy; it also includes traditional Ovambo food on its menu. N$454–483/689–719 sgl/dbl, B&B.

Okave Club (8 rondavels) Secondary Rd; \/f 065 220892. In the same part of town as the Santorini Inn, the bright-orange Okave Club is reached by turning left after the Engen station, then left again after the Bank of Namibia (onto a gravel road), & next right. The Okave Club started in 1990; its rondavels have AC, TV & phone, & there's also a pool, restaurant & bar. Reports suggest that it's not a place for a peaceful night, as it's close to a number of local *shebeens*. N$250/175 sgl/pp sharing, B&B.

WHERE TO EAT AND DRINK There is no shortage of places to eat which serve simple fare. The Portuguese Rochas restaurant is a favourite, and the restaurant at the Okave Club is also well frequented, whilst for fast food there's a popular Kentucky Fried Chicken in the Yetu shopping centre. Oshandira Lodge (see above) probably has the best food in town, or at least the most pleasant surroundings in which to eat it.

For an evening out, Oshakati can be excellent – provided that you enjoy joining in with the locals and don't demand anything too posh. Venues come and go so ask around for the current 'in' places.

GETTING ORGANISED Oshakati has all the major services that you might need. For car spares there is the large California Auto-spares dealer (\ 065 221240), a branch of Cymot (\ 065 220916) and many small garages. There are lots of fuel stations, including BP and Engen 24-hour stations, with a tyre place next door to Engen. For food shopping, the market on Main Street has a fairly extensive range of supplies, and there's also the Spar complex and a branch of Shoprite.

For money, there are major branches of Standard, Nedbank, Bank of Windhoek and First National, most with hole-in-the-wall ATMs.

If you need medicine there are several pharmacies, including Oshakati Pharmacy (\ 065 220964) on the main road, which has good basic supplies.

In an emergency, the police are reached on \ 065 10111, the ambulance on \ 065 220211, and the fire service on \ 065 220805. The hospital is on \ 065 223 3000.

THE ROAD TO RUACANA Continuing northwest towards Ruacana on the C46, you'll go through the small town of Ombalantu after about 86km. About a kilometre from here, on the M123 to the west of the town, is the Ombalantu Baobab Tree. A locally renowned hollow tree, it is today the site of a brave-new community-run venture (\ 064 251005) that incorporates a campsite, heritage centre and craft market. If you're planning to camp along this road, then this could be the place to head for.

RUACANA

This small town in the north of the country perches on the border with Angola, about 291km (mostly gravel) from Kamanjab and about 200km west of Oshakati. It owes its existence to the big hydro-electric dam that is built at a narrow gorge in the river and supplies over half of the country's electric power. This is of major economic and strategic importance, so the road from Tsumeb/Ondangwa is good tar all the way.

At Ruacana there's a BP petrol station, with the only fuel for miles, the Ruacana supermarket and a large school. The town's nucleus feels quite modern, but there are no other facilities, and few visitors pass through.

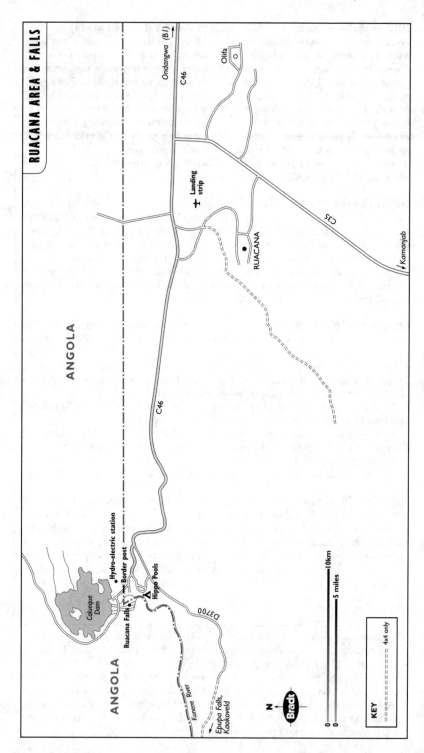

RUACANA AREA & FALLS

ANGOLA

ANGOLA

Caiueque Dam

Hydro-electric station

Border post

Ruacana Falls

Hippo Pools

Kunene River

D3700

Epupa Falls, Kaokoveld

C46

Landing strip

RUACANA

C46

Ondangwa (B1)

Olifa

C35

Kamanjab

N

Bradt

KEY

4x4 only

0   5 miles

0   10km

The Ruacana Falls used to be an attraction for visitors, but now the water flows over them only when the dam upstream in Angola allows it to, and even then much is diverted through a series of sluices to the hydro-electric station on the border. Between June and December, the falls are dry. They are well signposted in no man's land, so technically you have to exit the country to see them. However, at the large and under-used border post (*open 08.00–18.00*) you can do so temporarily, signing a book rather than going through the full emigration procedures. Be careful when taking photographs: ask permission and don't take pictures of anything apart from the falls. This border area is still very sensitive.

WHERE TO STAY

Ruacana Eha Lodge (21 rooms, 1 suite, camping) 065 270031/271500; f 065 270095; e info@ruacanaehalodge.com.na; www.ruacanaehalodge.com.na. This new lodge 20km from the falls is an unexpected find in an area which hitherto had almost nowhere to stay. Its en-suite rooms all have AC, TV, phone, tea/coffee facilities & fridge, as well as a private veranda. The grassy campsite has 15 pitches with individual braais, water & electricity, & there are also traditional huts, each with 2 beds. The shared ablution block also has facilities for paraplegics. In addition to a restaurant & bar, facilities include a swimming pool, squash court, gym & volleyball, so there's no excuse for remaining idle. Excursions to the falls, the hydro-electric station & a Himba village can be arranged with 48 hrs' notice. *N$630.26/864.09 sgl/dbl, B&B; 2-bed hut N$180 pp; camping N$50 pp.*

O'SheJa Guesthouse & Sunset Camp (7 rooms, camping) /f 065 270034; e anitad@iway.na. Recently taken over by Anita Devenish of the Santorini Inn in Oshakati, this guesthouse & separate camp are both situated in Ruacana. The guesthouse is a self-catering house with bedrooms, while Sunset Camp has 3 rooms & a campsite – plus a beautiful view of the villages down in the valley & great sunset vistas. The campsite has electricity & fresh water, & an ablution block with hot water via a donkey boiler; firewood is available. *O'SheJa N$150 pp; Sunset N$70 pp, camping N$35 pp.*

Hippo Pools Campsite (10 pitches) 065 270120; www.nacobta.com.na. Located next to the falls at the junction of the D3700 & the C46 to the west of Ruacana, this community campsite is also known as Otjipahulilo Campsite, & is a great place for birdwatchers. It's an attractive site, with pitches set out under trees overlooking the river, each with its own fireplace & BBQ facility. The central eco-friendly ablution block has toilets & showers, but there's no electricity or generator. You'll need to be totally self-sufficient except for firewood. Various trips can be arranged from here, including guided walks to the falls, & visits to local villages. *Camping N$45 pp. Guided trips from N$25 pp.*

We have also had reports of **Omunjandji Restcamp** about 10km west of Ruacana.

WEST OF RUACANA West of Ruacana is the Kaokoveld, covered in *Chapter 15*. There is a road directly from Ruacana along the Kunene, for about 125km as far as Epupa Falls. Its latter stages used to be very rough – taking me three days of painstaking driving on one occasion – and even now should not be taken lightly. Ideally, nothing west of Ruacana should be attempted without a self-sufficient two-vehicle party of rugged 4x4s.

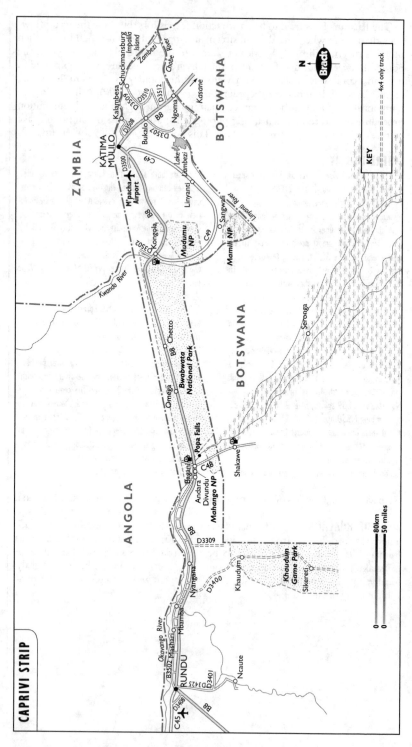

CAPRIVI STRIP

20

Rundu and the Caprivi Strip

The north of Namibia is generally very lush, watered by a generous annual rainfall. East of Owamboland – which means northeast of Grootfontein – lie the regions of Kavango and Caprivi.

These support a large population, and a surprising amount of wildlife. The wildlife has visibly increased in the national parks here in the last few years, helped enormously by various successful community-based game-guard and conservation/development programmes (see *Chapter 3*).

The main B8 road across the strip, or Golden Highway as it has sometimes been called, is now completely tarred. It is destined to become an increasingly important artery for trade with Zimbabwe and Zambia, and hence a busier road. It has come a long way since the dusty gravel road that I first crossed in 1989, when many viewed it as *terra incognita*.

Unlike much of the rest of Namibia, the Kavango and Caprivi regions feel like most Westerners' image of Africa. You'll see lots of circular huts, small kraals, animals, and people carrying water on their heads. These areas are probably what you imagined Africa to be like before you first arrived. By the roadside you'll find stalls selling vegetables, fruit or woodcarvings, and in the parks you'll find buffalo hiding in the thick vegetation. This area is much more like Botswana, Zimbabwe or Zambia than it is like the rest of Namibia. This is only what you'd expect if you look at a map of the subcontinent, or read the history of the area: it really is very different from the rest of the country.

KAVANGO REGION

East of Owamboland, and west of Caprivi, lies the region of Kavango – which broadly corresponds to the old region of Kavangoland. Within this, Rundu is the main town. It is a useful stopover for most visitors, but an end in itself for few. Further east is Popa Falls, a set of rapids on the Okavango River. These mark an important geological fault, where the Okavango starts to spread out across the Kalahari's sands, to form its remarkable delta in Botswana. Popa Falls has only a small waterfall, but a lovely little restcamp.

Just downstream from Popa, on the border with Botswana, Mahango National Park is tucked into a corner of the country. Bounded on one side by the broadening Okavango, it encompasses a very wide range of environments in its small area, and its game has improved vastly over the last decade. It now boasts Namibia's highest count of bird species in one park, and some prolific big game. With its expansive reedbeds, tall trees and lush vegetation, Mahango is typical of the game parks further east.

DRIVING FROM GROOTFONTEIN TO RUNDU The road between Grootfontein to Rundu is about 250km of good tar. Initially the only variation in the tree and bush thorn-scrub is an occasional picnic site by the roadside, or band of feathery makalani palms towering above the bush. About halfway to Rundu, however, you stop at a veterinary control post; a gap in the veterinary fence now known as the Mururani gate. This is the line where land-use changes drastically: from large, commercial ranches to small, subsistence farms. The fence is put there to stop the movement of cattle, and the transmission of foot-and-mouth and rinderpest disease. The difference is striking; the landscape changes drastically, becoming more like the stereotypical Western view of poor, rural Africa. Drivers should take care, as with more settlements there are now many more animals and people wandering across the road.

Gradually shops and bottle stalls appear, and eventually stalls selling woodcarvings, wooden aeroplanes and pots. Closer to Rundu, especially during the wet season, kiosks appear piled high with pyramids of tomatoes and exotic fruits – evidence of the agricultural potential in the rich alluvial soils and heavy rainfall.

Where to stay For a good place to stop along this road, you can't beat Roy's Camp (see page 411).

RUNDU Northeast of Grootfontein and about 520km west of Katima Mulilo, Rundu sits just above the beautiful Okavango floodplain and comes as a pleasant relief after the long, hot journey to reach it. Perhaps because of this distance, it feels like an outpost. It certainly has few specific attractions. But these distances also make it a prudent stopover, and most of the lodges expect visitors to spend just one night with them. Perhaps because it is across the river from Angola, Rundu has a relaxed, slightly Portuguese atmosphere.

Whilst the river itself is a powerful draw, with boat trips offered by many of the lodges, it is often so low from September to December that anything except, possibly, a shallow canoe will constantly ground on the sandbanks.

Getting there The main Engen fuel station is located at the four-way stop between the Shell garage (which is on the corner where you turn off the B8 and into Rundu) and town. If you are hitchhiking, then the Shell garage is the best place for lifts, as most people passing this will stop to fill up, or get a drink or food. Watch for thieves in the crowds here, as several problems have been reported in the past.

The Intercape Mainliner coach service, which links Windhoek with Victoria Falls, stops at the Engen garage on Tuesday, Thursday and Saturday at 07.45, en route for Victoria Falls. On the way back to Windhoek, it stops on Sunday and Wednesday and Friday at 13.55. Fares are around N\$185 to Victoria Falls, one way, and N\$495 to Windhoek. See pages 104–5 for details or, better, check their latest timetable using the search facility at www.intercape.co.za.

The 'airport' – little more than a military airstrip – is signposted off the main road to Grootfontein, to the west of the town, but no longer sees any regular, scheduled internal flights.

Orientation The B8 is the main artery on which people arrive and depart, though it actually skirts the town. You must turn off at the buzzing Shell petrol station to get into Rundu itself.

Taking this turning brings you past the sports stadium on your right and to a four-way stop junction. Continue straight on, and you eventually meet the old river road at right angles, opposite the police station and Omashare River Lodge. Turn left here for the Kavango River Lodge, and Hakusembe, and right for all the others. This old road used to be the main gravel road to Katima, and it runs more or less east, between the river and the new tar B8, all the way to Divundu.

Occasionally it connects with the new tar B8 by access roads numbered DR3402, DR3421, etc.

Getting around Rundu has no public transport network, but taxis congregate near the various supermarkets in town and may also be hailed on the streets. As an idea of fares, you can expect to pay around N$12 to Sarasungu Lodge, about 1km northeast of the town centre.

Where to stay Rundu has boomed in the last few years. The Caprivi has opened up more to tourism, and visitors need to stop over on their way there and back. Now there is a wide choice of places to stay, some in town, but most dotted along 30km of riverfront and clearly signposted from the road.

In town

Ngandu Safari Lodge (41 rooms, 4 houses, camping) Usivi Rd; ⤷ 066 256723; f 066 265999; e ngandu@mweb.com.na; http://resafrica.net/ngandu-safari-lodge. Just off the main road by the river, beside the turn-off to Sarasungu, Ngandu is an efficiently run complex originally intended as an affordable alternative for holidaymakers, but well suited to the business community. To its whitewashed A-frame chalets with thatched roofs, reminiscent of Cape Dutch style, have been added a range of smaller rooms in various configurations, clustered close together. 'Luxury' rooms have AC, DSTV, direct-dial phone, fridge & kettle. 'Semi-luxury' rooms are slightly smaller, while standard have no TV. There's also a campsite.

The lodge has a separate restaurant, a curio shop, a laundry, a swimming pool, internet access, shaded parking spots, braai facilities, a conference room & 24hr security. Boat trips & canoe trips are on offer at N$130 & N$115 pp per hour respectively.
Luxury N$390/530 sgl/dbl, semi-luxury N$320/460, standard N$280/430, all B&B. Camping N$55 pp.

Omashare River Lodge (20 rooms) ⤷ 066 256101; f 066 256111; e omashare@iway.na. Omashare is in the very centre of town, a convenient location that's popular with business travellers. Inside the main building are carpeted lounges, soft chairs, a restaurant, the Back Stage bar (the liveliest in town, open into the early hours), & casino with slot machines, as well as a conference room. Outside there's a large pool with banana trees planted to provide shade.

Rooms — all scheduled for an upgrade in 2006 — are built in a line facing sloping lawns, which overlook the Okavango to Angola beyond. They are small but comfortable, with AC, direct-dial phone, tea/coffee maker, flask with water, en-suite shower or bath & toilets, & TV; most are twin, but there are some family rooms.
N$440.75/608.95 sgl/dbl, inc b/fast.

Kavango River Lodge (14 chalets) ⤷ 066 255244; f 066 255013; e kavlodge@tsu.namib.com; www.discover-africa.com.na/kavango.php. Situated on a secure 3ha site on the western edge of Rundu, with superb views across the Okavango River, the long-established Kavango River Lodge is now owned by Jackie & Tulio Parreira. There's an ambitious programme of upgrading & development in progress, with the aim of 60 rooms & a caravan park. For now, there are dbl & family en-suite chalets, most with AC/ceiling fan, direct-dial phone & TV. Although some are newly built, the older ones — without AC & TV — appear more enticing.

The refurbished Riverview restaurant, set on a hill with stunning west-facing views, will be open to non-residents for b/fast & à-la-carte dinner (around N$60). Activities normally include fishing (for tigerfish & bream), sundowner cruises & canoeing — when there's enough water in the river. At present, though, all river trips must be pre-arranged as the lodge's own boats are not operating. The tennis courts next door can usually be used by arrangement.
N$350/550 sgl/dbl, B&B.

Tambuti Guesthouse (4 bungalows) ⤷/f 066 255711; e tambuti@iway.na; www.tambuti.com.na. This small, Swiss-owned guesthouse on the western edge of Rundu is perched above the river about 300m from the road leading down to the river, yet near the centre of town. Its whitewashed bungalows with tin roofs all overlook the river; they're clean, light & airy, with en-suite showers. At the back is a tree-shaded pool, & guests can make use of a braai area. No meals are served except b/fast.
N$320/420/520 sgl/dbl/family B&B.

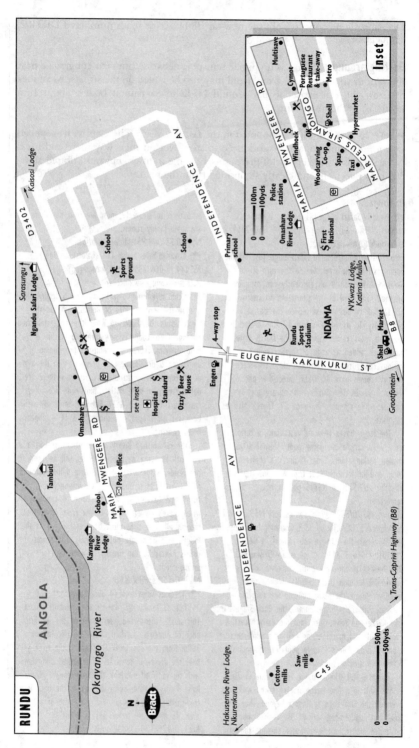

RUNDU

ANGOLA

Okavango River

Hakusembe River Lodge,
Nkurenkuru

Cotton mills

Saw mills

C45

Trans-Caprivi Highway (B8)

Kavango River Lodge

Tambuti

MWENGERE RD

MARIA

School

† Post office

Omashare RD

$ Standard

Hospital †

Ozzy's Beer House ✕

INDEPENDENCE AV

Engen ⓟ

EUGENE KAKUKURU ST

4-way stop

see inset

ⓔ

$ ✕

Ngandu Safari Lodge

Sarasungu

Kaisosi Lodge

D3402

Sports ground ✕

School

School

Primary school

INDEPENDENCE AV

Rundu Sports Stadium ✕

NDAMA

N'Kwazi Lodge,
Katima Mulilo

Shell ⓟ

Market

B8

Groatfontein

500m
500yds

0
0

Inset

0 100m
0 100yds

MARIA

MWENGERE RD

Police station

$ Omashare River Lodge

Windhoek $

Woodcarving Co-op

Spar

Taxi

MARCUS SIRANJO

OKONGO

✕ Portuguese Restaurant & take-away

Cymot

Multisave

ⓟ Shell

Metro

Hypermarket

ⓔ

$ First National

440

Further out along the river

Hakusembe River Lodge (8 chalets, floating bungalow, camping) 066 257010; f 066 257011; e hakusemb@mweb.com.na; www.natron.net/hakusembe. On the opposite side of town to virtually all the other lodges, Hakusembe is about 14km west of Rundu — off the main road to Nkurenkuru. To reach it, take a turning northwest off the main Rundu–Grootfontein road about 4km southwest of Rundu. Follow this towards Nkurenkuru for about 10km, until the lodge is signposted towards the river. The lodge is professionally managed by Lena Mudge.

Hakusembe's riverside location is enhanced by a beautiful flower garden, complete with carefully tended roses. Each of the chalets, named after one of the region's birds, has AC, mosquito nets, & en-suite shower & toilet. They are set amidst green lawns leading onto the river. Set back from these are 8 camping pitches, with power points & water. Unique to Hakusembe is a floating bungalow that occupies its own pontoon & has views of the river on three sides. Beautifully shipshape, with polished kyaak & Rhodesian teak, it has a huge dbl bed overlooking sliding doors to a private veranda. A corner bath brings an added touch of luxury (though at present there's a chemical toilet), while a combination of AC & netted windows keeps it all cool. There is also a swimming pool, & nearby, under thatch, a large bar (popular with residents) & dining area — though meals are often served on the terrace.

Boat trips are available Jan–Oct for N$80 pp/hr — options include fishing, birdwatching (with an excellent guide when we visited) & sightseeing trips by boat, as well as waterskiing (N$160 pp/20 mins), parasailing & kneeboarding. Sunset champagne cruises (N$120 pp) are also popular — & free to those spending a second night here.
N$830/640 sgl/pp sharing; floating bungalow N$830/640 sgl/pp sharing, all DBB.

Sarasungu River Lodge (9 bungalows) 066 255161; f 066 256238; e sarasungu@mweb.com.na; www.sarasunguriverlodge.com. One of the oldest lodges around Rundu, Sarasungu is by the river, just outside town. The well signposted turn-off from the main road leads down a hill, passing Ngandu on your left, before reaching the lodge a kilometre or so down a rutted, sandy track.

Large, comfortable en-suite bungalows, each named after a different animal, are spread out on green lawns. Brick-built 'luxury' bungalows with AC, TV, a veranda & river view have been added to the more traditional reed-&-thatch structures, most with

a small sitting area with chairs & coffee table & twin beds (beneath mosquito nets). Local fabrics & African artefacts bring an individual touch. Camping is by the river on a small, shady plot, but the ablution block has cold water only.

The Fish Trap restaurant & bar, with its TV loft area & rustic décor, is the focal point of the lodge, & its menu — including pizzas & pastas as well as more traditional grills — has acquired a good reputation locally (dinner around N$90), although service can be slow. Excursions include boat trips for around N$100 pp/hr, or fishing for N$120, while canoe hire is N$50 pp/hr.
Standard N$322/29/449.89/604.33 sgl/dbl/trpl; luxury N$455.40/617.76 sgl/dbl, B&B. Camping N$60 pp.

Kaisosi River Lodge (16 rooms, camping) 066 686012/3; f 066 686014; e kaisosi@iway.na; www.kaisosiriverlodge.com. Right on the river to the east of Rundu (take the first turning to the left as you head east out of town), Kaisosi is a smart, well-maintained hotel under new ownership since 2004. Upmarket rooms are housed in deep red, 2-storey chalets, & either have a fan & shower, or are larger, with AC & combined bath & shower. Each is carpeted, with twin or dbl beds, & direct-dial phone, & sliding doors opening to a patio or balcony overlooking the river. Perhaps surprisingly, there's also an excellent central campsite with private showers. The brick-built main building includes the reception, bar & dining area — all under a grand thatched roof. Just outside are a couple of pools overlooking the river, & a large area of wooden decking. Activities range from a champagne breakfast (N$150) or sunset cruise (N$105), to the more energetic *mokoro* trips N$60/hr or fishing (N$80/hr). It's a comfortable place for a stopover, if somewhat lacking in atmosphere.
N$450/700/820 sgl/dbl/trpl, B&B, exc levy. Camping N$60 pp.

n'Kwazi Lodge (13 chalets, camping) f 066 686006; m 081 242 4897; f 066 255452; e nkwazi@iafrica.com.na. About 22km east of Rundu, n'Kwazi is well signposted (with fish-eagle logos) from the main Rundu–Katima road. Take the tar road for 10km before turning left (it's the third left turning); 5km later, turn right onto the D3402, the old gravel Rundu–Katima road, then left after a further 3km. The lodge is about 4km along this dirt road. You'll need a 4x4 in the rainy season; if the water is up, keep to the left.

N'Kwazi was built in 1995 by Wynand & Valerie Peypers, & is still run by them & their family. It's a

20

relaxed, friendly place, with families particularly welcome. A couple of large thatched areas – one the main dining room, the other a bar, with ample comfortable seating & a central fire – are the focus of the lodge, both overlooking a pool & the river beyond. Good, home-cooked meals are available for N$20–60 (lunch) or N$110 (dinner).

The bungalows are large, comfortable wooden structures, with high thatched ceilings, large meshed windows & warm fabrics. They are lit by paraffin lamps when the generator stops. The adjacent campsite has ample space, showers & its own bar, with a pool in the offing.

In 2002, after the unrest in the Caprivi Strip, the Peypers turned their attention to supporting the local community through the villages, schools & churches. As part of this, they now run a scholarship project for children at local schools to enable them to progress to high school – so far, 11 children have benefited from the scheme, with one now attending university as a direct result. Visitors to the lodge can visit the local school on request, & local dancers sometimes perform at the lodge in aid of the community fund. *N$330/650 sgl/dbl, B&B. Camping N$50 pp.*

✗ Where to eat Rundu has few choices for eating out, and most people eat at their hotel or lodge. Of these, Omashare is the most central, while Sarasungu is also fairly close – both serve pizzas or more substantial mains from around N$50. Further afield, Hakusembe, n'Kwazi and Kaisosi also have good tables.

For low-budget bites, try **Ozzy's Beer House** (❨ 067 256735) at the entrance to town from the B8. Closer to the centre, there's the **Portuguese 'Restaurant' & Take-away** (❨ 067 255240/255792), which is actually just a takeway; it's almost opposite the Shell service station in the centre of town, near the Woodcarving Co-op. Alternatively, the **Hunter's Tavern** take-away at the Shell petrol station on the main road is the perfect choice for those just grabbing a bite on the run.

Getting organised There are several 24-hour **fuel stations** in town, including the main Shell and Engen stations, both of which have shops and a number of **garages**, including Gabus Garage (❨ 067 255641/255541), Kavango Mechanical Services in the industrial area (❨ 067 255474) and Dunlop Tyre Services (❨ 067 255445).

There are also branches of Bank Windhoek, Standard and First National banks.

Shopping For **food and supplies**, the best supermarkets are probably the OK or Spar, which are large and have a good selection of produce. Both are close to the Shell garage in town, where stallholders sell a range of fresh fruit and vegetables. Out of town, heading east on the old gravel road, 2km past the turning to Kaisosi River Lodge, is the **Vungu Vungu Dairy**. For those with a sophisticated line in camp cooking, this is a useful source of juices and fresh dairy produce like milk, butter and cream. On a more practical note, there's a branch of the cycle/outdoors specialists, Cymot (❨ 067 255668).

The **Mbangura Woodcarvers' Co-op** (*PO Box 86, Rundu;* ❨ 067 256170; f 067 256608) have a retail outlet next to OK Foods, in the centre of town. This large, thriving co-operative supplies many of the curio markets further south, including Okahandja's two large roadside markets. It is worth dropping into, although most of the carvings on display are larger items such as tables and chairs.

Internet café Sparks Enterprise (❨ 067 255752) is in the centre of town, close to the supermarkets.

Emergency The hospital and ambulance services are on ❨ 067 265500, and the police on ❨ 067 10111.

What to see and do While Rundu itself lacks any obvious attraction, the Okavango River more than makes up for it, so if the water is high enough (usually January to October), do make time for a river trip if you're staying a day or so.

On the Angolan bank, which at this point is generally steeper and more densely vegetated than its Namibian counterpart, numerous small villages line the river, with men, women and children constantly up and down the tracks to bathe and wash clothes. Tall reeds line the banks on the Namibian side, with villagers crossing between the two countries in *mokoros*.

In excess of 400 species of birds have been recorded along this part of the river, making it a haven for birders. The African fish eagle, no longer hunted now that the Angolan war is over, is returning to the river to breed. From its vantage point in the tall trees overlooking the river, it looks down on a domain that boasts several species of kingfisher (including the pied, giant, malachite and woodland), and two of jacana, as well as the swamp oboe, the wire-tailed swallow, and a range of colourful bee eaters. During one evening trip here in March 2006, all of these were seen, as well as Senegal coucal, black-crowned night heron, common sandpiper, wagtails, black-headed heron, little bittern and pygmy geese.

Hippos, too, are returning, though are less welcome to the villagers than to visitors seeking out the region's wildlife.

Sunset cruises are run by several of the lodges, with birdwatching trips a speciality of some. Typically, a trip will involve a slow meander against the current – which can run at up to 14km/h – then a leisurely drift back. For the more active, fishing for tigerfish or bream draws plenty of hopeful anglers, and when the water is sufficiently high, the river is also popular for watersports (see *Hakusembe River Lodge*, page 441, for details).

RUNDU TO DIVUNDU: 204KM While the new tar road lacks any real diversion, it is straight and even, allowing a consistent speed. The equivalent section of the old road makes a pleasant if considerably slower drive, as it is often surrounded by green, irrigated fields with the Okavango River as a backdrop. Do watch out for goats straying onto the road, though, even away from the villages.

Where to stay Should you wish to break the journey, there are a few places not far from the main road.

Mbamba Campsite (4 pitches) This immaculately kept community campsite about 35km east of Rundu was opened in 2006 in the Joseph Mbambangandu Conservancy. It occupies a deeply wooded, tranquil site close to the Shamange River, a tributary of the Okavango. To find it, follow the signposts for Shambyu off the B8 onto the D3402. After 3km on a tarred road, turn left (following the sign to the campsite), then at the fork over the river, bear left & follow the wooden poles. Firewood is available, & flush toilets are an unexpected bonus, but the site has no running water, so you'll need to fetch water from the river & bring absolutely all other supplies with you. N$35 pp.

Shankara Lodge (3 bungalows, camping) PO Box 1713, Rundu; \f 066 258616. About 50km east of Mbamba Campsite, this would make a reasonable stopover to break a journey. To get there, turn left off the B8 at the signpost, follow the tarred road about 3km to the T junction, then turn left again; the entrance is about 1km on your right. Simple, self-catering bungalows lie along the river; each is clean, with fridge/freezer & braai facilities. Camping is on a level site grazed by horses. The grounds are well kept, but the large pool could do with attention.
Bungalow N$450 (max 6 people); camping N$40 pp.

Divundu As the main road approaches Divundu, which is really little more than a road junction, it passes through several villages before it joins the old road just before a bridge. Cross the bridge and you'll find a 24-hour Shell garage, which also has a surprisingly well-stocked supermarket that sells made-up rolls and cold drinks. (The Engen garage just before the bridge was teetering on the brink of closure when last visited.)

Although administratively the boundary between the Kavango and Caprivi regions lies halfway across what used to be called the Caprivi National Park, and is now the Bwabwata National Park, the term 'Caprivi Strip' refers to the entire 450km strip of land that thrusts east between Angola and Botswana from Namibia's northeast corner, and continues to the Zambian border to the east of Katima Mulilo.

HISTORY OF THE STRIP On the map, the Caprivi Strip appears to be a strange appendage of Namibia rather than a part of it. It forms a strategic corridor of land, linking Namibia to Zimbabwe and Zambia, but seems somehow detached from the rest of the country. The region's history explains why.

When Germany annexed South West Africa (Namibia) in 1884, it prompted British fears that they might try to link up with the Boers, in the Transvaal, and thus drive a wedge between these territories and cut the Cape off from Rhodesia. Out of fear, the British negotiated an alliance with Khama, a powerful Tswana king, and proclaimed the Protectorate of Bechuanaland – the forerunner of modern Botswana. At that time, this included the present-day Caprivi Strip. Geographically this made sense if the main reason for Britain's claim was to block Germany's expansion into central Africa.

Meanwhile, off Africa's east coast, Germany laid claim to Zanzibar. This was the end game of the colonial 'scramble for Africa', which set the stage for the Berlin Conference of July 1890. Then these two colonial powers sat down in Europe to reorganise their African possessions with strokes of a pen.

Britain agreed to sever the Caprivi from Bechuanaland and give control of it to Germany, to add to their province of South West Africa (now Namibia). Germany hoped to use it to access the Zambezi's trade routes to the east, and named it after the German Chancellor of the time, Count George Leo von Caprivi. In return for this (and also the territory of Heligoland), Germany ceded control of Zanzibar to Britain, and agreed to redefine South West Africa's eastern border with Britain's Bechuanaland.

DIVUNDU TO POPA FALLS AND THE BOTSWANA BORDER A few hundred yards before the bridge over the Okavango, where the new road meets the old, there's a road junction. The road to the right – the C48/D3430 – leads to Botswana, via Popa Falls and Mahango National Park. Note that the only fuel in this area is on the east side of the bridge.

POPA FALLS RESERVE (*2WD. N$20 pp*) Popa Falls lie at a point where the Okavango River breaks up and drops 2.5m over a rocky section, caused by the first of five geological faults. Essentially they are a series of rapids, pretty rather than spectacular; even the warden at the entrance admits that many visitors are disappointed. After this point, the Okavango begins gradually to spread out across the Kalahari's sands until eventually, in Botswana, it forms its remarkable inland delta.

The area by the riverside at Popa Falls is thickly vegetated with tall riverine trees and lush green shrubs, which encourage waterbirds and a variety of small reptiles. Footbridges have been built between some of the islands, and it's worth spending a morning island hopping among the rushing channels, or walking upstream a little where there's a good view of the river before it plunges over the rapids. In a few hours you can see all of this tiny reserve, and have a good chance of spotting a leguvaan (water monitor), a snake or two, and many different frogs. The various birds include cormorants with a captivating technique of underwater fishing.

At the end of World War I the land was re-incorporated into Bechuanaland, but in 1929 it was again returned to South West Africa, then under South African rule. Hence it became part of Namibia.

More recently, during the late 1990s, cross-border skirmishes between Angolans and Namibians destabilised this whole area. Problems arose when Namibia's ruling SWAPO party went to the aid of Angola's MPLA (Popular Movement for the Liberation of Angola), in their civil conflict against the rebel UNITA party. An agreement between the Namibian government and the MPLA allowed Angolan troops to attack their rivals from Namibian soil, thus bringing the conflict over the border into Namibia. In 1999, the situation came to a head when members of a French family travelling through the Caprivi Region were unwittingly caught up in the conflict, and killed. As a result, the decision was taken that any traffic crossing the Caprivi Strip could proceed only in armed convoy. Thus, for the next few years, two armed convoys a day escorted all vehicles travelling between Kongola and Rundu.

Although the road across the Caprivi Strip is now safe to cross, travellers are still advised not to venture off road to the north.

DRIVING ACROSS THE STRIP: A SUMMARY The main B8 from Rundu to Katima, sometimes known as the 'Golden Highway', is now a good tarred road that runs parallel to the old gravel road. While the old road is scenic in parts, it's pot-holed and dusty: not for those in a hurry. A word of warning about the tar road, though. Do not underestimate the distances on the Caprivi: they are deceptively long. Driving in one day from Rundu to Mudumu, or from Popa Falls to Katima Mulilo, or Mudumu to Kasane or Victoria Falls, are the maximum distances that you should attempt as part of a normal holiday trip:

Rundu to Divundu: 204km (see page 443)
Divundu to Kongola: 198km (see pages 454–6)
Kongola to Katima Mulilo: 110km (see page 456)

Getting there The falls are right on the Okavango's western bank, south of the Divundu Bridge, near Bagani. Simply take the road signposted to Botswana which leaves the main B8 just west of the Bwabwata National Park, and the reserve is on the left after about 3.5km, immediately beside the road. Note that Popa's gates usually open at sunrise and close at sunset, so if you're planning on staying the night make sure you arrive before dark.

Where to stay and eat The restcamp at the falls is right on the spot. There are several alternative options, though, so there's plenty to choose from. They are listed below from north to south:

Popa Falls Restcamp (6 bungalows, camping)
Book via the NWR in Windhoek, page 124, or take pot luck. This neat, organised restcamp with a well-tended office lies right next to the falls. It has good sites, & excellent 4-bed bungalows. The camp's office includes a small shop with tinned food, cool drinks & postcards. There's also a surprisingly welcoming à-la-carte restaurant & bar that's open 07.00–09.00, 12.00–14.00 & 18.00–21.00.

Popa's bungalows are well built of local wild teak & come with their own bedding & gas lamps, but use communal kitchens & ablutions. If you are camping then walk around before you pitch camp: there are secluded sites as well as the more obvious ones. Try taking the main track down to the river, & turning right along the bank. Beware of the mosquitoes, which are numerous.
Camping N$30 pp; bungalow N$290, plus park fees.

Divava Okavango Lodge & Spa (25 chalets)
Contact Leading Lodges of Africa, ☎ 061 375300; f 061 375333; e res@leadinglodges.com; www.

leadinglodges.com. The former Suclabo Lodge was demolished in 2006 to make way for this entirely new lodge under the umbrella of Leading Lodges of Africa, to be opened in May 2007. It stands in a stunning position on a bend in the river, downstream of the main Popa Falls.

In keeping with the group's style, the new lodge will incorporate a restaurant, bar, lounge, pool & fully equipped wellness centre.

⌂ **Ngepi Camp** (7 tree houses, 2 bush huts, 3 tents, camping) ⌕ 066 259903; m 082 454844; f 066 259906; e bookings@ngepicamp.com, ngepi@getalifeplanet.com; www.ngepi.com. Signposted from the road between Suclabo & Ndhovu, Ngepi is 4km off the road, along a track that really needs negotiating with a high-clearance vehicle to avoid the sand traps.

From its inception as a sprawling, green, grassy campsite by the river under some shady trees, Ngepi seems to have grown in line with the enthusiasm of its managers & staff, with some quirky touches that add colour & humour to the place. Popular with overlanders & backpacker types, it's fun & lively, with something of a party atmosphere (the music is turned down after midnight). Aside from the campsite — which includes 8 very secluded pitches on the river, & a separate overlanders' site, with various ablution blocks — there are en-suite bush huts with their own braai areas, simply kitted out tents on high platforms, & colourful dbl or twin tree houses with reed walls, mossie nets & open-air showers with great river views. It's all very simple, but well thought out — & don't miss the throne room with its bathtub overlooking the river! For the active, there's volleyball, frisbee golf, & an innovative 'pool' in the form of an enclosure tied up alongside the riverbank, but a cool beer at the bar is equally attractive. Canoes can be hired, too, or there are mokoro trips (from N$80 pp for 2 hrs). Additional options range from boat cruises & fishing to game drives & guided walks, with day trips (from N$300 pp) including the Tsodilo Hills.
Tree houses N$330/220, huts N$255/170, tents N$150–180/100–120 sgl/pp sharing, camping N$60 pp, all exc VAT. B/fast N$45, dinner N$80.

⌂ **Ndhovu Lodge** (8 tents, camping) ⌕ 066 259901; f 064 066 259153; e ndhovu@iway.na; reservations ⌕ 061 224712; f 061 224217; e reservations@resdes.com.na. This long-established riverside lodge (the name means 'elephant') is clearly signposted 20km from the bridge at Divundu towards Popa Falls. It was taken over in 2004 by

Horst & Uisel Kock, who own a farm in the mountains around Windhoek, & bring their knowledge of the land to this very different part of Namibia. The lodge today has something of a guest-farm atmosphere, with home-cooked meals served *en famille* in the large, dark lapa. The attractive hand-painted crockery used for meals is also on sale in the curio shop.

Simple Meru-style walk-in tents are set on either side facing the river, with twin or dbl beds, & a bath or shower & toilet under thatch at the back. Mains electricity is backed up by solar power. Camping, limited to one group at a time, must be pre-booked. There's a small pool shaded by trees, while a wooden deck over the river is a good place to chill.

Activities include fishing trips, boat trips down the river (N$115 pp), 4x4 excursions into the nearby Mahango National Park or to Bwabwata West National Park (N$150 plus park fees), & trips to a local village.
N$970/N$795 sgl/pp sharing, DBB.

⌂ **Mahangu Safari Lodge** (7 bungalows, 4 tents, camping) ⌕ 066 259037; f 066 259115; www.mahangu.com.na. Reservations Eden Travel, ⌕ 061 234342; f 061 233872; e eden@mweb.com.na. The approach across a neat grassy lawn gives a slightly suburban feel to this thatched lodge, with its lime-green walls & reed fences. Situated adjacent to Ndhovu (bear right rather than left at the entrance), it was opened at the end of the 1990s, with German owner Ralf Walter aiming to make even the most nervous visitor feel entirely secure. Green-painted brick-built bungalows — including 1 for families — face the river; each is en suite, with animal-print fabrics, AC, TV & 24hr electricity. Camping is on the riverfront, with power available. Meru-style tents are backed by brick-built bathrooms with solid doors to keep out creepy crawlies.

Most meals are served outside beneath mature jackalberry trees. By the river, a couple of decks shelter under thatch, with the pool shaded by an amarula tree. Inside, photos & game trophies adorn the walls, so it's not to everyone's taste. Activities include game drives to Mahango & Bwabwata national parks (N$175–230), boat trips (N$90) & fishing (N$140).
Bungalows N$790/645 sgl/pp sharing, tents N$520 pp sharing, all DBB.

⋏ **N//goabaca, Community Campsite** ⌕ 061 255977; e nacobta@iafrica.com.na; www.nacobta.com.na. The turn-off for N//goabaca

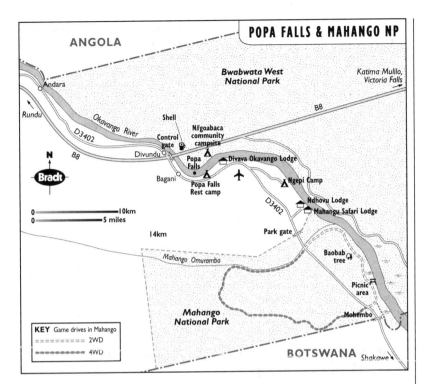

ANGOLA

Bwabwata West
National Park

Katima Mulilo,
Victoria Falls

Andara

Rundu

Okavango River

D3402

B8

B8

Shell

N//goabaca
community
campsite

Control
gate

Divundu

Popa
Falls

Bagani

Popa Falls
Rest camp

Divava Okavango Lodge

Ngepi Camp

D3402

Ndhovu Lodge

Mahangu Safari Lodge

Park gate

Baobab
tree

Picnic
area

Mohembo

Mahango
National Park

14km

Mahango Omuramba

KEY Game drives in Mahango
========== 2WD
---------- 4WD

N

Bradt

0 ————————10km
0 ————————5 miles

BOTSWANA Shakawe

(see page 420 for explanation of obliques) is 4km east of the bridge, & the campsite is 3km from the road – the last 500m along a sandy track. Each of the 4 private pitches has flush toilet, hot shower & a water tap; 2 have viewing decks, & all overlook the falls from the eastern bank. The site is run by Kxoe Bushmen, many of whom worked as trackers &

scouts for the South African Army during the war, but have subsequently been economically & politically marginalised. Tourism can not only pay them, but also encourages them to put a higher value on their traditional skills & bushcraft, so support them if you can.

MAHANGO NATIONAL PARK (2WD/4x4. *Open sunrise–sunset; N$40 pp & N$10 per vehicle, but no charge if you're driving straight through on the main road*) This small reserve is tucked away in a corner of the Caprivi Strip, bounded by the Botswana border. It is bisected by one of the main roads between Namibia and Botswana, a wide gravel artery from which two game drives explore the area.

Though forming its eastern boundary, the Okavango River is also the focus of this reserve. The eastern loop road passes beside the river and is normally the better one for game. Here the river forms channels between huge, permanent papyrus reedbeds. Adjacent are extensive floodplain areas, where you're quite likely to spot red lechwe or sable, a relatively scarce but beautiful antelope which seem to thrive here.

Beside these, on the higher and drier land of the bank, are wide belts of wild date palm-forest, as well as the lush riverine vegetation that you'd expect. Further from the river are dry woodlands and acacia thickets, dotted with a few large baobabs. This rich variety of greenery attracts an impressive range of animals including the water-loving buffalo, elephant, sable, reedbuck, bushbuck, waterbuck and the more specialist red lechwe and sitatunga. Good numbers of hippo and crocodile are also present.

Mahango is a great favourite with birdwatchers; more species can be found here than in any other park in Namibia. This variation should come as no surprise, as the reserve has one of Namibia's few wetland habitats, adjacent to large stretches of pristine Kalahari sandveld. Thus many water-loving ducks, geese, herons, plovers, egrets, kingfishers, and various waders occur here, along with the dry-country birds that you'll find in the rest of Namibia. Okavango specialities like the slaty egret can sometimes be spotted, and for many birds – including the lesser jacana, coppery-tailed coucal and racket-tailed roller – Mahango marks the western limit of their distributions.

Amongst the larger species, the uncommon western-banded snake eagles occur, though black-breasted and brown snake eagles are more frequently seen. Similarly, the park's Pel's fishing owls are rare compared with its marsh, giant eagle and spotted owls.

When to visit As with most parks, the game varies with the season. The dry season, July to October, tends to be better as the riverfront is at its busiest with animals drinking. Sometimes the park is inundated with elephants and buffalo. During the summer rains (from November to April) the big game here can be disappointing. When visiting in early March one year, the highlight of my day's game-viewing was a distant kudu, and a snatched glimpse of fleeing sable. Whilst game densities have improved since then, the vegetation is still thick and the animals elusive. However, summer migrants like the exquisite carmine bee-eaters are then in residence, making this the perfect time for birdwatching here.

 Where to stay There are no facilities in Mahango itself, so most people stay in one of the lodges or restcamps between the park and Popa Falls (see pages 445–7).

What to see and do
Game drives There are two game drives to explore, both branching from the main road about 800m south of the northern entrance to the park. The better, eastern road, which is good gravel, soon overlooks the floodplain, passing a picnic spot before returning to the main road farther south. The western course, suitable for high-clearance 4x4s only, follows a sandy omuramba away from the river, before splitting after about 10.7km. The right fork continues along the omuramba, terminating at a waterhole, while the left rejoins the main road again 19km later.

Bush walking One real bonus is that walking in the park is officially encouraged. However, beware – the summer's lush growth is far too thick to walk safely in, so it's better to visit when the plants and shrubs have died down during the winter and you are able to see for a good distance around you. Then you can get out of the car and go for it, but watch for the elephants, buffalo and occasional lion. (For comments on walking safely in the bush, see *Chapter 7*, pages 110–13.)

EXCURSIONS INTO BOTSWANA As you drive across the Caprivi Strip, Botswana's Okavango Delta can feel so near, and yet so far. However, just south of Mahango, within Botswana, are several small camps which are close enough to reach while crossing the Caprivi Strip. They offer a taste of the Okavango Delta, within easy reach of Namibia.

At the southern end of Mahango lies Namibia's Mohembo border post, followed by a new Botswana customs and immigration post. These are generally quiet posts, open 06.00–18.00. Staff on both sides seem pleasant and efficient, but you'll still need to allow around half an hour to clear the formalities in each direction. There are various forms to be filled out on both sides, so it's worth collecting these as you drive into Botswana, to save time on the return trip. In addition to the standard information required at border posts (passport details, vehicle registration, etc), you'll need to know your vehicle engine and chassis numbers, which are usually shown on the tax disk on the front windscreen; if it's not clear, the top number is probably the chassis number. The same information is required separately by the police, who rather unexpectedly may not be in uniform. On the Botswanan side, there's a charge of N$80 to 'import' a vehicle (valid for one year). When returning to Namibia, you'll be charged for a CBC (cross-border charges) permit, currently N$120 for a private car.

Prices within this section are in pula (£1 = P12.30, US$1 = P6.57; €1 = P8.33).

Mohembo border and ferry From the border, the road leads shortly to a T-junction, about 13km north of Shakawe. A left turn takes you to the (free) Mohembo ferry, which usually takes a few vehicles at a time across the river, including the occasional small truck. Expect to find a lot of people waiting around here – some to cross, others to meet those who have crossed, or to buy and sell things here. To continue to Shakawe, turn right at the junction.

Shakawe This very large fishing village stands east of the main road on the northern banks of the Panhandle of the delta, some 281km north of Sehithwa and 13km south of the Mohembo border post on the Caprivi Strip. Driving into the village always used to feel like entering a maze of reed walls, each surrounding a small kraal, as the track split countless ways between the houses. The odd trap of deep sand was enough to stop you for an hour, and thus serve up excellent entertainment to numerous amused locals.

Today, however, Shakawe is a bustling little place. Just a stone's throw from the tar road you'll find a significant base for the army (the Botswana Defence Force), as you'd expect in one of the country's more sensitive border areas, and a major police station. If you're going to be doing anything unusual here, then stopping to ask at the police station if it is OK to proceed is always a good idea. If you've the time, take a walk along the river that is just behind the police station. Sometimes there's a mokoro ferry shuttling local people to and from the eastern side of the river, full with their wares to sell or recent purchases to take back home.

Of particular importance to drivers is the Saoshoko filling station (*open daily 07.00–18.00*) close to the entrance to the village when heading north. There are also a few shops and a post office, many concentrated within the small shopping centre around the bus stop. And if you can't leave the modern world behind, then

Shakawe has mobile phone coverage which usually extends to Drotsky's, but not much further.

If you fancy a break before driving on, you could try a guided tour of Krokovango Crocodile Farm, 5km south of Shakawe, but there's little else to delay you here.

Getting there and getting away There are good daily bus services to Maun via the rest of the western Panhandle from the centre of town. Of these, the fastest is the Golden Bridge Express (P35 one way), which leaves at around 07.30 each morning, taking around 4½ hours to reach Maun. Zebra minibuses are cheaper (P28) but very cramped and take an hour longer; they also depart only when full. A third bus leaves a little later in the day. Return buses leave Maun at around the same time. Alternatively, hitchhiking is relatively easy.

On the west side of the main road, just 400m off the tarmac, you'll find a paved airstrip, with a very neat, round, thatched terminal building.

Where to stay There's nowhere practical to stay in Shakawe itself, but there are several water-based camps on the river south of town that cater mainly for fishing and birdwatching. Now that the Caprivi Strip is once more accessible to visitors, trade here has picked up so you will often need to book. Listed here are the three main options, from north to south.

Drotsky's Cabins (6 chalets, camping) ☎ +267 6875 035; f +267 687 5043; e drotskys@info.bw. Almost 8km south of the radio mast in Shakawe you'll find a left turn off the tar road. This sandy track will lead you east, crossing the old road up the Panhandle for about 3km to reach Drotsky's Cabins (⊕ DROTSK 18°24.868'S, 21°53.120'E). You should be able to drive across this in a normal 2WD car, though the sand can be very thick, so some driving skill is needed.

This long-established camp is run by the delightful Jan & Eileen Drotsky, & their family, who have seen the Shakawe area change from a remote outpost to a thriving little town. It stands on a high bank, overlooking the river, which is already several kilometres wide. Below is a network of deep-water channels & large beds of papyrus. It's excellent for birdwatching or fishing, though there's little game around except for hippos & crocodiles.

Drotsky's chalets are set amongst well-watered lawns in a shaded haven under a canopy of thick riverside trees. Colourful shrubs & banana trees have been planted between them, creating the welcoming impression of a green & tropical haven.

A-frame chalets sleep either 2 or 4 people: the latter are bigger & built on 2 levels. All have low brick sidewalls supporting a tall, steeply angled thatched roof. They all have simple furnishings, rugs on the floor, & a tabletop electric fan, & are lit by mains electricity. There's also a shady campsite with electric points. Central to the lodge is a bar (which

often seems to play host to an eclectic selection of local characters) & a very large dining area, built over the river. Look out for the rather beautiful wooden top to the bar!

Drotsky's is a genuine old camp, where hospitality hasn't been learned from a manual. If you are willing to take it on its own terms, then it can be a super lodge, & offer you fascinating insights into the area, its history & its ecosystems. P395/325 sgl/pp sharing; 4-person chalet P850; camping P85 pp, inc firewood. B/fast P66, lunch P77, dinner P110. Boat hire from P175 /hr per boat, plus fuel, depending on size of boat; rod hire P45 per day. Transfers to or from Shakawe Airport P25 pp.

Xaro Lodge (8 Meru tents) Book via Drotsky's Cabins, above. Xaro (⊕ XARO 18°25.423'S, 21°56.364'E) is about 8.5km downstream from Drotsky's Cabins, its parent camp, & is usually reached from there by a 15-min boat trip. The lodge is built on an outcrop from the mainland, amidst an old, established grove of knobthorn (Acacia nigrescens), mangosteen (Garcenia livingstonei) & jackalberry (Diospyros mespiliformis) trees.

It was originally built in about 1984 by Hartleys Safaris, before passing through several hands until it was acquired by Jan Drotsky, whose son, Donovan, now runs the camp with his wife, Yolande.

It's hard to escape the feeling that this was once an absolutely beautiful, old-style Okavango camp. You'll still find a thatched, stone dining area

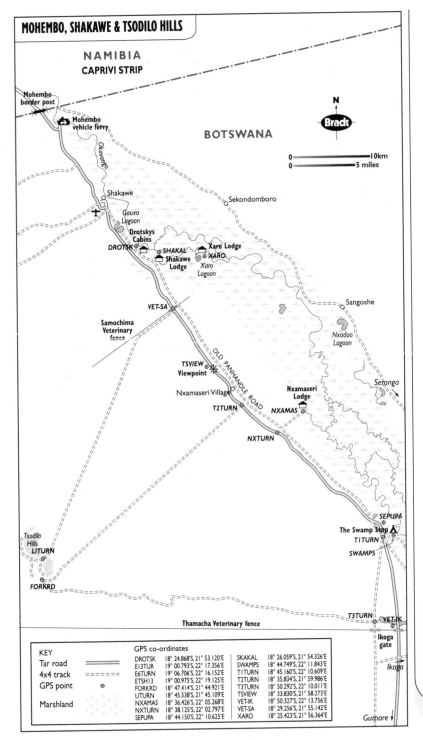

MOHEMBO, SHAKAWE & TSODILO HILLS

NAMIBIA
CAPRIVI STRIP

Mohembo
border post

Mohembo
vehicle ferry

BOTSWANA

Okavango

Shakawe

Sekondomboro

Gauxa
Lagoon

Drotskys
Cabins

DROTSK

SHAKAL
Shakawe
Lodge

Xaro Lodge

XARO

Xaro
Lagoon

VET-SA

Samochima
Veterinary
fence

TSVIEW
Viewpoint

OLD PANHANDLE ROAD

Nxamaseri Village

Sangoshe

Nxadao
Lagoon

Seronga

Nxamaseri
Lodge

T2TURN

NXAMAS

NXTURN

SEPUPA

The Swamp Stop

TITURN

SWAMPS

Tsodilo
Hills
LITURN

FORKRD

T3TURN **VET-IK**

Ikoga
gate

Thamacha Veterinary fence

Ikoga

Gumare

0 ————————— 10km
0 ————————— 5 miles

N

Bradt

KEY
Tar road	———
4x4 track	=====
GPS point	⊕
Marshland	

GPS co-ordinates
DROTSK	18° 24.868'S, 21° 53.120'E	SKAKAL	18° 26.059'S, 21° 54.326'E
E13TUR	19° 00.793'S, 22° 17.356'E	SWAMPS	18° 44.749'S, 22° 11.843'E
E6TURN	19° 06.706'S, 22° 16.152'E	TITURN	18° 45.160'S, 22° 10.609'E
ETSH13	19° 00.975'S, 22° 19.125'E	T2TURN	18° 35.834'S, 21° 59.986'E
FORKRD	18° 47.414'S, 21° 44.921'E	T3TURN	18° 50.292'S, 22° 10.011'E
LITURN	18° 45.538'S, 21° 45.109'E	TSVIEW	18° 33.830'S, 21° 58.273'E
NXAMAS	18° 36.426'S, 22° 05.268'E	VET-IK	18° 50.327'S, 22° 13.756'E
NXTURN	18° 38.125'S, 22° 02.797'E	VET-SA	18° 29.256'S, 21° 55.142'E
SEPUPA	18° 44.150'S, 22° 10.625'E	XARO	18° 25.423'S, 21° 56.364'E

with a large table in the centre & various old books on the bookshelves in the walls. Accommodation, though, is in new, Meru-style tents raised on stilts with en-suite facilities & sliding doors leading to a wooden deck. Look around & you'll also find a garden of succulents & cacti, banana trees & even a small baobab tree (*Adansonia digitata*) on the left of the camp as you look out onto the river.

Royal, one of the marvellous staff who has been with the family for years, recalls that the lodge has always been used for fishing & birdwatching from motorboats, never from mekoro – & that's still the situation, with birding from the lodge itself considered particularly good.

P370/300 sgl/pp sharing/sgl, inc transfer from Drotsky's. Transfers to or from Shakawe Airport P35 pp. Meals & activities as Drotsky's, above.

🏠 **Shakawe Lodge** (10 bungalows, camping) Contact via Travel Wild, Maun; ☎ +267 6860 822; f +267 6860 493; e win@travelwild.co.bw. Shakawe Lodge (⊕ SKAKAL 18°26.059'S, 21°54.326'E) was started in 1959, & was for decades known as Shakawe Fishing Camp. You'll find the turning to it on the east of the main road (⊕ SHAKAT 18°26.804'S, 21°53.654'E), about 5.5km north of the Samochima veterinary fence (⊕ VET-SA 18°29.256'S, 21°55.142'E) or 15km south of Shakawe village. The lodge stands on the bank of the Okavango River, a little less than 3km from the road. Its present owners, Barry & Elaine Price, took it over in 1975.

Now the lodge offers large, thatched, brick bungalows. Each has a fan & mains power throughout, & an en-suite bathroom. All are carpeted, though very basic. There's a circular thatched boma, used as a bar/dining room, adjacent to a small lily-covered lagoon that's behind the splash pool.

Under shady trees on the riverbank, a few metres south of the main lodge, is the campsite. This is a lovely, grassy site with simple ablutions & a few metal drums that act as braai stands for cooking.

Most visitors here come to fish, though birdwatching – through the riverside forest or from boats – is also popular. Although Mahango National Park is within reach of a day trip, most visitors would opt to stay there as a separate destination.

Beside the bank at the lodge, look for the Okavango's only Angolan houseboat, a relic of the Angolan war from the late 1970s. Apparently it was used by 32 Battalion of the South African forces, who were stationed in the Caprivi Strip, near the site where Ngepi Campsite is now. However, it broke loose & drifted south, & has been gently rusting in Botswana ever since! Barry has some stories to tell you about this if you ask him.

Chalet P350/P550/P836.50 sgl/dbl/trpl, camping P66 pp, all inc tax. B/fast P55, lunch P66, dinner P110. Boat hire P198 per hr, plus fuel.

Visa/MasterCard accepted; payment may be made in all convertible currencies.

Nxamaseri

Though the small village of Nxamaseri is not a stop for most visitors, I've included this section because the surrounding area is a very interesting one, offering an insight into the attractions of the delta that is on a par with most of the reserves further east. Like Guma Lagoon, further south, it's also fairly easily accessible due to the presence of a lodge.

The Nxamaseri Channel is a side channel of the main Okavango River. When water levels are high, there are plenty of open marshy floodplains covered with an apparently unblemished carpet of grass, and dotted with tiny palm islands. It's very like the Jao Flats, and is one of the Okavango's most beautiful corners.

If you want a real delta experience in the Panhandle, then this should be high on your list of places to visit – though getting here requires either your own vehicle or a flight.

Flora and fauna highlights

The Nxamaseri Channel is north of the point where the main Okavango River divides at the base of the Panhandle, and is a stretch of open, clear water up to about 30m wide in places. Beside the edges you'll find stands of papyrus and common reeds, whilst its quieter edges are lined by patches of waterlilies, including many night lilies, *Nymphaea lotus* (aka lotus lilies) as well as the more common day lilies, *Nymphaea nouchali caerulea*. Look out also for the heart-shaped floating leaves, and star-shaped white or yellow flowers, of the water gentian, *Nymphoides indica*.

As with the rest of the Panhandle, this isn't a prime area for game viewing. You may catch glimpses of the odd lechwe or the shy sitatunga, and you're almost bound to see hippo and crocodile, but big game is scarce. However, the channel is a super waterway for birdwatching; home to a tremendous variety of waterbirds. Without trying too hard, my sightings including many pygmy geese, greater and lesser jacanas, lesser galinules, colonies of reed cormorants, darters, several species of bee-eater and kingfisher, green-backed herons, a relaxed black crake, numerous red-shouldered widows and even (on a cloudy morning in February) a pair of Pel's fishing owls. Beside the channel are pockets of tall riverine trees and various real fan and wild date palms, whose overhanging branches house colonies of weavers (masked, spotted-backed and brown-throated). Upstream of the lodge, on the main Okavango River, there's a colony of carmine bee-eaters at a location known locally as 'the red cliffs'. This is occupied from around early September to the end of December, but is probably at its best in late September/early October (the best time for most migrant species here). While watching for birds, keep an eye out for the elusive spotted-necked otter, *Lutra maculicollis*, which also frequents these waters.

Getting there and away Nxamaseri lies about 37km south of Shakawe or 19km north of Sepupa. If you're approaching from the north, follow the tar road to the Somachima veterinary fence (⊕ VET-SA 18°29.256'S, 21°55.142'E), then after 10km you'll pass a slight rise marked by a sign as 'Tsodilo View' (⊕ TSVIEW 18°33.830'S, 21°58.273'E). From here, on a clear day, you can see the hills to the southwest. Less than 3km south of this viewpoint you'll pass a sign to Nxamaseri, which leads to the village of the same name. Nxamaseri Lodge's unmarked turning (⊕ NXTURN 18°38.125'S, 22°2.797'E) is almost 9km south of this; it's just a vague track in the deep sand leading northeast to the lodge (⊕ NXAMAS 18°36.426'S, 22°5.268'E), about 5.5km from the main road. However, the lodge is surrounded by water for most of the year and self-drivers will usually be met and transferred by boat for the final few kilometres. Advanced reservations are essential; this is not a lodge to try and drop into unannounced.

Where to stay

Nxamaseri Lodge (7 chalets) ☎ +267 6878 015; f +267 6878 016; e info@nxamaseri.com; www.nxamaweri.com. This long-established camp was started as a fishing camp in about 1980. Recently bought back by the original owners, P J & Barney Bestelink (who run Okavango Horse Safaris), it is now run by P J's son, Brad. It is claimed that fly-fishing in the Delta was pioneered at Nxamaseri, & certainly it remains an attraction for people who fish seriously, but to this have now been added birdwatching, visits to a local village to watch basket making, & day trips to the Tsodilo Hills, making this a wonderful all-round lodge justifying a stay of at least 2 days.

The lodge has been built within a wonderfully thick & tropical patch of riverine vegetation. All around are knobthorn (*Acacia nigrescens*), waterberry (*Syzygium cordatum*), sycamore fig (*Ficus sycomorus*), mangosteen (*Garcinia livingstonei*), jackalberries (*Diospyros mespiliformis*), sausage trees

(*Kigelia africana*) & some of the most wonderfully contorting python vines (*Cocculus hirsutus*) that you'll see anywhere. Sensitive refurbishment in 2006 means that the strong sense of place has been retained, but with higher standards of accommodation & food. Its wide, thatched lounge/dining area is built around a couple of lofty old jackalberry trees, with an open frontage to the river: it's comfortable & well thought out, but not ornate. Wooden walkways lead to a dbl chalet on one side; & twin-bedded chalets to the other. All are brick with high thatched roofs & wooden decks above the river. Each large, comfortable chalet has an en-suite shower & toilet, & bedside lights powered by a generator or batteries.

The boat trips for birdwatching are first class, & whilst there tends to be less emphasis on mokoro excursions, these are also possible (& magical) when the water levels are high & there are suitable areas of shallow water nearby. Fly-fishing & lure/spinning fishing with top-quality equipment are possible throughout the year under expert guidance at every level. The very best tiger-fishing months are Aug–Nov, while the best times for bream are Mar–Jun. During the first 3 months of the year the rain & new floodwaters are said to disturb the fish, which move out to the floodplains, so fishing in the channels can be more difficult. Nxamaseri's record tiger-fish catch is about 6.7kg, though in a normal season they'd expect to have 10–15 catches over the 6kg mark. Like most Okavango lodges, Nxamaseri operates a 'catch-&-release' system, except for the occasional bream taken for the table. They have two large, flat, barge-like boats which provide a very stable platform for several people fishing, & are also ideal for photography.

US$437/655 pp sharing/sgl, inc all meals & most activities, exc bar drinks & transfers. Day trips to Tsodilo Hills & full-day fishing US$50 pp. Open all year.

CAPRIVI REGION

The Caprivi Region's nerve-centre, Katima Mulilo, is closer to Lusaka, Harare or Gaborone than it is to Windhoek, and in many ways this region is more like the countries which surround it than like the rest of Namibia. For example, note the different designs of the rondavels and villages as you travel through. Some are identical to those in eastern Zimbabwe, whilst others resemble the fenced-in kraals in Botswana. Even the local language used in the schools, the Caprivi's *lingua franca*, is the Lozi language – as spoken by the Lozi people of Zambia.

Situated on the banks of the Zambezi, Katima Mulilo is a very lively, pleasant town with a bustling market and most of the facilities that you are likely to need. Away from the main town, the region has two established national parks, Mamili and Mudumu. These are both lush, riverside reserves with increasing numbers of animals, and a very bright future. Sadly, the Bwabwata National Park (formerly Caprivi Game Park) has still to live up to its name, having been badly abused during the war of independence and largely ignored since then. Right on the area's eastern tip, relying mainly on the riverside attractions of Botswana's Chobe National Park, several new lodges are now springing up.

For a history of the Caprivi Strip, see box pages 444–5.

DIVUNDU TO KONGOLA AND THE KWANDO RIVER: 198KM

Because it borders on Angola, this area was very sensitive and controlled by the military for many years (see page 445). Now only two control posts remain to remind you of Caprivi's past troubles: one at Divundu and another at Kongola. You do not need any permits to cross the strip and the people staffing the control posts will usually just ask where you are going and wave you on with a smile; alternatively, you may be asked to provide information about you and your trip, including your vehicle's engine and chassis number.

A large chunk of the Caprivi Strip is taken up by the **Bwabwata National Park** (frequently pronounced 'Babatwa'). The park is bordered to east and west by the Okavango and Kwando rivers, and is divided into two – Bwabwata West and Bwabwata East – with the boundary between them falling 40km west of the Susuwe information point (see page 456). The Golden Highway bisects this undeveloped park which, whilst it is home to much wildlife, has few facilities and little in the way of marked game-viewing side roads. As the game seems to avoid the main road, most visitors just pass through, saving their time for other parks. All that you can usually see from the road are a few raptors aloft and the occasional elephant dropping on the road – but drive carefully in case something does appear unexpectedly.

The western entry point to the park is technically at the checkpoint on the bridge at Divundu, just before the fuel station which is the only reliable source of fuel for hundreds of kilometres in each direction. For the majority of visitors, who

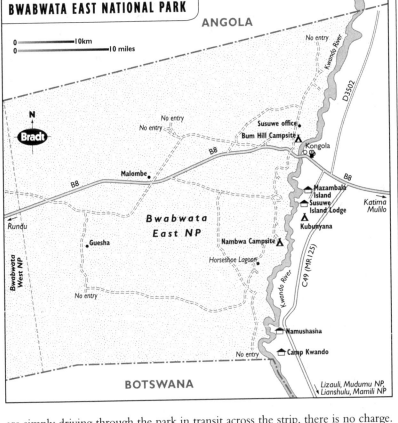

ANGOLA

0   10km
0   10 miles

N

Bradt

No entry

No entry
No entry

Susuwe office
Bum Hill Campsite

Kongola

B8

Malombe

B8

Bwabwata East NP

B8

Mazambala Island
Susuwe Island Lodge

Katima Mulilo

Kubunyana

Rundu

Guesha

Nambwa Campsite

Horseshoe Lagoon

C49 (MR 125)

Bwabwata West NP

No entry

Kwando River

Namushasha

No entry

Camp Kwando

BOTSWANA

Lizauli, Mudumu NP, Lianshulu, Mamili NP

are simply driving through the park in transit across the strip, there is no charge. Those planning to explore further, however, must purchase a permit. For Bwabwata West, permits are obtainable at Buffalo (stressed on the 'a', as Buffalo), a few kilometres east of the bridge at Divundu. There is nowhere to stay, but there is a map of the game drives in the vicinity. For permits for the eastern end of the park, visitors must go to Susuwe (see page 456).

The park is very sparsely populated, with only a few larger settlements: Omega, 70km from Divundu, then Chetto, 40km further on, and Omega III 60km to the east. Few visitors stop at any of these but they might be helpful in an emergency.

KWANDO RIVER AREA The southern border of the eastern Caprivi Region is defined rather indistinctly along the line of the Kwando, the Linyanti and the Chobe rivers. These are actually the same river in different stages. The Kwando comes south from Angola, meets the Kalahari's sands, and forms a swampy region of reedbeds and waterways called the Linyanti swamps. (To confuse names further, locals refer to sections of the Kwando above Lianshulu as 'the Mashi'.)

These swamps form the core of Mamili National Park. In good years a river emerges from here, called the Linyanti, and flows northeast into Lake Liambezi. It starts again from the eastern side of Lake Liambezi, renamed the Chobe. This beautiful river has a short course before it is swallowed into the mighty Zambezi, which continues over the Victoria Falls, through Lake Kariba, and eventually discharges into the Indian Ocean.

To explore any of these areas on your own, ensure that you have the relevant 1:250,000 maps from the Surveyor General (numbers 1723, 1724, 1823 and 1824), a compass and the normal tourist map of Namibia. Combine these with local guidance and you will find some interesting areas. If you are heading off into Mamili, then you should have some back-up help (eg: a second 4x4 vehicle) and a GPS might be very useful.

Kongola and environs

Though a large dot on most maps, Kongola is just a small settlement, about 7km east of the impressive new bridge that carries the B8 over the Kwando – tangible proof, in tar and concrete, that the Caprivi is regarded as a major trade artery of the future. Its centre, at the main road's junction with the C49 (confusingly marked on the ground as the MR125, but also labelled on maps as the D3501 or the D3511), is a fuel station. Fuel here, particularly unleaded, isn't entirely reliable, so do fill up earlier if you have a chance. There's also a shop on site selling freshly made bread, and a separate post office. On the opposite corner is **Mashi Crafts** (*open Mon–Fri during Feb–Dec; Sun only rest of year*), a community craft centre selling curios made by the local Kxoe community. It specialises in traditional baskets, beadwork and East Caprivian reed mats and carvings, each clearly labelled with the name of the maker, and his or her village.

The Intercape Mainliner bus between Windhoek and Victoria Falls stops at Kongola on Tuesday, Thursday and Saturday, at 06.45, with southbound buses stopping at 10.00 on Monday, Wednesday and Friday. One-way tickets cost N$230 to Victoria Falls, or N$240 to Windhoek.

From here, the MR125 heads south towards Linyanti and eventually loops round to come out near Katima Mulilo. Initially, it passes a number of lodges that line the eastern banks of the Kwando River, before going deep inside Mudumu National Park, and skirting Mamili. About 126km from the B8 turn-off is the village of Linyanti, where there may be fuel available; it is then a further 90km or so to Katima.

About 4km west of the fuel station in Kongola, between the river and the MR125, is a turn-off south to Mazambala Island Lodge.

Susuwe Triangle

To the west of the Kwando River, inside Bwabwata East National Park, is a narrow tract of land that is wide in the north, but becomes narrower towards the Botswana border. Known variously as 'the triangle', 'the Susuwe Triangle' or 'the Golden Triangle', it is rich in game.

To explore this area you'll need a 4x4, and some detailed maps; you'll also need a permit from the MET rangers' station (✪ 17° 51.703'S, 023° 19.159'E; *N$40 pp per day, plus N$10 per vehicle; open daily 08.00–17.00*). To find this, turn north from the western end of the Kongola Bridge, following the **i** sign to 'Information at Susuwe'; the rangers' station lies about 3km along this track, close to a bush airstrip. Here you can buy your permit and will be given a useful map; it's also wise to ask their advice on what you plan to do.

Well worth visiting is Horseshoe Lagoon, about 5km south of Nambwa Campsite. This stunning ox-bow lake set in riverine woodland attracts excellent game and numerous birds. Elephant are in abundance near here, their presence evident both in the damage to trees and in the cleared sandy area lining the shore: even if you see nothing, you can't miss the prints of various animals in the sand. The overhanging trees have been colonised by a large family of baboons, which makes for entertaining viewing. A word of caution, though: driving alone in this area during or just after the rainy season is ill advised. It's all too easy to get bogged down in the cottonsoil, and there are few people around to help out.

Where to stay There are several places to stay on the eastern bank of the Kwando River – some are just campsites; others are much more comfortable. There are also two community campsites on the western bank, within the national park. If you're driving yourself, be aware that the road south from Kongola is variously marked on the ground and on maps as the C49, the D3501 and the MR125.

In the park Both community campsites lie on the western bank of the Kwando River, with reservations through NACOBTA (☏ *061 255977;* e *nacobta@ iafrica.com.na; www.nacobta.com.na*) You'll need to be fully equipped with your own 4x4 vehicle, including all supplies and drinking water. That said, the sites are surprisingly well equipped, with cold and hot water (courtesy of solar panels), and plenty of tree shade.

⚠ **Bum Hill Campsite** (6 pitches) Owned & run by the Kwando Conservancy, the attractive Bum Hill site was opened in 2004. It's clearly signposted off the road to Susuwe information point (see page 456), north of the B8. In addition to 3 pitches sharing an ablution block, there are a further 3 set on a platform in a tree, reached by a ladder, & with toilet & shower beneath. *N$60 pp per day.*

⚠ **Nambwa Campsite** (4 pitches) Nambwa is south of the B8; the turn-off (⊕ 17°47.039'S, 23°20.141'E) is opposite the one to 'Information at Susuwe'. Follow the track parallel to the river until you reach a fork; here you bear right, following the signposts to the camp. This site is run by the Mayuni Conservancy. *N$60 pp per day.*

East of the Kwando River

⌂ Mazambala Island Lodge (12 chalets, camping) ☏/f 066 686041; e mazambala@mweb.com.na. Although Mazambala opened in June 1997, it has been closed for a while. Now it's back under the ownership of André Visser. The closest lodge to the main road, its turn-off is to the right, a few kilometres east of the Kongola Bridge. Follow this dirt road for about 4km south, past the campsite; it's accessible most of the year in a saloon car (when the river's in flood, guests are met at the campsite by boat). The lodge is carefully sited on slightly higher ground about 100m from the river – away from the mosquitoes & to avoid flooding. This position comes into its own when viewed from the large, open-sided bar & dining area, built high on stilts with views across the Kwando floodplain; there's also a river view from the 15m swimming pool. At the heart of the lodge is a magnificent sausage tree, around 500 years old, near which small thatched chalets form a tight circle. Recently built of brick & reeds, these are simply appointed with twin beds, netting windows & ceiling fans, & en-suite facilities at the back; electricity is available 24 hrs. The campsite is on the river, halfway between the road & the lodge, with its own ablution blocks & hot water. Activities comprise ½-day game drives (N$210 pp), boat trips (N$180 pp), fishing trips (N$100 pp/hr), & guided nature walks (N$60 pp/hr). *N$520/840/1,110/1,280 sgl/dbl/trpl/family, exc bed levy. Camping N$55 pp. B/fast N$60, lunch N$65, dinner N$125.*

⌂ Camp Kwando (3 tree houses, 11 chalets, camping) ☏/f 066 686021; m 081 124 5177; f 066 686023; e reservations@campkwando.com; www.campkwando.com. Completely rebuilt following a fire in October 2005, Camp Kwando lies 26km south of Kongola, along the C49/D3501, & then a further 3km west from that, past the 'traditional village' of Kwando, where visitors are welcome. The new camp, right by the river, makes good use of traditional design, its central area comprising a series of traditional rondavels interlinked in circles that include the lounge, dining & bar areas, plus a deck & fire pit. Furnished in solid wood & cream canvas, & decorated with local artefacts, it's stylish & comfortable, but not at all grand. Simple tented chalets on low stilts with a small veranda sit above the marshes; each has twin beds, mossie nets & electricity (from a generator on a timer), with pole-screened open-air toilet & shower at the back. Spacious tree houses, with wide staircase access & a higher specification that includes solid wood furniture & floors, overlook the river across to Botswana. The circular campsite benefits from tree shade, & there's a nearby pool. A highlight of Kwando is the opportunity for scenic flights across the delta; there are also boat trips at N$160 pp, fishing trips, museum visits, & game drives (N$180) to Mudumu &, in winter, Mamili. *Chalets N$550/460 sgl/pp sharing, tree house N$1,000/780 sgl/pp sharing, all DBB. Camping N$50 pp.*

🏠 **Susuwe Island Lodge** (6 chalets) ☎ +27 11 706 7207; f +27 11 463 8251; e info@impalila.co.za; www.islandsinafrica.com. Without doubt the best lodge in the area, Susuwe is set on an island in the Kwando River, with a strong design focus & the emphasis on service & flexibility. Built, owned & run by the team responsible for Impalila Island Lodge (see page 468), it was constructed with impressive faith at a time of great uncertainty over the Caprivi's future for tourism. Many fly in to Susuwe; if you're driving yourself you'll normally be met near the checkpoint. To drive direct, take the road towards Nambwa Campsite (see above) & follow the signs. After 10km of sandy track, you'll have to leave your vehicle & transfer by boat to the lodge.

Constructed around mature jackalberry & mangosteen trees on the banks of a tributary of the Kwando, Susuwe's attractive open central area is decorated with local artefacts & is deceptively spacious. Cool in summer & – courtesy of a welcoming central fire-pit – warm in winter, it's fronted by thickly intertwined vines that filter the sunlight but allow the occasional elephant to come right up to the wooden railing. No dining tables inhibit the sense of space – instead, squashy sofas create individual areas for relaxing, chairs surround the fire-pit, & tables are set up for meals according to the number & make-up of guests. Up in the trees, a large, high platform makes a great place for a relaxing lunch, or to spend time with a pair of binoculars.

Susuwe's impressive & beautifully designed chalets are entirely private, hidden among thick vegetation along the river. Each comes complete with a lounge area, leading out to a tiny private plunge pool set in a wooden veranda overlooking the river. The canopied king-size beds have mosquito nets, & electricity to power ceiling fans & even hairdryers, while huge bathrooms host twin basins, a large bath & separate shower. Intricate inlay details in doors & floors add a creative touch without losing the essence of space & of the environment.

Relaxed & attentive staff ensure that activities – which include game drives, night drives, boating trips, birding walks & picnics in the bush – are tailored to individual requirements. This is a lodge to savour – & a place to linger.
Dec–Mar US$355, Apr, May & Nov US$390, Jun–Oct US$530, all pp sharing, inc all meals, soft drinks, house wine during meals & local beers, laundry, activities & boat transfer from Kasane Immigration to lodge.

🏠 **Kubunyana Camp** (3 tents, camping) ☎ 061 255977; e nacobta@iafrica.com.na; www.nacobta.com.na. See also page 449. One of the Caprivi's community-run campsites, Kubunyana is reached by turning south onto the MR125 (aka D3501) from the B8 at the Kongola filling station. After 6km the camp is signposted to the right, & you'll reach it a further 4km along a narrow, winding track that floods when it's wet.

In addition to 4 private camping pitches, there are large, pre-erected tents under thatched shade covers, with basic beds but no linen. There's also a communal kitchen, & ablution block with flush toilets & hot showers. You'll need to bring all your own food & drinking water.
Tent N$70 pp, camping N$35. Canoe N$25 pp, guide N$30 per game drive.

🏠 **Namushasha Lodge** (27 chalets) ☎ 066 686024; f 066 686027; e namu@iway.na, afrideca@mweb.com.na; www.namibialodges.com. Standing above the Kwando River, overlooking the Bwabwata Game Park, Namushasha was completely rebuilt in August 2005. To get there, take the MR125 off the B8, then turn west at the signpost for a further 4km along the lodge's well-maintained drive. (The final kilometre of this is over a sandy ridge; saloon cars need to be driven carefully.)

From the baobab tree by the new arched entrance, it is clear that things have changed. Gone are the functional chalets; in their place are solid, brick-&-thatch chalets with cream-painted walls & toning fabrics; some are adjacent, others detached; all are very private. Twin or dbl beds have 4-poster mosquito nets, & each room has a private balcony, of which most look over the river. There's also a classy VIP suite with dbl bedroom, a modern living/dining room, & a huge shower & basin set into solid wood.

The central building features a lofty bar/lounge area under thatch, & a separate dining room with netting to protect from mosquitoes, all overlooking the river & park beyond. Steps lead down to a deck overlooking the water, with a fire-pit for chilly winter evenings. Nearby is a swimming pool, with dugout canoes modified into poolside seats, surrounded by green lawns. A small curio shop has basic toiletries.

Activities include boat trips, game drives & – more unusually – guided horse trails for all levels (hard hats included), as well as scenic flights organised through Kwando Camp (see above). There's also a 2.5km self-guided walking trail that circles the riverbank near camp. Namushasha is a good camp, professional & welcoming. The lodge is open to day visitors for lunch & activities.
N$760/540 sgl dbl pp, inc b/fast. Dinner N$125 pp. Game drive N$80.

Mudumu National Park (*N$40 pp, and N$10 per vehicle. Permits from the NWR in Windhoek or at the Nakatwa Camp in the park*) The more northerly of the region's two reserves, Mudumu, covers 850km² of riverine forest south of Kongola, either side of the C49. Bordered by the Kwando River on the west, the reserve has good populations of a large variety of animals. Together with Mamili and the Triangle, Mudumu is notable for its buffalo (otherwise uncommon in Namibia), roan and sable antelope (both generally uncommon species), the water-loving lechwe and sitatunga, and often large herds of elephant.

Mudumu can be explored on foot or by 4x4, though don't expect much organisation or many clearly marked game drives.

Where to stay To stay in the park, the choice is either an unfenced campsite with river water and basic sanitation, Nakatwa Nature Conservation Camp, or Lianshulu Lodge, by the river. If you opt to camp, then follow the signs to the camp and note that the reserve, which is not fenced or clearly demarcated, borders onto hunting areas. Ask the scouts *exactly* where the boundaries are. Some of the camps beside the Susuwe Triangle also run trips into Mudumu.

Lianshulu Lodge (8 chalets, 3 suites) Reservations ☏ 061 254317; f 061 254980; e lianshul@ mweb.com.na; www.lianshulu.com.na. Lianshulu was one of the first private lodges to be built inside a Namibian national park, in 1989, & was completely rebuilt in 2005. Now owned & run by Ralph Meyer-Rust, with a staff of around 50, it stands on the banks of a backwater of the Kwando River, about 5km down a good bush track off the C49 (D3511), 40km from the B8 turn-off. It's usually accessible with care in a saloon car. There is also a private airstrip.

The lodge is set on a 1,000-acre private concession beneath a canopy of mature jackalberry & mangosteen trees, giving an air of seclusion & ensuring that it blends into the surrounding bush. A discreet electric fence is in place in an attempt to deter elephants from damaging the trees, but other wildlife can come & go freely. An imposing entrance leads into a huge central area with an integral viewing platform looking west over the river, complete with fire-pit, & a second fire right at the back, well away from chilly night breezes. Despite the size, the layout of solid wood furniture & ethnic fabrics combines to create a more intimate series of 'rooms', with lounge, bar & dining areas. Painted chalets (with en-suite shower) & suites (with bath, capacious open-air shower & – coming soon – individual plunge pools) are well spaced along the river, affording a high standard of accommodation & privacy. Each is under thatch, with 2 dbl beds, mosquito nets, rugs on a solid-wood floor, a safe, a veranda overlooking the river, & lots of space. One of the rooms is designed for families, & is also wheelchair adapted.

Under the eye of a team of 6 guides, of whom 4 hail from Zimbabwe, visitors explore the river's channels afloat, go on game drives (including at night) & take walks through Mudumu, these last in an area that is exclusive to the lodge. For guests seeking to appreciate both the aquatic attractions of the Okavango Delta & the wildlife of Mudumu, Lianshulu offers packages with Kwando Lagoon Camp in Botswana, & even has a border post on the concession, to ensure a minimum of bureaucratic hassle during transfers.

Lianshulu is an efficiently run operation that maintains close links with the community, & is heavily involved with education at several levels. They are currently setting up links with the primary school at Lianshulu, building toilets & repainting school buildings. There are also open days to children from local schools, & talks about jobs in the tourism industry for community groups. *Chalets N$1,100–1,395 pp sharing DBB, suites N$2,165–3,005/1,915–2,580 sgl/pp sharing, inc all meals, drinks & activities, depending on season. Park fees extra.*

Lianshulu Bush Lodge (8 chalets) See above for contact details. The Bush Lodge, some 2km downstream from the main lodge, is essentially a slightly smaller version of the main lodge. It is currently booked exclusively by the American tour company, OAT, but may eventually be brought back within the main Lianshulu fold.

Lizauli Traditional Village This small village is well signposted on the C49, just to the north of Lianshulu, and is an important attraction for visitors. N$20 is

The solution tried at Lianshulu is simple: to link the success of the lodge and the national park with direct economic benefits for the local community, and thus to promote conservation of the local wildlife.

The problem with many national parks in Africa has been that the surrounding local communities feel little benefit from the tourists. However, they are affected by the park's animals, which raid their crops and kill their livestock. Thus the game animals are regarded as pests, and killed for their meat and skins whenever possible.

In the area around Mudumu and Mamili, the need to involve the communities in conservation is being directly addressed through at least four projects: the community game guard scheme, the bed-night levy, the Lizauli Traditional Village, and the thatching grass project.

Under the first, game guards are recruited from the local villages, to stem poaching and educate about conservation. They are paid by grants from the US, WWF and Namibia's own Endangered Wildlife Trust.

Second, there is a nominal charge to visitors for each night stayed on the reserve (already included in Lianshulu's prices), which goes directly to the communities most affected by the park. It aims to compensate for any loss of crops or stock caused by wild animals, and to show that the wildlife can be of direct financial benefit to the local people.

A third project focuses on Lizauli Traditional Village, an attraction by which the local people themselves can earn money directly from visitors. This inevitably depends upon the flow of visitors through the reserve. Since more animals should mean more visitors and hence more income for the village, so the local people benefit financially if the area's wildlife is preserved.

Finally, in 1994 Lianshulu started a scheme to transport thatching grass from the area further south, where there is a strong demand for its use in thatching new safari lodges and chalets. With the unrest in the Caprivi, customers looked to other sources, but now the development of local tourism is providing a new market, and the supply of thatching grass remains an ongoing business. The local communities all collect and bundle it, knowing that there's plenty of demand and it will sell. It is, of course, a truly sustainable resource, which can only be produced if the local communities continue to conserve the environment.

charged as an entrance fee, and visitors are guided around the village where traditional arts and crafts are being practised. Aside from the fascination of the actual attractions – an iron forge, a grain store, and various carvers and basket weavers – a visit here gives a good opportunity to sit down and talk to some local people about their way of life. This is just one of several important community projects in this area.

Sangwali Museum In 1999, Stella Kilby, a distant relative of some British missionaries, founded a small museum at Sangwali in memory of her ancestors To find the museum, continue along the C49 (D3511) from Lianshulu until you reach a sign indicating Sangwali, then a second pointing to Sangwali Health Clinic (this is about 50km south of the turning to Namushasha). To find the museum, take this road for about 5km, passing the clinic, and continuing towards Mamili as indicated by some rough handmade signs. About 500m before the log bridge, you'll see the museum on the left – it's the only white-painted concrete building in the area.

Inside the museum, large wall maps trace the route of Livingstone's travels from South Africa through the Botswanan desert until he reached the Linyanti

River at Sangwali in 1855. Here, he persuaded the London Mission Society to open a mission station. Four years later, two missionaries, Holloway Hellmore and Roger Price, arrived with their families in Sangwali, after a hard seven-month journey from South Africa. The local Makololo tribe, however, weren't overjoyed to have white missionaries among them, and eight of the travellers died after eating meat that had apparently been poisoned. The survivors turned their backs on the nascent mission, and trekked all the way back to South Africa.

The story is recorded in Stella's book, *No Cross Marks the Spot* (Galamena Press, Southend on Sea, 2001).

Mamili National Park (*N$40 pp, & N$10 per vehicle. Permits from the NWR in Windhoek, or the IRNDC or MET in Katima Mulilo*) This unfenced swampland reserve of about 350km^2 was created shortly before independence and consists largely of marshland, veined by a network of reed-lined channels. It includes two large islands: Nkasa and Lupala. Together with Mudumu National Park, it has the vast majority of Namibia's population of sitatunga, red lechwe and puku.

Mamili is located in the southwest corner of the eastern Caprivi Strip, where the Kwando sharply changes direction to become the Linyanti. As yet there are no facilities for visitors and few passable roads, even with a 4x4.

Approaching along the D3501, the turn-off to Mamili National Park is at Sangwali village. This community, together with the nearby villages of Samudono and Nongozi, is in the process of setting up a conservancy in the area just outside the park, where they plan to develop a simple campsite. There is already a small craft stall, Sheshe Crafts, about 4km from the D3501 as you head into Mamili. This sells locally produced baskets, carvings, reed mats and some very authentic fishing traps.

If you really want to see Mamili, and don't have a small expedition, then the easiest way is probably to stay on the other side of the river, in one of several exclusive camps in Botswana. Selinda, Linyanti, DumaTau and King's Pool are all in this area, overlooking the park from Botswana. For details of these, see my companon guide, *Botswana – Okavango, Chobe, Northern Kalahari: The Bradt Safari Guide.*

KATIMA MULILO Established originally by the British in 1935, Katima is the regional capital of the eastern Caprivi. It replaced the old German centre of Schuckmannsburg, which now consists of just a police post, a clinic and a few huts. Collectors of trivia note that the taking of Schuckmannsburg, on 22 September 1914, was the first Allied occupation of German territory during World War I.

Katima is a large town with good facilities, beautifully placed on the banks of the Zambezi. Leafy outskirts lead to an open central square, where you'll find useful places such as the post office and an internet café.

Recently, as western Zambia has started to open up, Katima has taken on the role of frontier town: a base for supplies and communication for the new camps on the Upper Zambezi River in Zambia. It has just a little of the Wild West air that Maun used to have a decade ago, when it was remote and the hub of the Okavango's safari industry.

Getting there
By air Katima's M'Pacha Airport lies about 18km west of town, towards Rundu, and doubles as the military airbase. There is currently just one Air Namibia service a week between Windhoek and Katima Mulilo, on Monday, costing N$3,540 one way. Otherwise, aside from the odd private flight for Lianshulu or Namushasha, the airport is deserted, with no facilities whatsoever apart from toilets. Tutwa

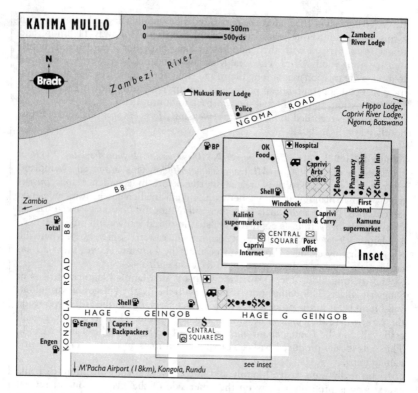

Tourism & Travel (see pages 464–5) runs a shuttle service to and from the airport on request.

By road Katima is about 69km from the Ngoma border post, and with only one road through the Caprivi Strip, **hitching**, at least as far as Grootfontein or Kasane in Botswana, is relatively easy. Lifts to Victoria Falls and Etosha have also been reported.

The Intercape Mainliner **bus** from Livingstone to Windhoek stops at the Shell Garage on Hage G Geingob Street. Buses for Windhoek leave Katima on Wednesday, Friday and Sunday at 15.30, arriving back on Monday, Wednesday and Friday at 08.00. Livingstone-bound buses leave Katima on Tuesday, Thursday and Saturday at 08.45, returning on Wednesday, Friday and Sunday between 11.00 and 15.00, depending on hold-ups at the border. Tickets cost N$435 through to Windhoek, and around N$195 to Livingstone, and may be purchased through Tutwa Tourism Travel (see pages 464–5), who charge a handling fee of N$10.

In addition, **minibuses** ply between Katima Mulilo and Windhoek, via Rundu (one way N$220), while others go to Livingstone or into Botswana.

To and from Zambia To reach the Zambian border, continue west past the Zambezi Lodge until the tar turns left towards Rundu. Instead of following it, continue straight onto a gravel road for about 6km, passing the (unpleasant) rubbish dump. The border post here at Wenella opens 06.00–18.00 every day.

Sesheke, the small Zambian settlement near the border, is split in half by the Zambezi. Either side makes Katima look like a thriving metropolis in comparison. Namibian dollars can usually be changed into Zambian kwacha here (try the green building with the Coca-Cola sign, opposite the Chuma Kweseka grocers), before continuing on the long gravel road north to Ngonye Falls and ultimately to Mongu.

Where to stay

🏠 **Zambezi River Lodge** (27 rooms, camping) ◣ 066 253149; f 066 253631; e gm-zambezi@ proteahotels.com.na; www.proteahotels.com. Zambezi River Lodge (formerly just Zambezi Lodge) was renamed at the end of 2006 when it was taken over by Protea Hotels. Just a few hundred metres off the main road as it enters Katima from Ngoma, it is the area's best hotel, boasting a swimming pool, restaurant & even a floating bar (which closes at a lamentably early 19.00).

The hotel caters mainly for business visitors & tourists who stop for a night. Though the service at its open-air restaurant is attentive, its chefs seem too used to mass catering to produce anything outstanding, but there's always a swim in the pool to make you feel better.

The large, comfortable rooms are spread out east in a long row along the river. All have been refurbished in a modern, quite German, style: tiled floors & walls throughout, en-suite toilet/shower, AC, minimalist desk & chair, direct-dial phone & tea/coffee-making facilities. Each has a wide dbl patio door overlooking the river — but with a pathway along the river, there's no privacy. Campers can stay on the west side of the lodge, on a small site with ablution block, fire-pits & electricity.

Zambezi River Lodge is pleasant, efficient & ideal for a one-night stop. However, its activities are limited to 1½hr cruises on the river (N$85 pp 4–6 people) & fishing trips (N$160 pp/hour, min 2) & it lacks the character or activities to entice visitors to stay longer.

High season (Jul–Nov) N$410/600/855 sgl/dbl/family of 4, low season N$370/540/770 sgl/dbl/family, all inc b/fast; camping N$45 pp, & N$40 per car

🏠 **Mukusi River Lodge** (10 rooms) ◣/f 066 252442; e mukusi@mweb.com.na; www.mukusi.com.na. Built on stilts over a tributary of the river, Mukusi is geared to guests in search of fishing. To get there, when coming from the west, take the turning before the police station & the lodge is at the end by the river. In addition to 3 floating rooms on 2 storeys, with sliding doors to a tiny platform, it has no-frills wooden cabins on dry land at the back, all with AC, TV, kettle, fridge & en-suite facilities. As you might expect, there's a distinctly nautical flavour about the bar & eating deck with its table & canvas chairs; there's also a small pool. Fishing trips (Jun–Aug only) cost N$150pp for the first hr, then N$100/hr pp; boat cruises are N$100 pp, or N$80 pp for 2; 'booze cruise' N$60 pp for 3 or more passengers. Sun–Thu N$340/460 sgl/dbl; Fri & Sat N$300/340 sgl/dbl. Floating rooms N$460 dbl bed (upstairs), N$380 twin.

🏠 **Mukusi Cabins** (29 rooms) Next to the Engen garage; ◣ 066 253255; f 252359. Under the same ownership as the river lodge, this also has the same facilities & prices, but without the riverside location.

🏠 **Caprivi Travellers' Backpackers Hostel** ◣ 066 252788; m 081 257 5048; Despite signposts indicating that this hostel is 900m from the main street, we were unable to find it — so any reports would be welcome.

Out of town Several lodges of different styles lie along the river east of town. They are listed here broadly in order of distance from Katima Mulilo.

🏠 **Hippo Lodge** (19 chalets) ◣ 066 253684 (⊕ S17°29.795'S, E024°20.019'E). Situated east of town, just beyond the turn to Caprivi Cabins, Hippo Lodge is 2km off the main road. It has some of the lushest gardens in Namibia & a laidback atmosphere.

Hippo's thatched rooms, with brick-&-reed walls painted purple or turquoise, are built in rows, some overlooking the river, others the gardens. They have en-suite shower & toilet, mosquito nets & fans, but are pretty basic & could do with sprucing up. Camping is a better option.

There is a pool to swim in, surrounded by green lawns & colourful herbaceous borders. A couple of decks overlooking the river in front of a rather dark but attractive lapa — with large TV — make this a pleasant spot for lunch or a light snack. N$200/300/450 sgl/dbl/family of 4; camping N$30 pp. B/fast from N$15.

🏠 **Caprivi River Lodge** (8 chalets) Ngoma Rd; ◣ 066 252288, 253300; f 066 253158; e mary@ capririverlodge.net; hakunamatat@iway.na; www.capririverlodge.net (⊕ S17°29.482'S, 024°18.952'E). Some 1.5km east of Zambezi Lodge, & about 800m down a wide sandy track (by the

Coca-Cola signboard), this lodge has literally blossomed in recent years under the ownership of Mary Rooken-Smith & her ex-army husband, Keith. Compact, spotlessly clean chalets are fronted by lush riverside gardens shared by a family of guinea fowl. Each of the chalets, upgraded in 2006, has its own patio, with sliding doors leading through to a room with stone-tiled floor, & beds whose intricately carved headboards, mostly of kiaat wood, are an attraction in their own right. A ceiling fan, fridge, kettle, telephone & en-suite shower (or bath) complete the picture. At the back of the site are some self-catering wooden cabins with AC & braai area: one is en suite with dbl bed, TV & sofa, while 'backpacker' cabins have a separate ablution block. Plans are in hand to develop a couple of upmarket camping pitches — but much more fun is the rather ramshackle 2-storey 'houseboat', with plenty of through breeze — just like camping on the river.

Lunch & dinner are served as a set menu in a large dining/bar area with high thatched ceiling; non-residents are welcome with a reservation. There's a cosy fire for the evenings, & a cool pool for hotter days. Trips include guided fishing & kayaking tours (there's a freezer for those fresh-caught fish). This is also the base for Hakuna Matata Adventures, which promotes tourism right across the region. *Chalets N$495/600 sgl/dbl B&B, cabins N$375 en suite, N$105–150/195–260 sgl/dbl, all exc levy. Substantial accommodation discounts for those arriving in a Land Rover (20%) or on a motorbike (50%) – Keith is an enthusiast!*

⌂ **Island View Lodge** (10 chalets, camping) ☎ 066 252801/686037; e tiger@islandvl.com; www.islandvl.com. Opened in 2001 by the Cavanagh family from Durban, Island View is primarily a fishing lodge, although the birding is considered to be an attraction, too. To get there, drive 13km from Katima towards Ngoma (about 56km from Ngoma), until the lodge is signposted off left on the D3508 (⊕ 17°33.692'S, 024°30.923'E).

Continue 2.5km down a gravel road, then follow the signs to the lodge (⊕ S17°32.731'S, 024°31.406'E); the road is passable all year in a 4x4, & accessible — if bumpy — by saloon car in the dry season. Transfers can be arranged from Livingstone, Victoria Falls & Kasane. It's a pleasant site, with rustic, black-painted reed-&-thatch chalets on concrete plinths right by the river. These have twin beds, fan, mossie nets, & private facilities, but are not en suite — only the chalets further back (with dbl bed) offer this. The tree-shaded campsite has its own ablutions, braai area & electricity. There's a pool set amid lawns & the central bar area has a pool table; there's also a small shop selling fishing tackle. The cost of fishing trips depends on fuel costs. *N$165/400 pp self-catering/FB; camping N$40 pp, all exc 2% levy. Fishing N$350/500–600 half/full day, plus fuel costs, or N$120/hr*

⌂ **Kalizo Lodge** (7 chalets, 4 self-catering rooms, camping) ☎ 066 686802/3; f 066 686804; e kalizo@mighty.co.za, bruno@iway.na; www.kalizolodge.com. The family-run Kalizo stands on the banks of the Zambezi, downstream from Katima. To reach it, drive 13km from Katima towards Ngoma (about 56km from Ngoma), until Kalizo is clearly signposted off left on the D3508. Continue 20km down a gravel road, then turn left at the sign indicating 5km & follow the signs; it's sandy in places so inexperienced drivers may need a high-clearance vehicle.

Set along the river, Kalizo's rustic thatched chalets are well furnished & comfortable, with twin beds & en-suite facilities. Each of the self-catering units has 2 or 3 bedrooms, a bathroom & kitchenette, & is equipped with linen, cutlery & crockery, while the shady campsite, also on the river, has power, water points & ablution block.

Much of the restcamp's original raison d'être was tiger-fishing, & this is still a feature; boats can be hired for N$70/hr, or N$300 for a full day, inc a guide & fuel; to hire equipment, add N$25 pp per day. It's now also popular with birders, with added interest provided by quad-biking, nature walks & the swimming pool. Trips further afield, to Chobe & Victoria Falls, can be organised too. *N$450 pp sharing, DBB; self-catering N$200 pp sharing; camping N$50 pp.*

✘ **Where to eat** If you are staying in Katima Mulilo, then you'll probably eat at your lodge. Alternative options are at present limited to just:

🍴 **Boabab Bistro** Hage G Geingob Rd; ☎ 081 127 8632. Centrally located café with b/fast & snack menus. Daily specials N$40. *Open Mon–Fri 07.00–18.00, Sat 08.00–15.00.*

Getting organised Your first port of call should be **Tutwa Tourism Travel** (*Hage G Geingob Rd;* ☎ *066 253048/ 252739;* m *081 127 7429;* f *066 252238;*

e tutwa@mweb.com.na), to the left of the pharmacy. A mine of useful information, it also sells postcards and souvenirs, acts as agent for Intercape Mainliner and has internet facilities (N$20 for ½ hr).

On the same parade are the practical Caprivi Cash & Carry, which carries all sorts of useful goods, including fishing equipment, and the **Air Namibia** office (*open Mon–Fri, 08.40–10.30, 13.40–16.30*).

For **food and provisions**, start just behind the square at the Katima bakery, which sells good fresh bread. Both the supermarkets – OK and Kalinki – have their own bakeries too. If you're after something more colourful, there's a busy market in the centre of town, near the craft centre. Should you be in need of **car repairs**, try Tractor and Truck Repairs on the main road in from Rundu.

The local **Bank Windhoek** has an ATM. Note that changing Zambian currency in Katima is likely to be a problem, so if you have kwacha you may need to cross the border and exchange currency with local traders on the Zambian side.

For permits for the national parks, contact the IRDNC (℄ *066 697052*) on the B8 towards Rundu, or try the MET on Ngana Road (℄ *066 253143*).

Internet
Caprivi Internet Café On the square. N$10 for ½ hr. *Open Mon–Sat 08.00–19.00.*

Emergency and health The police can be contacted on ℄ 066 10111. Should you be in need of medical treatment, the number for the ambulance/hospital is ℄ 066 251400, but you'd be better advised to contact one of the town's doctors, Dr Pretorius or Dr Badenhorst, either through the pharmacy (see below), or through Dr Sitengu (℄ *066 252083*), whose office is next to the pharmacy.

Caprivi Pharmacy Hage G Geingob Rd; ℄ 066 253446. *Open 08.00–13.00, 14.00–17.00 Mon–Fri, Sat 08.30–11.00.*

What to see and do Katima has few intrinsic attractions, although the lodges along the Zambezi are very pleasant places to stay. If you do have time here, then use it for trips on the river, or as a base for longer expeditions into Mudumu, Mamili, the upper Zambezi and Lake Liambezi.

The **Caprivi Arts Centre** on Olifant Street is a good outlet for the many local crafts and well worth a visit.

LAKE LIAMBEZI This large, shallow lake is located between the Linyanti and Chobe rivers, about 60km south of Katima Mulilo. When full, it covers some 10,000ha, although it has been dry (something of a dustbowl) since 1985. People and cattle now populate its bed.

Lake Liambezi's main source of water used to be the River Linyanti, but after this has filtered through the swamps it seems unable to fill the lake, even in recent years of good rain. However, next time the Zambezi is in flood it may be able fill the lake either via the Bukalo Channel, which runs southwest from the river to the lake, or even via the Chobe River – which can actually reverse its flow.

There is one new community campsite planned in this area (page 470), in the new Salambala Conservancy.

ZAMBEZI–CHOBE CONFLUENCE Two rivers bound the eastern end of the Caprivi Strip: the Chobe to the south, and the Zambezi to the north. Their confluence is at the end of Impalila Island, at the eastern tip of Namibia. The Zambezi flows relentlessly to the sea but, depending on their relative heights, the Chobe either contributes to that, or may even reverse its flow and draw water from the Zambezi.

Between the two rivers is a triangle of land, of about 700km², which is a mixture of floodplains, islands and channels which link the two rivers.

This swampy, riverine area is home to several thousand local people, mostly members of Zambia's Lozi tribe. (The main local languages here are Lozi and Sobia.) Most have a seasonal lifestyle, living next to the river channels, fishing and farming maize, sorghum, pumpkins and keeping cattle. They move with the water levels, transferring on to higher, drier ground as the waters rise.

Flora and fauna The area's ecosystems are similar to those in the upper reaches of the Okavango Delta: deep-water channels lined by wide reedbeds and rafts of papyrus. Some of the larger islands are still forested with baobabs, water figs, knobthorn, umbrella thorn, mopane, pod mahogany, star chestnut and sickle-leafed albizia, while jackalberry and Chobe waterberry overhang the rivers, festooned with creepers and vines.

Because of hunting by the local population, large mammals are scarce. Most that do occur come over from Botswana's Chobe National Park. Elephants and buffalo sometimes swim over, and even lion have been known to swim across into Namibia in search of the tasty domestic cattle kept there.

Even when there are no large mammals here, the birdlife is spectacular. Large flocks of white-faced ducks congregate on islands in the rivers, African skimmers nest on exposed sandbanks, and both reed cormorants and darters are seen fishing or perching while they dry their feathers. Kingfishers are numerous, from the giant to the tiny pygmy, as are herons and egrets. However, the area's most unusual bird is the unassuming rock pratincole with its black, white and grey body, which perches on the rocks of rapids, between hawking for insects in the spray.

Where to stay The largest island in this area, Impalila Island, is at the very tip of Namibia. It gained notoriety during the 1980s as a military base for the SADF (South African Defence Forces), as it was strategically positioned within sight of Botswana, Zambia and Zimbabwe. It still boasts a 1,300m-long runway of smooth tar, but now its barracks are a secondary school, serving most of the older children in the area.

There is a customs and immigration post on Impalila, which opens from 07.00 to 17.00. The lodges here all use this, and are usually reached by a short boat transfer from Kasane in Botswana.

Ichingo Chobe River Lodge (7 Meru tents) ℷ/f +267 6250 143 (on island); m 7131 8979; f +267 6250 223 (in Kasane town); e ichingo@ iafrica.com; www.ichingo.com. Ichingo was the brainchild of Dawn & Ralph Oxenham, who since 1996 have run the lodge themselves. Occupying a secluded site on the south side of Impalila Island, it overlooks the quiet backwaters of some of the Chobe River's rapids, a world away from busy Kasane just across the water. It makes a super base for river trips & game-viewing from boats along the Chobe River, & offers some excellent birdwatching too.

Accommodation, which was renovated in 2006, is in rustic walk-in Meru tents, each set high above the flood levels – important in a location where

the rise & fall of water is up to 2m. En-suite showers are at the back under thatch, & there's a balcony at the front, with views of the water through thick vegetation, dominated by the water-tolerant waterberry trees, *Syzygium guineese*, with the orange-fruited mangosteen, *Garcinea livinstonei*. A generator in the evening ensures a steady power supply, backed up by battery lights in each tent. Meals are taken around a large, solid wooden table in the thatched dining area/bar/lounge that fronts onto the river.

Activities are run individually, with a guide allocated to each tent for the duration of the guests' stay. Not surprisingly, the river is the main focus, with game-viewing, birdwatching & fishing from motorboats, & fly-fishing in the rapids, as well as

EASTERN CAPRIVI'S WETLANDS

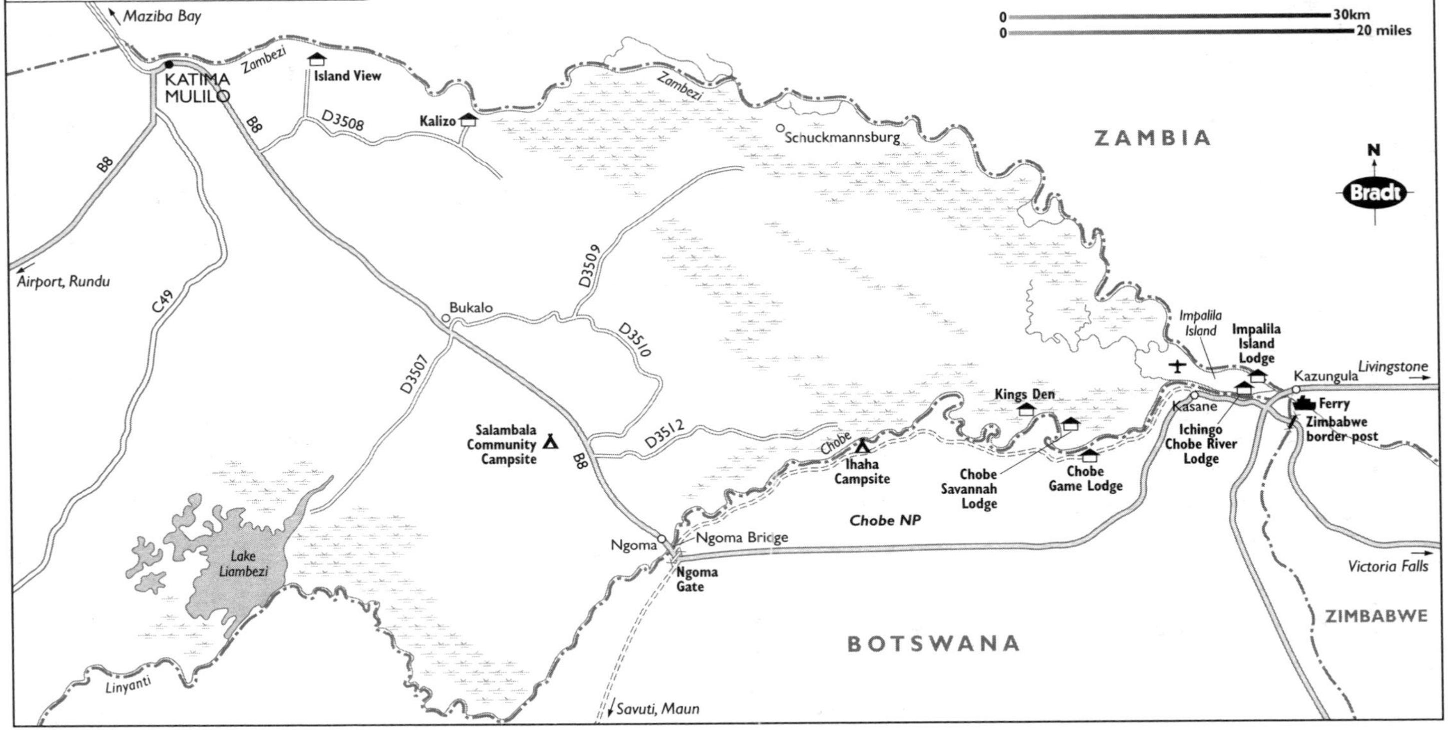

N

Bradt

0 — 30km
0 — 20 miles

ZAMBIA

Livingstone
Kazungula
Ferry
Zimbabwe border-post

Victoria Falls

ZIMBABWE

Impalila Island Lodge
Impalila Island
Kasane
Ichingo Chobe River Lodge

Chobe Game Lodge
Kings Den
Chobe Savannah Lodge

Chobe NP

Ihaha Campsite

Chobe

BOTSWANA

Schuckmannsburg

Zambezi

Ngoma Bridge
Ngoma Gate
Ngoma

Savuti, Maun

D3510
D3512
D3509

Bukalo

B8

Salambala Community Campsite

D3507

Kalizo

Island View

D3508

B8

Zambezi

Maziba Bay

KATIMA MULILO

C49

B8

Airport, Rundu

Lake Liambezi

Linyanti

island walks through local villages to a giant baobab. Unusually for a bush lodge, the camp actively welcomes children of all ages, even when not accompanied by adults, as craft activities can usually be organised for them.

US$340 pp sharing, inc all meals & activities & airport transfer. Closed Jan.

🏠 **Ichobezi** (4 cabins) ☎ +27 (0)7120 2439; e info@ichobezi.co.za; www.ichobezi.co.za. For those seeking to spend longer on the river, Ichingo has introduced the 8-berth *Ichobezi*, a luxury 'safari' boat that cruises on the Zambezi & Chobe rivers, as well as into the contiguous wetlands of Namibia's Caprivi Strip. As a Namibian registered vessel, it is permitted to cruise the waters of the Chobe when the national park is closed, & all Botswanan vessels must leave, so it offers a unique opportunity to watch game & experience the tranquillity of the river after dark & at sunrise.

With its crew of 5, the boat is considered an extension of the lodge, with small groups & personal attention. Each en-suite cabin has huge picture windows, so guests can sit & watch wildlife from their rooms or up on deck. This is the chance for total relaxation with a drink or in the on-board plunge pool, but for more involvement tender boats are available for fishing or birdwatching with an experienced guide.

US$340 pp sharing, inc all meals & activities & airport transfer.

🏠 **Impalila Island Lodge** (8 chalets) Islands in Africa, South Africa; ☎ +27 11 706 7207; f +27 11 463 8251; e info@islandsinafrica.com; www.islandsinafrica.com; lodge ☎ 6250 795. Situated on the northwest side of Impalila Island, overlooking the Zambezi's Mambova Rapids, Impalila Island Lodge has in many ways brought the island to people's attention.

Accommodation is in wooden chalets, each with twin beds or a king-sized double. It is fairly luxurious, with much made of polished local mukwa wood, with its natural variegated yellow & brown colours. The raised-up chalets have a square design, enclosing a bathroom in one corner, giving blissfully warm showers from instant water heaters. Below the high thatch ceilings are fans for warmer days, & mosquito nets. Large adjacent dbl doors open one corner of the room onto a wide wooden veranda, overlooking the rapids. These doors have an optional mosquito-net screen for when it's hot, though are more usually glass. Being next to the river can be quite cold on winter mornings.

Activities include guided motorboat trips on the

Zambezi & Chobe: the Zambezi mainly for birdwatching & fishing, whilst longer boat trips to Chobe offer remarkable game-viewing on the edge of the national park there. Mokoro trips explore the shallower channels, & even run the gentle rapids, whilst guided & independent walks are possible on the island. Superb fishing (especially for tiger-fish, best caught on a fly-rod) is all around, & the guides are experienced enough to take beginners or experts out to try their luck.

Since the lodge was merely a project on the drawing board, the team at Impalila has worked in a very low-key, but positive way to involve the local community. Currently the lodge pays into a 'community development fund' that is utilised by the community for various projects — the clinic, the school, measures to encourage preservation of wildlife & to conserve the local environment — & administered by Dusty & the local chief. Now there are long-term plans to start a wildlife conservancy including Impalila Island, but these could take years to realise. However, because of their excellent approach, don't miss the visits that the lodge organises to local villages, as they can be very rewarding. (Note that Impalila has a super sister-lodge, Susuwe Island Lodge, in Namibia's Caprivi Strip (see page 458). It's on an island in the Kwando River, just northeast from the Kwando concession in Botswana, & is also a first-rate spot with an equally progressive approach to community involvement.)

The main part of the lodge is a large thatched bar/dining area & comfortable lounge built around a huge baobab. This is open to the breeze, though can be sheltered when cold. The wooden pool deck has reclining loungers, umbrellas & a great view of the river. Impalila's food is excellent & candle-lit 3- or 4-course meals around the baobab make a memorable scene. It is a stylish, well-run lodge ideal for fishing, birding or just relaxing, with the added bonus of game-viewing from the river in Chobe.

N$305–455 pp sharing, inc all meals, drinks (except spirits & non-house wines), laundry & activities; 30% sgl supplement. Open all year.

🏠 **Ntwala** (4 suites) Ntwala Island; contact as for Impalila (above). The ultra-exclusive camp operated by Impalila is run on country-house lines. The style, though, combines a distinctly modern approach, white & angular, with a loose mokoro theme, & the corrugated-iron roof may come as a surprise. Each chalet has all that you would expect — & more — in the way of luxury, & comes complete with a

The precise boundary between Namibia and Botswana in this area has been defined to follow the deepest channel of the Chobe River – a definition which works well for most river boundaries. However, the Chobe splits into many streams, whose strengths and depths seem to gradually alter over the years.

Kasikili Island is a very low, flat island which covers about 3.5km² when the waters are low, but shrinks to a much smaller size when it is flooded. It's used mainly for grazing cattle. For many years, it was regarded as South West African and then Namibian territory. However, around the time of Namibian independence, it was occupied by Botswana, which calls it Sedudu Island. The Botswana Defence Force (BDF) built several watchtowers on it – chunky structures towering over the island's grassy plains, and cunningly disguised with variegated military-pattern netting. In early 1995, both Botswana and Namibia agreed to put the issue before the International Court of Justice (ICJ) in The Hague, and in February 1996 they both agreed to abide by its eventual judgement.

Botswana argued that the northern channel was the main river channel, while Namibia maintained that southern channel was the larger one. Finally, in December 1999, the ICJ pronounced that the border should 'follow the line of the deepest soundings in the northern channel of the Chobe River around Kasikili-Sedudu Island'.

That said, the court also diplomatically ruled that 'in the two channels around Kasikili-Sedudu Island, the nationals of, and vessels flying the flags of, the Republic of Botswana and the Republic of Namibia shall enjoy equal national treatment'.

For visitors, this means that game-viewing boats from both countries are allowed on both sides of this tiny, troublesome patch of floodplain!

---

private pool & deck with hammock, all open to the river. Guests in each suite are allocated their own boat & a personal guide, too. Facing the rapids, the central building continues the mokoro theme; guests come together here for evening meals. *N$305–585 pp sharing, inc all meals, drinks (except spirits & non-house wines), laundry & activities; 30% sgl supplement. Open all year.*

⌂ **King's Den** (10 chalets, riverboat) ✆/f Botswana +267 6250 814; e kingsden@botsnet.bw. Owned by the Namib Sun Hotel group, King's Den overlooks Chobe National Park from Kasikili (Sedudu) Island. It can be reached by taking a boat west from Kasane, & is nearer to the park than any of Impalila Island's lodges.

It has wooden chalets constructed on stilts on the edge of the island, all with en-suite facilities. In addition, there is a 13-cabin riverboat, the *Zambezi Queen*.

Options for guests include game-viewing boat excursions on the Chobe River or through the Chassai Channel, as well as fishing, a visit to a traditional village, & day trips to Victoria Falls. *N$1,080/1,720 sgl/dbl, inc all meals & boat cruise.*

NGOMA BORDER The conversion of the gravel road from Katima to Ngoma into tar is at last complete. At Ngoma itself, there's little apart from the border post, a smart office next to the bridge by the Chobe River. About 2km further on, over the river, Botswana's border post is a newer building perched high above the water. Both seem efficient, pleasant and generally quiet. This crossing is fine for 2WD vehicles, and opens 06.00–18.00.

Beyond is a good gravel road to Kasane, which cuts through the Chobe National Park, or a choice of much slower, but more scenic routes. One leads to Kasane, for game-viewing along the Chobe riverfront; the other heads through forested and communal lands towards Savuti and Maun. Both the scenic options require park permits and a 4x4 vehicle.

✕ Where to stay

✕ Salambala Community Campsite (4 pitches) 〄 061 255977; e nacobta@iafrica.com.na; www.nacobta.com.na. The turn-off for Salambala from the main B8, is about 15km north of Ngoma or 46km south of Katima Mulilo. This is another of the Caprivi's excellent community campsites (see page 49). It has 3 separate pitches for tents & a fourth better suited to larger groups, each with a private flush toilet & a shower with hot water. All profits from this camp go back to the community. *N$40 pp.*

Appendix I

WILDLIFE GUIDE

This wildlife guide is designed in a manner that should allow you to name most large mammals that you see in Namibia. Less common species are featured under the heading *Similar species* beneath the animal to which they are most closely allied, or bear the strongest resemblance.

CATS AND DOGS

Lion *Panthera leo* Shoulder height 100–120cm. Weight 150–220kg.
Africa's largest predator, the lion is the animal that everybody hopes to see on safari. It is a sociable creature, living in prides of five to ten animals and defending a territory of between 20 and 200km². Lions often hunt at night, and their favoured prey is large or medium antelope such as wildebeest and impala. Most of the hunting is done by females, but dominant males normally feed first after a kill. Rivalry between males is intense and takeover battles are frequently fought to the death, so two or more males often form a coalition. Young males are forced out of their home pride at three years of age, and male cubs are usually killed after a successful takeover.

When not feeding or fighting, lions are remarkably indolent – they spend up to 23 hours of any given day at rest – so the anticipation of a lion sighting is often more exciting than the real thing. Lions naturally occur in any habitat, except desert or rainforest. They once ranged across much of the Old World, but these days they are all but restricted to the larger conservation areas in sub-Saharan Africa (one remnant population exists in India).

In Namibia, lions are occasionally reported in the Kaokoveld or in the central highlands, but Etosha and Caprivi's parks are the most reliable places to see them. Occasionally, they used to find their way down river valleys and take seals on the coast as prey. However, there are no reliable reports of this in recent years.

Leopard *Panthera pardus* Shoulder height 70cm. Weight 60–80kg.
The powerful leopard is the most solitary and secretive of Africa's big cats. It hunts at night, using stealth and power, often getting to within 5m of its intended prey before pouncing. If there are hyenas and lions around then leopards habitually move their kills up into trees to safeguard them. The leopard can be distinguished from the cheetah by its rosette-like spots, lack of black 'tearmarks' and more compact, low-slung, powerful build.

The leopard is the most common of Africa's large felines, yet a good sighting in the wild is extremely unusual – in fact there are many records of individuals living for years undetected in close proximity to humans. They occur everywhere apart from the desert, though they favour habitats with plenty of cover, like riverine woodlands and rocky

kopjes. Namibia's central highlands are perfect for leopard, which are common on the farms there. Some lodges, like Okonjima, encourage sightings by offering them food.

Cheetah *Acynonix jubatus* Shoulder height 70–80cm. Weight 50–60kg.

This remarkable spotted cat has a greyhound-like build, and is capable of running at 70km/hr in bursts, making it the world's fastest land animal. Despite superficial similarities, you can

easily tell a cheetah from a leopard by the former's simple spots, disproportionately small head, streamlined build, diagnostic black tearmarks, and preference for relatively open habitats. It is often seen pacing the plains restlessly, either on its own or in a small family group consisting of a mother and her offspring. A diurnal hunter, cheetah favour the cooler hours of the day to hunt smaller antelope, like steenbok and duiker, and small mammals like scrub hares. Namibia probably has Africa's highest cheetah population – estimated at 25% of the world's population. This is largely due to the

eradication of lion and spotted hyena from large areas of commercial farmland, where cheetah are not usually regarded (by enlightened farmers) as a threat to cattle.

Etosha is Namibia's best park for cheetah in the wild, though there's probably a higher density of them on many farms.

Similar species: The **serval** (*Felis serval*) is smaller than a cheetah (shoulder height 55cm) but has a similar build and black-on-gold spots giving way to streaking near the head. Seldom seen, it is widespread and quite common in moist grassland, reedbeds and riverine habitats throughout Africa, including Owamboland, Etosha, Bushmanland and the Caprivi Strip. It preys on mice, rats and small mammals, but will sometimes take the young of small antelope.

Caracal *Felis caracal* Shoulder height 40cm. Weight 15–20kg.

The caracal resembles the European lynx with its uniform tan coat and tufted ears. It is a solitary hunter, feeding on birds, small antelope and young livestock. Found throughout the subcontinent, it thrives in Namibia's relatively arid savanna habitats, and occurs everywhere except the far western coastal strip of the Namib. It is nocturnal and rarely seen.

Similar species: The smaller **African wild cat** (*Felis sylvestris*) ranges from the Mediterranean to the Cape of Good Hope, and is similar in appearance to the domestic tabby cat. It has an unspotted torso, which should preclude confusion with the even smaller **small spotted cat** (*Felis nigripes*), a relatively rare resident of southeastern Namibia which has a more distinctively marked coat. Both species are generally solitary and nocturnal, often utilising burrows or termite mounds as daytime shelters. They prey upon reptiles, amphibians and birds as well as small mammals.

African wild dog *Lycaon pictus* Shoulder height 70cm. Weight 25kg.

Also known as the painted hunting dog, the wild dog is distinguished from other African dogs by its large size and mottled black, brown and cream coat. Highly sociable, living in packs of up to 20 animals, wild dogs are ferocious hunters that literally tear apart their prey on the run. They are now threatened with extinction, the most endangered of Africa's great predators. This is the result of relentless persecution by farmers, who often view the dogs as dangerous vermin, and their susceptibility to diseases spread by domestic dogs. Wild dogs are now extinct in many areas where they were formerly abundant, like the Serengeti, and they are common nowhere. The global population of fewer than 3,000 is concentrated in southern Tanzania, Zambia, Zimbabwe, Botswana, South Africa and Namibia.

Wild dogs prefer open savanna with only sparse tree cover, if any, and packs have enormous territories, typically covering 400km² or more. They travel huge distances in search of prey and so few parks are large enough to contain them. In Namibia wild dogs are sometimes seen in Khaudum or on the Caprivi Strip. Botswana's nearby parks of Chobe and Moremi are one of their last strongholds, and so they certainly move across the border. Attempts to reintroduce them to Etosha have so far failed.

Black-backed jackal *Canis mesomelas* Shoulder height 35–45cm. Weight 8–12kg.

The black-backed jackal is an opportunistic feeder capable of adapting to most habitats. Most often seen singly or in pairs at dusk or dawn, it is ochre in colour with a prominent black saddle flecked by a varying amount of white or gold. It is probably the most frequently observed small predator in Africa south of the Zambezi, and its eerie call is a characteristic sound of the bush at night. It is found throughout Namibia, excluding the Caprivi Strip, and is particularly common in Etosha, where it is frequently seen inside the restcamps at night, scavenging for scraps.

Similar species: The similar **side-striped jackal** (*Canis adustus*) is more cryptic in colour, and has an indistinct pale vertical stripe on each flank and a white-tipped tail. Nowhere very common, in Namibia it is found in the Caprivi Strip and occasionally Khaudum or Owamboland.

Bat-eared fox *Otocyon megalotis* Shoulder height 30–35cm. Weight 3–5kg.

This endearing small, silver-grey insectivore is unmistakable with its huge ears and black eye-mask. It is relatively common throughout Namibia, anywhere that the harvester termite is found. It is mostly nocturnal, but can sometimes be seen in pairs or small family groups during the cooler hours of the day, usually in dry open country. It digs well, and if seen foraging then it will often 'listen' to the ground (its ears operating like a radio-dish) while wandering around, before stopping to dig with its forepaws. As well as the termites, bat-eared foxes will eat lizards, gerbils, small birds, scorpions and beetle larvae.

Similar species: The **Cape fox** (*Vulpes chama*) is an infrequently seen dry-country predator which occurs throughout Namibia, but is absent from the Caprivi Strip. The Cape fox lacks the prominent ears and mask of the bat-eared fox, and its coat is a uniform sandy grey colour. I once had a Cape fox approach me cautiously, after dusk, while camping at Bloedkoppie in the northern section of the Namib-Naukluft Park, but have never seen another.

Spotted hyena *Crocuta crocuta* Shoulder height 85cm. Weight 70kg.
Hyenas are characterised by their bulky build, sloping back, rough brownish coat, powerful jaws and dog-like expression. Contrary to popular myth, spotted hyenas are not exclusively scavengers; they are also adept hunters which hunt in groups and kill animals as large as wildebeests. Nor are they hermaphroditic, an ancient belief that stems from the false scrotum and penis covering the female hyena's vagina. Sociable animals, hyenas live in loosely structured clans of about ten animals, led by females who are stronger and larger than males, based in a communal den.

Hyenas utilise their kills far better than most predators, digesting the bones, skin and even teeth of antelope. This results in the distinctive white colour of their faeces – which is an easily identified sign of them living in an area.

The spotted hyena is the largest hyena, identified by its light brown, blotchily spotted coat. It is found in the wetter areas of northern Namibia, most of the national parks and reserves devoted to game, and occasionally in eastern parts of the Namib Desert. Although mainly nocturnal, spotted hyenas can often be seen around dusk and dawn in protected areas like Etosha. Their distinctive, whooping calls are a spine-chilling sound of the African night.

Similar species: The secretive **brown hyena** (*Hyaena brunnea*) occurs in arid parts of Namibia, and has a shaggy, unmarked dark brown coat – not unlike a large, long-haired German shepherd dog. In contrast to the spotted hyena, brown hyenas tend to scavenge rather than hunt, and are generally solitary while doing so. They are the dominant carnivore in the drier areas of the Namib, and are even seen scavenging on the beaches and around seal colonies. Because of this, the local name for them is *strandwolf,* or beach-wolves.

Normally they forage for whatever they can, from small birds and mammals to the remains of kills and even marine organisms cast up upon the beaches. During drier, leaner periods they will eat vegetable as well as animal matter, and can go without water for long periods by eating nara melons.

Aardwolf *Proteles cristatus* Shoulder height 45–50cm. Weight 7–11kg.
With a tawny brown coat and dark, vertical stripes, this insectivorous hyena is not much bigger than a jackal and occurs in low numbers in most parts of Namibia. It is active mainly at night, gathering harvester termites, its principal food, with its wide, sticky tongue. These termites live underground (not in castle-like termite mounds) and come out at night to cut grass, and drag it back down with them.

Thus open grassland or lightly wooded areas form the typical habitat for aardwolves, which can sometimes be spotted around dusk, dawn, or on very overcast days, especially during the colder months. They seem to be thriving in Namibia's central ranchland, giving you better chances of glimpsing them on many guest farms than anywhere else in Africa.

PRIMATES
Chacma baboon *Papio cynocephalus ursinus* Shoulder height 50–75cm. Weight 25–45kg.
This powerful terrestrial primate, distinguished from any other monkey by its much larger size, inverted 'U' shaped tail and distinctive dog-like head, is fascinating to watch from a behavioural perspective. It lives in large troops which boast a complex, rigid social structure characterised by a matriarchal lineage and plenty of inter-troop movement by males seeking social dominance. Omnivorous and at home in almost any habitat, the baboon is the most

widespread primate in Africa, frequently seen in most game reserves.

There are three African races, of which the chacma baboon is the only one occurring in Namibia. With a highly organised defence system, the only predator that seriously affects them is the leopard, which will try to pick them off at night, while they are roosting in trees or cliffs.

Vervet monkey *Cercopithecus aethiops* Length (excluding tail) 40–55cm. Weight 4–6kg.
Also known as the green or grivet monkey, the vervet is probably the world's most numerous monkey and certainly the most common and widespread representative of the *Cercopithecus* guenons, a taxonomically controversial genus associated with African forests. An atypical guenon in that it inhabits savanna and woodland rather than true forest, the vervet spends a high proportion of its time on the ground. In Namibia, it is found only around the narrow belts of woodland beside the Orange and Kunene rivers, and in the lush areas of Mahango and the Caprivi Strip.

The vervet's light grey coat, black face and white forehead band are distinctive – as are the male's garish blue genitals. The only animal that is even remotely similar is the baboon, which is much larger and heavier.

Vervets live in troops averaging about 25 animals. They are active during the day and roost in trees at night. They eat mainly fruit and vegetables, though are opportunistic and will take insects and young birds, and even raid tents at campsites (usually where ill-informed visitors have previously tempted them into human contact by offering food).

Lesser bushbaby *Galago senegalensis* Length (without tail) 17cm. Weight 150g.
The lesser bushbaby is the most widespread and common member of a group of small and generally indistinguishable nocturnal primates, distantly related to the lemurs of Madagascar. In Namibia they occur throughout the north, from northern Kaokoland and Etosha to Khaudum and the Caprivi Strip.

More often heard than seen, the lesser bushbaby is nocturnal but can sometimes be picked out by tracing a cry to a tree and shining a torch into the branches; its eyes reflect as two red dots. These eyes are designed to function in what we would describe as total darkness, and they feed on insects – some of which are caught in the air by jumping – and also eating sap from trees, especially acacia gum.

They inhabit wooded areas, and prefer acacia trees or riverine forests. I remember being startled while lighting a braai at Halali restcamp, in Etosha, by a small family of bushbabies. They raced through the trees above us, bouncing from branch to branch while chattering and screaming out of all proportion to their size.

LARGE ANTELOPE
Sable antelope *Hippotragus niger* Shoulder height 135cm. Weight 230kg.
The striking male sable is jet black with a distinct white face, underbelly and rump, and long decurved horns – a strong contender for the title of Africa's most beautiful antelope. The female is chestnut brown and has shorter horns, whilst the young are a lighter red-brown colour. Sable are found throughout the wetter areas of southern and east Africa. In Namibia, a thriving herd frequents the floodplain beside the Okavango River in Mahango National Park, and there are other groups further east in the Caprivi Strip's other parks.

Sable are normally seen in small herds: either bachelor herds of males, or breeding herds of females and young which are often accompanied by the dominant male in that territory. The breeding females drop their calves around February or March, the calf remaining hidden away from the herd, for its first few weeks. Sable are mostly grazers, though will browse, especially when food is scarce. They need to drink at least every other day, and seem especially fond of low-lying dewy vleis in wetter areas.

Roan antelope *Hippotragus equinus* Shoulder height 120–150cm. Weight 250–300kg.

This handsome horse-like antelope is uniform fawn-grey with a pale belly, short decurved horns and a light mane. It could be mistaken for the female sable antelope, but this has a well-defined white belly, and lacks the roan's distinctive black-and-white facial markings. The roan is a relatively rare antelope; common almost nowhere in Africa (Malawi's Nyika Plateau being one obvious exception). In Namibia small groups of roan are found in Etosha, Waterberg, Khaudum and the Caprivi.

Roan need lots of space if they are to thrive and breed; they don't generally do well where game densities are high. Game farms prize them as one of the most valuable antelope (hence expensive to buy). They need access to drinking water, but are adapted to subsist on relatively high plateaux with poor soils.

Oryx or gemsbok *Oryx gazella* Shoulder height 120cm. Weight 230kg.
This is the quintessential desert antelope; unmistakable with its ash-grey coat, bold black facial marks and flank strip, and unique long, straight horns. Of the three races of oryx in Africa, the gemsbok is the largest and most striking. It occurs throughout the Kalahari and Namib and is widespread all over Namibia, from the coast to the interior highlands.

As you might expect, gemsbok are very adaptable. They range widely and are found in areas of dunes, alkaline pans, open savanna and even woodlands. Along with the much smaller *springbok*, they can sometimes even be seen tracking across flat desert plains with only dust-devils and mirages for company. Gemsbok can endure extremes of temperature, helped by specially adapted blood capillaries in their nasal passages which can cool their blood before it reaches their brains. Thus although their body temperature can rise by up to 6°C, their brains remain cool and they survive. They do not need drinking water and will eat wild melons and dig for roots, bulbs and tubers when grazing or browsing becomes difficult.

Waterbuck *Kobus ellipsiprymnus* Shoulder height 130cm. Weight 250–270kg.
The waterbuck is easily recognised by its shaggy brown coat and the male's large lyre-shaped horns. The common race of southern Africa and areas east of the Rift Valley has a distinctive white ring around its rump, while the defassa race of the Rift Valley and areas further west has a full white rump. In Namibia, waterbuck are very uncommon, only

occasionally seen on the eastern fringes of the Caprivi Strip. They need to drink very regularly, so usually stay within a few kilometres of water, where they like to graze on short, nutritious grasses. At night they may take cover in adjacent woodlands. It is often asserted that waterbuck flesh is oily and smelly, which may discourage predators.

Blue wildebeest *Connochaetes taurinus* Shoulder height 130–150cm. Weight 180–250kg.
This ungainly antelope, also called the brindled gnu, is easily identified by its dark coat and bovine appearance. The superficially similar buffalo is far more heavily built. When they have enough space, blue wildebeest can form immense herds – as perhaps a million do for their annual migration from Tanzania's Serengeti Plains into Kenya's Masai Mara. In Namibia they naturally occur north of Etosha and east into the Caprivi Strip. They are also found in the Kalahari, Khaudum and the far eastern borders of Namibia. They are adaptable grazers, but prefer short grass plains and need access to drinking water. They have been introduced onto several game ranches.

Similar species: The **black wildebeest** *Connochaetes gnou*, endemic to South Africa's central highveld, now numbers a mere 4,000. It is seen most easily in South Africa's Golden Gate National Park, though has also been introduced into several private game areas in Namibia. It differs from the blue wildebeest in having a white tail, a defined black-on-white mane, and horns that slope sharply down then rise to form a 'U' when seen from the side.

Hartebeest *Alcelaphus buselaphus* Shoulder height 125cm. Weight 120–150kg.
Hartebeests are ungainly antelopes, readily identified by the combination of large shoulders, a sloping back, a glossy, red-brown coat and smallish horns in both sexes. Numerous sub-species are recognised, all of which are generally seen in small family groups in reasonably open country. Though once hartebeest were found from the Mediterranean to the Cape, only isolated populations still survive.
The only one native to Namibia is the red hartebeest, which is found throughout the arid eastern side of the country, and north into Etosha and Owamboland. They have been introduced onto the NamibRand Nature Reserve but are absent from the Caprivi Strip, and common nowhere. Hartebeests are almost exclusively grazers; they like access to water though will eat melons, tubers and rhizomes when it is scarce. Etosha's waterholes, especially those in areas of mopane sparse woodland, probably offer your best chance to see hartebeest in Namibia.

Similar species: The **tsessebe** *Damaliscus lunatus* is basically a darker version of the hartebeest with striking yellow lower legs. (Related sub-species are known as *topi* in east Africa.) Widespread but thinly and patchily distributed, the tsessebe occurs occasionally in the Caprivi Strip. Its favourite habitat is open grassland, where it is a selective grazer, eating the newer, more nutritious grasses. The tsessebe is one of the fastest antelope species, and jumps very well.

Bontebok *Damaliscus dorcas dorcas* Shoulder height 850–95cm. Weight 60–70kg.
Though endemic to the fynbos areas of the Western Cape in South Africa, bontebok have

been introduced into many private reserves in Namibia. They look like particularly striking small hartebeest, with a distinctive white face, chestnut back, black flanks and white belly and rump. Bontebok were hunted close to extinction in the early 20th century, and now they are largely found in private protected areas – like the grounds of Mokuti Lodge, or the NamibRand Nature Reserve.

Similar species: The duller but more common **blesbok** (*Damaliscus dorcas phillipsi*) is, in essence, the highveld race of bontebok native to eastern South Africa. That, too, has occasionally been introduced onto the odd private reserve in Namibia.

Kudu *Tragelaphus strepsiceros* Shoulder height 140–155cm. Weight 180–250kg.

The kudu (or, more properly, the greater kudu) is the most frequently observed member of the genus tragelaphus. These medium-size to large antelopes are characterised by the male's large spiralling horns and dark coat, which is generally marked with several vertical white stripes. They are normally associated with well-wooded habitats.

The kudu is very large, with a grey-brown coat and up to ten stripes on each side. The male has magnificent double-spiralled corkscrew horns. Occurring throughout Mozambique, Zimbabwe, Zambia, Botswana and Namibia, kudu are widespread and common, though not in dense forests or open grasslands. In Namibia they are absent only from the Namib Desert – though they are found in the river valleys and are very common on farmland, where their selective browsing does not compete with the indiscriminate grazing of the cattle.

Sitatunga *Tragelaphus spekei* Shoulder height 85–90cm. Weight 105–115kg.

The semi-aquatic antelope is a widespread but infrequently observed inhabitant of west and central African swamps from the Okavango in Botswana to the Sudd in Sudan. In Namibia it occurs in the Okavango River beside Mahango, and in protected areas of the Kwando–Linyanti–Chobe–Zambezi river system where there are extensive papyrus reedbeds. Because of its preferred habitat, the sitatunga is very elusive and seldom seen, even in areas where it is relatively common.

Eland *Taurotragus oryx* Shoulder height 150–175cm. Weight 450–900kg.

Africa's largest antelope, the eland is light brown in colour, sometimes with a few faint white vertical stripes. Its somewhat bovine appearance is accentuated by relatively short horns and a large dewlap. It was once widely distributed in east and southern Africa, but in Namibia it is now found only in isolated Kalahari areas, Etosha and Waterberg.

Small herds of eland frequent grasslands and light woodlands, often fleeing at the slightest provocation. (They have long been hunted for their excellent meat, so perhaps this is not surprising.)

Eland are opportunist browsers and grazers, eating fruit,

berries, seed pods and leaves as well as green grass after the rains, and roots and tubers when times are lean. They run slowly, though can trot for great distances and jump exceedingly well.

MEDIUM AND SMALL ANTELOPE

Bushbuck *Tragelaphus scriptus* Shoulder height 70–80cm. Weight 30–45kg.
This attractive antelope, a member of the same genus as the kudu, is widespread throughout Africa and shows great regional variation in its colouring. It occurs in forest and riverine woodland, where it is normally seen singly or in pairs. The male is dark brown or chestnut, while the much smaller female is generally a pale reddish brown. The male has relatively small, straight horns and both sexes are marked with white spots and sometimes stripes, though the stripes are often indistinct.

Bushbuck tend to be secretive and very skittish, except when used to people. They depend on cover and camouflage to avoid predators, and are often found in the thick, herby vegetation around rivers. They will freeze if disturbed, before dashing off into the undergrowth. Bushbuck are both browsers and grazers, choosing the more succulent grass shoots, fruit and flowers. In Namibia they have a very limited distribution around the Okavango River in Mahango National Park, and beside the Chobe and Kwando rivers on the eastern side of the Caprivi Strip.

Impala *Aepeceros melampus* Shoulder height 90cm. Weight 45kg.
This slender, handsome antelope is superficially similar to the springbok, but in fact belongs to its own separate family. Chestnut in colour, and lighter underneath than above, the impala has diagnostic black and white stripes running down its rump and tail, and the male has large lyre-shaped horns. One of the most widespread and successful antelope species in east and southern Africa, the impala is normally seen in large herds in wooded savanna habitats. It is the most common antelope in the Caprivi Strip, and throughout much of the country further east, although it is absent from much of Namibia.

However, a separate sub-species, the **black-faced impala** (*A. m. petersi*), occurs in Etosha, the Kaokoveld and southern Angola. This is almost identical to the normal impala, and distinguished only by extra black stripes on its face, including a prominent one down the front of its nose. The total population of black-faced impalas is about a thousand individuals, but with a few days spent in Etosha you have a surprisingly good chance of spotting some.

As expected of such a successful species, it both grazes and browses, depending on what fodder is available.

Springbok *Antidorcas marsupilis* Shoulder height 60cm. Weight 20–25kg.
Springbok are graceful, relatively small antelope – members of the gazelle family – which generally occur in large herds. They have finely marked short coats: fawn-brown upper parts and a white belly, separated by a dark brown band. Springbok occur throughout Namibia; they are often the most common small antelope. They can be seen by the thousand in Etosha.

They favour dry, open country, preferring open plains or savanna, and avoiding thick woodlands and mountains. They can subsist without water for long periods, if there is moisture in the plants they graze or browse; I have even seen springbok amongst the dunes at Sossusvlei on occasions.

Reedbuck *Redunca arundinum* Shoulder height 80–90cm. Weight 45–65kg.

Sometimes referred to as the southern reedbuck (as distinct from mountain and Bohor reedbucks, found further east), these delicate antelope are uniformly fawn or grey in colour, and lighter below than above. They are generally found in reedbeds and tall grasslands, often beside rivers, and are easily identified by their loud, whistling alarm call and distinctive bounding running style. In Namibia they occur only on the Caprivi Strip and a few riverine areas in the far north.

Klipspringer *Oreotragus oreotragus* Shoulder height 60cm. Weight 13kg.
The klipspringer is a stongly built little antelope, normally seen in pairs, and easily identified by its dark, bristly grey-yellow coat, slightly speckled appearance and unique habitat preference. Klipspringer means 'rockjumper' in Afrikaans and it is an apt name for an antelope which occurs exclusively in mountainous areas and rocky outcrops from Cape Town to the Red Sea.

They are common throughout Namibia, wherever rocky hills or kopjes are found – which means most of the central highlands and western escarpment, but not in the far north or the Caprivi Strip. Klipspringers are mainly browsers, though they do eat a little new grass. When spotted they will freeze, or bound at great speed across the steepest of slopes.

Lechwe *Kobus leche* Shoulder height 90–100cm. Weight 80–100kg.
Otherwise known as the red lechwe, this sturdy, shaggy antelope has a reddish coat and beautiful lyre-shaped horns. They are usually found only in moist, open environments and in Namibia they are found only beside the great rivers of the Caprivi Strip.

Lechwe need dry land on which to rest, but otherwise will spend much of their time grazing on grasses and sedges, standing in water if necessary. Their hooves are splayed, adapted to bounding through their muddy environment when fleeing from the lion, hyena and wild dog that hunt them.

Steenbok *Raphicerus cempestris* Shoulder height 50cm. Weight 11kg.
This rather nondescript small antelope has red-brown upper parts and clear white underparts, and the male has short straight horns. It is probably the most commonly observed small antelope; if you see a small antelope fleeing from you across farmland in Namibia, it is likely to be a steenbok. Like most other small antelopes, the steenbok is normally encountered singly or in pairs and tends to 'freeze' when disturbed, before taking flight.

Similar species: **Sharpe's grysbok** (*Raphicerus sharpei*) is similar in size and appearance, though it has a distinctive white-flecked coat. It occurs alongside the steenbok in the far eastern reaches of the Caprivi Strip, but is almost entirely nocturnal in its habits and so very seldom seen. The **Oribi** (*Ourebia ourebi*) is a widespread but very uncommon antelope, which is usually found only in large, open stretches of grassland. It looks much like a steenbok but stands about 10cm higher at the shoulder and has an altogether more upright bearing. In Namibia you have a chance of seeing these only on the Caprivi Strip, and you'll need to look hard.

The **Damara dik-dik** (*Madoqua kirki*) occurs in central-north Namibia, Etosha and the Kaokoland, as well as parts of east Africa where it is known as Kirk's dik-dik. It is Namibia's smallest antelope; easily identified from steenbok by its much smaller size. It is adapted to arid areas and prefers a mixture of bushes and spare grassland cover. Damara dik-diks are common in Etosha, and will often sit motionless beside the road while they are passed by without ever being seen. They are active during the cooler hours of the day as well as the night and are almost exclusively browsers.

Common duiker *Sylvicapra grimmia* Shoulder height 50cm. Weight 20kg.

This anomalous duiker holds itself more like a steenbok or grysbok and is the only member of its (large) family to occur outside of forests. Generally grey in colour, the common duiker can most easily be separated from other small antelopes by the black tuft of hair that sticks up between its horns. It occurs throughout Namibia, everywhere except the Namib Desert. Common duikers tolerate most habitats except for true forest and very open country, and are tolerant of nearby human settlements. They are opportunist feeders, taking fruit, seeds and leaves, as well as crops, small reptiles and amphibians.

OTHER LARGE HERBIVORES

African elephant *Loxodonta africana* Shoulder height 2.3–3.4m. Weight up to 6,000kg.
The world's largest land animal, the African elephant is intelligent, social and often very entertaining to watch. Female elephants live in close-knit clans in which the eldest female plays matriarch over her sisters, daughters and granddaughters. Mother–daughter bonds are strong and may last for up to 50 years. Males generally leave the family group at around 12 years to roam singly or form bachelor herds. Under normal circumstances, elephants range widely in search of food and water, but when concentrated populations are forced to live in conservation areas their habit of uprooting trees can cause serious environmental damage. Elephants are widespread and common in habitats ranging from desert to rainforest. In Namibia they are common in the Caprivi Strip and Etosha, and in Kalahari areas around Khaudum.

Read about the history of Etosha, and you'll realise that the park used to cover much of the present Kaokoveld. Until about 50 years ago Etosha's elephants used to migrate, spending the wetter parts of the year in the Kaokoveld and the drier months nearer to Etosha's permanent waterholes. Etosha's boundary fence has stopped that. However, the herds still tend to head to the hills of western Etosha during the rains, returning to the pan several months later as the bush dries out. Every year a few break out of the park's elaborate fences.

The isolated population which frequents the river valleys of the Kaokoveld are commonly known as 'desert elephants' – though desert-adapted might be a more accurate term. These family groups have learnt where the rivers and waterholes are, probably from their elders, and can navigate through the Kaokoveld's mountains and dunes to find water. The community game guard scheme, amongst others, has rescued this population from the

edge of oblivion; it is thriving to the point of conflict with the area's human population. After several decades of persecution by humans, these elephants are now (understandably) noted for their aggression. Even visitors in sturdy vehicles should treat them with exceptional respect (see *Driving near elephants*, page 96).

Black rhinoceros *Diceros bicornis* Shoulder height 160cm. Weight 1,000kg.
This is the more widespread of Africa's two rhino species, an imposing and rather temperamental creature. It has been poached to extinction in most of its former range, but still occurs in *very* low numbers in many southern African reserves; Namibia offers its best chance of long-term survival – thanks in no small measure to the work of Namibia's Save the Rhino Trust.

Black rhinos exploit a wide range of habitats from dense woodlands and bush, through to the very open hillsides of the Kaokoveld. Often (and descriptively) referred to as the hook-lipped rhino, the black rhino is adapted to browse. Over its range it utilises hundreds of different plants, though local populations are often more specific in their diet: in the Kaokoveld, for example, *Euphorbia damarana* is a great favourite.

Black rhinos are generally solitary animals and can survive without drinking for 4–5 days. However, they will drink daily if they can, and individuals often meet at waterholes – as visitors to the floodlit waterholes at Okaukuejo and Halali will usually see to their delight. They are often territorial and have very regular patterns of movement, which make them an easy target for poachers. Black rhinos can be very aggressive when disturbed and will charge with minimal provocation. Their hearing and sense of smell is acute, whilst their eyesight is poor (so they often miss if you keep a low profile and don't move).

White rhinoceros *Ceratotherium simum* Shoulder height 180cm. Weight 1,500–2,000kg.
No paler in colour than the black rhino – the 'white' derives from the Afrikaans *weit* (wide) and refers to its flattened mouth, an ideal shape for cropping grass. This is the best way to tell the two rhino species apart, since the mouth of the black rhino, a browser in most parts of its range, is more rounded with a hooked upper lip. (Note that there is *no colour difference at all* between these two species of rhino; 'white' and 'black' are not literal descriptions.)

Aside from a relic population of some 30 animals in the northern Congo, the white rhino is now restricted to southern African reserves. There are thriving populations in many South African parks, especially the Umfolozi and Hluhluwe parks, which have effectively saved the species and started to re-populate many of southern Africa's parks. They were reintroduced to Waterberg years ago, and about a dozen have recently been introduced back into Etosha – where they seem to frequent the areas between Namutoni and Springbokfontein waterhole. Unlike their smaller cousins, white rhino are generally placid grazing animals which are very rarely aggressive. They prefer open grassy plains and are often seen in small groups.

Hippopotamus *Hippopotamus amphibius* Shoulder height 150cm. Weight 2,000kg.
Characteristic of Africa's large rivers and lakes, this large, lumbering animal spends most of the day submerged but emerges at night to graze. Strongly territorial, herds of ten or more animals are presided over by a dominant male who will readily defend his patriarchy to the death. Hippos are abundant in most protected rivers and water bodies, and they are still quite common outside of reserves, where they are widely credited with killing more people than any other African mammal.

In Namibia they occur only in the great rivers of the Caprivi Strip, and occasionally in the Kunene River, at the north end of the Kaokoveld. Otherwise you won't generally see them.

Cape buffalo *Syncerus caffer* Shoulder height 140cm. Weight 700kg.

Frequently and erroneously referred to as a water buffalo (an Asian species), the Cape, or African, buffalo is a distinctive, highly social ox-like animal that lives as part of a herd. It prefers well-watered savanna, though also occurs in forested areas. Common and widespread in sub-Saharan Africa, in Namibia it is limited to the Caprivi Strip, largely by the absence of sufficient water in the rest of the country.

Buffalo are primarily grazers and need regular access to water, where they swim readily. They smell and hear well, and old bulls have a reputation for charging at the slightest provocation. Lion often follow herds of buffalo, their favourite prey.

Giraffe *Giraffa camelopardis* Shoulder height 250–350cm. Weight 1,000–1,400kg.

The world's tallest and longest-necked land animal, a fully grown giraffe can measure up to 5.5m high. Quite unmistakable, the giraffe lives in loosely structured herds of up to 15, though herd members often disperse and then they are seen singly or in smaller groups. Formerly distributed throughout east and southern Africa, these great browsers are found in the north of Namibia, from northern Damaraland and Kaokoland, to the Caprivi. Etosha has a thriving population, many of which are very relaxed with cars and allow visitors in vehicles to approach very closely.

Common zebra *Equus burchelli* Shoulder height 130cm. Weight 300–340kg.

Also known as Burchell's or plains zebra, this attractive striped horse is common and widespread throughout most of east and southern Africa, where it is often seen in large herds alongside wildebeest. It is common in most conservation areas from northern South Africa, Namibia and Botswana all the way up to the southeast of Ethiopia. Southern races, including those in Namibia, have paler brownish 'shadow stripes' between the bold black stripes that are present in all races.

Similar species: The **Hartmann's mountain zebra** (*Equus grevyi hartmannae*), is confined to Namibia's western escarpment and the plains nearby. It is very closely related to the Cape mountain zebra which occurs in South Africa. Mountain zebra have a slightly lighter frame than the Burchell's, their underparts are not striped, the striping on their legs extends all the way to their hooves, and they have a dewlap which the Burchell's lack.

They occur from the conservation area around the Fish River Canyon to the Hartmann Valley in the Kaokoveld, and have been introduced onto several private reserves away from the escarpment area.

Warthog *Phacochoreus africanus* Shoulder height 60–70cm. Weight up to 100kg.

This widespread and often conspicuously abundant resident of the African savanna is grey in colour with a thin covering of hairs, wart-like bumps on its face, and rather large upward curving tusks. Africa's only diurnal swine, the warthog is often seen in family groups, trotting around with its tail raised stiffly (a diagnostic trait) and a determinedly nonchalant air. They occur everywhere in Namibia apart from the far south and the western desert areas, although I have often seen them grazing, on bended knee, where the C36 cuts through the Namib-Naukluft National Park.

Similar species: Bulkier, hairier and more brown, the **bushpig** (*Potomochoerus larvatus*) is only known to occur in Namibia in the Caprivi Strip. It is very rarely seen due to its nocturnal habits and preference for dense vegetation.

SMALL MAMMALS

African civet *Civettictis civetta* Shoulder height 40cm. Weight 10–15kg.

This bulky, long-haired, rather feline creature of the African night is primarily carnivorous, feeding on small animals and carrion, but will also eat fruit. It has a similarly coloured coat to a leopard, which is densely blotched with large black spots becoming stripes towards the head. Civets are widespread and common in many habitats, but very rarely seen. In Namibia, it is restricted to the far north.

Similar species: The **small-spotted genet** (*Genetta genetta*) and **large-spotted genet** (*Genetta tigrina*) are the most widespread members of a group of similar small predators. All of these are slender and rather feline in appearance (though they are *not* cats), with a grey to gold-brown coat marked with black spots and a long ringed tail. Most likely to be seen on nocturnal game drives or scavenging around game-reserve lodges, the large-spotted genet is gold-brown with very large spots and a black-tipped tail, whereas the small-spotted genet is greyer with rather small spots and a pale-tipped tail. Exact identification is a job for experts. The small-spotted genet is found all over Namibia, whilst the large-spotted genet is restricted to the Caprivi Strip and the area adjacent to the Okavango River.

Banded mongoose *Mungos mungo* Shoulder height 20cm. Weight around 1kg.

The banded mongoose is probably the most commonly observed member of a group of small, slender, terrestrial carnivores. Uniform dark grey-brown except for a dozen black stripes across its back, it is a diurnal mongoose occurring in playful

family groups, or troops, in most habitats north and east of Okahandja. They feed on insects, scorpions, amphibians, reptiles and even carrion and bird's eggs, and can move across the veld at quite a pace.

Similar species: Another eight or so mongoose species occur in Namibia; some are social and gather in troops, others solitary. Several are too scarce and nocturnal to be seen by casual visitors. Of the rest, the water or **marsh mongoose** (*Atilax paludinosus*) is large, normally solitary and has a very scruffy brown coat; it's widespread along the Caprivi Strip, the Kunene and the Orange. The **white-tailed ichneumon** (*Ichneumia albicauda*) is another mongoose that is widespread in the Caprivi. It is a solitary, large brown mongoose, easily identified by its bushy white tail.

The **slender mongoose** (*Galerella sanguinea*) is as widespread and also solitary, but it is very much smaller (shoulder height 10cm) and has a uniform brown or reddish coat and blackish tail tip. It is replaced in the far south of Namibia by the **small grey mongoose** (*Galerella pulveruntela*), similar in size but grey with white flecks on its coat.

The **yellow mongoose** (*Cynitis penicillata*) is a small, sociable mongoose with a tawny or yellow coat, and is commonly found across most of Namibia. It normally forages alone and is easily identified by the white tip on the end of its tail.

Finally, **the dwarf mongoose** (*Helogate parvula*) is a diminutive (shoulder height 7cm), highly sociable light brown mongoose often seen in the vicinity of the termite mounds where it nests.

Meerkat or suricate
Suricata suricatta Shoulder height 25–35cm. Weight 650–950g.

Found throughout the Kaokoveld and southern Namibia, meerkats are only absent from the driest western areas of the Namib and the wetter parts of northeast Namibia. These small animals are sandy- to silvery-grey in colour, with dark bands running across their backs. They are exclusively diurnal and have a distinctive habit of sitting upright on their hind legs. They do this when they first emerge in the morning, to sun themselves, and throughout the day.

Living in complex social groups, meerkats are usually seen scratching around for insects, beetles and small reptiles in dry, open, grassy areas. While the rest forage, one or two of the group will use the highest mound around as a sentry-post – looking out for predators using their remarkable eyesight. Meerkats' social behaviour is very complex: they squeak constantly to communicate and even use different alarm calls for different types of predators. Because of their photogenic poses and fascinating social behaviour, they have been the subject of several successful television documentaries filmed in the southern Kalahari.

Honey badger
Mellivora capensis Shoulder height 30cm. Weight 12kg.

Also known as the ratel, the honey badger is black with a puppyish face and grey-white back. It is an opportunistic feeder best known for its symbiotic relationship with a bird called the honeyguide which leads it to a beehive, waits for it to tear it open, then feeds on the scraps. The honey badger is among the most widespread of African carnivores, and also amongst the most powerful for its size; it occurs all over Namibia. However, it is thinly distributed and rarely seen, except when it has been tamed enough to turn up on cue to artificial feedings at safari camps (Okonjima's nightly feeding session used to get occasional visits from honey badgers).

Similar species: Several other mustelids occur in the region, including the **striped polecat** (*Ictonyx striatus*), a common but rarely seen nocturnal creature with black underparts and a bushy white back, and the similar but much scarcer striped weasel (*Poecilogale albincha*). The **Cape clawless otter** (*Aonyx capensis*) is a brown freshwater mustelid with a white collar, which is found in the Caprivi area, the Kunene and the Orange River. The smaller **spotted-necked otter** (*Lutra maculicollis*) is darker with light white spots on its throat, and is restricted to the Caprivi and Okavango River.

Aardvark
(*Orycteropus afer*) Shoulder height 60cm. Weight up to 70kg.

This singularly bizarre nocturnal insectivore is unmistakable with its long snout, huge ears and powerful legs, adapted to dig up the nests of termites, on which it feeds. Aardvarks occur throughout southern Africa, except the driest western areas of the Namib. Though their distinctive three-toed tracks are often seen, and they are not uncommon animals, sightings of them are rare.

Aardvarks prefer areas of grassland and sparse scrub, rather than dense woodlands, and Namibia's ranchland suits them well – although their excavations into roads and dam walls are not appreciated by farmers.

Pangolin *Manis temmincki* Total length 70–100cm. Weight 8–15kg.

Sharing the aardvaak's diet of termites and ants, pangolins are another very unusual nocturnal insectivore – with distinctive armour-plating and a tendency to roll up in a ball when disturbed. Sometimes known as Temminck's pangolin, or scaly anteaters, these strange animals walk on their hind legs, using their tail and front legs for balance. They occur in eastern and northern Namibia, but not in the Namib Desert, and are both nocturnal and rare – so sightings are exceedingly unusual.

In some areas further east, particularly Zimbabwe, local custom is to make a present of any pangolin found to the paramount chief (often taken to mean the president), which has caused great damage to their population.

Porcupine *Hystrix africaeaustralis* Total length 80–100cm. Weight 15–25kg.
This is the largest rodent found in the region, and occurs all over southern Africa, except for the western reaches of the Namib Desert. It easily identified by its black and white striped quills, generally black hair, and shambolling gait. If heard in the dark, then the rustle of its foraging is augmented by the slight rattle of its quills. These drop off fairly regularly, and are often found in the bush.

The porcupine's diet is varied, and they are fairly opportunistic when it comes to food. Roots and tubers are favourites, as is the bark of certain trees; they will also eat meat and small reptiles or birds if they have the chance.

Similar species: Also spiky, the **southern African hedgehog** is found in north-central areas, including the Kaokoveld and Owamboland. This species is much smaller than the porcupine (about 20cm long), but is also omnivorous. They are not common.

Rock hyrax *Procavia capensis* Shoulder height 35–30cm. Weight 4kg.
Rodent-like in appearance, hyraxes (also known as dassies) are claimed to be the closest living relative of elephants. The rock hyrax and similar **Kaokoveld rock hyrax** (*Heterohyrax welwitschii*) are often seen sunning themselves in rocky habitats, and become tame when used to people.

They are social animals, living in large groups, and largely herbivorous, eating leaves, grasses and fruits. Where you see lots of dassies, watch out for black eagles and other raptors which prey extensively on them.

Scrub hare *Lepus saxatilis* Shoulder height 45–60cm. Weight 1–4.5kg.
This is the largest and commonest African hare or rabbit, occurring everywhere in Namibia except the far west and south. In some areas a short walk at dusk or after nightfall might reveal three or four scrub hares. They tend to freeze when disturbed.

Ground squirrel *Xerus inauris* Shoulder height 20–30cm. Weight 400–700g.
This terrestrial rodent is common in most arid parts of Namibia, except the far west of the desert. The ground squirrel is grey to grey-brown with a prominent white eye ring and silver-black tail. Within its range, it might be confused with the meerkat, which also spends much time on its hind legs. Unlike the meerkat, ground squirrels have a characteristic squirrel mannerism of holding food in their forepaws.

The ground squirrel is a social animal; large groups share one communal burrow. It can often be spotted searching for vegetation, seeds, roots and small insects, whilst holding its tail aloft as a sunshade.

Appendix 2

LANGUAGE

There isn't the space here to include a guide to Namibia's many languages, although, if you are staying in a community for longer than a few days, then you should try to learn a few local greetings from your hosts. Do note, too, the cultural guidelines on pages 24–5. For background details on language, see *Chapter 2*.

While travelling, you are likely to come across unfamiliar words that are in common use in southern African English, many of Afrikaans origin. These include:

apteek	chemist or pharmacy (most towns have one)
bakkie	pick-up truck, with open back
berg	mountain, or mountain range
boerewors (or *wors*)	sausage – an essential component of any *braai*
boma	traditional enclosure, often used at safari camps to mean the area around the fire where everyone gathers.
braaivleis (*braai*)	barbecue
the bush	generic term for any wild area, usually implying some thick vegetation cover
bundu	the bush (see above) – more often used in Zimbabwe
donga	small ravine, sometimes caused by water erosion
dorp	small rural town, though often implies a place with small-minded, reactionary attitudes
kantoor	an office
klippe	rock or stone (as used in *klip*springer)
kloof	ravine, often with a small river at the bottom
kopje (or *koppie*)	rocky hill, often alone in an otherwise flat area.
kraal	cattle enclosure or group of African huts (Owambo)
lekker	good, nice – now slang, typically used to describe food
mielie	corn or maize, the staple for most of the subcontinent
mieliepap	maize flour porridge, often eaten for breakfast
mokoro	dugout canoe (plural *mekoro*)
orlag	war
pad	road or track
ompad	diversion, often used on road signs
rivier	river
robots	traffic lights (ie: 'turn left at the *robots*, then …')
rondavel	traditional African hut (usually round)
tackies	running shoes or trainers
veld	grassland – like 'the bush', this term is used for wide open wilderness areas, but implies mostly low vegetation cover
vlei	depression, valley, lake or low-lying place where water gathers, this term is used throughout the subcontinent
werft	traditional settlement (often Herero)

A2

Appendix 3

BOOKS
History

Hansheinrich von Wolf and Duwisib Castle by Dr N Mossolow. Society for Scientific Development, Swakopmund, 1995. This neat 20-page account of the castle and its founder is half in German and half in English, and often available from the castle itself. The middle eight pages are black-and-white photographs of the castle and its characters. Worth buying while you are there.

Africa: A Biography of the Continent by John Reader. Penguin Books, London, 1997. Over 700 pages of highly readable history, interwoven with facts and statistics, to make a remarkable overview of Africa's past. Given that Namibia's boundaries were imposed from Europe, its history *must* be looked at from a pan-African context to be understood. This book can show you that wider view; it is compelling and essential reading.

The Bushman Myth: The Making of a Namibian Underclass by Robert J Gordon. Westview Press Inc, Colorado and Oxford, 1992. If you, like me, had accepted the received wisdom that Bushmen are the last descendants of Stone Age man, pushed to living in splendid isolation in the Kalahari, then you must read this. It places the Bushmen in an accurate historical context and deconstructs many of the myths we have created about them.

Rivers of Blood, Rivers of Gold: Europe's Conflict with Tribal Peoples by Mark Cocker. Jonathan Cape, London, 1998. This highly readable book explores four colonial episodes: the conquest of Mexico, the British onslaught in Tasmania, the uprooting of the Apache in north America, and the German campaign in South West Africa during the early 20th century. It gives an excellent, detailed account of the 1904–7 war, and examines the conflict, and the main characters, in the context of contemporary world politics.

Lake Ngami and *The River Okavango* by Charles John Andersson. Originally published in the late 1850s; republished as a facsimile reprint by Struik, Cape Town, 1967. These two fascinating books record Namibia in the 1850s through the eyes of one of the first traders and hunters in the area.

Explorations in South-West Africa by Thomas Baines. London, 1864. Although linked more with the countries further east, the travels of Baines, as he accompanied Livingstone and others, make fascinating reading.

Namibia – The Facts. IDAF Publications, London, 1989. Concentrates mainly on the liberation struggle over the last ten years. Highly emotive text and pictures.

History of Resistance in Namibia by Peter H Katjavivi. Co-published by James Currey, London; OAU in Addis Ababa; Unesco Press in Paris. Rather more scholarly than *Namibia – The Facts*, it's impressive in its detail.

The History of Rehoboth by Robert Camby. A very useful pamphlet for understanding Rehoboth's history.

The Price of Freedom by Ellen Ndeshi Namhila. New Namibia Books, Windhoek, 1997. A biographical account of 19 years spent in exile by a young Namibian woman.

'Why gossip is good for you' by R I M Dunbar. Article in *New Scientist*, 21 November 1992.

'Franz or Klikko, the Wild Dancing Bushmen: A Case Study in Khoisan Stereotyping' by Q N Parsons. Published in *Botswana Notes & Records*, vol 20 (1989), pages 71–6.

Photography

The Skeleton Coast by Amy Schoeman. Struik, Cape Town, 2003. Involving, well-informed text and superb photographs make this an excellent read, and easily the definitive work on the coast. Amy's late husband was the legendary Louw Schoeman, and she remains involved with Skeleton Coast Fly-in Safaris, though she now concentrates on travel writing and photography.

Namib by David Coulson. Sidgwick & Jackson, London, 1991. This stunning coffee-table book doubles as a readable travelogue. Published 18 years after Coulson's first visit, its insight tells much of his love for Namibia's wilderness.

Namibia – Africa's Harsh Paradise by Anthony Bannister and Peter Johnson. New Holland, London, 1990. Yet another for the coffee table, this covers the whole country and concentrates on the Bushman and Himba people.

'Etosha: Namibia's Kingdom of Animals' article in *National Geographic*, vol 163, no 3, March 1983. A general article about managing the park – with discussion of the problems of waterholes, anthrax, and too many lions!

'Elephant Talk' article in *National Geographic*, vol 176, no 2, August 1989, pages 264–77. On infrasound communication in elephants, with some interesting comments about desert elephants in the Hoarusib River.

Guidebooks

Discovering Southern Africa by T V Bulpin. Discovering Southern Africa Productions, South Africa, 1970. In this part guidebook and part history book, Bulpin covers mainly South Africa but also extends into Namibia and Zimbabwe. A weighty tome with useful background views and information, written from a South African perspective.

Travelogues

The Lost World of the Kalahari by Laurens van der Post. First published by the Hogarth Press, 1958, subsequently many reprints by Penguin. Laurens van der Post's classic account of how he journeyed into the heart of the Kalahari Desert in search of a 'pure' Bushman group – eventually found at the Tsodilo Hills. His almost mystical description of the Bushmen is fascinating, so long as you can cope with the rather dated turgid prose. You then need to read Robert J Gordon's very different book (see page 488) to put it in perspective.

Sheltering Desert by Henno Martin. First English edition published by William Kimber, London, 1957. The story of two German geologists who lived out World War II by hiding in the Kuiseb Canyon – holiday reading if you're visiting the Namib-Naukluft National Park.

Natural history

The Namib by Dr Mary Seely. Shell Oil Namibia, Windhoek. A detailed work on the desert's origins, with descriptions of many sites and the animals and plants that live there. This paperback is well worth getting when you arrive in Namibia. Also in this series is *Waterberg*.

Field Guide to Mammals of Southern Africa by Chris and Tilde Stuart. Struik Publishers, South Africa, revised 2007.

Namib Flora by Patricia Craven and Christine Marais. Gamsberg Macmillan, Windhoek, 1986. This delightful little hardback covers a small area 'from Swakopmund to the giant *welwitschia* via Goanikontes', though many of the plants that it so beautifully illustrates will be found elsewhere.

Damaraland Flora by Patricia Craven and Christine Marais. Gamsberg Macmillan, Windhoek, 1992. Similar to the *Namib Flora*, and equally well illustrated, this volume covers Spitzkoppe, Brandberg and Twyfelfontein, but is invaluable anywhere in the Kaokoveld.

Birds of Southern Africa by Kenneth Newman. Published in numerous editions from 1983 by Southern Books, South Africa. Probably the best identification field guide to birds in southern Africa, including Namibia.

The Living Deserts of Southern Africa by Dr Barry Lovegrove. Fernwood Press, South Africa, 1993. A beautifully illustrated book with a scholarly text that is both informative and accessible.

Fascination of Geology by Nicole Grunert. Klaus Hess Publishers, Namibia.

The Harsh and Forbidden Sperrgebiet Rediscovered by Sakkie & Theresa Rothmann, Namibia.

Kalahari: Life's Variety in Dune and Delta by Michael Main. Southern Books, Johannesburg, 1987. Though primarily concerned with Botswana, this is a superb, highly readable, treatise on the Kalahari. It covers the origins and ecology of this thirstland and even tackles some of the more sticky political and human questions facing the region. The many marvellous details in the book, and Main's general clarity on the issues, come from personal experience – he's lived in Botswana and travelled there very extensively. But even if you're heading for Namibia's Kalahari, it's still worth getting a copy. The only problem is that it will, of course, captivate you and make a subsequent visit to Botswana essential.

Wild Flowers of the Central Namib by Antje Burke. Namibia Scientific Society, 2003.

Art and culture

The Rock Paintings of Southern Africa by the Abbé Henri Breuil. Trianon Press Ltd, Paris, 1955–60. These large volumes cover some of Namibia's major rock-art sites, including the controversial 'white lady' of Brandberg.

Rural Art in Namibia Rössing Foundation of Namibia, 1993. A 25-page colour booklet, categorised by region, illustrating traditional Namibian arts and crafts, including interviews with artists about their work.

Peoples of Namibia by Professor J S Malan. Rhino Press, Pretoria, 1995.

Art in Namibia by Adelheid Lilienthal. National Art Gallery of Namibia.

Ongoma! – Notes on Namibian Musical Instruments by Minette Mans. Gamsberg Macmillan, Windhoek, 2000. Although written as a resource book for teachers, this practical little book contains a wealth of information on traditional instruments that deserves a wider readership.

Health/reference

An Explorer's Handbook – Travel, Survival and Bush Cookery by Christina Dodwell. Hodder and Stoughton, London, 1984. Over 170 pages of both practical and amusing anecdotes, including chapters on 'unusual eatables', 'building an open fire', and 'tested exits from tight corners'. Practical advice for both plausible and most unlikely eventualities – and it's a great read.

Bugs, Bites & Bowels by Dr Jane Wilson-Howarth. Cadogan Books, London, 2006. An amusing and erudite overview of the hazards of tropical travel.

Your Child Abroad: A Travel Health Guide by Dr Jane Wilson-Howarth and Dr Matthew Ellis. Bradt Travel Guides, Chalfont St Peter, 2005. Full of practical first-hand advice from two leading medical experts. An indispensable guide if you plan to travel abroad with young children.

Fiction

The Purple Violet of Oshaantu by Neshani Andreas. Heinemann, London, 2001. A Namibian woman's perspective on love and marriage in the context of traditional values and beliefs.

Meekulu's Children by Kaleni Hiyalwa. New Namibia Books, Windhoek, 2000. Reads more like a biography of a child growing up during Namibia's struggle for independence than a novel. Powerful stuff.

WEBSITES

www.airnamibia.com Air Namibia's site includes schedules and fares.

www.grnnet.gov.na The official website of the Namibian government.

www.holidaytravel.com.na Links to various tourism magazines, including *Flamingo*, the in-flight magazine of Air Namibia.

www.met.gov.na Ministry of Environment and Tourism website.

www.nacobta.com.na The overview of the community-orientated tourism projects run under the auspices of NACOBTA.

www.namibian.com.na *The Namibian* newspaper online.

www.namibiatourism.com.na Namibia Tourism Board's official site.

www.namibia-travel-guide.com The online version of this guide.

www.namibweb.com A rather ramshackle site focused on travel around Namibia.

www.nbc.com.na The government-sponsored Namibia Broadcasting Corporation (NBC)

www.nwr.com.na Namibia Wildlife Resorts (NWR). Essential for booking accommodation in national parks.

To convert	Multiply by
Inches to centimetres	2.54
Centimetres to inches	0.3937
Feet to metres	0.3048
Metres to feet	3.281
Yards to metres	0.9144
Metres to yards	1.094
Miles to kilometres	1.609
Kilometres to miles	0.6214
Acres to hectares	0.4047
Hectares to acres	2.471
Imperial gallons to litres	4.546
Litres to imperial gallons	0.22
US gallons to litres	3.785
Litres to US gallons	0.264
Ounces to grams	28.35
Grams to ounces	0.03527
Pounds to grams	453.6
Grams to pounds	0.002205
Pounds to kilograms	0.4536
Kilograms to pounds	2.205
British tons to kilograms	1016.0
Kilograms to British tons	0.0009812
US tons to kilograms	907.0
Kilograms to US tons	0.000907

5 imperial gallons are equal to 6 US gallons
A British ton is 2,240 lbs. A US ton is 2,000 lbs.

TEMPERATURE CONVERSION TABLE The bold figures in the central columns can be read as either centigrade or fahrenheit.

°C		°F	°C		°F
−18	**0**	32	10		
−15	**5**	41	13	**50**	122
−12	**10**	50	16	**55**	131
−9	**15**	59	18	**60**	140
−7	**20**	68	21	**65**	149
−4	**25**	77	24	**70**	158
−1	**30**	86	27	**75**	167
2	**35**	95	32	**80**	176
4	**40**	104	38	**90**	194
7	**45**	113	40	**100**	212
				104	219

WIN £100 CASH!

READER QUESTIONNAIRE

Send in your completed questionnaire for the chance to win £100 cash in our regular draw

All respondents may order a Bradt guide at half the UK retail price – please complete the order form overleaf.

(Entries may be posted or faxed to us, or scanned and emailed.)

We are interested in getting feedback from our readers to help us plan future Bradt guides. Please answer ALL the questions below and return the form to us in order to qualify for an entry in our regular draw.

Have you used any other Bradt guides? If so, which titles? . . . .
. . . .
What other publishers' travel guides do you use regularly? . . . .
. . . .
Where did you buy this guidebook? . . . .
What was the main purpose of your trip to Namibia (or for what other reason did you read our guide)? eg: holiday/business/charity etc.. . . . .
. . . .
What other destinations would you like to see covered by a Bradt guide?
. . . .
Would you like to receive our catalogue/newsletters?

YES / NO (If yes, please complete details on reverse)

If yes – by post or email? . . . .

Age (circle relevant category) 16–25   26–45   46–60   60+

Male/Female (delete as appropriate)

Home country . . . .

Please send us any comments about our guide to Namibia or other Bradt Travel Guides. . . . .
. . . .
. . . .
. . . .

Bradt Travel Guides

23 High Street, Chalfont St Peter, Bucks SL9 9QE, UK
☎ +44 (0)1753 893444 f +44 (0)1753 892333
e info@bradtguides.com
www.bradtguides.com

CLAIM YOUR HALF-PRICE BRADT GUIDE!

Order Form

To order your half-price copy of a Bradt guide, and to enter our prize draw to win £100 (see overleaf), please fill in the order form below, complete the questionnaire overleaf, and send it to Bradt Travel Guides by post, fax or email.

Please send me one copy of the following guide at half the UK retail price

Title	Retail price	Half price
...	....	......

Please send the following additional guides at full UK retail price

No	Title	Retail price	Total
...	....	....	....
...	....	....	....
...	....	....	....

Sub total ....
Post & packing ....
(£1 per book UK; £2 per book Europe; £3 per book rest of world)
Total ....

Name ....

Address...

Tel .... Email ....

☐ I enclose a cheque for £........ made payable to Bradt Travel Guides Ltd

☐ I would like to pay by credit card. Number: ....

Expiry date: ... / ...   3-digit security code (on reverse of card) .....

☐ Please add my name to your catalogue mailing list.

☐ I would be happy for you to use my name and comments in Bradt marketing material.

Send your order on this form, with the completed questionnaire, to:

Bradt Travel Guides NAM3
23 High Street, Chalfont St Peter, Bucks SL9 9QE
☏ +44 (0)1753 893444   f +44 (0)1753 892333
e info@bradtguides.com   www.bradtguides.com

Bradt Travel Guides

Africa

Africa Overland	£15.99
Benin	£14.99
Botswana: Okavango, Chobe,	£15.99
Northern Kalahari	
Burkina Faso	£14.99
Cape Verde Islands	£13.99
Canary Islands	£13.95
Cameroon	£13.95
Eritrea	£15.99
Ethiopia	£15.99
Gabon, São Tomé, Príncipe	£13.95
Gambia, The	£13.99
Ghana	£15.99
Johannesburg	£6.99
Kenya	£14.95
Madagascar	£15.99
Malawi	£13.99
Mali	£13.95
Mauritius, Rodrigues & Réunion	£13.99
Mozambique	£13.99
Namibia	£15.99
Niger	£14.99
Nigeria	£15.99
Rwanda	£14.99
Seychelles	£14.99
Sudan	£13.95
Tanzania, Northern	£13.99
Tanzania	£16.99
Uganda	£15.99
Zambia	£15.95
Zanzibar	£12.99

Britain and Europe

Albania	£13.99
Armenia, Nagorno Karabagh	£14.99
Azores	£12.99
Baltic Capitals: Tallinn, Riga,	£12.99
Vilnius, Kaliningrad	
Belarus	£14.99
Belgrade	£6.99
Bosnia & Herzegovina	£13.99
Bratislava	£6.99
Budapest	£8.99
Cork	£6.99
Croatia	£13.99
Cyprus see North Cyprus	
Czech Republic	£13.99
Dresden	£7.99
Dubrovnik	£6.99
Eccentric Britain	£13.99
Eccentric Cambridge	£6.99
Eccentric Edinburgh	£5.95
Eccentric France	£12.95
Eccentric London	£13.99
Eccentric Oxford	£5.95
Estonia	£13.99
Faroe Islands	£13.95
Georgia	£14.99
Helsinki	£7.99
Hungary	£14.99
Kiev	£7.95
Kosovo	£14.99

Krakow	£7.99
Latvia	£13.99
Lille	£6.99
Lithuania	£13.99
Ljubljana	£7.99
Macedonia	£14.99
Montenegro	£13.99
North Cyprus	£12.99
Paris, Lille & Brussels	£11.95
Riga	£6.95
River Thames,	£10.95
In the Footsteps of the Famous	
Serbia	£14.99
Slovakia	£14.99
Slovenia	£12.99
Spitsbergen	£14.99
Switzerland: Rail, Road, Lake	£13.99
Tallinn	£6.99
Ukraine	£14.99
Vilnius	£6.99
Zagreb	£6.99

Middle East, Asia and Australasia

China: Yunnan Province	£13.99
Great Wall of China	£13.99
Iran	£14.99
Iraq	£14.95
Maldives	£13.99
Mongolia	£14.95
North Korea	£13.95
Oman	£13.99
Sri Lanka	£13.99
Syria	£14.99
Tibet	£13.99
Turkmenistan	£14.99

The Americas and the Caribbean

Amazon, The	£14.99
Argentina	£15.99
Bolivia	£14.99
Cayman Islands	£12.95
Costa Rica	£13.99
Chile	£16.95
Eccentric America	£13.95
Eccentric California	£13.99
Falkland Islands	£13.95
Panama	£13.95
Peru & Bolivia: Backpacking and Trekking	£12.95
St Helena	£14.99
USA by Rail	£13.99

Wildlife

Antarctica: Guide to the Wildlife	£14.95
Arctic: Guide to the Wildlife	£15.99
Galápagos Wildlife	£15.99
Madagascar Wildlife	£14.95
Peruvian Wildlife	£15.99
Southern African Wildlife	£18.95
Sri Lankan Wildlife	£15.99

Health

Your Child Abroad: A Travel Health Guide	£10.95

Index

Page numbers in italics indicate maps